Mnemonic	Operands	Descripti[illegible]	[illegible]	[illegible]	[illegible]
bra	label	Branch to labeled instruction (within ±64 one-wor[illegible]	[illegible]	[illegible]	[illegible]
goto	label	Go to labeled instruction (anywhere)	[illegible]	[illegible]	[illegible]
bc	label	If carry (C=1), then branch to labeled instruction (w[illegible]	1	1/2	-
bnc	label	If no carry (C=0), then branch to labeled instruction (within ±64 one-word instructions)	1	1/2	-
bz	label	If zero (Z=1), then branch to labeled intruction (within ±64 one-word instructions)	1	1/2	-
bnz	label	If not zero (Z=0, then branch to labeled instruction (within ±64 one-word instructions)	1	1/2	-
bn	label	If negative (N=1), then branch to labeled instruction (within ±64 one-word instructions)	1	1/2	-
bnn	label	If not negative (N=0), then branch to labeled instruction (within ±64 one-word instructions)	1	1/2	-
bov	label	If overflow (OV=1), then branch to labeled instruction (within ±64 one-word instructions)	1	1/2	-
bnov	label	If no overflow (OV=0), then branch to labeled instruction (within ±64 one-word instructions)	1	1/2	-
cpfseq	f(, BANKED)	Skip if f is equal to WREG	1	1/2	-
cpfsgt	f(, BANKED)	Skip if f is greater than WREG (unsigned compare)	1	1/2	-
cpfslt	f(, BANKED)	Skip if f is less than WREG (unsigned compare)	1	1/2	-
tstfsz	f(, BANKED)	Test f; skip if zero	1	1/2	-
decfsz	f, F/W(, BANKED)	Decrement f, putting result in F or WREG; skip if zero	1	1/2	-
dcfsnz	f, F/W(, BANKED)	Decrement f, putting result in F or WREG; skip if not zero	1	1/2	-
incfsz	f, F/W(, BANKED)	Increment f, putting result in F or WREG; skip if zero	1	1/2	-
infsnz	f, F/W(, BANKED)	Increment f, putting result in F or WREG; skip if not zero	1	1/2	-
rcall	label	Call labeled subroutine (within ±512 one-word instructions)	1	2	-
call	label	Call labeled subroutine (anywhere)	2	2	-
call	label, FAST	Call labeled subroutine (anywhere); copy state to shadow registers: (WREG)→WS, (STATUS)→STATUSS, (BSR)→BSRS	2	2	-
return		Return from subroutine	1	2	-
return	FAST	Return from subroutine; restore state from shadow registers: (WS)→WREG, (STATUSS)→STATUS, (BSRS)→BSR	1	2	C, DC, Z, OV, N
retlw	k	Return from subroutine, putting literal value in WREG	1	2	-
retfie		Return from interrupt; reenable interrupts	1	2	-
retfie	FAST	Return from interrupt; restore state from shadow registers: (WS)→WREG, (STATUSS)→STATUS, (BSRS)→BSR; reenable interrupts	1	2	C, DC, Z, OV, N
push		Push address of next instruction onto stack	1	1	-
pop		Discard address on top of stack	1	1	-
clrwdt		Clear watchdog timer	1	1	-
sleep		Go into standby mode	1	1	-
reset		Software reset to same state as is achieved with the MCLR input	1	1	C, DC, Z, OV, N
nop		No operation	1	1	-
tblrd*		Read from program memory location pointed to by TBLPTR into TABLAT	1	2	-
tblrd*+		Read from program memory location pointed to by TBLPTR into TABLAT, then increment TBLPTR	1	2	-
tblrd*-		Read from program memory location pointed to by TBLPTR into TABLAT, then decrement TBLPTR	1	2	-
tblrd+*		Increment TBLPTR, then read from program memory location pointed to by TBLPTR into TABLAT	1	2	-

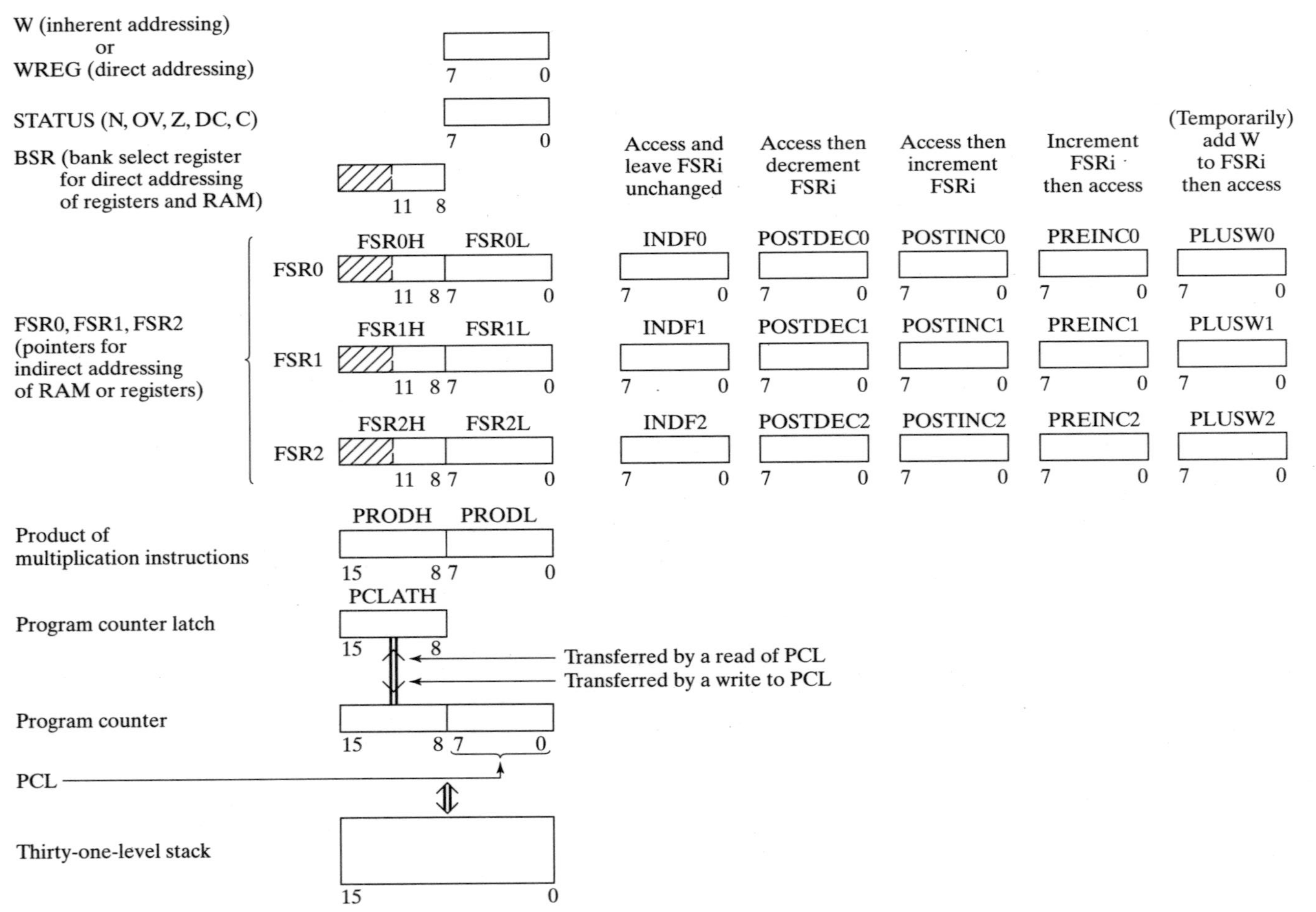

W (inherent addressing)
or
WREG (direct addressing)
STATUS (N, OV, Z, DC, C)
BSR (bank select register for direct addressing of registers and RAM)
FSR0, FSR1, FSR2 (pointers for indirect addressing of RAM or registers)
FSR0
FSR1
FSR2
FSR0H
FSR0L
FSR1H
FSR1L
FSR2H
FSR2L
Access and leave FSRi unchanged
Access then decrement FSRi
Access then increment FSRi
Increment FSRi then access
(Temporarily) add W to FSRi then access
INDF0
POSTDEC0
POSTINC0
PREINC0
PLUSW0
INDF1
POSTDEC1
POSTINC1
PREINC1
PLUSW1
INDF2
POSTDEC2
POSTINC2
PREINC2
PLUSW2
Product of multiplication instructions
PRODH
PRODL
Program counter latch
PCLATH
Transferred by a read of PCL
Transferred by a write to PCL
Program counter
PCL
Thirty-one-level stack

Embedded Design with the PIC18F452 Microcontroller

John B. Peatman

Department of Electrical and Computer Engineering
Georgia Institute of Technology

Pearson Education, Inc.
Upper Saddle River, New Jersey

Library of Congress Cataloging-in-Publication Data
Peatman, John B.
Embedded design with the PIC18F452 Microcontroller / John B. Peatman.
p. cm.
ISBN 0-13-046213-6
1. Programmable controllers. 2. Embedded computer systems—Design and construction. I. Title.

TJ223.P76 P42 2003
629.89—dc21

2002070432

Vice President and Editorial Director, ECS: *Marcia J. Horton*
Publisher: *Tom Robbins*
Editorial Assistant: *Jody McDonnell*
Vice President and Director of Production and Manufacturing, ESM: *David W. Riccardi*
Executive Managing Editor: *Vince O'Brien*
Managing Editor: *David A. George*
Production Editor: *Cindy Miller*
Director of Creative Services: *Paul Belfanti*
Creative Director: *Carole Anson*
Art Director: *Jayne Conte*
Cover Designer: *Bruce Kenselaar*
Art Editor: *Greg Dulles*
Manufacturing Manager: *Trudy Pisciotti*
Manufacturing Buyer: *Lynda Castillo*
Marketing Manager: *Holly Stark*

Pearson Education, Inc.
Upper Saddle River, NJ 07458

Printed in the United States of America
10 9 8 7 6 5 4 3 2 1

ISBN 0-13-046213-6

Pearson Education Ltd., *London*
Pearson Education Australia Pty. Ltd., *Sydney*
Pearson Education Singapore, Pte. Ltd.
Pearson Education North Asia Ltd., *Hong Kong*
Pearson Education Canada, Inc., *Toronto*
Pearson Educación de Mexico, S.A. de C.V.
Pearson Education—Japan, *Tokyo*
Pearson Education Malaysia, Pte. Ltd.
Pearson Education, *Upper Saddle River, New Jersey*

To
Lyndsey, David, John, Rebecca, Carter and Hunter

CONTENTS

APPENDICES

PREFACE

The evolution of microcontrollers (i.e., single-chip microcomputers) has been driven by two strong trends. One trend is the demand for a low-cost means of putting intelligence into a product. When a product is produced in quantities of millions, a small savings in component cost will drive component selection decisions. Another trend is the demand for a programmable solution when an application has severe timing constraints, such as those in automobile engine control. This demand has led to ever faster, more sophisticated microcontroller architectures. Microchip Technology has evolved its product line of PIC microcontrollers from simple, low-cost devices. Subsequent generations of PIC microcontrollers have included enhancements to meet the needs of an increasing circle of applications. At the same time, Microchip has never lost sight of the value of introducing new technology at the lowest possible cost and thereby "buying" market share. As pointed out in Chapter 1 of this text, Microchip has followed this strategy to the point where it is now the number two producer of eight-bit microcontrollers in the world, with a market share that continues to rise each year. Because eight-bit microcontrollers span the needs of most applications, "eight-bitters" dominate the world of microcontrollers.

This book is developed around Microchip's latest family of parts, the PIC18FXXX family. It focuses on the PIC18F452, a new part brought to market in May 2002. It is a 40-pin microcontroller upgrade of their earlier PIC16C74 and PIC16F877 microcontrollers. This upgrade will be familiar to users of those parts, but with myriad enhancements. Virtually all of the quirks that characterized earlier PIC microcontroller parts have been eliminated. The flash program memory of the PIC18F452 microcontroller makes low-cost development possible. Not only is the part inexpensive (less than $10 in single quantities), but it is supported by Microchip's free assembler and by a free QwikBug monitor program. QwikBug, once programmed into the chip, supports the downloading of successive iterations of a user program and supports the ability to debug the user program with the help of running to a breakpoint, monitoring/changing watch variables, and single-stepping.

To provide a "learning by doing" environment, a QwikFlash development board is included inside the back cover of this first printing of the book. A photograph of the populated board is shown in Figure 4–1. Readers not interested in using this board may wish to know that the board is included, *gratis,* courtesy of a friend of the author. Parts for populating the board can be purchased under a special arrangement with the Digi-Key Corporation. Appendix A1 includes the Digi-Key parts list as well as construction hints, intended both for the novice who has never soldered before and for the experienced student, professional, and hobbyist. Alternatively, a populated board can be purchased from MICRODESIGNS, Inc. via their Web site, **www.microdesignsinc.com**.

Throughout this book, the approach taken is to introduce a *template* of assembly language code that encompasses a set of features of the PIC18F452 plus its interactions with some of the I/O devices resident on the QwikFlash board. In this way, it is intended that the reader will find a smooth path to the creative process of writing enhanced application code. There is no end to the variety of such enhancements, many of which are suggested in the end-of-chapter problems. Others are listed in Appendix A10 as a set of suggested lab projects that might accompany the first offering of a college or university course organized around this book. Still other project enhancements are suggested by the presence of the many features of the microcontroller and by the versatility of the QwikFlash board's I/O devices themselves.

Many years ago, Skip Addison impressed me with the clarity that his *structured* assembler could bring to the writing of code. Its implementation of nested IF . . . ELSE. . . ENDIF, WHILE . . . ENDWHILE, and REPEAT . . . UNTIL constructs gave assembly language the clean control flow normally associated with a compiled language such as C. At this time, Jessica Meremonte has prepared a free structured assembly preprocessor that, together with Microchip's free (and excellent) assembler, does this same thing for code writing with the PIC18F452 microcontroller. Introduced in Chapter 6, the use of Jessica's *sasm* utility acts like a one-step assembler. It enhances the code writing process, and code understandability, for the remaining 14 chapters of the book.

To utilize a microcontroller effectively, a designer should develop at least three capabilities, each of which is addressed in this book. First, he or she must understand available components. This begins with the microcontroller itself, with its CPU register structure, its instruction set, its addressing modes, and its on-chip resources. It extends to user I/O devices such as keypads and displays and sensing/control devices such as temperature transducers and stepper motor actuators. Using interrupt control, a microcontroller can juggle many real-time activities simultaneously. To achieve this without error, the designer must understand how the microcontroller handles interrupts and the timing issues related to them.

Second, the designer must thoroughly understand the algorithmic processes required by each aspect of the design and be able to translate them into the language of the microcontroller. For example, the design of an antilock brake system for an automobile involves an understanding of both the brake system dynamics and the implementation of a suitable control algorithm.

Third, the designer must understand how the extensive requirements of an instrument or device can be broken down into manageable parts. Almost any project can be likened to the process of jumping from boulder to boulder to cross a stream. Each boulder may represent the design ideas needed to understand and use a device such as a liquid crystal display. But in addition to studying boulders, the designer must pay attention to how streams are crossed. Through examples, both with the template programs and with complete designs available on the author's web site (e.g., the source code for the QwikFlash instrument described in Section 4.3), the reader can view the structure of several projects.

This book attempts to organize and unify the development of these three capabilities: to understand and use components, to exploit powerful algorithmic processes, and to break down the complexity of an instrument or device so as to meet its specifications.

ABOUT THE BOOK

This book will typically be used in a one-semester course at the senior level. Alternatively, it might be used at the junior level if it is deemed worthwhile to trade the increased engineering experience of seniors for the opportunity to follow this course with other design-oriented courses and individual project activities. Although the context of the book is electrical, each component is sufficiently explained to permit the book to be used in a variety of curricula as an introduction to design using a microcontroller. The incentive to so use the book lies in the diverse applications made possible by the availability of a "controller on a chip."

There has been an attempt to make many parts of the book self-contained. A reader might scan Chapter 1 to gain the perspective of Steve Sanghi, CEO and President of Microchip Technology. Chapters 2 and 3 describe the PIC18F452's CPU structure, instructions, and addressing modes. The brief Chapter 4 describes the features of the QwikFlash board (i.e., the built-up version of the bare board located on the inside back cover of the book). This description includes one application of the board as a QwikFlash instrument to measure frequencies and time intervals with uncanny accuracy, using a free program available from the author's web site.

Chapters 5 and 6 present the first template of code and a discussion of development alternatives. This latter discussion is augmented in the appendices. Appendix sections A1.2 and A4.3 describe Microchip's ICD2 in-circuit debugger. Appendix A4 describes the free QwikBug on-chip monitor program and what it takes to program it into a chip. Appendix A3 describes how the free *sasm* structured assembler utility can be used with or without the support of Microchip's MPLAB facility. Appendix section A5.2 describes the free QwikAddress utility and the help it provides in conjunction with the sasm utility.

Chapter 7 develops the use of the liquid-crystal display built into the QwikFlash board. A second template of code is presented, serving as a stepping stone for subsequent project work. Chapters 8 and 12 augment the discussion of user I/O available on the board. Chapter 8 discusses a widely used input device, the rotary pulse generator (RPG). Chapter 12 develops what amounts to an allocation scheme for the display and the RPG, for user input.

Chapter 9 discusses the timing and the *critical region* issues associated with interrupts. It describes the high- and low-priority mechanisms built into the chip to field interrupts and explains how to allocate interrupt sources between the two so as to be most effective in meeting the timing requirements of an application.

The remaining chapters of the book can be "mixed and matched" to meet the needs of a course and its sequencing of lab projects. Chapters 13 and 16 explain in detail how to use the PIC18F452's superb timers for capturing the timing of input events and for controlling the timing for output events. Chapters 10 and 11 describe the nuances of using the chip's analog and digital input pins. Chapter 14 explains how to use any of Microchip's library of 36 integer subroutines for dealing with the multiplication and division of multiple-byte unsigned and signed numbers. It also explains how to use their eight floating-point subroutines and the role of these subroutines in retaining the precision of a computation. Chapters 15 and 17 delve into two approaches for expanding the number of I/O pins available as well as two convenient means for enhancing the peripheral capabilities of the chip beyond those peripherals already built into the chip. Chapter 18 discusses the use of the UART built into the chip while Chapter 19 looks at how a low-end PIC microcontroller can be used as a smart peripheral, connecting to the PIC18F452 through one of its UART pins. Chapter 20 discusses a variety of disparate but significant features of the chip, including the use of its non-volatile data EEPROM, its watchdog timer and brownout reset circuits, and how it can be operated to achieve an exceedingly low battery supply current.

The last two template programs, P3 and P4, are recast as C programs written by Mike Chow and included in Appendix A7. Each one is written for both Microchip Technology's C compiler and Hi-Tech Software's C compiler, two high-quality C compilers. A class that makes the switch from assembly coding can benefit from the use of the P3 template, cast in C. As a template for subsequent work, it encompasses many issues that will arise as further code is written. The P4 template illustrates how to handle interrupts.

This book is directed toward a specific goal of engineering studies—the development of creative design capability. Given a powerful, low-cost microcontroller chip, a low-cost development board, and the development tools needed to develop and debug program code, we are able to focus the design process on the microcontroller chip itself and a variety of I/O devices, thereby giving zest to the process of learning. While some of these I/O devices are available on the QwikFlash board itself, the laboratory for a college or university course can make use of a second QwikProto board to expand the variety of I/O resources easily, as described in Appendix A2 and illustrated, by example, in the photograph of Figure A2-5. Other I/O possibities are described there and in Appendix section A10.2. Also refer to the author's web site, **www.picbook.com**, for URLs pointing to I/O device information and project ideas being employed at other universities. To help readers take advantage of the opportunities for developing microcontroller design capability, most chapters close with an assortment of problems, many having a design flavor. A suggested course calendar is included at the beginning of Appendix A10 along with 10 "starter" lab projects.

ACKNOWLEDGMENTS

I have had the good fortune to have the counsel and support of Roger Webb and Bill Sayle, Chair and Associate Chair, respectively, of the School of Electrical and Computer Engineering at the Georgia Institute of Technology. At the same time, I have been aided over many years by some outstanding students who have shared my interests and passions. Chris Twigg has been prominent during this past year in a dozen endeavors involved with this book and with the switching of my lab, and its supporting utilities, over to the PIC18F452. He has developed the code presented in this book for the I^2C interface of Chapter 17, for the creative Bargraph subroutine of Figure 7-17, for the transformation of the math subroutines prepared for use by Microchip's C compiler into a library of subroutines easily accessible for assembly programming use, and for the QwikPH utility for updating the *Program Hierarchy* included in an application program. He has developed the **www.picbook.com** web site. He, Cory Hawkins, and Paul Nichols have developed the QwikFlash instrument described in Section 4.3. Jessica Meremonte's handiwork with her *sasm* structured assembler utility reaches throughout the book. David Flowers QwikAddress utility resolves several issues arising from the use of the *sasm* utility in an elegant fashion. The team of students listed at the end of Appendix A4, culminating with the work of Burt Sims and then Rawin Rojvanit, have developed the QwikBug resident debugger utility. This combination of capabilities provides complete, and free, support for developing applications with the QwikFlash development board.

Rick Farmer and I have had a cooperative relationship in the development of PC boards for my lab over the last several years. Rick has worked with PIC microcontrollers for years and has been a productive, insightful designer for even more years. His insights through three iterations of the QwikFlash board have resulted in a fine, solid design. His original *PICloader* "load and go" resident utility for the PIC16F877 microcontroller provided the impetus for QwikBug development.

Microchip, through its ever helpful personnel have been invaluable in the development of this book about a chip yet to be introduced commercially at the time of this writing. Scott Fink's early suggestion that I learn about the forthcoming PIC18F452 lay the foundation for this project and for our development activities. Al Lovrich's support with every request armed me with the tools and the information needed to carry out this work. Carol Popovich and Paul Landino have supported my every request for the tools and the pre-production chips needed for an early switch of my instructional lab over to the PIC18F452. Craig Miller and Greg Robinson have been free with their knowledge of the chip's background debug mode (used by its in-circuit debugger) to help us develop QwikBug. Josh Conner and (outside consultant) Frank Testa aided in our acquisition and understanding of the math routines. Brett Duane helped me understand some of the issues that arose in my early experimentation with the microcontroller. Steve Sanghi and Eric Sells provided valuable material and insights for Chapter 1.

Digi-Key has helped to expedite the ordering of all the parts for stuffing the QwikFlash board. They identified parts available from Digi-Key that I had overlooked, making possible one single-source order. They set up the single identifying kit number, 18F452-KIT, that acts as an alias for the one-by-one enumeration of each part listed in Figure A1-1. Simplicity and accuracy in placing the order as well as significantly reduced parts cost are the result.

I am grateful to Bill Kaduck and Dave Cornish of MICRODESIGNS, Inc. for making a low-cost, built-up QwikFlash board available to readers of this book via their Web site, **www.microdesignsinc.com**. See Appendix section A1.1. Doug Armstrong of AppForge has been involved with cutting-edge design work for years and has generously helped with applications for my instructional laboratory. Leland Strange of Intelligent Systems Corp. has long been a source of insight and counsel. Skip Addison's photography gives the clarity of a visual perspective throughout this book.

At Prentice Hall I have been fortunate to have had two fine editors, first Eric Frank and presently Tom Robbins. When we first discussed how the QwikFlash board might be included with the book, Eric even pursued his creative idea of die-cutting the front cover to hold the board in a transparent pocket. I am grateful to Tom Robbins for including the board with the first printing of the book, on the basis that readers would not have to bear the cost of the board in the cost of the book. With that as a given, I am grateful to Jim Carreker for his support in paying for these first-printing PC boards. As a spellbindingly energetic undergraduate, he was responsible for a major redirection in my professional life. It is a delight to me that he has once again been able to impact my life in this way.

Also, at Prentice Hall I have been fortunate to work with Lynda Castillo and David George on the production of this book. Cindy Miller of Clarinda Publications has done a fine and careful job as production editor for the book. Laserwords of Chennai, India holds my gratitude for their accurate and expeditious rendering of all my pencil-drawn figures. This is my first experience with artwork corrections being expedited by the instantaneous transfer of pdf files, and I could not be more satisfied.

Finally, on the publication of this, my sixth textbook, I am again grateful to my wife, Marilyn, for a partnership that has been in place for each book. We pace each other, with Marilyn graciously clarifying my stilted sentences as she enters handwritten text into her word processor. Throughout my career I have been fortunate that we both enjoy this form of working together.

John B. Peatman
Georgia Institute of Technology

Chapter

1

INTRODUCTION

1.1 A REVOLUTION IN INFORMATION PROCESSING[1]

The embedded information processing revolution is happening all around us. Electronics intelligence is hidden inside the products we use in our daily lives. As the cost of the integrated circuits that provide this intelligence has dropped over the years, the number of manufacturers using these devices—and their diverse applications—has exploded.

Competitive pressures require manufacturers to expand product functionality and provide differentiation while maintaining or reducing cost. To address these requirements, manufacturers use integrated circuit-based embedded control systems that provide an integrated solution for application-specific control requirements. Embedded control systems enable manufacturers to differentiate their product, replace less efficient electromechanical control devices, add product functionality, and significantly reduce product costs. In addition, embedded control systems facilitate the emergence of complete new classes of products. Embedded control systems typically incorporate microcontrollers for the principle activity, and sometimes are the sole component.

A microcontroller is a self-contained computer-on-a-chip consisting of a central processing unit, nonvolatile program memory, random access memory for data storage, and various input-output capabilities. In addition to the microcontroller, a complete embedded control system incorporates application-specific software and may include specialized peripheral device controllers and external, nonvolatile memory components, such as EEPROMs to store additional program software.

[1]This section was written by Steve Sanghi, CEO and President of Microchip Technology Inc., Chandler, Arizona.

Embedded control solutions have been incorporated into thousands of products and subassemblies in a wide variety of markets worldwide. Some of these applications include

- Automotive air bag systems
- Remote control devices
- Handheld tools
- Appliances
- Portable computers
- Cordless and cellular telephones
- Motor controls
- Security systems

The increasing demand for embedded control has made the market for microcontrollers one of the largest segments of the semiconductor market. Microcontrollers are currently available in 4-bit through 32-bit architectures. Although 4-bit microcontrollers are relatively inexpensive, typically costing under $1.00 each, they generally lack the minimum performance and features required by today's design engineers for product differentiation and are typically used only to produce basic functionality in products. Although 16-bit and 32-bit architectures provide very high performance, they can be expensive for most high-volume embedded control applications, typically costing $6.00 to $12.00 each. As a result, manufacturers of competitive, high-volume products have increasingly found 8-bit microcontrollers, which typically cost $1.00 to $8.00 each, to be the most cost-effective embedded control solution.

For example, a typical new automobile may include one 32-bit microcontroller for engine control; three 16-bit microcontrollers for transmission control, audio systems, and antilock braking; and up to fifty 8-bit microcontrollers to provide other embedded control functions, such as door locking, automatic windows, sun roof, adjustable seats, electric mirrors, air bags, fuel pump, speedometer, and the security and climate control systems.

The uses for 8-bit microcontrollers are multiplying, targeting many high-volume, low-cost applications and limited only by the imagination. Because 8-bit microcontrollers are so ubiquitous, successful engineers need to comprehend the many complexities of designing with these devices.

Microchip Technology Inc. designed the PIC18F452 to help embedded control engineers explore the many benefits of differentiating their end-product design by incorporating a very flexible, easy-to-use, flash-based microcontroller. The PIC18F452 is loaded with peripherals and comes with a comprehensive suite of development tools. This book will help readers learn the PIC18FXXX architecture rapidly and use the PIC18F452 device to differentiate products and enhance their end-market appeal.

1.2 THE LEARNING CURVE

A manufacturing principle that Microchip Technology handles adroitly is its use of learning curve economies. This principle states that each doubling of the quantity of parts produced results in a fixed percentage decrease in the unit cost of a part. Coupled with passing along the reduced costs to customers, these economies are used by a company to gain market share. In Microchip Technology's case, it shows up as what might otherwise seem to be an unusual pricing of parts. A new part such as the PIC18F452 microcontroller, for all of its new and attractive features, does not carry an elevated price relative to older PIC® microcontroller parts. Instead, it carries a price that reflects its manufacturing cost and follows a pricing regimen reflecting the reduction in that manufacturing cost as quantities increase. The result is illustrated in Figure 1-1, which shows Microchip's gain in market share in the world of 8-bit microcontrollers relative to other manufacturers. This is a world that has been dominated for years

1990 Rank	1993 Rank	1996 Rank	2000 Rank
Motorola	Motorola	Motorola	Motorola
Mitsubishi	Mitsubishi	Mitsubishi	Microchip
NEC	NEC	SGS-Thomson	NEC
Intel	Hitachi	NEC	Hitachi
Hitachi	Philips	Microchip	ST-Micro
Philips	Intel	Philips	Infineon
Matsushita	SGS	Zilog	Mitsubishi
National	Microchip	Hitachi	Philips
Siemens	Matsushita	Fujitsu	Toshiba
TI	Toshiba	Intel	Atmel
Sharp	National	Siemens	Zilog
Oki	Zilog	Toshiba	Fujitsu
Toshiba	TI	Matsushita	Matsushita
SGS-Thomson	Siemens	TI	Realtek
Zilog	Sharp	National	Samsung
Matra MHS	Oki	Temic	National
Sony	Sony	Sanyo	Sanyo
Fujitsu	Sanyo	Ricoh	Elan
AMD	Fujitsu	Oki	TI
Microchip	AMD	Sharp	Sony

Figure 1-1 Worldwide market share for producers of 8-bit microcontrollers, sorted by units shipped (Dataquest).

by Motorola. As shown in Figure 1-2, Microchip's market share has grown significantly relative to Motorola's, supporting Microchip's stated goal of becoming the number-one supplier of 8-bit microcontrollers in the world. And while the technical press regularly touts the features of new 16-bit and 32-bit microcontrollers, in fact the world of microcontrollers is dominated by 8-bit microcontrollers such as the PIC18F452 discussed in this book, as illustrated in Figure 1-3.

What this means for readers of this book is that their learning is focused on a family of parts that finds wide industrial use and is price competitive. Furthermore, the emphasis on Microchip's latest microcontroller architecture is well placed, given Microchip's propensity to gain market share with competitively priced new parts.

1.3 FLASH MEMORY TECHNOLOGY

The flash program memory in the PIC18F452 microcontroller permits the microcontroller to be programmed, erased, and programmed again repeatedly. In contrast to its windowed EPROM counterpart, the PIC18C452 microcontroller, it does not need a special programmer and an ultraviolet eraser to

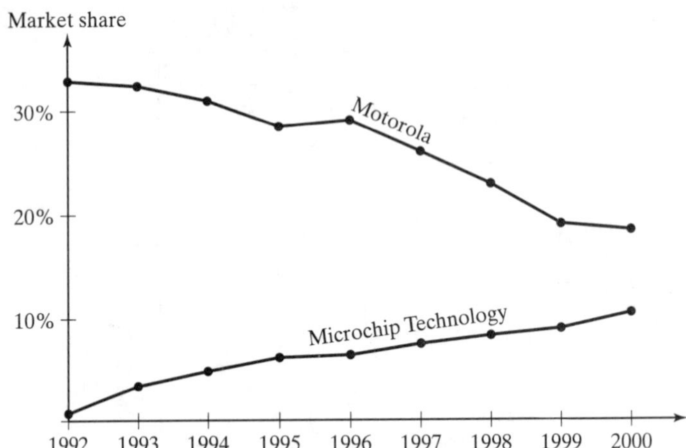

Figure 1-2 Market share of total number of 8-bit microcontrollers shipped per year (Dataquest).

achieve this reprogramming capability. The cost of its plastic package also contrasts favorably with the expensive ceramic package plus quartz window of the windowed PIC18C452 microcontroller. Some observers predict a major migration in microcontroller program memory technology to flash program memory. This migration is certainly happening for reprogrammable parts. For OTP (one-time programmable) parts made with an EPROM part in a windowless plastic package, such a migration would seem to depend on the equalization of the die sizes for the two technologies as well as on learning curve considerations.

The flash memory technology of the PIC18F452 microcontroller also has a profound effect on the cost of the development tools required in the implementation of an application. The "low-cost" approach

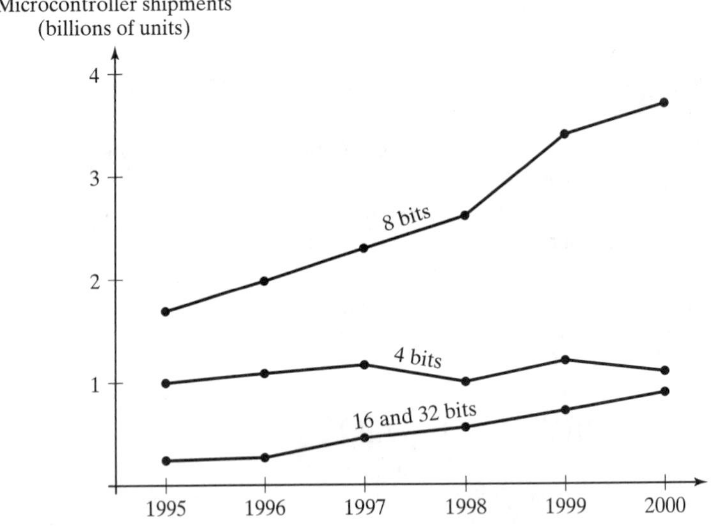

Figure 1-3 Microcontroller unit shipments per year, as distinguished by data word length (Dataquest).

to code development with a windowed EPROM part calls for a programmer and an ultraviolet eraser. It also inserts into the program-test-erase-reprogram-test code development cycle the need to shuffle among several parts to deal efficiently with an erase time of several minutes. In contrast, as will be seen in this book, a flash part can be reprogrammed in seconds in its target system environment with a low-cost "in-circuit debugger" that interacts with the microcontroller via three of its pins plus power and ground. Alternatively, it can be reprogrammed in seconds in its target system environment with the zero-cost *QwikBug* monitor program discussed in this book. This program, resident in the chip, uses the on-chip UART to establish communications with a PC.

1.4 MICROCONTROLLER FEATURE SET

The PIC18F452 microcontroller is actually one of a family of parts distinguished from each other on the basis of

- The number of pins available for inputs and outputs
- The amount of memory available for programs and for variables

The part distinctions are listed in Figure 1-4. The package alternatives are shown in Figure 1-5. Because of the package alternatives available to this family of parts, it is interesting to note that in spite of its 40 or 44 pins, the PIC18F452 microcontroller has both the largest and the smallest footprint, compared with the 28-pin parts.

A block diagram of the PIC18F452 (and the PIC18F442) is shown in Figure 1-6. The use of the various features of this chip forms the heart of this book. For now, it is enough to understand that this chip has a rich feature set, permitting it to meet a wide range of applications.

A block diagram of the 28-pin PIC18F252 (and the PIC18F242) is shown in Figure 1-7. It is identical to the block diagram of the PIC18F452 except for the absence of PORTD and PORTE and the resources attached to the pins of these two ports.

Features of this PIC18FXXX family of microcontroller parts that designers find attractive are

- *Speed:* With its maximum internal clock rate of 10 MHz and its 16-bit-wide instruction bus, the CPU can execute most of its instructions in 0.1 μs, or ten instructions per microsecond.
- *Flexible timer resources:* Four independent timers plus two capture/compare/pulse-width-modulation modules support timing measurements and output interval control with a timing resolution as fine as 0.1 μs.
- *Interrupt control:* Seventeen independent interrupt sources control when the CPU deals with each source.

Part Number	Program Memory (16-bit words)	RAM Bytes	Total Pins	I/O Pins	Package size—length × width, including pins				
					40-pin DIP	44-pin PLCC	44-pin TQFP	28-pin DIP	28-pin SOIC
PIC18F452	16384	1536	40/44	33	2.058″ × 0.600″	0.690″ × 0.690″	0.472″ × 0.472″		
PIC18F442	8192	768	40/44	33	2.058″ × 0.600″	0.690″ × 0.690″	0.472″ × 0.472″		
PIC18F252	16384	1536	28	22				1.345″ × 0.300″	0.704″ × 0.407″
PIC18F242	8192	768	28	22				1.345″ × 0.300″	0.704″ × 0.407″

Figure 1-4 Alternative family member parts.

Figure 1-5 PIC18FXXX family parts.

- *Robustness:* I/O pins can drive loads of up to 25 mA as outputs and are protected against static electricity damage as inputs.
- *Error recovery:* The built-in watchdog timer, brown-out reset circuitry, and low-voltage detect circuitry provide alternative means for detecting an actual or impending malfunction and dealing with it.
- *Support of low-power operation:* In addition to being an exceedingly power-stingy part, the PIC18F452 microcontroller can greatly extend battery life by alternating intervals of low-power sleep mode with intervals of normal operation. The watchdog timer can be used to produce a low duty cycle and, thereby, a low average power dissipation (Section 20.7).
- *I/O expansion:* The built-in serial peripheral interface (Chapter 15) can make use of standard 16-pin shift-register parts to add any number of I/O pins. The built-in I^2C interface (Chapter 17) supports the addition of specialty peripheral parts.
- *Math support:* Microchip supports the PIC18F452 microcontroller with a variety of multiplication and division subroutines for multiple-byte, fixed-point numbers and for floating-point numbers (Chapter 14).
- *Mail-order support:* Digi-Key Corporation (www.digikey.com) and Newark Electronics (www.newark.com) provide both on-line and telephone purchasing of PIC18FXXX microcontroller parts as well as development tools.
- *Free software tools:* To encourage new users and to support upgrades to veteran users, Microchip makes its MPLAB® Integrated Development Package (consisting of assembler, simulator, and user interface) as well as all manuals and application notes available at no cost from their Web site (www.microchip.com).
- *Development tool versatility:* The PIC18F452 microcontroller's flash program memory supports not only a standard emulator that includes the ability to capture trace information, it also supports a low-cost in-circuit debugger and a zero-cost *QwikBug* monitor program. Each of these permits the loading and execution of a user program as well as the use of breakpoints, memory/register modification, and single stepping (Section 4.4).

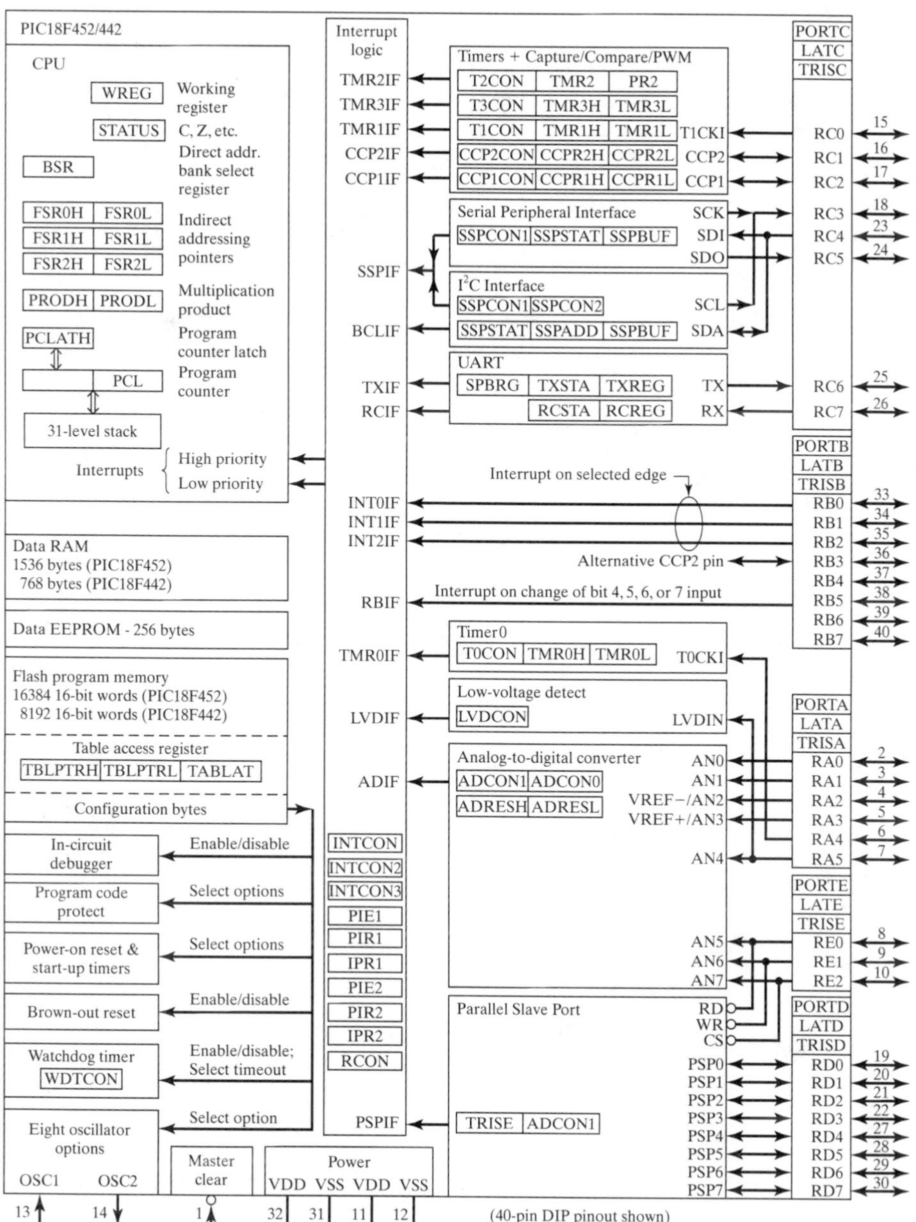

Figure 1-6 PIC18F452/442 block diagram.

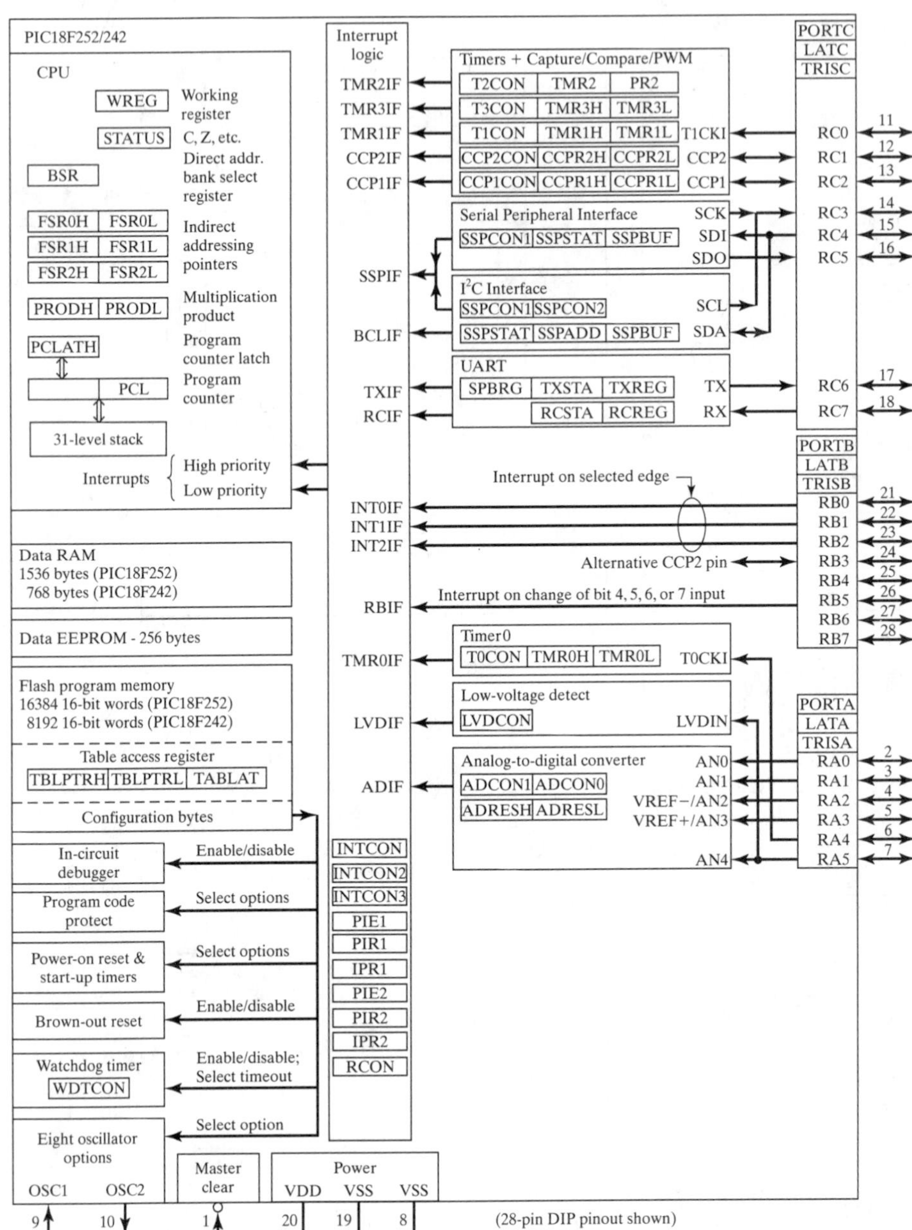

Figure 1-7 PIC18F252/242 block diagram.

Chapter 2

CPU ARCHITECTURE

2.1 OVERVIEW

This chapter begins with a look at the *Harvard architecture* of the PIC18F452 microcontroller, which allows extraordinary execution speed via separate buses for program memory and for operand memory. Next, the alternative means for accessing operands will be examined. Program memory will be considered in light of the several ways in which program instruction sequencing can be controlled. Finally, these considerations will be combined into a programmer's view of the CPU (central processing unit) registers.

2.2 HARVARD ARCHITECTURE

The PIC18F452 microcontroller employs the two buses shown in Figure 2-1. The program memory bus employs a 16-bit-wide path for fetching instructions. Because all but 5 of the 75 instructions are contained in a single 16-bit instruction word, most instructions require just one fetch from program memory to complete an instruction fetch. The 5 two-word instructions (e.g., the subroutine *call* instruction with an address field large enough to reach any program memory address) require two fetches from program memory to complete an instruction fetch. Except for these 5 instructions, a new instruction is fetched during each cycle of the internal clock. With its maximum internal clock rate of 10 MHz, the PIC18F452 executes close to ten million instructions every second.

Having these two separate buses and a *pipelined* architecture, the CPU fetches a new instruction even as it executes the previously fetched instruction. This is illustrated in Figure 2-2a. In the case of any two-word instruction that requires two cycles for the instruction fetch, such an instruction executes in two

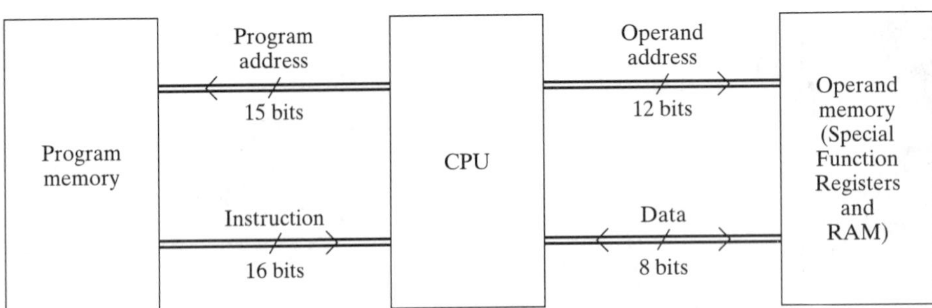

Figure 2-1 Harvard architecture.

cycles, as shown in Figure 2-2b. Finally, any instruction that changes the program counter also flushes the pipeline and executes in two cycles. This is shown in Figure 2-2c.

2.3 DIRECT ADDRESSING

The PIC18F452 employs any of three methods for addressing an operand:

1. Literal addressing
2. Direct addressing
3. Indirect addressing

An instruction that uses literal addressing contains the operand value in the instruction itself. For example, the instruction

```
movlw 5
```

will move the literal value, 5, into the CPU's working register, **WREG**. After the execution of this instruction, **WREG** will contain the number 5.

To understand how *direct* addressing works, first consider the operand memory map, shown in Figure 2-3. Each instruction that makes use of direct addressing uses 8 bits of its 16-bit instruction word to specify any one of 256 locations as the address of the operand. A 9th bit of the instruction word selects either the *Access Bank* of Figure 2-3a or one of the banks shown in Figure 2-3b. For any, the instruction that accesses any variable assigned to an address in the range 0x000 to 0x07f, the assembler will assign Access Bank direct addressing to that instruction. For any instruction that accesses any variable assigned to an address of 0x080 or higher, the assembler will assign Banked direct addressing to that instruction. In this case, it is the code writer's responsibility to ensure that the **BSR** register is correctly set before that instruction is executed.

Because of this handling of addresses, the **BSR** register can be left at its power-on default value of 0x00 and code can be written to deal with up to 256 RAM variables assigned to addresses extending from 0x000 up to 0x0ff. Direct addressing will reach every one without changing the **BSR** register. Any instruction that accesses a variable in the range of 0x000 up to 0x07f will be assigned Access Bank direct addressing for that instruction, while any instruction accessing a variable in the range of 0x080 up to 0xff will be assigned Banked direct addressing.

This idea can be extended one step further for more than 256 variables but less than 128 + 256 = 384 variables. Up to 128 variables can be assigned to the addresses between 0x000 and 0x07f, while up

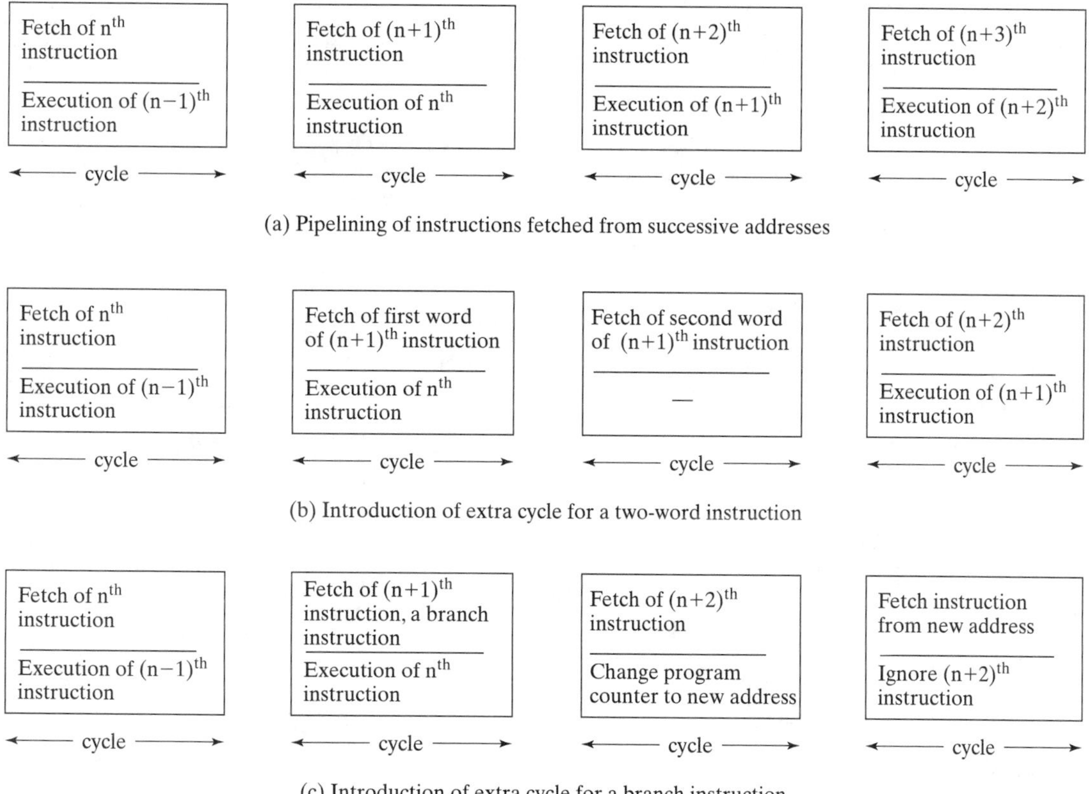

Figure 2-2 Instruction pipelining.

to 256 variables are assigned to the Bank 1 addresses extending from 0x100 to 0x1ff. Once the **BSR** register is initialized to 0x01, direct addressing will correctly access every variable. The assembler will assign the correct direct addressing mode to every instruction automatically.

Every one of the Special Function Registers (e.g., every I/O port, every timer register, and the status, control, and data registers associated with the chip's UART) is assigned an Access Bank address by the assembler, as shown in Figure 2-3a. In this manner, the Microchip designers have eliminated the tedious bank switching needed to reach Special Function Registers (SFRs) in earlier-generation parts.

2.4 INDIRECT ADDRESSING

Some data types are best accessed by means of a variable pointer. For example, whereas the PIC18F452 operates on numbers a byte at a time, larger numbers can often be most easily operated on within a loop of instructions. Figure 2-4a illustrates two 3-byte binary numbers, **NUM1** and **NUM2**, which are to be added together. The PIC18F452 instruction set expedites such operations. One instruction can load one of the three 12-bit pointers, say **FSR0**, with the address of the low byte of one of the numbers:

```
lfsr  0,NUM1
```

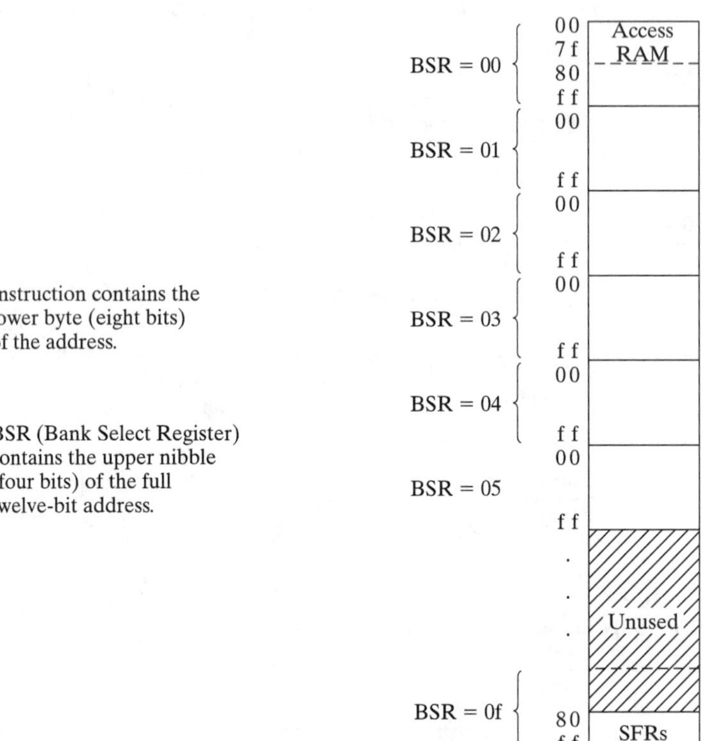

Figure 2-3 Direct addressing options for accessing the operand memory space.

A second instruction can do the same with **FSR1**:

```
lfsr  1,NUM2
```

A RAM variable, **COUNT**, can be initialized to 3:

```
movlw  3
movwf  COUNT
```

The carry bit can be cleared:

```
bcf  STATUS,C
```

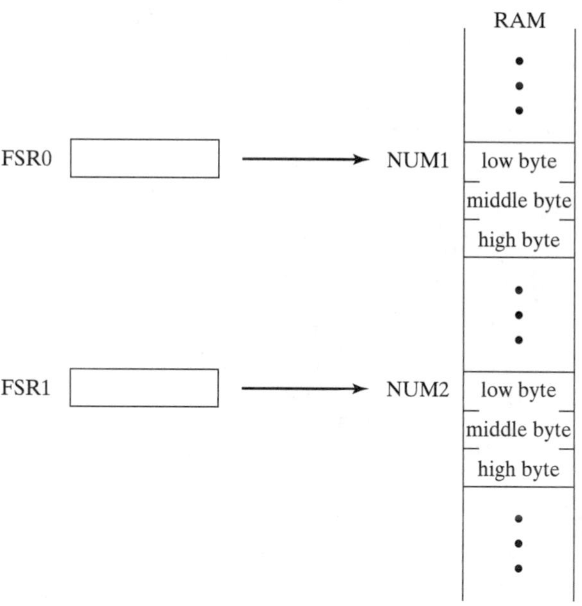

(a) Use of pointers to help form NUM1 ← NUM1 + NUM2

```
        lfsr  Ø,NUM1          ;Load FSRØ with address of NUM1
        lfsr  1,NUM2          ;Load FSR1 with address of NUM2
        movlw  3              ;Set COUNT = 3
        movwf  COUNT
        bcf  STATUS,C         ;Clear carry bit
Again
        movf  POSTINC1,W      ;Copy byte of NUM2 to WREG, then increment pointer
        addwfc  POSTINCØ,F    ;Byte of NUM1 = byte of NUM1 + byte of NUM2 + carry
        decfsz  COUNT,f       ;Decrement loop counter (without changing carry bit)
        bra  Again            ;Repeat if COUNT does not equal zero
```

(b) Assembly code implementation

Figure 2-4 Indirect addressing application.

The byte of **NUM2** pointed to by **FSR1** can be loaded into **WREG**, the "working register," and **FSR1** automatically incremented:

```
movf  POSTINC1,W
```

The byte in **WREG**, the byte pointed to by **FSR0**, and the carry bit can be added together and the sum returned to the location pointed to by **FSR0** and then **FSR0** can be incremented:

```
addwfc  POSTINCØ,F
```

Finally, this process can be repeated two more times:

```
decfsz  COUNT,F
bra  Again
```

These two instructions decrement **COUNT** (without changing the carry bit) and repeat the loop of instructions until **COUNT** has been decremented to zero. The addition is repeated on the middle two

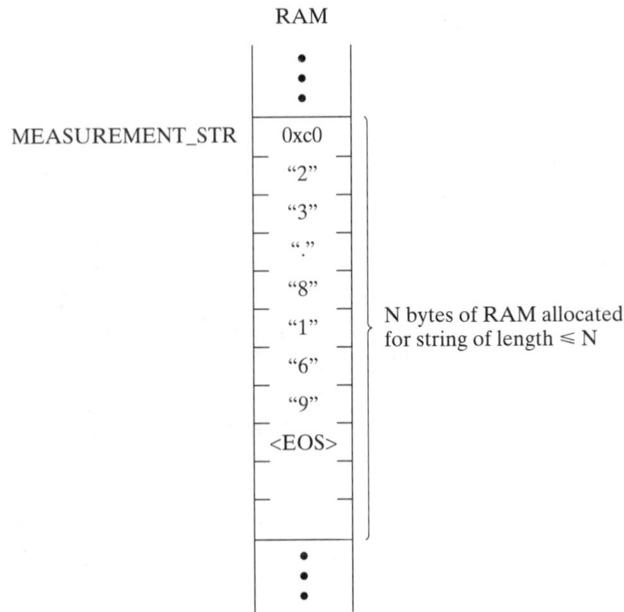

(a) A "display string", used to display a variable on an LCD

```
        lfsr  0,MEASUREMENT_STR  ;Load FSR0, with address of string
        movf  INDF0,W            ;Copy first string character to WREG
Again
        call  LCD                ;Write WREG out to the display
        movf  PREINC0,W          ;Increment FSR0, then get next string character
        bnz   Again              ;Repeat until End-of-String character (0x00) is reached
```

(b) Assembly code to update display

Figure 2-5 Another indirect addressing application.

bytes and then the high bytes, adding in the carry between bytes. The entire sequence is shown in Figure 2-4b. In Chapter 3, the operation of these instructions will be clarified. They are used here only to illustrate the power of indirect addressing together with a loop of instructions to extend the instruction set to handle multiple-byte numbers.

Another common application of indirect addressing occurs when dealing with a *string* variable. This is illustrated in Figure 2-5a, where a string consisting of ASCII-coded characters is stored beginning at the RAM address labeled **MEASUREMENT_STR**. This might be a variable "display string" representing the result of a measurement made by the microcontroller to be displayed on a liquid-crystal display (LCD). The 0xc0 in the first byte of the string might indicate at which character position on the LCD the string should begin. The subsequent bytes hold the ASCII codes for the digits and decimal point shown. The end-of-string designator, <EOS>, is coded as the number zero. This distinguishes <EOS> from the ASCII code for displayable characters. The code in Figure 2-5b uses an LCD subroutine to send each ASCII-coded character to the LCD.

The operand memory space of Figure 2-3 is shown again in Figure 2-6. Now the addresses are recast into the 12-bit addresses employed by indirect addressing, extending from 0x000 to 0xfff. Operands

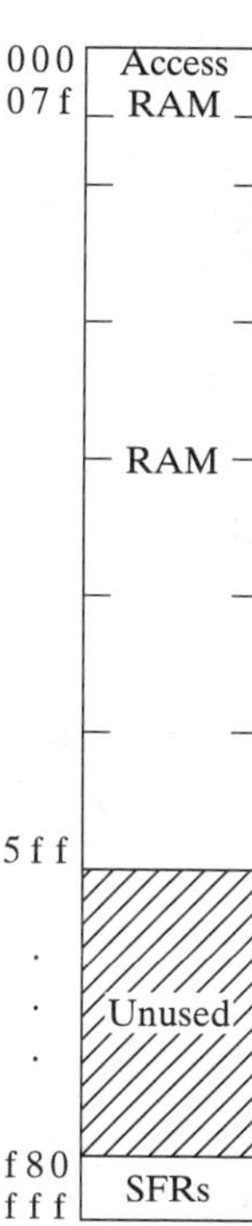

Figure 2-6 Indirect addressing of operand space.

are accessed via one of the three pointers—**FSR0**, **FSR1**, or **FSR2**—shown in Figure 2-7. Each pointer contains the full 12-bit address needed to reach from the lowest address in RAM (0x000) up to the highest address in the Special Function Registers (0xfff).

When accessing an operand via indirect addressing, the CPU starts with the address in the **FSRi** register (where **i** = 0, 1, or 2). If the operand name is either **INDFi**, **POSTDECi**, or **POSTINCi** (where **i** = 0, 1, or 2), then the CPU accesses the location pointed to by **FSRi**. For **INDFi**, **FSRi** is left unchanged. For **POSTDECi**, the pointer is decremented after the instruction has been executed, and for **POSTINCi**, the pointer is incremented after execution. If the operand name is **PREINCi**, the pointer is *first* incremented and then used as the address of the actual operand.

The **PLUSWi** operand name temporarily adds **WREG** (treated as a signed number) to the address in **FSRi** to form the address of the operand to be used by the instruction. On completion of the instruction execution, the address in **FSRi** is the same value as it was prior to the addition of **WREG**.

Because of the auto-increment and auto-decrement options associated with indirect addressing, not only can any address in operand memory be reached via a 12-bit pointer but also the automatic increment or decrement of the pointer ensures that the full 12-bit number is handled correctly. For example, if **FSR0** contains 0x3ff, the auto-increment will correctly produce 0x400. In contrast, using the PIC® microcontroller's instructions to increment **FSR0** via direct addressing leads to the following two-instruction sequence:

```
infsnz  FSR0L,F            ;Increment lower byte, skip if not zero
incf  FSR0H,F              ;Increment upper byte
```

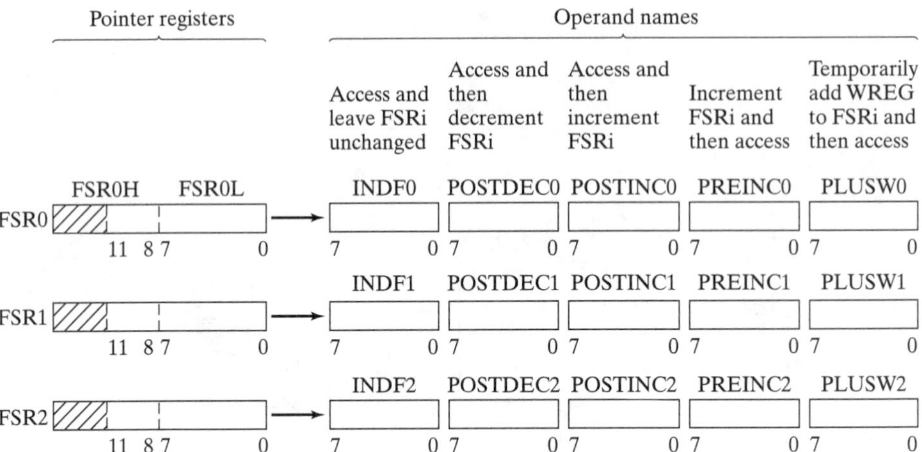

Figure 2-7 Indirect addressing registers and operand names.

Decrementing one of the pointers via direct addressing is somewhat more roundabout.

```
          movf  FSRØL,F          ;Set Z = 1 if lower byte = Ø
          bnz  Skip              ;If so, decrement upper byte
          decf  FSRØH,F
Skip
          decf  FSRØL,F          ;In either case, decrement lower byte
```

These are the sequences that auto-incrementing and auto-decrementing bypass.

2.5 READING OPERANDS FROM PROGRAM MEMORY

Because of its Harvard architecture, a PIC18F452 microcontroller needs a special mechanism for program instructions to read operands from program memory. This relationship between the Harvard architecture and the special mechanism is illustrated in Figure 2-8a. Because the instructions access the operand memory shown to the right of the CPU in that figure, the special mechanism uses a 16-bit address register called **TBLPTR** (i.e., TaBLe PoinTeR) that can be written to, thereby selecting the program address to read. Execution of any of the four instructions shown in Figure 2-8b will invoke the special mechanism to read from the selected program memory address and put its contents into **TABLAT** (i.e., TABle LATch).

To take full advantage of this mechanism, the designers of the chip have addressed program memory in 8-bit bytes, not 16-bit words. This is illustrated in Figure 2-9a. Each instruction occupies two of these bytes, beginning at an even address. In the case of a 2-byte instruction, 4 bytes are occupied, again beginning at an even address. The program counter increments from even address to even address as successive instructions are fetched 16 bits at a time. The mechanisms for storing tables and strings in program memory are designed to ensure that an even number of bytes will be assigned to the table or string, perhaps filling in a final byte with 0x00 to ensure that an even number of bytes will be used. Any program instructions that follow such a table or string in program memory will be assured of beginning at an even address. Figure 2-9b illustrates how the assembler might expect a table of hexadecimal numbers to be entered in an assembly language program. In this table, each of the 4-byte entries is the floating-point representation of a power of 10, starting with the representation of 1,000,000 and ending with the representation of 1. Figure 2-9c illustrates a constant "display string" that can be used to write the message

```
FREQ  Hz
```

to a liquid-crystal display. The quotes tell the assembler to translate each character into its ASCII code. The four-character sequence \x80 within the quotes tells the assembler to treat the hexadecimal number 80 as 1 byte in the string. This initial byte in the string might specify the location on the LCD where the string should begin. The \x00 is the end-of-string designator. The assembly language code of Figure 2-10 illustrates how the constant string of Figure 2-9c, located in program memory, might be sent to the LCD, in a manner analogous to the code of Figure 2-5b for a variable string.

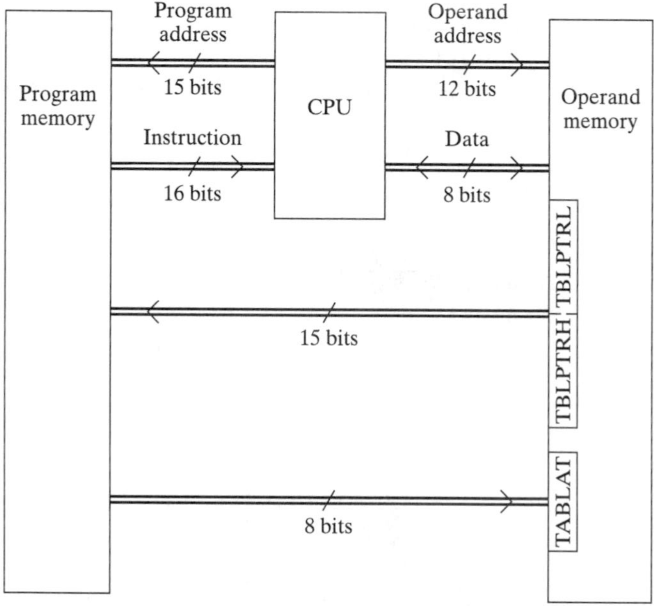

(a) Special mechanism for reading from program memory

```
tblrd*     Read from program memory location pointed to by TBLPTR into TABLAT

tblrd*+    Read from program memory location pointed to by TBLPTR into TABLAT,
           then increment TBLPTR

tblrd*-    Read from program memory location pointed to by TBLPTR into TABLAT,
           then decrement TBLPTR

tblrd+*    Increment TBLPTR, then read from program memory location pointed to
           by TBLPTR into TABLAT
```

(b) Special instructions for reading from program memory

Figure 2-8 Reading operands from program memory.

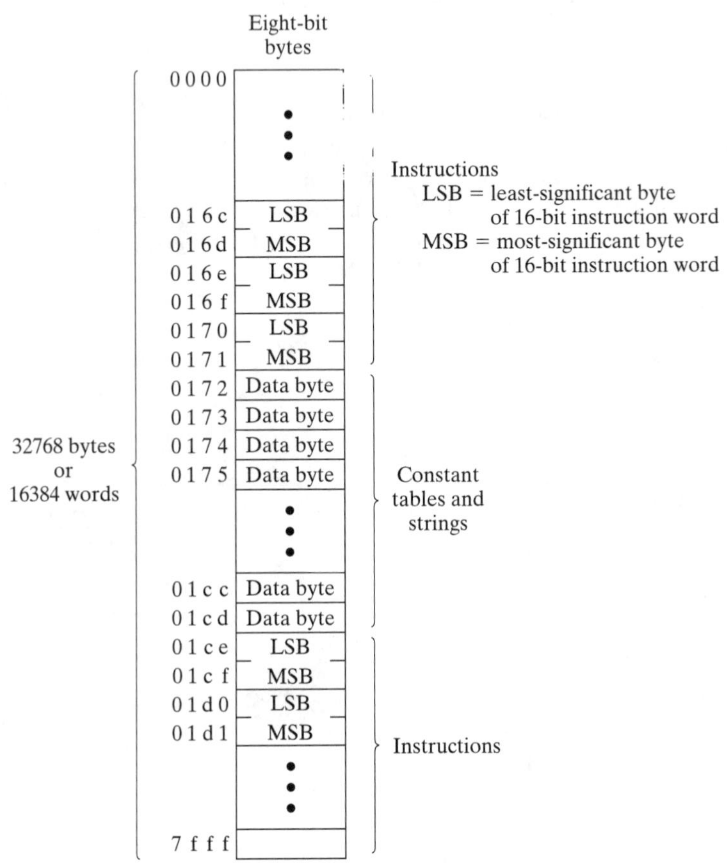

(a) Byte addressing

```
PowTen  db      0x92, 0x74, 0x24, 0x00      ;Floating point representation of 1000000
        db      0x8f, 0x43, 0x50, 0x00      ;100000
        db      0x8c, 0x1c, 0x40, 0x00      ;10000
        db      0x88, 0x7a, 0x00, 0x00      ;1000
        db      0x85, 0x48, 0x00, 0x00      ;100
        db      0x82, 0x20, 0x00, 0x00      ;10
        db      0x7f, 0x00, 0x00, 0x00      ;1
```

(b) Assembly code entry of a table

```
Freq_Hz db      "\x80FREQ  Hz\x00"
```

(c) Assembly code entry of a constant string

Figure 2-9 Byte addressing of program memory.

```
           movlw  high Freq_Hz     ;Get high byte of string address
           movwf  TBLPTRH          ; and load it into high byte of TBLPTR
           movlw  low Freq_Hz      ;Get low byte of string address
           movwf  TBLPTRL          ; and load it into low byte of TBLPTR
           tblrd*                  ;Read into TABLAT
           movf  TABLAT.W          ; and from there to WREG
   Again
           call  LCD               ;Sent WREG to display
           tblrd+*                 ;Increment TBLPTR and then read byte from string
           movf  TABLAT.W          ; and into WREG
           bnz  Again              ;If not zero, then repeat
```

Figure 2-10 Assembly code to display a constant string.

2.6 PROGRAM INSTRUCTION SEQUENCING

The PIC18F452 has three special program addresses:

- Address 0x0000, the reset vector
- Address 0x0008, the high-priority interrupt vector
- Address 0x0018, the low-priority interrupt vector

The chip incorporates a variety of mechanisms for resetting itself. It will reset itself when power is first applied to it or when its $\overline{\text{MCLR}}$ (i.e., its active-low master clear) pin is driven low, perhaps when a user presses a "reset" pushbutton. An optionally enabled watchdog timer will reset the chip if the CPU goes awry and stops executing its program correctly. An optionally enabled brownout reset will reset the chip if the supply voltage drops below some specified level (e.g., 4.5 V). A stack overflow or underflow also can cause a reset of the chip. In all of these cases, the program counter will be cleared to zero so that the first instruction fetch will occur from address 0x0000.

The PIC18F452 has 17 separate interrupt sources, each of which can be assigned to be either a high-priority interrupt source, a low-priority interrupt source, or disabled (which is the reset state). This interrupt capability gives the chip the ability to respond to the demands of one of its resources within microseconds. A strategy for assigning priority is to assign low priority to *all* interrupts. If the timing requirements of one of the interrupt sources cannot be met in this way, the interrupt source can be raised to high-priority. It will then have the benefit of obtaining immediate service, even if it means suspending, momentarily, the execution of the interrupt service routine for the low-priority sources.

When an interrupt occurs, several things happen automatically:

- The program counter contents are set aside on the stack.
- Further low-priority interrupts are disabled.
- If it is a high-priority interrupt that has occurred, further high-priority interrupts are also disabled.
- The contents of several key registers are copied into *shadow* registers, from which they can later be restored.
- The program counter will be set to 0x0018 in the case of a low-priority interrupt or 0x0008 in the case of a high-priority interrupt.

Because of these automatic operations, the assembly code for a program might begin with

```
          org  0x0000
          goto  Mainline
          org  0x0008
          goto  HiPriISR
          org  0x0018
          goto  LoPriISR
Mainline
          .
          .
          .
```

As the CPU fetches one instruction, it automatically increments its program counter so it will be ready to fetch the next instruction from the next address. This lockstep sequencing of instructions can be disrupted by a **goto** instruction or a **bra** instruction, either of which changes the contents of the program counter. The two-word **goto** instruction contains the complete address of the destination, so it can reach to any location in program memory. The one-word **bra** instruction adds an 8-bit signed value to the program counter, so it can reach anywhere within the ±128 addresses surrounding the present contents of the program counter. This is sufficient for all branches within all subroutines. (If a subroutine is so large that this is no longer true, it should probably be broken into a hierarchy of smaller subroutines. This hierarchy helps provide the clarity that eliminates obscure bugs in the code.)

Subroutine calls and returns provide another mechanism for disrupting the lockstep progression of instruction sequencing. Again, there are two versions of subroutine calls. The two-word

```
call   <subroutine name>
```

instruction pushes a return address (i.e., the address of the next instruction in line) onto the stack and then loads the program counter with the complete address of the subroutine. The one-word

```
rcall   <subroutine name>
```

also pushes the return address onto the stack and then adds an 11-bit signed value to the program counter, reaching up to ±1024 addresses (or ±512 one-word instructions) away from the present address. It is not always clear when the one-word **rcall** instruction will reach the desired subroutine. If it is always assumed that the **rcall** instruction will work, the assembler will flag the few cases where it does not. These can then be changed to **call** instructions.

The **return** instruction at the end of a subroutine pops the full return address from the stack back into the program counter. Because both the **call** and the **rcall** instructions push the full return address onto the stack, there is never a problem of the **return** instruction being able to reach to anywhere in program memory.

The **retfie** (return from interrupt and reenable interrupts) instruction also pops a return address from the stack to the program counter. With room for up to 31 return addresses on the stack, subroutine calls can be nested with virtually no concern for overflowing the stack. That is, a subroutine can call another subroutine, which in turn calls another, and so on, with hardly a worry that this process will overflow the stack. It is only an erroneous recursive call (wherein a subroutine calls itself) that is likely to cause a problem until it has been debugged.

One further mechanism for altering the flow of program execution arises when an instruction writes to the program counter. With a 15-bit address needed to access any location in the PIC18F452's program memory and with instructions that produce 8-bit results, the CPU needs help from the hardware to change every bit of the program counter during a single 8-bit write. The mechanism supporting this is shown in Figure 2-11. At the same time that an instruction writes to **PCL** (the lower 8 bits of the program counter), the content of **PCLATH** is written to the "high" bits of the program counter (i.e., bits 15 to 8). A read of **PCL** will copy bits 15 to 8 of the program counter to **PCLATH**. To support future growth to larger program memory, the Microchip designers have implemented a 21-bit program counter. Bits 20 to 16 of this extended program

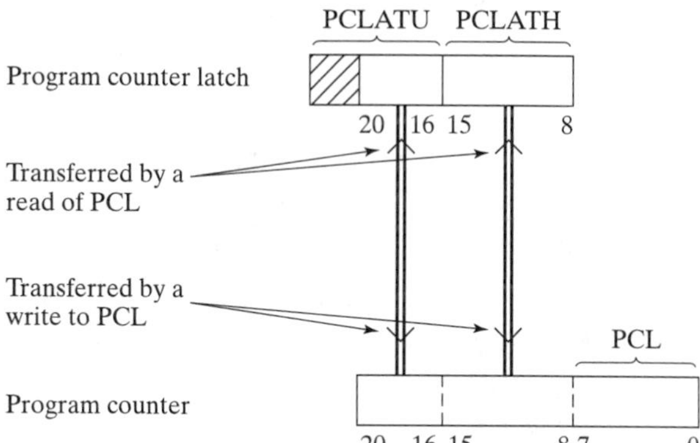

Figure 2-11 Program counter and PC latch.

counter are supported by **PCLATU,** a latch for the "upper" bits of the program counter. Because **PCLATU** (as well as **PCLATH**) is cleared to zero at reset, this extension can be ignored by PIC18F452 applications.

2.7 THE CPU AND ITS STATUS BITS

The job of the CPU is to execute the instructions of an application program. In doing this, it uses the registers shown in Figure 2-12. As will be seen in Chapter 3, the **STATUS** register contains bits that are set or cleared in response to the execution of various instructions.

C is the carry bit that is set when the addition of two 8-bit unsigned binary numbers (ranging between 0 and 255) produces an overflow (i.e., a sum greater than 255); otherwise, **C** is cleared. It is the complement of a borrow bit, being cleared when the subtraction of two 8-bit unsigned binary numbers produces a borrow. It is set when an increment instruction causes the operand to roll over from 255 to 0. The two instructions that rotate a register through the carry bit will also change the carry bit, as shown in Figure 2-13.

The **OV**, or overflow, bit responds to additions, subtractions, increments and decrements. Just as the carry bit responds to these operations on unsigned binary numbers, the overflow bit responds to these operations on twos-complement-coded signed binary numbers (ranging from −128 to +127). Thus, when an operand is incremented from +127 (B′01111111′) to −128 (B′10000000′), the **OV** bit is set.

The **Z**, or zero, bit is set when an instruction's 8-bit result is B′00000000′; otherwise, the **Z** bit is cleared. In writing code, it is important to check the instruction table of Figure 3-1to determine whether a specific instruction affects the **Z** flag *at all.* For example,

```
movwf  TEMP
```

will move the contents of **WREG** to a RAM variable called **TEMP.** However, as the table indicates, this instruction does not affect the **Z** flag. If **Z** = 0 before the execution of this instruction, then **Z** = 0 afterwards; if **Z** = 1 beforehand, then **Z** = 1 afterwards.

The rationale for which instructions affect which flags is somewhat arbitrary. In fact, the **incf** and **decf** instructions, when executed on earlier generations of PIC microcontrollers, did not affect any status bits other than the **Z** bit, whereas these two instructions affect all five status bits in the PIC18F452.

The **N**, or negative, bit echoes the sign bit resulting from an arithmetic operation on twos-complement-coded signed binary numbers. A negative number will have its most significant bit set, and the operation that produced this result will also set the **N** bit. Some nonarithmetic instructions likewise will echo the most-significant bit (MSb) of a result in the **N** bit.

The **DC**, or decimal carry, bit helps with arithmetic operations on *packed BCD* (binary-coded-decimal) numbers. With this code, a decimal digit is coded with its 4-bit binary equivalent (e.g., 5 is coded

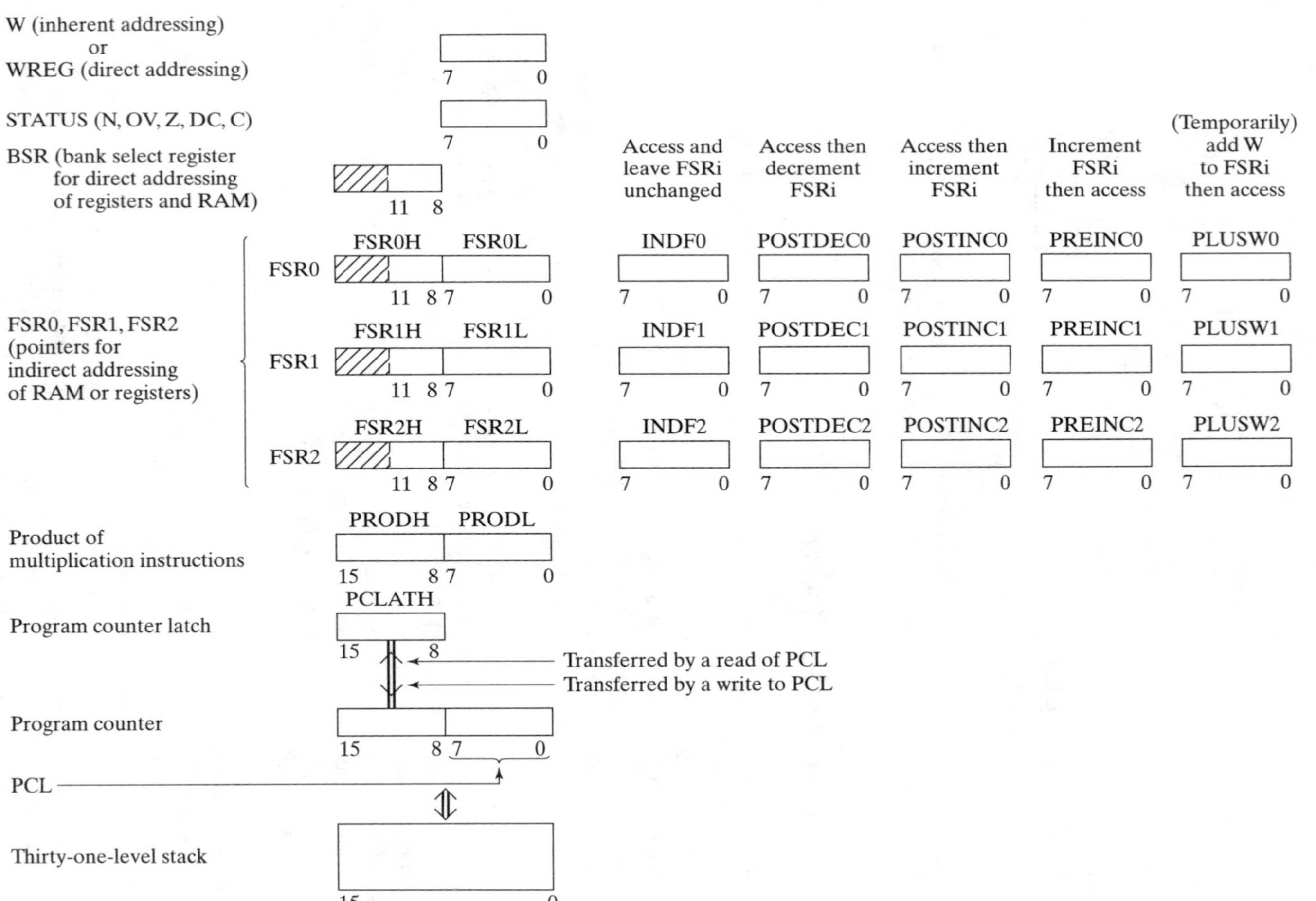

Figure 2-12 CPU registers.

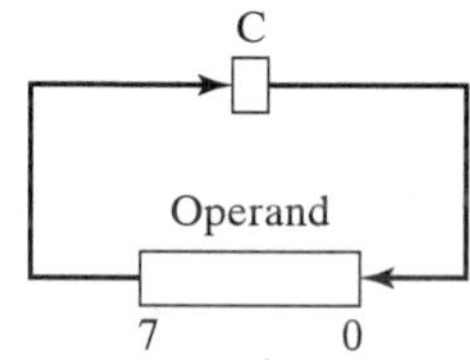

(a) rlcf, rotate left through carry, instruction

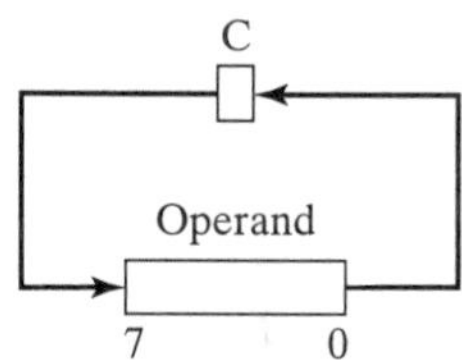

(b) rrcf, rotate right through carry, instruction

Figure 2-13 Effect of "rotate through carry" instructions upon the carry bit.

as B'0101'). Packed BCD code packs two digits in each byte of a number. When two packed BCD-encoded numbers are added together as if they were binary numbers, any carry from bit 3 to bit 4 will be echoed into the **DC** bit. The execution of a **daw** instruction will take **DC**, **C**, and the 8-bit result in **WREG** into consideration and will return the correct BCD result in **WREG** and **C**.

2.8 THE SPECIAL FUNCTION REGISTERS (SFRs)

The Special Function Registers are listed in Figure 2-14. They are located in the operand memory space between addresses 0xf80 and 0xfff. Note that all 2-byte registers are located in memory least-significant byte (LSB) first.

PROBLEMS

2-1 Pipelined instructions If each one-word instruction requires both a fetch cycle and an execute cycle, what is meant when it is said that the CPU executes a new instruction every cycle (with a few exceptions)?

2-2 Execution cycles It is clear that a two-word instruction will require one more cycle than a one-word instruction. But why does a one-word branch instruction, which changes the program counter, also require one more cycle than other one-word instructions?

2-3 Direct addressing For this problem, the bank select register, **BSR**, is initialized to 0x00 and not changed thereafter. How many RAM locations can program instructions reach with direct addressing, without changing **BSR**?

2-4 Direct addressing Repeat Problem 2-3, but with **BSR** initialized to 0x01. How many RAM locations can be reached with instructions of the form

```
clrf <variable name>
```

f8Ø	PORTA	faØ	PIE2	fcØ		feØ	BSR
f81	PORTB	fa1	PIR2	fc1	ADCON1	fe1	FSR1L
f82	PORTC	fa2	IPR2	fc2	ADCONØ	fe2	FSR1H
f83	PORTD	fa3		fc3	ADRESL	fe3	PLUSW1
f84	PORTE	fa4		fc4	ADRESH	fe4	PREINC1
f85		fa5		fc5	SSPCON2	fe5	POSTDEC1
f86		fa6		fc6	SSPCON1	fe6	POSTINC1
f87		fa7		fc7	SSPSTAT	fe7	INDF1
f88		fa8		fc8	SSPADD	fe8	WREG
f89	LATA	fa9		fc9	SSPBUF	fe9	FSRØL
f8a	LATB	faa		fca	T2CON	fea	FSRØH
f8b	LATC	fab	RCSTA	fcb	PR2	feb	PLUSWØ
f8c	LATD	fac	TXSTA	fcc	TMR2	fec	PREINCØ
f8d	LATE	fad	TXREG	fcd	T1CON	fed	POSTDECØ
f8e		fae	RCREG	fce	TMR1L	fee	POSTINCØ
f8f		faf	SPBRG	fcf	TMR1H	fef	INDFØ
f9Ø		fbØ		fdØ	RCON	ffØ	INTCON3
f91		fb1	T3CON	fd1	WDTCON	ff1	INTCON2
f92	TRISA	fb2	TMR3L	fd2	LVDCON	ff2	INTCON
f93	TRISB	fb3	TMR3H	fd3	OSCCON	ff3	PRODL
f94	TRISC	fb4		fd4		ff4	PRODH
f95	TRISD	fb5		fd5	TØCON	ff5	TABLAT
f96	TRISE	fb6		fd6	TMRØL	ff6	TBLPTRL
f97		fb7		fd7	TMRØH	ff7	TBLPTRH
f98		fb8		fd8	STATUS	ff8	TBLPTRU
f99		fb9		fd9	FSR2L	ff9	PCL
f9a		fba	CCP2CON	fda	FSR2H	ffa	PCLATH
f9b		fbb	CCPR2L	fdb	PLUSW2	ffb	PCLATU
f9c		fbc	CCPR2H	fdc	PREINC2	ffc	STKPTR
f9d	PIE1	fbd	CCP1CON	fdd	POSTDEC2	ffd	TOSL
f9e	PIR1	fbe	CCPR1L	fde	POSTINC2	ffe	TOSH
f9f	IPR1	fbf	CCPR1H	fdf	INDF2	fff	TOSU

Figure 2-14 The Special Function Registers.

2-5 Indirect addressing A queue, or first-in, first-out data structure, is a mechanism for buffering between two data transfer rates. For example, the microcontroller might receive bytes of data in response to a fast burst of interrupts. It might process these bytes, 128 at a time, every 10 milliseconds, even as more bytes are arriving. Assume that the input rate averages less than 128 bytes every 10 milliseconds, so that the queue is not overrun by input data. Consider what would be involved using the 256 bytes of RAM between 0x400 and 0x4ff as a queue. **FSR1** is to be used as an input pointer, to indicate where the next input byte is to be stored. Note that each time the lower byte of **FSR1**, called **FSR1L**, rolls over during an auto-increment, **FSR1H** must be decremented from 0x06 to 0x05. **FSR2** is to be used as an output pointer.

(a) How should the pointers be initialized?
(b) Describe what happens as each new byte is entered into the queue.
(c) Describe how bytes are read out of the queue.
(d) Describe how the CPU can tell if the queue has been emptied after each byte has been removed from the queue.

2-6 Execution cycles The one-word instructions listed in Figure 2-8b for reading from program memory require two cycles for execution. Describe what is happening to program memory during the execution of one of these instructions, why it affects the fetch of a new instruction during that cycle, and therefore why it adds an extra cycle to the instruction's execution time.

2-7 Table access Consider the PowTen table of Figure 2-9b. Assume that four bytes of the nth table entry are to be loaded into the 4-byte RAM variable located in Access RAM:

BEXP BARGB0 BARGB1 BARGB2

Assume that **WREG** contains the value of n (where $n = 0, 1, 2, 3, 4, 5$, or 6). Describe what must be done.

2-8 PCLATH Consider the instruction

```
addwf  PCL,F
```

This instruction reads **PCL** into a "hidden" register (i.e., a register inaccessible to program instructions), adds **WREG** to it, and puts the result back into **PCL**.

(a) What happens to **PCLATH** during the read of **PCL**?
(b) What happens to bits 15–8 of the program counter when the addition result is written back to **PCL**?
(c) Must **PCLATH** be initialized appropriately just before a read-modify-write instruction operating on **PCL** is executed?
(d) Must **PCLATH** be initialized appropriately just before the execution of an instruction that just writes to **PCL**?

2-9 Jump table implementation *A jump table* uses an index value to jump to one address if the index is zero, another address if the index is 1, another if 2, etc. The index value might be doubled and then added to **PCL** to change the program counter to the next address (for index = 0), two addresses beyond that (for index = 1), etc. If a sequence of **goto** instructions follows the instruction that adds into **PCL**, then the intent is to jump to a different arbitrary address for each value of the index. With the index located in **WREG**, code to implement a jump table might be

```
JmpTbl
        addwf  WREG,W            ;Double index
        addwf  PCL,F
        goto  <address if index = 0>
        goto  <address if index = 1>
        goto  <address if index = 2>
```

If this jump table is located at an arbitrary location in a program, it may not work as intended. The add instruction

```
        addwf  PCL,F
```

will read **PCL,** add **WREG** to it, and write the result back to **PCL**.

(a) Consider Figure 2-12. What will happen if the assembler just happened to assign the instruction labeled JmpTbl to (byte) addresses 0x25f6 and 0x25f7 and (for example)?

(b) Alternatively, any jump tables might be located at the beginning of the program, after

```
        org  0x0018        ;Low-priority interrupt vector
        goto  LoPriISR
```

Now the jump table is accessed with a **goto JmpTbl**. Why does this alleviate the potential problem of part (a)?

2-10 Carry bit operation Changing the carry bit in response to an **incf** instruction or a **decf** instruction is a feature absent from earlier PIC microcontrollers and not well documented in the PIC18F452 data manual.

(a) Knowing that code can be written to test the carry bit and to set or clear one pin of an output port, describe a sequence of instructions to test what happens to the carry bit when a **decf** instruction causes the operand to roll over from 0x00 to 0xff.

(b) If the carry bit is copied to the output pin each time the **decf** is decremented, and if this instruction sequence is repeated endlessly, what would you expect to see on a scope display of the output pin?

Chapter

3

INSTRUCTION SET

3.1 OVERVIEW

The complete PIC18F452 instruction set is tabulated in Figure 3-1. The role of this chapter is to explain the cryptic entries in the table and to describe some of the common roles played by specific instructions.

3.2 F/W DISTINCTION

When the assembly code for a typical microcontroller application is examined, it is immediately apparent that a major activity throughout is the moving of operands from one place to another. For many microcontrollers, this is accentuated by an architecture that carries out most operations on the contents of an *accumulator*. An operand is moved from RAM to the accumulator, the operation is executed, and the result moved back to RAM. The PIC18F452 treats all 256 locations making up the Access Bank (i.e., 128 RAM locations plus all of the Special Function Registers) as accumulators. That is, most operations can deal with operands in place. If two operands are needed, then one will first be moved to **WREG**, the CPU's working register. Consider the code to add two 8-bit numbers:

```
movf   NUM2,W          ;Move NUM2 to WREG
addwf  NUM1,F          ;NUM1 = NUM1 + NUM2
```

If this seems like the same thing as is done with an accumulator-centered microcontroller, then consider the PIC microcontroller's code to emulate such a microcontroller for this same operation:

Mnemonic	Operands	Description	Words	Cycles	Status bits affected
movlw	k	Move literal value to WREG	1	1	-
movwf	f(, BANKED)	Move WREG to f	1	1	-
movff	f_S, f_D	Move f_S to f_D (both with full 12-bit addresses)	2	2	-
movf	f, F/W(, BANKED)	Move f to F or WREG	1	1	Z, N
lfsr	i, k	Load FSRi with full 12-bit address, where i = 0 to 2	2	2	-
clrf	f(, BANKED)	Clear f	1	1	Z
setf	f(, BANKED)	0xff → f	1	1	-
movlb	k	Move literal value to BSR<3 : 0> , where k = 0 to 15, to set the bank for direct addressing	1	1	-
swapf	f, F/W(, BANKED)	Swap nibbles of f, putting result in F or WREG	1	1	-
bcf	f, b(, BANKED)	Clear bit b of register f, where b = 0 to 7	1	1	-
bsf	f, b(, BANKED)	Set bit b of register f, where b = 0 to 7	1	1	-
btg	f, b(, BANKED)	Toggle bit b of register f, where b = 0 to 7	1	1	-
rlcf	f, F/W(, BANKED)	Copy f into F or WREG; rotate F or WREG left through carry bit (9-bit rotate left)	1	1	C, N, Z
rlncf	f, F/W(, BANKED)	Copy f into F or WREG; rotate F or WREG left without carry bit (8-bit rotate left)	1	1	N, Z
rrcf	f, F/W(, BANKED)	Copy f into F or WREG; rotate F or WREG right through carry bit (9-bit rotate right)	1	1	C, N, Z
rrncf	f, F/W(, BANKED)	Copy f into F or WREG; rotate F or WREG right without carry bit (8-bit rotate right)	1	1	N, Z
incf	f, F/W(, BANKED)	Increment f, putting result in F or WREG	1	1	C, DC, Z, OV, N
decf	f, F/W(, BANKED)	Decrement f, putting result in F or WREG	1	1	C, DC, Z, OV, N
comf	f, F/W(, BANKED)	Complement f, putting result in F or WREG	1	1	Z, N
negf	f(, BANKED)	Change sign of a twos-complement-coded number	1	1	C, DC, Z, OV, N
andlw	k	AND literal value into WREG	1	1	Z, N
andwf	f, F/W(, BANKED)	AND WREG with f, putting result in F or WREG	1	1	Z, N
iorlw	k	Inclusive-OR literal value into WREG	1	1	Z, N
iorwf	f, F/W(, BANKED)	Inclusive-OR WREG with f, putting result in F or WREG	1	1	Z, N
xorlw	k	Exclusive-OR literal value into WREG	1	1	Z, N
xorwf	f, F/W(, BANKED)	Exclusive-OR WREG with f, putting result in F or WREG	1	1	Z, N
addlw	k	Add literal value into WREG	1	1	C, DC, Z, OV, N
addwf	f, F/W(, BANKED)	Add WREG and f, putting result in F or WREG	1	1	C, DC, Z, OV, N
addwfc	f, F/W(, BANKED)	Add WREG and f and carry bit, putting result in F or WREG	1	1	C, DC, Z, OV, N
daw		Decimal adjust sum of two packed BCD digits to correct packed BCD result in WREG	1	1	C
sublw	k	Subtract WREG from literal value, putting result in WREG	1	1	C, DC, Z, OV, N
subwf	f, F/W(, BANKED)	Subtract WREG from f, putting result in f or WREG	1	1	C, DC, Z, OV, N
subwfb	f, F/W(, BANKED)	Subtract WREG and borrow bit from f, putting result in F or WREG	1	1	C, DC, Z, OV, N
subfwb	f, F/W(, BANKED)	Subtract f and borrow bit from WREG, putting result in F or WREG	1	1	C, DC, Z, OV, N
mullw	k	Multiply WREG with literal value, putting result in PRODH : PRODL (WREG remains unchanged)	1	1	-
mulwf	f(, BANKED)	Multiply WREG with f, putting result in PRODH : PRODL (WREG and f remain unchanged)	1	1	-
btfsc	f, b(, BANKED)	Test bit b of register f, where b = 0 to 7 ; skip if clear	1	1/2	-
btfss	f, b(, BANKED)	Test bit b of register f, where b = 0 to 7; skip if set	1	1/2	-

Figure 3-1 Instruction set (1 of 2).

Mnemonic	Operands	Description	Words	Cycles	Status bits affected
bra	label	Branch to labeled instruction (within ±64 one-word instructions)	1	2	-
goto	label	Go to labeled instruction (anywhere)	2	2	-
bc	label	If carry (C=1), then branch to labeled instruction (within ±64 one-word instructions)	1	1/2	-
bnc	label	If no carry (C=0), then branch to labeled instruction (within ±64 one-word instructions)	1	1/2	-
bz	label	If zero (Z=1), then branch to labeled intruction (within ±64 one-word instructions)	1	1/2	-
bnz	label	If not zero (Z=0, then branch to labeled instruction (within ±64 one-word instructions)	1	1/2	-
bn	label	If negative (N=1), then branch to labeled instruction (within ±64 one-word instructions)	1	1/2	-
bnn	label	If not negative (N=0), then branch to labeled instruction (within ±64 one-word instructions)	1	1/2	-
bov	label	If overflow (OV=1), then branch to labeled instruction (within ±64 one-word instructions)	1	1/2	-
bnov	label	If no overflow (OV=0), then branch to labeled instruction (within ±64 one-word instructions)	1	1/2	-
cpfseq	f(, BANKED)	Skip if f is equal to WREG	1	1/2	-
cpfsgt	f(, BANKED)	Skip if f is greater than WREG (unsigned compare)	1	1/2	-
cpfslt	f(, BANKED)	Skip if f is less than WREG (unsigned compare)	1	1/2	-
tstfsz	f(, BANKED)	Test f; skip if zero	1	1/2	-
decfsz	f, F/W(, BANKED)	Decrement f, putting result in F or WREG; skip if zero	1	1/2	-
dcfsnz	f, F/W(, BANKED)	Decrement f, putting result in F or WREG; skip if not zero	1	1/2	-
incfsz	f, F/W(, BANKED)	Increment f, putting result in F or WREG; skip if zero	1	1/2	-
infsnz	f, F/W(, BANKED)	Increment f, putting result in F or WREG; skip if not zero	1	1/2	-
rcall	label	Call labeled subroutine (within ±512 one-word instructions)	1	2	-
call	label	Call labeled subroutine (anywhere)	2	2	-
call	label, FAST	Call labeled subroutine (anywhere); copy state to shadow registers: (WREG)→WS, (STATUS)→STATUSS, (BSR)→BSRS	2	2	-
return		Return from subroutine	1	2	-
return	FAST	Return from subroutine; restore state from shadow registers: (WS)→WREG, (STATUSS)→STATUS, (BSRS)→BSR	1	2	C, DC, Z, OV, N
retlw	k	Return from subroutine, putting literal value in WREG	1	2	-
retfie		Return from interrupt; reenable interrupts	1	2	-
retfie	FAST	Return from interrupt; restore state from shadow registers: (WS)→WREG, (STATUSS)→STATUS, (BSRS)→BSR; reenable interrupts	1	2	C, DC, Z, OV, N
push		Push address of next instruction onto stack	1	1	-
pop		Discard address on top of stack	1	1	-
clrwdt		Clear watchdog timer	1	1	-
sleep		Go into standby mode	1	1	-
reset		Software reset to same state as is achieved with the MCLR input	1	1	C, DC, Z, OV, N
nop		No operation	1	1	-
tblrd*		Read from program memory location pointed to by TBLPTR into TABLAT	1	2	-
tblrd*+		Read from program memory location pointed to by TBLPTR into TABLAT, then increment TBLPTR	1	2	-
tblrd*-		Read from program memory location pointed to by TBLPTR into TABLAT, then decrement TBLPTR	1	2	-
tblrd+*		Increment TBLPTR, then read from program memory location pointed to by TBLPTR into TABLAT	1	2	-

Figure 3-1 Instruction set (2 of 2).

```
movf   NUM1,W              ;Move NUM1 to WREG
addwf  NUM2,W              ;WREG = NUM1 + NUM2
movwf  NUM1                ;Return result to NUM1
```

Every two-operand instruction sequence runs 33% faster (for the same clock rate) and uses 33% less program memory with a PIC microcontroller than with an accumulator-centered microcontroller. For the PIC18F452 running at its maximum internal clock rate, the two-instruction, two-cycle add operation takes just 0.2 microseconds.

For the large number of instructions listed in Figure 3-1 that include "F/W" as part of the operand, this designation specifies whether the result of the operation should be returned to its source or, alternatively, to **WREG.** For example,

```
decf  COUNT,F
```

will decrement the contents of **COUNT**, whereas

```
decf  COUNT,W
```

will, in effect, move **COUNT** to **WREG** and decrement **WREG**, leaving the contents of **COUNT** unchanged.

3.3 ",BANKED" OPTION

Microchip's excellent, and free, assembler looks at the address that has been assigned to an instruction's operand before deciding how to treat the instruction's ",BANKED" option. For any instruction that directly accesses a variable that has been assigned to an address ranging from 0x000 to 0x07f as well as for all of the Special Function Registers (e.g., **PORTB**) for which the addresses range from 0xf80 to 0xfff, the assembler will assign Access Bank direct addressing to the instruction. As pointed out in Section 2.3, when the instruction is executed, the CPU will take the 8-bit operand and convert it to the actual full operand address of 0x000 to 0x07f if its 8-bit value is 0x7f or less. The CPU will convert the operand to the actual full operand address of 0xf80 to 0xfff if its 8-bit value is 0x80 or more.

For any instruction that directly accesses a RAM variable that has been assigned an address of 0x080 or higher, the assembler will assign Banked direct addressing to the instruction. Before the instruction can be executed correctly, the program must have executed a **movlb** instruction to load the **BSR** register with the bank address. Because of this automatic handling by the assembler, it is never necessary to append the **",BANKED"** designation to the operand of an instruction.

Again as pointed out in Section 2.3, up to 256 variables (with addresses ranging from 0x000 up to 0x0ff) can be accessed using direct addressing without ever changing the **BSR** register from its power-on default value of zero. Instructions accessing variables having addresses ranging from 0x000 to 0x07f will be assigned Access Bank direct addressing. Instructions accessing variables having addresses ranging from 0x080 to 0x0ff will be assigned Banked direct addressing and will take advantage of the default **BSR** value of zero.

3.4 MOVE INSTRUCTIONS

Even with the "F/W" feature helping to reduce the need to move operands from one location to another, the instructions that move operands nevertheless pervade the code for a given application. Of these instructions, four are dominant: **movlw**, **movwf**, **movff**, and **movf**. The instruction

```
movlw  5
```

will load a 1-byte *literal* value, ranging from 0 to 255, into **WREG**.

The Microchip assembler understands number formats expressed in any of the following forms:

```
0x7f           hexadecimal
H'7f'          alternative hexadecimal form
B'10011100'    binary
D'32'          decimal
O'777'         octal
A'C'           ASCII representation for a character
'C'            alternative form for ASCII
```

The assembler accepts hexadecimal numbers by default. That is, unless the default is changed (as will be done for examples later in this text), a number expressed without any clarifying prefix will be treated as a hexadecimal number. Thus

```
movlw  20
```

will load 0x20 (i.e., D′32′) into **WREG**.

The assembler treats a number expressed with no sign as an unsigned number. For example, D′128′ is treated as B′10000000′. On the other hand, a number expressed with a minus sign is treated as a twos-complement-coded signed number. For example,

```
movlw  -2
```

will load B′11111110′ into **WREG**.
Finally,

```
movlw  0x1234
```

will load 0x34 into WREG. That is, it forms the operand, modulo 0x100, when it is expecting a 1-byte operand but is given a larger operand.

More often than not in typical application code, a **movlw** instruction is immediately followed by a **movwf** instruction in order to initialize a 1-byte variable or register. For example,

```
movlw  B'11100000'
movwf  TRISB
```

will initialize **PORTB**'s data direction register so that **PORTB**'s upper three bits will become inputs while the remaining bits will be outputs. This is such a common instruction sequence that it might be represented by the *macro* expression

```
MOVLF  B'11100000',TRISB
```

as will be done in Section 5.6.

The **movlw** and **movwf** instructions are joined by the **movff** instruction as dominant instructions in typical application code. This latter instruction is a two-word instruction for copying a 1-byte source operand to a destination operand, using the full 12-bit address for each. The instruction

```
movff  PORTB,PORTB_COPY
```

will read **PORTB** and save the value read to a RAM variable called **PORTB_COPY**.

The last of the four main move instructions is **movf**. It is the only one of the four that affects any of the flags in the **STATUS** register. It is commonly used to move one of the operands of a two-operand instruction sequence into **WREG**. Thus the sequence

```
movf   NUM2,W
addwf  NUM1,F
```

first copies **NUM2** into **WREG**, where it can be added to **NUM1**. It is also occasionally used with **movwf** in place of a **movff** instruction if it is desired to put the operand not only in the destination location but also in **WREG**. Another occasional use occurs when a further test will check whether the operand has reached a value of zero (because the **movf** instruction affects the **Z** flag). In fact, it is sometimes used solely for this purpose:

```
movf   COUNTL,F
```

This example might arise in the process of decrementing a 2-byte variable

```
COUNTH:COUNTL
```

If the **movf** instruction indicates that the lower byte is initially zero, both bytes must be decremented; otherwise, just the lower byte must be decremented.

The remaining five "move" instructions carry out specialty operations. The **lfsr** instruction loads an address identified by a label into one of the three indirect addressing pointers (**FSR0**, **FSR1**, or **FSR2**). For example,

```
lfsr   Ø,NUM1
```

was used in Figure 2-4b to load **FSR0** with the address of the low byte of the 2-byte binary number **NUM1**.

Sometimes it is useful to set aside, and later restore, the value of one of the three pointers. For example, **FSR0** might be used in the UART's interrupt service routine to store a received byte into the next location of a "line buffer" located in RAM. If the interrupted mainline code also uses **FSR0**, the interrupt service routine first sets aside the present value of **FSR0** to two RAM variables:

```
movff  FSRØL,FSRØL_TEMP
movff  FSRØH,FSRØH_TEMP
```

Then it loads **FSR0** with the value saved by the last execution of the UART interrupt service routine:

```
movff  FSRØL_UART,FSRØL
movff  FSRØH_UART,FSRØH
```

Although the **MOVLF** two-instruction macro will be used for most initializations, three one-word instructions carry out special initialization tasks:

```
clrf  TEMP                    ;Load ØxØØ into TEMP
setf  TEMP                    ;Load Øxff into TEMP
movlb  2                      ;Load ØxØ2 into BSR
```

Finally, the **swapf** instruction carries out an occasionally needed operation expeditiously. In Chapter 7, a "nibble" interface to a liquid-crystal display will be used to reduce from ten to six the number of microcontroller pins needed for transfers. A byte will be sent to the LCD by writing one 4-bit nibble to four output pins, executing a **swapf** instruction, and writing the other 4-bit nibble to the same four output pins. If the other pins of the port are configured as inputs, the 8-bit write to the port will change the four pins connected to the LCD, while the other four bits written to the port will be ignored.

3.5 SINGLE OPERAND INSTRUCTIONS

Three instructions permit a single bit of an operand to be set, cleared, or toggled while the other bits of the operand remain unchanged. For example,

```
bsf  PORTB,0
```

will set the least-significant bit (i.e., bit 0) of **PORTB**. The CPU does this within a single cycle as follows. Each internal clock cycle is broken into four quarter-cycles. The CPU reads the port (or other operand) into a hidden CPU register during one of the quarter-cycles. Then it ORs the hidden register with a binary number having zeros in all bits other than the bit being set. Finally, it writes the result back to the port, thereby setting the specified pin while at the same time writing back to any other output pins exactly what was read earlier in the clock cycle.

The *bit clear* instruction

```
bcf  PORTB,1
```

operates in much the same way. The CPU reads the port into a hidden register, ANDs this with a binary number having 1s in all bits other than the bit being cleared, and writes the result back out to the port. The *bit toggle* instruction

```
btg  PORTB,2
```

exclusive-ORs what is read from the port with a binary number having zeros in all bits other than the bit being toggled, writing the result back to the port. Note that exclusive-ORing with a zero leaves a bit unchanged; exclusive-ORing with a one complements (i.e., toggles) it.

Four *rotate* instructions move the bits of an operand one place to the left or right. Two of these, **rlcf** and **rrcf**, implement a 9-bit rotate through the carry bit, as shown in Figure 2-13. They are *building-block* instructions, supporting the left-shifting or right-shifting of a multiple-byte number, operations that will multiply or divide a binary number by 2. Figures 3-2a and 3-2b illustrate the multiplication by 2 of a 24-bit binary number. This figure makes use of a strange terminology for naming the bytes of a 3-byte variable called **AARG** ("A argument"). **AARGB0** ("byte zero") is designated as the most-significant byte (MSB). It is the terminology Microchip uses with their extensive library of multiple-byte multiplication and division subroutines; accordingly, the terminology will be used throughout this text.

The division of a multiple-byte number by 2 is illustrated in Figures 3-2c and 3-2d. In the case of the twos-complement-coded (signed) number of Figure 3-2d, it is necessary to maintain the sign bit in the leftmost bit position. Hence, the first step is to copy the sign bit into the carry bit, and only then proceed with shifting the resulting 25-bit number to the right.

The two 8-bit rotate instructions, **rlncf** and **rrncf**, are illustrated in Figure 3-3. These instructions are especially useful when the bits of a byte not only need to be shifted but also retained for subsequent use. If the instruction

```
swapf  TEMP,F
```

were not a part of the instruction set, the following sequence would serve the same purpose:

```
rrncf  TEMP,F
rrncf  TEMP,F
rrncf  TEMP,F
rrncf  TEMP,F
```

The variation

```
swapf  TEMP,W
```

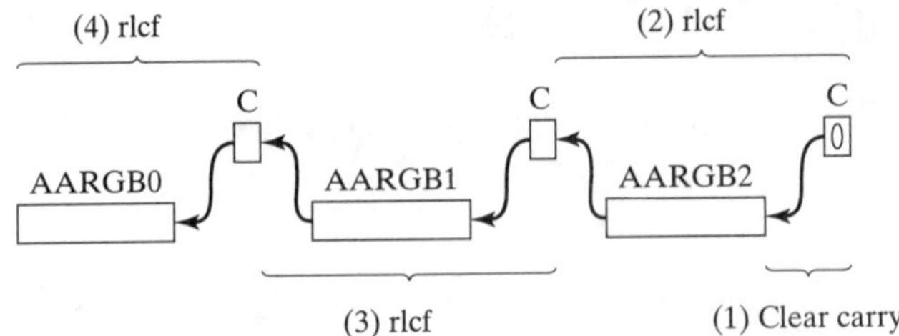

(a) Use of rlcf instruction to multiply the 24-bit binary number in AARG (i.e., ARRGB0: AARGB1: AARGB2) by two

```
bcf   STATUS,C          ;Clear the carry bit
rlcf  AARGB2,F          ;Rotate least-significant byte
rlcf  AARGB1,F          ;Rotate middle byte
rlcf  AARGBØ,F          ;Rotate most-significant byte
```

(b) Instruction sequence to multiply the three-byte number, AARG, by two

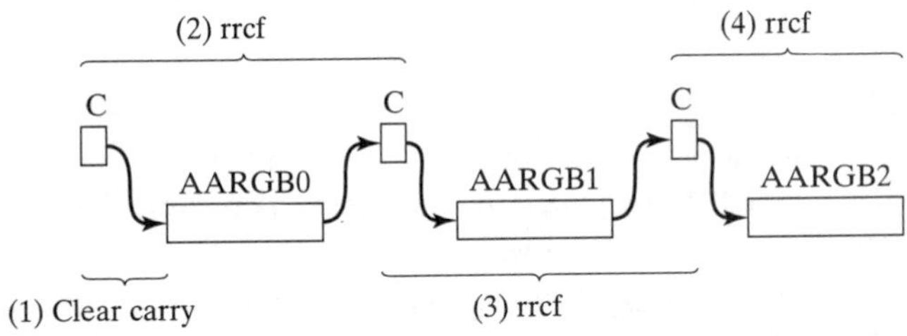

(c) Division of an unsigned 24-bit number by two

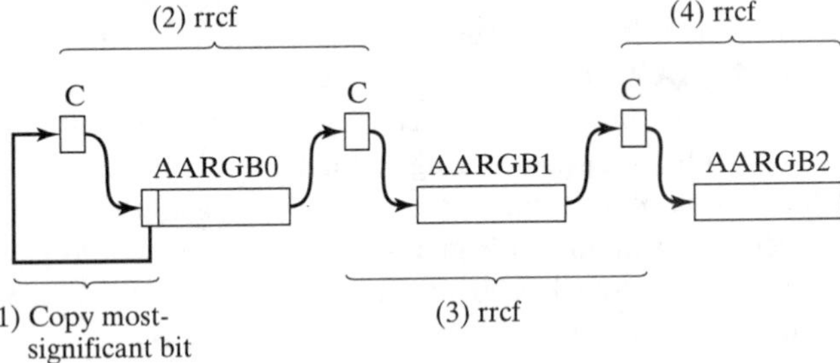

(d) Division of a twos-complement-coded, 24-bit signed number by two

Figure 3-2 Use of rotate-through-carry instructions with multiple-byte numbers.

is equivalent to

```
rrncf  TEMP,W
rrncf  WREG,W
rrncf  WREG,W
rrncf  WREG,W
```

The remaining four single-operand instructions are **incf**, **decf**, **comf**, and **negf**. With these, a 1-byte operand can be incremented, decremented, complemented, or negated. The latter operation changes the

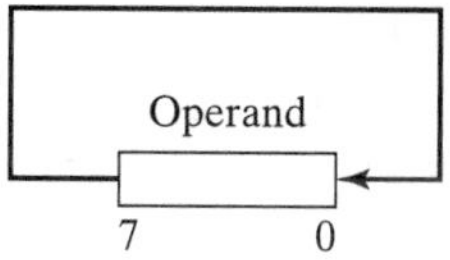

(a) rlncf, rotate left with no carry, instruction

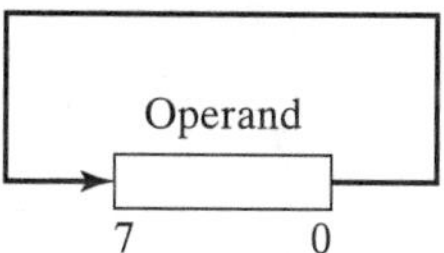

(b) rrncf, rotate right with no carry, instruction

Figure 3-3 8-bit rotate instructions.

sign of a twos-complement-coded number. It is equivalent to complementing the number (i.e., complementing each bit of the number) and then adding 1 to the result. Figure 3–4 illustrates the extension of each of these operations to a 3-byte number. The implementations shown make use of the PIC18F452's add-with-carry and subtract-with-borrow instructions.

3.6 AND, OR, EXCLUSIVE-OR INSTRUCTIONS

The bit clear instruction, **bcf**, the bit set instruction, **bsf**, and the bit toggle instruction, **btg**, have counterparts for changing any number of bits in an operand. Thus, the **andlw** and the **andwf** instructions are used to force selected bits to zero while leaving the remaining bits unchanged. For example, the following instruction will *mask off* the upper bits of **WREG**:

```
andlw  B'00001111'          ;Force upper 4 bits of WREG to 0
```

The following two-instruction sequence will carry out the same operation on any other variable:

```
movlw  B'00001111'          ;Load WREG with mask
andwf  TEMP,F               ;AND TEMP with mask
```

The **iorlw** and **iorwf** instructions are used to force selected bits of an operand to 1 while leaving the remaining bits unchanged. For example, the following instruction sequence will set the most-significant three bits of **PORTB** while leaving any other output pins unchanged:

```
movlw  B'11100000'
iorwf  PORTB,F
```

The **xorlw** and **xorwf** instructions will toggle selected bits of an operand by exclusive-ORing the selected bits with 1s. The unselected bits are exclusive-ORed with zeros, leaving them unchanged. Thus

```
xorlw  B'11111000'
```

will toggle the upper five bytes of **WREG**, leaving the remaining three bits unchanged.

(a) A three-byte binary number, AARG

```
clrf    WREG                ;First clear WREG
incf    AARGB2,F            ;Increment the least-significant byte
addwfc  AARGB1,F            ;Add carry (and WREG=Ø) to middle byte
addwfc  AARGBØ,F            ;Add carry to most-significant byte
```

(b) Incrementing AARG

```
clrf    WREG                ;First clear WREG
decf    AARGB2,F            ;Decrement the least-significant byte
subwfb  AARGB1,F            ;Subtract borrow (and WREG=Ø) from middle byte
subwfb  AARGBØ,F            ;Subtract borrow from most-significant byte
```

(c) Decrementing AARG

```
comf    AARGB2,F            ;Toggle ones and zeros
comf    AARGB1,F
comf    AARGBØ,F
```

(d) Complementing AARG

```
comf    AARGB2,F            ;First complement
comf    AARGB1,F
comf    AARGBØ,F
clrf    WREG                ;Then add one
incf    AARGB2,F
addwfc  AARGB1,F
addwfc  AARGBØ,F
```

(e) Negating AARG

Figure 3-4 Incrementing, decrementing, complementing, and negating of a multiple-byte number.

3.7 ARITHMETIC INSTRUCTIONS

In addition to the two instructions, **addlw** and **addwf**, for adding two 1-byte binary numbers together, the PIC18F452 has the *building-block* add-with-carry instruction used in Figure 3-4. When adding multiple-byte binary numbers, this **addwfc** instruction simplifies the handling of the carry bit, as was exemplified in Figure 2–4. Not having this instruction, designs using earlier PIC microcontrollers required the following steps:

- Add the least-significant bytes of the two numbers.
- If a carry resulted, increment the second byte of the "destination" number (**NUM1** in Figure 2-4).
- If this, in turn, caused this second byte of the destination number to roll over to zero, the third byte of the destination number would be incremented.

This would be repeated through the entire destination number. The addition process would then continue with the addition of the second bytes of the two numbers and the attendant handling of any carry. What a difference is made with this add-with-carry enhancement of the instruction set.

The subtract instructions, **sublw** and **subwf**, have this same enhancement. In fact, because of the asymmetry of the subtract instruction (i.e., $A - B$ is not the same as $B - A$), the instruction set benefits from the inclusion of *two* subtract-with-borrow instructions, **subwfb** and **subfwb**.

One potential bug in the code of a designer who is new to the use of the PIC microcontroller chip is exemplified by

```
sublw  2
```

Contrary to expectations, this instruction does not subtract 2 from **WREG**, but rather subtracts **WREG** from 2! The intended operation can usually be accomplished with

```
movlw  2
subwf  NUMBER,F
```

where **NUMBER** contains the number to be decreased by 2.

The **daw** (decimal-adjust **WREG**) instruction is designed to support the addition of *packed-BCD* (i.e., binary-coded decimal) numbers. In this packed-BCD representation of a decimal number, each digit is represented by its 4-bit binary equivalent, and two coded digits are stored in a single byte. Thus, the decimal number 1234 would be coded

```
00010010  00110100
```

Two multiple-byte packed BCD numbers, **NUM1** and **NUM2**, can be added by adding the two least-significant bytes as if they were binary numbers, putting the result in **WREG**. This is followed by the **daw** instruction that looks for either of the two 4-bit sums to be greater than 9 or the 4-bit carry (DC or C) to be 1. For any of these cases, the **daw** instruction corrects **WREG** to the correct BCD value and the correct carry out of the byte. The corrected byte in **WREG** can be saved (e.g., in the least-significant byte of **NUM1**) before proceeding to the next bytes. This process is illustrated in Figure 3-5 for two 2-byte numbers.

The final arithmetic instructions, **mullw** and **mulwf**, multiply two unsigned 1-byte numbers. Both instructions expect that **WREG** will contain one of the numbers. If the other number is a constant, this constant is used as the literal value with the **mullw** instruction. Thus, for example, the contents of **WREG** can be multiplied by 10 with

```
mullw  D'10'
```

The 16-bit result will appear after the one-cycle execution in **PRODH:PRODL**. The original number remains in **WREG**.

The **mulwf** instruction multiplies the contents of any variable with **WREG**. The result is again placed in **PRODH:PRODL**, and again the original operands remain unchanged.

In Chapter 14, the use of Microchip's library of multiplication and division subroutines for both unsigned and signed numbers will be considered. These subroutines use the **mulwf** instruction as a building block to enhance their speed of execution.

3.8 CONDITIONAL AND UNCONDITIONAL BRANCHES

The following instructions,

```
bc     bnc     bz     bnz     bn     bnn     bov     bnov
```

carry out the most commonly occurring tests of the **STATUS** register bits

C Z N OV

```
NUM1        Ø 1   2 3
NUM2        5 8   9 6
----        ---------
NUM1        6 Ø   1 9
```

(a) Two-byte packed BCD numbers, **NUM1** and **NUM2**, to be added back into **NUM1**.

```
         C=0    DC=0
             0010    0011
             1001    0110
             ------------
addwf        1011    1001
daw
C=1          0001    1001   =   19 (packed BCD code)
```

(b) Binary addition of lower bytes into **WREG**, followed by **daw** instruction

```
         C=0    DC=0    C=1
             0000    0001
             0101    1000
             ------------
addwfc       0101    1010
daw
C=0          0110    0000   =   60 (packed BCD code)
```

(c) Binary addition, with carry, of upper bytes into **WREG**, followed by **daw** instruction

Figure 3-5 Addition of packed BCD numbers.

and either branch to a "nearby" program address (within ±64 one-word instructions) or go on to the next instruction in sequence. As program code is developed in small, testable subroutines that are nested together to achieve the functionality of an application, being limited to branches to "nearby" addresses is not a serious limitation. If the assembler indicates that a specific branch instruction has tried to reach beyond its limit, the code can be modified, as illustrated by the following example:

```
        bnz  DoItAgain
```

This can be changed to

```
        bz   Next
        goto  DoItAgain
Next
```

The two-word **goto** instruction will reach anywhere in the entire program address range.

In addition to these conditional branch instructions, a **bra** instruction can be used to branch unconditionally. For example, a subroutine might contain the following structure to do "OneThing" if **C** = 0 and "AnotherThing" if **C** = 1:

```
        bc  AnotherThing
OneThing
        .
        .
        .
        bra  Done
AnotherThing
        .
        .
        .
Done
```

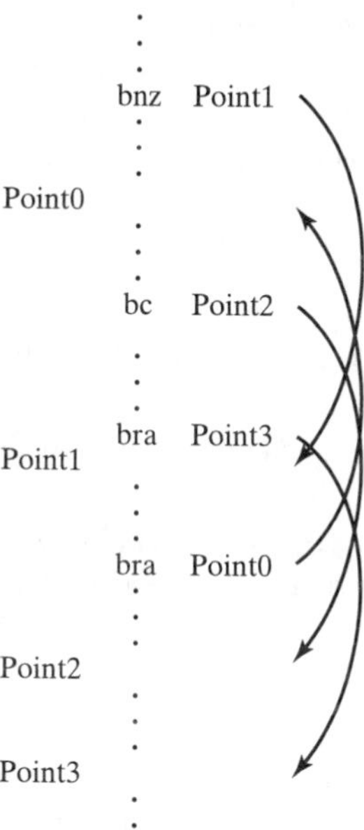

Figure 3-6 Spaghetti code.

In Chapter 6, a structured assembly preprocessor will be considered that will support rewriting this code as

```
IF_  .NC.
     .
     .          (code for OneThing)
     .
ELSE_
     .
     .          (code for AnotherThing)
     .
ENDIF_
```

Such structures support a discipline on the code-writing process that eliminates the worst attribute of many assembly language programs—their tangled, "spaghetti-code" use of interlocked (rather than nested) loops of instructions. An example is shown in Figure 3-6. Debugging spaghetti code requires that attention be directed not only toward the requirements of the application but also toward untangling the awkward flow of program execution.

3.9 CONDITIONAL SKIP INSTRUCTIONS

In addition to the ability to test **STATUS** bits, the PIC18F452 has ten further instructions that test for a condition and skip over the next instruction if the condition is met. That next instruction is typically a **bra** (branch always) instruction or an **rcall** (subroutine call) instruction, but it can actually be *any* instruction. It can even be one of the two-word instructions (e.g., **goto** or **movff**), because the second word of all five of these instructions is of the form

```
B'1111 bbbb bbbb bbbb'
```

The CPU treats any one-word instruction having B′1111′ in the most-significant four bits as a **nop** (no operation) instruction. Consequently, when the CPU skips over the first word of a two-word instruction, it executes a one-cycle **nop** instruction and then proceeds to the next instruction.

The two most widely used of the ten skip instructions are **btfsc** and **btfss**. Each of these tests one bit of an operand and skips the next instruction if the test condition is met. For example, consider

```
btfss  PORTB,2
```

This instruction tests bit 2 (or any bit from 0 to 7) of **PORTB**. If bit 2 is set, the next instruction will be skipped; otherwise, it will be executed.

Three skip instructions compare an unsigned binary operand against **WREG**. These instructions are **cpfslt**, **cpfseq**, and **cpfsgt**. The first skips if the operand is less than **WREG**, the second skips if they are equal, and the third skips if the operand is greater than **WREG**.

A **tstfsz** instruction skips the next instruction if the operand equals zero. For example,

```
tstfsz  TABLAT
```

will test the byte returned from a string stored in program memory (refer to Section 2-5). It will skip the next instruction if the end-of-string byte (coded as 0x00) is returned, breaking out of a loop of instructions that reads the entire string, one byte each time around the loop.

The last four skip instructions will increment or decrement an operand and skip if the result is, or is not, zero. Consider the following examples.

```
decfsz  COUNT,F          ;Decrement COUNT, skip if zero
decfsnz  COUNT,W         ;Copy COUNT to WREG, decrement WREG,
                         ; skip if not zero
incfsz  COUNT,F          ;Increment COUNT, skip if zero
incfsnz  COUNT,F         ;Increment COUNT, skip if not zero
```

3.10 SUBROUTINE CALL AND RETURN INSTRUCTIONS

As discussed in Section 2.6, subroutines can often be called with the one-word **rcall** instruction that can reach anywhere within ±512 one-word instructions. Unlike the conditional *branch* instructions that are usually located within the same small subroutine as their destination, the code for a subroutine will often be located far (i.e., more than 512 one-word instructions away) from the calling instruction. The two-word **call** instruction will reach to a subroutine regardless of where it is located in program memory. Although the subroutine call and return instructions possess a FAST option, this option should usually be ignored. High-priority interrupts use the FAST option automatically and will corrupt any other use, as will be seen in Section 9.4.

A variation of the subroutine return is the **retlw** instruction. If a subroutine ends with

```
retlw  5
```

then the value 5 will be returned to the calling program in **WREG**. This may appear to be just a shortcut in place of the sequence

```
movlw  5
return
```

In actuality, it is a relic of earlier-generation PIC microcontrollers where it served as the only mechanism for accessing tables stored in program memory. Now, the approach of Section 2.5 provides a more versatile alternative for achieving this capability.

3.11 REMAINING INSTRUCTIONS

The remaining instructions of Figure 3-1 can be considered to be specialty instructions, designed to support some feature of the hardware. The **push** and **pop** instructions support the extension of the CPU's 31-level stack to a larger array in RAM. The **clrwdt** instruction serves a role specific to the watchdog timer and will be explained later in that context. The **sleep** instruction is used in some battery-operated applications to conserve battery life and will be considered in that context in Section 20.9.

The **reset** instruction initiates exactly the same initialization of registers as occurs when the $\overline{\text{MCLR}}$ (master clear) pin is driven low. Although it is probably not an instruction that will find its way into application code, it provides a hard-to-duplicate function to a program such as the QwikBug monitor that allows the QwikFlash board discussed throughout this book to have the support of most of the functions of Microchip's in-circuit debugger but without the cost of the extra ICD2 module.

The PIC18F452 instruction set includes four **tblwt** instructions to support writes to the flash program memory. These are analogous to the four **tblrd** instructions of Figure 3-1. The flash program memory must be erased in blocks of 64 bytes at a time and programmed in blocks of 8 bytes at a time. Each erase operation halts CPU execution for (about) 4 milliseconds, while each write operation halts CPU execution for (about) 2 milliseconds. The details of the complex protocol are beyond the scope of this text. Accordingly, the four **tblwt** instructions are omitted from the table of instructions in Figure 3-1.

To support nonvolatile data retention, the PIC18F452 includes a block of data EEPROM consisting of 256 (8-bit) bytes. This data EEPROM handles writes without halting the CPU and is written to, and read, a byte at a time. Its use is discussed in Section 20.11.

PROBLEMS

3-1 F/W distinction. A common error in writing PIC microcontroller code is to forget to specify the destination of an instruction, when such a specification is required. The assembler will post a warning when this is done, but it is up to the code writer to pay attention to such warnings. Usually, a posted warning indicates that an omitted option was filled with a default value and then the assembly process completed. It only takes the default choice to differ from the designer's assumed choice for the warning to be identifying what is actually an error. What will be the consequence if an

```
incf  COUNT
```

instruction is interpreted by the assembler as

```
incf  COUNT,W
```

when, in fact, what was intended was

```
incf  COUNT,F
```

if this instruction is used as a loop counter with the intention of looping until COUNT = 4?

3-2 Move instructions. What value, expressed as a binary number, will be loaded into **WREG** by the following instruction if the assembler's default radix has been changed to decimal?

```
movlw  10000000
```

What is strange about this result?

3-3 Move instructions. In what sense does the two-word instruction

```
movff  <operand1>, <operand2>
```

avoid side effects better than the two-word instruction sequence

```
movf  <operand1>,W
movwf  <operand2>
```

3-4 Multiple-byte increment. Figures 3-4a and 3-4b illustrate one way to increment a 3-byte number. Write an alternative instruction sequence to increment **AARG** using nothing but **incf** instructions and either **bz** or **bnz** instructions. Is there any reason to prefer the scheme of Figure 3-4b? Is there any reason to prefer your scheme?

3-5 Bit manipulation. Assume that all eight pins of **PORTB** are set up as outputs. Also assume that **WREG** contains a number of the form

$B'00000b_2b_1b_0'$

Using a sequence of the following three instructions—**xorwf, andlw, xorwf**—update the lower three bits of **PORTB** with the $b_2b_1b_0$ bits in **WREG** while leaving the upper five bits of **PORTB** unchanged. *Hint:* Note that if a bit is exclusive-ORed with itself, the result will be zero.

3-6 Bit manipulation. Assume that two bytes of a string variable are labeled **D10** and **D1** and that they contain the ASCII code for two digits. If the upper four bits of the ASCII code for a digit are forced to zero, what remains will be the binary value of the digit. Minimizing instructions, write an instruction sequence to form the "packed-BCD" version of this two-digit number into a 1-byte variable called **D10_1**. Leave the original string variable unchanged. For example, if **D10** = B′00110101′ (i.e., ASCII code for 5) and **D1** = B′00111001′ (i.e., ASCII code for 9), then your code sequence should leave **D10** and **D1** unchanged while forming **D10_1** = B′01011001′ (i.e., the packed-BCD encoding of the decimal number 59).

3-7 Bit manipulation. Minimizing instructions, write an instruction sequence that reverses the operation of the last problem. Note that the upper 4-bit "nibble" of the ASCII encoding of a digit is B′0011′.

3-8 Sublw instruction. To form

```
WREG - <literal value>
```

the following two-instruction sequence has been suggested.

```
sublw  <literal value>      ;Form literal-WREG
negf  WREG,F                ;Form -(literal-WREG)
```

This certainly works if **WREG** contains a twos-complement-coded signed number (between +127 and −128) and the literal value expresses a twos-complement-coded number, because it forms

```
-(<literal value> - WREG)
```

However, it also seems to work if **WREG** contains an unsigned number (between 0 and 255) and the literal value is an unsigned number less than or equal to **WREG** so that the result is still an unsigned number. Try this for the following pairs:

(a) **WREG** = 5, literal = 3, so the result should be 2.
(b) **WREG** = 255, literal = 3, so the result should be 252.

3-9 Fast shifting. Because it is so fast, the multiply instruction can be used as a swifter shifter, throwing away bits at one end of the number and filling in zeros at the other end. The operand is moved to **WREG** and multiplied by a power of 2 corresponding to the desired number of shifts. For example, if the number B'11000101' is multiplied by 8, then **PRODH** will equal B'00000110' and **PRODL** will equal B'00101000'. Note that **PRODH** contains the original number shifted right five places. **PRODL** contains the original number shifted left three places. The selected byte can finally be written back to the original operand.

(a) What is the general rule for shifting a number left n places (where $2 \leq n \leq 7$)?
(b) What is the general rule for shifting a number right n places (where $2 \leq n \leq 7$)?
(c) Write the code to shift the 1-byte variable **TEMP** left three places, using "rotate left" instructions and then clearing the three least-significant bits.

3-10 Conditional branch instructions. Show the code that a structured assembly preprocessor would create from the following code:

```
WHILE_  .C.
    .
    .              (Code to be executed)
    .
    .
ENDWHILE_
```

3-11 Conditional skip instructions. Show the code that a structured assembly preprocessor would create from the following code:

```
REPEAT_
    .
    .              (Code to be executed)
    .
    .
UNTIL_  PORTB,6 == 1
```

This structure should execute the block of code once and then continue to execute the block repeatedly until finally bit 6 of **PORTB** equals 1.

Chapter

4

QWIKFLASH TARGET BOARD

4.1 OVERVIEW

A microcontroller finds its role in any application through sensing inputs and controlling outputs. Learning to design with a microcontroller involves developing skills in three main areas:

1. Sensing inputs. These include user-interface inputs (e.g., switches and knobs), analog voltage inputs (e.g., the output of a temperature or pressure transducer), and timed-transition inputs (e.g., serial data inputs and time-interval measurements).
2. Controlling outputs. These include user-interface outputs (e.g., annunciator LEDs, buzzers, and alphanumeric displays), voltage outputs (e.g., a "tweaking" input to an analog circuit), and timed-transition outputs (e.g., serial communications and pulses with required pulse widths).
3. Developing algorithms. These include interpreting inputs (e.g., deciphering the serial protocol of a magnetic card reader), manipulating data (e.g., finding a worst-case event time), and formatting outputs (e.g., scaling a frequency display into Hz, kHz, or MHz).

To give substance to the development of these skills, many of the design ideas arising in this book will be applied to the circuitry and devices on the target board shown in Figure 4-1. Whether or not the reader uses the actual board, the intent throughout the book will be to ensure that all of the issues involved in a real application are addressed.

The first printing of this book includes a complimentary, unstuffed PC board for building this *QwikFlash* development board. It is located at the back of the book. Appendix A1 has construction hints plus a parts list, with all of the parts available from just one mail-order distributor, Digi-Key. The entire list of parts is available at a significant discount from Digi-Key as Part Number "18F452-KIT."

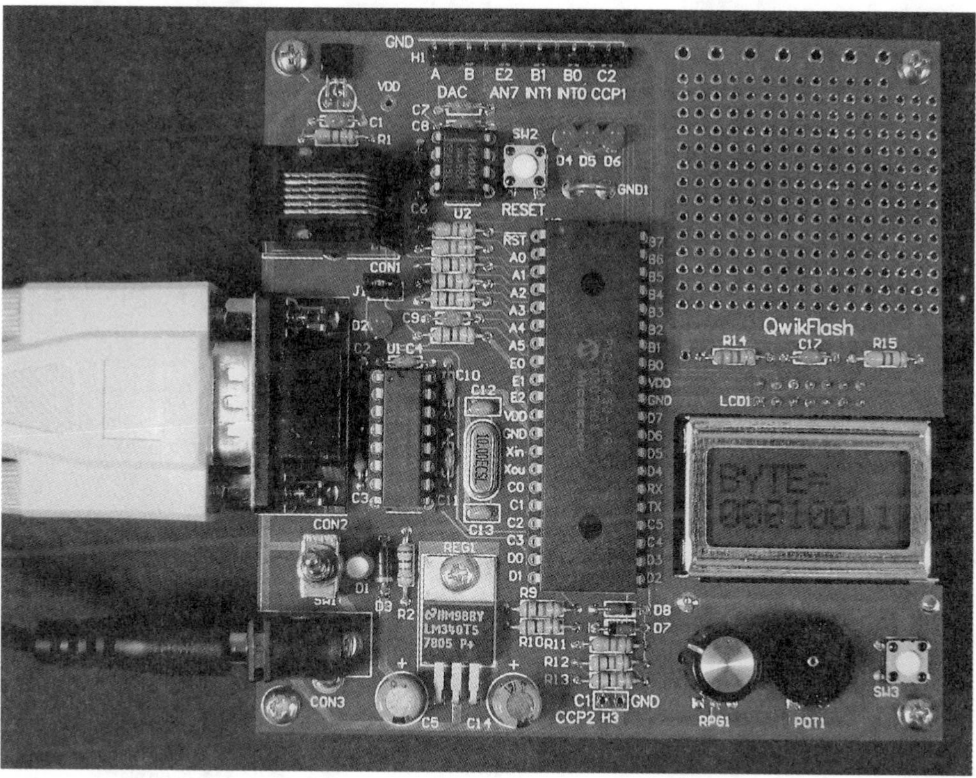

Figure 4-1 *QwikFlash* target board.

The board permits PIC18F452 code development and testing to be carried out wherever the reader has access to an IBM-compatible computer. Initially, and once only, the PIC18F452 must be programmed with the *QwikBug* monitor program. In a college environment, an entire class can take advantage of a single low-cost (about $150) in-circuit debugger (ICD2) from Microchip, via Digi-Key, for this step.

The QwikFlash board provides a low-cost, versatile vehicle for learning to use the PIC18F452. It avoids the use of tiny surface-mount parts. A built-up version of the board, complete with QwikBug monitor, can be purchased from *www.microdesignsinc.com.*

In this chapter, the features of the board will be examined. This includes not only the various I/O devices and their interconnection to the PIC18F452 but also the support provided by the board for debugging user code.

4.2 QWIKFLASH I/O CIRCUITRY

The input and output circuitry of the PIC18F452 on the QwikFlash board is shown in somewhat simplified form in Figure 4-2. The complete board circuitry and parts list are available in Appendix A1. The I/O resources on the board provide a wide range of design opportunities in spite of being relatively

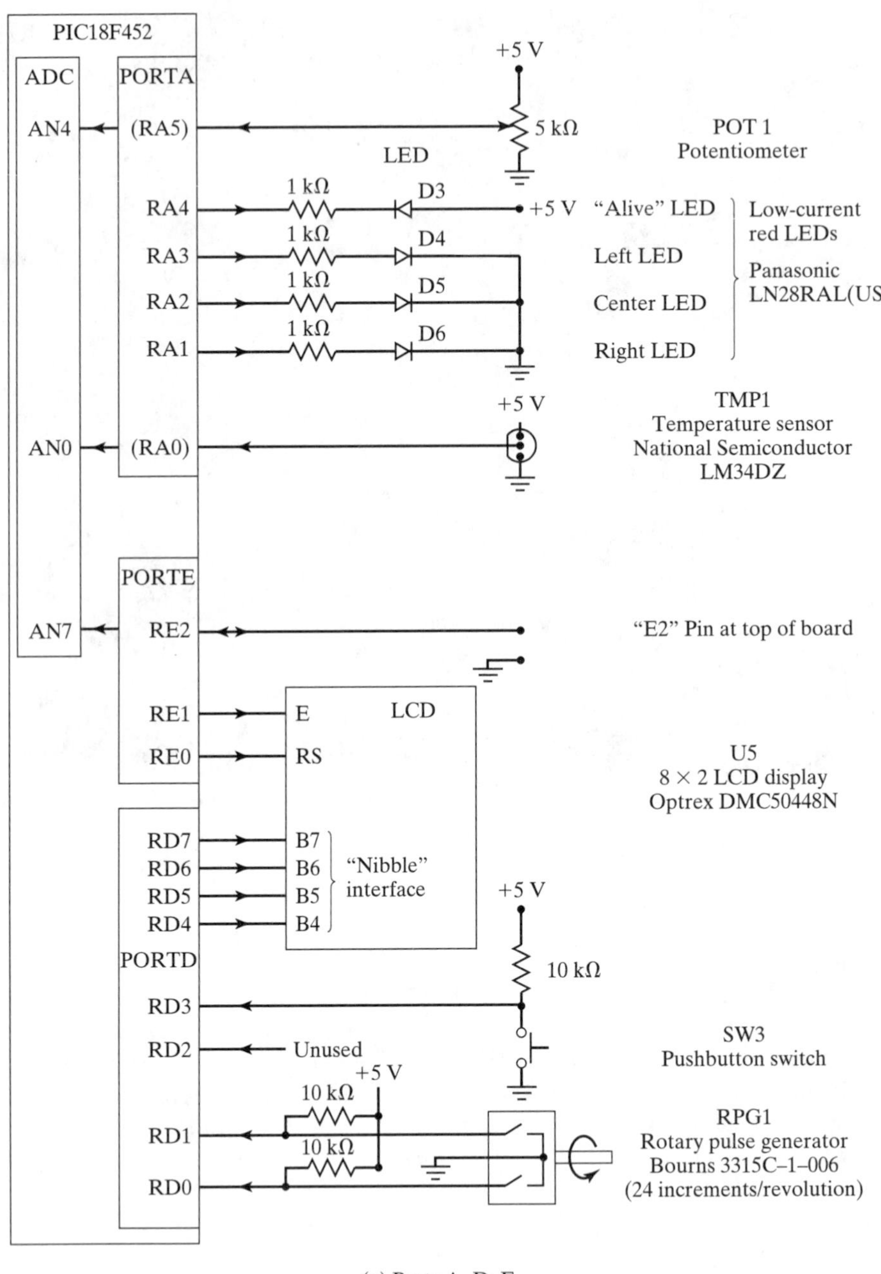

(a) Ports A, D, E

Figure 4-2 QwikFlash I/O.

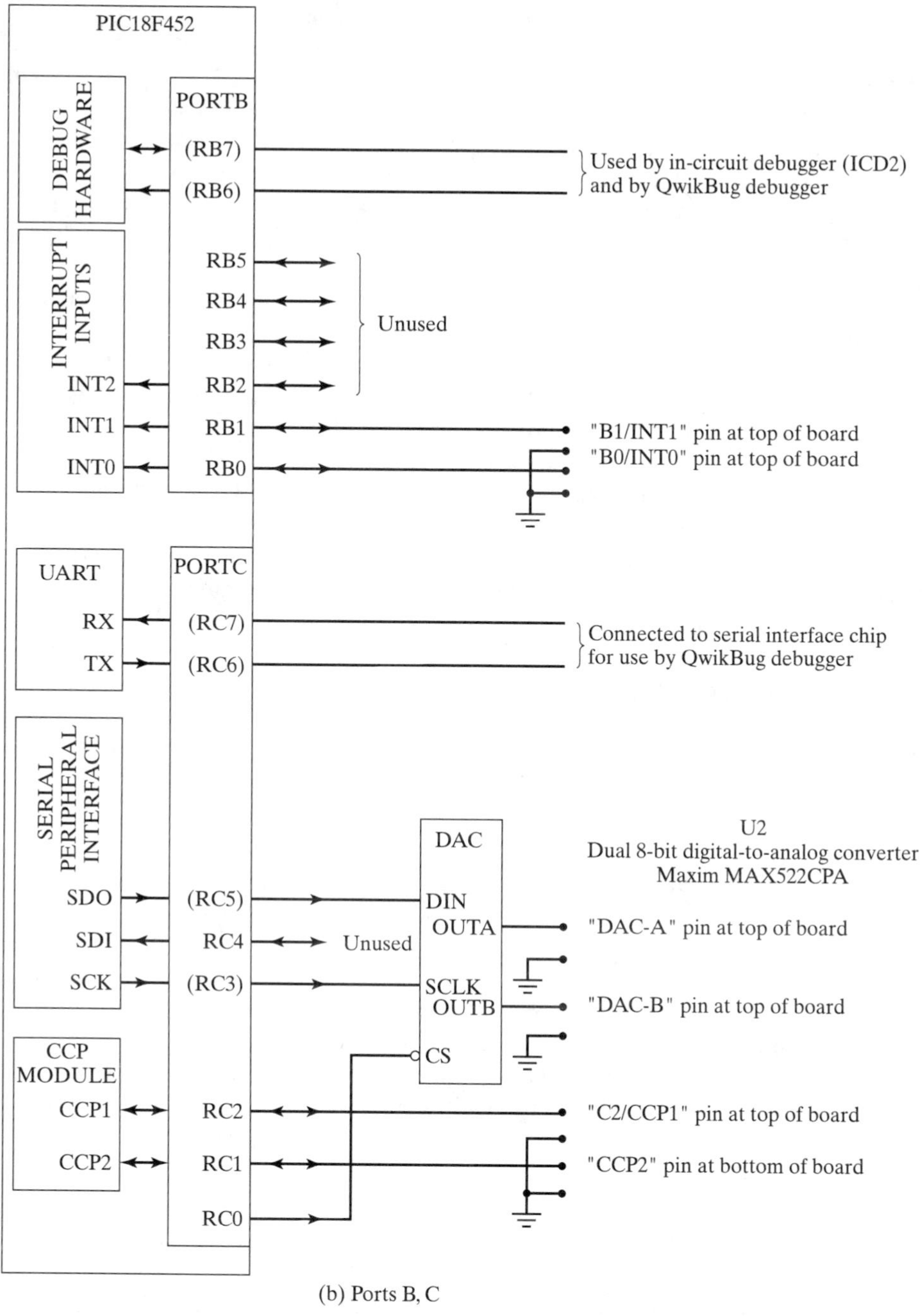

(b) Ports B, C

Figure 4-2 QwikFlash I/O.

inexpensive. In particular, the LCD together with the three components located just beneath it (a push-button switch, a rotary pulse generator, and a potentiometer) provide a versatile user interface, even given such a tiny display. An application program will blink the "Alive" LED connected to RA4 (i.e., bit 4 of PORTA) briefly but periodically. It gives a simple but valuable indication that program execution is progressing, at least to some degree, as expected. Bit 4 of PORTA, when configured as an output, is the chip's only open-drain output. It can drive the output to ground when a zero is written to it. It becomes a high-impedance output, unable to drive anything, when a 1 is written to it. Accordingly, the Alive LED is turned on by driving RA4 low. The *annunciator* LEDs are turned on by driving their output pins high. They are typically used in an application to signal (i.e., annunciate) that a specified condition has occurred. The potentiometer and the temperature sensor serve as inputs to the chip's analog-to-digital converter, whereas the dual DAC serves two functions: It generates two analog outputs, and it also serves as an example of a peripheral device connected to the microcontroller via its *serial peripheral interface,* a shift-register interface often used to gain extra I/O pins for an application.

Six I/O pins are brought out to a terminal strip at the top of the board for ease of monitoring. For example, to meet the specifications for an application, the execution time of an event may be required to be less than some specified value. If the "B0" pin (i.e., bit 0 of PORTB) is set at the beginning of the event and cleared at the end of the event, its pulse width can be measured to determine the duration of the event. An oscilloscope connected to this pin can be used to measure this time. Alternatively, as will be discussed in the next section, a second QwikFlash board can measure the maximun duration of a repetitive event.

The final user feature of the QwikFlash board is its prototyping area working in conjunction with the PIC18F452's 11 undedicated I/O pins. These can be used to support a variety of other I/O facilities, discussed later in the book, such as a stepper motor driver or the connection to a magnetic card reader. Devices connected to the microcontroller via its I^2C bus interface will be examined. The prototype area has sufficient room to handle such additions.

4.3 THE QWIKFLASH INSTRUMENT

The CCP2 and ground pins at the bottom of the board facilitate the use of one QwikFlash board as an instrument to monitor the performance of code running on another QwikFlash board. This connection is illustrated in Figure 4-3. The application program that resides in the QwikFlash instrument will measure frequency or period with the 50-parts-per-million accuracy of the on-board crystal oscillator. It will determine the maximum pulse width of a varying input pulse. Even with its limited capabilities, it is well suited to the kinds of measurements useful for code development. The code for the QwikFlash instrument can be downloaded from www.picbook.com.

4.4 DEBUGGING SUPPORT

The QwikFlash board includes a modular connector for debugging support via Microchip's in-circuit debugger. The ICD2 module is shown in Figure 4-4. It is connected to a PC through a serial cable. It connects to just three pins of the PIC18F452 (RB7, RB6, and the master clear/programming voltage pin). This three-pin connection and the "hooks" internal to the chip are sufficient to

- Program user code into the chip.
- Reset, run, single-step, and run to a breakpoint

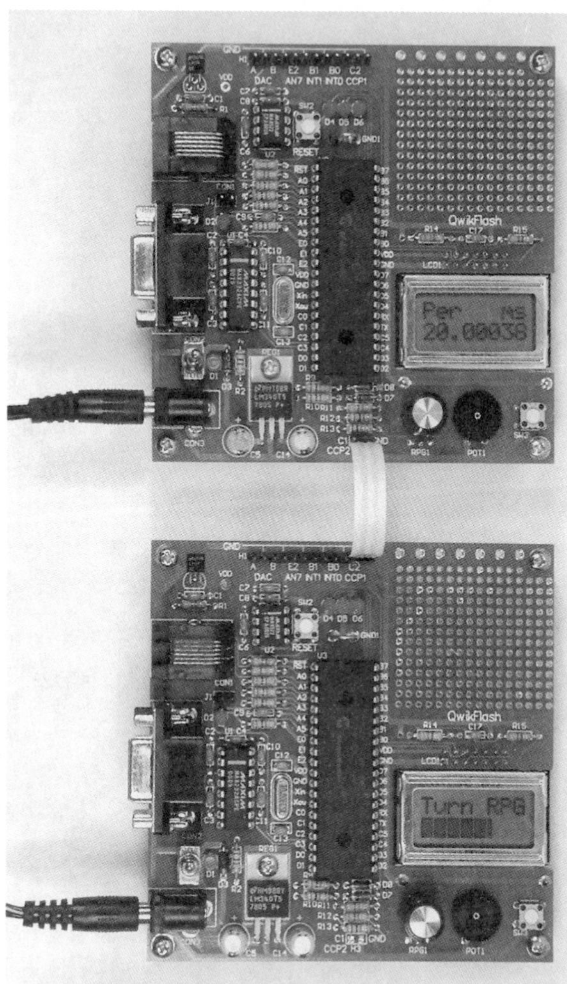

Figure 4-3 The QwikFlash instrument, top, measuring twice the loop time generated by another QwikFlash board.

- Display selected "watch" variables
- Examine and change a register or RAM variable.

This is almost the same feature set as that of the much more expensive Microchip ICE2000 emulator shown in Figure 4-5. Because the emulator actually uses fast RAM to hold the user program, it can "instantaneously" download a large user program each time through the debugging cycle of run-debug-modify-reload-run, whereas the low-cost ICD2 module requires a noticeable amount of time to download a large program. The emulator also includes a logic analyzer to capture real-time activity for subsequent examination and debugging.

The QwikFlash board's built-in *QwikBug* debugger program resides in the upper memory of the PIC18F452. It provides almost the same feature set as that of the ICD2 module but requires nothing more than a serial cable from the DB-9 on-board connector to the PC's serial port. However, whereas Microchip's ICD2 support software is built into their MPLAB® integrated design environment user interface, *QwikBug* interacts with the PC through a terminal emulator program such as the free **Tera Term Pro**. Refer to Appendix A4 for details on the installation and use of the *QwikBug* debugger.

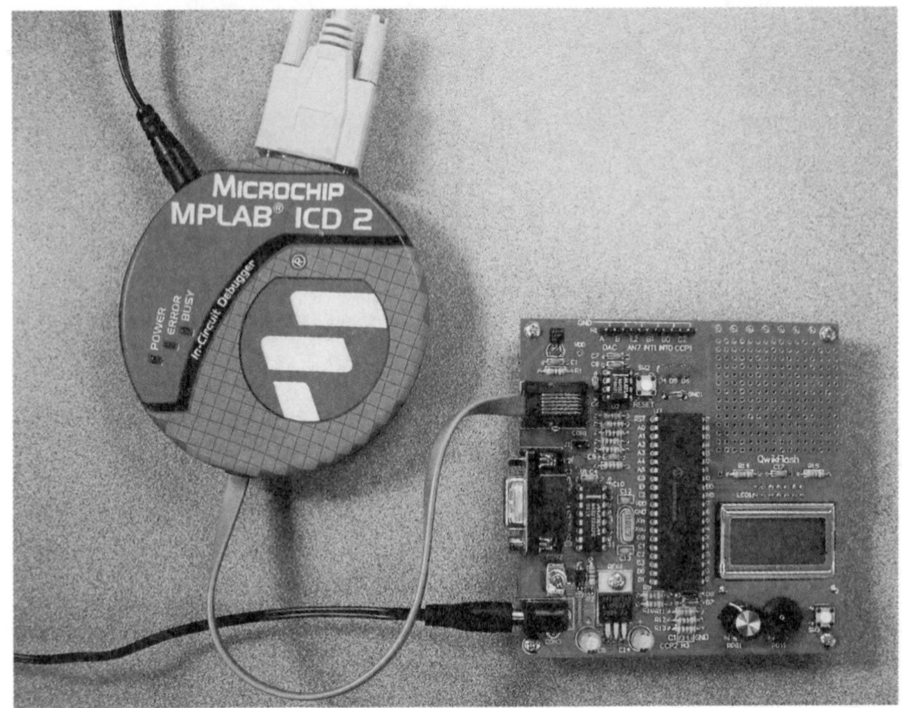

Figure 4-4 Microchip Technology's in-circuit debugger (ICD2).

Figure 4-5 Microchip Technology's MPLAB ICE 2000 emulator.

Chapter

5

PROGRAM DEVELOPMENT (P1 TEMPLATE)

5.1 OVERVIEW

In this chapter, the process of program development will be considered. The chapter begins with the use of one of the PIC18F452's timers as a precise scale-of-*N* counter, with *N* having any value up to the 65,536 scale of its 16-bit binary counter. A counter that cycles through its count sequence every 10 milliseconds will be created.

A program structure will be developed that uses the 10-millisecond "ticks" so derived to control the timing of slow events. A simple application of the timing control will produce a faint blink of an "Alive" LED every 2.5 seconds. The blinking serves as a simple, but effective, indication that any application code subsequently being developed is running with a basic level of functionality.

The structure of a program is developed, including the entire infrastructure needed by the assembler to produce code that meets the constraints imposed by the hardware of the PIC18F452. Microchip supports this process with their excellent, free assembler. Obtaining this assembler and its manual as well as some other tools over the Internet is described.

The Microchip assembler is a *macro* assembler, permitting the extension of the PIC18F452's instruction set to include new *macro* instructions. When such a macro is invoked, it causes a sequence of instructions to be executed. A specific macro, **MOVLF**, will be defined and will become a cornerstone of code development.

This chapter concludes with a brief discussion of the assembly of an application program, how it is carried out, and the files generated by the process. Loading and running the code on the QwikFlash board can be supported with Microchip's in-circuit debugger, their emulator, or the *QwikBug* debugger. The use of the *QwikBug* debugger for this purpose is described.

5.2 TIMER0 OPERATION

The PIC18F452 includes four 16-bit counters: Timer0, Timer1, Timer2, and Timer3. Each of these is especially well suited for certain jobs. Thus, Timer1 and Timer3 can each be coupled to capture/compare/pulse-width-modulation (CCP1 or CCP2) circuitry for measuring and controlling the timing of external events precisely. Timer2 is also used with the CCP circuitry for generating a pulse-width-modulated output. Timer0 is the least versatile of the four counters and can be dedicated to the role of timing slow events.

To gain some idea of Timer0's alternative function as a high-speed counter, consider Figure 5-1a. When operated in this mode, bit 4 of **PORTA** is dedicated as Timer0's clock input (T0CKI). A prescaler value is selected that will scale the external input (of up to 50 MHz) down to a frequency of less than the internal clock rate of the PIC18F452. The scaled frequency input is synchronized to the internal clock, as shown in Figure 5-1b, so that the 16-bit timer, **TMR0H:TMR0L**, can be read from or written to reliably under program control (without violating setup-time and hold-time requirements). The output edges occur after a delay of two internal clock cycles and are synchronized to the internal clock.

The control registers for setting up the mode of operation of Timer0 are shown in Figure 5-1c. A discussion of the **INTCON** register's interrupt enable bits will be discussed in Chapter 9.

For the illustrative code used throughout this book, Timer0 will be clocked with the internal clock (**T0CS** = 0 in the **T0CON** register) and with the prescaler bypassed (**PSA** = 1 in the **T0CON** register). Given this, the time between successive settings of the **TMR0IF** flag as the **TMR0H:TMR0L** rolls over from 0xffff to 0x0000 can be made equal to *exactly N* clock cycles. The circuit is shown in Figure 5-2.

Figure 5-2 illustrates the sophisticated circuitry used by the Microchip designers to permit a 16-bit counter to be read from and written to without error, even though the reads and writes take place 8 bits at a time. At the exact moment that **TMR0L** is read, the contents of the upper counter are copied into a buffer register. A subsequent read of **TMR0H** is actually a read of the buffer register. It holds what was in the upper counter at the precise moment **TMR0L** was read.

In like manner, a 16-bit value can be written into Timer0 at a precise moment. First, the upper byte is written into the buffer register, **TMR0H**. Then, at the exact moment when the lower byte is written to **TMR0L**, the buffer register (**TMR0H**) will be written to the upper byte of the counter.

With no prescaler, Timer0 normally rolls over every 65,536 clock cycles. To make it count with a scale of 25,000 so that the microcontroller's internal clock period of 0.4 microseconds produces a setting of **TMR0IF** precisely every 10 milliseconds, it is necessary to remove

$$65{,}536 - 25{,}000 = 40{,}536$$

counts from the sequence. However, because the process of reading **TMR0H:TMR0L**, adding to the value read, and writing back to **TMR0H:TMR0L** takes some number of clock cycles, M, it is actually necessary to add

$$65{,}536 - 25{,}000 + M$$

If any potential interrupt sources are enabled, they must be disabled during the modification of Timer0 to maintain M as a constant, known value. In addition, two extra cycles must be added because writing to **TMR0L** resets the synchronizer, causing the loss of two counts between its input and its output. So, finally, the value to be added is

$$65{,}536 - 25{,}000 + M + 2$$

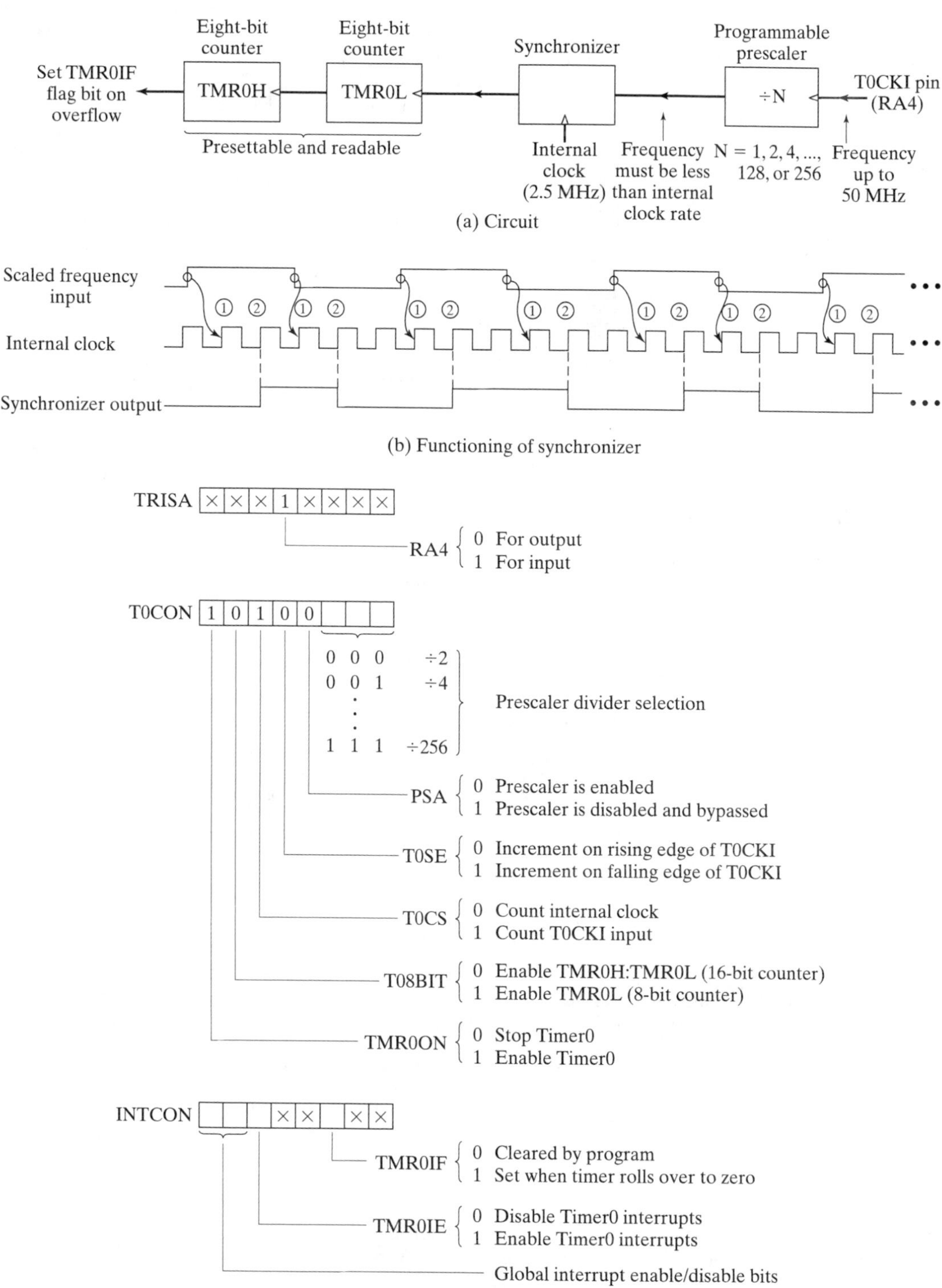

Figure 5-1 Use of Timer0 as a high-speed counter.

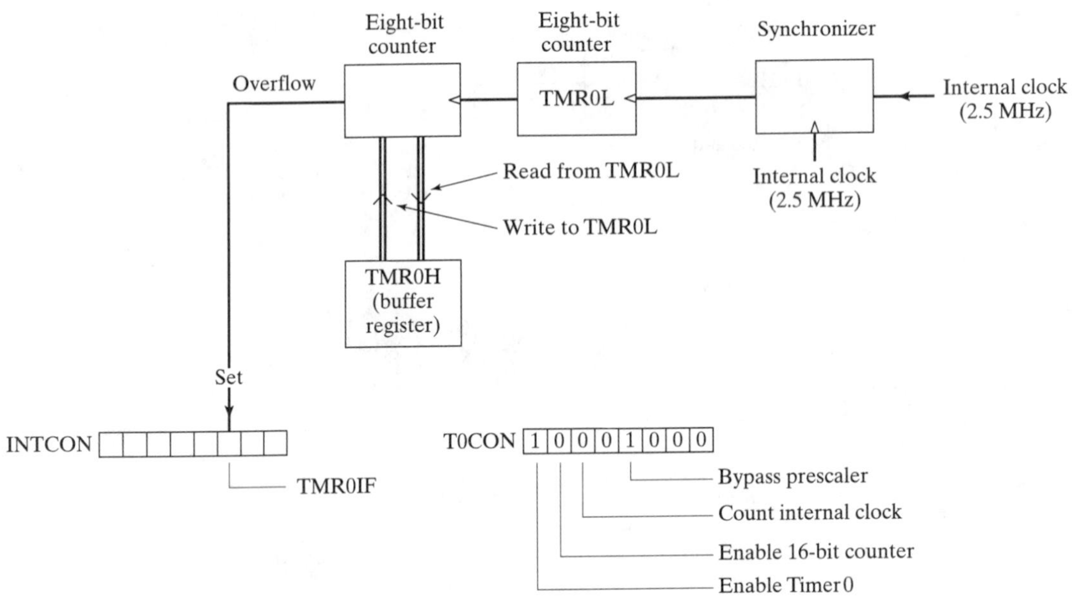

Figure 5-2 Use of Timer0 to implement a scale-of-*N* counter.

```
movff  TMRØL,TMRØLCOPY   ;Read 16-bit counter at this moment
movff  TMRØH,TMRØHCOPY
movlw  low  Bignum
addwf  TMRØLCOPY,F
movlw  high  Bignum
addwfc  TMRØHCOPY,F
movff  TMRØHCOPY,TMRØH
movff  TMRØLCOPY,TMRØL   ;Write 16-bit counter at this moment
```

(a) Instruction sequence.

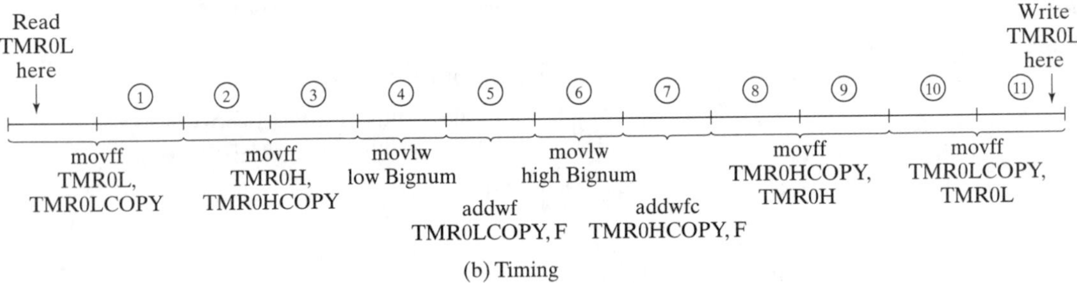

(b) Timing

Figure 5-3 Read-add-write timing for Timer0.

where *M* is the number of cycles between the reading of **TMR0L** and the writing back to **TMR0L**. The code to carry out this read-add-write operation is shown in Figure 5-3a, and a timing diagram is shown in Figure 5-3b. Although only 11 clock cycles transpire between the read of **TMR0L** and the write back to **TMR0L**, the counter itself has actually incremented 12 times between these two events. To understand why this is so, note that each instruction is executed over four quarter-cycles. When an instruction does a read, the read occurs during the second quarter-cycle. When it does a write, the write occurs during the fourth quarter-cycle. Timer0 is incremented between these two events leading to $M = 12$ or

$$65{,}536 - 25{,}000 + 12 + 2 = 40{,}550$$

Although the prescaler can be used to extend this scheme and create a scale-of-N counter for values of N up to

$$65{,}536 \times 256$$

or over 16 million, the scale is no longer exact. Each write to **TMR0L** also resets the prescaler, extending the period from the intended value by the number in the prescaler. However, even with this discrepancy, the period is within one part in 65,536 of the intended value.

5.3 PROGRAM STRUCTURE

Consider the program structure of Figure 5-4. As the microcontroller comes out of reset, it first initializes appropriate registers and variables. Then it enters a loop of instructions consisting of subroutine calls. These subroutines carry out the action of the microcontroller. The **LoopTime** subroutine uses Timer0 to fill out each loop to 10 milliseconds. With a 10 MHz crystal and an internal clock period of 0.4 microseconds, this means that the mainline subroutines have up to 25,000 cycles available for their execution each time around the loop. Algorithms that must act more slowly can obtain their timing information by acting only every Nth time their subroutines are called. For example, an LED can be toggled every second with a subroutine that implements a scale-of-100 counter and increments the counter each time the subroutine is called. Each time the counter resets, the LED is toggled.

With the simple scheme of Figure 5-4, real-time tasks that are served by subroutines in the mainline loop may have that service delayed for up to 10 milliseconds. For faster service, they can trigger an interrupt and be serviced by an interrupt handler. With its plethora of interrupt sources associated with its many internal facilities as well as its three external interrupt pins, the PIC18F452 is well equipped to achieve sophisticated real-time operation with the simple program structure of Figure 5-4.

5.4 LOOPTIME SUBROUTINE

The task of the **LoopTime** subroutine in the mainline loop of Figure 5-4 is to link how long it takes to traverse the loop to the period of Timer0. The subroutine is listed in Figure 5-5. Each time Timer0 rolls over from 0xffff to 0x0000, it automatically sets the **TMR0IF** flag in the **INTCON** register. The **LoopTime** subroutine begins by waiting for this event to occur. Then it disables all interrupts, does the read-add-write operation, reenables interrupts, clears the **TMR0IF** flag, and returns.

```
Mainline
        rcall  Initial
Loop
        call   Subroutine1
        call   Subroutine2
         .
         .
         .
        call   SubroutineN
        call   LoopTime
        bra  Loop
Initial
         .
         .
         .
        return
Subroutine1
         .
         .
         .
        return
Subroutine2
         .
         .
         .
        return
         .
         .
         .
SubroutineN
         .
         .
         .
        return
LoopTime
         .
         .
         .
        return
HiPriISR                 }
         .               }
         .               }  Instructions to be executed in response
         .               }  to a high-priority interrupt
         .               }
        retfie           }
LoPriISR                 }
         .               }
         .               }  Instructions to be executed in response
         .               }  to a low-priority interrupt
        retfie           }
```

Figure 5-4 A program structure.

Example 5-1 The simple change of one of the *configuration byte*[1] settings in the source file for an application will change the chip's internal clock rate from 10/4 = 2.5 MHz to 10 MHz. The 10 MHz crystal oscillator will be synced via a phase-locked loop to an internal 40 MHz VFO (variable frequency oscillator) divided by 4. In this way, and with no hardware change to the QwikFlash board, the PIC18F452 will run at an internal clock rate of 10 MHz, with the 40 MHz VFO providing the quarter-cycle timing.

[1]See Section 5.7

```
;;;;;;; LoopTime subroutine ;;;;;;;;;;;;;;;;;;;;;;;;;;;;;;;;;;;;;;;;;;;;;;;;;;;;;
;
; This subroutine waits for TimerØ to complete its ten millisecond count
; sequence. It does so by waiting for sixteen-bit TimerØ to roll over. To obtain
; a period of precisely 10000/0.4 = 25,000 clock periods, it needs to remove
; 65,536-25000 or 40536 counts from the sixteen-bit count sequence.  The
; algorithm below first copies TimerØ to RAM, adds "Bignum" to the copy, and
; then writes the result back to TimerØ. It actually needs to add somewhat more
; counts to TimerØ than 40536.  The extra number of 12+2 counts added into
; "Bignum" makes the precise correction.

Bignum  equ     65536-25000+12+2

LoopTime
        btfss  INTCON,TMRØIF      ;Wait until 10 milliseconds are up
        bra  LoopTime
        movff  INTCON,INTCONCOPY  ;Disable all interrupts to CPU
        bcf  INTCON,GIEH
        movff  TMRØL,TMRØLCOPY    ;Read 16-bit counter at this moment
        movff  TMRØH,TMRØHCOPY
        movlw  low  Bignum
        addwf  TMRØLCOPY,F
        movlw  high  Bignum
        addwfc  TMRØHCOPY,F
        movff  TMRØHCOPY,TMRØH
        movff  TMRØLCOPY,TMRØL    ;Write 16-bit counter at this moment
        movf  INTCONCOPY,W        ;Restore GIEH interrupt enable bit
        andlw  B'10000000'
        iorwf  INTCON,F
        bcf  INTCON,TMRØIF        ;Clear TimerØ flag
        return
```

Figure 5-5 LoopTime subroutine.

(a) Using as small a value of prescaler divider as possible and the information in Figure 5-1, determine the appropriate initialization of **T0CON** to continue to use Timer0 to obtain a looptime of 10 milliseconds, that is, to divide the internal clock rate by 10,000 microseconds/0.1 microsecond = 100,000.

(b) What should the **LoopTime** subroutine's value for **Bignum** be now?

Solution:

(a) By using the prescaler's ÷2 divider, Timer0 will roll over every $65{,}536 \times 2 = 131{,}072$ internal clock cycles. **T0CON** must be initialized to B′10000000′.

(b) **Bignum** $= 131072 - 100000 + 12 + 2$

5.5 BLINKALIVE SUBROUTINE

The **BlinkAlive** subroutine listed in Figure 5-6 takes advantage of the 10 millisecond looptime and a scale-of-250 counter to take action every 2 ½ seconds. The **ALIVECNT** variable is decremented each time the subroutine is called. When **ALIVECNT** is decremented to zero, it is reinitialized to 250 and the LED is turned on. Ten milliseconds later, the LED is turned off. Thus the LED is turned on for 10 milliseconds every 2 ½ seconds. Although this low duty cycle would seem to produce a hardly visible flicker of light, it is actually enough to indicate to a user that the code is being executed and thereby serve as a simple debugging aid.

```
;;;;;;; BlinkAlive subroutine ;;;;;;;;;;;;;;;;;;;;;;;;;;;;;;;;;;;;;;;;;;;;;;;;;;;;
;
; This subroutine briefly blinks the LED next to the PIC every 2.5
; seconds.

BlinkAlive
        bsf  PORTA,RA4            ;Turn off LED
        decf  ALIVECNT,F          ;Decrement loop counter and return if not zero
        bnz  BAend
        MOVLF  250,ALIVECNT       ;Reinitialize ALIVECNT
        bcf  PORTA,RA4            ;Turn on LED for 10 milliseconds every 2.5 sec
BAend
        return
```

Figure 5-6 BlinkAlive subroutine.

Example 5-2 What change in the **BlinkAlive** subroutine must be made so that the LED is toggled every half-second?

Solution:

The initial **bsf** instruction must be removed. The **bcf** instruction must be changed to a **btg** instruction, which will complement the bit each time the **ALIVECNT** variable is reinitialized. Finally, **ALIVECNT** should be reinitialized to 50 so that every 50×10 ms $= 500$ ms $= 0.5$ s the state of the LED will be changed.

5.6 MACROS

Microchip's free assembler, MPASMWIN.EXE, includes support for macros. This capability permits a recurring sequence of instructions to be given a nickname. For example, the PIC18F452 instruction set includes a

```
movff  <source>,<destination>
```

instruction to read a byte from a source location and copy it to a destination location. The related operation of loading a constant, or literal, value into a destination location is not supported by a single instruction. Instead, the following sequence appears repeatedly in user code:

```
movlw  <literal>
movwf  <destination>
```

It can be represented by a macro. To do so, the macro must first be *defined,* using the following assembler syntax:

```
MOVLF  macro  literal,dest
       movlw  literal
       movwf  dest
       endm
```

When it is subsequently *invoked* with

```
MOVLF  250,ALIVECNT
```

the assembler will replace this macro expression by the two-instruction sequence

```
movlw  250
movwf  ALIVECNT
```

Many code writers capitalize macro names so that they will stand out as something other than a normal instruction. One good reason to capitalize macros is to serve as a flag to the code writer to remember to watch out for any *side effects* of the macro. For example, this macro has the side effect of corrupting the contents of **WREG.** Note that the sequence

```
movlw  5
MOVLF  10,COUNT
call  Subroutine1
```

which might be intended to call **Subroutine1** with the value of 5 in **WREG** and the value of 10 in **COUNT,** will actually call **Subroutine1** with the value of 10 in both **WREG** and **COUNT**.

The structure of a macro definition begins with a line holding the name of the macro, the word "macro," and dummy names for any parameters used by the macro. The macro definition ends on a line with the single word "endm." In between these can be an arbitrary instruction sequence.

Example 5-3 The PIC18F452 instruction set includes **incf** and **decf** instructions to increment or decrement any single-byte register or RAM variable. It does not have specific instructions to increment or decrement the 12-bit pointers, **FSR0**, **FSR1**, and **FSR2**. Create two macros

INC0 and **DEC0**

to increment and decrement **FSR0**.

Solution: The autoincrement option associated with indirect addressing provides an opportunity:

```
INC0  macro
      movf  POSTINC0,F
      endm
```

The **movf** instruction will first copy the location pointed to by **FSR0** to itself and then automatically increment the 12-bit register, **FSR0**. Note that the alternative instruction

```
      incf  FSR0L,F
```

will malfunction if **FSR0** is pointing to RAM address 0x01ff. In this case, the result of the **incf** instruction will be 0x0100.

The **DEC0** macro employs the autodecrement feature of indirect addressing:

```
DEC0  macro
      movf  POSTDEC0,F
      endm
```

If a macro definition includes a label to identify the destination of a conditional branch instruction, the assembler will flag a "duplicate label" error for each invocation of the macro after the first, saying that the label has already been defined. One solution to this problem is to identify the target address of a branch instruction using an operand of the form

```
$±2N
```

The "$" sign represents the address of the present instruction. Thus

```
bra  $
```

is treated the same as

```
Stop  bra  Stop
```

The following sequence in a macro definition

```
btfss  register,bit
bra  $-2
```

will test "bit" and if it is clear, will branch back to the **btfss** instruction. Because program memory is addressed by 8-bit bytes, not 16-bit instruction words, a branch of *N* instruction words requires a value of *2N*.

5.7 P1.ASM PROGRAM

The code of Figure 5-7 brings these ideas together into a program that can be assembled and then executed by the PIC18F452. The program adds the infrastructure needed both for clarity and to fulfill the programming needs of the chip. It begins with brief comments describing the application. Note that the assembler ignores a line beginning with a semicolon. Consequently, such a line can be used for descriptive comments.

The *Program hierarchy* serves as a table of contents to show the relationship between the program's subroutines. The indentation indicates that **Mainline** calls **Initial**, **BlinkAlive**, and **LoopTime**. If **BlinkAlive** called a **Wait** subroutine, the word **Wait** would be indented beneath **BlinkAlive** to indicate this relationship.

The *Assembler directives* section begins with a *list* assembler directive that can be used in either of two ways. The Microchip assembler, MPASMWIN.EXE, uses

```
list  (without any parameters)
```

and

```
nolist
```

to bracket any lines of code that are not to be included in the list file generated by the assembler. For example, the second line in this section

```
#include  P18F452.inc
```

tells the assembler to find a file called P18F452.inc and insert its lines into the P1 file, ready to be assembled together. This *include* file is necessary to associate register names (e.g., **PORTB**) with their addresses (e.g., 0xf81), and also bit names (e.g., **Z**) with their bit position in the register holding them (e.g., 2). Because all of this information for all registers and all of their bit names would just clutter the list file, the PIC18F452.inc file has a *nolist* directive at its beginning and a *list* directive at its end, thereby removing its lines from the list file.

An alternative usage of the *list* assembler directive is shown in Figure 5-7. The parameters specify the following information:

P = PIC18F452	identifies the specific target microcontroller
F = INHX32	specifies that the output *hex* file should use the Intel 32-bit hexadecimal format
C = 160	formats the list file for a printer capable of printing 160 columns

```
;;;;;;; P1 for QwikFlash board ;;;;;;;;;;;;;;;;;;;;;;;;;;;;;;;;;;;;;;;;;;;;;;;;
;
; Use 10 MHz crystal frequency.
; Use Timer0 for ten millisecond looptime.
; Blink "Alive" LED every two and a half seconds.
; Toggle C2 output every ten milliseconds for measuring looptime precisely.
;
;;;;;;; Program hierarchy ;;;;;;;;;;;;;;;;;;;;;;;;;;;;;;;;;;;;;;;;;;;;;;;;;;;;;
;
; Mainline
;   Initial
;   BlinkAlive
;   LoopTime
;
;;;;;;; Assembler directives ;;;;;;;;;;;;;;;;;;;;;;;;;;;;;;;;;;;;;;;;;;;;;;;;;;

        list  P=PIC18F452, F=INHX32, C=160, N=0, ST=OFF, MM=OFF, R=DEC, X=ON
        #include P18F452.inc
        __CONFIG  _CONFIG1H, _HS_OSC_1H  ;HS oscillator
        __CONFIG  _CONFIG2L, _PWRT_ON_2L & _BOR_ON_2L & _BORV_42_2L  ;Reset
        __CONFIG  _CONFIG2H, _WDT_OFF_2H  ;Watchdog timer disabled
        __CONFIG  _CONFIG3H, _CCP2MX_ON_3H  ;CCP2 to RC1 (rather than to RB3)
        __CONFIG  _CONFIG4L, _LVP_OFF_4L  ;RB5 enabled for I/O

;;;;;;; Variables ;;;;;;;;;;;;;;;;;;;;;;;;;;;;;;;;;;;;;;;;;;;;;;;;;;;;;;;;;;;;;

        cblock  0x000           ;Beginning of Access RAM
        TMR0LCOPY               ;Copy of sixteen-bit Timer0 used by LoopTime
        TMR0HCOPY
        INTCONCOPY              ;Copy of INTCON for LoopTime subroutine
        ALIVECNT                ;Counter for blinking "Alive" LED
        endc

;;;;;;; Macro definitions ;;;;;;;;;;;;;;;;;;;;;;;;;;;;;;;;;;;;;;;;;;;;;;;;;;;;;

MOVLF   macro  literal,dest
        movlw  literal
        movwf  dest
        endm

;;;;;;; Vectors ;;;;;;;;;;;;;;;;;;;;;;;;;;;;;;;;;;;;;;;;;;;;;;;;;;;;;;;;;;;;;;;

        org  0x0000             ;Reset vector
        nop
        goto  Mainline

        org  0x0008             ;High priority interrupt vector
        goto  $                 ;Trap

        org  0x0018             ;Low priority interrupt vector
        goto  $                 ;Trap

;;;;;;; Mainline program ;;;;;;;;;;;;;;;;;;;;;;;;;;;;;;;;;;;;;;;;;;;;;;;;;;;;;;

Mainline
        rcall  Initial          ;Initialize everything
Loop
        btg  PORTC,RC2          ;Toggle pin, to support measuring loop time
        rcall  BlinkAlive       ;Blink "Alive" LED
        rcall  LoopTime         ;Make looptime be ten milliseconds
        bra  Loop

;;;;;;; Initial subroutine ;;;;;;;;;;;;;;;;;;;;;;;;;;;;;;;;;;;;;;;;;;;;;;;;;;;;
;
; This subroutine performs all initializations of variables and registers.

Initial
        MOVLF  B'10001110',ADCON1  ;Enable PORTA & PORTE digital I/O pins
        MOVLF  B'11100001',TRISA  ;Set I/O for PORTA
        MOVLF  B'11011100',TRISB  ;Set I/O for PORTB
        MOVLF  B'11010000',TRISC  ;Set I/O for PORTC
        MOVLF  B'00001111',TRISD  ;Set I/O for PORTD
        MOVLF  B'00000000',TRISE  ;Set I/O for PORTE
        MOVLF  B'10001000',T0CON  ;Set up Timer0 for a looptime of 10 ms
        MOVLF  B'00010000',PORTA  ;Turn off all four LEDs driven from PORTA
        return
```

Figure 5-7 P1.asm file.

```
;;;;;;; LoopTime subroutine ;;;;;;;;;;;;;;;;;;;;;;;;;;;;;;;;;;;;;;;;;;;;;;;;;;;
;
; This subroutine waits for Timer0 to complete its ten millisecond count
; sequence. It does so by waiting for sixteen-bit Timer0 to roll over. To obtain
; a period of precisely 10000/0.4 = 25000 clock periods, it needs to remove
; 65536-25,000 or 40536 counts from the sixteen-bit count sequence.  The
; algorithm below first copies Timer0 to RAM, adds "Bignum" to the copy, and
; then writes the result back to Timer0. It actually needs to add somewhat more
; counts to Timer0 than 40536.  The extra number of 12+2 counts added into
; "Bignum" makes the precise correction.

Bignum  equu    65536-25000+12+2

LoopTime
        btfss  INTCON,TMR0IF     ;Wait until ten milliseconds are up
        bra  LoopTime
        movff  INTCON,INTCONCOPY  ;Disable all interrupts to CPU
        bcf  INTCON,GIEH
        movff  TMR0L,TMR0LCOPY   ;Read 16-bit counter at this moment
        movff  TMR0H,TMR0HCOPY
        movlw  low  Bignum
        addwf  TMR0LCOPY,F
        movlw  high  Bignum
        addwfc  TMR0HCOPY,F
        movff  TMR0HCOPY,TMR0H
        movff  TMR0LCOPY,TMR0L   ;Write 16-bit counter at this moment
        movf  INTCONCOPY,W       ;Restore GIEH interrupt enable bit
        andlw  B'10000000'
        iorwf  INTCON,F
        bcf  INTCON,TMR0IF       ;Clear Timer0 flag
        return

;;;;;;; BlinkAlive subroutine ;;;;;;;;;;;;;;;;;;;;;;;;;;;;;;;;;;;;;;;;;;;;;;;;;;
;
; This subroutine briefly blinks the LED next to the PIC every two-and-a-half
; seconds.

BlinkAlive
        bsf  PORTA,RA4           ;Turn off LED
        decf  ALIVECNT,F         ;Decrement loop counter and return if not zero
        bnz  BAend
        MOVLF  250,ALIVECNT      ;Reinitialize ALIVECNT
        bcf  PORTA,RA4           ;Turn on LED for ten milliseconds every 2.5 sec
BAend
        return

        end
```

Figure 5-7 continued

N = 0	turns off headers otherwise intended to be printed at the top of each page of the list file
ST = OFF	turns off the inclusion of the symbol table in the list file
MM = OFF	turns off the inclusion of a memory map in the list file
R = DEC	specifies that the default radix is to be decimal (instead of hexadecimal)
X = ON	turns on macro expansion in the list file, thereby showing all instructions introduced each time that a macro is invoked.

The __CONFIG assembler directives specify settings that select among hardware options or enable/disable hardware features. For example, the PIC18F452 offers a user *eight* different oscillator circuits, one of which must be selected. It has a watchdog timer that must be either enabled or disabled.

The *Variables* section of Figure 5-7 uses the construct

```
cblock  0x000
   .
   .
   .
endc
```

to tell the assembler to assign successive addresses to each listed variable name, beginning with address 0, the beginning of the Access RAM of Figures 2-3 and 2-6.

As discussed in Section 2.6, the PIC18F452 has three special program addresses, called *vector* addresses. The first of these is address 0x0000, the reset vector address. The code of P1.asm lists

```
org  0x0000                    ;Reset vector
nop
goto  Mainline
```

Coming out of reset, the chip automatically clears the program counter to 0. The "org 0x0000" directive above tells the assembler to assemble the lines that follow beginning at hexadecimal address 0000. Although the initial **nop** instruction is not necessary, it hurts nothing.The **goto Mainline** instruction jumps over the two interrupt vector addresses, 0x0008 and 0x0018. Although these other two vectors are not used with the P1 code, they will be used in subsequent chapters.

The *Mainline program* section shows the overall structure of the entire program. Coming out of reset, the program will initialize registers and variables as appropriate. Then it will settle into the mainline loop, where it calls the **BlinkAlive** subroutine each time around the loop. The **LoopTime** subroutine forces that loop time to be 10 milliseconds.

The **Initial** subroutine begins with a cryptic initialization

```
MOVLF  B'10001110',ADCON1
```

The **ADCON1** register, used in conjunction with the PIC18F452's analog-to-digital converter, also specifies which pins of **PORTA** and **PORTE** are to be used as ADC analog inputs and which are to be used as digital I/O pins. The default, power-on state disables the digital circuitry associated with these pins. The initialization shown configures **PORTA**'s RA0/AN0 pin (i.e., bit 0 of **PORTA**) as an analog input and all the remaining pins as digital I/O pins. Referring back to Figure 4-2(a), it will be seen that the RA5/AN4 pin on the QwikFlash board is intended to be used as an ADC input from a potentiometer. The initialization of **ADCON1** selecting this pin as a digital I/O pin does not disable its analog function as long as the digital pin is set up as an *input* pin.

The **TRIS** initializations of Figure 5-7 set up every I/O line on the chip to match the surrounding circuitry of Figure 4-2. Each 0 in a **TRIS** bit specifies that the corresponding pin is to be configured as an output.

5.8 FREE TOOLS

Microchip's free assembler, MPASMWIN.EXE, and its manual are available for downloading from their Web site, www.microchip.com. Select *Developer's Toolbox—Development Tools.* Within the resulting Web page, select *PICmicro Tools—Development Environment* and download the "Integrated Development Environment," *MPLAB IDE,* as well as *MPLAB Manual and Tutorial.* Among all the files downloaded are the two needed in the next section, MPASMWIN.EXE and P18F452.INC. The manual on the assembler is reached from the Web page *PICmicro Tools—Code Generation Tools—MPASM Assembler.* Download *MPASM Assembler User's Guide with MPLINK and MPLIB.*

Use of the *QwikBug* debugger calls for a terminal emulator that can be set up to deal directly with a device connected to a PC's serial port. An excellent, free, and popular terminal emulator is Tera Term Pro. It is available from a variety of sources that can be found with the search engine www.google.com. Just search for *Tera Term Pro.*

```
PORT:              COM1:
Baud rate:         19200
Data:              8 bit
Parity:            none
Stop:              1 bit
Flow control:      none
Transmit delay
  0 msec/char       10 msec/line
                    (or 20 msec/line; see Appendix section A4.5)
```

Figure 5-8 Tera Term Pro's serial port setup for QwikBug.

After downloading and installing the utility, create a desktop icon for it. Using Windows Explorer, go to C:\Program Files\TTERMPRO folder, right-click on ttermpro.exe, and create a shortcut to it. Drag the shortcut to the Windows desktop. Double-click on the icon to open Tera Term Pro. To change the default folder for the files to be developed, click on the *Files* pull-down menu and double-click on the *Change folder*. . . entry. Enter C:\Work, or whatever is chosen as the folder name for source files to be developed for the PIC18F452. Close this window and click on *Setup,* followed by *Save setup* . . . , to save this folder information.

The *QwikBug* debugger expects the serial port parameters shown in Figure 5-8. The port should be switched from COM1: to whatever port is used to connect via a serial cable to the QwikFlash board. That board is set up to transfer data at 19,200 baud with the protocol shown.

The transmit delay of 10 msec/line is used during the download of a user program to the PIC18F452's flash memory under the control of *QwikBug.* The "hex" file (discussed in the next section) has eight instruction words in each line of the file. *QwikBug* reads an entire line and must verify a check sum and program the eight words before it is ready to receive the next line. The "10 msec/line" transmit delay provides time for the microcontroller to program the eight instruction words making up the line.

After entering the serial port setup of Figure 5-8, click on the *Save setup* . . . item in the setup pull-down menu. This will save the serial setup information for the next time Tera Term Pro is used.

One other utility that can be optimized for use with the assembler is the DOS utility itself. An MS-DOS icon can be added to the Windows desktop that opens directly into the folder containing files to be assembled as well as the assembler. Using Windows Explorer, click on the C:\WINDOWS folder. Click on the COMMAND.COM file and drag it to the desktop. Right-click on its name, "Shortcut to MS-DOS Prompt" and rename it "MS-DOS for PIC". Next, right-click on its icon and click on *Properties* and then the *Program* tab. Under *Working:,* enter the path to the folder used to hold source files and the assembler (e.g., C:\Work). Subsequent clicking on the desktop icon will open a DOS window into this folder, immediately ready to be used for assembly.

5.9 ASSEMBLY

The procedure for assembling the P1.asm file can be carried out from either the DOS prompt or from within Microchip's MPLAB. Given the simplicity of running the assembler from the DOS prompt, it will be described. With the following three files all present in the same Windows folder:

P1.asm
MPASMWIN.EXE
P18F452.INC

open a DOS window into this folder. Then execute

```
mpasmwin P1
```

```
:020000040000FA
:0600000000000EEF00F00D
:0400080004EF00F011
:080018000CEF00F004D8827423
:1000200029D812D8FCD78E0EC16EE10E926EDC0E6E
:10003000936ED00E946E0F0E956E000E966E880E17
:10004000D56E100E806E1200F2A4FED7F2CF02F031
:10005000F29ED6CF00F0D7CF01F0660E00269E0E9E
:10006000012201C0D7FF00C0D6FF0250800BF21260
:10007000F29412008088030603E1FA0E036E809862
:020080001200 6C
:020000040030CA
:08000000FFFAF6FEFFFFFBFF13
:00000001FF
```

Figure 5-9 P1.HEX file.

This *command-line interface* will generate several files. The *hex* file, P1.HEX, is the primary output of the assembler and is shown in Figure 5-9. It is the file to be downloaded to the PIC18F452's flash memory by the *QwikBug* monitor program or with Microchip's in-circuit debugger. Alternatively, it can be downloaded to an emulator or to a programmer. It is a file containing the hexadecimal-coded program instructions and their addresses.

The *error* file, P1.ERR, lists all warnings and errors found by the assembler. Each entry includes an error number and its brief description plus the line number in the source file containing the source of the warning or error. The P1.ERR file provides a shortcut between assembler errors and their removal from the source file, P1.asm.

The *list* file, P1.LST, shown in Figure 5-10, lists the source file together with the hex code generated by the assembler, instruction by instruction. It also shows the program address corresponding to each instruction.

The *cod* file, P1.COD, is used to pass labels and their addresses to the MPLAB software for use in debugging with the in-circuit debugger or with an emulator.

5.10 EXECUTION

Depending on what tools are available, execution of the P1 program on the QwikFlash board calls for a procedure that fits the tool. If that tool is the *QwikBug* monitor already residing in the PIC18F452 chip on the board, then a terminal emulator (e.g., Tera Term Pro) is started and power applied to the QwikFlash board. It sends a startup message, displayed on the PC's monitor, with a help screen for *QwikBug* commands. This help screen can also be displayed at any time by pressing the F1 function key. Press the F3 key to load the hex file. This sets up *QwikBug* to receive the hex file to be sent to it next. Press no other keyboard keys before clicking on Tera Term Pro's menu *File* and then the *Send File . . .* entry. Double-click on the hex file to send it to the QwikFlash board. Finally, as the *QwikBug* help screen (invoked by pressing the F1 function key) indicates, pressing F2 followed by F7 will reset the PIC18F452 and then run the downloaded code from reset. The "Alive" LED will blink briefly every 2.5 seconds. The period of the "C2" output at the top of the board can be monitored using a second QwikFlash board running the QwikFlash instrument described in Section 4.3. Because the mainline program toggles this pin every time around the 10 millisecond mainline loop, the period of the C2 output will be 20 milliseconds. This is the measurement shown in Figure 4-3. Alternatively, the period can be monitored using the period-measurement feature of an oscilloscope, such as that shown in Figure 5-11.

```
                  00001 ;;;;;;; P1 for QwikFlash board ;;;;;;;;;;;;;;;;;;;;;;;;;;;;;;;;;;;;;;;;;;;;;;;
                  00002 ;
                  00003 ; Use 10 MHz crystal frequency.
                  00004 ; Use Timer0 for ten millisecond looptime.
                  00005 ; Blink "Alive" LED every two and a half seconds.
                  00006 ; Toggle C2 output every ten milliseconds for measuring looptime precisely.
                  00007 ;
                  00008 ;;;;;;; Program hierarchy ;;;;;;;;;;;;;;;;;;;;;;;;;;;;;;;;;;;;;;;;;;;;;;;;;;;;
                  00009 ;
                  00010 ; Mainline
                  00011 ;   Initial
                  00012 ;   BlinkAlive
                  00013 ;   LoopTime
                  00014 ;
                  00015 ;;;;;;; Assembler directives ;;;;;;;;;;;;;;;;;;;;;;;;;;;;;;;;;;;;;;;;;;;;;;;;;
                  00016
                  00017         list  P=PIC18F452, F=INHX32, C=160, N=0, ST=OFF, MM=OFF, R=DEC, X=ON
                  00018         #include P18F452.inc
                  00001         LIST
                  00002 ; P18F452.INC  Standard Header File, Version 1.1   Microchip Technology, Inc.
                  00776         LIST
300000 FAFF       00019         __CONFIG  _CONFIG1H, _HS_OSC_1H  ;HS oscillator
                  00020         __CONFIG  _CONFIG2L, _PWRT_ON_2L & _BOR_ON_2L & _BORV_42_2L  ;Reset
300002 FEF6       00021         __CONFIG  _CONFIG2H, _WDT_OFF_2H  ;Watchdog timer disabled
300004 FFFF       00022         __CONFIG  _CONFIG3H, _CCP2MX_ON_3H  ;CCP2 to RC1 (rather than to RB3)
300006 FFFB       00023         __CONFIG  _CONFIG4L, _LVP_OFF_4L  ;RB5 enabled for I/O
                  00024
                  00025 ;;;;;;; Variables ;;;;;;;;;;;;;;;;;;;;;;;;;;;;;;;;;;;;;;;;;;;;;;;;;;;;;;;;;;;;
                  00026
                  00027         cblock  0x000             ;Beginning of Access RAM
  00000000        00028         TMR0LCOPY                 ;Copy of sixteen-bit Timer0 used by LoopTime
  00000001        00029         TMR0HCOPY
  00000002        00030         INTCONCOPY                ;Copy of INTCON for LoopTime subroutine
  00000003        00031         ALIVECNT                  ;Counter for blinking "Alive" LED
                  00032         endc
                  00033
                  00034 ;;;;;;; Macro definitions ;;;;;;;;;;;;;;;;;;;;;;;;;;;;;;;;;;;;;;;;;;;;;;;;;;;;
                  00035
                  00036 MOVLF   macro  literal,dest
                  00037         movlw  literal
                  00038         movwf  dest
                  00039         endm
                  00040
                  00041 ;;;;;;; Vectors ;;;;;;;;;;;;;;;;;;;;;;;;;;;;;;;;;;;;;;;;;;;;;;;;;;;;;;;;;;;;;;
                  00042
000000            00043         org  0x0000               ;Reset vector
000000 0000       00044         nop
000002 EF0E F000  00045         goto  Mainline
                  00046
000008            00047         org  0x0008               ;High-priority interrupt vector
000008 EF04 F000  00048         goto  $                   ;Trap
                  00049
000018            00050         org  0x0018               ;Low-priority interrupt vector
000018 EF0C F000  00051         goto  $                   ;Trap
                  00052
                  00053 ;;;;;;; Mainline program ;;;;;;;;;;;;;;;;;;;;;;;;;;;;;;;;;;;;;;;;;;;;;;;;;;;;;
                  00054
00001C            00055 Mainline
00001C D804       00056         rcall  Initial            ;Initialize everything
00001E            00057 Loop
00001E 7482       00058         btg  PORTC,RC2            ;Toggle pin, to support measuring loop time
000020 D829       00059         rcall  BlinkAlive         ;Blink "Alive" LED
000022 D812       00060         rcall  LoopTime           ;Make looptime be 10 milliseconds
000024 D7FC       00061         bra  Loop
                  00062
```

Figure 5-10 P1.LST file.

```
                     ;;;;;;; Initial subroutine ;;;;;;;;;;;;;;;;;;;;;;;;;;;;;;;;;;;;;;;;;;;;;;;;;;;
                     ;
                     ; This subroutine performs all initializations of variables and registers.

000026               Initial
                             MOVLF  B'10001110',ADCON1  ;Enable PORTA & PORTE digital I/O pins
000026 0E8E                M movlw  B'10001110'
000028 6EC1                M movwf  ADCON1
                             MOVLF  B'11100001',TRISA  ;Set I/O for PORTA
00002A 0EE1                M movlw  B'11100001'
00002C 6E92                M movwf  TRISA
                             MOVLF  B'11011100',TRISB  ;Set I/O for PORTB
00002E 0EDC                M movlw  B'11011100'
000030 6E93                M movwf  TRISB
                             MOVLF  B'11010000',TRISC  ;Set I/O for PORTC
000032 0ED0                M movlw  B'11010000'
000034 6E94                M movwf  TRISC
                             MOVLF  B'00001111',TRISD  ;Set I/O for PORTD
000036 0E0F                M movlw  B'00001111'
000038 6E95                M movwf  TRISD
                             MOVLF  B'00000000',TRISE  ;Set I/O for PORTE
00003A 0E00                M movlw  B'00000000'
00003C 6E96                M movwf  TRISE
                             MOVLF  B'10001000',T0CON  ;Set up Timer0 for a looptime of 10 ms
00003E 0E88                M movlw  B'10001000'
000040 6ED5                M movwf  T0CON
                             MOVLF  B'00010000',PORTA  ;Turn off all four LEDs driven from PORTA
000042 0E10                M movlw  B'00010000'
000044 6E80                M movwf  PORTA
000046 0012                  return

                     ;;;;;;; LoopTime subroutine ;;;;;;;;;;;;;;;;;;;;;;;;;;;;;;;;;;;;;;;;;;;;;;;;;;
                     ;
                     ; This subroutine waits for Timer0 to complete its ten millisecond count
                     ; sequence. It does so by waiting for sixteen-bit Timer0 to roll over. To obtain
                     ; a period of precisely 10000/0.4 = 25,000 clock periods, it needs to remove
                     ; 65,536-25000 or 40,536 counts from the sixteen-bit count sequence.  The
                     ; algorithm below first copies Timer0 to RAM, adds "Bignum" to the copy, and
                     ; then writes the result back to Timer0. It actually needs to add somewhat more
                     ; counts to Timer0 than 40,536.  The extra number of 12+2 counts added into
                     ; "Bignum" makes the precise correction.

  00009E66           Bignum  equ     65536-25000+12+2

000048               LoopTime
000048 A4F2                  btfss  INTCON,TMR0IF     ;Wait until ten milliseconds are up
00004A D7FE                  bra  LoopTime
00004C CFF2 F002             movff  INTCON,INTCONCOPY  ;Disable all interrupts to CPU
000050 9EF2                  bcf  INTCON,GIEH
000052 CFD6 F000             movff  TMR0L,TMR0LCOPY  ;Read 16-bit counter at this moment
000056 CFD7 F001             movff  TMR0H,TMR0HCOPY
00005A 0E66                  movlw  low  Bignum
00005C 2600                  addwf  TMR0LCOPY,F
00005E 0E9E                  movlw  high  Bignum
000060 2201                  addwfc  TMR0HCOPY,F
000062 C001 FFD7             movff  TMR0HCOPY,TMR0H
000066 C000 FFD6             movff  TMR0LCOPY,TMR0L  ;Write 16-bit counter at this moment
00006A 5002                  movf  INTCONCOPY,W      ;Restore GIEH interrupt enable bit
00006C 0B80                  andlw  B'10000000'
00006E 12F2                  iorwf  INTCON,F
000070 94F2                  bcf  INTCON,TMR0IF      ;Clear Timer0 flag
000072 0012                  return

                     ;;;;;;; BlinkAlive subroutine ;;;;;;;;;;;;;;;;;;;;;;;;;;;;;;;;;;;;;;;;;;;;;;;;;
                     ;
                     ; This subroutine briefly blinks the LED next to the PIC every two-and-a-half
                     ; seconds.

000074               BlinkAlive
000074 8880                  bsf  PORTA,RA4          ;Turn off LED
000076 0603                  decf  ALIVECNT,F        ;Decrement loop counter and return if not zero
000078 E103                  bnz  BAend
                             MOVLF  250,ALIVECNT     ;Reinitialize ALIVECNT
00007A 0EFA                M movlw  250
00007C 6E03                M movwf  ALIVECNT
00007E 9880                  bcf  PORTA,RA4          ;Turn on LED for 10 milliseconds every 2.5 sec
000080               BAend
000080 0012                  return

                             end
Errors   :    0
Warnings :    0 reported,    0 suppressed
Messages :    0 reported,    0 suppressed
```

Figure 5-10 continued

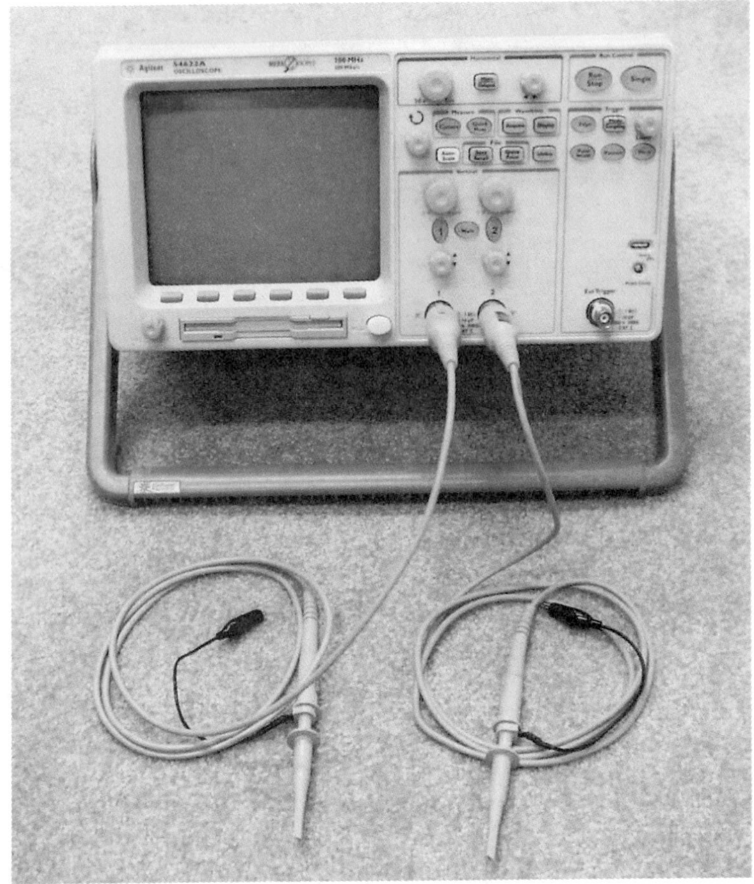

Figure 5-11 An oscilloscope for making timing measurements. (Agilent Technologies)

PROBLEMS

5-1 Timer0 as a high-speed counter. The counter circuit of Figure 5-1 illustrates the use of Timer0 with an input having a higher frequency than the microcontroller's internal clock rate.

(a) For input frequencies up to 50 MHz, what is the smallest prescaler divider that will provide satisfactory operation of Timer0?

(b) With this divider and with an actual input frequency of 50 MHz, what will be the interval between successive settings of the **TMR0IF** flag?

5-2 Synchronizer. The synchronizer of Figure 5-1 prevents a read of the contents of **TMR0H:TMR0L** from occurring at a time when an erroneous value might be read, caused by a violation of setup-time/hold-time specifications. If, for example, there were no synchronizer and **TMR0L** were to change from B′01111111′ to B′10000000′ at the precise moment it is read into **WREG**, what might be the result? Explain.

5-3 Twelve-count adjustment. Figure 5-3a shows the instruction sequence to read the **TMR0H:TMR0L** counter, add a value called "Bignum" to the read value, and write the result back to the counter. Figure 5-3b shows the timing diagram accorded to this instruction sequence. The read of **TMR0L** is shown occurring in the second quarter of the first clock cycle shown. The write back to **TMR0L** is shown occurring in the fourth quarter of the last clock cycle shown. The counter itself is incremented during the third quarter of every cycle.

(a) Assume the beginning of the sequence reads **TMR0L** = D′83′. What will be the contents of **TMR0L** after the completion of the third quarter of that same first clock cycle shown, expressed as a decimal number?
(b) What will be the content of **TMR0L** after the completion of the third quarter of the last clock cycle shown, expressed as a decimal number?
(c) What value would have to be written to **TMR0L** during that last clock cycle shown (expressed as a decimal number) to write a value that is exactly equal to the value already there (because of the incrementing of the counter)?
(d) What is the decimal difference between the answer in Part *(c)* and the D′83′ value read at the beginning of the sequence?
(e) What is the significance of this difference when using Timer0 to implement a scale-of-N scaler?

5-4 LoopTime subroutine. The **LoopTime** subroutine of Figure 5-5 disables interrupts while the read-add-write sequence of operations takes place.

(a) If this were not done and if the CPU digressed to an interrupt service routine for 15 microseconds before returning, what would be the effect on the loop time?
(b) Mainline code that must not be interrupted is called a *critical region* of code. One of its effects is to delay the servicing of an interrupt, increasing that interrupt source's *worst-case interrupt latency.* How much (in microseconds) does the critical region of Figure 5-5 increase worst-case interrupt latency?

5-5 BlinkAlive subroutine.

(a) Change the **BlinkAlive** subroutine of Figure 5-6 so that it simply toggles the LED every 2.5 seconds.
(b) Change it so that it briefly (and, therefore, faintly) blinks the LED once per second.

5-6 Macros. Write the definition for a macro called **BCOPY** that copies one bit in one register to a different bit in a different register without changing any of the other bits of either register. Begin the macro definition with

```
BCOPY  macro  source,sbit,dest,dbit
```

Minimize the instructions generated by each invocation of this macro. As an example of its use

```
BCOPY  PORTD,RDØ,PORTA,RA1
```

and

```
BCOPY  PORTD,RD1,PORTA,RA2
```

will copy the two outputs of the "RPG" of Figure 4-2a to two of the LEDs on the QwikFlash board so that the state of the RPG can be monitored by eye.

5-7 P1.asm program. Check the initialization of each **TRIS** register in Figure 5-7 against the corresponding requirements of the QwikFlash circuit of Figure 4-2.

(a) Are all pins tied to I/O devices set up correctly as inputs and outputs?
(b) Pencil arrowheads on all unused I/O pins of Figure 4-2 according to the initialization of Figure 5-7.

5-8 Tera Term Pro. Find Tera Term Pro on the Internet, download it, and install it with an icon on the desktop. Change the serial port setup to that of Figure 5-8. Create a C:\Work folder and set up Tera Term Pro to open directly into this folder.

5-9 MS-DOS. Create a desktop icon for MS-DOS. Rename it "DOS for PIC." Double-clicking on the desktop should be made to open a DOS window directly into the folder to be used for source files and their assembly.

5-10 Editor. If you do not already have a favorite text editor, you might get a copy of the popular freeware editor, PFE, *Programmer's File Editor.* The www.google.com search engine will find multiple sources for it. Install it and place its icon on the desktop. To have it open to your folder of choice, click on

Options → Preferences → Working Folder → Specified here,

and then enter your folder (e.g., C:\Work).

Chapter

6

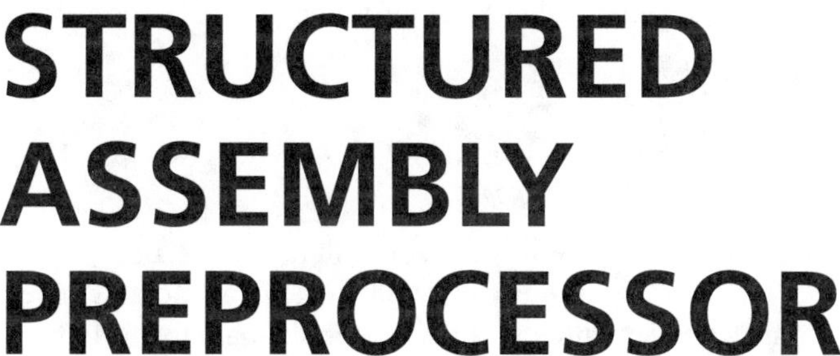

STRUCTURED ASSEMBLY PREPROCESSOR

6.1 OVERVIEW

A drawback of much assembly language coding is the confusing instruction sequencing that can arise with "spaghetti code," illustrated in Figure 3-6. The role of the structured assembly preprocessor introduced in this chapter is to make all flow control through the algorithms of subroutines immediately obvious by implementing the flow control with nested constructs such as

```
IF_ <test>    ...    ELSE_    ...    ENDIF_
```

and

```
WHILE_ <test>    ...    ENDWHILE_
```

In this chapter, a free *structured assembly preprocessor*

```
sasm  <source file>
```

will be introduced. It was developed by Jessica Meremonte while she was student at Georgia Tech. It is available from the author's Web site www.picbook.com. Interested readers can also obtain the C++ source code for the structured assembly preprocessor from the author's Web site.

One of the goals of this chapter is to develop the syntax of the structured assembly constructs. Another is to see how each construct is translated into assembly language. It will be found that these constructs give clarity to the flow control within subroutines and macros without adding superfluous instructions. That is, the code writer does not lose touch with exactly how the code will be executed, instruction by instruction.

The structured assembly preprocessor, SASM.EXE, is actually a program that preprocesses a source file by translating the structure constructs into labels and instructions that the Microchip assembler,

MPASMWIN.EXE, will understand. If the preprocessor detects one or more errors, it generates an error file and goes no further. If it detects no errors, its output ".apr" file will then be subjected to the Microchip assembler automatically.

6.2 CONDITIONAL ASSEMBLY VS. CONDITIONAL EXECUTION

The full-featured Microchip assembler includes the following directives for *conditional assembly:*

```
IF ‹test›    ...    ELSE    ...    ENDIF
```

and

```
WHILE ‹test›    ...    ENDW
```

Note the difference in the spelling of these constructs and the **IF_**, **ELSE_**, etc. of the last section. These are interpreted at the time of assembly to decide which code to assemble and which code to ignore. For example, consider code written for the QwikFlash board that is to be assembled correctly for running at an internal clock rate of either 2.5 MHz (using its 10 MHz crystal oscillator directly) or 10 MHz (using its 10 MHz oscillator together with its 40 MHz VFO and PLL combination, as described in Example 5-1). A **TENMHZ** constant can be defined at the beginning of the source file with

```
#define  TENMHZ  1          ;Assemble for 10 MHz
```

or

```
#define  TENMHZ  0          ;Assemble for 2.5 MHz
```

Then the construct

```
IF  TENMHZ
  __CONFIG  CONFIG1H, _HSPLL_OSC_1H
ELSE
  __CONFIG  CONFIG1H, _HS_OSC_1H
ENDIF
```

can be used in place of line 19 in the P1.asm file of Figure 5-7. Depending on whether **TENMHZ** has been defined as 1 (true) or 0 (false), one line will be assembled while the other is ignored.

The constructs used by the structured assembly preprocessor have nothing to do with conditional assembly. Rather they have everything to do with *conditional execution.* Their tests are carried out during execution of the program code by the PIC microcontroller. To ensure that this distinction is interpreted correctly, first by the structured assembly preprocessor and subsequently by the assembler, the names of the structured assembly constructs are followed by "_".

6.3 STRUCTURED ASSEMBLY CONSTRUCTS

The structured assembly preprocessor supports the six constructs shown in Figure 6-1a. The

```
IF_ ‹test›    ...    ENDIF_
```

construct allows an optional ELSE_ construct. The

```
IF_ ‹test› ... [ELSE_ ... ] ENDIF_

WHILE_ ‹test› ... ENDWHILE_

REPEAT_ ... UNTIL_ ‹test›

LOOP_ ... ENDLOOP_

CONTINUE_

BREAK_
```

Figure 6-1 Structured assembly constructs.

```
LOOP_

  IF_ ‹test whether interrupt #1 is ready for service›
    rcall Int1handler
    CONTINUE_
  ENDIF_

  IF_ ‹test whether interrupt #2 is ready for service›
    rcall Int2 handler
    CONTINUE_
  ENDIF_

  IF_ ‹test whether interrupt #3 is ready for service›
    rcall Int3handler
    CONTINUE_
  ENDIF_
   .
   .
   .
  IF_ ‹test whether interrupt #N is ready for service›
    rcall IntN handler
    CONTINUE_
  ENDIF_

  BREAK_

ENDLOOP_
```

Figure 6-2 Interrupt service routine's polling routine.

```
WHILE_ ‹test›   ...   ENDWHILE_
```

construct is similar in performance to the

```
REPEAT_   ...   UNTIL_ ‹test›
```

construct except that the **REPEAT_** construct will always execute the encompassed instructions one time before the test is applied, whereas the **WHILE_** construct will bypass the encompassed instructions altogether if the test is not satisfied when first encountered. Otherwise, the two constructs repeatedly execute the encompassed instructions, subject to the test condition.

The third looping construct

```
LOOP_   ...   ENDLOOP_
```

will be used in PIC18F452 code to implement the mainline loop. Also, when interrupts are discussed later in the book, the **LOOP_ . . . ENDLOOP_** construct will be used, together with the **CONTINUE_** and the **BREAK_** constructs, to implement the control flow required in the routine that polls each interrupt source and executes its handler if it is requesting service, as shown in Figure 6-2. After a handler has been executed, the **CONTINUE_** construct returns to the beginning of the loop. The **BREAK_**

```
IF_  <test1>
  IF_  <test2>
    <execute only if both conditions are met>
  ENDIF_
ENDIF_
```

(a) Nesting to meet multiple conditions.

```
MOVLF  10,COUNTH
clrf  COUNTL
REPEAT_
  REPEAT_
    decf  COUNTL,F
  UNTIL_  .Z.
  decf  COUNTH,F
UNTIL_  .Z.
```

Figure 6-3 Nesting constructs. (b) Nesting to implement a multiple-byte counter with a 256 × 10 count sequence.

construct at the end of the loop will only be reached after every interrupt flag has been tested, in order, and found to be zero. Only then will the interrupt service routine return to the mainline program.

These constructs may be nested, with no limit on the number of levels of nesting. Figure 6-3a illustrates how multiple **IF_** constructs can lead to the execution of code only if all conditions are met. Figure 6-3b illustrates how a multiple-byte counter can be implemented.

6.4 CONDITION TESTS

There are two types of tests that can be used with the conditional constructs: unary tests and bit tests. The unary tests are shown in Figure 6-4a. Each one tests a bit in the **STATUS** register. Because both carries and borrows are flagged by the carry bit, **C**, and because a carry sets **C** whereas a borrow clears **C**, the two tests .C. and .NB. are equivalent as are .NC. and .B.

The bit tests are shown in Figure 6-4b. When using the bit test, the only operator that can be used is "==", and the bit can only be compared to 1 or to 0. Any other operators or literal values will produce syntax errors.

The structured assembly preprocessor also supports the ANDing of multiple conditions, using the **AND_ . . . ENDAND_** structure of Figure 6-4c. In similar fashion, the ORing of multiple conditions is supported by the **OR_ . . . ENDOR_** structure of Figure 6-4d.

The **LoopTime** test of Figure 5-5 is shown implemented with a **REPEAT_ . . . UNTIL_** construct in Figure 6-5a. An alternative implementation using a **WHILE_ . . . ENDWHILE_** construct is shown in Figure 6-5b. A compound test to execute a segment of code if two conditions are *both* met is illustrated with two approaches in Figures 6-5c and 6-5d. Finally, a compound test to execute a segment of code if *either* of two conditions is met is illustrated in Figure 6-5e.

6.5 SASM INPUT PARAMETERS

The help message of Figure 6-6 will be displayed if

```
sasm
```

is executed with no parameters. The same result occurs in response to

```
sasm  -?
```

```
.Z.     True if the Z bit of STATUS is 1
.NZ.    True if the Z bit of STATUS is Ø
.C.     True if the last operation produced a carry
.NC.    True if last operation did not produce a carry
.B.     True if the last operation resulted in a borrow
.NB.    True if it did not result in a borrow
.N.     True if the N bit of STATUS is 1
.NN.    True if the N bit of STATUS is Ø
.OV.    True if the overflow bit of STATUS is 1
.NOV.   True if the overflow bit of STATUS is Ø
```

(a) Unary tests.

```
<register>,<bit> == Ø
<register>,<bit> == 1
```

(b) Bit tests.

```
AND_
  <test1>
  <test2>
  <test3>
ENDAND_
```

(c) **AND_ . . . ENDAND_** construct.

```
OR_
  <test1>
  <test2>
  <test3>
ENDOR_
```

(d) **OR_ . . . ENDOR_** construct.

Figure 6-4 Tests.

As an option, the preprocessor can be used to clean up the indenting of the source file. Two parameters must be invoked:

```
sasm  -tabs  -noasm  P1.asm
```

The P1.asm file will be left unchanged while, at the same time, being massaged into a reformatted P1.apr file. Assuming the result is an improvement, it can be renamed P1.asm. The "-noasm" parameter tells the sasm.exe utility not to preprocess and not to assemble. By not preprocessing, the structured assembler constructs are left intact and not translated into assembly code instructions and labels. The "-tabs" parameter does the following in forming the .apr file:

- All lines of code that are not comments or labels will start in column 9.
- Labels, which must begin in column 1, remain there.
- Comments (identified by ;) will start at column 33.
- For any line of source code that extends beyond column 33, the comment will start two spaces beyond the source code.
- Nested constructs will produce a two-column indentation.
- Whatever spacing/tabbing exists between the instruction mnemonic and its operand will be left unchanged.

This last condition means that the cleanest result will occur if tab characters have not been inserted in the line. The code of the P1.asm file has been entered with two spaces between mnemonic and operand in anticipation of adding the indention of structured assembler constructs and still having the indented file look consistent.

```
REPEAT_
UNTIL_  INTCON,TMRØIF == 1  ;Loop until TimerØ rolls over
```

(a) Wait for the setting of a flag.

```
WHILE_  INTCON,TMRØIF == Ø  ;Loop until TimerØ rolls over
ENDWHILE_
```

(b) Alternative approach to wait for the setting of a flag.

```
IF_  PIR1,CCP1IF == 1
  IF_  PIE1,CCP1IE == 1
    <statements to execute if both conditions are satisfied>
  ENDIF_
ENDIF_
```

(c) Compound test.

```
IF_
  AND_
    PIR1,CCP1IF == 1
    PIE1,CCP1IE == 1
  ENDAND_
  <statements to execute if both conditions are satisfied>
ENDIF_
```

(d) Use of **AND_ . . . ENDAND_** alternative for compound test.

```
IF_
  OR_
    .Z.
    PORTD,RD3 == Ø
  ENDOR_
  <statements to execute if either condition is satisfied>
ENDIF_
```

(e) Use of **OR_ . . . ENDOR_** compound test.

Figure 6-5 Test examples.

```
SASM                          Assembly Pre-Processor
Jessica Meremonte             Georgia Institute of Technology
Pre-processes and assembles a structured assembly file.
The file is output to a second file of the same name
but with the extension '.apr'.
This second file is then assembled using mpasm.
Usage: sasm [-options] filename
Options include:
-?       - display this message
-tabs    - format the .apr file with appropriate indention
-n<num>  - format the .apr file, with comments starting at column <num>
-18      - optimize for the PIC18CXX2/PIC18FXX2 series (default)
-16      - optimize for the PIC16F87X series
-noasm   - do not preprocess or assemble;
           use with -tabs or -n<num> option to format the .apr file
```

Figure 6-6 SASM help screen.

A variation of the "-tabs" parameter is the "-n<num>" parameter. This option allows the user to specify the column at which comments should begin. For example,

```
sasm  -n4Ø  -noasm  P1.asm
```

will produce a P1.apr file with comments beginning at column 40.

The sasm utility was designed to handle the PIC18F452's instruction set. However, it does include an option "-16" that lets it be applied to the earlier generation PIC16F877 and other PIC16-series microcontrollers that do not have the conditional branch instructions of the PIC18F452 (e.g., the **bz** instruction).

Finally, it should be noted that the sasm utility will look for, and use, the source file having the ".asm" extension if no extension is specified. That is,

```
sasm  P1
```

does the same thing as

```
sasm  P1.asm
```

6.6 SASM INSTALLATION AND EXECUTION, AND PROGRAM CODE DEBUGGING

Two files, SASM.EXE and PIC18.cfg, can be optained from the author's web site, www.picbook.com. They, along with the Microchip assembler, MPASMWIN.EXE, should be installed in the same folder with the source files to be processed. Alternatively, if Microchip's complete MPLAB software has already been downloaded and installed from www.microchip.com into their suggested folder, C:\Program Files\MPLAB, then these new files can be installed in this same folder.

Execution takes place from a DOS window opened to the folder containing the source files to be processed (e.g., C:\Work). The preprocessor will create a file with the .apr extension and pass that file to the assembler. The assembler will then generate .HEX, .LST, and .COD files.

If either preprocessor or assembler errors occur, a corresponding .ERR file will indicate the nature of the errors so the source file can be corrected. For errors uncovered while preprocessing, the .ERR file identifies the line number in the .asm file where the error was discovered, thereby helping with the correction of the error in that file. Unfortunately, for errors uncovered while assembling, the line number where the error occurred that is indicated in the .ERR file points back into the .apr file, not the original .asm source file. David Flowers has created a QwikAddress utility, described in Appendix A5, that translates the line numbers found in the .ERR file back to the corresponding line numbers in the .asm file. This fine utility also works with the free QwikBug monitor program, described in Appendix A4, to identify the addresses of variables and SFRs for setting "watch" variables and to identify program addresses for setting breakpoints.

6.7 P1.ASM REVISITED

With these structured assembler constructs in hand, the P1.asm file of Figure 5-7 has been rewritten as the P1_SA.asm file of Figure 6-7. This source file, when subjected to the sasm utility, generates the P1_SA.apr file of Figure 6-8. The mainline program's **LOOP_ . . . ENDLOOP_** construct has generated two labels, **L1** and **PL1**, and a

```
bra  L1
```

```
;;;;;;; P1_SA for QwikFlash board ;;;;;;;;;;;;;;;;;;;;;;;;;;;;;;;;;;;;;;;;;;;;;
;
; Use 10 MHz crystal frequency.
; Use Timer0 for ten millisecond looptime.
; Blink "Alive" LED every two and a half seconds.
; Toggle C2 output every ten milliseconds for measuring looptime precisely.
;
;;;;;;; Program hierarchy ;;;;;;;;;;;;;;;;;;;;;;;;;;;;;;;;;;;;;;;;;;;;;;;;;;;;;;
;
; Mainline
;   Initial
;   BlinkAlive
;   LoopTime
;
;;;;;;; Assembler directives ;;;;;;;;;;;;;;;;;;;;;;;;;;;;;;;;;;;;;;;;;;;;;;;;;;;

        list  P=PIC18F452, F=INHX32, C=160, N=0, ST=OFF, MM=OFF, R=DEC, X=ON
        #include P18F452.inc
        __CONFIG  _CONFIG1H, _HS_OSC_1H  ;HS oscillator
        __CONFIG  _CONFIG2L, _PWRT_ON_2L & _BOR_ON_2L & _BORV_42_2L  ;Reset
        __CONFIG  _CONFIG2H, _WDT_OFF_2H  ;Watchdog timer disabled
        __CONFIG  _CONFIG3H, _CCP2MX_ON_3H  ;CCP2 to RC1 (rather than to RB3)
        __CONFIG  _CONFIG4L, _LVP_OFF_4L  ;RB5 enabled for I/O

;;;;;;; Variables ;;;;;;;;;;;;;;;;;;;;;;;;;;;;;;;;;;;;;;;;;;;;;;;;;;;;;;;;;;;;;;

        cblock  0x000           ;Beginning of Access RAM
        TMR0LCOPY               ;Copy of sixteen-bit Timer0 used by LoopTime
        TMR0HCOPY
        ALIVECNT                ;Counter for blinking "Alive" LED
        endc

;;;;;;; Macro definitions ;;;;;;;;;;;;;;;;;;;;;;;;;;;;;;;;;;;;;;;;;;;;;;;;;;;;;;

MOVLF   macro  literal,dest
        movlw  literal
        movwf  dest
        endm

;;;;;;; Vectors ;;;;;;;;;;;;;;;;;;;;;;;;;;;;;;;;;;;;;;;;;;;;;;;;;;;;;;;;;;;;;;;;

        org  0x0000             ;Reset vector
        nop
        goto  Mainline

        org  0x0008             ;High priority interrupt vector
        goto  $                 ;Trap

        org  0x0018             ;Low priority interrupt vector
        goto  $                 ;Trap

;;;;;;; Mainline program ;;;;;;;;;;;;;;;;;;;;;;;;;;;;;;;;;;;;;;;;;;;;;;;;;;;;;;;

Mainline
        rcall  Initial          ;Initialize everything
        LOOP_
          btg  PORTC,RC2        ;Toggle pin, to support measuring loop time
          rcall  BlinkAlive     ;Blink "Alive" LED
          rcall  LoopTime       ;Make looptime be ten milliseconds
        ENDLOOP_

;;;;;;; Initial subroutine ;;;;;;;;;;;;;;;;;;;;;;;;;;;;;;;;;;;;;;;;;;;;;;;;;;;;;
;
; This subroutine performs all initializations of variables and registers.

Initial
        MOVLF  B'10001110',ADCON1  ;Enable PORTA & PORTE digital I/O pins
        MOVLF  B'11100001',TRISA  ;Set I/O for PORTA
        MOVLF  B'11011100',TRISB  ;Set I/O for PORTB
        MOVLF  B'11010000',TRISC  ;Set I/O for PORTC
        MOVLF  B'00001111',TRISD  ;Set I/O for PORTD
        MOVLF  B'00000000',TRISE  ;Set I/O for PORTE
        MOVLF  B'10001000',TOCON  ;Set up Timer0 for a looptime of 10 ms
        MOVLF  B'00010000',PORTA  ;Turn off all four LEDs driven from PORTA
        return
```

Figure 6-7 P1_SA.asm file with structured assembler constructs.

```
;;;;;;; LoopTime subroutine ;;;;;;;;;;;;;;;;;;;;;;;;;;;;;;;;;;;;;;;;;;;;;;;;;;;;;
;
; This subroutine waits for Timer0 to complete its ten millisecond count
; sequence. It does so by waiting for sixteen-bit Timer0 to roll over. To obtain
; a period of precisely 10000/0.4 = 25000 clock periods, it needs to remove
; 65536-25000 or 40536 counts from the 16-bit count sequence.  The
; algorithm below first copies Timer0 to RAM, adds "Bignum" to the copy, and
; then writes the result back to Timer0. It actually needs to add somewhat more
; counts to Timer0 than 40,536.  The extra number of 12+2 counts added into
; "Bignum" makes the precise correction.

Bignum  equ     65536-25000+12+2

LoopTime
        REPEAT_
        UNTIL_  INTCON,TMR0IF == 1  ;Wait until ten milliseconds are up
        bcf   INTCON,GIE          ;Disable all interrupts from CPU
        movff  TMR0L,TMR0LCOPY    ;Read 16-bit counter at this moment
        movff  TMR0H,TMR0HCOPY
        movlw  low  Bignum
        addwf  TMR0LCOPY,F
        movlw  high  Bignum
        addwfc  TMR0HCOPY,F
        movff  TMR0HCOPY,TMR0H
        movff  TMR0LCOPY,TMR0L    ;Write 16-bit counter at this moment
        bcf  INTCON,TMR0IF        ;Clear Timer0 flag
        bsf  INTCON,GIE           ;Reenable interrupts to CPU
        return

;;;;;;; BlinkAlive subroutine ;;;;;;;;;;;;;;;;;;;;;;;;;;;;;;;;;;;;;;;;;;;;;;;;;;;;
;
; This subroutine briefly blinks the LED next to the PIC every two-and-a-half
; seconds.

BlinkAlive
        bsf  PORTA,RA4            ;Turn off LED
        decf  ALIVECNT,F          ;Decrement loop counter and return if not zero
        IF_  .Z.
          MOVLF  250,ALIVECNT     ;Reinitialize ALIVECNT
          bcf  PORTA,RA4          ;Turn on LED for ten milliseconds every 2.5 sec
        ENDIF_
        return

        end
```

Figure 6-7 continued

instruction.

The LoopTime subroutine's **REPEAT_ . . . UNTIL_** construct has generated two labels, **L2** and **RL2**, and the instruction sequence

```
btfss  INTCON,TMR0IF
bra  L2
```

The construct has produced exactly the same two instructions that would have been developed by virtually any designer without the help of the preprocessor, but its use avoids any tendency to get the sense of the test wrong (i.e., accidentally using **btfsc** instead of the correct **btfss**).

The **BlinkAlive** subroutine's **IF_ . . . ENDIF_** construct translates into a label, L3, and the single instruction

```
bnz  L3
```

Each of the ten unary tests of Figure 6-4 could have been treated as one of the bit tests of Figure 6-5a. They are not treated as bit tests because of the availability of the conditional branch instructions for these specific bits and for no others. For each of these **STATUS** register bits, a structured assembly construct will translate the test into a single instruction. For any other bit in any other register, the test

```
;;;;;;; P1_SA for QwikFlash board ;;;;;;;;;;;;;;;;;;;;;;;;;;;;;;;;;;;;;;;;;;;;;
;
; Use 10 MHz crystal frequency.
; Use Timer0 for ten millisecond looptime.
; Blink "Alive" LED every two and a half seconds.
; Toggle C2 output every ten milliseconds for measuring looptime precisely.
;
;;;;;;; Program hierarchy ;;;;;;;;;;;;;;;;;;;;;;;;;;;;;;;;;;;;;;;;;;;;;;;;;;;;;;
;
; Mainline
;   Initial
;   BlinkAlive
;   LoopTime
;
;;;;;;; Assembler directives ;;;;;;;;;;;;;;;;;;;;;;;;;;;;;;;;;;;;;;;;;;;;;;;;;;;

        list  P=PIC18F452, F=INHX32, C=160, N=0, ST=OFF, MM=OFF, R=DEC, X=ON
        #include P18F452.inc
        __CONFIG  _CONFIG1H, _HS_OSC_1H  ;HS oscillator
        __CONFIG  _CONFIG2L, _PWRT_ON_2L & _BOR_ON_2L & _BORV_42_2L  ;Reset
        __CONFIG  _CONFIG2H, _WDT_OFF_2H  ;Watchdog timer disabled
        __CONFIG  _CONFIG3H, _CCP2MX_ON_3H  ;CCP2 to RC1 (rather than to RB3)
        __CONFIG  _CONFIG4L, _LVP_OFF_4L  ;RB5 enabled for I/O

;;;;;;; Variables ;;;;;;;;;;;;;;;;;;;;;;;;;;;;;;;;;;;;;;;;;;;;;;;;;;;;;;;;;;;;;;

        cblock  0x000           ;Beginning of Access RAM
        TMR0LCOPY               ;Copy of sixteen-bit Timer0 used by LoopTime
        TMR0HCOPY
        ALIVECNT                ;Counter for blinking "Alive" LED
        endc

;;;;;;; Macro definitions ;;;;;;;;;;;;;;;;;;;;;;;;;;;;;;;;;;;;;;;;;;;;;;;;;;;;;;

MOVLF   macro  literal,dest
        movlw  literal
        movwf  dest
        endm

;;;;;;; Vectors ;;;;;;;;;;;;;;;;;;;;;;;;;;;;;;;;;;;;;;;;;;;;;;;;;;;;;;;;;;;;;;;;

        org  0x0000             ;Reset vector
        nop
        goto  Mainline

        org  0x0008             ;High-priority interrupt vector
        goto  $                 ;Trap

        org  0x0018             ;Low-priority interrupt vector
        goto  $                 ;Trap

;;;;;;; Mainline program ;;;;;;;;;;;;;;;;;;;;;;;;;;;;;;;;;;;;;;;;;;;;;;;;;;;;;;;

Mainline
        rcall  Initial          ;Initialize everything
        ;LOOP_
L1
          btg  PORTC,RC2        ;Toggle pin, to support measuring loop time
          rcall  BlinkAlive     ;Blink "Alive" LED
          rcall  LoopTime       ;Make looptime be ten milliseconds
        ;ENDLOOP_
        bra      L1
PL1

;;;;;;; Initial subroutine ;;;;;;;;;;;;;;;;;;;;;;;;;;;;;;;;;;;;;;;;;;;;;;;;;;;;;
;
; This subroutine performs all initializations of variables and registers.

Initial
        MOVLF  B'10001110',ADCON1  ;Enable PORTA & PORTE digital I/O pins
        MOVLF  B'11100001',TRISA  ;Set I/O for PORTA
        MOVLF  B'11011100',TRISB  ;Set I/O for PORTB
        MOVLF  B'11010000',TRISC  ;Set I/O for PORTC
        MOVLF  B'00001111',TRISD  ;Set I/O for PORTD
        MOVLF  B'00000000',TRISE  ;Set I/O for PORTE
        MOVLF  B'10001000',T0CON  ;Set up Timer0 for a looptime of 10 ms
        MOVLF  B'00010000',PORTA  ;Turn off all four LEDs driven from PORTA
        return
```

Figure 6-8 P1_SA.apr file with structured assembler constructs.

```
;;;;;;; LoopTime subroutine ;;;;;;;;;;;;;;;;;;;;;;;;;;;;;;;;;;;;;;;;;;;;;;;;;;;;
;
; This subroutine waits for Timer0 to complete its ten millisecond count
; sequence. It does so by waiting for sixteen-bit Timer0 to roll over. To obtain
; a period of precisely 10000/0.4 = 25000 clock periods, it needs to remove
; 65536-25000 or 40536 counts from the sixteen-bit count sequence.  The
; algorithm below first copies Timer0 to RAM, adds "Bignum" to the copy, and
; then writes the result back to Timer0. It actually needs to add somewhat more
; counts to Timer0 than 40,536.  The extra number of 12+2 counts added into
; "Bignum" makes the precise correction.

Bignum  equu    65536-25000+12+2

LoopTime
        ;REPEAT_
L2
        ;UNTIL_  INTCON,TMR0IF == 1  ;Wait until ten milliseconds are up
        btfss INTCON,TMR0IF
        bra      L2
RL2
        bcf  INTCON,GIE          ;Disable all interrupts from CPU
        movff  TMR0L,TMR0LCOPY   ;Read 16-bit counter at this moment
        movff  TMR0H,TMR0HCOPY
        movlw  low  Bignum
        addwf  TMR0LCOPY,F
        movlw  high  Bignum
        addwfc  TMR0HCOPY,F
        movff  TMR0HCOPY,TMR0H
        movff  TMR0LCOPY,TMR0L   ;Write 16-bit counter at this moment
        bcf  INTCON,TMR0IF       ;Clear Timer0 flag
        bsf  INTCON,GIE          ;Reenable interrupts to CPU
        return

;;;;;;; BlinkAlive subroutine ;;;;;;;;;;;;;;;;;;;;;;;;;;;;;;;;;;;;;;;;;;;;;;;;;;
;
; This subroutine briefly blinks the LED next to the PIC every two-and-a-half
; seconds.

BlinkAlive
        bsf  PORTA,RA4           ;Turn off LED
        decf  ALIVECNT,F         ;Decrement loop counter and return if not zero
        ;IF_  .Z.
        bnz      L3
          MOVLF  250,ALIVECNT    ;Reinitialize ALIVECNT
          bcf  PORTA,RA4         ;Turn on LED for ten milliseconds every 2.5 sec
        ;ENDIF_
L3
        return

        end
```

Figure 6-8 continued

will translate into two instructions having the same form as those generated by the **REPEAT_... UNTIL_** construct's test of

```
INTCON,TMR0IF == 1
```

PROBLEMS

6-1 Conditional assembly. Section 6.2 utilized the example of the two oscillator options available to the QwikFlash board. If the name **TENMHZ** were defined to be 1, then the PIC18F452 would be programmed to run at an internal clock rate of 10 MHz. If **TENMHZ** were defined to be 0, then the chip would be programmed to run at an internal clock rate of 2.5 MHz.

Using the P1.asm file available over the Internet from the author's Web site, modify this file as needed for either frequency. In addition to handling the **_CONFIG1** byte, be sure to handle both the initialization of **T0CON** and the definition of **Bignum** so as to keep a loop time of 10 milliseconds. Note that the *QwikBug* monitor program prevents the reprogramming of the configuration bytes. Therefore, the new P1.HEX file will only work with the in-circuit debugger or with an emulator.

6-2 Structured assembly constructs. Show how each of the six constructs of Figure 6-1 will be translated by the assembler preprocessor. To show the structure, surround each construct with a **nop** instruction. Use generic labels for each case, understanding that the preprocessor has a sophisticated scheme for generating labels that can handle the nesting of the constructs.

6-3 Structured assembly constructs. Show how the polling routine of Figure 6-2 will be translated by the preprocessor. Again, use generic labels for handling each construct.

6-4 Tests. Show the code leading up to and including the **IF_** test that will execute the code encompassed by the **IF_ . . . ENDIF_** construct

(a) if the upper nibble of **WREG** equals 0 (that is, if **WREG** = B('0000bbbb')
(b) if **PORTB** = B'bbbbbb10'
(c) if **COUNT** = 5

6-5 Tests. Execute a block of code at least once and then repeatedly until

(a) **WREG** = B'0000bbbb'
(b) **PORTB** = B'bbbbbb10'
(c) **COUNT** = 5

6-6 Formatting. Copy the P1.asm file to P1a.asm. Modify the **BlinkAlive** subroutine by nesting its

```
bcf  PORTA,RA4
```

instruction within the following construct

```
IF_  PORTD,RD3 == 0
ENDIF_
```

(a) Referring to Figure 4-2a, what will be the effect of pressing the pushbutton switch upon the blinking of the "Alive" LED.
(b) Remove all indenting and then add extra spaces and a tab or two here and there between the different fields of the **BlinkAlive** subroutine's lines of code. Now execute

```
sasm  -tabs  -noasm  P1a
```

and check the effect of the preprocessor's formatting of the resulting P1a.apr file. Go back and rework the P1a.asm file until you like what the preprocessor produces. Rename the P1a.apr file to become the new P1a.asm file.

Chapter

7

ALPHANUMERIC LIQUID-CRYSTAL DISPLAYS (P2 TEMPLATE)

7.1 OVERVIEW

A display forms an integral part of the interface for many microcontroller applications. Alphanumeric liquid-crystal displays (LCDs) are widely used in this role. They are versatile, low-powered devices. At a cost of a fraction of a cent per bit of information, they offer a low-cost solution to the need for a moderate amount of user information in an instrument or device. They are widely available from many manufacturers and in a variety of configurations. For example, the little 8x2-character Optrex LCD module used on the QwikFlash board is one of a family of Optrex alphanumeric LCD modules ranging up to a 40x4-character LCD and is readily available from the major mail-order distributor Digi-Key (www.digikey.com).

Years ago, Hitachi developed its HD44780 LCD controller chip, which became the de facto standard interface employed by virtually all alphanumeric LCDs. A common configuration, used by the QwikFlash display shown in Figure 4-1, has the display itself mounted on a somewhat larger printed circuit board. A metal bezel protects the glass edges of the display. The PC board provides interconnections for the display, the controller chip (mounted on the back of the board), and a 14-pin pattern of pads for connecting to a microcontroller.

This chapter will explore two microcontroller interface alternatives and will examine the initialization and data transfer protocol required for each. A simple "display string" message protocol will be introduced, together with a **DisplayC** subroutine for sending a constant display string residing in the PIC18F452's program memory to the display. A **DisplayV** subroutine for displaying a variable string residing in RAM is a slight variation of **DisplayC**. Finally, the generation and use of special characters will be discussed.

7.2 LCD INTERFACE ALTERNATIVES

All of the many alphanumeric LCD modules that employ the Hitachi HD44780 onboard controller chip have a 14-pad pattern for making the interface connections. Figure 7-1 illustrates the 2x7 pattern of 100-mil-spaced pads for two popular displays. Another common configuration is a 1x14 pattern of 100-mil-spaced pads, usually located along the top edge of the display. The connection between the little 8x2 LCD of Figure 7-1 and the QwikFlash board is made with a 14-pin header that also serves to lock the top edge of the display in place. The two bottom tabs of the display are locked in place with pins soldered between the display and the PC board.

The LCD module's Hitachi controller offers the option of either 8-bit or 4-bit data transfers. An 8-bit interface is illustrated in Figure 7-2a. ASCII-encoded displayable characters and control codes are transferred a byte at a time under control of an "RS" (register select) input and an "E" (clock) input, as described in Figure 7-2b. For example, if a *cursor-position* control code of 0xc0 is sent to the display with RS = 0, then the next displayable ASCII-encoded character sent to the display with RS = 1 will appear at the left-most position on the second line of the display.

Each transfer to the display must meet the timing specifications of Figure 7-3a. Even with the PIC18F452 running at an internal clock rate of 10 MHz (i.e., with 100 nanoseconds per instruction cycle), these timing specifications are easily met. The forty *microseconds* (not nanoseconds) of Figure 7-3b are needed by the Hitachi controller to act upon the reception of each byte before it will be ready to receive the next byte.

The 4-bit interface of Figure 7-4 offers the benefit of freeing four of the microcontroller's I/O pins for other uses. After being initialized to expect incoming data to arrive a 4-bit nibble at a time, the Hitachi controller rebuilds each pair of nibbles into a byte and then responds to the byte.

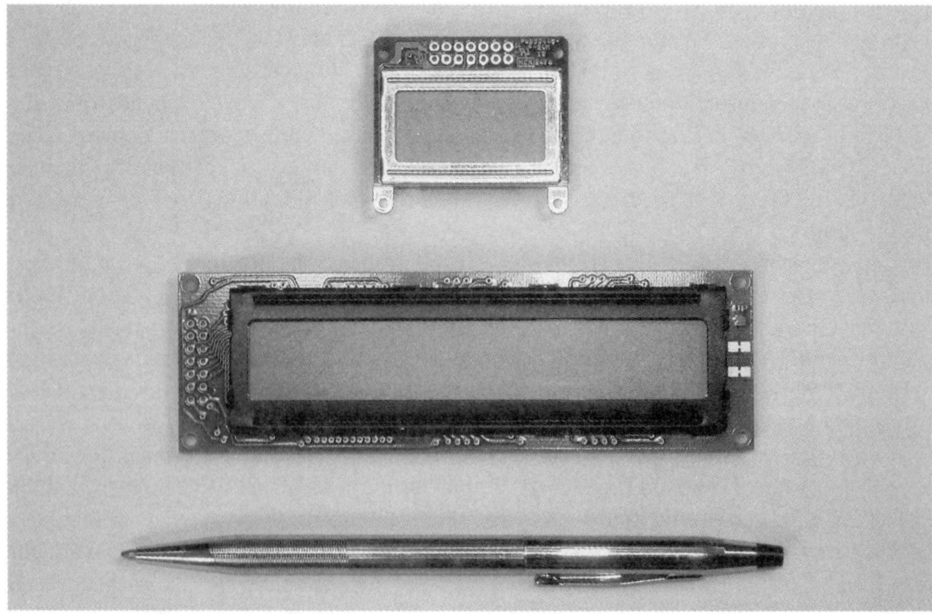

Figure 7-1 Optrex DMC-50448N (8x2) and DMC-24227 (24x2) LCD Modules.

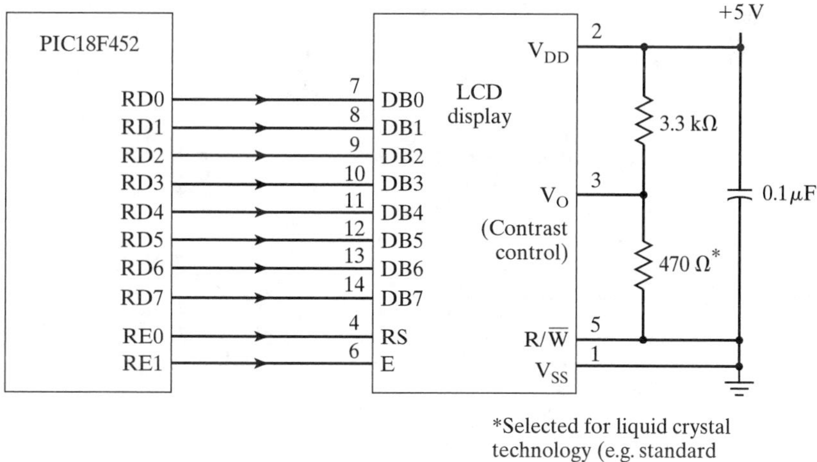

(a) Interface

```
RS = { Ø for control codes
     { 1 for displayable characters
Falling edge of E triggers the display to deal with data byte and RS
```

(b) Role of RS (register select) and E (clock).

Figure 7-2 8-bit interface.

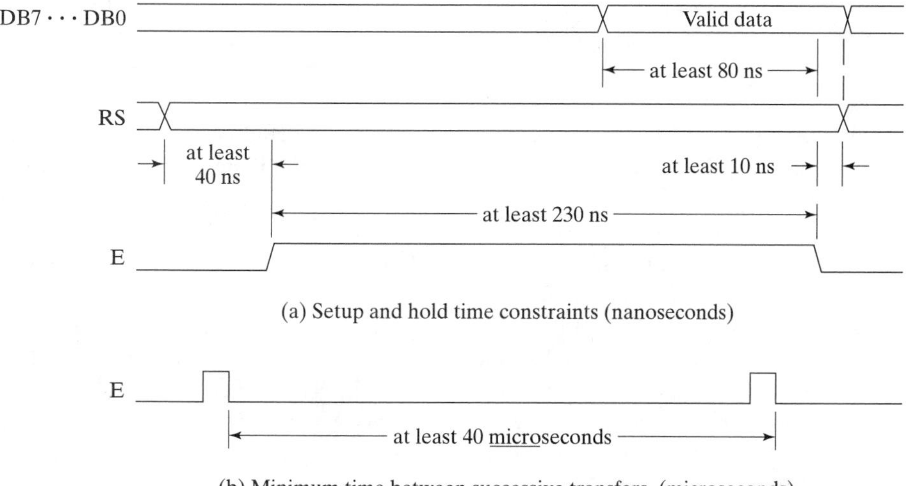

(a) Setup and hold time constraints (nanoseconds)

(b) Minimum time between successive transfers (microseconds)

Figure 7-3 LCD timing specifications.

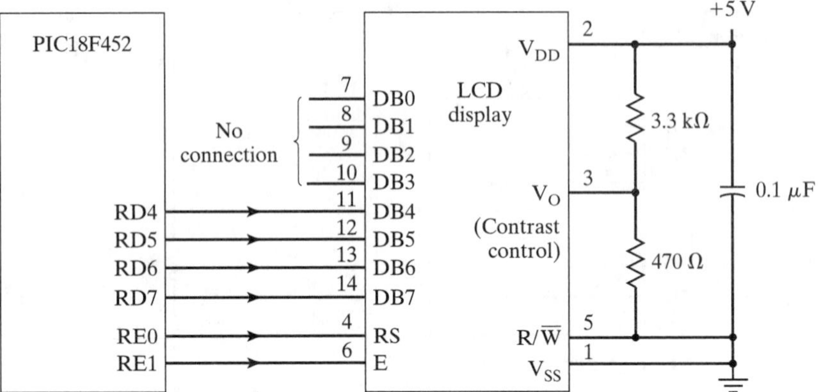

Figure 7-4 4-bit interface

7.3 INITIALIZATION

The Hitachi designers created a versatile LCD controller. It can be used with one-line, two-line, or four-line displays. A visible cursor, indicating where the next character will be entered, can be suppressed (as is appropriate for an instrument display). As characters are entered, they can be displayed in successive positions to the right. Alternatively, the already-entered characters can be shifted to the left to form a scrolling "Times Square" display.

The options selected are specified by the microcontroller when it initializes the LCD module. A potential problem occurs when power is first turned on. Both the PIC microcontroller and the Hitachi controller have their own power-on reset circuits. If the PIC microcontroller begins initializing the LCD as soon as the PIC microcontroller comes out of reset, it may send initialization commands to the LCD while the Hitachi chip is still being held at reset. The commands will be ignored, and the display will be turned off by its own power-on initialization sequence. Subsequent characters sent by the PIC microcontroller will not be displayed. The microcontroller's initialization routine for the LCD can resolve this potential problem simply by waiting for a tenth of a second before sending initialization commands to the display.

There must be pauses between some of the initialization commands sent to the LCD. Because the initialization sequence only occurs at power-up, a call of the **LoopTime** subroutine after each LCD command will insert a sufficient, hardly noticeable, pause. The initialization sequence for the 4-bit interface used by the QwikFlash board is shown in Figure 7-5.

For handling this initialization sequence as well as subsequent constant strings, the **db** assembler directive will be used. The assembler will take an expression such as that in Figure 7-6a and pack 2 bytes into each 16-bit program word. If the number of bytes specified by a **db** directive is odd, the assembler will add an extra 0x00 byte to maintain word alignment for whatever follows. In this way, a **db** directive can be followed by an instruction (which must always begin at an even address).

The mechanism for reading bytes from program memory was discussed in conjunction with Figure 2-8. First, the address of the byte to be read is loaded into the program memory pointer, **TBLPTRH:TBLPTRL**. The **POINT** macro of Figure 7-6b will help with this loading of **TBLPTRH:TBLPTRL**. Thus, the line

```
POINT  LCDstr
```

1. After PIC comes out of reset, wait 0.1 second before beginning the LCD initialization (to make certain its controller chip has exited its own power-on reset and initialization).
2. Drive RS low and leave it low for the entire initialization (since all bytes sent to the LCD module during initialization are command bytes).
3. Raise E, send 0x3, drop E, wait one loop time.
4. Raise E, send 0x3, drop E, wait one loop time.
5. Raise E, send 0x3, drop E, wait one loop time.
6. Raise E, send 0x2, drop E, wait one loop time. (Sets 4-bit interface.)
7. Raise E, send 0x2, drop E, wait one loop time.
8. Raise E, send 0x8, drop E, wait one loop time. (Sets two-line display.)
9. Raise E, send 0x0, drop E, wait one loop time.
10. Raise E, send 0x1, drop E, wait one loop time. (Clears display.)
11. Raise E, send 0x0, drop E, wait one loop time.
12. Raise E, send 0xc, drop E, wait one loop time. (Turns off cursor, turns on display.)
13. Raise E, send 0x0, drop E, wait one loop time.
14. Raise E, send 0x6, drop E, wait one loop time. (Increments cursor automatically.)

Figure 7-5 Initialization for 4-bit interface.

will load the pointer with the address of **LCDstr**. During an invocation of this macro, the assembler will form the 2-byte hex address of **LCDstr**. The *high* operator extracts the high byte of this 2-byte address, while the *low* operator extracts the low byte.

With **TBLPTRH:TBLPTRL** pointing to the byte to be read, the execution of the **tblrd*+** instruction will load the latch, **TABLAT**, with the byte. Then it will increment the address, ready for the next read.

The **InitLCD** subroutine of Figure 7-6c first pauses one-tenth of a second. Then it reads a byte from the **LCDstr** string and sends it to the display a nibble at a time. After each byte has been sent, a new byte is retrieved from program memory. The subroutine terminates when the byte retrieved is 0x00, representing an *end-of-string terminator*. The code of **InitLCD** has been written to meet the timing specifications of Figure 7-3a, whether the internal clock is 2.5 MHz or 10 MHz.

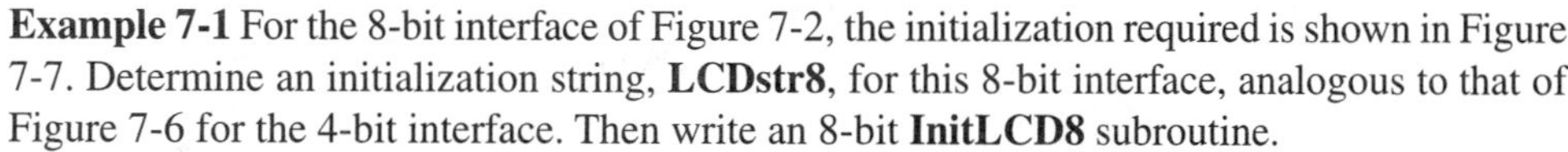

Example 7-1 For the 8-bit interface of Figure 7-2, the initialization required is shown in Figure 7-7. Determine an initialization string, **LCDstr8**, for this 8-bit interface, analogous to that of Figure 7-6 for the 4-bit interface. Then write an 8-bit **InitLCD8** subroutine.

Solution

The initialization string is shown in Figure 7-8a. The change for InitLCD8 is minimal. It only requires the removal of the second write to PORTD and its attendant delay. The result is shown in Figure 7-8b.

7.4 CURSOR-POSITIONING CODES

The Hitachi controller's command set includes a command of the form

```
B'1bbbbbbb'
```

which, if sent to the display with RS = 0, will set the cursor position. It thereby specifies the position of the next displayable character sent to the display. This 8-bit value sent to the display with RS = 0 will

```
LCDstr  db  0x33,0x32,0x28,0x01,0x0c,0x06,0x00
```

(a) Initialization string for the LCD.

```
POINT   macro  stringname
        MOVLF  high stringname, TBLPTRH
        MOVLF  low stringname, TBLPTRL
        endm
```

(b) POINT macro definition.

```
;;;;;;; InitLCD subroutine ;;;;;;;;;;;;;;;;;;;;;;;;;;;;;;;;;;;;;;;;;;;;;;;;;;;;;
;
; Initialize the Optrex 8x2 character LCD.
; First wait for 0.1 second, to get past display's power-on reset time.
; Then send each nibble of each byte in string.

InitLCD
        MOVLF  10,COUNT              ;Wait 0.1 second
        REPEAT_
          rcall  LoopTime            ;Call LoopTime 10 times
          decf  COUNT,F
        UNTIL_  .Z.

        bcf  PORTE,0                 ;RS=0 for command
        POINT  LCDstr                ;Set up table pointer to initialization string
        tblrd*                       ;Get first byte from string into TABLAT
        REPEAT_
          bsf  PORTE,1               ;Drive E high
          movff  TABLAT,PORTD        ;Send upper nibble
          bcf  PORTE,1               ;Drive E low so LCD will process input
          rcall  LoopTime            ;Wait ten milliseconds
          bsf  PORTE,1               ;Drive E high
          swapf  TABLAT,W            ;Swap nibbles
          movwf  PORTD               ;Send lower nibble
          bcf  PORTE,1               ;Drive E low so LCD will process input
          rcall  LoopTime            ;Wait ten milliseconds
          tblrd+*                    ;Increment pointer and get next byte
          movf  TABLAT,F             ;Is it zero?
        UNTIL_  .Z.
        return
```

(c) InitLCD subroutine.

Figure 7-6 LCD initialization for 4-bit interface.

1. After PIC comes out of reset, wait 0.1 second before beginning the LCD initialization (to make certain its controller chip has exited its own power-on reset and initialization).
2. Drive RS low and leave it low for the entire initialization (since all bytes sent to the LCD module during initialization are command bytes).
3. Raise E, send 0x38, drop E, wait one loop time.
4. Raise E, send 0x38, drop E, wait one loop time.
5. Raise E, send 0x38, drop E, wait one loop time.
6. Raise E, send 0x38, drop E, wait one loop time. (Sets 8-bit interface, two-line display.)
7. Raise E, send 0x01, drop E, wait one loop time. (Clears display.)
8. Raise E, send 0x0c, drop E, wait one loop time. (Turns off cursor, turns on display.)
9. Raise E, send 0x06, drop E, wait one loop time. (Increments cursor automatically.)

Figure 7-7 Initialization for 8-bit interface.

```
LCDstr8 db  0x38,0x38,0x38,0x38,0x01,0x0c,0x06,0x00
```

(a) Initialization string for the LCD.

```
;;;;;;; InitLCD8 subroutine ;;;;;;;;;;;;;;;;;;;;;;;;;;;;;;;;;;;;;;;;;;;;;;;;;;;;
;
; Initialize the Optrex 8x2 character LCD display with eight-bit interface.
; First wait for 0.1 second, to get past display's power-on reset time.
; Then send each byte in string.

InitLCD8
        MOVLF  10,COUNT             ;Wait 0.1 second
        REPEAT_
          rcall  LoopTime           ;Call LoopTime 10 times
          decf  COUNT,F
        UNTIL_  .Z.

        bcf  PORTE,0                ;RS=0 for command
        POINT  LCDstr8              ;Set up table pointer to initialization string
        tblrd*                      ;Get first byte from string
        REPEAT_
          bsf  PORTE,1              ;Drive E high
          movff  TABLAT,PORTD       ;Send byte to display
          bcf  PORTE,1              ;Drive E low so LCD will process input
          rcall  LoopTime           ;Wait 10 milliseconds
          tblrd+*                   ;Increment pointer and get new byte
          movf  TABLAT,F            ;Is it zero?
        UNTIL_  .Z.
        return
```

(b) **InitLCD8** subroutine.

Figure 7-8 LCD initialization for 8-bit interface.

0x80	0x81	0x82	0x83	0x84	0x85	0x86	0x87
0xc0	0xc1	0xc2	0xc3	0xc4	0xc5	0xc6	0xc7

Figure 7-9 QuikFlash cursor-positioning codes.

be referred to as a *cursor-positioning code.* The cursor-positioning codes for the little 8x2 LCD on the QwikFlash board are shown in Figure 7-9.

Example 7-2 Write the units of frequency, kHz, to the right edge of the first line of the display.

Solution

The first of the three displayable characters is to be positioned with a cursor-positioning code of 0x85. The ASCII code for a displayable character such as "k" can be represented to the assembler as A'k'. So the display needs to be sent the sequence

```
RS    Code
 0    0x85
 1    A'k'
 1    A'H'
 1    A'z'
```

Virtually the entire family of LCD displays uses the same scheme for assigning cursor-positioning codes to character positions:

- Row 1 begins with 0x80. Successive positions to the right have successive cursor-positioning codes.
- Row 2 begins with 0xc0. Again, successive positions to the right have successive cursor-positioning codes.
- If there is a third row, it is a continuation of the first row. For example, a 20x4 LCD will have first-row codes of 0x80 to 0x93 and third-row codes of 0x94 to 0xa7.
- If there is a fourth row, it is a continuation of the second row.

7.5 DISPLAY STRINGS

Messages to be sent to an LCD must address two questions:

- Where should the message begin?
- What characters should be displayed?

A *display string* will be defined to begin with a cursor-positioning code, followed by the ASCII-encoded characters to be displayed, and ending with an end-of-string terminator, coded as 0x00. A constant display string can be stored in the program area using the same **db** directive discussed earlier. For this purpose, it is helpful to express the operand as a string. The assembler permits the following representation:

```
kHz  db  "\x85kHz\x00"
```

This is a string named "kHz." Characters within the quotes are normally converted to their ASCII-coded values. However, the hex value for a byte can be entered into the string with the four-character sequence

```
\xhh
```

If the number of bytes in the string is odd, the assembler will add an extra zero byte to the end of the string, thereby assigning an integral number of 16-bit words to the string. A **DisplayC** subroutine must be developed that can be passed a pointer to a display string located in the program memory. The **POINT** macro of Figure 7-6b facilitates this operation. Thus, the sequence

```
POINT  kHz
rcall  DisplayC
```

will load **TBLPTRH:TBLPTRL** with the address of the **kHz** string. The **DisplayC** subroutine must then retrieve successive bytes from the string and send them to the display one nibble at a time, inserting the 40 microsecond delay required by the timing specification of Figure 7-3b after each byte has been delivered to the LCD. The register select bit, RS, must be cleared to zero for the cursor-positioning byte and then set to one for the subsequent displayable characters. The resulting **DisplayC** subroutine and its **T40** subroutine are listed in Figure 7-10. Note the use of the **tblrd*** instruction at the beginning to read the program address pointed to by **TBLPTRH:TBLPTRL** into the **TABLAT** register, as described in conjunction with Figure 2-8. Note also the use of the **tblrd+*** instruction near the end of the subroutine to first increment the pointer and then to do the read.

Example 7-3 Write the code for a **DisplayV** subroutine that has passed to it in **FSR0** the address of a display string located in RAM.

```
;;;;;;;DisplayC subroutine;;;;;;;;;;;;;;;;;;;;;;;;;;;;;;;;;;;;;;;;;;;;;;;;;;;;;;;;
; This subroutine is called with TBLPTR containing the address of a constant
; display string.  It sends the bytes of the string to the LCD.  The first
; byte sets the cursor position.  The remaining bytes are displayed, beginning
; at that position.
; This subroutine expects a normal one-byte cursor-positioning code, Øxhh, or
; an occasionally used two-byte cursor-positioning code of the form ØxØØhh.

DisplayC
        bcf   PORTE,Ø             ;Drive RS pin low for cursor-positioning code
        tblrd*                    ;Get byte from string into TABLAT
        movf  TABLAT,F            ;Check for leading zero byte
        IF_  .Z.
          tblrd+*                 ;If zero, get next byte
        ENDIF_
        REPEAT_
          bsf   PORTE,1           ;Drive E pin high
          movff  TABLAT,PORTD     ;Send upper nibble
          bcf   PORTE,1           ;Drive E pin low so LCD will accept nibble
          bsf   PORTE,1           ;Drive E pin high again
          swapf  TABLAT,W         ;Swap nibbles
          movwf  PORTD            ;Write lower nibble
          bcf   PORTE,1           ;Drive E pin low so LCD will process byte
          rcall  T4Ø              ;Wait 4Ø usec
          bsf   PORTE,Ø           ;Drive RS pin high for displayable characters
          tblrd+*                 ;Increment pointer, then get next byte
          movf  TABLAT,F          ;Is it zero?
        UNTIL_  .Z.
       return

;;;;;;; T4Ø subroutine ;;;;;;;;;;;;;;;;;;;;;;;;;;;;;;;;;;;;;;;;;;;;;;;;;;;;;;;;;;;;
;
; Pause for 4Ø microseconds  or 4Ø/Ø.4 = 1ØØ clock cycles.
; (Assumes a 1Ø/4 = 2.5 MHz internal clock rate with an Ø.4 microsecond
; internal clock period.)

T4Ø
        movlw  1ØØ/3              ;Each REPEAT loop takes 3 cycles
        movwf  COUNT
        REPEAT_
          decf  COUNT,F
        UNTIL_  .Z.
        return
```

Figure 7-10 DisplayC and **T40** subroutines.

Solution

The **DisplayV** subroutine, shown in Figure 7-11, substitutes RAM accesses, using **FSR0** as a pointer, for program memory accesses, using **TBLPTRH:TBLPTRL** as a pointer.

A call of the **DisplayV** subroutine takes the form

```
lfsr  Ø,FREQ
rcall  DisplayV
```

where **FREQ** might be a display string to display a frequency value. The string must first be initialized with the cursor-positioning code at the beginning, the end-of-string terminator at the end, and the ASCII representation of the frequency in between.

Example 7-4 Show the code to initialize **FREQ** to display a three-digit frequency value to the left of the "kHz" display discussed earlier. Assume that a **Frequency** subroutine computes the three-digit ASCII value and inserts it into the string.

```
;;;;;;; DisplayV subroutine ;;;;;;;;;;;;;;;;;;;;;;;;;;;;;;;;;;;;;;;;;;;;;;;;;;;;;
;
; This subroutine is called with FSR0 containing the address of a variable
; display string.  It sends the bytes of the string to the LCD.  The first
; byte sets the cursor position.  The remaining bytes are displayed, beginning
; at that position.

DisplayV
        bcf  PORTE,0              ;Drive RS pin low for cursor-positioning code
        REPEAT_
          bsf  PORTE,1            ;Drive E pin high
          movff  INDF0,PORTD      ;Send upper nibble
          bcf  PORTE,1            ;Drive E pin low so LCD will accept nibble
          bsf  PORTE,1            ;Drive E pin high again
          swapf  INDF0,W          ;Swap nibbles
          movwf  PORTD            ;Write lower nibble
          bcf  PORTE,1            ;Drive E pin low so LCD will process byte
          rcall  T40              ;Wait 40 usec
          bsf  PORTE,0            ;Drive RS pin high for displayable characters
          movf  PREINC0,W         ;Increment pointer, then get next byte
        UNTIL_  .Z.               ;Is it zero?
       return
```

Figure 7-11 DisplayV subroutine.

Solution

To display the three digits, a 5-byte string must be defined. If it is called **FREQ**, then the 5 bytes of RAM can be set aside for this use by adding

```
FREQ:5
```

to the **cblock . . . endc** construct used to define variables (see Figure 5-7). The "kHz" string uses the last three character positions of the first line of the QwikFlash display. Referring to Figure 7-9, it is seen that if 0x81 is used as the cursor-positioning code for the **FREQ** string, then the three digits will be followed by a space followed by "kHz". The initialization code then becomes

```
MOVLF  0x81,FREQ             ;Cursor-positioning code
clrf  FREQ+4                 ;End of string
```

The string can be displayed with the instruction sequence

```
rcall  Frequency
lfsr  0,FREQ
rcall  DisplayV
```

7.6 LCD CHARACTER SET

The LCD family of displays supported by the Hitachi HD44780 controller has three groups of character sets:

1. Codes between 0x20 and 0x7f produce the standard displayable ASCII character set.
2. Codes between 0xa0 and 0xff produce Japanese characters.
3. Codes between 0x00 and 0x07 produce eight user-defined characters. These are also available with codes between 0x08 and 0x0f.

The first set is listed in Figure 7-12a. Only codes 0x5c, 0x7e, and 0x7f differ from their normal ASCII meanings of "\", "~", and "delete." The second set contains a few occasionally useful codes, some of

Lower nibble of character code	Upper nibble of character code: 2	3	4	5	6	7
0		0	@	P	`	p
1	!	1	A	Q	a	q
2	"	2	B	R	b	r
3	#	3	C	S	c	s
4	$	4	D	T	d	t
5	%	5	E	U	e	u
6	&	6	F	V	f	v
7	'	7	G	W	g	w
8	(	8	H	X	h	x
9	)	9	I	Y	i	y
a	*	:	J	Z	j	z
b	+	;	K	[	k	{
c	,	<	L	***	l	|
d	-	=	M	]	m	}
e	.	>	N	^	n	→
f	/	?	O	_	o	←

*** Japanese symbol

(a) 0x20-0x7f (ASCII codes)

0xdf	°(degree symbol for temperature)
0xe0	α
0xe2	β
0xf7	π
0xf6	Σ
0xf4	Ω

(b) Some other characters and their character codes.

Figure 7-12 Character codes for displayable characters.

which are listed in Figure 7-12b. The user-defined characters mentioned as the third set of LCD characters will be explained in the next section.

7.7 USER-DEFINED CHARACTERS

The Hitachi controller chip supports the generation of up to eight user-defined characters. Once defined, these eight characters can be accessed with character codes between 0x01 and 0x0f, as shown in Figure 7-13.

Before these characters can be used, they must first be defined by writing the pixel pattern for each character to a special *character-generating RAM* (CGRAM) in the Hitachi chip. Although each of the normal displayable ASCII characters (accessed with character codes 0x20 to 0x7f) is generated with a 5x7 array of pixels, there is actually an eighth row of five pixels below each character, used for the optional cursor display. This eighth row is available, along with the other seven, when creating a user-defined character. The same **DisplayC** subroutine used to send a display string to the Hitachi chip's *data-display RAM* can also be used to write to the character-generating RAM. A write to the data-display RAM begins with a cursor-positioning command of the form

```
B'1bbbbbbb'  (with RS=0)
```

A write to the character-generating RAM begins with a CGRAM-positioning command of the form

```
B'01bbbbbb'  (with RS=0)
```

The bytes that follow this (with RS = 1) will be treated as writes to successive rows of a character, beginning with the top row. Figure 7-13 shows the CGRAM-positioning code for each character. After the 8 bytes have been written to define one character, the Hitachi chip is ready to receive the 8 bytes for the next character without the need for an intervening CGRAM-positioning code.

Of each byte sent to the CGRAM, only the least-significant 5 bits are used to define the 5 pixels of one row of the 5x8-character pattern. The Hitachi chip ignores the other three bits.

A "display string," which begins with one of the CGRAM-positioning codes of Figure 7-13, can be sent to the LCD via the **DisplayC** subroutine. The one string can write, or rewrite, the pixel pattern for any number of the eight user-defined characters. However, a row with all pixels turned off must not be represented by 0x00 in the "display string" because that will be interpreted, by the **DisplayC** subroutine, as an end-of-string terminator.

Example 7-5 Create a "block" character consisting of a 3x3 array of 1s centered on the 5x7-pixel array of the user-defined character having the character code 0x01.

User-defined character number	Character code (for using character)			CGRAM-positioning code (for defining character)
0	0x00*	or	0x08	0x40
1	0x01	or	0x09	0x48
2	0x02	or	0x0a	0x50
3	0x03	or	0x0b	0x58
4	0x04	or	0x0c	0x60
5	0x05	or	0x0d	0x68
6	0x06	or	0x0e	0x70
7	0x07	or	0x0f	0x78

* 0x00 should not be used as a character code in a display string since 0x00 is reserved for use as the end-of-string terminator

Figure 7-13 Character codes and CGRAM-positioning codes for eight user-defined characters.

Ignored bits			← 5 →						Hexadecimal representation of row
1	0	0	0	0	0	0	0	↑	0x80
1	0	0	0	0	0	0	0		0x80
1	0	0	0	1	1	1	0		0x8e
1	0	0	0	1	1	1	0	7	0x8e
1	0	0	0	1	1	1	0		0x8e
1	0	0	0	0	0	0	0		0x80
1	0	0	0	0	0	0	0	↓	0x80
1	0	0	0	0	0	0	0	Cursor row	0x80

BlockStr db 0x48, 0x80, 0x80, 0x8e, 0x8e, 0x8e, 0x80, 0x80, 0x80, 0x00

(a) "Display string" for creating a block character having a character code of 0x01

```
BlockOn    db 0x83, 0x01, 0x01, 0x00
```

(b) Display string to write two block characters to the center of line 1 of the QwikFlash display.

```
BlockOff   db 0x83, A' ', A' ', 0x00
```

(c) Display string to blank the two character positions.

Figure 7-14 LCD character creation.

Solution

The pixel pattern for the block character is shown in Figure 7-14a for the actual 5x8 array that includes the cursor row. The hexadecimal representation for each row of pixels is shown to the right. To create this pattern for the user-defined character having character code 0x01, a "display string" begins with the CGRAM-positioning code of 0x48 that corresponds to character code 0x01 in Figure 7-13. The "display string," also shown in Figure 7-14a, continues with the bytes for all eight rows of pixels, followed by the 0x00 end-of-string terminator.

An example display string that will write this block character twice in the center of the first line of the QwikFlash display is shown in Figure 7-14b. Another display string that will blank the two character positions is shown in Figure 7-14c.

Example 7-6 Write a **BlinkBlock** subroutine, called from the 10-millisecond mainline loop, that will continuously blink the two block characters in the center of line 1 of the display.

Solution

Assume that the LCD is initially blanked, or at least that line 1 is initially blanked. The two character positions might be rewritten every half-second to cause a 1 Hz blink rate. The code shown in Figure 7-15a can be added to the **Initial** subroutine to create the block character. The **BlinkBlock** subroutine is listed in Figure 7-15b. It uses a variable, **LCDCOUNT**, as a scale-of-100 scaler.

```
        POINT  BlockStr
        rcall  DisplayC
```

(a) Code to be added to the **Initial** subroutine to create a block character having a character code of 0x01.

```
BlinkBlock
        decf  LCDCOUNT,F            ;Decrement counter
        IF_  .Z.                    ;Turn on blocks when LCDCOUNT=100
          MOVLF  100,LCDCOUNT
          POINT  BlockOn
          rcall  DisplayC
        ELSE_                       ;Turn off blocks when LCDCOUNT=50
          movf  LCDCOUNT,W
          sublw  50
          IF_  .Z.
            POINT  BlockOff
            rcall  DisplayC
          ENDIF_
        ENDIF_
        return
```

(b) **BlinkBlock** subroutine, called in the mainline loop, to blink two block characters on and off every second.

Figure 7-15 Code for Example 7.6.

```
BarChars
        db  0x00,0x48               ;CGRAM-positioning code
        db  0x90,0x90,0x90,0x90,0x90,0x90,0x90,0x90  ;Column 1
        db  0x98,0x98,0x98,0x98,0x98,0x98,0x98,0x98  ;Columns 1,2
        db  0x9c,0x9c,0x9c,0x9c,0x9c,0x9c,0x9c,0x9c  ;Columns 1,2,3
        db  0x9e,0x9e,0x9e,0x9e,0x9e,0x9e,0x9e,0x9e  ;Columns 1,2,3,4
        db  0x9f,0x9f,0x9f,0x9f,0x9f,0x9f,0x9f,0x9f  ;Columns 1,2,3,4,5
        db  0x00                    ;End-of-string terminator
```

(a) "Display string" for creating bar graph characters.

```
        POINT  BarChars
        rcall  DisplayC
```

(b) Code to add to the **Initial** subroutine to create the bar graph characters.

Figure 7-16 Example 7.7.

Example 7-7 One of the rows of the 8x2-character LCD display can be used as an (8x5 =) 40-segment bar graph display. Each segment is to consist of a single 8x1 column of pixels. A bar graph value of 23 segments will be implemented by turning on every pixel of the (23/5=) 4 left-most characters, turning on every pixel of the (23 mod 5=) 3 left-most columns of the next character, and blanking the remaining characters. Create the characters needed to implement the bar graph display.

Solution

Five user-defined characters are needed.

- A single left-justified column of pixels
- Two left-justified columns of pixels
- Three left-justified columns of pixels

- Four left-justified columns of pixels
- All five columns of pixels.

These can be conveniently assigned to character codes 0x01, 0x02, 0x03, 0x04, and 0x05. The **BarChars** "display string" of Figure 7-16a contains so many bytes that is has been divided into successive **db** directives. Because the assembler will pad each of these to an even number of bytes (i.e., an integral number of 16-bit words), the CGRAM-positioning code has been written as

```
db   0x00,0x48
```

The **DisplayC** subroutine has been written to ignore an initial 0x00 byte solely to handle this representation of the display string's "cursor-positioning" code as a word whose first byte is 0x00.

The code to be added to the **Initial** subroutine to support this creation of the five user-defined characters is shown in Figure 7-16b.

Example 7-8 Write a **Bargraph** subroutine that will translate **WREG** into a 40-segment bar graph display for values between 0 and 40. For larger values, turn on all 40 segments.

Solution

A variable display string can be created and filled and then passed to **DisplayV** for sending to the display. Alternatively, the **Bargraph** subroutine might handle each byte individually. As each byte is formed, it is immediately sent to the display. The solution of Figure 7-17 uses this latter approach.

Bargraph first truncates the content of **WREG** into a number in **TEMP** between 0 and 40. Then it sends the cursor-positioning code, 0x80, for the beginning of row 1 of the display. The first

```
WHILE_   .NB.         ...         ENDWHILE_
```

construct will send the user-defined character coded as 0x05 to the display if **TEMP** is greater than, or equal to, 5. This will send a character with all five segments turned on. 5 is then subtracted from **TEMP** and the process repeated.

When **TEMP** becomes less than 5, a check is made to see if 1, 2, 3, or 4 segments are called for. If so, one character with a character code of 1, 2, 3, or 4 (the user-defined characters for these segments) is sent. The remaining character positions of the line are sent blank characters to complete the display.

7.8 DISPLAY DEBUGGING AID

Some microcontroller development boards include an 8-bit LED display of a port. As an application program is being developed, the state of a variable or register of concern can be monitored by writing it to the port. For example, if PORTB drives an array of eight LEDs, then

```
movff <register>,PORTB        ;Display register state
```

will display the state of the selected register or RAM location as a binary number.

```
        BGCOUNT                 ;Bargraph character position counter
        TEMP                    ;Temporary variable
```

(a) New variables.

```
        POINT  BarChars         ;Create bargraph characters
        call  DisplayC
```

(b) New initialization.

```
        movf  <variable to be displayed>,W
        call  Bargraph
```

(c) Addition to mainline loop.

```
;;;;;;; Bargraph subroutine ;;;;;;;;;;;;;;;;;;;;;;;;;;;;;;;;;;;;;;;;;;;;;;;;;;;;;
;
; This subroutine uses line 1 of the LCD display as a 40-segment bargraph
; display of WREG.  As the number of segments for each character position is
; determined, the corresponding user-defined character code is sent to the
; display, a single character at a time using the SendByte subroutine.

Bargraph
        movwf  TEMP             ;Store W
        sublw  40               ;Check for valid value <= 40
        IF_  .B.
          MOVLF  40,TEMP        ;Cap at 40
        ENDIF_

        bcf  PORTE,0            ;Drive RS pin low for cursor-positioning code
        movlw  0x80
        rcall  SendByte         ;Send cursor-positioning code
        bsf  PORTE,0            ;Drive RS pin high for displayable characters

        MOVLF  8,BGCOUNT        ;Set BGCOUNT for 8 chars
        movlw  5
        subwf  TEMP,F           ;Subtract 5 from value

        WHILE_  .NB.            ;While resulting TEMP is 0 or greater,
          rcall  SendByte       ;send user-defined character 5 (all segments)
          decf  BGCOUNT,F       ;Decrement char counter
          movlw  5
          subwf  TEMP,F         ;Subtract 5 from value
        ENDWHILE_
        addwf  TEMP,W           ;Restore value

        IF_  .NZ.               ;If non-zero, send character 1,2,3,or 4
          rcall  SendByte
          decf  BGCOUNT,F       ;Decrement char counter
        ENDIF_

        movf  BGCOUNT,F
        WHILE_  .NZ.            ;Fill remaining LCD characters with blanks
          movlw  A' '
          rcall  SendByte       ;Send blank to LCD
          decf  BGCOUNT,F
        ENDWHILE_
        return

;;;;;;; SendByte subroutine ;;;;;;;;;;;;;;;;;;;;;;;;;;;;;;;;;;;;;;;;;;;;;;;;;;;;;;
;
; This subroutine sends a single character from WREG to the LCD.

SendByte
        bsf  PORTE,1            ;Drive E pin high
        nop                     ;Delay needed if internal clock period = 0.1us
        movwf  PORTD            ;Send upper nibble
        bcf  PORTE,1            ;Drive E pin low so LCD will accept nibble
        bsf  PORTE,1            ;Drive E pin high again
        swapf  WREG,W           ;Swap nibbles
        movwf  PORTD            ;Write lower nibble
        bcf  PORTE,1            ;Drive E pin low so LCD will process byte
        rcall  T40              ;Wait 40 usec
        return
```

(d) Subroutines.

Figure 7-17 Bargraph subroutine.

```
        BYTE                    ;Eight-bit byte to be displayed
        BYTESTR:10              ;Display string for binary version of BYTE
```

(a) Variables.

```
BYTE_1  db  "\x80BYTE=   \x00"  ;Write "BYTE=" to first line of LCD
```

(b) Constant string.

```
DISPLAY macro  register
        movff  register,BYTE
        call  ByteDisplay
        endm
```

(c) **DISPLAY** macro definition.

```
        DISPLAY  PORTD          ;Display PORTD as a binary number
```

(d) Example of the use of the **DISPLAY** macro.

```
;;;;;;; ByteDisplay subroutine ;;;;;;;;;;;;;;;;;;;;;;;;;;;;;;;;;;;;;;;;;;;;;;;;
;
; Display whatever is in BYTE as a binary number.

ByteDisplay
        POINT  BYTE_1           ;Display "BYTE="
        rcall  DisplayC
        lfsr  0,BYTESTR+8
        REPEAT_
          clrf  WREG
          rrcf  BYTE,F          ;Move bit into carry
          rlcf  WREG,F          ;and from there into WREG
          iorlw  0x30           ;Convert to ASCII
          movwf  POSTDEC0       ; and move to string
          movf  FSR0L,W         ;Done?
          sublw  low BYTESTR
        UNTIL_  .Z.

        lfsr  0,BYTESTR         ;Set pointer to display string
        MOVLF  0xc0,BYTESTR     ;Add cursor-positioning code
        clrf  BYTESTR+9         ;and end-of-string terminator
        rcall  DisplayV
        return
```

(e) **ByteDisplay** subroutine.

Figure 7-18 Support for the **DISPLAY** macro to display an arbitrary register as a binary number.

During code development, the QwikFlash's LCD display can be used for the same purpose. In this case, the binary display of a register or RAM variable can be invoked with

```
DISPLAY  <register>
```

where **DISPLAY** is a macro that inserts into the code the two-line sequence

```
movff  <register>,BYTE
call  ByteDisplay
```

The net effect, if the register contains B′00101111′, is to produce

```
BYTE=
00101111
```

on the little 8x2 LCD display.

Example 7-9 Develop the **DISPLAY** debugging aid.

Solution

The variables to be added to the **cblock ... endc** construct are shown in Figure 7-18a. The **BYTE_1** display string of Figure 7-18b can be used to write "BYTE=" to line 1 of the display. The **DISPLAY** macro definition is shown in Figure 7-18c. An example of its use to monitor the state of the "RPG" inputs connected to bits 1 and 0 of **PORTD** is shown in Figure 7-18d. Refer to Figure 4-2a for the external connections to **PORTD**. Finally, the **ByteDisplay** subroutine is listed in Figure 7-18e. The first line of the display becomes

```
BYTE=
```

Then the subroutine peels off each bit of **BYTE**, beginning with the right-most bit, converts it to the ASCII code for 0 or 1 (i.e., 0x30 or 0x31), and writes it into the string, beginning with the right-most byte. It terminates when the low byte of the pointer register, **FSR0L**, matches the low byte of the address **BYTESTR**. Then this display string is sent to the display.

7.9 P2.ASM, A DISPLAY TEMPLATE PROGRAM

The display utilities developed in this chapter have been used to create the "template" program, P2.asm, of Figure 7-19. In addition to the **DisplayC** and **DisplayV** utilities, it includes the **DISPLAY** debugging aid of the last section.

```
;;;;;;; P2 for QwikFlash board ;;;;;;;;;;;;;;;;;;;;;;;;;;;;;;;;;;;;;;;;;;;;;;;;
;
; Use 10 MHz crystal frequency.
; Use Timer0 for ten millisecond looptime.
; Blink "Alive" LED every two and a half seconds.
; Display PORTD as a binary number.
; Toggle C2 output every ten milliseconds for measuring looptime precisely.
;
;;;;;;; Program hierarchy ;;;;;;;;;;;;;;;;;;;;;;;;;;;;;;;;;;;;;;;;;;;;;;;;;;;;
;
; Mainline
;   Initial
;     InitLCD
;       LoopTime
;   BlinkAlive
;   ByteDisplay (DISPLAY macro)
;     DisplayC
;       T40
;     DisplayV
;       T40
;   LoopTime
;
;;;;;;; Assembler directives ;;;;;;;;;;;;;;;;;;;;;;;;;;;;;;;;;;;;;;;;;;;;;;;;;

        list  P=PIC18F452, F=INHX32, C=160, N=0, ST=OFF, MM=OFF, R=DEC, X=ON
        #include P18F452.inc
        __CONFIG  _CONFIG1H, _HS_OSC_1H  ;HS oscillator
        __CONFIG  _CONFIG2L, _PWRT_ON_2L & _BOR_ON_2L & _BORV_42_2L  ;Reset
        __CONFIG  _CONFIG2H, _WDT_OFF_2H  ;Watchdog timer disabled
        __CONFIG  _CONFIG3H, _CCP2MX_ON_3H  ;CCP2 to RC1 (rather than to RB3)
        __CONFIG  _CONFIG4L, _LVP_OFF_4L  ;RB5 enabled for I/O

;;;;;;; Variables ;;;;;;;;;;;;;;;;;;;;;;;;;;;;;;;;;;;;;;;;;;;;;;;;;;;;;;;;;;;;

        cblock  0x000           ;Beginning of Access RAM
        TMR0LCOPY               ;Copy of sixteen-bit Timer0 used by LoopTime
        TMR0HCOPY
        INTCONCOPY              ;Copy of INTCON for LoopTime subroutine
        COUNT                   ;Counter available as local to subroutines
        ALIVECNT                ;Counter for blinking "Alive" LED
        BYTE                    ;Eight-bit byte to be displayed
        BYTESTR:10              ;Display string for binary version of BYTE
        endc

;;;;;;; Macro definitions ;;;;;;;;;;;;;;;;;;;;;;;;;;;;;;;;;;;;;;;;;;;;;;;;;;;;


MOVLF   macro  literal,dest
        movlw  literal
        movwf  dest
        endm

POINT   macro  stringname
        MOVLF  high stringname, TBLPTRH
        MOVLF  low stringname, TBLPTRL
        endm

DISPLAY macro  register
        movff  register,BYTE
        call  ByteDisplay
        endm

;;;;;;; Vectors ;;;;;;;;;;;;;;;;;;;;;;;;;;;;;;;;;;;;;;;;;;;;;;;;;;;;;;;;;;;;;;

        org  0x0000             ;Reset vector
        nop
        goto  Mainline
        org  0x0008             ;High priority interrupt vector
        goto  $                 ;Trap
        org  0x0018             ;Low priority interrupt vector
        goto  $                 ;Trap
```

Figure 7-19 P2.asm file.

```
;;;;;;; Mainline program ;;;;;;;;;;;;;;;;;;;;;;;;;;;;;;;;;;;;;;;;;;;;;;;;;;;;;;

Mainline
        rcall  Initial            ;Initialize everything
        LOOP_
          btg  PORTC,RC2          ;Toggle pin, to support measuring looptime
          rcall  BlinkAlive       ;Blink "Alive" LED
          DISPLAY  PORTD          ;Display PORTD as a binary number
          rcall  LoopTime         ;Make looptime be ten milliseconds
        ENDLOOP_

;;;;;;; Initial subroutine ;;;;;;;;;;;;;;;;;;;;;;;;;;;;;;;;;;;;;;;;;;;;;;;;;;;;;;
;
; This subroutine performs all initializations of variables and registers.

Initial
        MOVLF  B'10001110',ADCON1  ;Enable PORTA & PORTE digital I/O pins
        MOVLF  B'11100001',TRISA  ;Set I/O for PORTA
        MOVLF  B'11011100',TRISB  ;Set I/O for PORTB
        MOVLF  B'11010000',TRISC  ;Set I/O for PORTC
        MOVLF  B'00001111',TRISD  ;Set I/O for PORTD
        MOVLF  B'00000000',TRISE  ;Set I/O for PORTE
        MOVLF  B'10001000',T0CON  ;Set up Timer0 for a looptime of 10 ms
        MOVLF  B'00010000',PORTA  ;Turn off all four LEDs driven from PORTA
        rcall  InitLCD
        return

;;;;;;; InitLCD subroutine ;;;;;;;;;;;;;;;;;;;;;;;;;;;;;;;;;;;;;;;;;;;;;;;;;;;;;;
;
; Initialize the Optrex 8x2 character LCD.
; First wait for 0.1 second, to get past display's power-on reset time.

InitLCD
        MOVLF  10,COUNT           ;Wait 0.1 second
        REPEAT_
          rcall  LoopTime         ;Call LoopTime 10 times
          decf  COUNT,F
        UNTIL_  .Z.

        bcf  PORTE,0              ;RS=0 for command
        POINT  LCDstr             ;Set up table pointer to initialization string
        tblrd*                    ;Get first byte from string into TABLAT
        REPEAT_
          bsf  PORTE,1            ;Drive E high
          movff  TABLAT,PORTD     ;Send upper nibble
          bcf  PORTE,1            ;Drive E low so LCD will process input
          rcall  LoopTime         ;Wait ten milliseconds
          bsf  PORTE,1            ;Drive E high
          swapf  TABLAT,W         ;Swap nibbles
          movwf  PORTD            ;Send lower nibble
          bcf  PORTE,1            ;Drive E low so LCD will process input
          rcall  LoopTime         ;Wait ten milliseconds
          tblrd+*                 ;Increment pointer and get next byte
          movf  TABLAT,F          ;Is it zero?
        UNTIL_  .Z.
        return

;;;;;;; T40 subroutine ;;;;;;;;;;;;;;;;;;;;;;;;;;;;;;;;;;;;;;;;;;;;;;;;;;;;;;;;;;
;
; Pause for 40 microseconds  or 40/0.4 = 100 clock cycles.
; Assumes 10/4 = 2.5 MHz internal clock rate.

T40
        movlw  100/3              ;Each REPEAT loop takes 3 cycles
        movwf  COUNT
        REPEAT_
          decf  COUNT,F
        UNTIL_  .Z.
        return
```

Figure 7-19 continued

```
;;;;;;;DisplayC subroutine;;;;;;;;;;;;;;;;;;;;;;;;;;;;;;;;;;;;;;;;;;;;;;;;;;;;;
;
; This subroutine is called with TBLPTR containing the address of a constant
; display string.  It sends the bytes of the string to the LCD.  The first
; byte sets the cursor position.  The remaining bytes are displayed, beginning
; at that position.
; This subroutine expects a normal one-byte cursor-positioning code, Øxhh, or
; an occasionally used two-byte cursor-positioning code of the form ØxØØhh.

DisplayC
        bcf  PORTE,Ø              ;Drive RS pin low for cursor-positioning code
        tblrd*                    ;Get byte from string into TABLAT
        movf  TABLAT,F            ;Check for leading zero byte
        IF_  .Z.
          tblrd+*                 ;If zero, get next byte
        ENDIF_
        REPEAT_
          bsf  PORTE,1            ;Drive E pin high
          movff  TABLAT,PORTD     ;Send upper nibble
          bcf  PORTE,1            ;Drive E pin low so LCD will accept nibble
          bsf  PORTE,1            ;Drive E pin high again
          swapf  TABLAT,W         ;Swap nibbles
          movwf  PORTD            ;Write lower nibble
          bcf  PORTE,1            ;Drive E pin low so LCD will process byte
          rcall  T4Ø              ;Wait 4Ø usec
          bsf  PORTE,Ø            ;Drive RS pin high for displayable characters
          tblrd+*                 ;Increment pointer, then get next byte
          movf  TABLAT,F          ;Is it zero?
        UNTIL_  .Z.
       return

;;;;;;; DisplayV subroutine ;;;;;;;;;;;;;;;;;;;;;;;;;;;;;;;;;;;;;;;;;;;;;;;;;;;;
;
; This subroutine is called with FSRØ containing the address of a variable
; display string.  It sends the bytes of the string to the LCD.  The first
; byte sets the cursor position.  The remaining bytes are displayed, beginning
; at that position.

DisplayV
        bcf  PORTE,Ø              ;Drive RS pin low for cursor-positioning code
        REPEAT_
          bsf  PORTE,1            ;Drive E pin high
          movff  INDFØ,PORTD      ;Send upper nibble
          bcf  PORTE,1            ;Drive E pin low so LCD will accept nibble
          bsf  PORTE,1            ;Drive E pin high again
          swapf  INDFØ,W          ;Swap nibbles
          movwf  PORTD            ;Write lower nibble
          bcf  PORTE,1            ;Drive E pin low so LCD will process byte
          rcall  T4Ø              ;Wait 4Ø usec
          bsf  PORTE,Ø            ;Drive RS pin high for displayable characters
          movf  PREINCØ,W         ;Increment pointer, then get next byte
        UNTIL_  .Z.               ;Is it zero?
       return

;;;;;;; BlinkAlive subroutine ;;;;;;;;;;;;;;;;;;;;;;;;;;;;;;;;;;;;;;;;;;;;;;;;;;
;
; This subroutine briefly blinks the LED next to the PIC every two-and-a-half
; seconds.

BlinkAlive
        bsf  PORTA,RA4            ;Turn off LED
        decf  ALIVECNT,F          ;Decrement loop counter and return if not zero
        IF_  .Z.
          MOVLF  25Ø,ALIVECNT     ;Reinitialize ALIVECNT
          bcf  PORTA,RA4          ;Turn on LED for ten milliseconds every 2.5 sec
        ENDIF_
        return
```

Figure 7-19 continued

```
;;;;;;; LoopTime subroutine ;;;;;;;;;;;;;;;;;;;;;;;;;;;;;;;;;;;;;;;;;;;;;;;;;;;;;
;
; This subroutine waits for Timer0 to complete its ten millisecond count
; sequence. It does so by waiting for sixteen-bit Timer0 to roll over. To obtain
; a period of precisely 10000/0.4 = 25000 clock periods, it needs to remove
; 65536-25000 or 40536 counts from the sixteen-bit count sequence.  The
; algorithm below first copies Timer0 to RAM, adds "Bignum" to the copy ,and
; then writes the result back to Timer0. It actually needs to add somewhat more
; counts to Timer0 than 40536.  The extra number of 12+2 counts added into
; "Bignum" makes the precise correction.

Bignum  equu    65536-25000+12+2

LoopTime
        REPEAT_
        UNTIL_  INTCON,TMR0IF == 1  ;Wait until ten milliseconds are up
        movff  INTCON,INTCONCOPY  ;Disable all interrupts to CPU
        bcf  INTCON,GIEH
        movff  TMR0L,TMR0LCOPY  ;Read 16-bit counter at this moment
        movff  TMR0H,TMR0HCOPY
        movlw  low  Bignum
        addwf  TMR0LCOPY,F
        movlw  high  Bignum
        addwfc  TMR0HCOPY,F
        movff  TMR0HCOPY,TMR0H
        movff  TMR0LCOPY,TMR0L  ;Write 16-bit counter at this moment
        movf  INTCONCOPY,W      ;Restore GIEH interrupt enable bit
        andlw  B'10000000'
        iorwf  INTCON,F
        bcf  INTCON,TMROIF      ;Clear Timer0 flag
        return

;;;;;;; ByteDisplay subroutine ;;;;;;;;;;;;;;;;;;;;;;;;;;;;;;;;;;;;;;;;;;;;;;;;;;
;
; Display whatever is in BYTE as a binary number.

ByteDisplay
        POINT  BYTE_1           ;Display "BYTE="
        rcall  DisplayC
        lfsr  0,BYTESTR+8
        REPEAT_
          clrf  WREG
          rrcf  BYTE,F          ;Move bit into carry
          rlcf  WREG,F          ;and from there into WREG
          iorlw  0x30           ;Convert to ASCII
          movwf  POSTDEC0       ; and move to string
          movf  FSR0L,W         ;Done?
          sublw  low BYTESTR
        UNTIL_  .Z.

        lfsr  0,BYTESTR         ;Set pointer to display string
        MOVLF  0xc0,BYTESTR     ;Add cursor-positioning code
        clrf  BYTESTR+9         ;and end-of-string terminator
        rcall  DisplayV
        return

;;;;;;; Constant strings ;;;;;;;;;;;;;;;;;;;;;;;;;;;;;;;;;;;;;;;;;;;;;;;;;;;;;;;;;

LCDstr  db  0x33,0x32,0x28,0x01,0x0c,0x06,0x00  ;Initialization string for LCD
BYTE_1  db  "\x80BYTE=   \x00"  ;Write "BYTE=" to first line of LCD
BarChars                        ;Bargraph user-defined characters
        db  0x00,0x48           ;CGRAM-positioning code
        db  0x90,0x90,0x90,0x90,0x90,0x90,0x90,0x90  ;Column 1
        db  0x98,0x98,0x98,0x98,0x98,0x98,0x98,0x98  ;Columns 1,2
        db  0x9c,0x9c,0x9c,0x9c,0x9c,0x9c,0x9c,0x9c  ;Columns 1,2,3
        db  0x9e,0x9e,0x9e,0x9e,0x9e,0x9e,0x9e,0x9e  ;Columns 1,2,3,4
        db  0x9f,0x9f,0x9f,0x9f,0x9f,0x9f,0x9f,0x9f  ;Column 1,2,3,4,5
        db  0x00                ;End-of-string terminator

;;;;;;;;;;;;;;;;;;;;;;;;;;;;;;;;;;;;;;;;;;;;;;;;;;;;;;;;;;;;;;;;;;;;;;;;;;;;;;;;

        end
```

Figure 7-19 continued

PROBLEMS

7-1 Timing specifications. Referring to the timing specifications of Figure 7-3a, consider the **InitLCD** subroutine of Figure 7-6c. Are the timing specifications met, even if the PIC18F452 chip is operated at an internal clock rate of 10 MHz (i.e., with an internal clock period of 100 ns)?

7-2 LCD potential bug. The **InitLCD** subroutine includes a 0.1 second pause at its beginning. It has been found that with this 0.1 second pause omitted from the code, a user application would work correctly if run from the QwikBug monitor or under control of Microchip's in-circuit debugger or their emulator. However, a PIC18F452 programmed with the same application code would operate everything but the display when power is turned on to the QwikFlash board.

(a) What is happening?
(b) If the board's pushbutton reset button is pressed, will the LCD display now work correctly? Explain.

7-3 Timing specifications. Repeat Problem 7-1 for the **InitLCD8** subroutine of Figure 7-8b.

7-4 Cursor-positioning codes. Assuming that the 24x2 LCD module shown in Figure 7-1 follows the rules for its cursor-positioning codes outlined at the end of Section 7.4 (which it does), what should the cursor-positioning code be to place a three-character message

(a) at the upper left-hand corner of the display?
(b) at the upper right-hand corner of the display?
(c) at the lower left-hand corner of the display?
(d) at the lower right-hand corner of the display?

7-5 Display string. Write the code for a display string called **"TIMEinit"** that is to be stored in the program area. If

```
POINT  TIMEinit
rcall  DisplayC
```

is executed, the following should appear on the second row of the QwikFlash display:

```
ΔΔΔ:ΔΔAM
```

where "Δ" represents a blank character.

7-6 Display string. Show two display strings, **ColonOn** and **ColonOff,** which can be used to turn the colon of Problem 7-5 on or off, leaving the remainder of the display unchanged.

7-7 BlinkColon subroutine

(a) Write a **BlinkColon** subroutine, called from the mainline loop, to toggle the colon in the display of Problem 7-5 every half-second. Be sure to return from the subroutine after the minimum amount of time needed to toggle the colon.
(b) If a

```
bsf  PORTC,RC2
```

instruction were placed at the beginning of the subroutine and a

```
bcf   PORTC,RC2
```

instruction were placed at the end, and the QwikFlash instrument were used to measure the maximum pulse width on the RC2 pin, then roughly what value would it measure?

(c) What minimum pulse width would it measure?

7-8 CopyString subroutine

(a) Write a **CopyString** subroutine that can be used to initialize a display string in RAM by copying one from the program memory. Assume the **POINT** macro and the **lfsr** instruction are used to initialize the two pointers used by the subroutine before the subroutine is called. Terminate the subroutine when the end-of-string terminator has been copied.

(b) Assume that 10 bytes of RAM have been assigned with

```
TIMESTR:10
```

in the **cblock . . . endc** construct used to assign RAM to variables. Copy the **TIMEinit** string of Problem 7-5 into **TIMESTR** to initialize it.

7-9 Timing specifications. Repeat Problem 7-1 on the **DisplayC** subroutine of Figure 7-10.

7-10 T40 subroutine

(a) Examine the **DisplayC** and the **DisplayV** subroutines and determine the worst-case (i.e., minimum) time from the falling edge of the E pin after both nibbles have been sent to the LCD to the next falling edge of the E pin, assuming the

```
rcall   T40
```

subroutine has been removed from the code. It is *this* time that must actually be no shorter than 40 microseconds.

(b) How short can the inserted time be, beginning with the execution of

```
rcall   T40
```

and ending with the execution of

```
return
```

at the end of the **T40** subroutine?

(c) Rewrite the **T40** subroutine of Figure 7-10, taking advantage of this slightly reduced time.

(d) How much shorter is it?

7-11 T40 subroutine

(a) Rewrite the **T40** subroutine of Figure 7-10 to operate correctly if the microcontroller's internal clock rate is switched to 10 MHz. Incorporate the ideas of Problem 7-10.

(b) Using the conditional assembly ideas of Problem 6-1 and its named constant, **TENMHZ**, rewrite **T40** so that it will assemble correctly for either internal clock rate (i.e., 10 MHz or 2.5 MHz).

7-12 FAHRinit constant display string

(a) Create a **FAHRinit** constant display string for use with a display of Fahrenheit temperature of the form

```
ΔΔΔΔ.Δ°F
```

for the second line of the 2x8 LCD display, where "Δ" represents a blank.

(b) Using the **CopyString** subroutine of Problem 7-8, initialize a 10-byte string in RAM called **FAHRTEMP**.

7-1 Backslash character

(a) Create a constant "display string" called **BSlashStr** analogous to that of Figure 7-14a with a character code of 0x08 that can be used to define a backslash character in the 5x7 pixel matrix.

(b) Show the code to be added to the **Initial** subroutine to create this character.

(c) Create a constant string called **DemoStr** that can be used to write

```
//\\//\\
```

on the first line of the LCD so that the forward and back slashes can be visually compared.

(d) Show the code to display the characters in part (c).

7-14 Vertical bar graph. A 16-segment vertical bar graph can be created on a two-row LCD by creating eight characters.

(a) Create a **VbarChars** "display string" analogous to that of Figure 7-16a such that character code 0x01 will turn on the bottom row of pixels, character code 0x02 will turn on the bottom two rows of pixels, . . . , character code 0x07 will turn on the bottom seven rows of pixels, and character code 0x08 will turn on all 5x8 pixels.

(b) Show the code to be added to the **Initial** subroutine to create the eight bar graph characters.

7-15 Vertical bar graph

(a) Create and initialize two 3-byte display strings called **VBARU** and **VBARL** (vertical bar graph, upper and lower) that can be used to write a single character to the right-most character position on the first and second lines of the display.

(b) Write a **Vbargraph** subroutine that has passed to it an arbitrary value in **WREG**. The subroutine is to ignore the upper 4 bits of **WREG** and display the lower 4-bit value as a vertical bar graph between 0 and 15.

Chapter

8

ROTARY PULSE GENERATORS

8.1 OVERVIEW

For user entry of a parameter value, one of the most widely used devices is a rotary pulse generator (RPG), also known as a rotary encoder. It is used as the tuning or volume control for many automobile radios and home receivers. It is universally used as the frequency control input for function generators and for other instruments with a wide parametric range (e.g., for setting a frequency output that ranges from Hz to MHz). With just two outputs, the device is deceptively simple.

In this chapter, the use of the low-cost RPG employed by the QwikFlash board will be explored. It shares the same features of versatility and sensitivity as the more robust RPGs used in instrument design.

8.2 RPG RESOLUTION

Figure 8-1 shows two RPGs. The little Bourns RPG on the right uses three internal electrical contacts to three tracks of a coded wheel, as illustrated in Figure 8-2a. With the pullup resistors and the ground connection shown in that figure, the Channel A and B outputs traverse through six cycles per revolution. Each cycle produces 4 output states, giving 24 states per revolution, as shown in Figure 8-2b.

The Agilent Technologies RPG shown on the left in Figure 8-1 does much the same thing but with the benefit of optical reflective technology to give it a minimum specified life of one million revolutions. The Bourns unit has the lower minimum specified life of 100,000 cycles, or 17,000 revolutions, befitting its electromechanical technology. The Agilent unit is available with resolutions of 16, 32, 64, or 120 cycles per revolution (CPR), whereas the Bourns unit is manufactured with a resolution of either 6 or 16 CPR.

Figure 8-1 Agilent Technologies HRPG-AS32#13F rotary pulse generator and Bourns 3315C-001-006 rotary encoder.

The QwikFlash board uses the Bourns 6 CPR unit for 24 counts per revolution. This resolution is suitable for human interactions and is roughly equivalent to the resolution used in the design of many instruments. Although it might seem that "finer is better," it is frustrating to have a resolution so fine that a parameter value entered by an instrument user increments or decrements one or more counts when the RPG's knob is released.

8.3 RPG FUNCTIONALITY

As an RPG is turned, its output sequence traverses the 2-bit Gray code values

```
... → 00 → 01 → 11 → 10 → 00 → ...
```

when turned in one direction and

```
... → 00 → 10 → 11 → 01 → 00 → ...
```

when turned in the other direction. By reading the RPG outputs at a faster rate than they change, the resulting changes can be used to increment or decrement the parameter being controlled. The Bourns unit has a specified maximum turning rate of 120 RPM, or two revolutions per second. At this maximum rate, the minimum time between increments is about 20 milliseconds. By reading the RPG every time around the mainline loop (i.e., every 10 milliseconds), every change of state will be detected. Also, with a maximum contact bounce-time specification of 5 milliseconds, reading its output every 10 milliseconds effectively debounces it.

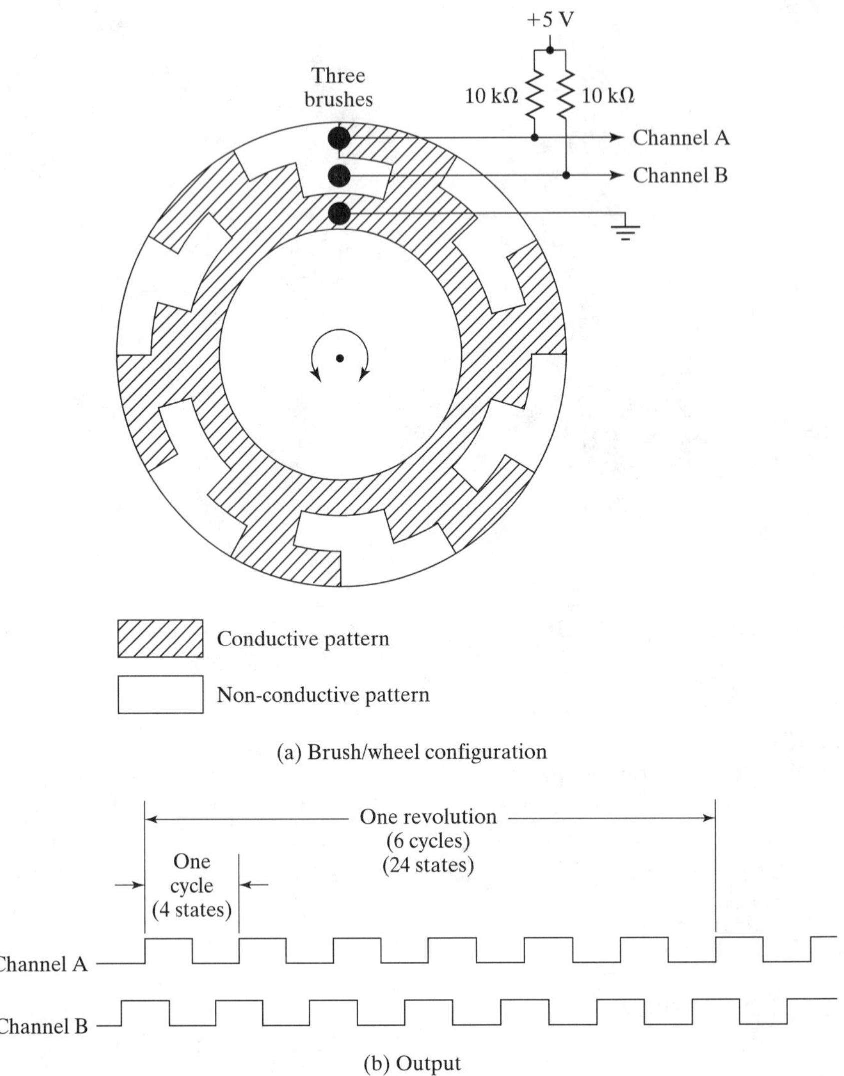

Figure 8-2 RPG's encoding wheel and brushes.

8.4 RPG SUBROUTINE

As shown in Figure 4-2a, the RPG on the QwikFlash board is sensed by reading bits 1 and 0 of **PORTD**. Each time around the mainline loop their state is compared with their state 10 milliseconds ago. This can be done in an **RPG** subroutine, called within the mainline loop. The subroutine returns with

```
DELRPG = 0x00, if no change
```

```
= Ø×Ø1, if CW change
= Øxff, if CCW change
```

Note that 0xff is the twos-complement coding of −1. If added to a 1-byte parameter, the parameter will be decremented.

Other subroutines called from within the mainline loop can use the value of **DELRPG** to increment or decrement a parameter value, as appropriate. In this way, the **RPG** subroutine stands as a general utility, deciphering changes on the two **PORTD** input pins for the subsequent benefit of any other interested subroutines.

When reading external pins from within a subroutine, care should be taken to read the pins just once. If within the subroutine the pins are read a second time just microseconds after the first read, code written assuming that the pins have remained unchanged over that short interval will work correctly almost all of the time—but not *all* the time. The bug-free approach is to copy the port to a RAM variable. Rather than read the port a second time, read the RAM variable instead.

The **RPG** subroutine of Figure 8-3a first clears the parameter, **DELRPG**, to zero, the value to be returned by the subroutine if no change is noted on the two RPG outputs. Then **PORTD** is copied into both **WREG** and **TEMP**. **OLDPORTD** holds the value of **PORTD** read 10 milliseconds ago. If bits 1 and 0, the RPG bits, have not changed, the **xorwf** instruction will produce zeros in these two bits of **WREG**. The **andlw** instruction will force the remaining bits of **WREG** to zero. In this way, the question "Have the two bits of **PORTD** remained unchanged since 10 milliseconds ago?" has been transformed into the *testable* question, "Is the **Z** flag set?" This is a technique used again and again in microcontroller code. In this case, if the two bits remain unchanged, **TEMP** is copied to **OLDPORTD**, and the subroutine returns with **DELRPG** = 0x00.

If the bits have changed, the assumption is that the new state is one Gray code count from the old state. The **RPG** subroutine manipulates the two bits of **OLDPORTD** to what they would be if the RPG had turned in a counterclockwise direction. If this matches the actual new state, the subroutine registers this by decrementing **DELRPG** to 0xff. Otherwise, the assumption is that the RPG turned in a clockwise direction. The little algorithm to change the old Gray code value to the new value after a CCW change is

```
new bØ = old b1 (implemented with rrcf)
new b1 = complement of old bØ (implemented with  IF_ .C.  block)
```

This changes

```
ØØ → 1Ø
1Ø → 11
11 → Ø1
Ø1 → ØØ
```

The operation of this subroutine can be monitored by adding the test code of Figure 8-3b to the mainline loop. The variables of Figure 8-3c must be added to the **cblock . . . endc** construct, and the initialization of Figure 8-3d must be added to the **Initial** subroutine.

8.5 RATE-SENSITIVE RPG

If the parameter value being changed with the RPG extends over a large range (e.g., a frequency value anywhere between 1 Hz and 1 MHz), it helps a user if fast turning of the RPG is treated differently from slow turning. The threshold between slow and fast turning can be implemented by counting the

```
;;;;;;; RPG subroutine ;;;;;;;;;;;;;;;;;;;;;;;;;;;;;;;;;;;;;;;;;;;;;;;;;;;;;;;;;;;
;
; This subroutine decyphers RPG changes into values of DELRPG of 0, +1, or -1.
; DELRPG = +1 for CW change, 0 for no change, and -1 for CCW change.

RPG
        clrf  DELRPG            ;Clear for "no change" return value
        movf  PORTD,W           ;Copy PORTD into W
        movwf  TEMP             ; and TEMP
        xorwf  OLDPORTD,W       ;Any change?
        andlw  B'00000011'      ;If not, set Z flag
        IF_  .NZ.               ;If the two bits have changed then...
          rrcf  OLDPORTD,W      ;Form what a CCW change would produce
          IF_  .C.              ;Make new bit 1 = complement of old bit 0
            bcf  WREG,1
          ELSE_
            bsf  WREG,1
          ENDIF_
          xorwf  TEMP,W         ;Did the RPG actually change to this output?
          andlw  B'00000011'
          IF_  .Z.              ;If so, then change  DELRPG to -1 for CCW
            decf  DELRPG,F
          ELSE_                 ;Otherwise, change DELRPG to  +1 for CW
            incf  DELRPG,F
          ENDIF_
        ENDIF_
        movff  TEMP,OLDPORTD    ;Save PORTD as OLDPORTD for ten ms from now
        return
```

(a) The subroutine.

```
        rcall  RPG              ;Decypher RPG inputs into DELRPG
        movf  DELRPG,W
        addwf  RPGCNT,F         ;Increment or decrement RPGCNT from RPG
        DISPLAY  RPGCNT         ;Display RPGCNT as a binary number
```

(b) Test code for mainline loop.

```
        OLDPORTD                ;Holds previous value of RPG inputs
        TEMP                    ;Temporary local variable
        DELRPG                  ;Generated by RPG
        RPGCNT                  ;Used to display RPG changes
```

(c) Variables.

```
        movff  PORTD,OLDPORTD   ;Initialize "old" value
        clrf  RPGCNT            ;Clear counter to be displayed
```

(d) Initialization.

Figure 8-3 RPG subroutine.

number of loop times between changes of the RPG. If that number is less than some threshold value, a fast change has occurred.

A new **RateRPG** subroutine can distinguish between slow and fast turning and signal five possible turning rates with the **DELRPG** value:

```
DELRPG = +2  fast CW change
         +1  slow CW change
          0  no change
         -1  slow CCW change
         -2  fast CCW change
```

This coded value can be interpreted by the subroutine expecting an RPG input.

```
;;;;;;; RateRPG subroutine ;;;;;;;;;;;;;;;;;;;;;;;;;;;;;;;;;;;;;;;;;;;;;;;;;;;;;;
;
; This subroutine decyphers RPG changes into values of DELRPG.
; DELRPG = +2 for fast CW change, +1 for slow CW change, Ø for no change,
;          -1 for slow CCW change and -2 for fast CCW change.

Threshold equ  3              ;Value to distinguish between slow and fast

RateRPG
        bcf  PORTA,RA2        ;Turn LED off
        clrf  DELRPG          ;Clear for "no change" return value
        movf  PORTD,W         ;Copy PORTD into W
        movwf  TEMP           ; and TEMP
        xorwf  OLDPORTD,W     ;Any change?
        andlw  B'ØØØØØØ11'    ;If not, set Z flag
        IF_  .NZ.             ;If the two bits have changed then...
          rrcf  OLDPORTD,W    ;Form what a CCW change would produce
          IF_  .C.            ;Make new bit 1 = complement of old bit Ø
            bcf  WREG,1
          ELSE_
            bsf  WREG,1
          ENDIF_
          xorwf  TEMP,W       ;Did the RPG actually change to this output?
          andlw  B'ØØØØØØ11'
          IF_  .Z.            ;If so, then change  DELRPG to -1 for CCW
            decf  DELRPG,F
            movf  THR,F
            IF_  .NZ.
              decf  DELRPG,F  ;If fast turning, decrement again
              bsf  PORTA,RA2  ;Turn LED on
            ENDIF_
          ELSE_               ;Otherwise, change DELRPG to  +1 for CW
            incf  DELRPG,F
            movf  THR,F
            IF_  .NZ.
              incf  DELRPG,F  ;If fast turning, increment again
              bsf  PORTA,RA2  ;Turn LED on
            ENDIF_
          ENDIF_
          MOVLF  Threshold+1,THR  ;Reinitialize THR
        ENDIF_
        movf  THR,F           ;Does THR equal zero
        IF_  .NZ.             ;If not, then decrement it
          decf  THR,F
        ENDIF_
        movff  TEMP,OLDPORTD  ;Save PORTD as OLDPORTD for ten ms from now
        return
```

Figure 8-4 Rate-sensitive **RateRPG** subroutine with **Threshold** = 3.

Example 8-1 Create a new **RateRPG** subroutine to exhibit rate sensitivity.

Solution

The threshold can be implemented with the help of a "down" counter called **THR**, initialized to zero. Each time that the **RateRPG** subroutine detects an RPG change, it looks at the value of **THR**. If it is zero, a slow change is noted. If, on the other hand, **THR** has a nonzero value, a fast change is noted. In either case, **THR** is initialized to a threshold value. Each time **RateRPG** detects *no change,* it decrements **THR** unless it is already equal to zero. In that case, it leaves **THR** unchanged.

The **RateRPG** subroutine of Figure 8-4 differs in two ways from that of Figure 8-3a. First, the code includes modifications to deal with **THR.** Second, any time a fast turn is detected, the middle of the three LEDs on the board (driven from **PORTA**, bit **RA2**) is blinked on for 10 milliseconds. It is used to give a visual indication of the efficacy of a given threshold value.

PROBLEMS

8-1 Agilent RPG. The Agilent RPG shown in Figure 8-1 uses its optical technology to generate higher resolutions than are feasible with brushes and a conductive disk. It also generates a bounceless output. This makes it possible to use one of the interrupt inputs to the microcontroller to sense RPG changes.

(a) If the microcontroller's RB2/INT2 pin is set up so that each falling edge from the RPG's Channel A output triggers an interrupt, what will be the resolution (interrupts/revolution) of Agilent's 32-CPR RPG?
(b) If the RPG's Channel B output were connected to the RD2 input, it is proposed that each interrupt can signal an increment of the RPG and that reading the state of RD2 in response to the interrupt can be used to distinguish between CW and CCW rotation. Referring to the timing diagram of Figure 8-2b, which is common to all RPGs, explain what is involved.
(c) If progressing to the right in Figure 8-2b represents moving in a clockwise direction, explain how to tell that an interrupt is caused by CW rotation.
(d) Explain how to tell that an interrupt is caused by CCW rotation.

8-2 Debugging an RPG output. Draw a timing diagram for one of the RPG's outputs as the RPG is slowly turned. The output is high for 100 ms and then goes low for the following 100 ms. However, when going from high to low, it exhibits 5 ms of contact bounce, where it bounces back and forth between 0 V and 5 V several times during this interval. The **RPG** subroutine samples each input every 10 milliseconds.

(a) What is the effect of contact bounce if a sample is taken during that time?
(b) Can it result in a lost count?
(c) Can it result in an extra count?

8-3 RPG operation. Make the changes to P2.asm, as suggested at the end of Section 8.4. Start execution on the QwikFlash board with the RPG knob's reference dot toward the top of the board and a display of B'00000000'. After turning the RPG back and forth and then returning to this position, the display should be B'00000000'. Now quickly turn the knob clockwise about a quarter of a turn and return more slowly to the zero position. Repeat this, rotating the quarter-turn clockwise faster and faster until counts are lost when the RPG is returned to the "straight up" position. Roughly how fast a turning rate can be tolerated before counts are lost?

8-4 Rate-sensitive RPG. With P2.asm modified with the test code of Figure 8-3b and with the rate-sensitive **RateRPG** subroutine of Figure 8-4, modify the subroutine so that it produces **DELRPG** values of +8, +1, 0, −1, and −8. Now fast turning will produce large steps.

(a) Use this to change the display as fast as you can back and forth between B'00000000' and B'10000000'.
(b) Reassemble with the "Threshold" value changed to 4 or 5. Does this help or hurt the operation of part (a)?
(c) Reassemble with Threshold = 2. Does this help or hurt the operation of part (a)?

8-5 Effect of threshold value. The rate-sensitive **RateRPG** subroutine of Figure 8-4 uses Threshold = 3. Note that when **THR** is reinitialized with the macro

```
MOVLF   Threshold+1,THR
```

THR will momentarily have a value of 4. A couple of instructions later, it is decremented to 3. It will still be 3 ten milliseconds later when the **RateRPG** subroutine is entered. Ten milliseconds later, it will be 2 when **RateRPG** is entered. After another 10 milliseconds **RateRPG** will be entered with **THR** = 1. Finally, after one more 10 millisecond interval, **THR** will equal 0 and will remain 0 thereafter until an RPG change occurs.

(a) Draw a time line with 10 millisecond ticks extending over 50 milliseconds. Assume initially that **THR** = 0. Mark an RPG change occurring just after the first tick. Then mark the value **THR** = 0 as the **RateRPG** subroutine is entered at the next tick. Continue with **THR** = 3 as the **RateRPG** subroutine is entered at the following tick. Continue with the value of **THR** as the **RateRPG** subroutine is entered at each subsequent tick. What is the *longest* interval between the initial RPG change and the next RPG change that will be registered by the **RateRPG** subroutine as a "fast" interval?

(b) Draw another time line like the one in part a. This time, mark an RPG change occurring just before the second tick. Mark **THR** values as the **RateRPG** subroutine is entered at the ticks to the right of this. What is the *shortest* interval between the initial RPG change and the next RPG change that will be registered by the **RateRPG** subroutine as a "slow" interval?

8-6 Rate-sensitive RateRPG for parameter entry

(a) Create a variable display string called **FREQSTR** of the form

```
ΔddddΔHz      (where "Δ" represents a blank character)
```

to display a frequency value ranging from 1 Hz to 9999 Hz on the second line of the LCD. Initialize it to 100 Hz. Create a **Frequency** subroutine that will update the second line of the display with this string every 0.1 s.

(b) Write a **BLZ** subroutine that the **Frequency** subroutine can use to blank leading zeros in the **FREQSTR** display string (e.g., change "00120ΔHz" to "ΔΔ120ΔHz") by replacing leading ASCII codes of 0x30 with 0x20.

(c) Modify the **Frequency** subroutine so that it uses the value of **DELRPG** each time around the mainline loop to update the string. For "slow" RPG changes, increment or decrement the value represented by the string. For "fast" RPG changes, increment or decrement the value by 10.

(d) Try running the program and changing from 123 to 7654 and back to 123. Does this fast/slow algorithm seem to give a satisfactory performance? What would you suggest as an improvement?

Chapter

9

INTERRUPTS AND INTERRUPT TIMING

9.1 OVERVIEW

Many microcontroller tasks can be monitored, and paced, by mainline loop timing. Inputs can be sensed for changes every 10 milliseconds. Output changes can be made to occur in response to input changes or in multiples of the 10 millisecond loop time. There are other tasks, however, that require faster handling. For example, transfers taking place at 19,200 baud from the serial port of a computer will present the microcontroller with a new byte of data to be handled every half-millisecond.

To handle this and other tasks requiring a fast response, the PIC18F452 microcontroller contains a wealth of resources. For example, as bits arrive from the serial port of a computer every 50 microseconds or so, the microcontroller's UART (**U**niversal **A**synchronous **R**eceiver **T**ransmitter) proceeds to build the received bits into successive bytes of data. Only as each byte is thus formed does the UART seek the support of the CPU to deal with the received byte. It does so by sending an interrupt signal to the CPU, asking the CPU to suspend what it is doing, deal with the received byte, and then resume the suspended task.

This UART example illustrates two facets of support that the microcontroller gives to fast events. First, built-in modules, operating independently of the CPU, are able to handle a burst of activity before turning to the CPU for help. In addition to the UART, the SPI (**S**erial **P**eripheral **I**nterface) does the same buffering of a byte of data for a shift register interface. The I^2C (**I**nter-Integrated **C**ircuit) interface uses a special protocol to transfer bytes to or from one of several I^2C devices using just two pins of the microcontroller.

Second, a built-in module such as the UART, or one of the timer resources, or even a change on an external interrupt pin can send an interrupt signal to the CPU asking for help. With 17 different interrupt sources, the PIC18F452 provides the designer with a broad range of resources for managing fast events. To give just one example of this breadth, an application requiring a second UART receiver can build one with an external interrupt pin (e.g., RB1/INT1) to signal the start of each new byte and an internal timer mechanism (e.g., CCP1) to provide an interrupt when each new bit of the received byte is to be read.

This chapter will begin with an examination of the timing issues involved with multiple interrupt sources. Next it will explore how to use a single interrupt source and then multiple interrupt sources. The PIC18F452's two interrupt priority levels will be examined. Working together, they can reduce the *latency* for a high-priority interrupt. The final sections deal with *critical regions* of the mainline code and with the use of external interrupt pins.

9.2 INTERRUPT TIMING FOR LOW-PRIORITY INTERRUPTS

An interrupt source can be characterized by two parameters:

- **TPi**, the time interval between interrupts from interrupt source #i. If this varies from interrupt to interrupt, then **TPi** represents the *shortest* (i.e., the worst-case) interval.
- **Ti**, the time during which the CPU digresses from the execution of the mainline program to handle this one interrupt source. If this varies, then **Ti** represents the *longest* (i.e., the worst-case) value.

For an application with a single interrupt source, the needs of that source will be met if

$$T1 < TP1$$

as illustrated in Figure 9-1. This means that the CPU will complete the execution of the interrupt source's *handler* before it is asked to execute the handler again. The needs of the mainline program will be met if the slices of time left for its execution, TP1 − T1, are sufficient to execute the mainline subroutines during each 10 millisecond loop time. One of the strengths of the PIC18F452's derivation of its 2.5 MHz internal clock rate from a 10 MHz crystal (as on the QwikFlash board) is that both the interrupt source's timing needs and those of the mainline program can be ameliorated *by a factor of 4* simply by changing the programming of a configuration byte so that the chip will run at an internal clock rate of 10 MHz.

In the following discussion, all interrupt sources will be assumed to be fielded with the low-priority interrupt service routine. This is the normal scheme, leaving the PIC18F452's high-priority interrupt service routine available to ameliorate interrupt timing constraints without changing the chip's internal clock rate. Section 9.4 will explore the help provided by high-priority interrupts.

The worst-case timing diagrams for *two* interrupt sources are illustrated in Figure 9-2. The first is the worst-case timing diagram for interrupt source #1 (IS#1). Just before it requests service, IS#2 requests and gets service. Because the CPU's servicing of IS#2 automatically disables, temporarily, all other interrupts, IS#1 is put off until the handler for IS#2 has run to completion. This time is labeled T2, the duration of the handler. Thus the *worst-case latency* for IS#1 is this same value, T2. It can be seen that even in this worst case for IS#1, it is serviced well before it requests service again. In general, the condition IS#1 must meet is

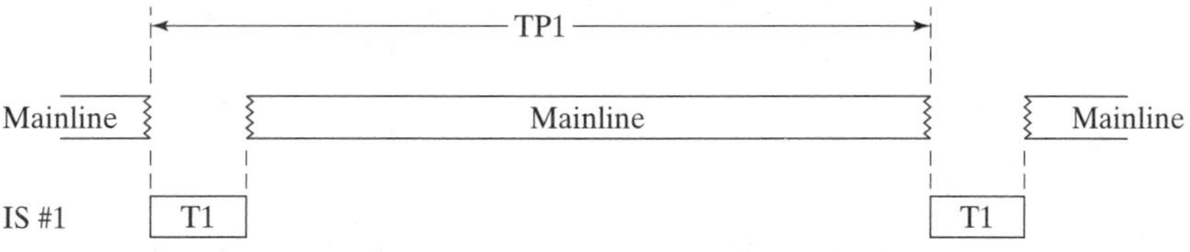

Figure 9-1 Interrupt timing parameters.

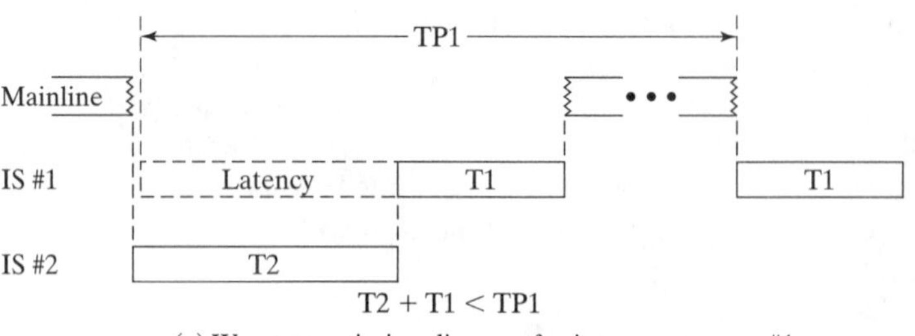

(a) Worst-case timing diagram for interrupt source #1

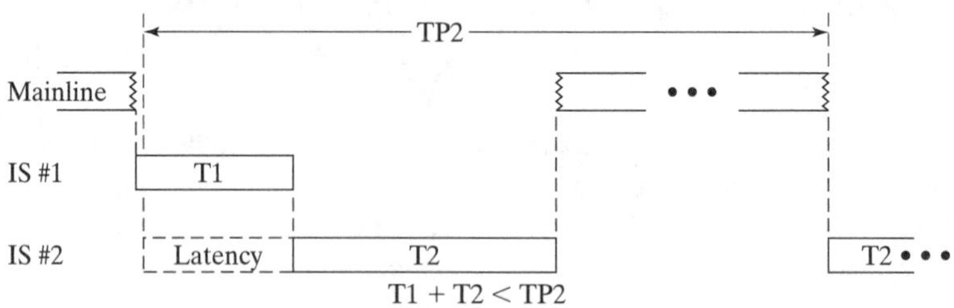

(b) Worst-case timing diagram for interrupt source #2

Figure 9-2 Worst-case timing diagrams for two interrupt sources.

$$T2 + T1 < TP1$$

Figure 9-2b illustrates the worst-case timing diagram for IS#2. In this case, IS#2 requests service just after IS#1 has requested, and received, service. Again, so long as IS#2 receives service before it requests service again, it satisfies its timing requirements. In this case of two interrupt sources, the requirement can be expressed

$$T1 + T2 < TP2$$

For three or more interrupt sources, the test that each interrupt source must satisfy depends on the assignment of its handler in the interrupt service routine's polling routine listed in Figure 6-2 and repeated in Figure 9-3. Reassigning the order in which interrupt sources are polled can sometimes rectify an assignment that produces a worst-case timing problem. Two factors account for the worst-case timing constraint for each interrupt source:

1. In the worst case, an interrupt source will ask for service *just after* the longest handler further down the polling routine has begun.
2. In addition, all handlers above it will also be serviced first.

The first condition occurs because once the execution of *any* handler has begun, further interrupts are automatically disabled. Therefore, the execution of the handler (regardless of where it ranks in the polling routine) will play out to completion. The second condition is a result of the

```
CONTINUE_
```

construct being executed after each handler. This construct causes execution to revert to the beginning of the polling routine where, in the worst case, all interrupt sources above the source in question will be waiting for service.

```
LOOP_

  IF_  ‹test whether interrupt #1 is ready for service›
    rcall  Int1handler
    CONTINUE_
  ENDIF_

  IF_  ‹test whether interrupt #2 is ready for service›
    rcall  Int2handler
    CONTINUE_
  ENDIF_

  IF_  ‹test whether interrupt #3 is ready for service›
    rcall  Int3handler
    CONTINUE_
  ENDIF_
   .
   .
   .
  IF_  ‹test whether interrupt #N is ready for service›
    rcall  IntNhandler
    CONTINUE_
  ENDIF_

  BREAK_

ENDLOOP_
```

Figure 9-3 Interrupt service routine's polling routine.

These considerations lead to the following interrupt timing constraints for four interrupt sources:

$$\begin{aligned}(\text{maximum of T2,T3,T4}) + \text{T1} &< \text{TP1}\\ (\text{maximum of T3,T4}) + \text{T1} + \text{T2} &< \text{TP2}\\ \text{T4} + \text{T1} + \text{T2} + \text{T3} &< \text{TP3}\\ \text{T1} + \text{T2} + \text{T3} + \text{T4} &< \text{TP4}\end{aligned} \tag{9-1}$$

The low-priority interrupt service routine is shown in its entirety in Figure 9-4. When an interrupt occurs (with interrupts enabled to the CPU), the following sequence of events takes place automatically:

- The CPU completes the execution of its present mainline instruction.
- The low-priority global interrupt enable bit (**GIEL**) is cleared, thereby disabling further low-priority interrupts.
- The contents of the program counter (containing the address of the next mainline program instruction to be executed upon return from the interrupt service routine) is stacked.
- The program counter is loaded with 0x0018, the low-priority interrupt vector.

In order not to cause erroneous operation of the mainline code it is interrupting, the interrupt service routine must be sure to return CPU registers the way they were found. Because it is difficult to do *anything* without changing the contents of **WREG** and the **STATUS** register, these are set aside at the beginning of the interrupt service routine and restored at the end. Note the order of restoration: first **WREG** and then **STATUS**. This order matters because the

```
movf  WREG_TEMP,W
```

instruction affects the **Z** and the **N** bits of the **STATUS** register. By restoring **STATUS** last, the mainline code will get these bits back *exactly* as they were left by the last instructions executed in the mainline code before the interrupt occurred.

The assumptions listed in Figure 9-4c are suggested simply to reduce the number of *other* CPU registers that must be set aside and restored. As suggested in Section 2-3, the **BSR** register can be set to 0x01

```
;;;;;; Vectors ;;;;;;;;;;;;;;;;;;;;;;;;;;;;;;;;;;;;;;;;;;;;;;;;;;;;;;;;;;;;;;;
        org  0x0000             ;Reset vector
        nop
        goto  Mainline

        org  0x0008             ;High-priority interrupt vector address
        goto  $                 ;Trap

        org  0x0018             ;Low-priority interrupt vector address
        goto  LoPriISR
```

(a) Vectors.

```
LoPriISR                        ;Low-priority interrupt service routine
        movff  STATUS,STATUS_TEMP  ;Set aside STATUS and WREG
        movwf  WREG_TEMP

        LOOP_
          IF_  <test whether interrupt #1 is ready for service>
            rcall  Int1handler
            CONTINUE_
          ENDIF_

          IF_  <test whether interrupt #2 is ready for service>
            rcall  Int2handler
            CONTINUE_
          ENDIF_

          IF_  <test whether interrupt #3 is ready for service>
            rcall  Int3handler
            CONTINUE_
          ENDIF_
            .
            .
          IF_  <test whether interrupt #N is ready for service>
            rcall  IntNhandler
            CONTINUE_
          ENDIF_

          BREAK_
        ENDLOOP_

        movf  WREG_TEMP,W       ;Restore WREG and STATUS
        movff  STATUS_TEMP,STATUS
        retfie                  ;Return from interrupt, reenabling GIEL
```

(b) Low-priority interrupt service routine.

BSR is never changed throughout the application.
FSR0 and **FSR1** are used only in the mainline code.
FSR2 is used only in interrupt handlers.
PCL is never used as an operand in an interrupt handler.

(c) Assumptions.

Figure 9-4 Low-priority interrupt mechanism.

in the **Initial** subroutine and thereafter never changed. This will make 128 + 256 = 384 bytes of RAM reachable by direct addressing, an adequate number for most application programs. The remaining RAM is still reachable, but by means of indirect addressing with **FSR0**, **FSR1**, or **FSR2**.

It is quite common to use indirect addressing within an interrupt handler. For example, successive characters received by the UART might be written into a *line buffer* with the

```
movwf  POSTINC2
```

instruction. If the interrupt handlers all avoid using **FSR0** and **FSR1**, and if the mainline code avoids using **FSR2**, then none of these 2 byte registers need be set aside and restored.

The last assumption of Figure 9-4c of never using PCL as an operand in an interrupt handler is listed as a reminder that such an operation may change the content of **PCLATH**. If it is desired to build a *jump table* (see Problem 2-9) into an interrupt handler, it is only necessary to set aside and restore **PCLATH**.

The interrupt timing constraints for four interrupt sources listed earlier as (9-1) correctly identify items that must be considered in each case. However, in the interest of keeping the explanation simple, some small items were left out. For example, the polling routine of Figure 9-3 adds a few cycles as each test is carried out and the associated branch instruction executed. Likewise, the automatic vectoring from mainline code to interrupt service routine inserts a couple of cycles, as does the setting aside and restoring of **WREG** and **STATUS**. Nevertheless, the timing constraints of (9-1) keep the focus on the dominant factors that a designer can do something about if the timing is close.

9.3 LOW-PRIORITY INTERRUPT STRUCTURE

Using the high-priority/low-priority interrupt scheme built into the PIC18F452 begins with the setting of the **IPEN** bit shown in Figure 9-5a with

```
bsf   RCON,IPEN              ;Enable priority levels
```

The alternative, **IPEN** = 0, causes the chip to revert to the single interrupt level scheme of earlier-generation PIC microcontrollers, discarding a valuable feature of this chip.

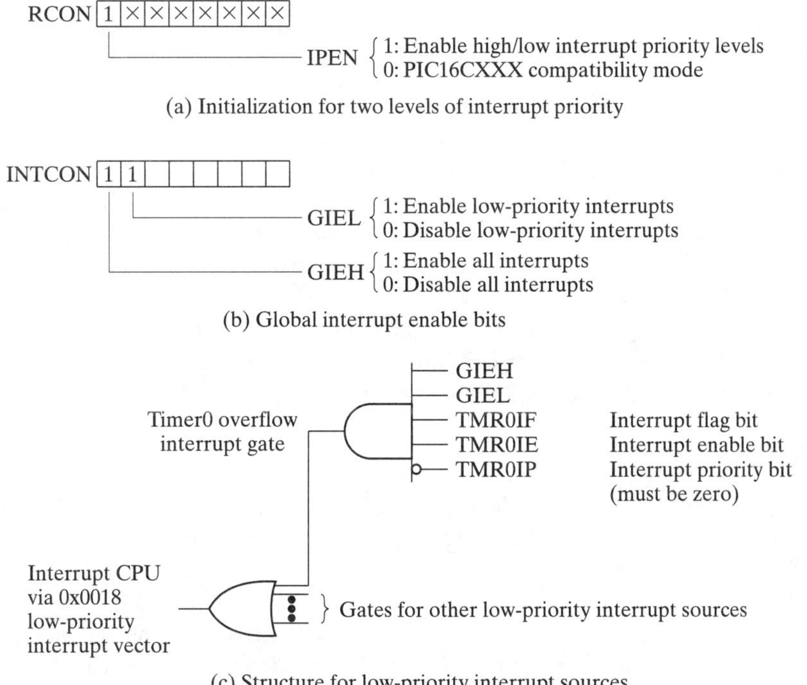

Figure 9-5 Low-priority interrupt structure.

The **GIEH** (**G**lobal **I**nterrupt **E**nable for **H**igh-priority interrupts) bit gates *all* interrupts to the CPU, both high priority and low priority. It is usually set by the last instruction before the **return** from the **Initial** subroutine, after each interrupt source being used in an application has been initialized.

The **GIEL** (**G**lobal **I**nterrupt **E**nable for **L**ow-priority interrupts) bit gates all low-priority interrupts to the CPU. It, too, is set by one of the last instructions in the **Initial** subroutine. It is automatically cleared when a low-priority interrupt occurs, blocking further automatic vectoring if a second low-priority interrupt occurs while a first one is being serviced. The **GIEL** bit is automatically set again by the execution of the

```
        retfie                  ;Return from interrupt
```

instruction at the close of the interrupt service routine.

The **GIEL** bit can also be used within the mainline code to disable low-priority interrupts while a *critical region* of code extending over a handful of instructions is executed, followed by the reenabling of interrupts by setting the **GIEL** bit again. One occasion that called for such treatment arose in conjunction with the **LoopTime** subroutine of Section 5-4.

Each interrupt source has associated with it an interrupt priority bit that assigns the interrupt source to either the high-priority interrupt structure (discussed in Section 9.4) or the low-priority interrupt structure discussed here. The default state of these interrupt-priority bits at power-on reset assigns every interrupt source to the high-priority interrupt structure. Accordingly, the "IP" bit for each interrupt source to be assigned to the low-priority interrupt structure must be *cleared* in the **Initial** subroutine. For example,

```
        bcf  INTCON2,TMRØIP
```

will assign Timer0 overflow interrupts to the low-priority interrupt structure.

Because the default state of the "IP" bit must be changed under the normal circumstance of assigning an interrupt source to the low-priority interrupt structure, it becomes necessary to know where each of these bits is located. Figure 9-6 lists them all, along with each interrupt source's local enable bit and its flag bit.

Example 9-1 The **LoopTime** subroutine discussed in Section 5.4 was able to use the setting of the **TMR0IF** flag to obtain precise timing for a 10 millisecond loop time with an internal clock rate of 2.5 MHz and the use of Timer0 as a scale-of-25,000 counter. Some precision was lost in trying to achieve a 10 millisecond loop time with an internal clock rate of 10 MHz and the use of Timer0 as a scale-of-100,000 counter. The counter required use of Timer0's prescaler, and the write to the timer reset the prescaler. For most applications, the resulting error is miniscule. With the help of Timer0 overflow interrupts, the error can be eliminated. Develop the interrupt routine and the modified **LoopTime** subroutine.

Solution

A **TMR0handler** interrupt handler can be made to set the **TMR0IF** flag precisely every 50,000 cycles, or 5 microseconds. Each time it does so, it decrements a **TMR0CNT** variable. The **LoopTime** subroutine now waits for **TMR0CNT** to be equal to zero as its signal that 10 milliseconds have elapsed. It then simply reinitializes **TMR0CNT** to 2. The resulting subroutine is listed in Figure 9-7a. The initialization for Timer0 interrupts is shown in Figure 9-7b. The **TMR0handler** is listed in Figure 9-7c. The **LoPriISR** interrupt service routine is shown in Figure 9-7d, assuming there are no other interrupt flags to poll.

Name	Priority Bit	Local Enable Bit	Local Flag Bit
INT0 external interrupt	*	INTCON,INT0IE	INTCON,INT0IF
INT1 external interrupt	INTCON3,INT1IP	INTCON3,INT1IE	INTCON3,INT1IF
INT2 external interrupt	INTCON3,INT2IP	INTCON3,INT2IE	INTCON3,INT2IF
RB port change interrupt	INTCON2,RBIP	INTCON,RBIE	INTCON,RBIF
TMR0 overflow interrupt	INTCON2,TMR0IP	INTCON,TMR0IE	INTCON,TMR0IF
TMR1 overflow interrupt	IPR1,TMR1IP	PIE1,TMR1IE	PIR1,TMR1IF
TMR3 overflow interrupt	IPR2,TMR3IP	PIE2,TMR3IE	PIR2,TMR3IF
TMR2 to match PR2 int.	IPR1,TMR2IP	PIE1,TMR2IE	PIR1,TMR2IF
CCP1 interrupt	IPR1,CCP1IP	PIE1,CCP1IE	PIR1,CCP1IF
CCP2 interrupt	IPR2,CCP2IP	PIE2,CCP2IE	PIR2,CCP2IF
A/D converter interrupt	IPR1,ADIP	PIE1,ADIE	PIR1,ADIF
USART receive interrupt	IPR1,RCIP	PIE1,RCIE	PIR1,RCIF
USART transmit interrupt	IPR1,TXIP	PIE1,TXIE	PIR1,TXIF
Sync. serial port int.	IPR1,SSPIP	PIE1,SSPIE	PIR1,SSPIF
Parallel slave port int.	IPR1,PSPIP	PIE1,PSPIE	PIR1,PSPIF
Low-voltage detect int.	IPR2,LVDIP	PIE2,LVDIE	PIR2,LVDIF
Bus-collision interrupt	IPR2,BCLIP	PIE2,BCLIE	PIR2,BCLIF

* INT0 can only be used as a high-priority interrupt

Figure 9-6 Register and bit names for every interrupt source.

Example 9-2 Determine the "T1" and "TP1" values for the Timer0 interrupts of the last example. Also determine the percentage of the CPU's time spent handling these interrupts.

Solution

The interval between interrupts, TP1, is 50,000 cycles or 5,000 microseconds, given the 10 MHz internal clock rate of the chip. When a Timer0 overflow interrupt occurs, the CPU takes two cycles after executing the last mainline instruction before it executes the interrupt vector instruction

```
goto  LoPriISR
```

Consequently,

$$T1 = 2 + 12 + 18 = 32 \text{ cycles}$$

The percentage of the CPU's time spent handling Timer0 interrupts is

$$(32/50000) \times 100 = 0.064\%$$

Example 9-3 If another low-priority interrupt were added to the Timer0 interrupts of the last problem, and if the Timer0 interrupts were placed second in the polling routine, what would be the new interrupt source's worst-case latency because of the Timer0 interrupts?

```
LoopTime
        REPEAT_                 ;Wait until interrupt decrements TMRØCNT to zero
          movf  TMRØCNT,F
        UNTIL_  .Z.
        MOVLF  2,TMRØCNT
        return
```

(a) **LoopTime** subroutine.

```
        bsf  RCON,IPEN          ;Enable two interrupt priority levels
        bcf  INTCON2,TMRØIP     ;Assign TMRØ low interrupt priority
        bcf  INTCON,TMRØIF      ;Clear TMRØ overflow flag
        bsf  INTCON,TMRØIE      ;Enable TMRØ overflow interrupt source
        MOVLF  2,TMRØCNT        ;Initialize counter
        bsf  INTCON,GIEL        ;Enable low-priority interrupts to CPU
        bsf  INTCON,GIEH        ;Enable all interrupts to CPU
```

(b) Instructions to be added to the **Initial** subroutine.

```
Bignum  equ  65536-5ØØØØ+12+2
TMRØhandler
        decf  TMRØCNT,F         ;Decrement counter                        (1)
        bcf  INTCON,GIEH        ;Disable interrupts                       (1)
        movff  TMRØL,TMRØLCOPY  ;Read 16-bit counter at this moment       (2)
        movff  TMRØH,TMRØHCOPY  ;                                         (2)
        movlw  low  Bignum      ;                                         (1)
        addwf  TMRØLCOPY,F      ;                                         (1)
        movlw  high  Bignum     ;                                         (1)
        addwfc  TMRØHCOPY,F     ;                                         (1)
        movff  TMRØHCOPY,TMROH  ;                                         (2)
        movff  TMRØLCOPY,TMROL  ;Write 16-bit counter at this moment      (2)
        bsf  INTCON,GIEH        ;Reenable interrupts                      (1)
        bcf  INTCON,TMRØIF      ;Clear TimerØ flag                        (1)
        return                  ;                                         (2)
```

(c) **TMR0handler** subroutine (18 cycles).

```
        org  Øx ØØ18            ;Low-priority interrupt vector address
        goto  LoPriISR          ;Jump                                     (2)
          .
          .
LoPriISR                        ;Low-priority interrupt service routine
        movff  STATUS,STATUS_TEMP  ;                                      (2)
        movwf  WREG_TEMP        ;                                         (1)
        rcall  TMRØhandler      ;                                         (2)
        movf  WREG_TEMP,W       ;                                         (1)
        movff  STATUS_TEMP,STATUS  ;                                      (2)
        retfie                  ;                                         (2)
```

(d) **LoPriISR** routine (12 cycles).

Figure 9-7 Example 9-1.

Solution

In the worst case, a Timer0 interrupt would have occurred, **STATUS** and **WREG** set aside, and the polling routine would have found the new interrupt source *not* asking for service. At that precise moment (in the worst case), the new interrupt source would set its flag, asking for service. Meanwhile, in **LoPriISR**, where interrupts are disabled, the CPU would execute

- The branch associated with the **IF_** construct for the new interrupt (2 cycles)
- The test of the **TMR0IF** flag (2 cycles)

- The call of **TMR0handler** (2 cycles)
- The handler itself (18 cycles)
- The branch for the **CONTINUE_** construct following the return to the polling routine (2 cycles)
- The test of the new interrupt's flag (2 cycles)
- The call of the new interrupt's handler (2 cycles)

After this worst-case latency of 30 cycles, or 3 microseconds, the CPU would execute the first instruction of the new interrupt's handler.

9.4 HIGH-PRIORITY INTERRUPT STRUCTURE

An interrupt source assigned with its "IP," interrupt priority, bit to the high-priority interrupt structure gains the benefit of being able to suspend the execution of the mainline code and to disable all low-priority interrupts. Furthermore, it can even suspend the execution of the low-priority interrupt service routine, **LoPriISR**. Except for any brief disabling of high-priority interrupts to protect a critical region of code, a *single* interrupt source assigned to the high-priority interrupt structure experiences *no* latency at all! This benefit quickly dissipates as soon as a second interrupt source is also assigned high priority.

The designers of the PIC18F452 added one further feature to minimize the latency of a high-priority interrupt. As shown in Figure 9-8a, when a high-priority interrupt occurs, the contents of **STATUS**, **WREG**, and **BSR** are automatically copied to *shadow registers*. Once the interrupt source has been serviced, the execution of

```
retfie  FAST
```

tells the CPU to automatically

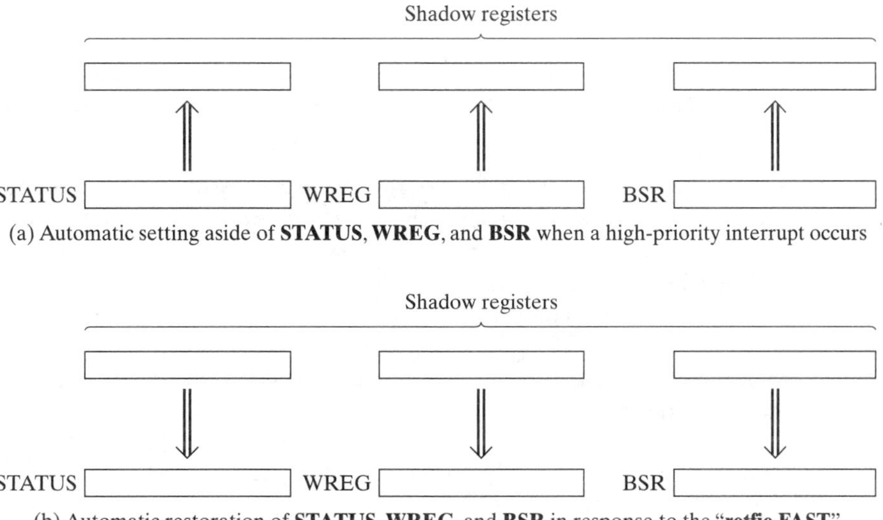

(a) Automatic setting aside of **STATUS**, **WREG**, and **BSR** when a high-priority interrupt occurs

(b) Automatic restoration of **STATUS**, **WREG**, and **BSR** in response to the "**retfie FAST**" instruction.

Figure 9-8 Use of high-priority interrupt's shadow registers.

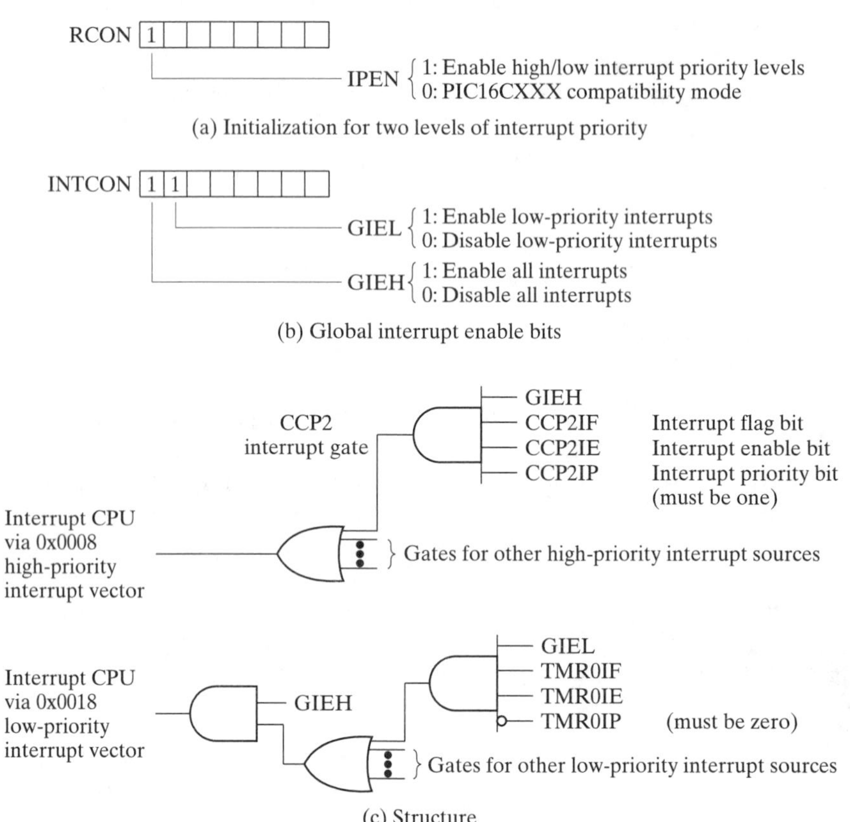

Figure 9-9 High-priority/low-priority interrupt structure.

1. Restore not only the program counter, but also **STATUS**, **WREG**, and **BSR**
2. Restore the **GIEH** bit, reenabling both high- and low-priority interrupts, as shown in Figure 9-9

Example 9-4 In Section 13.9, it will be seen that the frequency of a square wave can be measured with the 50 parts-per-million accuracy of the microcontroller's crystal oscillator. The PIC18F452's "CCP2" input will be used to generate a high-priority interrupt for every 16th rising edge of the input waveform. These interrupts will be counted over an interval of about 1 second. Knowing the exact number of internal clock cycles (e.g., 2500540) over which an integral number of periods of the input waveform takes place (e.g., $16 \times 123456 = 1975296$) gives the information needed to calculate the input frequency. If the microcontroller's internal clock period is 0.4 microseconds, the frequency is given by

$$\text{Frequency} = \frac{1975296}{2500540 \times 0.4} = 1.97487 \text{ MHz}$$

The time required to count every 16th input edge will determine the maximum frequency that can be measured. Show the high-priority interrupt service routine to increment a 3 byte counter,

FCOUNTU:FCOUNTH:FCOUNTL

```
            org  0x0008                ;High-priority interrupt vector address
            goto  HiPriISR             ;                                       (2)
             .
             .
             .
    HiPriISR                           ;High-priority interrupt service routine
            bcf  PIR2,CCP2IF           ;Clear interrupt flag                    (1)
            clr  WREG                  ;Clear WREG for subsequent adds with carry (1)
            incf  FCOUNTL,F            ;Add 1 to three-byte value in FCOUNT      (1)
            addwfc  FCOUNTH,F          ;                                        (1)
            addwfc  FCOUNTU,F          ;                                        (1)
            retfie  FAST               ;Return and restore from shadow registers (2)
```

Figure 9-10 Example 9-4.

Solution

The high-priority interrupt service routine is shown in Figure 9-10. With two cycles to get from the execution of interrupted code to execution of the

```
goto  HiPriISR
```

two more cycles for this **goto** instruction, and seven cycles for the **HiPriISR**, the CPU digresses from the interrupted code for eleven cycles, or

$$11 \times 0.4 = 4.4 \text{ microseconds}$$

The maximum frequency that can be measured is

$$\frac{16}{4.4} = 3.6 \text{ MHz}$$

9.5 CRITICAL REGIONS

A *critical region* of code is a sequence of program instructions that *must not* be interrupted if erroneous operation is to be avoided. An example arose in the **LoopTime** subroutine. Timer0 was read, manipulated, and rewritten. Correct operation required that exactly 12 cycles occurred between the read and the rewrite. An intervening interrupt would have thrown off this count, causing an extension of the loop time.

A resource accessed by both the mainline code and an interrupt handler may have the potential for a malfunction.

Example 9-5 Consider the three-LED array of the QwikFlash board driven from **PORTA**, as shown in Figure 4-2a. An interrupt routine is to set **RA3** when a rarely occurring condition occurs. If the LED is on, the user knows that the condition has occurred. Meanwhile, suppose that **RA2** and **RA1** are used by the mainline code to echo the state of the RPG (**PORTD**'s **RD1** and **RD0**) to give a visual indication of RPG changes. Show the code to echo the RPG state on the LEDs, describe the possible malfunction, and provide a solution.

Solution

One solution to echoing the RPG output to the two LEDs is shown in Figure 9-11a. **PORTA** is copied to **WREG**, the two bits that will hold the RPG bits are cleared to zero, and the result saved to **TEMP**. Next **PORTD** is copied to **WREG**, shifting bits 1 and 0 of **PORTD** to bits 2

```
movf   PORTA,W            ;Read PORTA and mask off bits 2 and 1
andlw  B'11111001'
movwf  TEMP               ;and save the result in TEMP
rlncf  PORTD,W            ;Shift PORTD one place left and into WREG
andlw  B'00000110'        ;Mask off all but bits 2 and 1
iorwf  TEMP,W             ;OR TEMP into this
movwf  PORTA              ;and return it to PORTA
```

(a) Original code with critical region problem.

```
bcf   <register>,<bit>    ;Disable the local interrupt enable bit
movf   PORTA,W            ;Read PORTA and mask off bits 2 and 1
andlw  B'11111001'
movwf  TEMP               ;and save the result in TEMP
rlncf  PORTD,W            ;Shift PORTD one place left and into WREG
andlw  B'00000110'        ;Mask off all but bits 2 and 1
iorwf  TEMP,W             ;OR TEMP into this
movwf  PORTA              ;and return it to PORTA
bsf   <register>,<bit>    ;Reenable local interrupt enable bit
```

(b) Solution by disabling the interrupt source that changes RA3.

```
movlw  B'11111001'        ;Force RA2 and RA1 to zero
andwf  PORTA,F
rlncf  PORTD,W            ;Move RD1 and RD0 to bits 2 and 1 of WREG
andlw  B'00000110'        ;Force all other bits to zero
iorwf  PORTA,F            ;and OR this back into PORTA
```

(c) Solution by changing **PORTA** with read-modify-write instructions.

```
IF_  PORTD,RD1 == 1       ;Copy RD1 to RA2
  bsf  PORTA,RA2
ELSE_
  bcf  PORTA,RA2
ENDIF_
IF_  PORTD,RD0 == 1       ;Copy RD0 to RA1
  bsf  PORTA,RA1
ELSE_
  bcf  PORTA,RA1
ENDIF_
```

(d) Alternative solution changing **PORTA** with read-modify-write instructions.

Figure 9-11 Example 9-5.

and 1 of **WREG**. The remaining bits of **WREG** are forced to zero, the result is ORed with the manipulated copy of **PORTA** located in **TEMP**, and the result returned to **PORTA**.

Note that if the interrupt occurs and sets bit 3 of **PORTA** anytime after the read of **PORTA** and before the write back to **PORTA**, then bit 3 of **PORTA** will be cleared back to its original state by the write back to **PORTA**.

The chance of the interrupt occurring at the precise moment this mainline sequence is being executed is remote. Consequently, the resulting code bug is difficult to find. Better solutions exist that absolutely avoid the problem. Figure 9-11b treats the mainline code as a critical region and postpones for just a few microseconds the execution of the specific interrupt handler that deals with the rarely occurring condition. An even better solution is to access **PORTA** with nothing but the microcontroller's read-modify-write instructions. The problem in Figure 9-11a arose because an interrupt could intervene between the initial read of **PORTA** and the final write to **PORTA**. In the code of Figure 9-11c the

```
andwf  PORTA,F
```

reads **PORTA**, modifies it, and writes the result back to **PORTA**, all in one instruction. Because an interrupt will not break into the middle of an instruction, the integrity of the read-modify-write sequence is not compromised. A little later in the sequence of Figure 9-11c, **PORTA** is again subjected to a read-modify-write instruction with the same result.

A third solution is shown in Figure 9-11d. In this case, only the read-modify-write

```
bsf
```

and

```
bcf
```

instructions are used to change **PORTA**, with the same error-free result.

A fourth solution would have the interrupt service routine set one bit of a flag variable (rather than RA3 directly). Then each time around the mainline loop, the CPU can check the flag bit. If it is set, then the CPU sets RA3.

9.6 EXTERNAL INTERRUPTS

The PIC18F452 has three external interrupt inputs:

INT0 INT1 INT2

These are shared with bits 0, 1, and 2 of **PORTB**. To use one of these as an interrupt source, its control bits must be set up, using the information of Figure 9-12.

Example 9-6 Set up INT1 as a falling-edge-sensitive interrupt input having low priority.

Solution

The following code will suffice:

```
bsf  TRISB,1            ;Input
bcf  INTCON2,INTEDG1    ;Falling-edge sensitive
bcf  INTCON3,INT1IP     ;Low priority
bcf  INTCON3,INT1IF     ;Clear flag
bsf  INTCON3,INT1IE     ;Enable interrupt source
bsf  INTCON,GIEL        ;Enable low-priority interrupts
bsf  INTCON,GIEH        ;Enable all interrupts
```

When a falling edge occurs on the INT1 input, the CPU will set aside what it is doing and vector through the low-priority interrupt vector at 0x0018 to the low-priority interrupt service routine, as described in Figure 9-4. Within the **INT1handler** subroutine, the interrupt flag can be cleared with

```
bcf  INTCON3,INT1IF
```

along with the code whose execution has been triggered by the falling edge on the INT1 input pin.

Example 9-7 Use the INT1 pin to generate a low-priority interrupt on both falling and rising edges.

Solution

Within the INT1 handler include

```
btg  INTCON2,INTEDG1    ;Toggle edge sensitivity
```

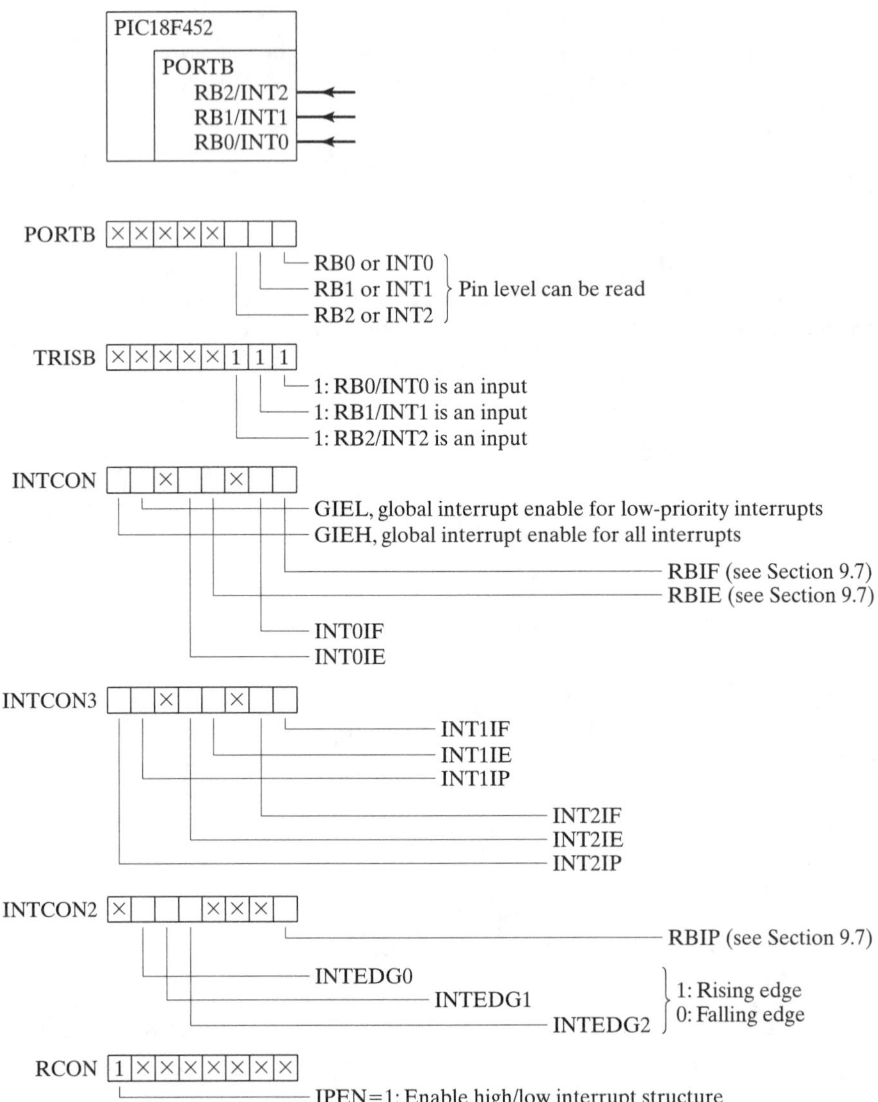

Figure 9-12 External interrupts.

9.7 PORTB-CHANGE INTERRUPTS (PINS RB7:RB4)

A low-to-high change or a high-to-low change on any of the upper four pins of **PORTB** *that are set up as inputs* can be used to generate an interrupt. Circuitry associated with **PORTB** keeps a copy of the state of these four pins as they were when the port was last read from or written to. Any subsequent mismatch caused by the change of an *input* pin among bits 7, 6, 5, 4 of **PORTB** will set the **RBIF** (register B interrupt flag) bit in the **INTCON** register. If interrupts have been set up appropriately (with **RBIE**,

RBIP, **GIEL**, and **GIEH**), then the CPU will be interrupted. An interrupt handler will respond to the **PORTB** change. The **RBIF** flag is cleared by a two-step process:

1. Read **PORTB** (or write to it) to copy the upper four bits of **PORTB** into the hardware copy, thereby removing the mismatch condition.
2. Execute

```
bcf  INTCON,RBIF
```

Note that once the **RBIF** flag has been set, the first step in clearing it may be carried out unintentionally if some unrelated routine accesses **PORTB**. For example,

```
bsf  PORTB,2
```

will carry out the first step needed to clear the **RBIF** bit. However, until the second step

```
bcf  INTCON,RBIF
```

is carried out, the flag will remain set. Consequently, a polling routine will work correctly in spite of reads and writes of **PORTB** by unrelated code.

A problem can arise if one of the inputs among the upper 4 bits of **PORTB** should happen to change at *the exact moment* that **PORTB** is being accessed by unrelated code. In this rarely occurring case, **RBIF** may not get set. This problem is a potential source of system malfunction any time **PORTB**-change interrupts are used. A better use of this facility arises when the microcontroller is put into its power-saving sleep mode. All code execution stops. A change on one of the **PORTB** upper pins can be used to awaken the microcontroller. Because there will never be a conflict between this occurrence and the execution of an instruction accessing **PORTB** (because code execution is stopped), the change on the **PORTB** pin will *never go* unnoticed.

PROBLEMS

9-1 Polling sequence. An application requires three interrupt sources having the following characterizing times:

TA = 10 μs	TPA = 2500 μs
TB = 10 μs	TPB = 250 μs
TC = 10 μs	TBC = 25 μs

For simplicity, assume that these times are the only times arising in the interrupt service routine (e.g., that all the extra tests and branches of the polling routine take no time).

(a) Show the worst-case timing diagram for IS#C if the interrupts are assigned to the polling routine in the order A, B, C. Will IS#C be serviced properly under all circumstances?
(b) Repeat with the polling routine order C, B, A.

9-2 Worst-case interrupt timing constraints. Consider the interrupt timing constraints for the four interrupt sources labeled (9-1) in Section 9-2.

(a) Why does the second constraint, imposed by IS#2, depend on the maximum of T3 and T4?
(b) Why does the constraint imposed by IS#3 equal that imposed by IS#4 if TP3 = TP4? That is, why does the higher position in the polling sequence not help IS#3?

9-3 LoPriISR. In the discussion of Figure 9-4, it was mentioned that the *order* of restoration of **WREG** and **STATUS** at the end of the interrupt service routine matters. Does the order of setting aside **WREG** and **STATUS** at the beginning of the interrupt service routine matter? Explain.

9-4 LoPriISR assumptions. Consider the assumptions of Figure 9-4c. If several interrupt handlers need to use indirect addressing, then **FSR2** (consisting of the two bytes, **FSR2H** and **FSR2L**) must be shared between them.

(a) Show the code used by IS#1 at the beginning of its handler to load its own pointer from **FSR21H:FSR21L** into **FSR2**.
(b) Show the code used by IS#1 at the end of its handler to save the content of **FSR2** back in **FSR21H:FSR21L**.
(c) How may cycles does this juggling of the content of **FSR2** add to the handler for IS#1?

9-5 LoopTime subroutine for 10 MHz operation. The **LoopTime** subroutine of Figure 9-7a causes **TMR0CNT** to count . . . , 1, 0 → 2, 1, 0 → 2, 1, 0 → 2, . . . in a two-state sequence.

(a) If the rest of the mainline code takes only 2 milliseconds to execute during a given pass around the mainline loop, what will be the state of **TMR0CNT** when the **LoopTime** subroutine is entered?
(b) Answer part (a) if the rest of the mainline code takes 7 milliseconds to execute.
(c) Answer part (a) if, on rare occasions, the rest of the mainline code takes 12 milliseconds to execute. What will be the effect of this on the performance of the **LoopTime** subroutine?
(d) Rewrite the **LoopTime** subroutine to test the most-significant bit (MSb) of **TMR0CNT**. When this bit becomes set, as **TMR0CNT** decrements from 0x00 to 0xff, increment **TMR0CNT** twice and then return from the subroutine.
(e) Given this change in the **LoopTime** subroutine, reanswer parts (a), (b), and (c).

9-6 Worst-case latency. Example 9-3 asked for the worst-case latency experienced by a second low-priority interrupt due to the Timer0 interrupts of Figure 9-7. This ignored the effect of a high-priority interrupt service routine. If, in fact, the high-priority interrupt service routine of Figure 9-10 were also employed in the application, then what would be the worst-case latency experienced by the second low-priority interrupt? Show a worst-case timing diagram.

9-7 Minimum latency. The text at the beginning of Section 9.4 implied that zero latency could be attained for an interrupt source if the application code never needed to disable high-priority interrupts to protect a critical region of code and if the "zero latency" interrupt source were made a high-priority interrupt. Actually, the **HiPriISR** code of Figure 9-10 exhibits a nonzero fixed latency, from the time the interrupt's flag is set until it is executing the first instruction of **HiPriISR**. Three cycles are automatically inserted by the CPU between the flag setting at the end of one cycle and the execution of a 1 byte instruction at vector address 0x0008. Four cycles are automatically inserted between the flag setting and the execution of a 2 byte "goto" instruction. Thus, the first (1 byte) instruction of **HiPriISR** is executed on the fourth or fifth cycle after the flag is set.

(a) What will be the latency if the

```
        goto   HiPriISR
```

of Figure 9-10 is replaced by the **HiPriISR** interrupt service routine itself?

(b) In general, how many instruction words can **HiPriISR** contain before it impinges on the low-priority ISR vector?

9-8 Shadow registers. The shadow register mechanism of Figure 9-8 can be used by a high-priority interrupt simply by terminating **HiPriISR** with the instruction

```
retfie  FAST
```

Assuming that **LoPriISR** is terminated (as it should be) with

```
retfie
```

would it matter whether the shadow register mechanism actually worked as in Figure 9-8a for low-priority interrupts as well as high-priority interrupts? Explain.

9-9 Measuring HiPriISR latency. With the QwikFlash board, jumper the output from **PORTB**, bit 1 (RB1) to the high-priority interrupt input, RB0/INT0.

(a) Write a high-priority interrupt service routine beginning directly at address 0x0008 with the instruction

```
bcf  PORTB,RB1
```

that simply clears the **INT0IF** flag and returns from the interrupt.

(b) Write a mainline program that initializes high-priority interrupts from rising edges on the INT0 input. A

```
bsf  INTCON2,INTEDG0
```

instruction will specify that INT0 interrupts are to occur on rising edges. After initialization has been completed, the mainline loop is to consist of

```
bsf  PORTB,RB1
```

followed by a dozen **nop** instructions. This will ensure that a single-word instruction is being executed when the CPU responds to the interrupt on INT0 caused by this rising edge on RB1. Then branch back to the

```
bsf  PORTB,RB1
```

to repeat the operation endlessly.

(c) Run the program and use a scope to monitor the RB1 pulse width. If zero latency is defined as the pulse width that would arise if the following sequence were executed:

```
bsf  PORTB,RB1
bcf  PORTB,RB1
```

then what is the latency measured by the RB1 pulse width due to the mainline/interrupt interactions?

9-10 Critical regions. Assume that a 1 byte variable called **FLAG** has been defined. Specific bits of **FLAG** are used to pass information from any one of several interrupt handlers back to the mainline code to indicate that its interrupt event has occurred and that the mainline code can take action accordingly, and then clear the specific **FLAG** bit. **FLAG** is thus a variable that is accessed and changed by multiple interrupt handlers as well as the mainline code. Why do the accesses and changes in the mainline code of this shared resource *not* constitute a critical region?

Chapter

10

ANALOG-TO-DIGITAL CONVERSION

10.1 OVERVIEW

The inclusion of a 10-bit analog-to-digital converter (ADC) in a low-cost microcontroller opens several opportunities. This chapter will consider a general examination of the features of the ADC and its use, including two applications built into the QwikFlash board.

10.2 ASSIGNMENT OF I/O PINS

Coming out of reset, eight pins of the PIC18F452 default to being analog inputs to the ADC. One of the frustrations of a new PIC microcontroller user occurs when writing code for a small application and finding that instructions that are intended to change an output pin produce no change at all. The problem arises when one of these eight pins is selected for the output and its setup has not included the initialization of a register called **ADCON1**. ("Why do I need to think about an ADC register when writing code for an application that does not use the analog-to-digital converter?")

The eight pins are shown in Figure 10-1, which is a block diagram for the ADC and for **PORTA** and **PORTE**. At reset, the eight pins default to being analog inputs. The digital I/O circuitry to the corresponding **PORTE** and **PORTA** pins is powered down and unable to transfer data either into or out of the chip. With a view of the options of Figure 10-2, the **Initial** subroutine for *any* application might begin with

```
MOVLF  B'11001110',ADCON1
```

whether or not the ADC facility will be used in the application. This choice powers the digital I/O circuitry for seven of the eight pins, leaving RA0/AN0 as an analog-only pin. Any of the seven pins with

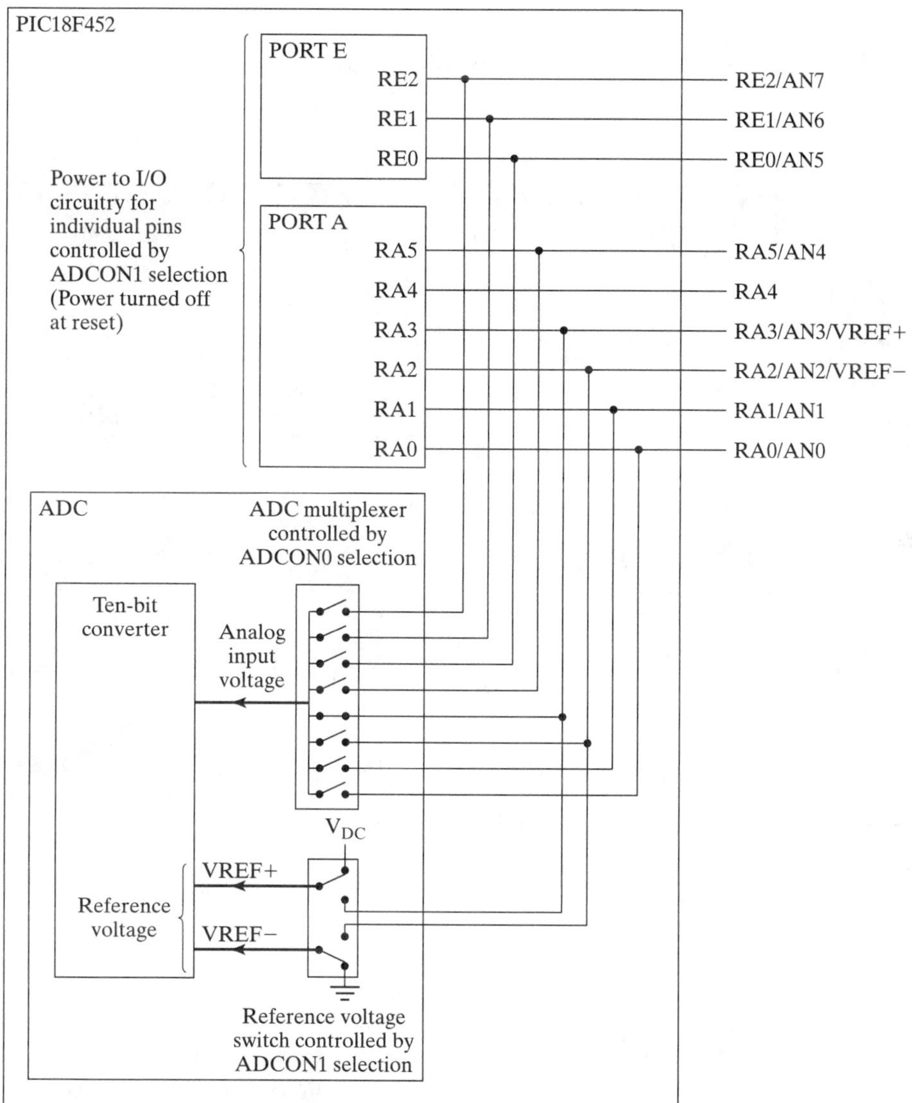

Figure 10-1 ADC/I/O-port block diagram.

powered digital I/O circuitry can *also* be used as an ADC input by keeping the pin's digital circuitry initialized as an *input.* The ADC conversion accuracy is unaffected by the pin being configured as a digital input. The pin's input impedance is likewise unaffected. It is only for a battery-powered application that it is wise to assign analog signals to pins configured as analog, not digital, pins. An "analog" pin draws less power than a "digital" pin because the pin's digital I/O circuitry will be shut down.

Another apparently good choice is

```
ADCON1 = B'----0111'
```

PCFG	AN7 (RE2)	AN6 (RE1)	AN5 (RE0)	AN4 (RA5)	AN3 (RA3)	AN2 (RA2)	AN1 (RA1)	AN0 (RA0)	VREF+	VREF−
0000	A	A	A	A	A	A	A	A	VDD	VSS
0001	A	A	A	A	VREF+	A	A	A	AN3	VSS
0010	D	D	D	A	A	A	A	A	VDD	VSS
0011	D	D	D	A	VREF+	A	A	A	AN3	VSS
0100	D	D	D	D	A	D	A	A	VDD	VSS
0101	D	D	D	D	VREF+	D	A	A	AN3	VSS
011x	D	D	D	D	D	D	D	D	-	-
1000	A	A	A	A	VREF+	VREF−	A	A	AN3	AN2
1001	D	D	A	A	A	A	A	A	VDD	VSS
1010	D	D	D	D	VREF+	A	A	A	AN3	VSS
1011	D	D	A	A	VREF+	VREF−	A	A	AN3	AN2
1100	D	D	D	A	VREF+	VREF−	A	A	AN3	AN2
1101	D	D	D	D	VREF+	VREF−	A	A	AN3	AN2
1110	D	D	D	D	D	D	D	A	VDD	VSS
1111	D	D	D	D	VREF+	VREF−	D	A	AN3	AN2

Figure 10-2 ADCON1 register.

because this configures all eight pins as digital pins. However, it also shuts down the reference voltage inputs, so ADC conversions no longer produce meaningful values.

Some ADC applications require the *accuracy* of a precision reference voltage rather than simply the 10-bit *resolution* obtained when the converter uses the microcontroller's supply voltage as its reference voltage. What would have been either the RA3 digital I/O pin or the AN3 analog input becomes the reference voltage input, as shown in Figure 10-3. With a 4.096 V reference voltage, each increment of the 10-bit ADC output represents

$$\frac{4096 \text{ mV}}{1024 \text{ increments}} = 4 \text{ millivolts}$$

In this case, the transfer function between input voltage and output number becomes that of Figure 10-4.

10.3 ADC OUTPUT FORMAT

The 10-bit output of the analog-to-digital converter can take either of two formats, depending on the initialization of the **ADFM** bit in the **ADCON1** register, as illustrated in Figure 10-5. The format of Figure 10-5a is the format of choice for applications making use of the output as a 2-byte integer, ranging be-

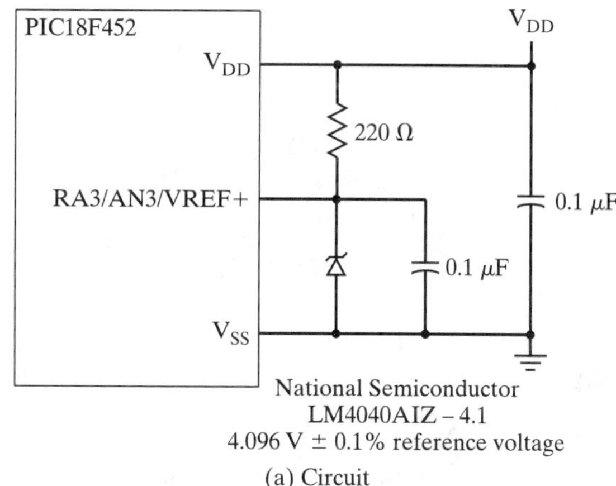

(a) Circuit

RA3/AN3/VREF+ pin becomes VREF+.
RA1/AN1 and RA0/AN0 pins become analog-only inputs.
Remaining five pins can be digital outputs, digital inputs, or analog inputs.

(b) ADCON1 = B'----0101' selection

Figure 10-3 Derivation of an accurate 4.096 V reference voltage.

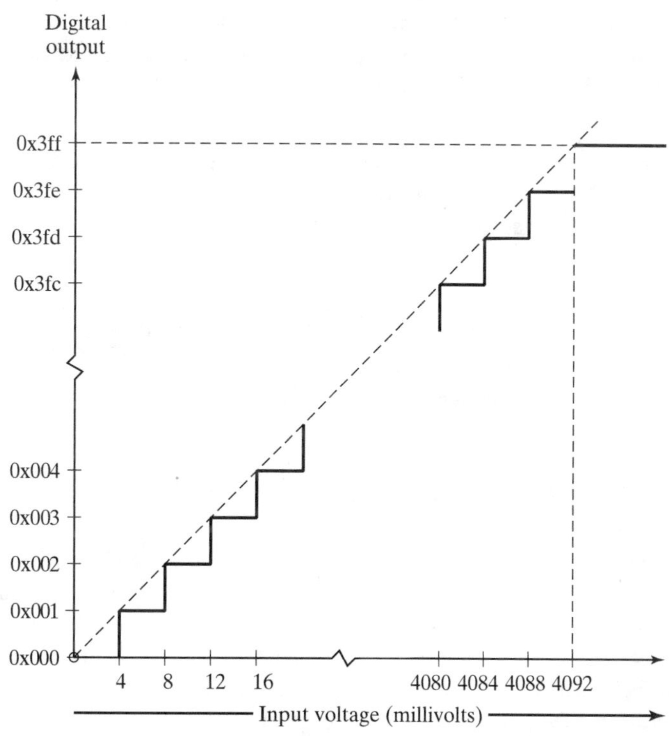

Figure 10-4 ADC transfer function with 4.096 V reference voltage.

ADRESH ADRESL

0	0	0	0	0	0	b_9	b_8

b_7	b_6	b_5	b_4	b_3	b_2	b_1	b_0

Ten-bit result

(a) Ten-bit output placement if **ADFM** = 1

ADRESH ADRESL

b_9	b_8	b_7	b_6	b_5	b_4	b_3	b_2

b_1	b_0	0	0	0	0	0	0

Ten-bit result

(b) Ten-bit output placement if **ADFM** = 0

Figure 10-5 Effect of **ADCON1** register's **ADFM** bit.

tween 0 and 1023. It can also be used to generate a 1-byte output in **ADRESL** if the input only varies over one the four restricted ranges:

$$0 \leq \text{Vin} < \text{VREF}/4$$
$$\text{VREF}/4 \leq \text{Vin} < \text{VREF}/2$$
$$\text{VREF}/2 \leq \text{Vin} < 3\text{VREF}/4$$
$$3\text{VREF}/4 \leq \text{Vin} < \text{VREF}$$

For example, the LM34 temperature sensor used on the QwikFlash board produces an output of 10 millivolts per degree Fahrenheit. Using the 5 volt power supply voltage as the reference voltage, one-quarter of the supply voltage is 1250 millivolts, corresponding to a temperature of 125°F. Although the LM34 is rated for measuring temperatures up to 300°F, if an application will never deal with temperatures over 125°F, the 1-byte output from **ADRESL** will serve the application without the need to handle a 2-byte value.

The QwikFlash board also employs a one-turn potentiometer to enter a voltage ranging between 0 V and +5 V, the supply voltage. Even 8-bit resolution is probably greater than an application can use, coming from a one-turn potentiometer. Thus the ADC output format of Figure 10-5b is most appropriate. The content of **ADRESH** will divide the 5 V range into 256 equal parts.

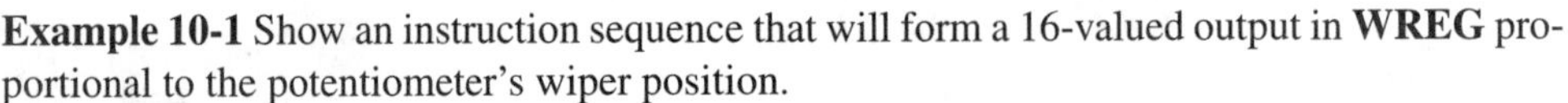

Example 10-1 Show an instruction sequence that will form a 16-valued output in **WREG** proportional to the potentiometer's wiper position.

Solution

Swap the nibbles of **ADRESH** into **WREG** and mask off the upper bits:

```
swapf  ADRESH,W
andlw  B'00001111'
```

10.4 ADC CHARACTERISTICS AND USE

The general transfer function for the ADC is shown in Figure 10-6. Its performance characteristics are delineated in Figure 10-7. Note the delay (i.e., minimum sample time) required after the analog multiplexer of Figure 10-1 has been switched to a new channel and before a conversion of the new channel is initiated. The delay gives the voltage on an internal sampling capacitor time to match the input voltage before it is disconnected from the input and used as a sampled surrogate of the input voltage during the conversion. The **GO_DONE** control bit that initiates a conversion and the multiplexer's channel

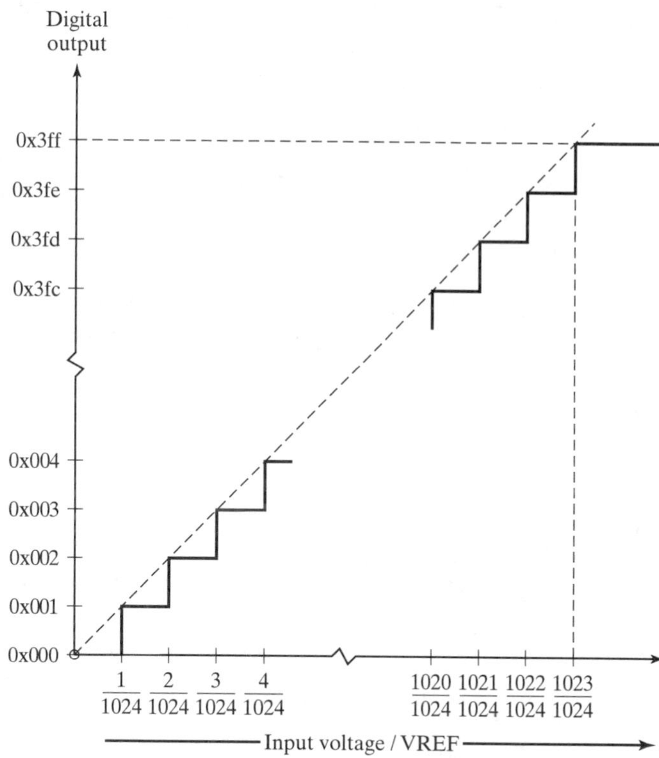

Figure 10-6 ADC transfer function.

selection bits are both located in the **ADCON0** register, shown in Figure 10-8. The temptation arises to do both the channel selection and conversion initiation at the same time, with the same instruction. The resulting erroneous output will be a conversion of a voltage close to that of the previous channel's input but changed somewhat toward the voltage of the newly selected channel's input.

The initialization of the ADC facility begins with the **ADCON1** register's initialization, to assign analog and digital pins, as already discussed in conjunction with Figure 10-2. Next, the ADC clock frequency must be set to meet the timing specification (neither too fast nor too slow) of Figure 10-9a. The three control bits of Figure 10-9b provide some alternatives.

The ADC clock is normally derived from the same clock oscillator from which the internal clocking of the chip is derived. The crystal frequency is divided down by as small a power of 2 as will yield an ADC clock frequency that meets the specifications of Figure 10-9a. The resulting divisor leads to the required setting of the three ADCSi bits, as listed in Figure 10-9b. For the 10 MHz crystal of the QwikFlash board with an internal clock rate of 2.5 MHz, the best divisor is 16. This gives an ADC clock frequency of 625 kHz and a conversion period equal to 12 ADC clock periods or 19.2 microseconds, as shown in Figure 10-9c.

Some battery-powered applications run at a reduced clock rate to save power (because the chip's battery current is proportional to frequency). A popular clock source for such an application is a 32768 Hz watch crystal. This clock frequency is too low for deriving the ADC clock because

$$32.768 \text{ kHz}/2 < 50 \text{ kHz}$$

The alternative in this case is to use the ADC's internal RC clock, resulting in the characteristics shown in Figure 10-9d.

Voltage reference	Internal: VREF = VDD (the PIC power supply voltage) External: VREF+ − VREF− > 3 V VREF+ < VDD + 0.3 V VREF− > VSS − 0.3 V
Error from idealized characteristic of Figure 10-6	Error < ±VREF/1024 (i.e., one increment)
Power supply current drawn by ADC	180 μA, typical (when powered on with ADON = 1 in ADCON0 register)
Maximum source impedance of analog input	2.5 kΩ
Minimum sample time	15 μs This is the time after an input channel has been selected and before a conversion is initiated.
Conversion time	19.2 μs—for 10 MHz crystal (with or without phase-locked loop) and ADC clock = $F_{osc}/16$ 24 μs—for 4 MHz crystal and ADC clock = $F_{osc}/8$

Figure 10-7 10-bit ADC performance characteristics.

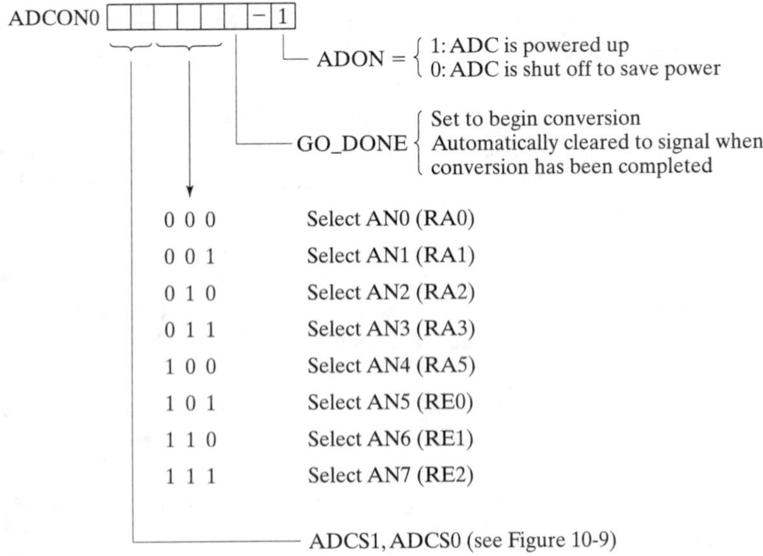

Figure 10-8 ADCON0 register.

50 kHz < ADC clock frequency < 625 kHz

(a) ADC clock frequency specification

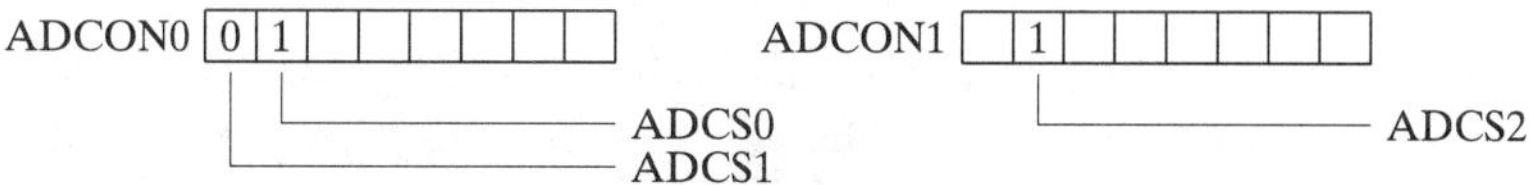

ADC Clock Frequency	ADCON0 ADCS1	ADCON0 ADCS0	ADCON1 ADCS2
$F_{OSC}/2$	0	0	0
$F_{OSC}/4$	0	0	1
$F_{OSC}/8$	0	1	0
$F_{OSC}/16$	0	1	1
$F_{OSC}/32$	1	0	0
$F_{OSC}/64$	1	0	1
F_{RC}	1	1	x

F_{OSC} is the oscillator frequency
(i.e., four times the chip's internal clock rate)

F_{RC} is the frequency of an internal RC oscillator.
(167 kHz < F_{RC} < 500 kHz)

(b) ADC clock frequency options

F_{osc} = 10 MHz
$F_{osc}/16$ = 625 kHz
ADC clock period = 1.6 μs
ADC conversion period = 12 × ADC clock period = 19.2 μs

(c) Selection for 10 MHz crystal oscillator

2 μs < ADC clock period < 6 μs
24 μs < ADC conversion period < 72 μs

(d) Use of the internal RC oscillator with its frequency between 167 kHz and 500 kHz

Figure 10-9 ADC clock frequency selection.

For the QwikFlash board, the **ADCON0** register can be initialized to

```
ADCON0 = B'01000001'    (Select AN0 for temperature sensor)
```

or

```
ADCON0 = B'01100001'    (Select AN4 for potentiometer)
```

whereas **ADCON1** can be initialized to

```
ADC0N1 = B'11001110'   (Use ADRESL for temperature sensor)
```

or

```
ADCON1 = B'01001110'    (Use ADRESH for potentiometer)
```

Before a conversion is carried out, the desired channel can be selected by rewriting **ADCON0**. The output format can be selected by setting or clearing the **ADFM** bit in the **ADCON1** register, as specified in Figure 10-5. Wait 15 microseconds for the ADC's sampling capacitor to settle. Then set the **GO_DONE** bit in the **ADCON0** register to initiate the conversion. Pause until **GO_DONE** returns to zero, signaling that the conversion is complete. Then read the result from **ADRESH** and/or **ADRESL**.

Note that no 15 microsecond pause is necessary if the input channel is not changed. For example, if the potentiometer's output on the QwikFlash board is read each time around the mainline loop and no other analog channels are used, it is only necessary to set the **GO_DONE** bit to start a conversion. Furthermore, no pause for the 19.2 μs conversion time is necessary if the **GO_DONE** bit is set just before calling the **LoopTime** subroutine. When the mainline subroutines are next executed, the ADC result will be available.

10.5 INTERRUPT CONTROL OF THE ADC

For slowly changing inputs, the interval between ADC samples is most easily controlled by counting loop times. For example, the temperature from the LM34 sensor of Figure 4-2a might be obtained and displayed every second by using the **BlinkAlive** subroutine of Figure 6-7 as a model.

For a fast-changing input to the ADC, the "A/D converter interrupt" of Figure 9-6 signals that a conversion has been completed. In Section 16.3, a "trigger special event" feature of the PIC18F452 chip will be discussed. It can use Timer3 together with the CCP2 facility, as shown in Figure 16-6,

- to implement a scale-of-*N* counter of the internal clock, with arbitrary scale, to set the ADC sample rate
- to initiate an ADC conversion by setting the **GO_DONE** bit once per cycle of the counter.

At the completion of the conversion, the ADC interrupt might take the sample and save it in an array of samples in RAM. Or it might average it with previous samples. In any case, the "trigger special event" feature yields precise control of the sampling interval.

PROBLEMS

10-1 Temperature measurement Modify the P2.asm code to display

```
ROOMTEMP
ΔΔΔΔdd°F
```

where Δ represents a blank character, coded as 0x20.

(a) Update the QwikFlash board's LCD display every second with a new LM34 reading using the internal reference voltage, VDD, assumed to be 5.00 V. At room temperature, the ADC result will be 1 byte.

(b) Normalize the 1-byte result by multiplying it times the "magic number" 125 and copying the upper byte of the product from **PRODH** to **TEMP**, a 1-byte RAM variable. This should be a close approximation to the temperature, expressed as a binary number.

(c) Convert **TEMP** to a packed-BCD representation as follows. Clear **WREG**. Then decrement **TEMP** once. Increment **WREG** once as a packed-BCD number with

```
incf  WREG,F
daw
```

Repeat this decrementing of **TEMP** and incrementing of **WREG** until **TEMP** = 0, at which point **WREG** should contain the packed-BCD representation of the temperature. For example, if **TEMP** initially contained 71 (expressed in binary), then **WREG** will end up holding 0x01110001, the packed-BCD representation of 71.

(d) Copy each BCD digit into the display string used to update the second line of the display. Convert each digit to its ASCII equivalent. Use the result in part *(a)* to update the display every second.

(e) After seeing that the display of temperature is approximately correct, explain why the "magic number" of 125 works in part *(b)*.

10-2 Potentiometer scaling Show the code to form a 16-valued output in **WREG** proportional to the potentiometer wiper position. Instead of using the scheme of Example 10-1, multiply **ADRESH** by an appropriate value so **PRODH** will be 0x00, 0x01, . . . , or 0x0f. One-sixteenth of the travel of the potentiometer is to translate into each value.

10-3 Potentiometer scaling Repeat Problem 10-2 to form a ten-valued output in **WREG** ranging from 0x00 to 0x09.

10-4 ADC clock frequency The PIC18F452 can use a 25 MHz crystal for its clock source, deriving an internal clock rate of 6.25 MHz.

(a) What is the highest ADC clock frequency that can be derived from this?
(b) To select this ADC clock frequency, what should the three **ADCS** bits be?
(c) What will be the ADC conversion period?

10-5 Conversion time The discussion at the end of Section 10.4 suggested that a conversion might be initiated just before calling the **LoopTime** subroutine.

(a) How long might pass before the converted value is used?
(b) If equally spaced samples are wanted, why is it better to start the conversion first thing in the mainline loop, wait for the short conversion time to play out, and then read the ADC output?

Chapter

11

I/O PIN CONSIDERATIONS

11.1 OVERVIEW

Each I/O pin of the PIC18F452 microcontroller generally serves at least two functions. If the specialty function (e.g., use of the RA1/AN1 pin's function as an input to the analog-to-digital converter) is not needed, the usefulness of the pin is not lost. Rather, it can become a general-purpose digital input or digital output pin (e.g., the RA1/AN1 pin's function as bit RA1 of **PORTA**). This chapter will examine the features of the general-purpose digital I/O pins. The designers of the PIC18F452 chip have designed digital I/O pin functionality that avoids quirks that could arise on earlier-generation parts. They have also designed protection circuitry into each I/O pin that permits it to shrug off conditions that would destroy the I/O pin of a less robust microcontroller, if not the microcontroller itself.

11.2 DIGITAL OUTPUT PIN FUNCTIONALITY

When a pin is used as an output and is driven low, it has the drive specification of Figure 11-1a. This specification can be interpreted as the Thévenin equivalent circuit of Figure 11-1b. Figures 11-1c and d show the specification and its Thévenin equivalent circuit when the pin is driven high.[3] Note that the output drive circuitry has significantly lower output impedance when driving low than when driving high.

[3]**PORTA**'s RA4 pin is an exception. Its open-drain output becomes an open circuit.

With V_{DD} of 4.5 V or above and with temperature between −40°C and +85°C and with a load current of 8.5 mA, the output voltage will rise no more than 0.6 V

(a) Specification when output pin is driven low

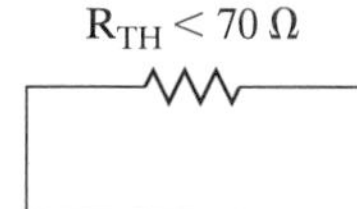

(b) Thévenin equivalent of output circuit when output is driven low

With V_{DD} of 4.5 V or above and with temperature between −40°C and +85°C and with a load current of 3.0 mA, the output voltage will drop no more than 0.7 V

(c) Specification when output pin is driven high

$R_{TH} < 233\ \Omega$

$E_{TH} = V_{DD}$

(d) Thévenin equivalent of output circuit when output is driven high

Figure 11-1 Specifications for output pin drive capability.

Example 11-1 The QwikFlash board uses aluminum gallium arsenide low-current LEDs in series with 1 kilohm resistors. The "Alive" LED turns on when RA4 is driven low. Each of the other three LEDs driven from **PORTA** turn on when the pin is driven high. If the output circuits exhibit their worst-case characteristics, how much of an effect does the output impedance have on the LED current and, thereby, the brightness? Assume $V_{DD} = 5$ V.

Solution

Figure 11-2 lists typical characteristics of two aluminum gallium arsenide low-current LEDs plus those of a standard-current LED. Figure 11-3a shows the equivalent circuit for the "Alive" LED, with its output pin driven low. The resulting LED current is 3.2 mA.

Figure 11-3b shows the equivalent circuit for each of the other three LEDs with the output pin driven high. The resulting LED current in this case drops slightly, to 2.8 mA. The 1 kΩ current-limiting resistor is large enough to dominate the port's output impedance. This resistor, the supply voltage, and the relatively constant forward-voltage drop of the LED are the dominant factors in setting the LED current in either case.

Example 11-2 The characteristics of a low-cost, standard-current LED are shown in Figure 11-2. Consider the drive circuit to turn the LED on with 15 mA of current from an output port. How much effect does the port's output impedance have on the LED current?

Solution

Figure 11-4 shows the circuit and the equivalent circuit when the LED is turned on by driving the output pin low. A current-limiting resistance value of 123 Ω will set the LED current to 15 mA. A PIC18F452 with a lower output impedance of 35 Ω (instead of the worst-case value of 70 Ω) would produce a LED current of 18 mA.

Description	Part Number	Maximum dc Current	Typical Brightness	Typical Voltage Drop	Source
Low-current LED	Agilent Technologies HLMP-1700	7 mA	3.5 mcd @ 3 mA	1.8 V @ 3 mA	Newark No. 06F6620 ($0.26)
Low-current LED	Panasonic LN28RAL(US)	30 mA	3.5 mcd @ 3 mA	1.6 V @ 3 mA	Digi-Key No. P403 ($0.35)
Standard-current LED	Panasonic LN28RPP	25 mA	0.4 mcd @ 3 mA 1.0 mcd @ 15 mA 1.5 mcd @ 25 mA	1.85 V @ 3 mA 2.10 V @ 15 mA 2.25 V @ 25 mA	Digi-Key No. P363 ($0.17)

Figure 11-2 Typical characteristics of low-current (aluminum gallium arsenide) and standard-current LEDs in small T-1 package.

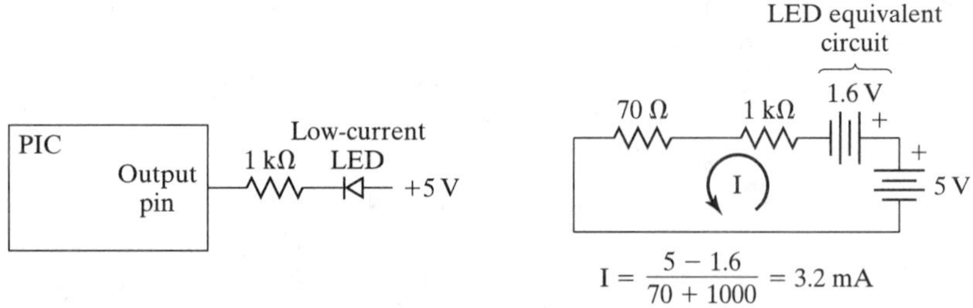

$$I = \frac{5 - 1.6}{70 + 1000} = 3.2 \text{ mA}$$

(a) Circuit and equivalent circuit for the "Alive" LED that is turned on when pin is driven low.

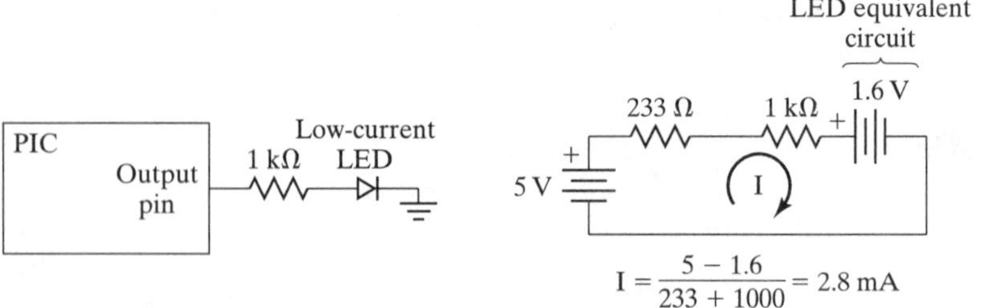

$$I = \frac{5 - 1.6}{233 + 1000} = 2.8 \text{ mA}$$

(b) Circuit and equivalent circuit for each of the three LEDs turned on when pin is driven high.

Figure 11-3 Drive circuits for low-current LEDs of Example 11-1.

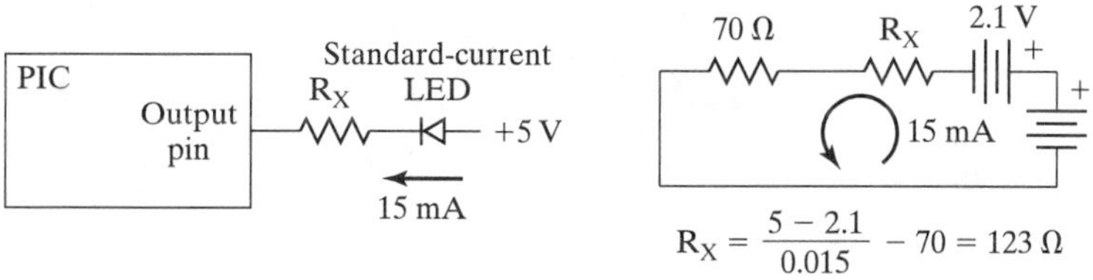

Figure 11-4 Drive circuit for standard-current LED of Example 11-2.

If the circuit is changed to turn on the LED when the output pin is driven high, the port's worst-case output impedance limits the LED current to just 12 mA, even with the current-limiting resistor removed entirely from the circuit. With *no* current-limiting resistor in the circuit, the LED current's sensitivity to output impedance variations from pin to pin or from chip to chip reaches its maximum:

$$\frac{\Delta(\text{LED current})}{\text{LED current}} = -\frac{\Delta(\text{Output impedance})}{\text{Output impedance}}$$

That is, a decrease in the output impedance by N percent will result in an increase in the LED current of the same N percent.

From these examples, the benefit afforded by a low-current LED and the resulting high value of its current-limiting resistor becomes apparent.

11.3 DIGITAL I/O CIRCUITRY

Each I/O pin is configured as shown in Figure 11-5. This sophisticated circuit is designed not only to accomplish the normal tasks of an I/O pin but also to overcome several subtle malfunction mechanisms. The pin is set up as an input or an output by writing a 1 or a 0 to the **TRIS** flip-flop. For example,

```
bcf  TRISD,2
```

sets up bit 2 of **PORTD** to be an output.

Once a pin is set up as an output, a write to either **LATi** or **PORTi** will write the value to the Data flip-flop, whose output is passed along to the I/O pin through the Output tristate buffer. A read of **PORTi** will read the state of each pin of **PORTi** whether that pin has been set up as an input or an output. A read of **LATi** will read the state of the Data flip-flop, not the state of the pin. As a general rule, the presence of the **LATi** instruction operand for each port can be ignored. It is only when one or more pins of the port are being used as bidirectional pins that a potential problem can arise. Any read-modify-write instructions intended to change *other* pins of the port should use **LATi**, not **PORTi**. In this way, whatever was previously written to the bidirectional pin will remain unchanged in the Data flip-flop for that pin.

Each I/O pin includes circuitry to help inputs to be read reliably. The first step for many of the chip's inputs is to pass through a Schmitt trigger. A slowly changing input to a Schmitt trigger will cause the output to *snap,* going from low-to-high or high-to-low in nanoseconds. This minimizes the time during which the digital circuitry will see an input in the threshold region, where a distinction between a 1 and a 0 will be made. Figure 11-6 shows which input functions employ a Schmitt-trigger input.

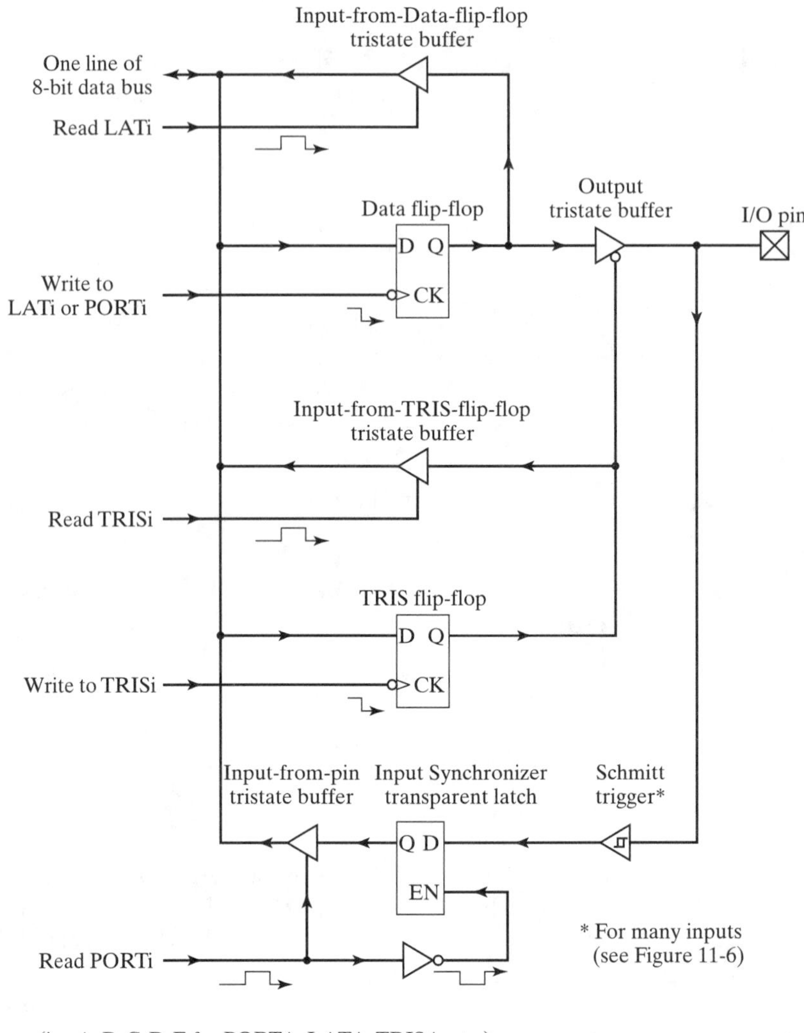

Figure 11-5 I/O pin configuration.

The Input Synchronizer transparent latch[4] shown in Figure 11-5 is designed to ameliorate the inevitable *metastability* problem associated with a digital input pin. When an instruction reads a port, an internal "Read **PORTi**" pulse is generated. The leading edge of this pulse captures the digital input into the Input Synchronizer transparent latch. If the input is passing through the 0 → 1 or 1 → 0 threshold at that precise moment, the Input Synchronizer, exhibiting metastability, may take some number of nanoseconds to settle to one state or the other. However, as long as it has settled some nanoseconds before the end of the "Read **PORTi**" pulse, the Input-from-pin tristate buffer will read the settled value from the

[4]A transparent latch passes the D input along to the Q output, unimpeded, as long as its EN input is high. When EN goes low, the input connection is broken and the Q output retains its last value until EN goes high again.

Pin	Function with Schmitt-Trigger Input
OSC1/CLKI	RC clock circuit input
MCLR/V_{PP}	Master clear (reset) input
RA4/TØCKI	T0CKI (Timer0 external clock input)
RA5/AN4/SS/LVDIN	SS (SPI's slave-select input)
RBØ/INTØ	INT0 (external interrupt 0)
RB1/INT1	INT1 (external interrupt 1)
RB2/INT2	INT2 (external interrupt 2)
RB3/CCP2	Capture2 input (if CCP2 is assigned to this pin)
RB6 and RB7	When used for programming the chip
RCØ/T1OSO/T1CKI	RC0 input and Timer1/Timer3 external clock input
RC1/T1OSI/CCP2	RC1 input and Capture2 input (if CCP2 is assigned to this pin)
RC2/CCP1	RC2 input and Capture1 input
RC3/SCK/SCL	RC3 input and Slave clock input for SPI and I^2C
RC4/SDI/SDA	RC4 input and SPI/I^2C data input
RC5/SDØ	RC5 input
RC6/TX/CK	RC6 input and Slave clock input for USART
RC7/RX/DX	RC7 input and USART receiver
RDØ/PSPØ	RD0 input
RD1/PSP1	RD1 input
RD2/PSP2	RD2 input
RD3/PSP3	RD3 input
RD4/PSP4	RD4 input
RD5/PSP5	RD5 input
RD6/PSP6	RD6 input
RD7/PSP7	RD7 input
REØ/AN5	RE0 input
RE1/AN6	RE1 input
RE2/AN7	RE2 input

Figure 11-6 Schmitt-trigger inputs.

Input Synchronizer into the executed instruction's destination register. In the rare event that the value has not settled, the metastability problem is passed along to the destination register. As long as the destination register settles out after this write and before it is next read, the ambiguity associated with metastability will be resolved satisfactorily.

For an example of metastability translating into a problem, consider

```
movf   PORTB,W
movwf  PORTB_COPY
```

If one of the bits of **WREG** is still in a metastable state when the write to **PORTB_COPY** takes place, then it is possible that **WREG** may end up in one state (e.g., B'11110000') while **PORTB_COPY** may end up in another state (e.g., B'11110001'). A *test* of **WREG** that controls the *use* of **PORTB_COPY** can, possibly, produce an erroneous result.

This may seem like a far-fetched error mechanism. On the other hand, Microchip has sold more than *1.5 billion* microcontrollers during its life as a company. With those huge numbers of chips executing millions of instructions a second, what seems like a far-fetched possibility will occur on rare occasions. The inclusion of the Input Synchronizer in the circuit of Figure 11-5 greatly reduces the probability that an application will *ever* experience an error from this source. Note also that the PIC18F452's new

```
movff   PORTB,PORTB_COPY
```

instruction takes the metastability issue one level further out because this 2-byte, two-cycle instruction reads **PORTB** into a hidden register in the CPU during one cycle and writes it to **PORTB_COPY** during the second cycle. For a problem to arise, the *following* instruction would have to find a bit of **PORTB_COPY** still in the metastable state so that it could *interpret* **PORTB_COPY** as being in one state even as **PORTB_COPY** settled out to another state.

11.4 INPUT CONSIDERATIONS

Input pins exhibit the exceptionally high input impedance associated with CMOS inputs. The input leakage current is less than ±1 μA, producing about the same inconsequential loading to any device driving an input as a 5 megohm resistor would.

Each input pin is protected against input voltages above V_{DD} and below V_{SS} with clamping diodes, as shown in Figure 11-7. If an input is driven above 5 V or below 0 V, a current will flow into or out of the pin through one of the clamping diodes in an attempt to protect the pin from a destructive breakdown voltage. If the driver does not have a high enough source impedance to limit this current to less than 20 mA, then a protection resistor should be interposed between the driver and the input pin, as in Figure 11-7.

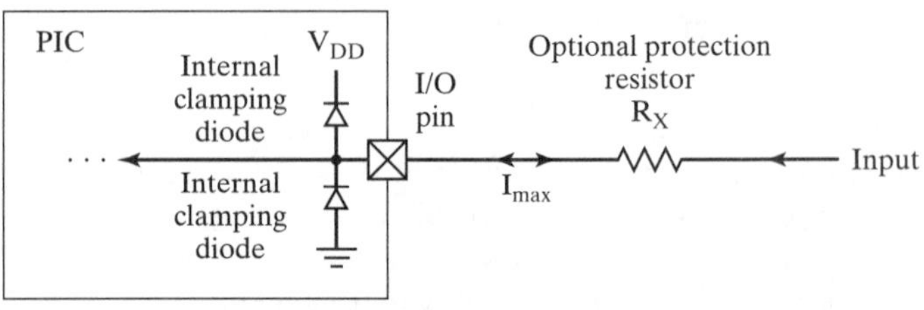

Figure 11-7 Clamping diodes on I/O pins.

Input pins are sometimes inadvertently exposed to an overvoltage when power to the board containing the microcontroller is turned off while other parts of the target application or test signal sources remain powered. Fortunately, if such a problem arises, it usually arises during development, when the target circuitry may still be in pieces and still subject to testing. Once the application reaches customers, the embedded microcontroller in the target application is spared from this problem except for a malfunction, an unprotected power-line voltage surge, or poor protection against static electricity voltages. Any of these are likely to destroy much more than an input pin.

PROBLEMS

11-1 Thévenin equivalent circuits The Thévenin equivalent is a linear representation of a circuit.

(a) Noting that an unloaded CMOS output will rise to the supply voltage, explain why the Thévenin voltage source in Figure 11-1d is equal to V_{DD}.
(b) Given this Thévenin voltage source, explain why a voltage drop of 0.7 V on the output pin when the load current is 3.0 mA translates into a Thévenin resistance (i.e., a source resistance) of 233 Ω.
(c) Explain why the Thévenin voltage source when the output is driven low is 0 V, as in Figure 11-1b.
(d) Explain why a rise of 0.6 V on the output pin when the output sinks 8.5 mA translates into a Thévenin resistance of 70 Ω.

11-2 LED Thévenin equivalent circuit For Example 11-1, the Panasonic low-current LED was represented by a voltage source of 1.6 V. This implies that its voltage does not vary with current. Actually, a closer approximation can be made by noting that between 1.5 mA and 8 mA, the forward-voltage drop varies almost linearly, from 1.60 V @ 1.5 mA to 1.70 V @ 8mA.

(a) Plot this voltage versus current characteristic.
(b) Thinking in terms of a Thévenin equivalent of the LED, what is the significance of the point on the straight line where the current is zero?
(c) What is the significance of the slope of the straight line?
(d) Repeat Example 11-1 with the Thévenin equivalent for the LED determined here. Does the more accurate LED model make much difference?

11-3 Sensitivity The *sensitivity* of LED current to output impedance of a port is defined as the ratio of the percentage change in current caused by some small percentage change in the output impedance. For example, if a 1.0% increase in the output impedance results in a 0.5% decrease in LED current, then it is said that the sensitivity of LED current to output impedance is $-0.5/1.0 = -0.5$.

(a) For Problem 11-2, when the output is driven low, what is the sensitivity of LED current to output impedance?
(b) What is the sensitivity of LED current to supply voltage?
(c) What is the sensitivity of LED current to current-limiting resistance value?
(d) If a current-limiting resistor with a ±5% tolerance in resistance value is used, how much will this affect the LED current?

11-4 Protection resistor Refer to the full schematic for the QwikFlash board in Appendix A1. Note that the CCP2/RC1 input, which serves as the board's input when used as the instrument described in Section 4.3, has both a 1 kilohm protection resistor and two external protection 1N4148 diodes (characterized by a 0.7 V forward-voltage drop).

(a) How far below 0 V must the input go before the current through the protection diode exceeds 20 mA?

(b) If the power to the QwikFlash board were turned off while the square wave oscillator driving CCP2 between 0 V and +5 V were left on, what would be the maximum current flowing through the protection diode?

Chapter

12

LCD SCREENS (P3 TEMPLATE)

12.1 OVERVIEW

With its little 8x2-character display, the QwikFlash board can benefit from a formal mechanism for sequencing through its alternate uses. One aspect of the approach to be introduced will permit the sequencing to help set up and monitor various aspects of a single overall job controlled by the microcontroller. An example is a function generator, with its setup of frequency, peak-to-peak voltage, dc offset, waveform choice (e.g., square wave, sine wave, triangle wave) and output on or off.

A second aspect occurs when the application involves the microcontroller in any one of several *alternate* uses. The QwikFlash instrument mentioned in Section 4.3 is an example. It can be an instrument to measure frequency, period, or maximum pulse width. The display can help with the measurement selection as well as the display of the measurement result.

The approach taken to sequencing will be to use the pushbutton switch beneath the LCD on the QwikFlash board to sequence through successive choices, using the LCD to indicate each choice (e.g., "Freq," "Period," "PWmax"). If one of the choices requires a "reset and start over" command, it will be triggered by a short press of the pushbutton switch, with longer presses used for sequencing. If sequencing is used for parameter entry, as for the function generator, then the RPG can be used to enter a parameter, with the changing parametric value displayed on the LCD.

For a user, what is displayed on the LCD "screen" indicates the state of the application. Accordingly in this chapter, the term *screen* will be used to denote

- How the LCD is being used
- How RPG entries are being interpreted
- Which of several possible application programs are being executed

12.2 PUSHBUTTON ENTRY

To draw a distinction between short and long presses of the pushbutton switch, the QwikFlash instrument counts loop times from the leading edge of the pushbutton pulse to its trailing edge. A pulse width of more than 0.3 seconds is treated as a long press. The **Pbutton** subroutine of Figure 12-1 responds by setting an Initiate Screen Change (**ISC**) bit in a 1-byte RAM variable, **PBSTATE**. A quick press, with a pulse width of less than 0.3 seconds, results in the setting of an Initiate Secondary Action (**ISA**) bit, also located in **PBSTATE**. Both **ISC** and **ISA** serve as flags to the **Screens** subroutine discussed in the next section. In response to the setting of the **ISC** flag by a long pushbutton press, the **Screens** subroutine will change screens. The setting of the **ISA** flag by a quick pushbutton press will be used, optionally, within a screen application. For example, the QwikFlash instrument of Section 4.3 uses this response to a quick press of the pushbutton while it is being used to determine the maximum pulse width of the input to the instrument. The quick press and release begins the maximum pulse width determination anew.

The **Pbutton** subroutine implements these two responses to pushbutton presses. If the **Pbutton** subroutine is called each time around the mainline loop, each press of the pushbutton will set either the **ISC** bit or the **ISA** bit for exactly one pass of the mainline loop. To maintain state information between one call of the **Pbutton** subroutine and the next call 10 milliseconds later, **Pbutton** uses a 1-byte variable, **PBSTATE**, and a 1-byte counter, **PBCOUNT**. The 5 bits used in **PBSTATE** are defined in Figure 12-1b. In addition to **ISC** and **ISA**, **PBSTATE** holds a **PDONE** bit that is used to disable more than one **ISC** pulse per long press. As soon as the press duration equals the threshold signified by **PBCOUNT** = 0, both **ISC** and **PDONE** are set. When **Pbutton** is entered again, **ISC** will be reset, but **PDONE** remains set, blocking further settings of the **ISC** bit until the pushbutton is released.

The state of the pushbutton connected to the **RD3** pin is copied into **NEWPB**. Note that all subsequent reads of the pushbutton are obtained by reading **NEWPB**, not the **RD3** bit of **PORTD**, thereby avoiding an occasional bug. The remainder of the subroutine consists of five independent parts:

- Initialize **PBCOUNT** to the threshold value, **PBthres**, upon detecting the leading edge of the pushbutton pulse.
- Set **ISC** = 1 if the pushbutton is pressed, the threshold time has been exceeded, and **ISC** has not already been set on a previous pass around the mainline loop.
- Set **ISA** = 1 on detecting the trailing edge of the pushbutton pulse if the threshold has not been reached.
- Decrement **PBCOUNT**, stopping at 0 to distinguish between short and long pauses.
- Save the present pushbutton state (**NEWPB**) in the **OLDPB** bit of **PBSTATE**.

Example 12-1 What modification can be made to the **Pbutton** subroutine so that the screen will change state in response to a fast press of the pushbutton while the secondary action will be triggered by a slow press?

Solution

In the one place where **ISC** is presently set, set **ISA** instead. In the one place where **ISA** is presently set, set **ISC** instead.

```
        PBSTATE                 ;Control/status byte for pushbutton
        PBCOUNT                 ;Counter for measuring duration of press
```

(a) Variables

```
ISC     equ  0                  ;Initiate screen change for long press
ISA     equ  1                  ;Initiate secondary action for short press
PDONE   equ  2                  ;Pushbutton action has been taken
OLDPB   equ  3                  ;Old state of pushbutton
NEWPB   equ  4                  ;New state of pushbutton
PBthres equ  30                 ;Pushbutton threshold for a long press
```

(b) Equates for bits of **PBSTATE** and threshold for long press (0.3 second)

```
        MOVLF  B'00001000',PBSTATE  ;Initialize pushbutton state
        clrf  PBCOUNT               ;and pushbutton count
```

(c) Initialization

```
;;;;;;; Pbutton subroutine ;;;;;;;;;;;;;;;;;;;;;;;;;;;;;;;;;;;;;;;;;;;;;;;;;;;;;;
;
; This subroutine sorts out long and short pushbutton presses into two outputs:
;       ISC=1: Initiate screen change for slow press
;       ISA=1: Initiate secondary action for fast press
;       PDONE=1: One of the above actions has occurred for this press

Pbutton
        bcf PBSTATE,ISC          ;Clear Initiate Screen Change bit (if set)
        bcf  PBSTATE,ISA         ;Clear Initiate Secondary Action bit (if set)
        IF_  PORTD,RD3 == 1      ;Copy pushbutton state to NEWPB
          bsf  PBSTATE,NEWPB
        ELSE_
          bcf  PBSTATE,NEWPB
        ENDIF_

        IF_  PBSTATE,OLDPB == 1 ;Look for leading edge (OLDPB=1, NEWPB=0)
          IF_  PBSTATE,NEWPB == 0
             MOVLF  PBthres,PBCOUNT  ;Start counter
          ENDIF_
        ENDIF_

        IF_  PBSTATE,NEWPB == 0 ;Pushbutton is still pressed
          movf  PBCOUNT,F
          IF_  .Z.               ;and counter has passed threshold
            IF_  PBSTATE,PDONE == 0 ;and no action has yet been taken
              bsf  PBSTATE,ISC    ;Initiate screen change
              bsf  PBSTATE,PDONE  ;Done with pulse
            ENDIF_
          ENDIF_
        ELSE_                    ;Pushbutton has been released
          bcf  PBSTATE,PDONE     ;so clear PDONE
        ENDIF_

        IF_  PBSTATE,OLDPB == 0  ;Look for trailing edge (OLDPB=0, NEWPB=1)
          IF_  PBSTATE,NEWPB == 1
            movf  PBCOUNT,F
            IF_  .NZ.            ;Fast pulse
              bsf  PBSTATE,ISA   ;Initiate secondary action
            ENDIF_
            bcf  PBSTATE,PDONE   ;Done with pulse
            clrf  PBCOUNT        ;Finish counting
          ENDIF_
        ENDIF_

        movf  PBCOUNT,F          ;Has counter reached zero?
        IF_  .NZ.                ;If not, then decrement it
          decf  PBCOUNT,F
        ENDIF_

        IF_  PBSTATE,NEWPB == 1 ;Copy NEWPB to OLDPB
          bsf  PBSTATE,OLDPB
        ELSE_
          bcf  PBSTATE,OLDPB
        ENDIF_
        return
```

(d) Subroutine

Figure 12-1 Pbutton subroutine

12.3 SCREENS SUBROUTINE

The **Screens** subroutine is called each time around the mainline loop. It employs a 1-byte variable called **SCREEN** to identify the state of the display and, thereby, the state of the application. **SCREEN** is initially cleared to 0. Whatever startup message has been written to the screen initially will remain there until the pushbutton is first pushed, and the **Pbutton** subroutine returns with **ISC** = 1. At that time, **SCREEN** will be incremented to one. Each subsequent time that the **Screens** subroutine is entered with **ISC** = 1, **SCREEN** will be incremented to its next state. When **SCREEN** equals its maximum value and **ISC** = 1, **SCREEN** returns to **SCREEN** = 1 to recycle through its states.

In addition to cycling the value of **SCREEN**, the **Screens** subroutine provides the option of executing selected subroutines each time around the mainline loop that are specific to the state specified by the **SCREEN** number. For example, the QwikFlash instrument uses

- **SCREEN** = 1 to select frequency measurement
- **SCREEN** = 2 to select period measurement
- **SCREEN** = 3 to select maximum-pulse-width measurement

With **SCREEN** = 3, the CPU acts as if neither the frequency nor the period measurement routine is even installed in the microcontroller. Each time around the mainline loop, the CPU calls the maximum-pulse-width measurement subroutine. Every second, this subroutine updates the display with the maximum pulse width found to that point. If the pushbutton is quickly pressed and released, the maximum-pulse-width measurement is begun anew. If the pushbutton is pressed more slowly, the instrument switches measurement modes and initiates its frequency measurement mode.

The **Screens** subroutine is listed in Figure 12-2. It uses the **TESTSCREEN** macro (defined in Figure 12-2b) as follows

```
TESTSCREEN 3
```

This will set the **Z** bit if **SCREEN** = 3. Another macro, **DISPLAYONCE** (defined in Figure 12-2c), tests the **ISC** flag passed to it by the **Pbutton** subroutine. The flag is used by the **Screens** subroutine to display a constant string just once when the screen is first entered.

When power is first turned on, the **Initial** subroutine writes an initial startup message to the LCD, as shown in Figure 12-2d. That message remains displayed until the pushbutton is pressed, setting **ISC** and incrementing **SCREEN** as shown at the beginning of the **Screens** subroutine of Figure 12-2f. Then, the block of code that begins

```
TESTSCREEN 1
```

is executed. Because the **ISC** bit remains set, the constant string called **FreqStr** is displayed (just once). While this screen remains active, the **Frequency** subroutine is called each time around the mainline loop. The frequency measurement is thus carried out until a long press of the pushbutton changes the screen to **SCREEN** = 2. At that point, the period measurement begins.

Example 12-2 Add a fourth screen to the **Screens** subroutine. This new application is to call the **RateRPG** subroutine of Figure 8-4 and use it to increment or decrement **RPGCNT** and display **RPGCNT** as a binary number, using the **DISPLAY** macro of Section 7.8. A quick press of the pushbutton is to reset **RPGCNT** to zero.

Solution

The revised **Screens** subroutine is shown in Figure 12-3.

```
        SCREEN                    ;State of LCD subroutine
```

(a) Variable

```
TESTSCREEN  macro  literal
        movf  SCREEN,W
        sublw  literal
        endm
```

(b) Macro definition to set the **Z** bit if **SCREEN** =2 when "**TESTSCREEN 2**" is executed

```
DISPLAYONCE  macro  stringname
        btfss  PBSTATE,ISC
        bra  $+14
        MOVLF  high stringname, TBLPTRH
        MOVLF  low stringname, TBLPTRL
        call  DisplayC
        endm
```

(c) Macro definition to update LCD with a constant string just once when the screen is changed

```
        POINT  StrtStr          ;Display startup message
        rcall  DisplayC
        clrf  SCREEN            ;Initialize Screen's SCREEN variable
```

(d) Initialization

```
StrtStr db   "\x80Push PB \x00"  ;Startup screen
Clear1  db   "\x80        \x00"  ;Clear line 1
Clear2  db   "\xc0        \x00"  ;Clear line 2
FreqStr db   "\x80Freq kHz\x00"  ;Frequency instrument
PerStr  db   "\x80Per   us\x00"  ;Period instrument
PWmaxStr db   "\x80PWmax us\x00" ;Maximum pulse width instrument
```

(e) Constant string definitions

Figure 12-2 Screens subroutine

```
;;;;;;; Screens subroutine ;;;;;;;;;;;;;;;;;;;;;;;;;;;;;;;;;;;;;;;;;;;;;;;;;;;;;;;;
;
; This subroutine uses the ISC bit from the Pbutton subroutine to cycle the
; state of SCREEN and to take action based upon its value.
; Initially SCREEN=0, so that whatever screen is displayed by the Initial
; subroutine is not changed until a PB switch press.  Then the screen
; corresponding to SCREEN=1 is displayed.  Subsequent PB switch
; presses cycle through SCREEN=2, 3, etc., recycling back to SCREEN=1.

Screens
        IF_  PBSTATE,ISC == 1
          incf  SCREEN,F
          movlw  NumberOfScreens+1  ;Check if past last screen
          subwf  SCREEN,W
          IF_  .Z.               ;Cycle back to SCREEN=1
            MOVLF  1,SCREEN
          ENDIF_

          POINT  Clear1          ;Clear the display when switching screens
          rcall  DisplayC
          POINT  Clear2
          rcall  DisplayC
        ENDIF_

        TESTSCREEN  1
        IF_  .Z.
          DISPLAYONCE  FreqStr
          rcall  Frequency       ;Frequency-measuring utility
        ENDIF_

        TESTSCREEN  2
        IF_  .Z.
          DISPLAYONCE  PerStr
          rcall  Period          ;Period-measuring utility
        ENDIF_

        TESTSCREEN  3
        IF_  .Z.
          DISPLAYONCE  PWmaxStr
          rcall  PWmax           ;Maximmum-pulse-width measuring utility
          IF_  PBSTATE,ISA == 1 ;Fast pulse, toggle RA1
            btg  PORTA,RA1
          ENDIF_
        ENDIF_

        return

NumberOfScreens  equ  3          ;Change this value if new screens are added
```

(f) Subroutine

Figure 12-2 continued

12.4 P3.ASM, A SCREENS TEMPLATE PROGRAM

Figures 12-1 and 12-2 are useful for seeing the incremental changes needed to implement screens. For *using* screens, it is helpful to have a complete program from which to work. The P3.asm program of Figure 12-4 includes not only the code of Figures 12-1 and 12-2, but also the **RateRPG** subroutine of Figure 8-4. It is intended to serve as a template for further code development.

```
;;;;;;; Screens subroutine ;;;;;;;;;;;;;;;;;;;;;;;;;;;;;;;;;;;;;;;;;;;;;;;;;;;;;;;;
;
; This subroutine uses the ISC bit from the Pbutton subroutine to cycle the
; state of SCREEN and to take action based upon its value.
; Initially SCREEN=Ø, so that whatever screen is displayed by the Initial
; subroutine is not changed until a PB switch press.  Then the screen
; corresponding to SCREEN=1 is displayed.  Subsequent PB switch
; presses cycle through SCREEN=2, 3, etc., recycling back to SCREEN=1.

Screens
        IF_  PBSTATE,ISC == 1
          incf  SCREEN,F
          movlw  NumberOfScreens+1  ;Check if past last screen
          subwf  SCREEN,W
          IF_  .Z.                  ;Cycle back to SCREEN=1
            MOVLF  1,SCREEN
          ENDIF_

          POINT  Clear1             ;Clear the display when switching screens
          rcall  DisplayC
          POINT  Clear2
          rcall  DisplayC
        ENDIF_

        TESTSCREEN  1
        IF_  .Z.
          DISPLAYONCE  FreqStr
          rcall  Frequency          ;Frequency-measuring utility
        ENDIF_

        TESTSCREEN  2
        IF_  .Z.
          DISPLAYONCE  PerStr
          rcall  Period             ;Period-measuring utility
        ENDIF_

        TESTSCREEN  3
        IF_  .Z.
          DISPLAYONCE  PWmaxStr
          rcall  PWmax              ;Maximum-pulse-width measuring utility
          IF_  PBSTATE,ISA == 1 ;Fast pulse, toggle RA1
            btg  PORTA,RA1
          ENDIF_
        ENDIF_

        TESTSCREEN  4
        IF_  .Z.
          rcall  RateRPG            ;Decipher RPG inputs into DELRPG
          movf  DELRPG,W
          addwf  RPGCNT,F           ;Increment or decrement RPGCNT from RPG
          DISPLAY  RPGCNT           ; and display as a binary number
          IF_  PBSTATE,ISA == 1 ;Fast pulse, reset RPGCNT
            clrf  RPGCNT
          ENDIF_
        ENDIF_

        return

NumberOfScreens  equ  4             ;Change this value if new screens are added
```

Figure 12-3 Solution to Example 12-2

```
;;;;;;; P3 for QwikFlash board ;;;;;;;;;;;;;;;;;;;;;;;;;;;;;;;;;;;;;;;;;;;;;;;;;;
;
; Use 10 MHz crystal frequency.
; Use Timer0 for ten millisecond looptime.
; Blink "Alive" LED every two and a half seconds.
; Use pushbutton to exercise Screens utility.
;
;;;;;;; Program hierarchy ;;;;;;;;;;;;;;;;;;;;;;;;;;;;;;;;;;;;;;;;;;;;;;;;;;;;;
;
; Mainline
;   Initial
;     InitLCD
;       LoopTime
;     DisplayC
;       T40
;   BlinkAlive
;   Pbutton
;   Screens
;     DisplayC
;       T40
;     Frequency
;     Period
;     PWmax
;     RateRPG
;     ByteDisplay
;       DisplayC
;         T40
;       DisplayV
;         T40
;   LoopTime
;
;;;;;;; Assembler directives ;;;;;;;;;;;;;;;;;;;;;;;;;;;;;;;;;;;;;;;;;;;;;;;;;;

        list  P=PIC18F452, F=INHX32, C=160, N=0, ST=OFF, MM=OFF, R=DEC, X=ON
        #include P18F452.inc
        __CONFIG  _CONFIG1H, _HS_OSC_1H  ;HS oscillator
        __CONFIG  _CONFIG2L, _PWRT_ON_2L & _BOR_ON_2L & _BORV_42_2L  ;Reset
        __CONFIG  _CONFIG2H, _WDT_OFF_2H  ;Watchdog timer disabled
        __CONFIG  _CONFIG3H, _CCP2MX_ON_3H  ;CCP2 to RC1 (rather than to RB3)
        __CONFIG  _CONFIG4L, _LVP_OFF_4L  ;RB5 enabled for I/O
        errorlevel -314, -315    ;Ignore lfsr messages

;;;;;;; Variables ;;;;;;;;;;;;;;;;;;;;;;;;;;;;;;;;;;;;;;;;;;;;;;;;;;;;;;;;;;;;;

        cblock  0x000                ;Beginning of Access RAM
        TMR0LCOPY                    ;Copy of sixteen-bit Timer0 used by LoopTime
        TMR0HCOPY
        INTCONCOPY                   ;Copy of INTCON for LoopTime subroutine
        COUNT                        ;Counter available as local to subroutines
        TEMP                         ;Temporary local variable
        ALIVECNT                     ;Counter for blinking "Alive" LED
        BYTE                         ;Eight-bit byte to be displayed
        BYTESTR:10                   ;Display string for binary version of BYTE
        OLDPORTD                     ;Holds previous value of inputs
        DELRPG                       ;Generated by RPG
        RPGCNT                       ;Used to display RPG changes
        PBSTATE                      ;Control/status byte for pushbutton
        PBCOUNT                      ;Counter for measuring duration of press
        SCREEN                       ;State of LCD subroutine
        LOOP10                       ;Scale of ten loop counter
        THR                          ;Threshold value used by Pbutton
        endc

;;;;;;; Equates ;;;;;;;;;;;;;;;;;;;;;;;;;;;;;;;;;;;;;;;;;;;;;;;;;;;;;;;;;;;;;;;

ISC     equ  0                       ;Initiate screen change for slow press
ISA     equ  1                       ;Initiate secondary action for fast press
PDONE   equ  2                       ;Pushbutton action has been taken
OLDPB   equ  3                       ;Old state of pushbutton
NEWPB   equ  4                       ;New state of pushbutton

PBthres equ  30                      ;Pushbutton threshold for a long press
```

Figure 12-4 P3.asm file

```
;;;;;;; Macro definitions ;;;;;;;;;;;;;;;;;;;;;;;;;;;;;;;;;;;;;;;;;;;;;;;;;;;;

MOVLF   macro  literal,dest
        movlw  literal
        movwf  dest
        endm

POINT   macro  stringname
        MOVLF  high stringname, TBLPTRH
        MOVLF  low stringname, TBLPTRL
        endm

DISPLAY  macro  register
        movff  register,BYTE
        call  ByteDisplay
        endm

TESTSCREEN  macro  literal
        movf  SCREEN,W
        sublw  literal
        endm

DISPLAYONCE macro stringname
        btfss  PBSTATE,ISC
        bra  $+14
        MOVLF  high stringname, TBLPTRH
        MOVLF  low stringname, TBLPTRL
        call  DisplayC
        endm

;;;;;;; Vectors ;;;;;;;;;;;;;;;;;;;;;;;;;;;;;;;;;;;;;;;;;;;;;;;;;;;;;;;;;;;;;;

        org  0x0000             ;Reset vector
        nop
        goto  Mainline

        org  0x0008             ;High priority interrupt vector
        goto  $                 ;Trap

        org  0x0018             ;Low priority interrupt vector
        goto  $                 ;Trap

;;;;;;; Mainline program ;;;;;;;;;;;;;;;;;;;;;;;;;;;;;;;;;;;;;;;;;;;;;;;;;;;;;

Mainline
        rcall  Initial          ;Initialize everything
        LOOP_
          rcall  BlinkAlive     ;Blink "Alive" LED
          rcall  Pbutton        ;Check pushbutton
          rcall  Screens        ;Deal with SCREEN state
          rcall  LoopTime       ;Make looptime be ten milliseconds
        ENDLOOP_

;;;;;;; Initial subroutine ;;;;;;;;;;;;;;;;;;;;;;;;;;;;;;;;;;;;;;;;;;;;;;;;;;;
;
; This subroutine performs all initializations of variables and registers.

Initial
        MOVLF  B'10001110',ADCON1  ;Enable PORTA & PORTE digital I/O pins
        MOVLF  B'11100001',TRISA  ;Set I/O for PORTA
        MOVLF  B'11011100',TRISB  ;Set I/O for PORTB
        MOVLF  B'11010000',TRISC  ;Set I/O for PORTC
        MOVLF  B'00001111',TRISD  ;Set I/O for PORTD
        MOVLF  B'00000000',TRISE  ;Set I/O for PORTE
        MOVLF  B'10001000',T0CON  ;Set up Timer0 for a looptime of 10 ms
        MOVLF  B'00010000',PORTA  ;Turn off all four LEDs driven from PORTA
        rcall  InitLCD            ;Initialize LCD
        movff  PORTD,OLDPORTD     ;Initialize "old" value
        clrf  RPGCNT              ;Clear counter to be displayed
        MOVLF  B'00001000',PBSTATE  ;Initialize pushbutton state
        clrf  PBCOUNT             ;and pushbutton count
        POINT  StrtStr            ;Display startup message
        rcall  DisplayC
        clrf  SCREEN              ;Initialize Screen's SCREEN variable
        clrf  THR                 ;Initialize Pbutton's THR variable
        return
```

Figure 12-4 continued

```
;;;;;;; InitLCD subroutine ;;;;;;;;;;;;;;;;;;;;;;;;;;;;;;;;;;;;;;;;;;;;;;;;;;;;;;;;;;
;
; Initialize the Optrex 8x2 character LCD.
; First wait for Ø.1 second, to get past display's power-on reset time.

InitLCD
        MOVLF  1Ø,COUNT            ;Wait Ø.1 second
        REPEAT_
          rcall  LoopTime          ;Call LoopTime 1Ø times
          decf  COUNT,F
        UNTIL_  .Z.

        bcf  PORTE,Ø               ;RS=Ø for command
        POINT  LCDstr              ;Set up table pointer to initialization string
        tblrd*                     ;Get first byte from string into TABLAT
        REPEAT_
          bsf  PORTE,1             ;Drive E high
          movff  TABLAT,PORTD      ;Send upper nibble
          bcf  PORTE,1             ;Drive E low so LCD will process input
          rcall  LoopTime          ;Wait ten milliseconds
          bsf  PORTE,1             ;Drive E high
          swapf  TABLAT,W          ;Swap nibbles
          movwf  PORTD             ;Send lower nibble
          bcf  PORTE,1             ;Drive E low so LCD will process input
          rcall  LoopTime          ;Wait ten milliseconds
          tblrd+*                  ;Increment pointer and get next byte
          movf  TABLAT,F           ;Is it zero?
        UNTIL_  .Z.
        return

;;;;;;; T4Ø subroutine ;;;;;;;;;;;;;;;;;;;;;;;;;;;;;;;;;;;;;;;;;;;;;;;;;;;;;;;;;;;;;
;
; Pause for 4Ø microseconds  or 4Ø/Ø.4 = 1ØØ clock cycles.
; Assumes 1Ø/4 = 2.5 MHz internal clock rate.

T4Ø
        movlw  1ØØ/3               ;Each REPEAT loop takes 3 cycles
        movwf  COUNT
        REPEAT_
          decf  COUNT,F
        UNTIL_  .Z.
        return

;;;;;;;DisplayC subroutine;;;;;;;;;;;;;;;;;;;;;;;;;;;;;;;;;;;;;;;;;;;;;;;;;;;;;;;;;;
;
; This subroutine is called with TBLPTR containing the address of a constant
; display string.  It sends the bytes of the string to the LCD.  The first
; byte sets the cursor position.  The remaining bytes are displayed, beginning
; at that position.
; This subroutine expects a normal one-byte cursor-positioning code, Øxhh, or
; an occasionally used two-byte cursor-positioning code of the form ØxØØhh.

DisplayC
        bcf  PORTE,Ø               ;Drive RS pin low for cursor-positioning code
        tblrd*                     ;Get byte from string into TABLAT
        movf  TABLAT,F             ;Check for leading zero byte
        IF_  .Z.
          tblrd+*                  ;If zero, get next byte
        ENDIF_
        REPEAT_
          bsf  PORTE,1             ;Drive E pin high
          movff  TABLAT,PORTD      ;Send upper nibble
          bcf  PORTE,1             ;Drive E pin low so LCD will accept nibble
          bsf  PORTE,1             ;Drive E pin high again
          swapf  TABLAT,W          ;Swap nibbles
          movwf  PORTD             ;Write lower nibble
          bcf  PORTE,1             ;Drive E pin low so LCD will process byte
          rcall  T4Ø               ;Wait 4Ø usec
          bsf  PORTE,Ø             ;Drive RS pin high for displayable characters
          tblrd+*                  ;Increment pointer, then get next byte
          movf  TABLAT,F           ;Is it zero?
        UNTIL_  .Z.
        return
```

Figure 12-4 continued

```
;;;;;;; DisplayV subroutine ;;;;;;;;;;;;;;;;;;;;;;;;;;;;;;;;;;;;;;;;;;;;;;;;;;;;;
;
; This subroutine is called with FSRØ containing the address of a variable
; display string.  It sends the bytes of the string to the LCD.  The first
; byte sets the cursor position.  The remaining bytes are displayed, beginning
; at that position.

DisplayV
        bcf  PORTE,Ø             ;Drive RS pin low for cursor positioning code
        REPEAT_
          bsf  PORTE,1           ;Drive E pin high
          movff  INDFØ,PORTD     ;Send upper nibble
          bcf  PORTE,1           ;Drive E pin low so LCD will accept nibble
          bsf  PORTE,1           ;Drive E pin high again
          swapf  INDFØ,W         ;Swap nibbles
          movwf  PORTD           ;Write lower nibble
          bcf  PORTE,1           ;Drive E pin low so LCD will process byte
          rcall  T4Ø             ;Wait 4Ø usec
          bsf  PORTE,Ø           ;Drive RS pin high for displayable characters
          movf  PREINCØ,W        ;Increment pointer, then get next byte
        UNTIL_  .Z.              ;Is it zero?
       return

;;;;;;; BlinkAlive subroutine ;;;;;;;;;;;;;;;;;;;;;;;;;;;;;;;;;;;;;;;;;;;;;;;;;;;
;
; This subroutine briefly blinks the LED next to the PIC every two-and-a-half
; seconds.

BlinkAlive
        bsf  PORTA,RA4           ;Turn off LED
        decf  ALIVECNT,F         ;Decrement loop counter and return if not zero
        IF_  .Z.
          MOVLF  25Ø,ALIVECNT    ;Reinitialize ALIVECNT
          bcf  PORTA,RA4         ;Turn on LED for ten milliseconds every 2.5 sec
        ENDIF_
        return

;;;;;;; LoopTime subroutine ;;;;;;;;;;;;;;;;;;;;;;;;;;;;;;;;;;;;;;;;;;;;;;;;;;;;;
;
; This subroutine waits for TimerØ to complete its ten millisecond count
; sequence. It does so by waiting for sixteen-bit TimerØ to roll over. To obtain
; a period of precisely 1ØØØØ/Ø.4 = 25ØØØ clock periods, it needs to remove
; 65536-25ØØØ or 4Ø536 counts from the sixteen-bit count sequence.  The
; algorithm below first copies TimerØ to RAM, adds "Bignum" to the copy ,and
; then writes the result back to TimerØ. It actually needs to add somewhat more
; counts to TimerØ than 40536.  The extra number of 12+2 counts added into
; "Bignum" makes the precise correction.

Bignum  equu     65536-25ØØØ+12+2

LoopTime
        REPEAT_
        UNTIL_  INTCON,TMRØIF == 1  ;Wait until ten milliseconds are up
        movff  INTCON,INTCONCOPY  ;Disable all interrupts to CPU
        bcf  INTCON,GIEH
        movff  TMRØL,TMRØLCOPY  ;Read 16-bit counter at this moment
        movff  TMRØH,TMRØHCOPY
        movlw  low  Bignum
        addwf  TMRØLCOPY,F
        movlw  high  Bignum
        addwfc  TMRØHCOPY,F
        movff  TMRØHCOPY,TMRØH
        movff  TMRØLCOPY,TMRØL  ;Write 16-bit counter at this moment
        movf  INTCONCOPY,W      ;Restore GIEH interrupt enable bit
        andlw  B'1ØØØØØØØ'
        iorwf  INTCON,F
        bcf  INTCON,TMRØIF      ;Clear TimerØ flag
        return
```

Figure 12-4 continued

```
;;;;;;; ByteDisplay subroutine ;;;;;;;;;;;;;;;;;;;;;;;;;;;;;;;;;;;;;;;;;;;;;;;;
;
; Display whatever is in BYTE as a binary number.

ByteDisplay
        POINT  BYTE_1               ;Display "BYTE="
        rcall  DisplayC
        lfsr  0,BYTESTR+8
        REPEAT_
          clrf  WREG
          rrcf  BYTE,F              ;Move bit into carry
          rlcf  WREG,F              ;and from there into WREG
          iorlw  0x30               ;Convert to ASCII
          movwf  POSTDEC0           ; and move to string
          movf  FSR0L,W             ;Done?
          sublw  low BYTESTR
        UNTIL_  .Z.
        lfsr  0,BYTESTR             ;Set pointer to display string
        MOVLF  0xc0,BYTESTR         ;Add cursor-positioning code
        clrf  BYTESTR+9             ;and end-of-string terminator
        rcall  DisplayV
        return

;;;;;;; RateRPG subroutine ;;;;;;;;;;;;;;;;;;;;;;;;;;;;;;;;;;;;;;;;;;;;;;;;;;;
;
; This subroutine decyphers RPG changes into values of DELRPG.
; DELRPG = +2 for fast CW change, +1 for slow CW change, 0 for no change,
;          -1 for slow CCW change and -2 for fast CCW change.

Threshold equ  3                    ;Value to distinguish between slow and fast

RateRPG
        bcf  PORTA,RA2              ;Turn LED off
        clrf  DELRPG                ;Clear for "no change" return value
        movf  PORTD,W               ;Copy PORTD into W
        movwf  TEMP                 ; and TEMP
        xorwf  OLDPORTD,W           ;Any change?
        andlw  B'00000011'          ;If not, set Z flag
        IF_  .NZ.                   ;If the two bits have changed then...
          rrcf  OLDPORTD,W          ;Form what a CCW change would produce
          IF_  .C.                  ;Make new bit 1 = complement of old bit 0
            bcf  WREG,1
          ELSE_
            bsf  WREG,1
          ENDIF_
          xorwf  TEMP,W             ;Did the RPG actually change to this output?
          andlw  B'00000011'
          IF_  .Z.                  ;If so, then change  DELRPG to -1 for CCW
            decf  DELRPG,F
            movf  THR,F
            IF_  .NZ.
              decf  DELRPG,F        ;If fast turning, decrement again
              bsf  PORTA,RA2        ;Turn LED on
            ENDIF_
          ELSE_                     ;Otherwise, change DELRPG to  +1 for CW
            incf  DELRPG,F
            movf  THR,F
            IF_  .NZ.
              incf  DELRPG,F        ;If fast turning, increment again
              bsf  PORTA,RA2        ;Turn LED on
            ENDIF_
          ENDIF_
          MOVLF  Threshold+1,THR  ;Reinitialize THR
        ENDIF_
        movf  THR,F                 ;Does THR equal zero
        IF_  .NZ.                   ;If not, then decrement it
          decf  THR,F
        ENDIF_
        movff  TEMP,OLDPORTD        ;Save PORTD as OLDPORTD for ten ms from now
        return
```

Figure 12-4 continued

```
;;;;;;; Pbutton subroutine ;;;;;;;;;;;;;;;;;;;;;;;;;;;;;;;;;;;;;;;;;;;;;;;;;;;
;
; This subroutine sorts out long and short pushbutton presses into two outputs:
;       ISC=1: Initiate screen change for slow press
;       ISA=1: Initiate secondary action for fast press
;       PDONE=1: One of the above actions has occurred for this press

Pbutton
        bcf PBSTATE,ISC           ;Clear Initiate Screen Change bit (if set)
        bcf  PBSTATE,ISA          ;Clear Initiate Secondary Action bit (if set)
        IF_  PORTD,RD3 == 1       ;Copy pushbutton state to NEWPB
          bsf  PBSTATE,NEWPB
        ELSE_
          bcf  PBSTATE,NEWPB
        ENDIF_

        IF_  PBSTATE,OLDPB == 1 ;Look for leading edge (OLDPB=1, NEWPB=Ø)
          IF_  PBSTATE,NEWPB == Ø
             MOVLF  PBthres,PBCOUNT  ;Start counter
          ENDIF_
        ENDIF_

        IF_  PBSTATE,NEWPB == Ø ;Pushbutton is still pressed
          movf  PBCOUNT,F
          IF_  .Z.                ;and counter has passed threshold
            IF_  PBSTATE,PDONE == Ø ;and no action has yet been taken
              bsf  PBSTATE,ISC    ;Initiate screen change
              bsf  PBSTATE,PDONE  ;Done with pulse
            ENDIF_
          ENDIF_
        ELSE_                     ;Pushbutton has been released
          bcf  PBSTATE,PDONE      ;so clear PDONE
        ENDIF_

        IF_  PBSTATE,OLDPB == Ø ;Look for trailing edge (OLDPB=Ø, NEWPB=1)
          IF_  PBSTATE,NEWPB == 1
            movf  PBCOUNT,F
            IF_  .NZ.             ;Fast pulse
              bsf  PBSTATE,ISA    ;Initiate secondary action
            ENDIF_
            bcf  PBSTATE,PDONE    ;Done with pulse
            clrf  PBCOUNT         ;Finish counting
          ENDIF_
        ENDIF_
        movf  PBCOUNT,F           ;Has counter reached zero?
        IF_  .NZ.                 ;If not, then decrement it
          decf  PBCOUNT,F
        ENDIF_

        IF_  PBSTATE,NEWPB == 1 ;Copy NEWPB to OLDPB
          bsf  PBSTATE,OLDPB
        ELSE_
          bcf  PBSTATE,OLDPB
        ENDIF_
        return
```

Figure 12-4 continued

```
;;;;;;; Screens subroutine ;;;;;;;;;;;;;;;;;;;;;;;;;;;;;;;;;;;;;;;;;;;;;;;;;;;;
;
; This subroutine uses the ISC bit from the Pbutton subroutine to cycle the
; state of SCREEN and to take action based upon its value.
; Initially SCREEN=0, so that whatever screen is displayed by the Initial
; subroutine is not changed until a PB switch press.  Then the screen
; corresponding to SCREEN=1 is displayed.  Subsequent PB switch
; presses cycle through SCREEN=2, 3, etc., recycling back to SCREEN=1.

Screens
        IF_  PBSTATE,ISC == 1
          incf  SCREEN,F
          movlw  NumberOfScreens+1  ;Check if past last screen
          subwf  SCREEN,W
          IF_  .Z.              ;Cycle back to SCREEN=1
            MOVLF  1,SCREEN
          ENDIF_

          POINT  Clear1         ;Clear the display when switching screens
          rcall  DisplayC
          POINT  Clear2
          rcall  DisplayC
        ENDIF_

        TESTSCREEN  1
        IF_  .Z.
          DISPLAYONCE  FreqStr
          rcall  Frequency      ;Frequency-measuring utility
        ENDIF_

        TESTSCREEN  2
        IF_  .Z.
          DISPLAYONCE  PerStr
          rcall  Period         ;Period-measuring utility
        ENDIF_

        TESTSCREEN  3
        IF_  .Z.
          DISPLAYONCE  PWmaxStr
          rcall  PWmax          ;Maximum-pulse-width measuring utility
          IF_  PBSTATE,ISA == 1 ;Fast pulse, toggle RA1
            btg  PORTA,RA1
          ENDIF_
        ENDIF_

        TESTSCREEN 4
        IF_  .Z.
          rcall  RateRPG        ;Decipher RPG inputs into DELRPG
          movf  DELRPG,W
          addwf  RPGCNT,F       ;Increment or decrement RPGCNT from RPG
          DISPLAY  RPGCNT       ; and display as a binary number
          IF_  PBSTATE,ISA == 1 ;Fast pulse, reset RPGCNT
            clrf  RPGCNT
          ENDIF_
        ENDIF_

        return

NumberOfScreens  equ  4         ;Change this value if new screens are added

;;;;;;; Stubs for measurement subroutines ;;;;;;;;;;;;;;;;;;;;;;;;;;;;;;;;;;;;

Frequency  return
Period  return
PWmax  return

;;;;;;; Constant strings ;;;;;;;;;;;;;;;;;;;;;;;;;;;;;;;;;;;;;;;;;;;;;;;;;;;;;

LCDstr  db  0x33,0x32,0x28,0x01,0x0c,0x06,0x00  ;Initialization string for LCD
BYTE_1  db  "\x80BYTE=    \x00"  ;Write "BYTE=" to first line of LCD
StrtStr db  "\x80Push PB \x00"  ;Startup screen
Clear1  db  "\x80        \x00"  ;Clear line 1
Clear2  db  "\xc0        \x00"  ;Clear line 2
FreqStr db  "\x80Freq kHz\x00"  ;Frequency instrument
PerStr  db  "\x80Per   us\x00"  ;Period instrument
PWmaxStr db  "\x80PWmax us\x00"  ;Maximum pulse width instrument

        end
```

Figure 12-4 continued

PROBLEMS

12-1 Pbutton subroutine If the pushbutton were connected to bit 5 of **PORTB** instead of bit 3 of **PORTD**, what change(s) would need to be made so that the **Pbutton** subroutine would operate correctly?

12-2 Contact bounce The pushbutton on the QwikFlash board has a maximum contact bounce time specification of 5 milliseconds.

(a) Note that the **Pbutton** subroutine reads the pushbutton just once, saving its value as the **NEWPB** bit in the **PBSTATE** variable. What will be the effect of reading the pushbutton while it is exhibiting contact bounce as its output changes from a 1 to a 0 (the leading edge of the pushbutton pulse)? Is it possible for this single pushbutton press to be interpreted as either zero or two key presses? Explain.
(b) Answer part (a) if the pushbutton exhibits contact bounce as its output changes from a 0 to a 1 (the trailing edge of the pushbutton pulse).
(c) Instead of first copying the pushbutton state into **NEWPB**, and then using **NEWPB** thereafter, the four places in **Pbutton** that use **NEWPB** could, instead, have read bit **RD3** of **PORTD** four separate times. Describe an example, if possible, where contact bounce could lead a single key press to be interpreted as no key press.
(d) Answer part (c) for a single key press to be interpreted as two key presses.

12-3 Pbutton modification What modification can be made to the **Pbutton** subroutine so that a "slow" press becomes any press longer than 0.2 seconds?

12-4 Threshold experiment A good procedure for deciding on the duration of a pushbutton press that distinguishes between a slow press and a fast press is to have a method to vary the threshold while the program is running. Modify the code of Figure 12-4 so that one LED blinks briefly each time **ISC** is set and another LED blinks briefly each time **ISA** is set. Use the RPG to vary **RPGCNT.** Display and use its value as the threshold between slow and fast pushbutton presses. What value seems about right?

12-5 Pbutton subroutine The second, third, and fourth blocks of code in the **Pbutton** subroutine look for

- The leading edge of the pushbutton pulse
- A "pushbutton still pressed" condition
- The trailing edge of the pulse

Does the sequence of these three blocks matter? Explain your answer.

12-6 Screens program Consider the **Screens** subroutine of Figure 12-3. Assume screen 4 is being executed and the **RPG** has been turned such that the display now shows the value of **RPGCNT** as

```
11001111
```

(a) If the pushbutton is pressed repeatedly to change screens until once again screen 4 is displayed, will **RPGCNT**'s value still be displayed as

```
11001111
```

(b) Would it have made any difference to this value if the RPG had been turned while passing through screen 2? Explain.

(c) Modify the code for screen 4, so that when changing to screen 4, the value of **RPGCNT** will be initialized to

```
00000000
```

Chapter

13

TIME-INTERVAL MEASUREMENTS

13.1 OVERVIEW

A task common to many microcontroller applications is the measurement of a time interval. This might be an internally generated interval such as the duration of a subroutine. It might be the interval between two edges of a waveform, or between the edge of a "triggering" signal and the delayed output edge of a responding device. The PIC18F452 offers superb capabilities for carrying out time-interval measurements. This chapter will be devoted to this widely used and fundamentally important topic.

13.2 TIMER1 AND INTERNAL MEASUREMENTS

For internal time-interval measurements, the circuitry of Timer1, shown in Figure 13-1a, is quite similar to that of Timer0, shown in Figures 5-1 and 5-2. Not shown is the optional use of an external clock input, to be discussed in Section 20.10. Also not shown is Timer1's overflow flag and interrupt mechanism, which will be discussed in Section 13.4, to extend timing measurements to time intervals requiring 3 bytes for their expression. Finally, Timer1's interactions with its closely coupled CCP1 facility will be deferred to Section 13.5 for *external* time-interval measurements.

Reads from, and writes to, the 16-bit **TMR1H:TMR1L** register are supported by the same mechanism used to read from and write to **TMR0H:TMR0L**. As was discussed in Section 5.2, at the precise moment that the lower byte of the counter is read, the upper byte is copied into a buffer register. Thus, a subsequent read of **TMR1H** will yield a correct value corresponding to the earlier moment when **TMR1L** was read. This is true even if an intervening interrupt occurred, and the upper byte of the

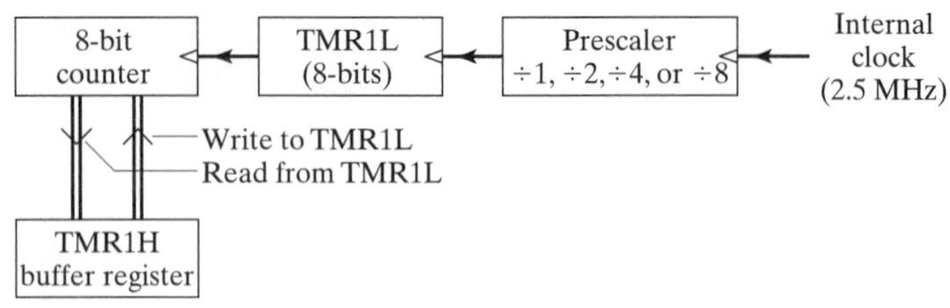

(a) Counter configuration

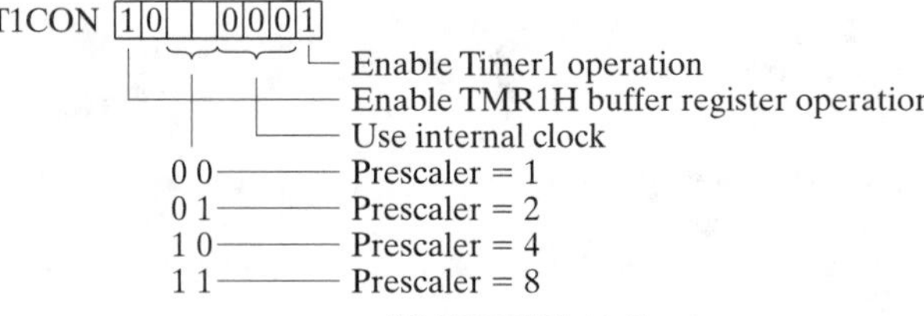

(b) **T1CON** initialization

Prescaler	Timing Resolution	Maximum Measurement
÷ 1	0.4 μs	26 ms
÷ 2	0.8 μs	52 ms
÷ 4	1.6 μs	104 ms
÷ 8	3.2 μs	208 ms

(c) Role of prescaler

Figure 13-1 Timer1 for time-interval measurements.

counter (but not the buffer register) incremented between the read of **TMR1L** and **TMR1H**. Even without an intervening interrupt, a read of **TMR1L** when its value is 0xff followed by a read of **TMR1H** will yield the correct 16-bit value even though the upper byte of the counter (but, again, not the buffer register) incremented between the two reads.

The maximum interval to be measured can be extended in either of two ways. The simpler of the two is to initialize Timer1's control register, **T1CON**, to select an appropriate prescaler value, as specified in Figures 13-1b and c. Selecting a divider value of 1 will yield time-interval measurements of up to 26 milliseconds (with an internal clock of 2.5 MHz) having a measurement resolution of 0.4 microseconds, the internal clock period of the chip. Selecting a larger divider will yield a resolution of 3.2 microseconds for measurements up to 208 milliseconds.

In Section 13.4, Timer1 will be extended from its inherent 2-byte counter to a 3-byte counter by incrementing a 1-byte RAM variable each time the 2-byte counter rolls over from 0xffff to 0x0000. This will allow time-interval measurements to extend beyond 6 seconds, even with 0.4 microsecond resolution.

One measurement of interest is the amount of time it takes to execute a specific subroutine. A more useful measurement result, usually, is the *maximum* time it takes to execute the subroutine as its input parameters are varied.

Example 13-1 Microchip's **FXD0808U** subroutine will divide an 8-bit unsigned number by an 8-bit unsigned number. It will be used to convert a number as large as 255 into an ASCII string, using successive divides by 10. How long might an experiment take to check the published maximum execution time of this subroutine for *all* parameter values when it is used to divide a 1-byte number by 10?

Solution

The maximum execution time of the **FXD0808U** subroutine in this case can be found by trying all 256 cases and picking out the maximum. Even if each trial takes the published maximum of 31 cycles (i.e., 12.4 microseconds) for *all* parameter values, the maximum time will be found in 3.2 milliseconds.

Example 13-2 How long will it take to check the maximum execution time for *all* parameter variations?

Solution

Even if the time to try each divisor possibility on all 256 dividend values takes 3.2 milliseconds, the total time will be less than a second.

One of the crowning achievements of the engineering profession is its development of the very tools needed to carry out its various design activities. Two tools of help here are a **START** macro and a **STOP** macro that can be used in the code sequence

```
START
rcall   FXD0808U
STOP
```

to measure the execution time to the code between two macros. The **START** macro, listed in Figure 13-2b, simply copies the value read from **TMR1H:TMR1L** to the 2-byte RAM variable **TIMEH:TIMEL**. The **STOP** macro of Figure 13-2c has a two-step job. First, it subtracts the value collected by the **START** macro from a new "snapshot" of the timer, taken at the moment that the

```
subwf   TMR1L,W
```

instruction is executed. Second, it subtracts a small correction, **Magic**. such that the sequence

```
START
STOP
```

produces a value of 0 in **TIMEH:TIMEL.**

Example 13-3 Determine the correction value, **Magic**.

Solution

One way to get this value is to run the **START/STOP** macros with no intervening code and with **Magic** = 0. The small resulting value in **TIMEL** is equal to the required value of **Magic**. That is, if the word **Magic** is replaced by this value, then the execution of **START** followed immediately by **STOP** will yield a result of **TIMEH:TIMEL** = 0.

Another way to determine the value of **Magic** is to count cycles from the read of **TMR1L** in the **START** macro to the read of **TMR1L** in the **STOP** macro. As shown in Figure 13-2d, this produces **Magic** = 5.

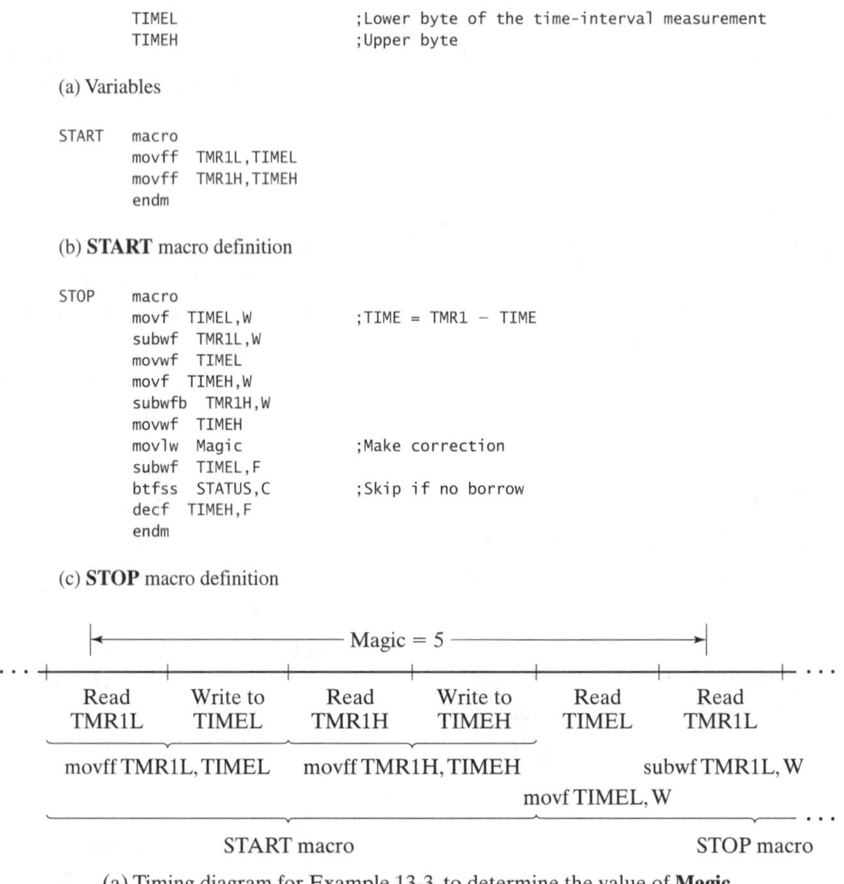

```
        TIMEL                   ;Lower byte of the time-interval measurement
        TIMEH                   ;Upper byte
```

(a) Variables

```
START   macro
        movff  TMR1L,TIMEL
        movff  TMR1H,TIMEH
        endm
```

(b) **START** macro definition

```
STOP    macro
        movf  TIMEL,W           ;TIME = TMR1 - TIME
        subwf  TMR1L,W
        movwf  TIMEL
        movf  TIMEH,W
        subwfb  TMR1H,W
        movwf  TIMEH
        movlw  Magic            ;Make correction
        subwf  TIMEL,F
        btfss  STATUS,C         ;Skip if no borrow
        decf  TIMEH,F
        endm
```

(c) **STOP** macro definition

(a) Timing diagram for Example 13-3, to determine the value of **Magic**

Figure 13-2 START and **STOP** macro definitions

Measuring the maximum of successively collected time intervals requires that each new value be compared with the previous high value. The new value is discarded until it exceeds the previous high, in which case it becomes the new high. Figure 13-3 lists a **MAX** macro to form the maximum in **MAXH:MAXL**.

13.3 DISPLAYMAX SUBROUTINE

In this section, a **DisplayMax** subroutine will be developed. It will make use of two general-purpose utility subroutines to carry out its function:

- **CyclesToMicrosec**—This subroutine converts the number of instruction cycles in the 3-byte variable **AARGB0:AARGB1:AARGB2** into microseconds. It assumes that each cycle lasts 0.4 microseconds. For its use within the **DisplayMax** subroutine, the 2-byte **MAXH:MAXL** will be copied into **AARGB1:AARGB2**, the upper byte **AARGB0** will be cleared, and then the

```
        MAXL                        ;Lower byte of the maximum time-interval
        MAXH                        ;Upper byte
```

(a) Variables

```
        clrf  MAXL                  ;Start maximum time interval at zero
        clrf  MAXH
```

(b) Initialization

```
MAX     macro
        movf  TIMEL,W               ;Form MAX - TIME
        subwf  MAXL,W
        movf  TIMEH,W
        subwfb  MAXH,W
        btfss  STATUS,C             ;If TIME > MAX, then update MAX with TIME
        movff  TIMEL,MAXL
        btfss  STATUS,C
        movff  TIMEH,MAXH
        endm
```

(c) The macro definition

Figure 13-3 MAX macro definition.

CyclesToMicrosec subroutine will be called. The number of microseconds will be returned in **AARGB0:AARGB1:AARGB2**.

- **DecimalDisplay**—This subroutine will take the 3-byte number in **AARGB0:AARGB1:AARGB2** and display its value (ranging from 0 to 6,710,886 microseconds) on the second line of the QwikFlash display.

The **CyclesToMicrosec** subroutine of Figure 13-4 carries out the conversion

$$\text{Microseconds} = (\text{Cycles}/10) \times 4$$

Microchip's **FXD2408U** subroutine will divide the number of cycles in **AARGB0:AARGB1:AARGB2** by the number 10 in **BARGB0**. It returns a quotient in **AARGB0:AARGB1:AARGB2** and a remainder with a value between 0 and 9 in **REMB0**. The quotient is then multiplied by 2 by shifting it left one place. Repeating this gives the needed

$$\text{Quotient} \times 4$$

However, the remainder, **REMB0**, from the division by 10 when multiplied by 4 also contributes to the total result. For example, if **REMB0** = 4, then

$$\textbf{REMB0} \times 4 = 16$$

This should be rounded to the nearest multiple of 10,

$$\textbf{REMB0} \times 4 = 20$$

and then the tens digit added to

$$\text{Quotient} \times 4$$

formed earlier. The **CyclesToMicrosec** subroutine treats the **REMB0** value as a BCD number and doubles it twice by adding it to itself twice, using BCD addition. Five is added to the result, using BCD addition, so that the tens digit will represent the correct rounded value. The units digit is cleared and the tens digit is swapped to the units digit position in **WREG**. This is added to **AARGB0:AARGB1:AARGB2** to produce the final result.

```
;;;;;;; CyclesToMicrosec subroutine ;;;;;;;;;;;;;;;;;;;;;;;;;;;;;;;;;;;;;;;;;;;;;;;;;
;
;  This subroutine converts AARGB0:AARGB1:AARGB2 from cycles to microseconds.
;            Microseconds = 0.4 Cycles = (Cycles/10)x4

CyclesToMicrosec
        MOVLF  10,BARGB0        ;Divide by 10
        call  FXD2408U
        bcf  STATUS,C           ;Multiply by two
        rlcf  AARGB2,F
        rlcf  AARGB1,F
        rlcf  AARGB0,F
        rlcf  AARGB2,F          ;Do it again
        rlcf  AARGB1,F
        rlcf  AARGB0,F
        movf  REMB0,W           ;Get remainder and double it
        addwf  WREG,W           ; as a BCD number
        daw
        addwf  WREG,W           ;Double it again
        daw
        addlw  5                ;Round off
        daw
        andlw  0xf0             ;Keep just tens digit
        swapf  WREG,W           ; and move it to the units position
        addwf  AARGB2,F         ; and add it to AARG
        clrf  WREG
        addwfc  AARGB1,F
        addwfc  AARGB0,F
        return
```

Figure 13-4 CyclesToMicrosec subroutine.

The other general-purpose utility subroutine, **DecimalDisplay**, does a job similar to that of the **ByteDisplay** subroutine of Figure 7-18e, which writes a binary representation of the variable, **BYTE**, to the LCD. The **DecimalDisplay** subroutine writes a decimal representation of **AARGB0:AARGB1:AARGB2** to the second line of the display.

As shown in Figure 13-5, the **DecimalDisplay** subroutine divides the number by 10, converts the one-digit remainder to ASCII, and inserts it into the string at the right-most character position. This is repeated seven more times to fill the eight character positions of the string.

Next, leading zeros are blanked. The cursor-positioning code for the second line of the LCD is written to the beginning of the string and the ‹EOS› character (0x00) is tacked onto the end of the string. Finally, the string is sent to the display.

Given the **CyclesToMicrosec** and the **DecimalDisplay** subroutines as building blocks, the **DisplayMax** subroutine to display the value of **MAXH:MAXL** is easily obtained. It is shown in Figure 13-6.

13.4 EXTENDED INTERNAL MEASUREMENTS

The range of Timer1 can be extended by incrementing a 1-byte RAM variable, **TMR1X** ("Timer1 extension"), each time **TMR1H:TMR1L** overflows from 0xffff to 0x0000. At that moment, the **TMR1IF** flag will be set, as shown in Figure 13-7, and can be used to generate either a high-priority or a low-priority interrupt. If no other interrupt sources require fast service, then the simplicity of a single high-priority interrupt service routine affords the solution shown in Figure 13-8.

```
;;;;;;; DecimalDisplay subroutine ;;;;;;;;;;;;;;;;;;;;;;;;;;;;;;;;;;;;;;;;;;;;;;
;
; Display whatever is in AARGBØ:AARGB1:AARGB2 as a decimal number on line 2
; of the LCD

DecimalDisplay
        lfsr  Ø,BYTESTR+8
        REPEAT_
          MOVLF  1Ø,BARGBØ        ;Divide AARG by ten
          call  FXD24Ø8U
          movf  REMBØ,W           ;Get digit
          iorlw  Øx3Ø             ;Convert to ASCII
          movwf  POSTDECØ         ; and move to string
          movf  FSRØL,W           ;Done?
          sublw  low BYTESTR
        UNTIL_  .Z.

        REPEAT_                   ;Blank leading zeros
          movlw  A'Ø'             ;ASCII code for zero
          subwf  PREINCØ,W        ;Leading zero?
          IF_  .Z.                ;If so, then blank it
            MOVLF  A' ',INDFØ
          ELSE_                   ;Otherwise, done with blanking
            BREAK_
          ENDIF_
          movf  FSRØL,W           ;In any case, stop at least-significant digit
          sublw  low BYTESTR+7
        UNTIL_  .Z.

        lfsr  Ø,BYTESTR           ;Set pointer to display string
        MOVLF  ØxcØ,BYTESTR       ;Add cursor-positioning code
        clrf  BYTESTR+9           ;and end-of-string terminator
        rcall  DisplayV
        return
```

Figure 13-5 DecimalDisplay subroutine.

```
;;;;;;; DisplayMax subroutine ;;;;;;;;;;;;;;;;;;;;;;;;;;;;;;;;;;;;;;;;;;;;;;;;;;
;
; This subroutine takes MAXH:MAXL, converts it to microseconds, and displays
; it on the second line of the LCD.

DisplayMax
        movff  MAXL,AARGB2
        movff  MAXH,AARGB1
        clrf  AARGBØ
        rcall  CyclesToMicrosec
        rcall  DecimalDisplay
        return
```

Figure 13-6 DisplayMax subroutine.

Reading the 3-byte value of **TMR1X:TMR1H:TMR1L** requires care to obtain a correct reading under worst-case circumstances.

Example 13-4 Assuming that the 3 bytes are read in the order **TMR1L**, **TMR1H**, and *then* **TMR1X**, give an example of an invalid reading.

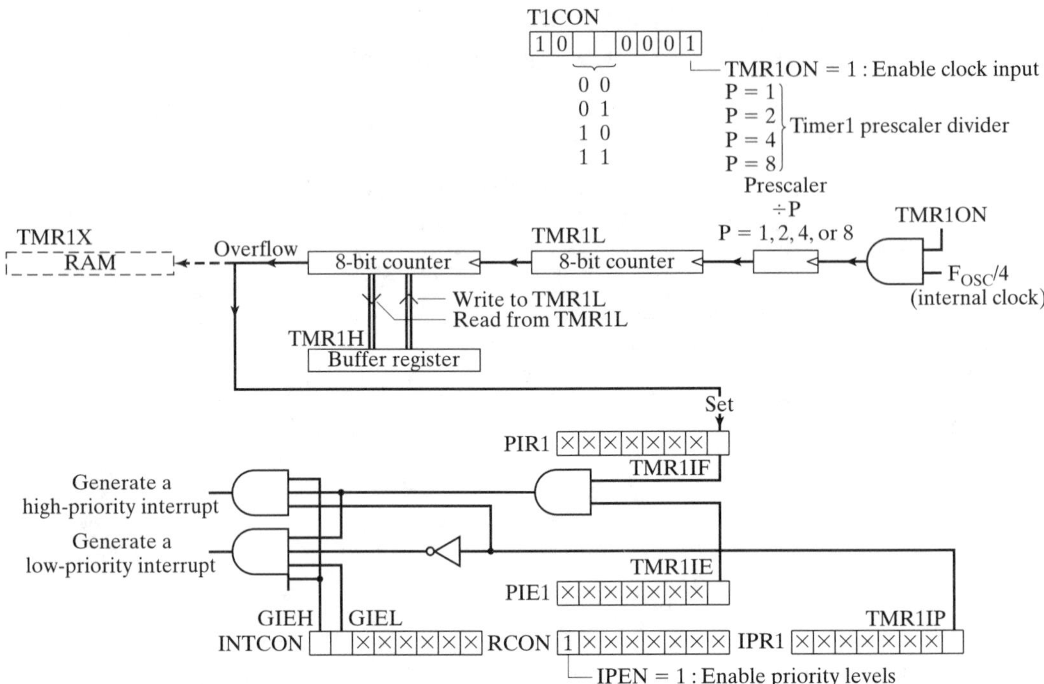

Figure 13-7 Timer1 for extended time-interval measurements.

```
TMR1X                   ;Extension of TMR1
```

(a) Variable

```
bsf  IPR1,TMR1IP        ;Assign high priority to TMR1 overflow interrupt
bcf  PIR1,TMR1IF        ;Clear flag
bsf  PIE1,TMR1IE        ;Enable TMR1 overflow interrupts
bsf  RCON,IPEN          ;Enable high/low interrupt structure
bsf  INTCON,GIEH        ;Enable high priority interrupts to CPU
return
```

(b) Last six instructions of the **Initial** subroutine, setting up the high-priority interrupt

```
org  0x0008             ;High priority interrupt vector
bcf  PIR1,TMR1IF        ;Clear flag
incf  TMR1X,F           ;and increment TMR1 extension
retfie  FAST
```

(c) High-priority interrupt service routine

Figure 13-8 Incrementing **TMR1X**, the extension of **TMR1H:TMR1L**.

Solution

If the three registers are read in this order, and produce a hex value of 35:ff:ff, the correct value is actually 34:ff:ff. The interrupt occurring as the hardware counter rolls over increments **TMR1X** from 0x34 to 0x35. Therefore, by the time **TMR1X** is read, the wrong value is read.

A solution to this ambiguity is to read the 3 bytes in the order **TMR1X**, **TMR1L**, **TMR1H**. If the most-significant bit (MSb) of **TMR1H** is 1, then the **TMR1X** value is valid because it was read sometime during the 32,768 counts before the overflow, when **TMR1H:TMR1L** was equal to B'1bbbbbbb bbbbbbbb'. On the other hand, if the MSb of **TMR1H** is 0, the value of **TMR1X** has the possibility of being invalid. This would be the case if the 3-byte hex number were read as 43:00:00 because the 0x43 was read first, before the hardware counter rolled over. The correct value of the counter at the instant that **TMR1L** was read is 44:00:00. A correct reading is assured when the MSb of **TMR1H** is 0 if **TMR1X** is simply read again. Observe that the instruction sequence

```
movf   TMR1H,W
movwf   TIMEH
```

will set the **STATUS** register's **N** bit if the MSb of **TMR1H** is set, while at the same time copying **TMR1H** to **TIMEH**. These considerations lead to the **STARTX** macro of Figure 13-9c, which copies the 3-byte **TMR1** (i.e., **TMR1X:TMR1H:TMR1L**) to the 3-byte RAM variable **TIME** (i.e., **TIMEX:TIMEH:TIMEL**).

The **STOPX** macro determines the number of cycles that have been executed since the **STARTX** macro was executed, putting this value into the 3-byte variable, **TIME**. It first reads **TMR1** into **TMR1BUF**. Then it subtracts **TIME** (collected by the **STARTX** macro) from **TMR1BUF**, putting the result into **TIME**. Finally, it subtracts from **TIME** the "Magic number," 9, so that the back-to-back execution of

```
STARTX
STOPX
```

will produce **TIME** = 0.

The **MAX3** macro ratchets the 3-byte **MAX** variable (i.e., **MAXX:MAXH:MAXL**) up to the maximum value of **TIME**. When a new value of **TIME** is formed, it is compared with the previous highest value, located in **MAX**. If the new value of **TIME** is larger, this new value replaces the previous value of **MAX**. Thus, the sequence

```
STARTX
<code whose maximum duration is to be determined>
STOPX
MAX3
```

forms the maximum duration in **MAXX:MAXH:MAXL**.

13.5 CCP1 AND EXTERNAL MEASUREMENTS

The PIC18F452 includes a capture/compare/pulse-width-modulation facility called CCP1 that can be closely coupled to Timer1 to measure time intervals between signal edges occurring on the RC2/CCP1 pin. Figure 13-10 illustrates the connection and its setup. With **T1CON** initialized to B'10000001' and with **CCP1CON** initialized to B'00000101', both prescalers will be bypassed. The **CCP1IF** flag in the **PIR1** register will be set when a rising edge occurs on the CCP1 input pin. In addition, **TMR1H:TMR1L** will be copied to **CCPR1H:CCPR1L** at that precise moment.

In the case of an internal time-interval measurement, the code to be executed to make the measurement is executed automatically at the beginning of each measurement (with the **START** macro) and at the end of each measurement (with the **STOP** and **MAX** macros). The CPU has all the time it needs to do the task being measured.

```
        TMR1X                ;Extension of TMR1
        TMR1LBUF             ;Temporary buffer for TMR1L
        TMR1HBUF             ;Temporary buffer for TMR1H
        TMR1XBUF             ;Temporary buffer for TMR1X
        TIMEL                ;Lower byte of the time-interval measurement
        TIMEH                ;Upper byte
        TIMEX                ;Extension byte
        MAXL                 ;Lower byte of maximum measurement
        MAXH                 ;Upper byte
        MAXX                 ;Extension byte
```

(a) Variables

```
        clrf  MAXL           ;Start maximum time interval at zero
        clrf  MAXH
        clrf  MAXX
```

(b) Initialization

```
STARTX  macro                ;Save TMR1 in TIME
        movff  TMR1X,TIMEX
        movff  TMR1L,TIMEL
        movf  TMR1H,W        ;Copy TMR1H to TIMEH and copy bit 7 to N
        movwf  TIMEH
        btfss  STATUS,N      ;Does TMR1 = B'Øbbbbbbb bbbbbbbb'?
        movff  TMR1X,TIMEX   ;If so, then reread TMR1X
        endm
```

(c) **STARTX**

```
STOPX   macro                ;Form TIME = TMR1 - TIME
        movff  TMR1X,TMR1XBUF   ;Form valid reading in TMR1BUF
        movff  TMR1L,TMR1LBUF
        movf  TMR1H,W
        movwf  TMR1HBUF
        btfss  STATUS,N      ;Does TMR1 = B'Øbbbbbbb bbbbbbbb'?
        movff  TMR1X,TMR1XBUF   ;If so, then reread TMR1X

        movf  TIMEL,W        ;Form TIME = TMR1BUF - TIME
        subwf  TMR1LBUF,W
        movwf  TIMEL
        movf  TIMEH,W
        subwfb  TMR1HBUF,W
        movwf  TIMEH
        movf  TIMEX,W
        subwfb  TMR1XBUF,W
        movwf  TIMEX

        movlw  9             ;Magic = 9; Make correction
        subwf  TIMEL,F
        btfss  STATUS,C
        decf  TIMEH,F
        btfss  STATUS,C
        decf  TIMEX,F
        endm
```

(d) **STOPX**

```
MAX3    macro
        movf  TIMEL,W        ;Form MAX - TIME for three-byte numbers
        subwf  MAXL,W
        movf  TIMEH,W
        subwfb  MAXH,W
        movf  TIMEX,W
        subwfb  MAXX,W       ;C=Ø if TIME > MAX
        btfss  STATUS,C      ;Replace MAX with TIME if C=Ø
        movff  TIMEL,MAXL
        btfss  STATUS,C
        movff  TIMEH,MAXH
        btfss  STATUS,C
        movff  TIMEX,MAXX
        endm
```

(e) **MAX3**

Figure 13-9 STARTX, **STOPX**, and **MAX3** macros.

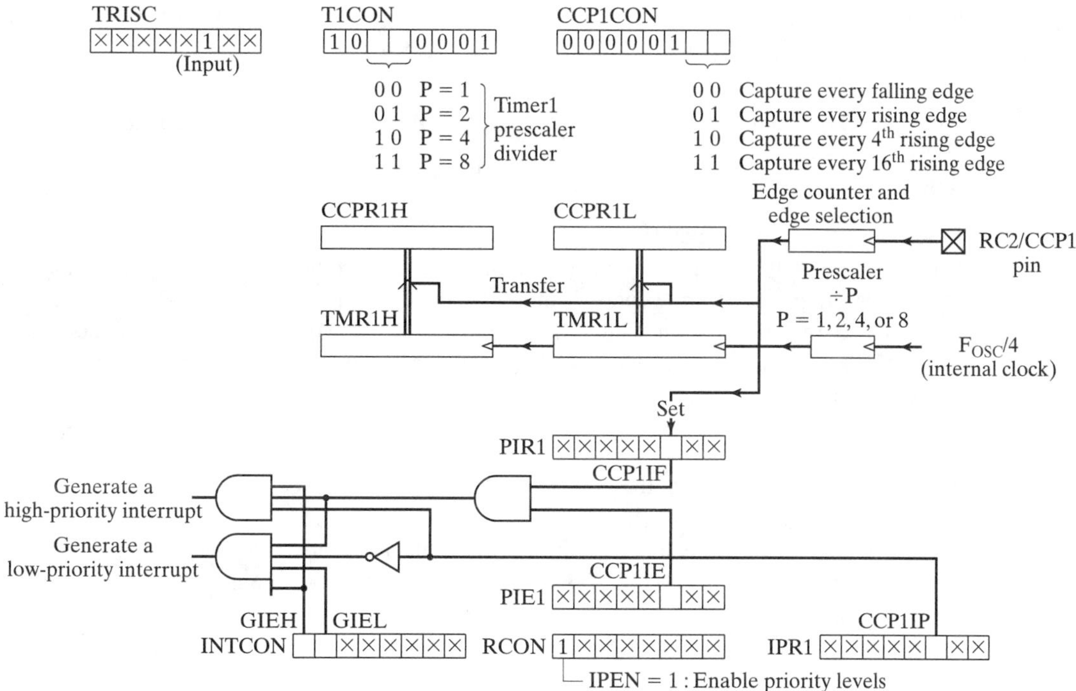

Figure 13-10 CCP1/Timer1 capture mode.

To achieve this same functionality for external time-interval measurements, both the start edge and the stop edge must generate an interrupt. Consider the measurement of a positive pulse (i.e., rising edge to falling edge). Within the CCP1 interrupt handler, if bit 0 of **CCP1CON** is set, then a rising-edge interrupt has occurred and the 2-byte **CCPR1** value can be copied into **TIME**. If it is cleared, then **TIME** can be replaced by **CCPR1** − **TIME**. The **MAX** macro of Figure 13-3 can then be invoked to ratchet up the maximum time interval whenever the latest measurement exceeds the previous maximum. Finally, the CCP1 interrupt handler can toggle bit 0 of **CCP1CON** in preparation for the next edge, clear the **CCP1IF** flag, and return.

Within the mainline loop, the display of the maximum value can be updated every second by counting loop times. Every 100th time around the mainline loop, **MAXH:MAXL** can be read by the **DisplayMax** subroutine of Figure 13-6 and displayed.

Example 13-5 Does the reading of **MAXH:MAXL** in this case constitute a critical region that should be protected by disabling interrupts, reading **MAXH:MAXL**, and then reenabling interrupts?

Solution

The reading does constitute a critical region. Between the reading of **MAXL** and the reading of **MAXH** in the **DisplayMax** subroutine, a CCP1 interrupt might change the value read. The result would be **MAXH(new):MAXL(old)**. If the old value was 00:fe and the new value is

01:02, then the value read would be 01:fe. It would be read and displayed, probably invalidating the on-going measurement.

Example 13-6 What determines the minimum pulse width of the pulse to be measured in this way?

Solution

In response to the leading edge of the pulse, the CPU must get to the CCP1 interrupt handler. If CCP1 is the only high-priority interrupt, then in the worst case, it is put off by the longest critical region in the mainline code. Within the handler, if bit 1 of **CCP1CON** equals 1, then this is the rising (i.e., leading) edge of the pulse. **CCPR1H:CCPR1L** must be copied to **TIMEH:TIMEL**, the bit 1 of **CCP1CON** toggled, and the **CCP1IF** flag bit cleared. At this point, even as the

```
retfie  FAST
```

instruction is being executed, the falling edge of the pulse can occur and its time will be successfully captured.

Since the time to respond to the trailing edge of the pulse takes somewhat longer, the minimum interval between pulses must be somewhat longer than the minimum pulse width asked for in this example.

13.6 CCP1 AND INTERNAL MEASUREMENTS

Internal time-interval measurements have already been examined in great detail. However, the use of the CCP1/Timer1 combination offers an interesting alternative. In support of this alternative, the RC2/CCP1 pin is initialized as an output, but with nothing connected to it. Then the **START** and **STOP** macros are redefined as

```
START  macro
       bsf   PORTC,RC2
       endm

 STOP  macro
       bcf   PORTC,RC2
       endm
```

The execution of the **START** macro will cause the output pin to go high and will trigger a CCP1 capture. The execution of the **STOP** macro will complete the measurement.

13.7 EXTENDED EXTERNAL MEASUREMENTS

By extending Timer1 to a 3-byte counter, as discussed in conjunction with Figure 13-7, external time-interval measurements can be extended to 3-byte values. Each Timer1 overflow can be handled with a low-priority interrupt. Each CCP1 interrupt might be handled with a high-priority interrupt if the minimum pulse width to be measured is less than 10 microseconds or so. For longer pulse-width measurements, CCP1 can be fielded with a low-priority interrupt, if the high-priority interrupt mechanism is to be reserved for some other application requiring its zero-latency feature.

Reading the Timer1 RAM extension variable, **TMR1X**, within the CCP1 handler requires the same care and technique used in Section 13.4. A valid 3-byte time stamp is thereby produced by each capture.

13.8 TIMER3 AND CCP2 USE

Timer3 has essentially the same capabilities as Timer1, as shown in Figure 13-11. Likewise, CCP2 has essentially the same capabilities as CCP1, as shown in Figure 13-12. As pointed out in Figure 13-11, **T3CON** contains two control bits that afford any one of three options:

- CCP1 and CCP2 can both be associated with Timer1.
- CCP1 and CCP2 can both be associated with Timer3.
- CCP1 can be associated with Timer1 while CCP2 is associated with Timer3.

Having two completely independent units can be useful for high-resolution measurements (with the timer's prescaler = 1) and for extended-range measurements (with the other timer's prescaler = 8). Another rationale for having two completely independent units arises when the CCP2/Timer3 is used in a "trigger special event" mode. It can trigger the analog-to-digital converter to start successive conversions automatically, with an arbitrary sample period, as will be discussed at the end of Section 16.3. Meanwhile, the CCP1/Timer1 combination can be used for captures or compares.

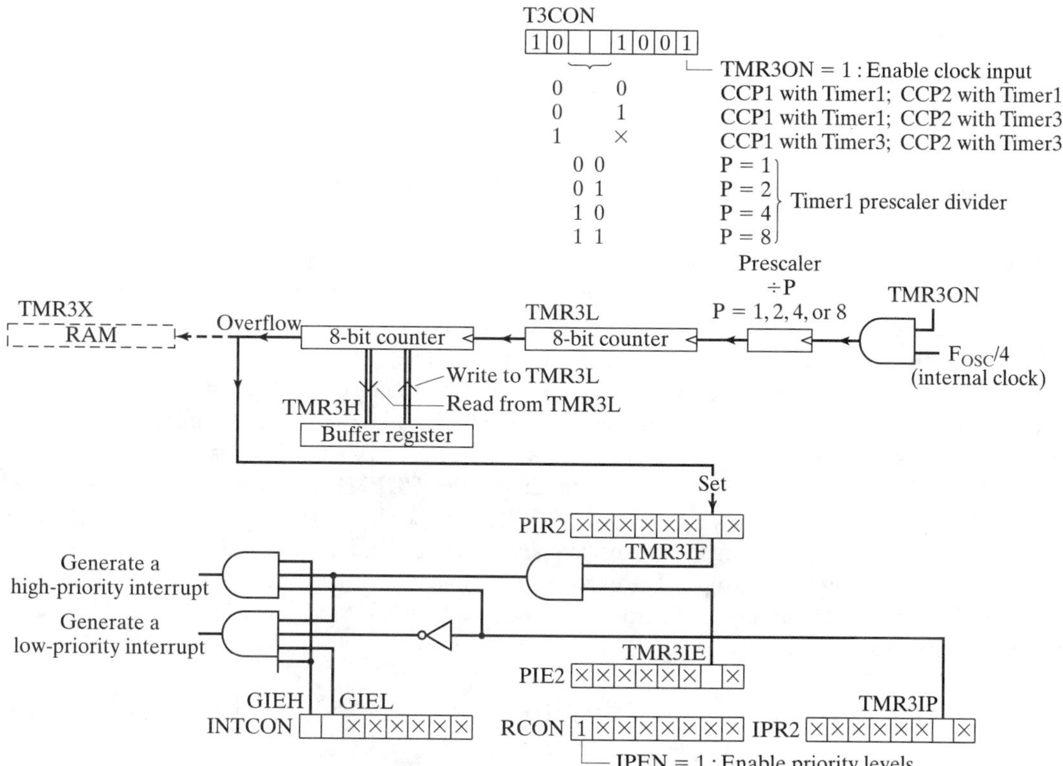

Figure 13-11 Timer3 operation.

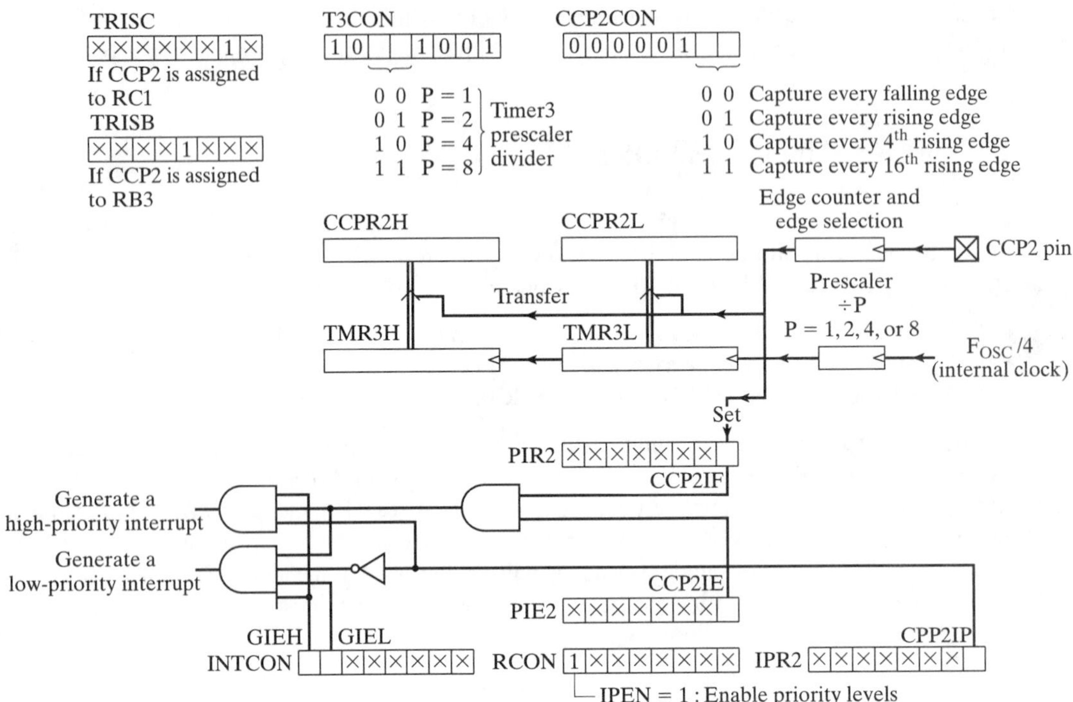

Figure 13-12 CCP2/Timer3 capture mode.

13.9 FREQUENCY MEASUREMENT

The QwikFlash instrument described in Chapter 4 will measure the frequency of the input to the RC1/CCP2 pin with the 50 parts-per-million accuracy afforded by the internal clock. A timing diagram of the measurement process is illustrated in Figure 13-13. Using the 3-byte **TMR3** (i.e., **TMR3X:TMR3H:TMR3L**) as a time base, the measurement begins when CCP2 is triggered by a rising edge of the input waveform to capture the start time (i.e., the value of **TMR3** at that time). Each successive rising edge of the input waveform must be counted. For high frequencies, this counting can be expedited by capturing every 16th rising edge with **CCP2CON** = B'00000111', as specified in Figure 13-12. Within the interrupt service routine for CCP2, the **CCP2IF** flag is cleared, and a 3-byte **MX:MH:ML** variable can be incremented by 16. **TMR3** must be checked to determine whether the gate time has been exceeded, signaling the end of the measurement. If so, the **CCP2IE** interrupt enable bit is cleared to turn off further interrupts. The captured start time is subtracted from the captured stop time to form **NX:NH:NL**, the number of internal clock periods between **MX:MH:ML** cycles of the input waveform. The frequency is then calculated as

$$\text{Frequency} = \frac{M}{N} \times 2{,}500{,}000 \text{ Hz}$$

The multiplication and division subroutines for carrying out this calculation will be discussed in the next chapter.

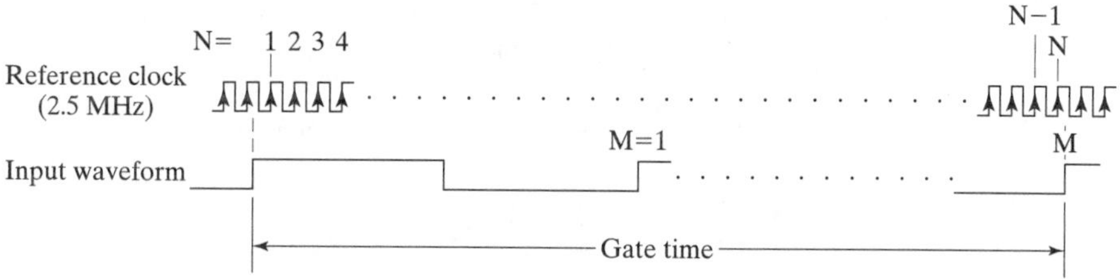

For a gate time of ≈ 0.4 seconds and a 2.5 MHz reference clock, n ≈ 1,000,000.
Start measurement on a rising edge of the input waveform.
Stop measurement on the first rising edge of the input waveform after the nominal gate time has been exceeded.
M equals the integral number of clock periods of the input waveform occurring between Start and Stop.
N equals the number of reference clock periods occurring between Start and Stop.
Period = (N/M) × 0.4 microseconds
Frequency = (M/N) × 2500000 Hz
Resolution = ±1 part in ≈ 1,000,000

Figure 13-13 Timing diagram for frequency measurement.

Determining when the gate time has been exceeded would seem to require that, within the CCP2 interrupt handler, the newly captured value of **TMR3** minus the start time be checked to see if it has exceeded the nominal gate time value of 1,000,000. If so, then the measurement has been completed. A simpler procedure entails noting that 1,000,000 = 0x0f4240. If **TMR3X** is initialized to 0x2f, then bit 6 of **TMR3X** will be set after as few as 0x400000 − 0x2fffff = D'1048577' clock cycles. Because the role of the gate time is to determine the resolution of the measurement, this will yield (slightly) better than one part-per-million resolution.

Within the mainline program, the **CCP2IE** interrupt enable bit can be monitored each time around the mainline loop. When the CCP2 interrupt handler clears it, signaling the end of the measurement, the mainline code takes the start time, the stop time, and **MX:MH:ML** and calculates and displays the frequency. A new measurement can be initiated by clearing the **CCP2IF** flag bit. Bit 7 of **TMR3X** can be set as a signal to the CCP2 interrupt handler that a new measurement has begun, so that it will, in turn, reinitialize **TMR3X** to the 0x2f value (discussed in the previous paragraph) and collect the start time. Finally, the **CCP2IE** bit is set, enabling CCP2 interrupts. The next rising edge of the input waveform will initiate a new measurement.

13.10 TEMPERATURE MEASUREMENT

In Section 10.3, the use of the voltage-output temperature transducer on the QwikFlash board was discussed in conjunction with the on-chip analog-to-digital converter. That transducer has a sensitivity of 10 millivolts per degree Fahrenheit while the ADC has a resolution of 5000 millivolts/1024. This translates into a measurement resolution of about half a degree Fahrenheit per increment. In Sections 15.8 and 17.9, two direct digital output temperature transducers will be considered, each using a serial output mechanism to transfer the temperature measurement back to the PIC18F452 microcontroller in Centigrade form.

An interesting alternative is presented by Analog Devices' TMP04 temperature transducer, available in the same TO-92 package as the LM34DZ part used on the QwikFlash board. Alternatively, it is

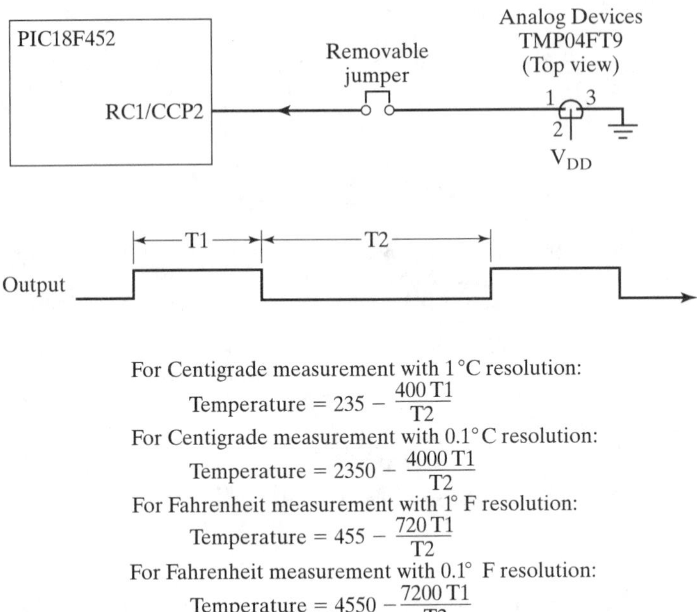

For Centigrade measurement with 1 °C resolution:

$$\text{Temperature} = 235 - \frac{400\,\text{T1}}{\text{T2}}$$

For Centigrade measurement with 0.1°C resolution:

$$\text{Temperature} = 2350 - \frac{4000\,\text{T1}}{\text{T2}}$$

For Fahrenheit measurement with 1° F resolution:

$$\text{Temperature} = 455 - \frac{720\,\text{T1}}{\text{T2}}$$

For Fahrenheit measurement with 0.1° F resolution:

$$\text{Temperature} = 4550 - \frac{7200\,\text{T1}}{\text{T2}}$$

Figure 13-14 Temperature measurement via time-interval measurements.

available in SO-8 and TSSOP-8 surface-mount packages. With a typical accuracy of ±1.5°C up to 100°C, it would seem to offer no advantage over the other choices. However, its output comes in the form of a pulse-width-modulated output having a nominal frequency of 35 Hz at room temperature. As shown in Figure 13-14, the output swings between 0 V and V_{DD}. The edges can be used to trigger CCP1 or CCP2 capture interrupts for time-interval measurements. Each period of the output consists of a "high" segment, denoted as T1, and a "low" segment, denoted as T2. T1 is nominally 10 milliseconds and is relatively insensitive to temperature change. (Analog Devices notes that T1 will not exceed 12 milliseconds over the rated temperature range of −25°C to +100°C.) With the equations of Figure 13-14, the nominal value of T2 at room temperature is about 19 milliseconds. These values for T1 and T2 mean that the measurements will be made with excellent resolution, better than 1 part in 10,000. Using the fixed-point multiplication and division subroutines of Sections 14.2 and 14.3 in the next chapter, the temperature is easily computed in either Centigrade or Fahrenheit and with a resolution that fits the application. Figure 13-14 lists the equations to compute the temperature so that each integer increment of the result represents 1 degree of temperature. The alternative equations produce a number wherein each integer increment of the result represents 0.1 degree of temperature. While these high-resolution results are unwarranted in terms of absolute temperature accuracy, they are quite accurate, and appropriate, for *incremental* temperature measurements.

PROBLEMS

13-1 Reading Timer1 What would be the consequence if all reads of the 2 bytes of Timer1 proceeded with a read of **TMR1H** followed immediately by a read of **TMR1L**?

13-2 CyclesToMicrosec subroutine

(a) Being sure to round off to the nearest integer, rewrite the subroutine of Figure 13-4 to implement the algorithm as

$$\text{Microseconds} = (\text{Cycles} \times 4)/10$$

(b) Which subroutine uses fewer instructions?
(c) What is the largest value of cycles that can be handled by each subroutine?

13-3 DecimalDisplay subroutine Rewrite the subroutine of Figure 13-5 as a new **DD1** subroutine that displays **AARGB0:AARGB1:AARGB2** as a decimal number on line 1 of the LCD. This new subroutine and the original, perhaps renamed **DD2**, can be used together to display two variables.

13-4 DisplayMax3 subroutine The **DisplayMax** subroutine of Figure 13-6 displays the 2-byte variable **MAXH:MAXL** in microseconds on the second line of the LCD. Write an expanded version, **DisplayMax3**, that will do the same for **MAXX:MAXH:MAXL**.

13-5 Incrementing TMR1X

(a) Using the low-priority interrupt's polling routine structure of Figure 9-4, show the modification to the polling sequence and create a **TMR1handler** subroutine to increment **TMR1X**.
(b) What is the effect of any *latency* introduced by using this low-priority interrupt to increment **TMR1X**?
(c) Are the **STARTX** and **STOPX** macros of Figure 13-9 still able to read **TMR1X:TMR1H:TMR1L** without error, even in the worst case? Explain.

13-6 CCP1handler subroutine Write a low-priority interrupt handler to form **MAXH:MAXL**, the maximum time interval between repeated rising and falling edges on the CCP1 input pin, as discussed in Section 13.5.

13-7 CCP1 high-priority interrupt service routine

(a) Recast the solution of Problem 13-6 as the sole source of high-priority interrupts.
(b) What is the minimum positive pulse width that can be measured? Explain.
(c) What is the minimum time between the trailing edge of one pulse and the leading edge of the next? Explain.

13-8 Internal time-interval measurements

(a) Compare measuring an internal time interval with the **START** and **STOP** macros of Figure 13-2 with your answer to part *(b)* of the last problem. Explain the difference.
(b) Section 13.6 offers an alternative scheme for measuring an internal time interval. What is the minimum time interval that can be measured in this way? Assume there are no other interrupt sources.

13-9 Extended external time-interval measurement

(a) With an internal 2.5 MHz clock and no prescaling, what is the maximum time interval that can be measured?
(b) With an internal 10 MHz clock and no prescaling, what is the maximum time interval that can be measured? What is the resolution of the measurement in this case?

Chapter

14

MATH SUBROUTINES

14.1 OVERVIEW

Microchip Technology has developed a set of subroutines for carrying out the fixed-point (i.e., integer) multiplications and divisions of multiple-byte numbers, both unsigned and signed. In addition, they have developed subroutines to deal with 32-bit floating-point numbers. These subroutines have been put into a form for use by Microchip's C18 compiler and are available for download with the free demo version of their C18 compiler. They have been modified and tested by Chris Twigg for stand-alone use in assembly code and are available from the author's Web site, www.picbook.com.

This chapter describes the available subroutines, their modification for assembly program use, and how to work with them. It also briefly describes how the PIC18FXXX microcontroller family's one-cycle 8×8 multiply instruction helps to accelerate the execution time not only of multiple-byte multiply subroutines but also of multiple-byte divide subroutines.

14.2 MULTIPLICATION

The instruction sequence

```
movf   AARGB0,W
mulwf  BARGB0
```

will form the 16-bit product of **AARGB0** and **BARGB0**, putting the result into **PRODH:PRODL** in a single cycle. Figure 14-1a shows the C18 compiler file, fxm0808u.asm. The **include**, **CODE**, **GLOB-**

```
;        RCS Header $Id: fxm0808u.asm,v 1.4 2000/09/20 22:13:33 ConnerJ Exp $
;        $Revision: 1.4 $
         include <P18C452.INC>            ; general Golden Gate definitions
         include <CMATH18.INC>            ; Math library definitions
         include <AARG.INC>               ; AARG declarations
         include <BARG.INC>               ; BARG declarations
;*******************************************************************************
;       8x8 Bit Unsigned Fixed Point Multiply 08 x 08 -> 16
;       Input:  8 bit unsigned fixed point multiplicand in AARGB0
;               8 bit unsigned fixed point multiplier in BARGB0
;       Use:    CALL     FXM0808U
;       Output: 16 bit unsigned fixed point product in AARGB0, AARGB1
;       Result: AARG  <--  AARG * BARG
;       Max Timing:     6 clks
;       Min Timing:     6 clks
;       PM: 5              DM: 3
PROG    CODE
FXM0808U
        GLOBAL    FXM0808U
        MOVF      BARGB0,W
        MULWF     AARGB0
        MOVFF     PRODH,AARGB0
        MOVFF     PRODL,AARGB1
        RETLW     0x00
        END
```

(a) C18 compiler's fxm0808u.asm file

```
;;;;;;; FXM0808U subroutine ;;;;;;;;;;;;;;;;;;;;;;;;;;;;;;;;;;;;;;;;;;;
;
;       8x8 Bit Unsigned Fixed Point Multiply 08 x 08 -> 16
;       Input:  8 bit unsigned fixed point multiplicand in AARGB0
;               8 bit unsigned fixed point multiplier in BARGB0
;       Use:    call     FXM0808U
;       Output: 16 bit unsigned fixed point product in AARGB0, AARGB1
;       Result: AARG  <--  AARG * BARG
;       Max Timing:     8 clks
;       Min Timing:     8 clks
;       PM: 7              DM: 3

FXM0808U
        MOVF       BARGB0,W
        MULWF      AARGB0
        MOVFF      PRODH,AARGB0
        MOVFF      PRODL,AARGB1
        RETLW      0x00
```

(b) Reformatted for use as a stand-alone FXM0808U subroutine.

Figure 14-1 FXM0808U subroutine.

AL, and **END** assembler directives have been stripped out to form the stand-alone **FXM0808U** subroutine of Figure 14-1b for inclusion in an assembly language source file.

Multiple-byte multiplication subroutines take advantage of the fast 8×8 multiply instruction, as illustrated in Figure 14-2a for **FXM1616U**, which multiplies **AARGB0:AARGB1** times **BARGB0:BARGB1**. The figure illustrates how the final product is implemented with four 8×8 multiplies plus the addition of the resulting bytes, weighted appropriately. Thus, the least-significant byte (the byte labeled 256^0) is the low byte of the 2-byte product resulting from multiplying **AARGB1** times **BARGB1**. The 256^1 byte is the sum of the high byte of **AARGB1** times **BARGB1** plus the low byte of **AARGB0** times **BARGB1** plus the low byte of **AARGB1** times **BARGB0**. Any carry resulting from

256^3	256^2	256^1	256^0
		AARGBØ :	AARGB1
		BARGBØ :	BARGB1
		high(AARGB1 × BARGB1)	low(AARGB1 × BARGB1)
	high(AARGBØ × BARGB1)	low(AARGBØ × BARGB1)	
	high(AARGB1 × BARGBØ)	low(AARGB1 × BARGBØ)	
high(AARGBØ × BARGBØ)	low(AARGBØ × BARGBØ)		

(a) Algorithm

```
;;;;;;; FXM1616U subroutine ;;;;;;;;;;;;;;;;;;;;;;;;;;;;;;;;;;;;;;;;;;;;;;;;;;;;
;
;       16x16 Bit Unsigned Fixed Point Multiply 16 x 16 -> 32
;       Input:  16 bit unsigned fixed point multiplicand in AARGBØ, AARGB1
;               16 bit unsigned fixed point multiplier in BARGBØ, BARGB1
;       Use:    call    FXM1616U
;       Output: 32 bit unsigned fixed point product in AARGBØ, AARGB1,
;               AARGB2, AARGB3
;       Result: AARG  <--  AARG * BARG
;       Max Timing:     31 clks
;       Min Timing:     31 clks
;       PM: 3Ø              DM: 7

FXM1616U
        MOVFF   AARGB1,TEMPB1

        MOVF    AARGB1,W
        MULWF   BARGB1
        MOVFF   PRODH,AARGB2
        MOVFF   PRODL,AARGB3
        MOVF    AARGBØ,W
        MULWF   BARGBØ
        MOVFF   PRODH,AARGBØ
        MOVFF   PRODL,AARGB1

        MULWF   BARGB1
        MOVF    PRODL,W
        ADDWF   AARGB2,F
        MOVF    PRODH,W
        ADDWFC  AARGB1,F
        CLRF    WREG
        ADDWFC  AARGBØ,F

        MOVF    TEMPB1,W
        MULWF   BARGBØ
        MOVF    PRODL,W
        ADDWF   AARGB2,F
        MOVF    PRODH,W
        ADDWFC  AARGB1,F
        CLRF    WREG
        ADDWFC  AARGBØ,F
        RETLW   ØxØØ
```

(b) Code

Figure 14-2 FXM1616U implementation.

the addition of these three terms is added into the 256^2 byte. The coded implementation is shown in Figure 14-2b.

Figure 14-3 lists the characteristics of all 16 multiply subroutines. Each signed number version expects the two inputs to be expressed in twos-complement code. Likewise, its output is expressed in twos-complement code.

Subroutine	Max. Cycles	Program Memory	Multiplicand	Multiplier	Product
FXM0808U	8	7	AARGB0	BARGB0	AARGB0:AARGB1
FXM0808S	13	12			
FXM1608U	15	14	AARGB0:AARGB1	BARGB0	AARGB0:AARGB1:AARGB2
FXM1608S	24	23			
FXM1616U	31	30	AARGB0:AARGB1	BARGB0:BARGB1	AARGB0:AARGB1:AARGB2:AARGB3
FXM1616S	45	44			
FXM2416U	46	45	AARGB0:AARGB1:AARGB2	BARGB0:BARGB1	AARGB0:AARGB1:AARGB2: AARGB3:AARGB4
FXM2416S	64	63			
FXM2424U	74	73	AARGB0:AARGB1:AARGB2	BARGB0:BARGB1:BARGB2	AARGB0:AARGB1:AARGB2: AARGB3:AARGB4:AARGB5
FXM2424S	90	89			
FXM3216U	61	60	AARGB0:AARGB1: AARGB2:AARGB3	BARGB0:BARGB1	AARGB0:AARGB1:AARGB2: AARGB3:AARGB4:AARGB5
FXM3216S	83	82			
FXM3224U	102	100	AARGB0:AARGB1: AARGB2:AARGB3	BARGB0:BARGB1:BARGB2	AARGB0:AARGB1:AARGB2: AARGB3:AARGB4:AARGB5: AARGB6
FXM3224S	120	119			
FXM3232U	139	138	AARGB0:AARGB1: AARGB2:AARGB3	BARGB0:BARGB1: BARGB2:BARGB3	AARGB0:AARGB1:AARGB2: AARGB3:AARGB4:AARGB5: AARGB6:AARGB7
FXM3232S	159	158			

Figure 14-3 Characteristics of multiply subroutines.

14.3 DIVISION

Unlike multiplication with its *building-block* **mulwf** instruction, division has no equivalent building-block instruction. However, each of the division subroutines uses a 256-entry table of 2-byte values called **IBXTBL256**. The most-significant byte (MSB) of the divisor is used as an index into the table. The table returns 0x10000 divided by this MSB of the divisor, rounded up.

Example 14-1 What is the table entry for 0x57?

Solution

0x10000/0x57 = 0x02f1.4a. . . , so the return from the table is 0x02f2.

Example 14-2 Consider the division of a 1-byte number, 0xc3, by another 1-byte number, 0x57. Form the quotient and the remainder.

Solution

An approximation to the quotient is first found from the inequality

$$\text{Quotient of } \frac{\text{0xc3}}{\text{0x57}} \leq \text{Integer part of} \left[\frac{\text{0x10000}}{\text{0x57}} \times \text{0xc3} \right] \div \text{0x10000}$$

The first term within the brackets is the quickly obtained table entry. Because the table entry corresponding to 0x10000/0x57 was rounded up, the expression

[Table entry × 0xc3] / 0x10000

will necessarily be equal to or greater than the quotient sought. In this case, the product to be formed is

Subroutine	Max. Cycles	Program Memory	Dividend	Divisor	Quotient	Remainder
FXD0808U	40	327	AARGB0	BARGB0	AARGB0	REMB0
FXD0808S	59	348				
FXD1608U	69	354	AARGB0:AARGB1	BARGB0	AARGB0:AARGB1	REMB0
FXD1608S	92	380				
FXD2408U	164	379	AARGB0:AARGB1:AARGB2	BARGB0	AARGB0:AARGB1:AARGB2	REMB0
FXD2408S	191	410				
FXD3208U	245	391	AARGB0:AARGB1:AARGB2:AARGB3	BARGB0	AARGB0:AARGB1:AARGB2:AARGB3	REMB0
FXD3208S	276	426				
FXD1616U	147	445	AARGB0:AARGB1	BARGB0:BARGB1	AARGB0:AARGB1	REMB0:REMB1
FXD1616S	176	479				
FXD2416U	326	649	AARGB0:AARGB1:AARGB2	BARGB0:BARGB1	AARGB0:AARGB1:AARGB2	REMB0:REMB1
FXD2416S	356	686				
FXD3216U	458	882	AARGB0:AARGB1:AARGB2:AARGB3	BARGB0:BARGB1	AARGB0:AARGB1:AARGB2:AARGB3	REMB0:REMB1
FXD3216S	491	923				
FXD2424U	341	797	AARGB0:AARGB1:AARGB2	BARGB0:BARGB1:BARGB2	AARGB0:AARGB1:AARGB2	REMB0:REMB1:REMB2
FXD2424S	362	838				
FXD3224U	459	1260	AARGB0:AARGB1:AARGB2:AARGB3	BARGB0:BARGB1:BARGB2	AARGB0:AARGB1:AARGB2:AARGB3	REMB0:REMB1:REMB2
FXD3224S	496	1306				
FXD3232U	390	1450	AARGB0:AARGB1:AARGB2:AARGB3	BARGB0:BARGB1:BARGB2:BARGB3	AARGB0:AARGB1:AARGB2:AARGB3	REMB0:REMB1:REMB2:REMB3
FXD3232S	422	1500				

Figure 14-4 Characteristics of divide subroutines.

$$0x02f2 \times 0xc3$$

Using the 8×8 multiply on the lower byte of 0x02f2:

$$0xf2 \times 0xc3 = 0xb856$$

For the upper byte, the 8×8 multiply produces

$$0x0200 \times 0xc3 = 0x100 \times (0x02 \times 0xc3) = 0x100 \times 0x0186 = 0x18600$$

Adding these together gives 0x023e56. Dividing by the 0x10000 outside of the brackets in the inequality gives an approximation to the quotient of 0x02.3e56. The number to the left of the hexadecimal point is the integer approximation to the quotient. It is the only part of this calculation that is of interest.

Multiplying this integer part, 0x02, by the divisor, 0x57, will produce a result of 0xae. The difference between the original dividend, 0xc3, and 0xae is 0x15, the remainder. That is

$$\frac{0xc3}{0x57} = 0x02 + \frac{0x15}{0x57}$$

$$\text{Quotient} = 0x02 \qquad \text{Remainder} = 0x15$$

All of the division subroutines operate with one or more iterations of this basic scheme, using the 256-entry table of reciprocal approximations together with fast 8×8 multiplications, additions, and subtractions to produce surprisingly fast divisions. Figure 14-4 lists the characteristics of the division subroutines.

14.4 USE OF MULTIPLICATION/DIVISION SUBROUTINES

These subroutines use a common set of variables (e.g., **AARGB0**). They also use a common set of equates, such as

```
LSB    equ  0
MSB    equ  7
```

The *include* file, MATHVARS.inc, shown in Figure 14-5, defines every one of these variables plus a few more variables (e.g., **AEXP**) and some constants (e.g., **MAXNUM24B0**) that are used by the floating-point subroutines of Section 14.6. The placement of the

```
#include  <C:\MATH18\MATHVARS.inc>
```

line in the source file is critical. Near the beginning of the P3.asm file of Figure 12-4, observe that the *Variables* section has the form

```
cblock  0x000
<user-defined variables>
endc
```

The **cblock** construct has associated with it, in this case, a parameter value of 0x000, which dictates that the first of the variables is to be assigned to RAM address 0x000. Now consider the **cblock** construct at the beginning of the MATHVARS.inc file of Figure 14-5 and observe that it has no such parameter value. Its variables will be assigned addresses beginning wherever a previous **cblock . . . endc** construct left off. Accordingly, the MATHVARS.inc file should be inserted into a source file just after that file's **cblock . . . endc** construct defining its variables:

```
cblock  0x000
<user-defined variables>
endc
#include  <C:\MATH18\MATHVARS.inc>
```

The multiply and divide subroutines expect these variables (i.e., **AARGB0**, etc.) to be assigned to Access RAM (0x000 to 0x07f) locations. The preceding construct will do this unless the application has already used more than $128 - 29 = 99$ RAM locations. In that case, some of the user-defined variables must be accessed using the **,BANKED** form of direct addressing discussed in Section 2.3, making room in Access RAM for the MATHVARS.inc variables.

To use one or more of the multiply or divide subroutines of Figures 14-3 and 14-4, just include it in the source file, perhaps just before the final **end** assembler directive. For example, an application program that uses the subroutines FXM1616U and FXD3208U can terminate with

```
#include  <C:\MATH18\FXM1616U.inc>
#include  <C:\MATH18\FXD3208U.inc>
end
```

14.5 RETAINING RESOLUTION

The fixed-point multiply and divide subroutines of the last several sections sometimes make it difficult to retain the resolution inherent in a calculation.

Example 14-3 Calculate the frequency obtained with the measurements described in Figure 13-13. Assume that M = 0x08a814 = D′567316′ and that N = 0x0f56c0 = D′1005248′.

```
       nolist
;;;;;;; MATHVARS.inc ;;;;;;;;;;;;;;;;;;;;;;;;;;;;;;;;;;;;;;;;;;;;;;;;;;;;;;;;;;;
;
;  Data memory required = 29 bytes
;
;;;;;;;;;;;;;;;;;;;;;;;;;;;;;;;;;;;;;;;;;;;;;;;;;;;;;;;;;;;;;;;;;;;;;;;;;;;;;;;;;

       list
       cblock
       AEXP                    ;AARG, floating-point exponent
       AARGBØ                  ;AARG, most-significant byte
       AARGB1
       AARGB2
       AARGB3
       AARGB4
       AARGB5
       AARGB6
       AARGB7

       BEXP                    ;BARG, floating-point exponent
       BARGBØ                  ;BARG, most-significant byte
       BARGB1
       BARGB2
       BARGB3

       CEXP
       CARGBØ                  ;CARG, most-significant byte
       CARGB1
       CARGB2
       CARGB3

       ZARGBØ                  ;ZARG, most-significant byte
       ZARGB1
       ZARGB2
       ZARGB3

       TEMPBØ                  ;Temporary variable, most-significant byte
       TEMPB1
       TEMPB2
       TEMPB3

       SIGN                    ;MSb = sign bit
       FPFLAGS                 ;Floating point options and exception flags
       endc

REMBØ  equ  AARGB4             ;Remainder, most-significant byte
REMB1  equ  AARGB5
REMB2  equ  AARGB6
REMB3  equ  AARGB7

TEMP   equ  TEMPBØ
       nolist

;;;;;;; General Literal Constants ;;;;;;;;;;;;;;;;;;;;;;;;;;;;;;;;;;;;;;;;;;;;;;

MSB    equ  7
LSB    equ  Ø

;;;;;;; Commonly Used Bits ;;;;;;;;;;;;;;;;;;;;;;;;;;;;;;;;;;;;;;;;;;;;;;;;;;;;;

#define  _C   STATUS,Ø
#define  _DC  STATUS,1
#define  _Z   STATUS,2
#define  _OV  STATUS,3

;;;;;;; Floating Point Specific Constants ;;;;;;;;;;;;;;;;;;;;;;;;;;;;;;;;;;;;;;

EXPBIAS  equ  D'127'

;;;;;;; FPFLAGS (floating point exception flags and options) ;;;;;;;;;;;;;;;;;;

IOV    equ  Ø               ; bitØ = integer overflow flag
FOV    equ  1               ; bit1 = floating point overflow flag
FUN    equ  2               ; bit2 = floating point underflow flag
FDZ    equ  3               ; bit3 = floating point divide by zero flag
NAN    equ  4               ; bit4 = not-a-number exception flag
DOM    equ  5               ; bit5 = domain error exception flag
RND    equ  6               ; bit6 = nearest neighbor rounding enable bit
                            ;        Ø: truncate, 1: round to nearest LSB
SAT    equ  7               ; bit7 = underflow/overflow control bit
                            ;        Ø: u/o produces spurious result
                            ;        1: u/o produces saturated value
```

Figure 14-5 MATHVARS.inc

```
;;;;;;; 32 Bit Floating Point Specific Constants ;;;;;;;;;;;;;;;;;;;;;;;;;;;;;;

; Machine precision

MACHEP32EXP  equ  Øx67          ; 5.96Ø46447754E-8 = 2**-24
MACHEP32BØ   equ  ØxØØ
MACHEP32B1   equ  ØxØØ
MACHEP32B2   equ  ØxØØ

; Maximum argument to EXP32

MAXLOG32EXP  equ  Øx85          ; 88.7228391117 = log(2**128)
MAXLOG32BØ   equ  Øx31
MAXLOG32B1   equ  Øx72
MAXLOG32B2   equ  Øx18

; Minimum argument to EXP32

MINLOG32EXP  equ  Øx85          ; -87.33654475Ø6 = log(2**-126)
MINLOG32BØ   equ  ØxAE
MINLOG32B1   equ  ØxAC
MINLOG32B2   equ  Øx5Ø

; Maximum argument to EXP1Ø32

MAXLOG1Ø32EXP  equ  Øx84        ; 38.531839445 = log1Ø(2**128)
MAXLOG1Ø32BØ   equ  Øx1A
MAXLOG1Ø32B1   equ  Øx2Ø
MAXLOG1Ø32B2   equ  Øx9B

; Minimum argument to EXP1Ø32

MINLOG1Ø32EXP  equ  Øx84        ; -37.9297794537 = log1Ø(2**-126)
MINLOG1Ø32BØ   equ  Øx97
MINLOG1Ø32B1   equ  ØxB8
MINLOG1Ø32B2   equ  Øx18

; Maximum representable number before overflow

MAXNUM32EXP  equ  ØxFF          ; 6.8Ø5647744Ø7E38 = (2**128) * (2 - 2**-23)
MAXNUM32BØ   equ  Øx7F
MAXNUM32B1   equ  ØxFF
MAXNUM32B2   equ  ØxFF

; Minimum representable number before underflow

MINNUM32EXP  equ  ØxØ1          ; 1.17549435Ø82E-38 = (2**-126) * 1
MINNUM32BØ   equ  ØxØØ
MINNUM32B1   equ  ØxØØ
MINNUM32B2   equ  ØxØØ

; Loss threshhold for argument to SIN32 and COS32

LOSSTHR32EXP  equ  Øx8A         ; LOSSTHR = sqrt(2**24)*PI/4
LOSSTHR32BØ   equ  Øx49
LOSSTHR32B1   equ  ØxØF
LOSSTHR32B2   equ  ØxDB
```

Figure 14-5 continued

```
;;;;;;; 24 Bit Floating Point Specific Constants ;;;;;;;;;;;;;;;;;;;;;;;;;;;;;;

; Machine precision

MACHEP24EXP  equ  0x6F         ; 1.52587890625e-5 = 2**-16
MACHEP24B0   equ  0x00
MACHEP24B1   equ  0x00

; Maximum argument to EXP24

MAXLOG24EXP  equ  0x85         ; 88.7228391117 = log(2*128)
MAXLOG24B0   equ  0x31
MAXLOG24B1   equ  0x72

; Minimum argument to EXP24

MINLOG24EXP  equ  0x85         ; -87.3365447506 = log(2*-126)
MINLOG24B0   equ  0xAE
MINLOG24B1   equ  0xAC

; Maximum argument to EXP1024

MAXLOG1024EXP  equ  0x84       ; 38.531839445 = log10(2**128)
MAXLOG1024B0   equ  0x1A
MAXLOG1024B1   equ  0x21

; Minimum argument to EXP1024

MINLOG1024EXP  equ  0x84       ; -37.9297794537 = log10(2**-126)
MINLOG1024B0   equ  0x97
MINLOG1024B1   equ  0xB8

; Maximum representable number before overflow

MAXNUM24EXP  equ  0xFF         ; 6.80554349248E38 = (2**128) * (2 - 2*-15)
MAXNUM24B0   equ  0x7F
MAXNUM24B1   equ  0xFF

; Minimum representable number before underflow

MINNUM24EXP  equ  0x01         ; 1.17549435082E-38 = (2**-126) * 1
MINNUM24B0   equ  0x00
MINNUM24B1   equ  0x00

; Loss threshhold for argument to SIN24 and COS24

LOSSTHR24EXP  equ  0x8A        ; LOSSTHR = sqrt(2**24)*PI/4
LOSSTHR24B0   equ  0x49
LOSSTHR24B1   equ  0x10
        list
```

Figure 14-5 continued

Solution

The frequency is given by

$$F = \frac{M}{N} 2{,}500{,}000 = \frac{M \times \text{0x2625a0}}{N}$$

The resolution of the input measurements will be retained if the multiplication, $M \times$ 0x2625a0, is carried out first, followed by the division by N. This requires the **FXM2424U** subroutine that produces a 6-byte result. What is needed next is **FXD4824U** to divide this 6-byte (i.e., 48-bit) result by the 3-byte (i.e., 24-bit) value of N. Unfortunately, such a 6-byte by 3-byte divide instruction is not a part of the Microchip assemblage of divide subroutines.

Another possibility is to calculate

$$\begin{aligned} \text{F} &= (((M \times 250)/N) \times 10{,}000) \\ &= (((M \times \text{0xfa})/N) \times \text{0x2710}) \\ &= (((\text{0x08a814} \times \text{0xfa})/\text{0x0f56c0}) \times \text{0x2710}) \\ &= ((\text{0x08742388}/\text{0x0f56c0}) \times \text{0x2710}) \\ &= \text{0x8d} \times \text{0x2710} \\ &= \text{0x1583d0} \\ &= \text{D'1410000'} \end{aligned}$$

The resolution of the final result was compromised by the division of one large number by another, producing a two-hex digit result, 0x8d. The actual frequency value is

$$\begin{aligned} F &= (567{,}316/1{,}005{,}248) \times 2{,}500{,}000 \\ &= 1{,}410{,}886 \text{ Hz} \end{aligned}$$

Example 14-3 illustrates what can be a difficult issue when using a succession of fixed-point multiplies and divides of large numbers. Floating-point calculations, discussed in the next section, provide a universally applicable solution for the retention of resolution.

14.6 FLOATING-POINT SUBROUTINES

In contrast to the myriad fixed-point multiply and divide subroutines, there are just seven floating-point subroutines. Each floating-point number is represented by a 24-bit mantissa and an 8-bit exponent for a total of 4 bytes. This number is normalized so that all 24 bits of the mantissa are significant. That is, the number is automatically aligned by the floating-point subroutine producing it so that the mantissa's most-significant bit (MSb) is a 1. Thus, any number of floating-point adds, subtracts, multiplies, and divides retain the one part in 2^{24} (i.e., one part in 16,777,216) resolution.

As shown in Figure 14-6a, a binary fraction having a 1 just to the right of the binary point represents a decimal value ranging between 0.5 and just under 1.0. The floating-point number representation shown in Figure 14-6b has a mantissa whose decimal value ranges between +0.5 and (virtually) +1.0 for positive numbers and between −0.5 and (virtually) −1.0 for negative numbers. The exponent accounts for the number of times the original number had to be divided by 2, or multiplied by 2, to get its magnitude to this range of 0.5 to 1.0. Given this normalization, *every* floating number has a 1 just to the right of the binary point. The floating-point *representation* suppresses this 1, using this bit position to hold a sign bit. Thus, a mantissa of 0x000000 represents the decimal number +0.5 and a mantissa of 0x800000 represents the decimal number −0.5.

The exponent used in the floating-point representation of a number has a built-in offset. Thus, the decimal number +0.5, with its mantissa represented by 0x000000, would seem to require an exponent of zero, since $2^0 = 1$. Instead, as shown in Figure 14-6c, the exponent in the floating-point representation of a number is coded with an offset of 0x7e. Numbers with a magnitude greater than 1 are represented with an exponent ranging from 0x7f up to 0xff. Numbers with a magnitude less than 1 are

Binary Fraction		Decimal
.10000000 00000000 00000000	=	0.50000000
.11111111 11111111 11111111	=	0.99999994

(a) 24-bit binary fractions

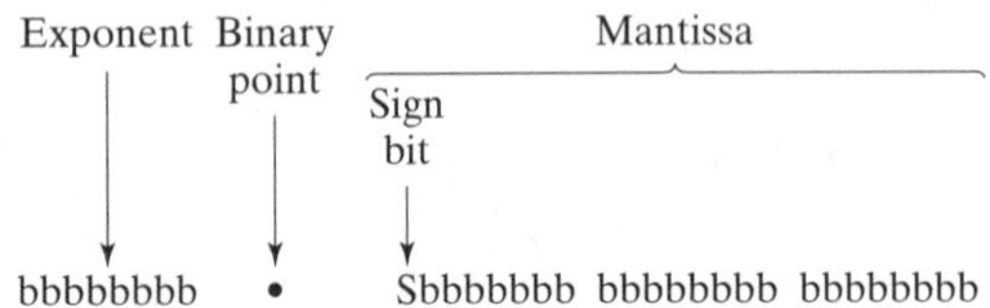

(b) Floating-point number representation (MSb of mantissa is implicitly equal to one and its bit position is occupied by the sign bit)

Decimal Representation	PIC Floating-Point Hexadecimal Representation
0.5	7e 000000
−0.5	7e 800000
1	7f 000000
−1	7f 800000
2	80 000000
−2	80 800000
1.7014117×10^{38}	ff 7fffff (largest positive number)
$2.9387359 \times 10^{-39}$	01 000000 (smallest positive number)

(c) Some examples

Figure 14-6 Floating-point number representation.

represented with an exponent ranging from 0x7e down to 0x01. The number 0 is given the unique floating-point representation

0x00 000000

The seven floating-point subroutines are listed in Figure 14-7a. Their expected input and output locations are posted in Figures 14-7b, c, and d. A floating-point calculation begins with the conversion of each 3-byte integer to floating-point form with either **FLO2432U** or **FLO2432S**. Three-byte resolution is maintained throughout the computations. The weak link with regard to resolution occurs on conversion back to integer form since the number is truncated at the binary point, with its fractional part being discarded. A scheme to retain an arbitrary number of decimal digits of resolution will be discussed in Section 14.8.

The variables used by these floating-point subroutines, listed in Figure 14-5, are a superset of the fixed-point multiply and divide variables. The additions are **AEXP**, **BEXP**, **CEXP**, **SIGN**, and **FPFLAGS**. The bits of **FPFLAGS** are defined in Figure 14-5. The two control bits (bit 7 and bit 6) of **FPFLAGS** deal with extreme conditions.

The maximum execution times listed in Figure 14-7a assume that the **Initial** subroutine includes

```
setf   FPFLAGS
```

so that results are rounded (rather than truncated) and so that an underflow or an overflow produces a saturated value (rather than a spurious result).

Name	Description	Max. Cycles	Program Memory
FLO2432U	Unsigned integer to floating-point conversion	57	
FLO2432S	Signed integer to floating-point conversion	67	
FPM32	Floating-point multiply	121	
FPD32	Floating-point divide	365	4140 words, total
FPA32	Floating-point add	141	
FPS32	Floating-point subtract	142	
INT3224	Floating point to signed integer conversion	89	

(a) The seven subroutines

```
Input:          AARGB0:AARGB1:AARGB2
Output:   AEXP:AARGB0:AARGB1:AARGB2
```

(b) Conversion from unsigned integer to floating point with FLO2432U
Conversion from twos-complement-coded, signed integer to floating point with FLO2432S

```
Inputs:   AEXP:AARGB0:AARGB1:AARGB2
          BEXP:BARGB0:BARGB1:BARGB2
Output:   AEXP:AARGB0:AARGB1:AARGB2
```

(c) Two-operand floating-point operations

```
Input:    AEXP:AARGB0:AARGB1:AARGB2
Output:        AARGB0:AARGB1:AARGB2
```

(d) Conversion from floating point to a twos-complement-coded integer

Figure 14-7 Floating-point subroutines.

14.7 USE OF FLOATING-POINT SUBROUTINES

For an application using fixed-point and/or floating-point subroutines, the **#include** assembler directive appends the variable list to the user-defined variable list with

```
cblock  0x000
<user-defined variables>
endc
#include  <C:\MATH18\MATHVARS.inc>
```

Again, a good out-of-the-way location in the source file for the floating-point subroutines is at the end of the file, using an *include* assembler directive:

```
#include  <C:\MATH18\FPSUBS.Inc>
end
```

The frequency-determining equation

$$\text{Frequency} = \frac{M}{N} \times 2{,}500{,}000$$

will now be revisited. The integer value of **NX:NH:NL** is first moved to **AARGB0:AARGB1:AARGB2**. Calling the **FLO2432U** subroutine will convert *N* to floating-point representation. The 4-byte value is moved to **BEXP:BARGB0:BARGB1:BARGB2**. Next, *M* is loaded into **AARGB0:AARGB1:AARGB2** and converted with a call of the **FLO2432U** subroutine to its 4-byte floating-point equivalent. The **FPD32** subroutine will form the quotient of *M/N* in **AARG**. This result is moved to **BARG**. Then **AARG** is loaded with the integer value, 2,500,000, converted to its floating-point equivalent, and multiplied by **BARG** with

```
MOVLF  upper 2500000,AARGB0
MOVLF  high 2500000,AARGB1
MOVLF  low 2500000,AARGB2
call  FLO2432U
call  FPM32
```

This sequence leaves the frequency, in floating-point form, in **AARG**. The resulting value retains its 24-bit resolution.

14.8 NORMALIZE SUBROUTINE

Retaining resolution while converting the floating-point representation of a number, *F*, back to a fixed-point representation can be handled in the following way. It will be assumed that the decimal equivalent of *F* ranges between 0.1 and 9,999,999. The **PowTen** table of Figure 14-8 contains the floating-point representation of eight decimal numbers

1,000,000   100,000   10,000   1000   100   10   1   0.1

This table is used to take a floating-point value of *F* and to multiply it by the one table entry that will result in a number whose decimal equivalent ranges between 1,000,000 and 9,999,999. The **INT3224** subroutine will convert this number to the three-byte hexadecimal representation of a seven-digit number. The number can be converted to a display string using the first part of the **DecimalDisplay** subroutine of Figure 13-5. The integer part of the original number can be shifted left one place to make room for the insertion of a decimal point. When sent to the LCD, this display string can fill out the second line that, together with the first line, might look like

```
Freq  Hz
123.4567
```

```
;;;;;;; Storage of floating point representation of powers of ten ;;;;;;;;;;;;;

PowTen  db  0x92,0x74,0x24,0x00 ;Floating point representation of 1000000
        db  0x8F,0x43,0x50,0x00 ;100000
        db  0x8C,0x1C,0x40,0x00 ;10000
        db  0x88,0x7A,0x00,0x00 ;1000
        db  0x85,0x48,0x00,0x00 ;100
        db  0x82,0x20,0x00,0x00 ;10
        db  0x7F,0x00,0x00,0x00 ;1
        db  0x7b,0x4c,0xcc,0xcd ;0.1
```

Figure 14-8 PowTen table.

The **Normalize** subroutine of Figure 14-9 carries out this operation, returning the normalized hexadecimal integer (with its decimal equivalent ranging between 1,000,000 and 9,999,999) in **AARG** and the number of digits to the left of the decimal point for the original number in the user-defined variable, **TMP0**.

Example 14-4 If the floating-point number passed to the **Normalize** subroutine in **AARG** has the number 123.4567 as its decimal equivalent, then what values will the subroutine return?

Solution

AARG will contain the hexadecimal equivalent of the decimal number 1234567. **TMP0** will contain the number 3, the number of digits to the left of the decimal point.

```
;;;;;;; Normalize subroutine ;;;;;;;;;;;;;;;;;;;;;;;;;;;;;;;;;;;;;;;;;;;;;;;;;;;;
;
; This subroutine normalizes AARG to an integer representation of its
; decimal equivalent with the decimal point moved to the right of a seven-digit
; number (i.e., a decimal number between 1,000,000 and 9,999,999).  It is
; assumed that the decimal equivalent of the actual number is less than
; 9,999,999 and more than 0.1000000.

; The location of the actual decimal point is returned in TMP0 with TMP0=0
; representing a number with no digits to the left of the decimal point.
; For example, if AARG is initially the floating point representation of
; 12.34567, then this subroutine will return with AARG holding the floating
; point representation of 1234567 and with TMP0 =2.

Normalize
        MOVLF  high PowTen, TBLPTRH  ;Point to first table entry
        MOVLF  low PowTen, TBLPTRL
        MOVLF  8,TMP0              ;Initialize return parameter
        REPEAT_
          decf  TMP0,F
          TBLRD*+
          movff  TABLAT,BEXP       ;First move table entry to BARG
          TBLRD*+
          movff  TABLAT,BARGB0
          TBLRD*+
          movff  TABLAT,BARGB1
          TBLRD*+
          movff  TABLAT,BARGB2
          movf  AARGB2,W           ;Subtract AARG from power of ten
          subwf  BARGB2,W
          movf  AARGB1,W
          subwfb  BARGB1,W
          movf  AARGB0,W
          subwfb  BARGB0,W
          movf  AEXP,W
          subwfb  BEXP,W
        UNTIL_  .NC.               ;Continue until AARG is larger than power of ten
                                   ;Form TBLPTR = PowTen + 4(TMP0)
        MOVLF  upper PowTen, TBLPTRU
        MOVLF  high PowTen, TBLPTRH
        MOVLF  low PowTen, TBLPTRL
        decf  TMP0,W
        bcf  STATUS,C
        rlcf  WREG,F
        rlcf  WREG,F
        addwf  TBLPTRL,F
        clrf  WREG
        addwfc  TBLPTRH,F
        addwfc  TBLPTRU,F
                                   ;Now retrieve this power of ten to BARG
        TBLRD*+
        movff  TABLAT,BEXP
        TBLRD*+
        movff  TABLAT,BARGB0
        TBLRD*+
        movff  TABLAT,BARGB1
        TBLRD*+
        movff  TABLAT,BARGB2
        rcall  FPM32               ;Multiply AARG by this power of ten
                                   ; to get a value greater than 1,000,000
        call  INT3224              ; and convert it to a three-byte integer
        return
```

Figure 14-9 Normalize subroutine.

PROBLEMS

14-1 FXD4824U subroutine

(a) Create the FXD4824U subroutine, wanted for Example 14-3, using code that includes four calls of the FXD3224U subroutine. Before doing this, you might carry out the following decimal division by the manual long-division method, just to refresh yourself on the steps involved:

$$987654 \div 123$$

(b) Initialize **AARG** and **BARG** with the values of Example 14-3. Calculate the frequency. Execute the **DecimalDisplay** subroutine of Figure 13-5. The LCD should show 1410886. Does it?

(c) Determine the time to carry out this calculation experimentally.

14-2 Floating-point calculation

(a) Carry out the calculation of Example 14-3 by using floating-point calculations. Then execute the **DecimalDisplay** subroutine to show the result. Does the LCD show 1410886?

(b) Determine the time to carry out this calculation experimentally.

14-3 Application Note AN575

(a) Find Application Note 575 "IEEE754 Compliant Floating-Point Routines" on Microchip Technology's Web site, www.microchip.com. This application note discusses the floating-point routines for earlier-generation PIC microcontrollers. The information is applicable to the PIC18 microcontroller family, but the subroutines for the PIC16 microcontroller family do not have the advantage of a multiply instruction, and those for the PIC17 microcontroller family use a somewhat different CPU architecture. Download the files anyway just to obtain a file called Fprep.exe. This utility will let you enter a decimal number. It will return the floating-point representation for that number.

(b) Use the Fprep utility to check the **PowTen** table entries of Figure 14-8.

(c) Extend the **PowTen** table down to 0.000001.

14-4 Normalize subroutine Rewrite this subroutine to handle any number over the range 0.000001 to 9,999,999. Return the normalized number in **AARG** and the twos-complement-coded *signed* number representing the position of the decimal point in **TMP0**. For numbers greater than 0.1, **TMP0** should produce the same value as that generated by the code of Figure 14-9. For numbers less than 0.1, the subroutine should return the appropriate new value.

14-5 Display Assume that the number to be normalized by the scheme of Problem 14-4 represents a voltage ranging anywhere from 1 microvolt to many volts. If the number is the floating-point representation of a voltage less than 1, create a display with (for example)

```
Input uV
123.4567
```

If the number is greater than 1, display (for example)

```
Input  V
4.973165
```

Chapter

15

SERIAL PERIPHERAL INTERFACE FOR I/O EXPANSION

15.1 OVERVIEW

The PIC18F452's Serial Peripheral Interface (SPI) is a *shift register* interface. It consists of a serial-clock line (SCK), a serial-data-out line (SDO), and a serial-data-in line (SDI). It supports both output port expansion and input port expansion using standard, low-cost, 74HCxxx shift register parts. Peripheral devices having an SPI interface (e.g., digital-to-analog converters and temperature sensors) can enhance the microcontroller's functionality. The microcontroller gains I/O capability with a conceptually simple interface, giving up very few pins to do so.

The SPI circuitry is part of the PIC18F452's Master Synchronous Serial Port (MSSP) module that supports either SPI or I2C bus transfers. Although this chapter focuses on the SPI bus, register names such as **SSPBUF**, **SSPSTAT**, and **SSPCON1** and bit names such as **SSPM3**, . . . , **SSPM0** reflect the dual role of these registers and bits.

15.2 SPI FUNCTIONALITY

The SPI interface functioning is illustrated with the simplified block diagram of Figure 15-1a. Notice that the SPI transfers an output byte and an input byte simultaneously. Also notice that each of these two bytes are transferred most-significant-bit (MSb) first. A typical timing diagram for the transfer is shown in Figure 15-1b. The **SSPIF** flag is first cleared. Then a *write* to (but *not* a read of) the **SSPBUF** register will initiate the transfer of **SSPBUF** out the SDO pin, MSb first. At the same time, the input on the SDI pin will be read in, MSb first. When the SSPIF flag goes high again, the transfer is complete. The byte received on the SDI pin can now be read out of **SSPBUF**.

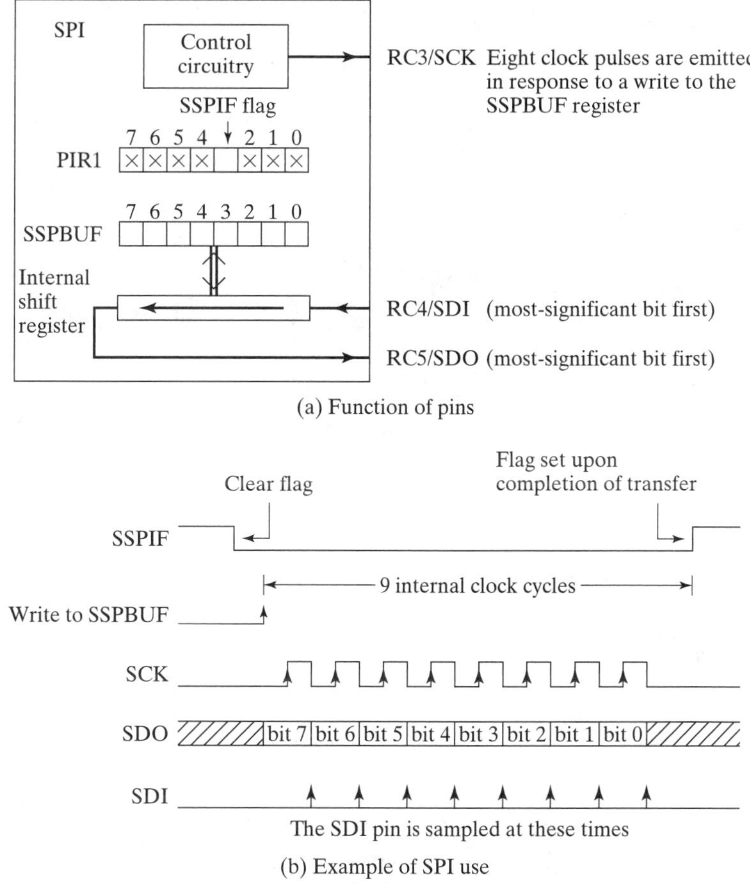

Figure 15-1 SPI functionality.

15.3 SPI SETUP

The SPI module's setup encompasses a variety of options, as shown in Figures 15-2 and Figure 15-3. The three pins associated with its *master mode* were shown in Figure 15-1a. Master mode refers to the ability of two (or more) microcontroller chips to communicate via the SPI bus. For this connection, one chip (the master) drives the SCK line. Because the slave chip receives its clock from the master, it can only respond to the master's commands and queries, never initiating a transfer. Most of this chapter focuses upon master-mode operation. The chapter concludes with a section that examines the use of the SPI interface to couple two or more PIC microcontrollers, with one configured as the SPI master and the others as SPI slaves.

Some applications use only two of the three SPI lines. For example, the SPI might be used to add two output ports and a DAC (digital-to-analog converter). The unused SDI pin can be used as a general-purpose output pin, RC4, by clearing bit 4 of the **TRISC** register. Likewise, an unused SDO pin can be used as a general-purpose input pin by setting bit 5 of **TRISC**.

The SPI clock rate is usually adjusted to the fastest rate that will work with the slowest connected device. For example, 74HCxxx shift register parts can be clocked well above 10 MHz. Consequently,

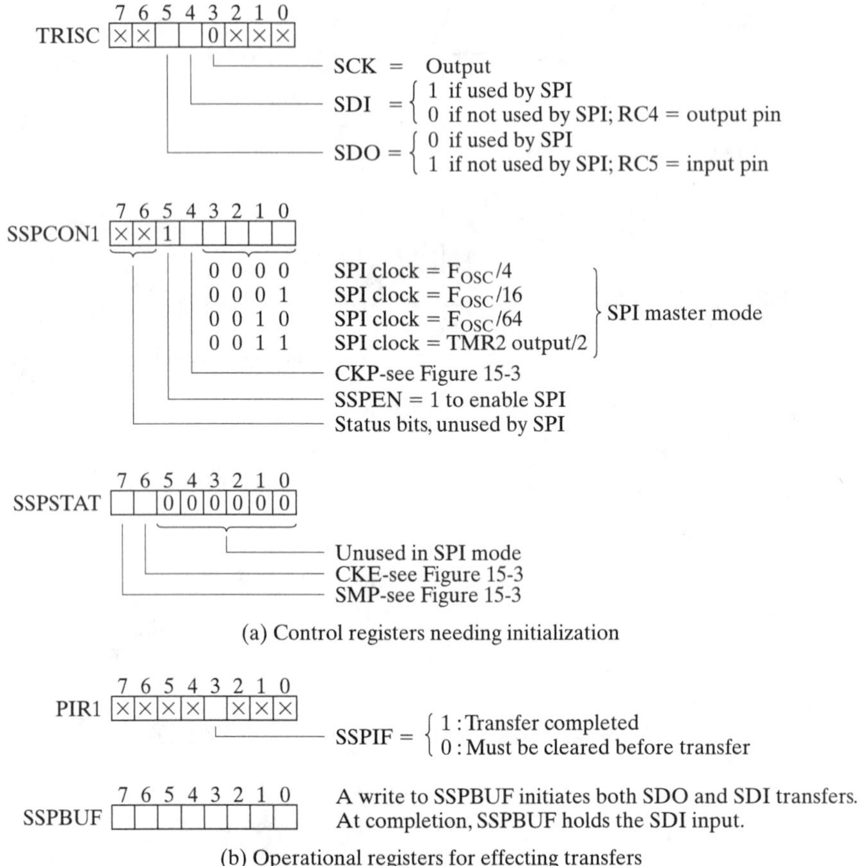

Figure 15-2 SPI setup and use.

even if the PIC18F452 is operated with a 10 MHz crystal and its PLL mode to yield F_{osc} = 40 MHz and an internal 10 MHz clock rate, the SPI's $F_{osc}/4$ option will carry out transfers at the 10 MHz rate. The DAC on the QwikFlash board has a maximum clock rate for its SPI interface of 5 MHz. If the microcontroller is operated with an internal clock rate of 2.5 MHz, then the SPI module's $F_{osc}/4$ clock option will provide a satisfactory 2.5 MHz SPI clock. On the other hand, an internal clock rate of 10 MHz can take advantage of the SPI module's $F_{osc}/16$ clock option and, again, use a 2.5 MHz SPI clock.

The three control bits, **CKP**, **CKE**, and **SMP**, give rise to the eight *phasing* options of Figure 15-3.

Example 15-1 A74HC595 shift register connected to SCK and *SDO* responds to rising edges on its clock input. Which phasing option of Figure 15-3 should be used for the microcontroller's SPI connection to the '595?

Solution

The SDO line must be stable (i.e., unchanging) at the time of rising edges on SCK. Accordingly, the timing of Figure 15-3a will work as will as that of Figure 15-3c. The other two options should be avoided because SDO is changing at the time of the rising edges on SCK.

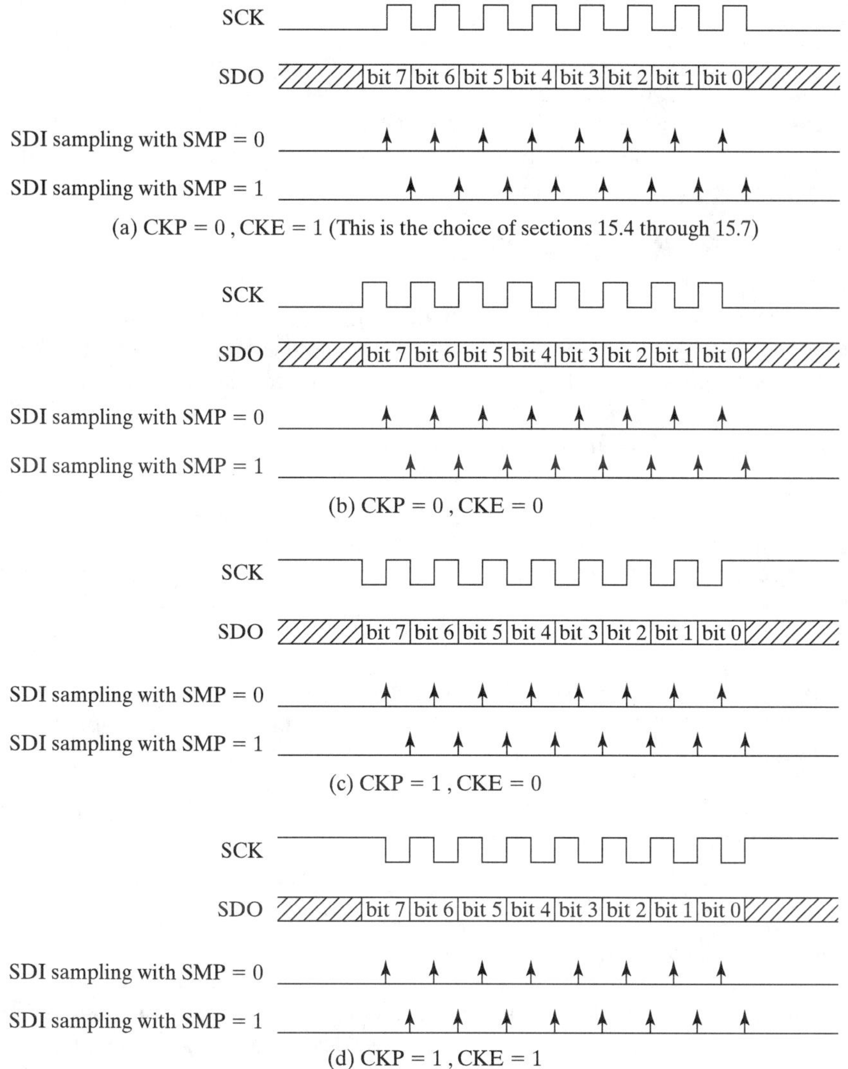

Figure 15-3 CKP, CKE, SMP options.

Example 15-2 A 74HC165 shift register connected to SCK and *SDI* responds to rising edges on its clock input. Which phasing option should be used?

Solution

In this case, the output of the '165 shift register should be sampled when it is not being shifted. Because of the **SMP** option in each of the four cases of **CKP** and **CKE**, all four can be made to work:

CKP = 0	CKE = 1	SMP = 1	works
CKP = 0	CKE = 0	SMP = 0	works

CKP = 1	CKE = 0	SMP = 1	works
CKP = 1	CKE = 1	SMP = 0	works

For some devices, the last case (from Figure 15-3d) has an advantage over the others in that the input is sampled before the shift register is first shifted. In any case, care must be taken to keep track of when the output of the external chip is sampled relative to when it is shifted.

15.4 OUTPUT PORT EXPANSION

The 74HC595 *double-buffered* shift register of Figure 15-4a serves as an ideal expansion output port, for most purposes. As a byte is shifted out of the SPI and into the '595's shift register, the output pins are isolated from the shifting data. Only when the byte is in place is the *latch clock* strobed, transferring the new byte to the output pins.

The timing diagram and the instruction sequence involved in effecting the transfer are shown in Figure 15-4c. Notice that the data is stable on the SDO line at the time of each rising edge of the SCK line. This ensures that the data bit will be reliably read by the shift-register input.

The transfer procedure begins with the clearing of the **SSPIF** flag bit so that it can subsequently be used to signal the completion of the transfer. If the RAM copy of the expansion port is called **OUT**, then the instruction

```
movff  OUT,SSPBUF
```

will initiate the clocking of the SCK line as the bits of **OUT** are shifted out the SDO line, MSb first. When **SSPIF** goes high again, the 8 bits will be sitting in the '595's shift register, ready for strobing into the D-type flip-flops that drive the output pins.

15.5 INPUT PORT EXPANSION

Using a parallel-in, serial-out 74HC165 shift register, the circuit of Figure 15-5 adds an input port to the microcontroller. The shift register is first loaded with the input port data by the active-low strobe pulse from an arbitrary output pin (RB4, in this case). The **SSPIF** flag is then cleared, initializing its use to signal when the serial transfer has been completed. Transmission is initiated by a write (of anything) to **SSPBUF**.

The SPI timing option selected, which is the same as that used in the last section for output port expansion, produces a rising edge on the SCK line that clocks the shift register *before* the shift register output is read by the SPI. Note the order,

```
b0, b7, b6, b5, b4, b3, b2, b1
```

in which the bits are initially strobed into the shift register by the RB4 pulse. The port's most-significant bit, b7, appears on the shift register output *after* that first SCK clock edge. The SPI module will read the bits in sequence: b7, b6, b5, b4, b3, b2, b1. Because the shift register's output is fed back to its input, the b0 bit, which initially appeared on the shift register output, will again be in place on the shift register output when the eighth bit is read by the SPI.

Upon completion of the transfer, as signaled by the setting of the **SSPIF** flag, the SPI's buffer register, **SSPBUF**, can be copied to a RAM variable, **IN**. If this reading of the input expansion port is executed at the beginning of the mainline loop, then mainline subroutines will always be served input data that is less than 10 milliseconds old.

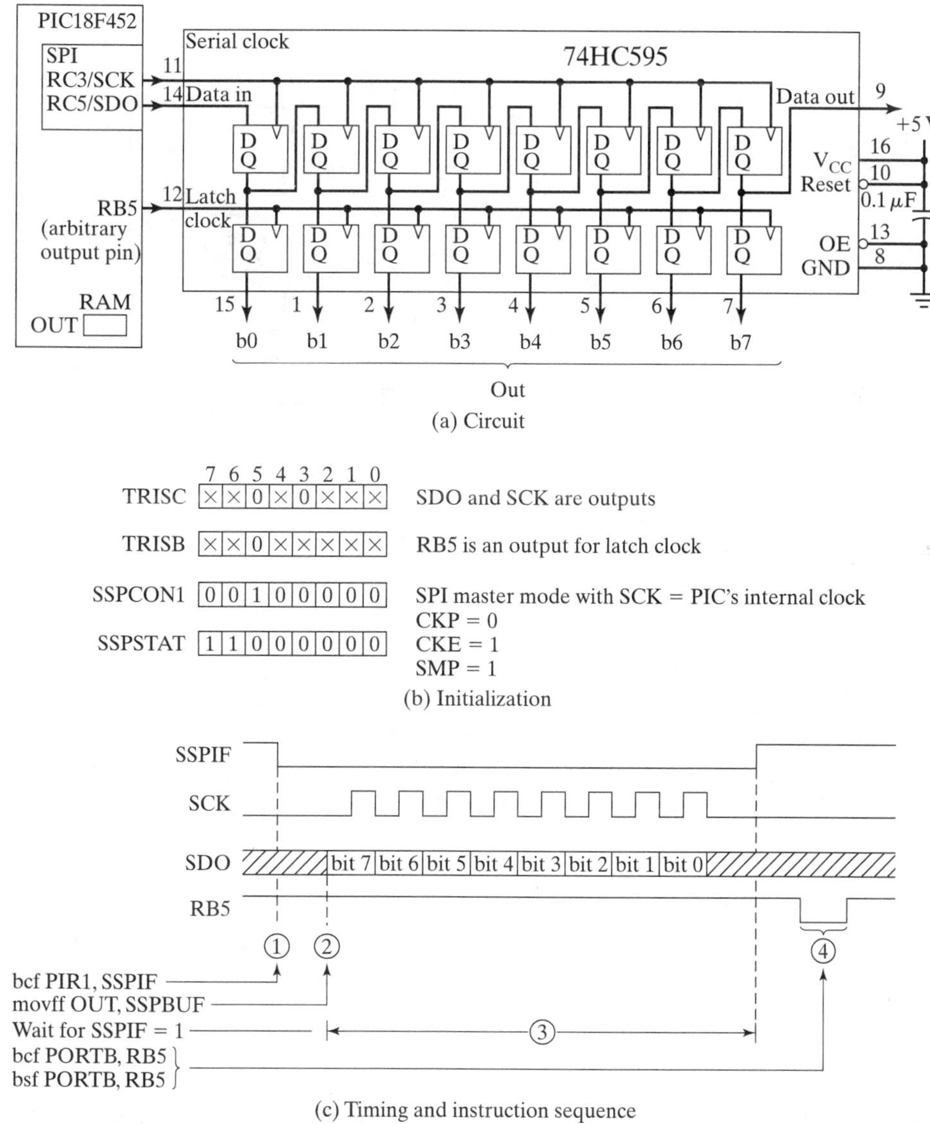

Figure 15-4 SPI use for output port expansion.

15.6 MULTIPLE I/O PORT EXPANSION

Because the same SPI timing option was used in the last two sections, the two circuits can be combined. Furthermore, because each shift-register part can be cascaded with one or more identical parts, any number of expansion ports can be implemented in this way. Figure 15-6a illustrates the interconnections to expand the microcontroller's I/O lines by 16 additional inputs and 16 additional outputs. To achieve this, the microcontroller gives up just five pins.

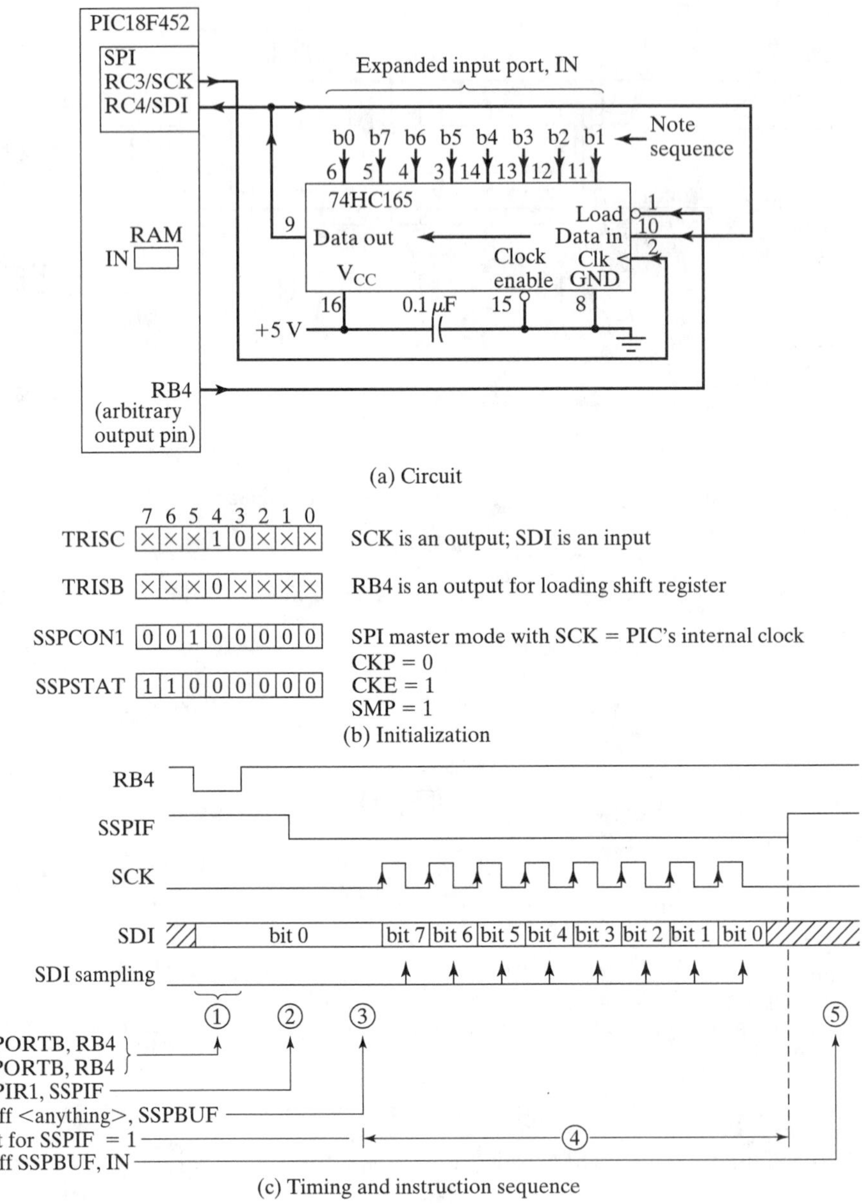

Figure 15-5 SPI use for input port expansion.

An update at the beginning of the mainline loop will transfer the two input ports, INH and INL, to two RAM variables, also called **INH** and **INL**. The timing for the transfers is illustrated in Figure 15-6b. The initial strobe pulse on RB4 (or any other output pin used for this process) initiates the sequence. It loads the two 74HC165 "input" shift registers.

The first SPI transfer is initiated by the write of the RAM variable, **OUTH**, to **SSPBUF**. Upon the completion of this transfer, the state of the INH input port is in **SSPBUF** and is copied to the RAM

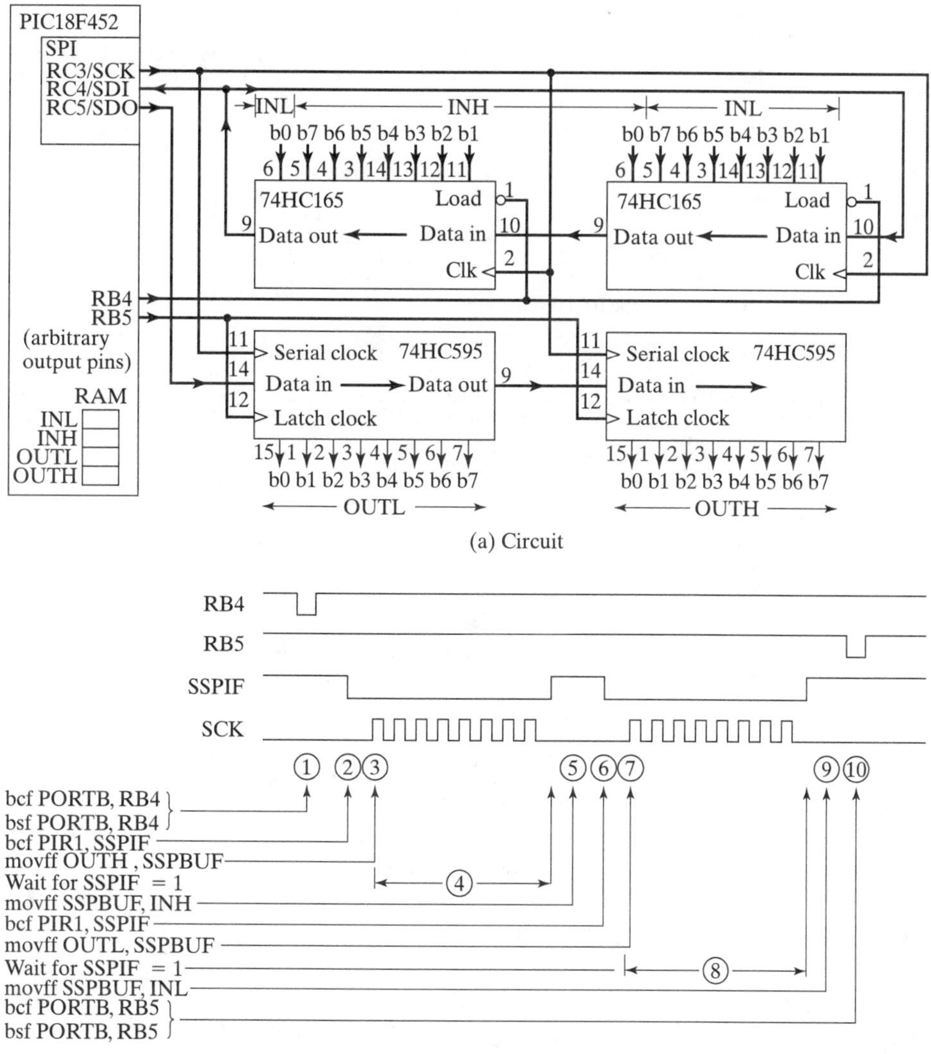

Figure 15-6 Four-port expansion circuit.

variable, **INH**. The state of the INL input port is now sitting in the left 74HC165 shift register. The contents of the RAM variable, **OUTH**, are sitting in the internal shift register of the left 74HC595 shift register.

The second transfer is initiated by the write of the RAM variable, **OUTL**, to **SSPBUF**. Upon its completion, the state of the INL input port has been moved to **SSPBUF**, ready to be copied to the RAM variable, **INL**. The 16 bits from **OUTH** and **OUTL** now reside in the internal shift registers of the two 74HC595 chips. The strobe pulse on RB5 copies the shift registers to the D-type flip-flops that drive the output pins, thus completing the operation.

An **IOupdate** subroutine to carry out the operation of Figure 15-6b is listed in Figure 15-7. If this subroutine is called at the beginning of each pass around the mainline loop, the four expansion ports will

```
INL                     ;Copy of input expansion port
INH
OUTL                    ;Copy of output expansion port
OUTH
```

(a) Variables

```
MOVLF  B'10010000',TRISC  ;See Figure 4-2b for other pins
bcf  TRISB,5              ;Output to strobe 74HC595's
bcf  TRISB,4              ;Output to strobe 74HC165's
MOVLF  B'00100000',SSPCON1 ;Set up SPI
MOVLF  B'11000000',SSPSTAT
```

(b) Code to be added to the **Initial** subroutine

```
;;;;;;; IOupdate subroutine ;;;;;;;;;;;;;;;;;;;;;;;;;;;;;;;;;;;;;;;;;;;;;;;;;;;;;;
;
; This subroutine copies the RAM variables OUTH and OUTL out to the two 74HC595
; expansion output ports.  It reads the inputs from the two 74HC165 expansion
; input ports into the two RAM variables INH and INL.
; It uses RB4 to load the 74HC165's at the beginning and RB5 to strobe the
; 74HC595 output registers at the end.

IOupdate
        bcf  PORTB,RB4          ;Strobe 74HC165 input ports to load them
        bsf  PORTB,RB4
        bcf  PIR1,SSPIF         ;Drive SSPIF low
        movff  OUTH,SSPBUF      ;Transfer OUTH out and INH in
        REPEAT_
        UNTIL_  PIR1,SSPIF == 1 ;Wait until transfer has been completed
        movff  SSPBUF,INH       ;Save expansion input port value to RAM
        bcf  PIR1,SSPIF         ;Get ready for next transfer
        movff  OUTL,SSPBUF      ;Transfer OUTL out and INL in
        REPEAT_
        UNTIL_  PIR1,SSPIF == 1 ;Wait until transfer has been completed
        movff  SSPBUF,INL       ;Save expansion input port value to RAM
        bcf  PORTB,RB5          ;Strobe 74HC595 output ports
        bsf  PORTB,RB5
        return
```

(c) The subroutine

Figure 15-7 IOupdate subroutine.

be updated every 10 milliseconds. The mainline subroutines will read the newly sampled input ports from the RAM variables, **INH** and **INL**. The OUTH and OUTL output ports will reflect all of the changes made to the **OUTH** and **OUTL** RAM variables during the last pass around the mainline loop.

15.7 DAC OUTPUT

The MAX522 dual DAC on the QwikFlash board employs the SPI interface to generate two analog outputs, each with 8-bit resolution between 0 V and 5 V, using the circuit of Figure 15-8a. Each output is buffered with an op-amp "follower" circuit, but the DAC-A output has the lower typical output impedance of 50 ohms, whereas the DAC-B's typical output impedance is 500 ohms.

Changing one of the DAC outputs requires the 2-byte command sequence shown in Figure 15-8c. The active-low chip select pin is first driven low by clearing the RC0 bit of **PORTC** (initialized as an output). To change the DAC-A output, 2 bytes are sent to the DAC. The first (control) byte is 0x21. The second (data) byte is, for example, 51, to set the output to

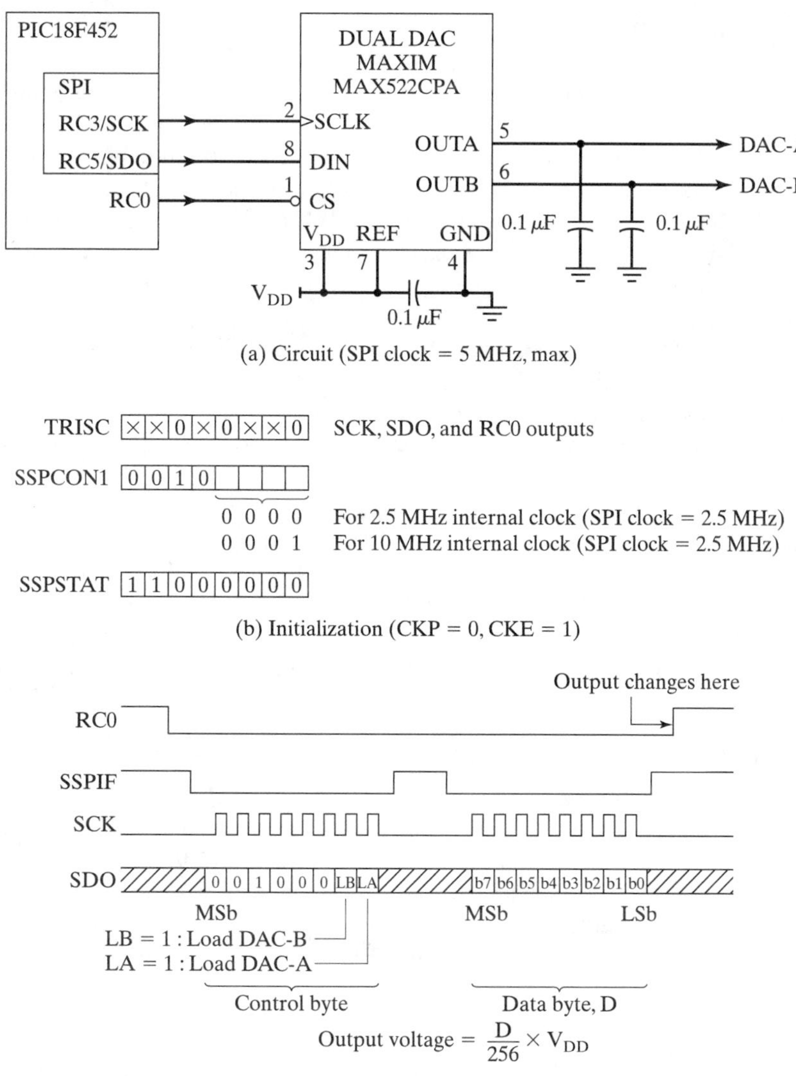

Figure 15-8 Dual DAC use.

$$\frac{51}{256} \times 5\text{ V} = 1.00\text{ V}$$

When the RC0 bit is set at the completion of the 2-byte transfer, the DAC-A pin will change to 1.00 volt. Changing the DAC-B output employs the same procedure, but with a control byte of 0x22.

15.8 TEMPERATURE INPUT

Dallas Semiconductor's DS1722 "digital thermometer" is a low-cost chip that digitizes temperatures over the range from −55°C (−67°F) to +120°C (+248°F). As is true for many new peripheral devices, it is *only* available in either of two tiny 8-pin surface-mount packages (150-mil SOIC and μ-SOP) and has thus not been used on the QwikFlash board. It has the interesting feature that a trade-off between measurement resolution and conversion time can be selected. Whereas the absolute accuracy of the device is ±2°C, a temperature *resolution* of 0.0625°C can be achieved, albeit with a conversion time of over a second. For temperature *difference* measurements, the measurement resolution is indeed the measurement accuracy.

As shown in Figure 15-9a, the part has the expected SPI connections. Note that the part's SDO output connects to the microcontroller's SDI input and that the part's SDI input connects to the microcontroller's SDO output. Also note that it uses an active-*high* chip enable (in contrast to many devices). The chip has separate power supply inputs to allow the analog supply to range over 2.65 V – 5.5 V while allowing the digital circuitry to range from 5.5 V all the way down to 1.8 V. The circuit of Figure 15-9a powers both supply inputs from V_{DD} = 5 V. With the SERMODE pin tied high, the chip implements MSb-first SPI protocol. (The alternative of tying SERMODE low produces an LSb-first serial protocol.)

Figure 15-9c shows the configuration alternatives, and Figure 15-9d illustrates the SPI protocol needed to set the configuration to perform a single 11-bit conversion. A mainline loop subroutine might read and display the temperature once a second and then send the configuration command shown in Figure 15-9d to initiate a new measurement. One second later, the new measurement will have been completed and be ready for display.

For 12-bit resolution with its attendant *maximum* conversion time of 1.2 seconds, a display of the temperature can be updated at the maximum rate afforded by the DS1722 part. Each time around the mainline loop, the Config/Status register is queried via the protocol of Figure 15-9e. If the conversion is complete, then the temperature is read and displayed and a new measurement initiated.

The SPI protocol to read the temperature is illustrated in Figure 15-9f. After sending out the 0x01 byte representing the read address of the low byte of the measurement, a dummy byte is sent out to elicit the return of the low byte of the measurement. Sending another dummy byte produces the return of the high byte of the measurement. The format of temperature output as a twos-complement-coded signed number is shown in Figures 15-9g and h.

Example 15-3 How many bits of resolution are needed to obtain a resolution of better than 0.1°F?

Solution

Because

$$F = \frac{18}{10}C + 32$$

as listed in Figure 15-9i, therefore

$$\Delta F = \frac{18}{10}\Delta C$$

and therefore

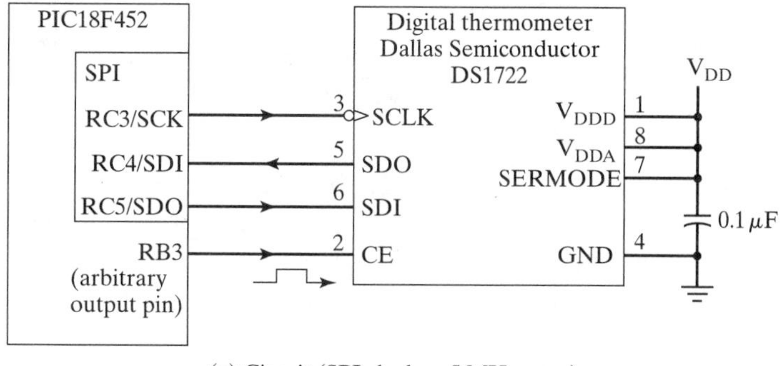

(a) Circuit (SPI clock = 5 MHz, max)

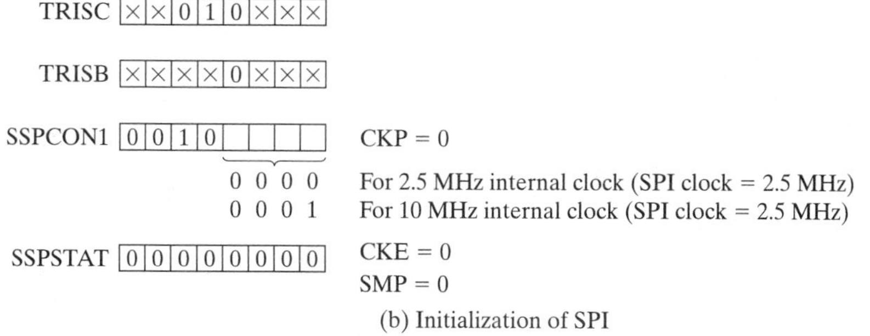

(b) Initialization of SPI

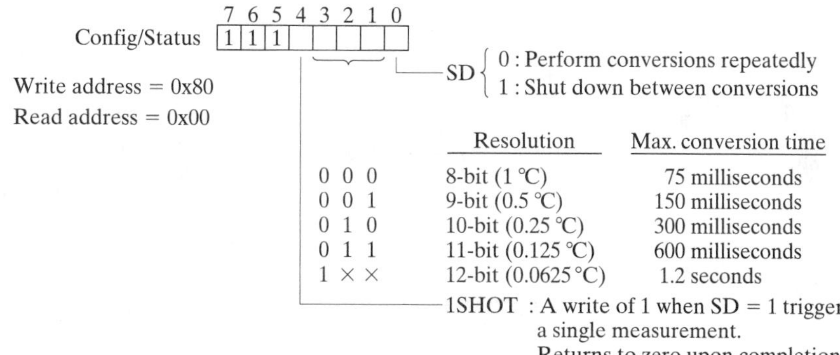

(c) DS1722 configuration

Figure 15-9 Digital thermometer use.

$$\Delta C = \frac{10}{18} \times 0.1 = \frac{1}{18} = 0.055°\text{C}$$

But 12-bit resolution produces increments of 0.0625°C. That is, even the maximum, 12-bit resolution does not quite yield 0.1°F resolution. In fact, it gives

$$\Delta F = \frac{18}{10} \times 0.0625 = 0.1125°\text{F}$$

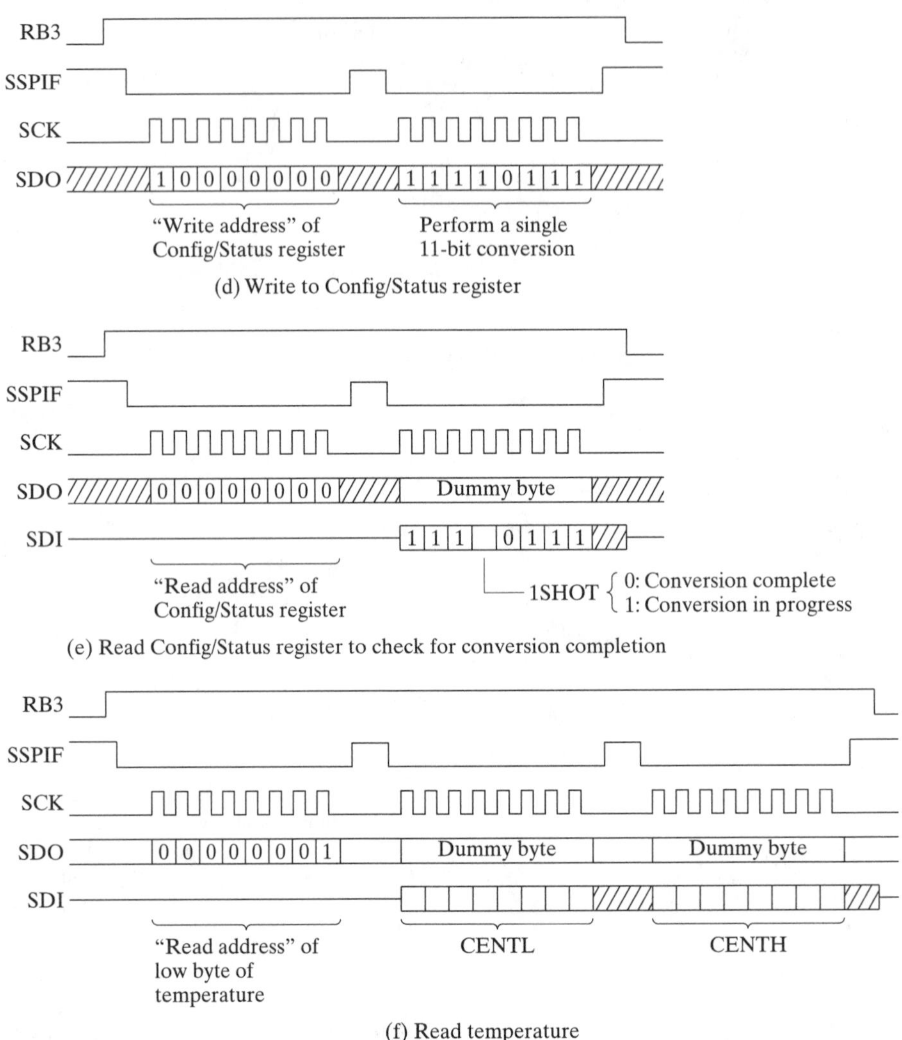

Figure 15-9 continued

15.9 MASTER–SLAVE INTERCONNECTIONS

Expansion beyond the resources of a single PIC18F452 can be achieved by interconnecting two or more PIC microcontrollers via the SPI lines. This might be done to implement a programmed peripheral chip (see Chapter 19), to gain extra CCP1/CCP2 timing facilities, or to partition a design to reduce the algorithmic complexity faced by a single CPU. The interconnections are shown in Figure 15-10. The SCK pin from the master is tied to each slave's SCK pin. Note that the master's SDO pin is connected to the SDI pin on the slave, or slaves. If more than one slave is employed, their SDO pins are tied together and to the master's SDI pin. This connection will work because before a transfer is carried out between the master and one of the slaves, the master will drive the slave's $\overline{\text{SS}}$ (slave-select) pin low. This does two things:

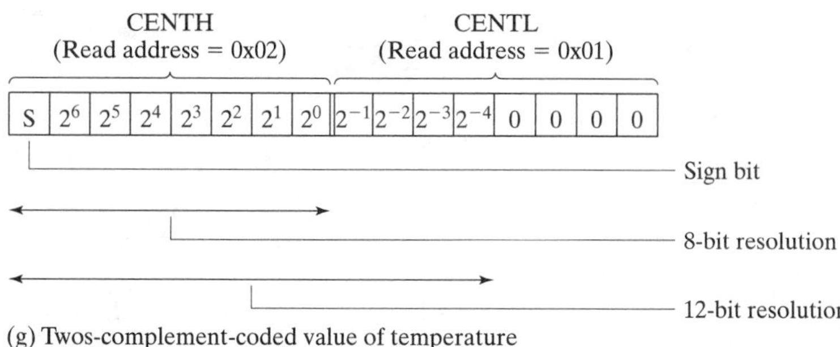

(g) Twos-complement-coded value of temperature

Temperature	CENTH: CENTL (binary)	CENTH: CENTL (hex)
+10.0625°C	0000 1010 0001 0000	0a 10
+1°C	0000 0001 0000 0000	01 00
+0.5°C	0000 0000 1000 0000	00 80
0°C	0000 0000 0000 0000	00 00
−0.5°C	1111 1111 1000 0000	ff 80
−1°C	1111 1111 0000 0000	ff 00
−10.0625°	1111 0101 1111 0000	f5 f0

(h) Examples

$$F = \frac{18}{10}C + 32$$

(i) Conversion to Fahrenheit

Figure 15-9 continued

- It enables the tristate buffer on the selected slave's SDO output pin.
- It enables the slave's SPI shift register and control of its SSPIF flag.

At the same time, the master leaves these functions disabled in the remaining slave chips by leaving their slave-select pins high. Each slave-select pin is driven by an otherwise unused output pin available on the master.

In addition to setting up the **TRIS** registers to select inputs and outputs appropriately, it is necessary to set up the **ADCON1** register according to the chart of Figure 10-2 so that the slave-select pin (which also can serve as RA5 or AN4) will be a digital I/O pin. Unless this is done, the slave's digital I/O circuitry will not be enabled and the slave's SPI function will not be controlled by the slave-select input. Furthermore, the slave's CPU will not be able to read the RA5 pin to know if a transfer is taking place.

The contents shown in Figure 15-10 for **SSPCON1** and **SSPSTAT** select the same CKP = 0, CKE = 1, and SMP = 0 in both the master and the slaves. Actually, any of the four combinations of CKP and CKE shown in Figure 15-10 will work as long as the selection for the slave or slaves matches the selection for the master. In every case, SMP = 0 must be used to ensure that incoming data is read in the middle of each clock period, when the data is not changing.

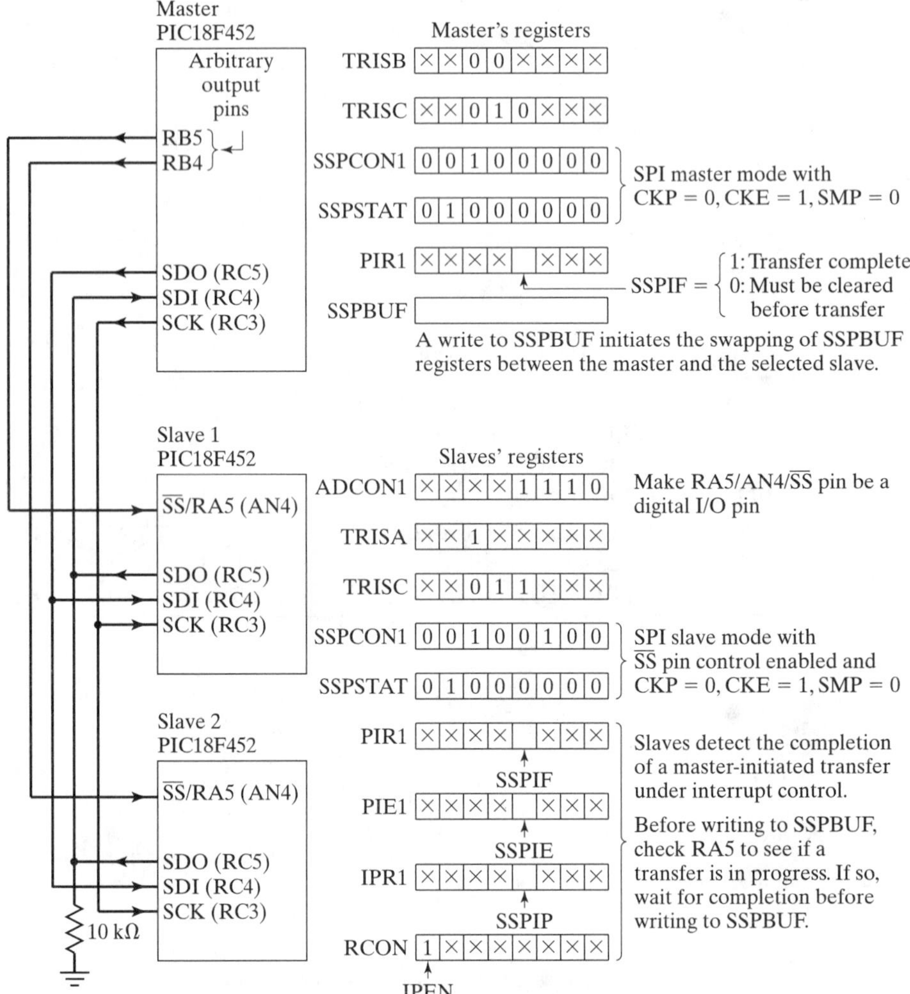

Figure 15-10 Master–slave SPI interconnections and registers.

Consider first the case for which the master is only sending data to a slave and never trying to receive data from that slave. It drives that slave's slave-select pin low, clears **SSPIF**, writes the data to be sent to the slave to **SSPBUF**, waits for the **SSPIF** flag to be set high again, and then drives the slave-select pin high again. For its part, the slave need not deal with the SPI facility until its **SSPIF** flag is set, generating an interrupt.

If the master is only receiving data from the slave and never trying to send information to the slave, then it can poll the slave periodically, perhaps every time around the mainline loop. The master can send a dummy byte that is different from what any slave data byte would be. If the slave's CPU does not write to its **SSPBUF** register before the master again polls the slave, then that dummy byte will be returned to the master. In this case, the master knows that the slave has not attempted to send a data byte. When the master's **SSPIF** flag is set at the end of the transfer, the master drives the slave-select pin high again and then reads **SSPBUF**. In this way, the master determines whether it has received a valid data byte on the one hand or a dummy byte on the other.

When the slave is ready to load a byte into **SSPBUF** (to be picked up when the master initiates the transfer), it must first check to make sure a transfer is not in progress. It can do this by reading RA5, the (active-low) slave-select pin. If it is high, then the write to **SSPBUF** can proceed. If it is low, then the slave must wait until RA5 goes high again before writing to **SSPBUF**. The wait will be no longer than 4 microseconds.

PROBLEMS

15-1 Heavy-duty output driver Allegro Microsystems has made their reputation with a wide variety of driver chips. Go to their Web site, www.allegromicro.com, and search for "5821." Download and print the data sheet for this part.

(a) Compare it with the 74HC595 "expansion output port" chip discussed in this chapter. What is the maximum SPI clock rate of the UCN5821A? What CKP and CKE combinations should be used with it? Is its "strobe" input active-low, active-high, rising-edge sensitive, or falling-edge sensitive? That is, what does it take to transfer its shift register contents to its output register?

(b) The driver for each output (shown on page 2 of the data sheet) is a bipolar Darlington circuit in which one transistor drives a second transistor to obtain a high sink current from its front-end CMOS shift register and control circuitry. Its open-collector output expects to drive a load whose other pin is connected to a supply voltage of up to 50 V with a load current of up to 500 mA. From the collector–emitter saturation voltage data for various current values, fit the data with a Thévenin equivalent that is more or less valid over the range of 100 mA to 350 mA.

(c) Check on the price and availability of the "UCN5821A" 16-pin-DIP version from the distributors covered by www.findchips.com.

15-2 LCD support The QwikFlash board uses six pins of the PIC18F452 to communicate with the LCD display (four pins for "nibble" transfers plus two more pins to drive the display's RS and E inputs). For an application that needs more I/O pins than the '452 offers, a 74HC164 serial-in, parallel-out shift register can help. Unlike the 74HC595, the 74HC164 shift register is not double buffered. Rather, the output pins are driven directly from the shift register flip-flops. If the application is already using the SPI interface, then the number of additional pins needed to drive the LCD is reduced to just two (to drive RS and E). The LCD's E pin serves the same role as the '595's latch clock input in that the LCD will not respond until the E pin sees a falling edge.

(a) Go to the Texas Instruments Web site, www.ti.com, search for 74HC164, and download the data sheet. Using Figure 7-2a for the LCD pinout, draw the complete interface circuit using RE0 and RE1 to drive RS and E.

(b) Will the same values of CKP and CKE work as for the 74HC595? What is the maximum SPI clock rate for the 74HC164 for supply voltages of at least 4.5 V?

(c) Rewrite the **InitLCD8** subroutine of Figure 7-8 for use with the SPI/74HC164 interface to the LCD.

(d) Rewrite the **DisplayC** and **DisplayV** subroutines of Figures 7-10 and 7-11 for use with this interface.

15-3 Digital potentiometer If an application involves analog circuitry, it will typically employ potentiometers in various roles. One use is to "tweak" small offset currents and voltages. Another is to compensate for unit-to-unit transducer sensitivity with a variable-gain op-amp circuit. Maxim Integrated Products makes a variety of digital potentiometers.

(a) Go to www.maxim-ic.com, search for "MAX5402," and download and print the data sheet for this tiny, eight-pin, surface-mount, 10 kΩ potentiometer with 256 taps. Check page 9 for the overall dimensions and for the pin spacing.

(b) Will the CKP = 0 and CKE = 1 SPI phasing alternative of Figure 15-3a used for the 74HC595 also work here? If not, what is needed?

(c) Check the application information on page 7 for the adjustable-gain, noninverting amplifier of Figure 5. If R1 is made equal to the potentiometer's end-to-end resistance (which is, nominally, 10 kΩ), then what are the minimum and maximum gains of the circuit? What is the incremental change in gain for each increment of the pot? Is this constant over the full range of pot settings?

(d) The end-to-end resistance of the pot is specified to have minimum and maximum values of 7.5 kΩ and 12.5 kΩ. Answer part *(c)* for each of these, assuming that the R1 value is 10 kΩ.

(e) In the final assembly of a device using this variable-gain circuit, *test code* would increment/decrement the pot until the optimum was achieved. The value to be written to the pot would be stored in the PIC18F452's nonvolatile data EEPROM. Thereafter, the application code would initialize the pot (once and for all) by copying the EEPROM value out to the pot. In Section 20.11, the storage and retrieval of data from the nonvolatile data EEPROM will be discussed. For this problem, a standard transducer input (e.g., a standard intensity light source) plus a transducer (e.g., a phototransistor) plus the variable op-amp circuit is to produce a voltage equal to $V_{DD}/2$, where V_{DD} is not only the PIC18F452's supply voltage but also that of the transducer.

The standard transducer input plus the transducer produces a voltage in the range of 0.5 V to 1.5 V. Choose the R1 value for the variable-gain amplifier of Figure 5 of the data sheet so that an output of 2.5 V is obtained whether the input is 0.5 V, 1.5 V, or anything in between. What is the maximum value of R1 that can be used, even with the part-to-part variations among MAX5402 parts?

15-4 Output port expansion Assume that the output port expansion circuit of Figure 15-6 is extended to *three* ports, labeled OUTU, OUTH, and OUTL. Also assume the SPI bus is not used for anything else, not even for the expanded input port circuitry of Figure 15-6.

(a) How many I/O pins are used so as to gain these 24 output pins?

(b) Write an **OUT** subroutine that copies the three RAM variables, **OUTU**, **OUTH**, and **OUTL**, to the expanded output ports.

15-5 Temperature display

(a) Initialize the SPI module as well as the DS1722 digital thermometer to initiate a single maximum-resolution temperature measurement.

(b) Write a **Fahrenheit** subroutine that will query the DS1722 and will return if a conversion is in progress. Otherwise, the subroutine is to read the temperature and convert it to an integer representing tenths of a degree Fahrenheit. Then write the temperature to the display's second line using the format

```
ddd.d °F
```

where the temperature is assumed to be a positive value (i.e., above freezing). If the hundreds' digit is 0, replace it with a blank. Then initiate a new measurement.

Chapter

16

OUTPUT TIME-INTERVAL CONTROL (P4 TEMPLATE)

16.1 OVERVIEW

When a microcontroller drives a peripheral device or peripheral circuitry, it has two requirements to fulfill. It must *sequence* the outputs appropriately. This was exemplified by the devices of the last chapter, especially the four-port expansion circuit of Figure 15-6. The microcontroller must also *time* the output changes appropriately.

For the fastest sequencing of events, the microcontroller paces the sequencing in either of two ways:

- Using the execution time of successive instructions and counting cycles (e.g., the **T40** subroutine employed by the **DisplayC** and **DisplayV** subroutines)
- Using internal or external circuits (e.g., the **SSPIF** flag control of the SPI module)

For slow sequencing, the microcontroller can pace the sequencing in either of two ways:

- By counting loop times of the mainline loop (e.g., the blinking of the "Alive" LED of Section 5.5)
- By checking an external flag each time around the mainline loop (e.g., the digital thermometer's "1SHOT" flag of Figure 15-9c).

This chapter addresses the sequencing of events in the vast middle ground between these two extremes. Sometimes the sequencing is orchestrated in response to external interrupts from a device via the INT0, INT1, or INT2 pin, as discussed in Section 9.6. An example of this sequencing will be illustrated in Section 16.2 for a magnetic card reader. In other cases, the timing is derived from periodically occurring interrupts generated by any one of three mechanisms discussed in Section 16.3:

- Timer2
- CCP1 and Timer1
- CCP2 and Timer3

Generating a *jitter-free* square wave output, wherein the period from one cycle of the waveform to the next is *precisely* the same, is a capability delivered by the PIC18F452's pulse-width-modulation (PWM) facility for output frequencies above 1 kHz or so, and with the compare-mode facility for any frequency lower than 1 kHz. As will be seen in Section 16.4, the PWM approach has the advantage of generating an output square wave with a frequency as high as the PIC18F452's internal clock rate and with no CPU intervention once the waveform has been initiated. The compare-mode approach of Section 16.5 has the advantage of permitting CPU interactions (e.g., counting the cycles and stopping after a precise number of cycles) even as the generated square wave is jitter free.

16.2 EXTERNAL CONTROL OF TIMING

The magnetic card reader of Figure 16-1 represents a good example of a device whose interactions with a microcontroller are timed by the device itself, not by the microcontroller. Whether the magnetic card is scanned quickly or slowly, the serial bit stream is reliably read. Figure 16-2a shows the connections between the card reader's active-low outputs and the microcontroller. The $\overline{\text{Strobe}}$ output is used as a rising-edge-sensitive interrupt input to the microcontroller's RB2/INT2 pin. The $\overline{\text{Data}}$ output produces a valid data bit at the time of each INT2 rising-edge interrupt. A third output, $\overline{\text{Card present}}$, is not needed, because the data is framed by a string of leading and trailing 0s. That is, when a card is scanned, the data

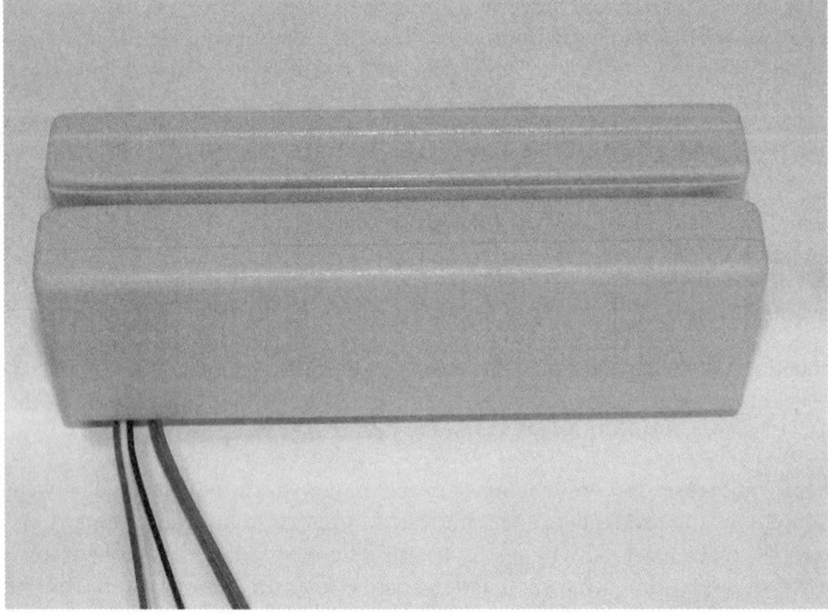

Figure 16-1 Magtek magnetic card reader.

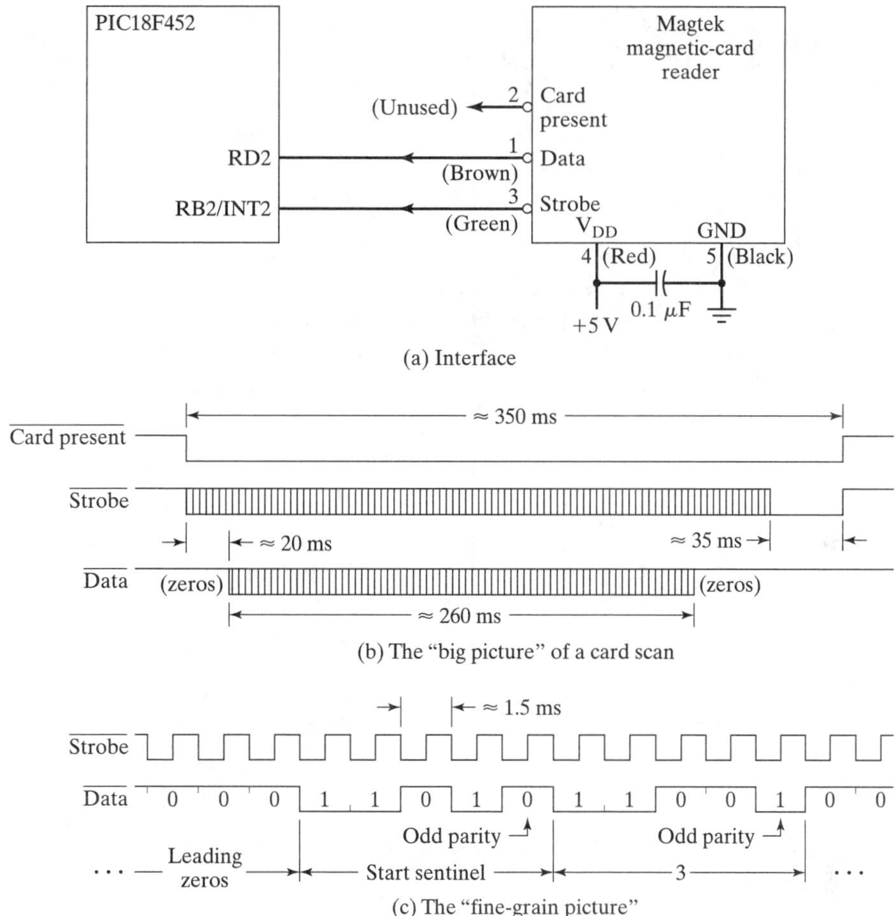

Figure 16-2 Magnetic card reader operation.

bits read in response to the first dozen or so interrupts will be 0s. The interrupt handler can initialize upon a sequence of more than five 0s and then wait for the first 1 to begin reading data.

The ANSI/ISO international standard for magnetic cards defines *three* tracks of data. The upper track, "Track 1," can hold up to 79 alphanumeric characters, each encoded with 6 data bits plus 1 parity bit. The middle track, "Track 2," is the most widely used track. It holds up to 40 numeric or control characters. It is the track read by the Magtek card reader of Figure 16-1 as well as bank card readers, gasoline pump readers, and myriad other commonly used readers. The bottom track, "Track 3," holds up to 107 numeric or control characters and is used for both reading and writing (by cards supporting this feature).

The timing diagram of Figure 16-2c illustrates the beginning of a card's data. Each group of 5 bits is read in least-significant bit (LSb) first. The ANSI/ISO standard specifies that the message string should begin with a "start sentinel," encoded as B′01011′, as shown in Figure 16-2c. The message string ends with two groups: an "end sentinel" encoded as B′11111′ and a Longitudinal Redundancy Check (LRC) character. The reading of a magnetic card is supported by strong error checking, implemented with the parity bit associated with each character and the LRC character (defined in Figure 16-2f).

Odd Parity	b3	b2	b1	b0	Meaning of Group	
0	1	0	1	1	b	Start sentinel
1	0	0	1	1	3	First data character
0	0	0	0	1	1	Second data character
0	0	0	1	0	2	Third data character
1	0	1	0	1	2	Fourth data character
		• • •				
0	0	1	1	1	7	Last data character
1	1	1	1	1	f	End sentinel
1	0	1	0	0		LRC character

(d) Message format

Display each four-bit "nibble" by appending an upper nibble of 0x3 and displaying the resulting byte (see Figure 7-12)
Start sentinel will be displayed as ";"
End sentinel will be displayed as "?"
Control characters and field separators will be displayed as : < = >

(e) Encoding of decimal digits plus six control characters

Parity bit produces odd parity on each row
LRC character produces even parity on each column

(f) Parity check and Longitudinal Redundancy Check (LRC)

Figure 16-2 continued

Example 16-1 Describe the operation of **INT2handler**, the interrupt handler for a magnetic card reader, ignoring the parity and LRC checks.

Solution

Maintain a **CHAR** variable for building each group of 5 bits of the data stream into an ASCII character. Maintain a **BITCNT** variable for counting the 5 data bits making up each character. After each group of 5 data bits has been shifted into bits 4, 3, 2, 1, 0 of **CHAR**, change the upper nibble of **CHAR** to B′0011′. Store the resulting ASCII character into a 40-byte **CARD_BUF** buffer using **FSR2** as an auto-incrementing pointer. When the received group of 5 bits is B′11111′ (representing the End Sentinel), set a flag for the mainline code indicating that a complete string has been received and is ready to be displayed.

Continue to read incoming bits with each successive interrupt. When 5-bit groups return to B′00000′, wait until a 1 appears in the data stream, signaling the start of the data for a new card scan. Clear the flag to the mainline code, reinitialize **FSR2** to the beginning of **CARD_BUF**, and begin receiving and counting the bits into **CHAR**.

This procedure assumes that **FSR2** is not used for any other tasks. If such is not the case, then save and restore **FSR2H:FSR2L** to and from a 2-byte RAM copy of its contents.

16.3 PERIODIC INTERRUPT GENERATOR

Timer2 provides a mechanism for obtaining periodic interrupts using the circuit shown in Figure 16-3a. The frequency of interrupts is

$$F = \frac{F_{osc}/4}{A \times B \times C}$$

where

$$A = 1, 4, \text{ or } 16$$
$$B = 1, 2, 3, 4, 5, \ldots, 255, \text{ or } 256$$
$$C = 1, 2, 3, 4, 5, \ldots, 15, \text{ or } 16$$

These three parameters are selected by initializing **PR2** and **T2CON**, as shown in Figure 16-3b. The Timer2 interrupt handler need only clear the **TMR2IF** flag, carry out the desired periodic action, and return.

These Timer2 interrupts can be used directly, to invoke a task every millisecond, for example. Alternatively, they can be used in much the same way as loop-time counting is used to time slow events. In this case, the Timer2 interrupts would give a finer timing resolution than loop-time counting would provide and would be used to support tasks having a shorter duration.

In Chapter 13, the CCP1 module was discussed in its role as a *capture* module (as was CCP2). In this section, its role as a periodic interrupt generator will be discussed. As shown in Figure 16-4, Timer1 with its prescaler, P, is clocked at the microcontroller's internal clock rate. **TMR1H:TMR1L** is compared with **CCPR1H:CCPR1L** every P^{th} clock period. When they are equal, **TMR1H:TMR1L** is reset to 0x0000 and the **CCP1IF** flag is set, generating an interrupt. Within the interrupt service routine, the **CCP1IF** flag is cleared and the desired periodic action taken.

Example 16-2 Consider the stepper-motor drive circuit of Figure 16-5. Each time the Allegro controller chip is pulsed, the motor takes a step either CW or CCW, depending on the state of the Direction input. With the scheme of Figure 16-4, what is the slowest stepping rate available? Assume a 2.5 MHz internal clock rate.

Solution

With CCPR1 set to 0xffff and with P = 8, the maximum period between steps is

$$\text{Period} = 65{,}536 \times 8 \times 0.4\ \mu\text{s} = 209{,}715.2\ \mu\text{s}$$

Consequently, the minimum stepping rate is

$$\text{Rate} = 1{,}000{,}000/209{,}715.2 = 4.8\ \text{steps/second}$$

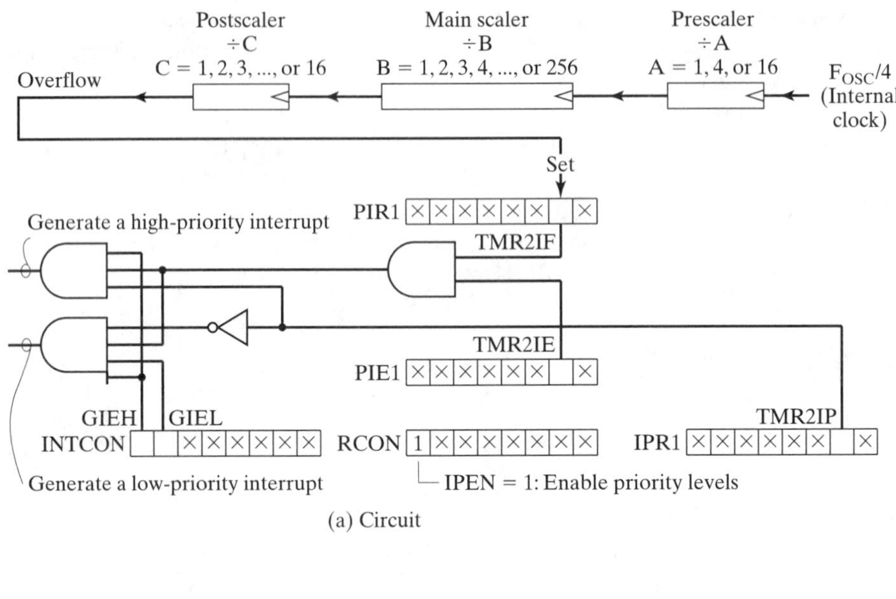

(a) Circuit

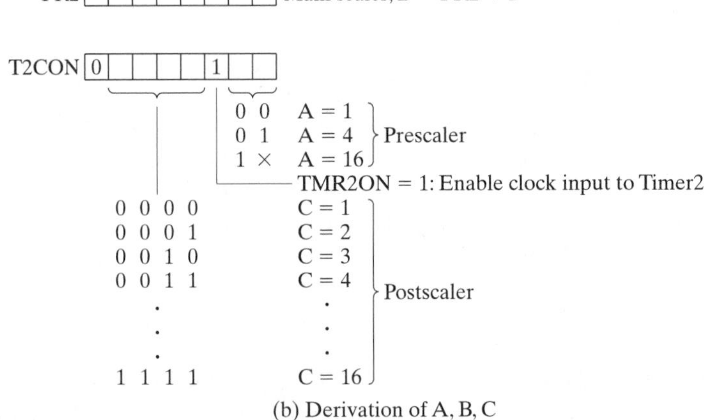

(b) Derivation of A, B, C

Figure 16-3 Timer2 use for generating periodic interrupts.

Example 16-3 With this prescaler value, P = 8, what should be loaded into **CCPR1** to step the stepper at a rate of 250 steps/second? At 1000 steps/second?

Solution

The relationship between the value of **CCPR1** and the step rate is given by

$$\text{Rate} = \frac{2{,}500{,}000}{(\text{CCPR1}+1) \times \text{P}} \text{ steps/second}$$

Therefore, **CCPR1** is given by

$$\textbf{CCPR1} = \frac{312{,}500}{\text{Rate}} - 1$$

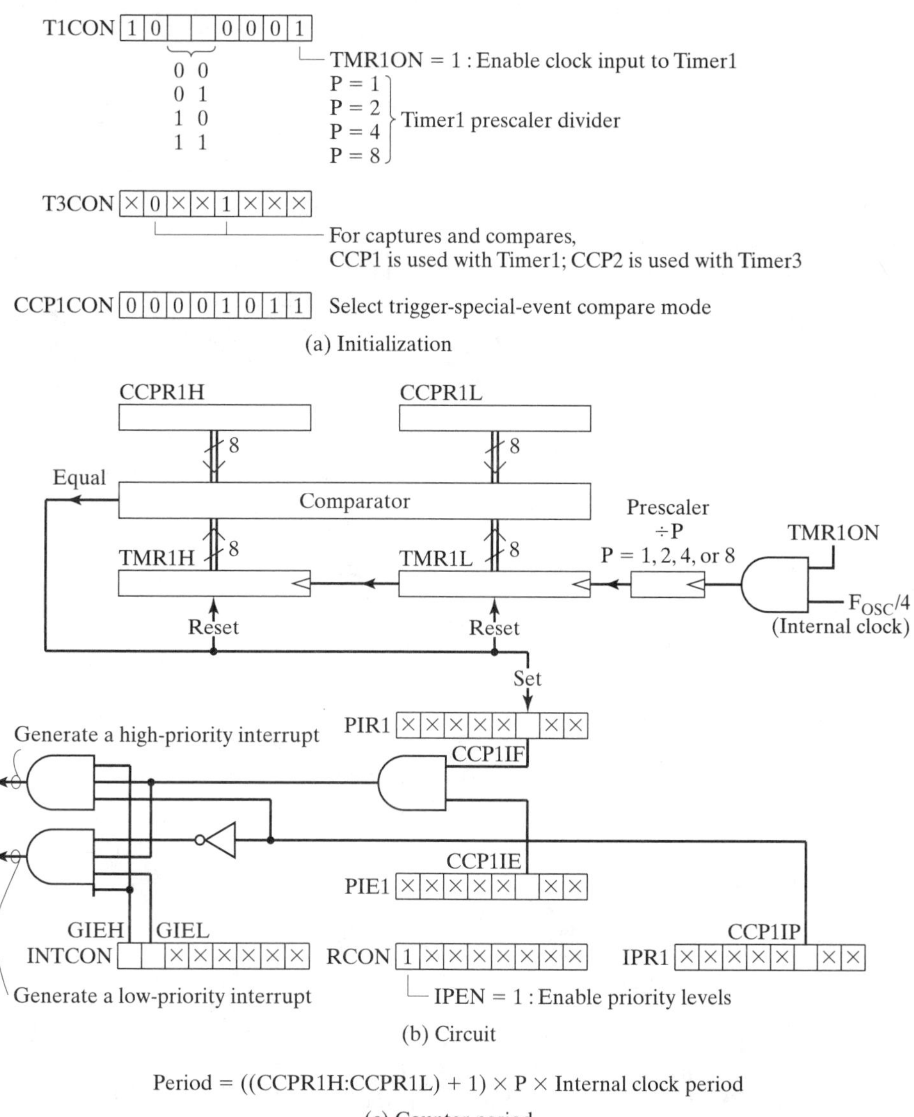

Figure 16-4 CCP1/Timer1 trigger-special-event compare mode.

For a rate of 250 steps/second, **CCPR1** = 1249.
For a rate of 1000 steps/second, **CCPR1** = 312.

Example 16-4 What might be the interactions between the mainline code and the **CCP1handler** interrupt handler so that a mainline routine can command the stepper motor to step a variable number of steps in a given direction?

Solution

Assume that when the stepper is stepped, the stepping rate is 250 steps/second. A 2-byte, twos-complement-coded variable, **NUMSTPSH:NUMSTPSL**, might be used for communication

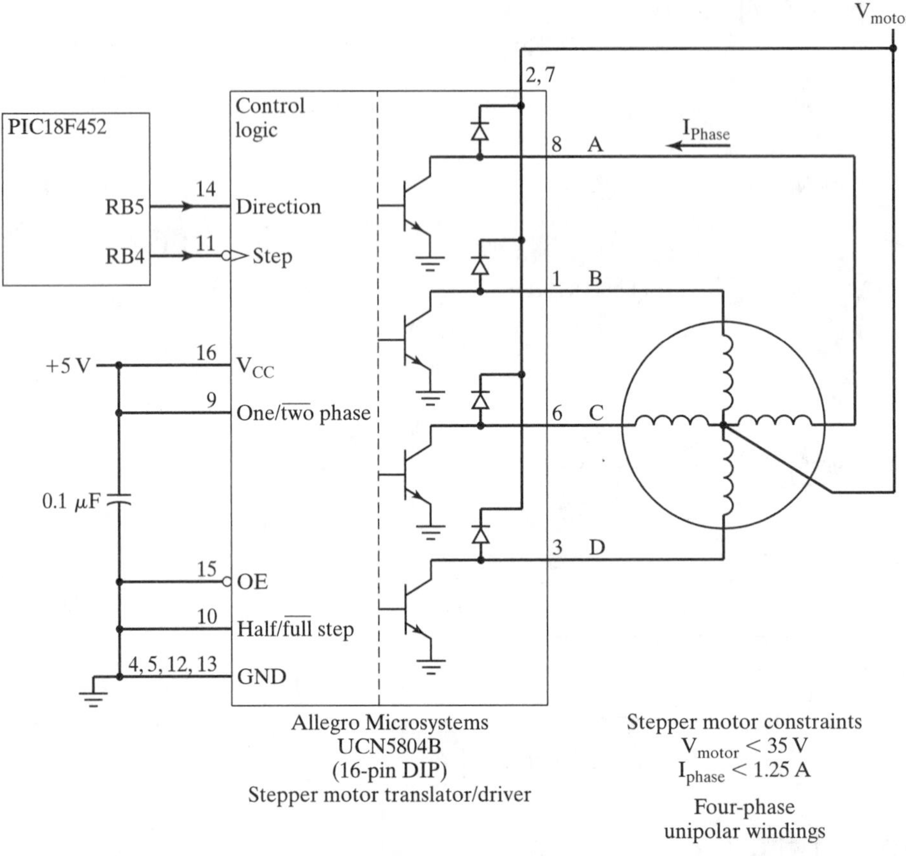

	Full-step, wave-drive sequence (Minimum power)				Full-step, two-phase sequence (Max. turning rate)				Half-step sequence (Max. resolution)			
	Half/$\overline{\text{full}}$ step = L One/$\overline{\text{two}}$ phase = H				Half/$\overline{\text{full}}$ step = L One/$\overline{\text{two}}$ phase = L				Half/$\overline{\text{full}}$ step = H One/$\overline{\text{two}}$ phase = L			
	A	B	C	D	A	B	C	D	A	B	C	D
Power-on reset state →	L	H	H	H	L	H	H	L	L	H	H	H
Direction = H	H	L	H	H	L	L	H	H	L	L	H	H
↕	H	H	L	H	H	L	L	H	H	L	H	H
	H	H	H	L	H	H	L	L	H	L	L	H
	L	H	H	H	L	H	H	L	H	H	L	H
Direction = L									H	H	L	L
									H	H	H	L
									L	H	H	L
									L	H	H	H

Figure 16-5 Stepper-motor interface.

between the mainline code and the interrupt handler. Every 4 milliseconds when a CCP1 interrupt occurs, the handler clears the **CCP1IF** flag and examines **NUMSTPSH:NUMSTPSL**. If it is 0, it simply returns without taking a step. If it is positive, it decrements **NUMSTPSH: NUMSTPSL** toward 0 and takes a CW step; if negative, it increments **NUMSTPSH: NUMSTPSL** toward 0 and takes a CCW step.

The mainline code treats the step request as a signed number to be *added* to **NUMSTPSH: NUMSTPSL**. Thus, this 2-byte number serves as an accumulator for the number of steps remaining to be taken. It removes the necessity of completing one mainline step command before initiating another.

Question

The mainline code adds a signed number to **NUMSTPSH:NUMSTPSL** to initiate a step command. The interrupt handler increments or decrements this number if it is not 0. It would seem that an interrupt occurring after the mainline code has added into **NUMSTPSL**, but before it has added into **NUMSTPSH**, could produce a net error. However, the author cannot find an example of an initial value plus a signed number to be added to it that produces a net error when the **CCP1** interrupt occurs between the two additions. Is this, in fact, generally true or should the 2-byte addition in the mainline code be treated as a critical region?

Example 16-5 Consider a stepper-motor application wherein the motor rotates continuously at a rate whose value is entered using the rate-sensitive RPG scheme of Section 8.5 and displayed on the LCD display. Why should the desired value of **CCPR1H:CCPR1L** be passed to the **CCP1handler** subroutine in **CCPR1HCOPY:CCPR1LCOPY** for the handler to read rather than having the mainline code load **CCPR1H:CCPR1L** directly?

Solution

If the value of **CCPR1H:CCPR1L** is decreased just before the moment when **TMR1H: TMR1L** reached the old value, then the compare might be skipped. In that case, the stepper motor will "hiccup" with a step that takes an extra 1/4.8 = 0.2 second. For example, if the rate is changed from 250 steps/second to 260 steps/second, then **CCPR1** must be changed from 1249 to 1201. If **TMR1** contains 1225 as **CCPR1** is loaded with the new value, **TMR1** will not equal **CCPR1** until it has incremented all the way up to 65,535, rolled over, and then incremented back up to 1201. Instead of 1250 × 8 or 1202 × 8 internal clock cycles between steps, during the transition from the old rate to the new rate, it goes from 0x4e1 (hex for 1249) to 0x04c9 (hex for 1201), or

$$0x04c9 - 0x04e1 = 0xffe8 = 65{,}512$$

internal clock cycles.

The interrupt handler is called as **TMR1** is reset to 0; therefore, at the time the interrupt handler changes **CCPR1** from 1249 to 1201 (or any other relatively large number), **TMR1** contains such a small number that the problem is avoided.

Just as the CCP1/Timer1 combination can be used as a periodic interrupt generator, so also can the CCP2/Timer3 combination, as shown in Figure 16-6. This mode of operation, with

```
CCP2CON = B'00001011
```

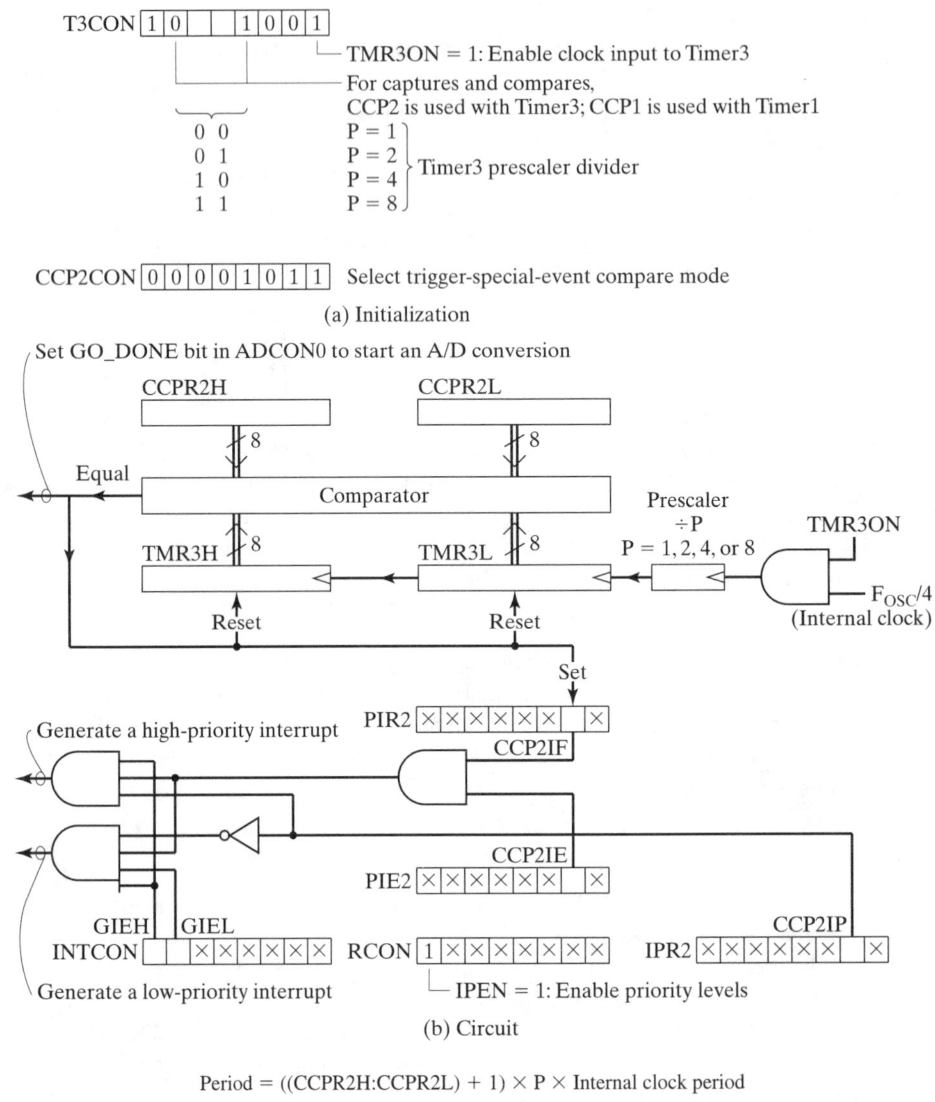

Figure 16-6 CCP2/Timer3 trigger-special-event compare mode.

has a "special event trigger" feature that will also initiate an analog-to-digital conversion if the ADC is enabled, as was mentioned in Section 10.5. In this way, the ADC can be set up to collect samples at a specified sample rate.

Slower periodic action than can be achieved using either CCP1/Timer1 or CCP2/Timer3 is generally accomplished in the mainline code by counting loop times. However, a variable period, with an arbitrary resolution in the period, can be obtained using CCP1/Timer1 (or CCP2/Timer3) just as was discussed at the beginning of this section using Timer2.

Example 16-6 Call an **Action** subroutine with any period up to 1 second and with a resolution in the period of 1 millisecond. The period is controlled by a mainline subroutine as it varies **PERIODH:PERIODL**.

Solution

First, set up CCP1/Timer1 to generate interrupts every millisecond. Within the interrupt handler, decrement a 2-byte variable, **CCP1CNTH:CCP1CNTL**, down to 0. When it reaches 0, call the **Action** subroutine. Also reload the counter with the value of the variable, **PERIODH:PERIODL**.

16.4 FAST JITTER-FREE SQUARE WAVE OUTPUT

The PIC18F452's pulse-width-modulation (PWM) facility can be used to generate a jitter-free square wave output with a frequency as high as the internal clock rate of the microcontroller and as low as 1/4096th of the internal clock rate (i.e., 610 Hz for an internal clock rate of 2.5 MHz). Once set up, the PWM circuit generates the output frequency with no further intervention by the CPU. The PWM facility includes the ability to vary the duty cycle (i.e., to modulate the pulse width), but for use here, the duty cycle will be set to 50%.

The PWM module is built from parts drawn from Timer2 and parts drawn from either CCP1 (to generate a square wave output on the CCP1 pin) or CCP2 (for an output on the CCP2 pin). Its circuit is shown in Figure 16-7. The oscillator frequency itself (i.e., four times the internal clock frequency) can be used as the PWMclock. Alternatively, the PWMclock can be ¼ or 1/16 of F_{osc}.

The heart of the PWM circuit is a 10-bit counter made up of the 8-bit **TMR2** counter preceded by a 2-bit counter. To gain insight into how this counter counts, consider the case that produces the highest frequency output, $F_{osc}/4$ (the same frequency as the chip's internal clock rate). **T2CON** is loaded with B′00000100′ to get PWMclock = F_{osc}. **PR2** is loaded with B′00000000′ so that **PR2** + 1, the input to the upper 8 bits of the 10-bit comparator is B′00000001′, and the full 10-bit comparator input is 4(**PR2** + 1) = B′0000000100′. The 10-bit counter made up of **TMR2** and its 2-bit front-end counter counts as follows:

```
              .
              .
              .
3 = 0000 0000 11
4 = 0000 0001 00        comparator sees a match and resets TMR2
1 = 0000 0000 01
2 = 0000 0000 10
3 = 0000 0000 11
4 = 0000 0001 00        another match and reset
              .
              .
              .
```

Notice that the period equals four PWMclock periods. The output flip-flop, which drives the output pin, is set as the 10-bit comparator detects equality.

To obtain a square wave, the lower 10-bit comparator must detect when the 10-bit counter reaches half of this value, 2(**PR2** + 1), and must reset the output flip-flop at that moment. The fixed 10-bit input to the lower comparator is the same as the fixed 10-bit input to the upper comparator shifted one place to the right.

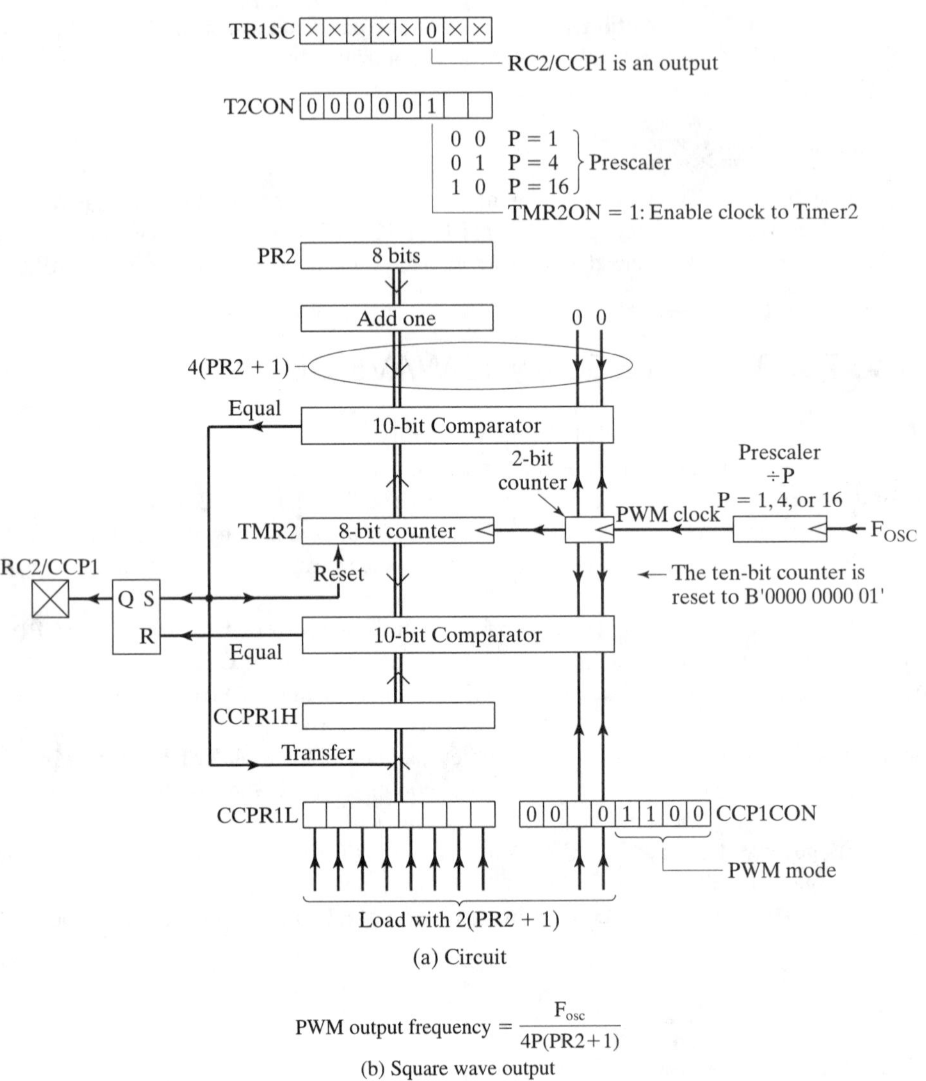

(a) Circuit

$$\text{PWM output frequency} = \frac{F_{osc}}{4P(PR2+1)}$$

(b) Square wave output

Figure 16-7 PWM square wave-generating circuit.

Notice that the **CCPR1H** input to the lower comparator is *not* loaded directly by an application program. Rather, it is loaded after a write by an application program to **CCPR1L** *and* a subsequent reset of **TMR2**. This mechanism solves, in hardware, the problem addressed in software in Example 16-5. Changing the duty cycle will never generate the kind of glitch discussed in that example.

To help make this use of the PWM facility more concrete, consider Figure 16-8. The left-hand column lists the PWM period as an integral number of internal clock periods, beginning with a value of 1, the highest output rate (i.e., 2.5 MHz for the QwikFlash board). Using a PWMclock divider of 1 and all 256 integer values of **PR2** produces output PWM periods of

$$N \times 0.4 \text{ microseconds} \quad \text{for } N = 1, 2, 3, \ldots, 256$$

PWM Period / Internal Clock Period	PR2	10-bit Value of 4 (PR2 + 1)	2 (PR2 + 1)		T2CON Prescaler
			CCPR1L	CCP1CON Bits	
1	00000000	0000000100	00000000	10	PWMclock = F_{osc} (Prescaler = 1)
2	00000001	0000001000	00000001	00	
3	00000010	0000001100	00000001	10	
4	00000011	0000010000	00000010	00	
•	•	•	•	•	
•	•	•	•	•	
255	11111110	1111111100	01111111	10	
256	11111111	0000000000	00000000	00	
260 = 65x4	01000000	0100000100	00100000	10	PWMclock = $F_{osc}/4$ (Prescaler = 4)
264 = 66x4	01000001	0100001000	00100001	00	
268 = 67x4	01000010	0100001100	00100001	10	
272 = 68x4	01000011	0100010000	00100010	00	
•	•	•	•	•	
•	•	•	•	•	
1020 = 255x4	11111110	1111111100	01111111	10	
1024 = 256x4	11111111	0000000000	00000000	00	
1040 = 65x16	01000000	0100000100	00100000	10	PWMclock = $F_{osc}/16$ (Prescaler = 16)
1056 = 66x16	01000001	0100001000	00100001	00	
1072 = 67x16	01000010	0100001100	00100001	10	
1088 = 68x16	01000011	0100010000	00100010	00	
•	•	•	•	•	
•	•	•	•	•	
4080 = 255x16	11111110	1111111100	01111111	10	
4096 = 256x16	11111111	0000000000	00000000	00	

Figure 16-8 PWM output period and the register contents that produce it.

Using a PWMclock divider of 4, longer periods can be obtained, all the way up to

$$1024 \times 0.4 \text{ microseconds}$$

but with a resolution of only

$$4 \times 0.4 = 1.6 \text{ microseconds}$$

While the chart indicates only the 192 values from

$$260 \times 0.4 = 104 \text{ microseconds}$$

up to

$$1024 \times 0.4 = 409.6 \text{ microseconds}$$

the PWMclock divider of 4 actually produces 256 values, beginning with 1.6 microseconds for PR2 = 0, 3.2 microseconds for PR2 = 1, 4.8 microseconds for PR2 = 2, etc. Finally, with a PWMclock divider of 16, the period extends up to

$$4096 \times 0.4 = 1638.4 \text{ microseconds}$$

for a frequency of 610 Hz.

Building a PWM circuit with CCP2 and Timer2 is virtually the same as the circuit of Figure 16-7, substituting CCP2 registers for CCP1 registers. The CCP2/Timer2 alternative does have one option not available to the CCP1/Timer2 PWM circuit. Whereas the pin associated with CCP1 is RC2 of **PORTC**, either one of *two* pins can be assigned to CCP2:

```
PORTC, bit RC1
```

or

```
PORTB, bit RB3
```

The selection is made with the **CCP2MX** bit of the **CONFIG3H** configuration byte (programmed into the chip along with the bits that select either the 10 MHz or the 2.5 MHz internal clock). Refer to Section 20.2 for the specification of the configuration bytes.

16.5 GENERAL JITTER-FREE SQUARE WAVE OUTPUT

The last section introduced a mechanism for producing a jitter-free square wave output *requiring no ongoing support.* In contrast, the periodic interrupt generator of Section 16.3 supports applications for which an action routine must be executed periodically (e.g., step a stepper motor). The timing jitter obtained in this latter case is determined by the varying latency experienced by the interrupt handler and is satisfactory for most applications. However, for an application requiring a periodic action and a jitter-free output, the PIC18F452's CCP1 or CCP2 module provides the mechanism.

Consider the compare-mode circuit of Figure 16-9. With an internal clock of 2.5 MHz and the Timer1 prescaler set to 1, **TMR1H:TMR1L** will increment every 0.4 microseconds, giving the maximum resolution for controlling output timing. During each clock cycle, **TMR1H:TMR1L** is incremented and compared with **CCPR1H:CCPR1L**. When **TMR1** eventually equals **CCPR1**, the **CCP1IF** flag is set and an interrupt is generated. At the precise moment of the compare, regardless of what the CPU is doing, the CCP1 module can be made to set, to clear, or to toggle the RC2/CCP1 pin.

Even when there is no action other than the toggling of the output pin, this approach can be used to generate a jitter-free square wave for frequencies below those that can be obtained using the PWM approach (e.g., below 610 Hz for a PIC18F452 with a 2.5 MHz internal clock rate).

Example 16-7 What is the minimum frequency of the jitter-free square wave that can be generated by the circuit of Figure 16-9?

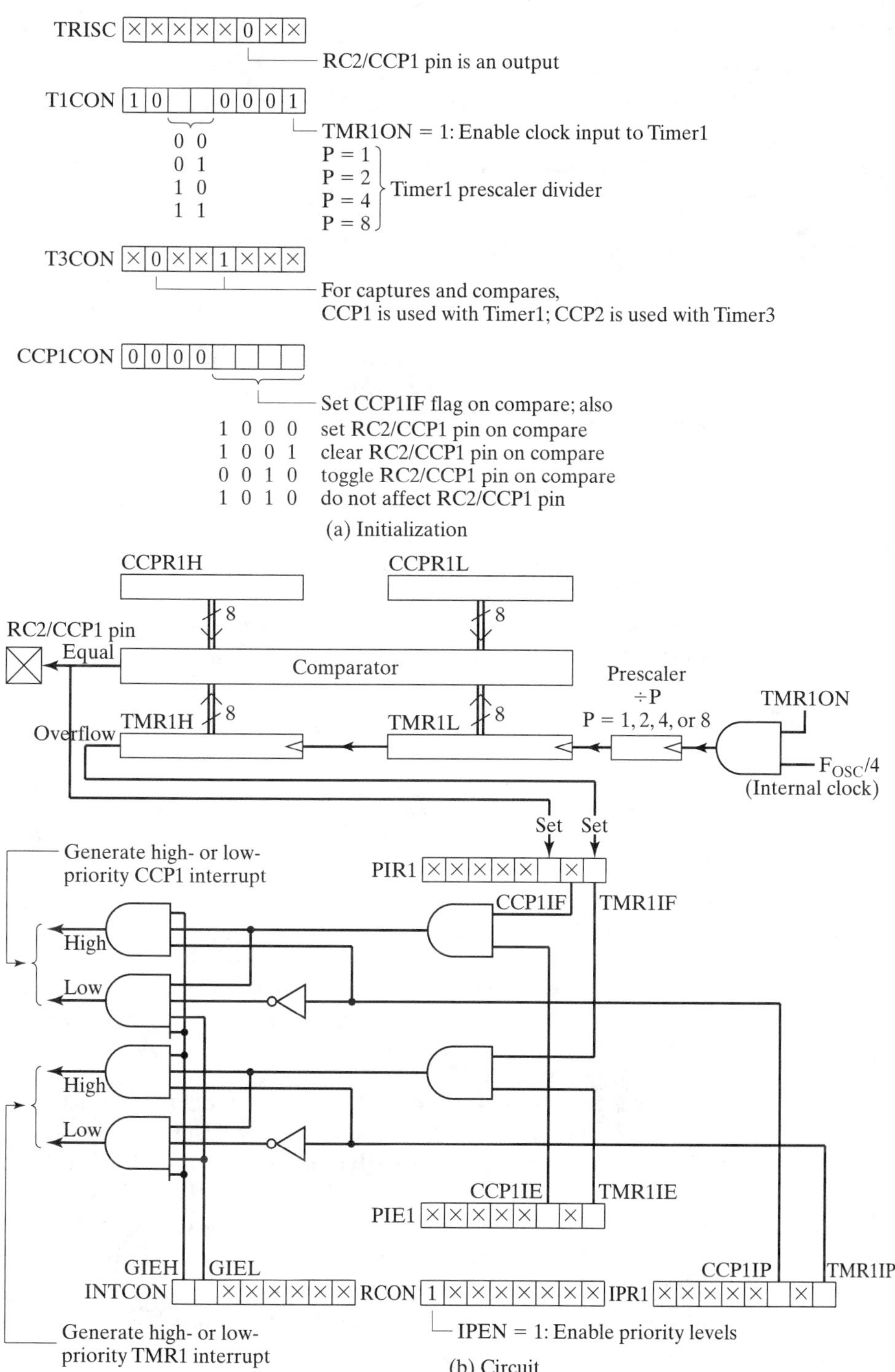

TRISC ×××××0××
RC2/CCP1 pin is an output
T1CON 10 0001
TMR1ON = 1: Enable clock input to Timer1
0 0 P = 1
0 1 P = 2
1 0 P = 4
1 1 P = 8
Timer1 prescaler divider
T3CON ×0××1×××
For captures and compares,
CCP1 is used with Timer1; CCP2 is used with Timer3
CCP1CON 0000
Set CCP1IF flag on compare; also
1 0 0 0 set RC2/CCP1 pin on compare
1 0 0 1 clear RC2/CCP1 pin on compare
0 0 1 0 toggle RC2/CCP1 pin on compare
1 0 1 0 do not affect RC2/CCP1 pin
(a) Initialization
CCPR1H
CCPR1L
RC2/CCP1 pin
Equal
Comparator
8
Prescaler
÷P
P = 1, 2, 4, or 8
TMR1ON
TMR1H
TMR1L
Overflow
FOSC/4
(Internal clock)
Set
Set
Generate high- or low-priority CCP1 interrupt
PIR1
CCP1IF
TMR1IF
High
Low
CCP1IE
TMR1IE
PIE1
GIEH
GIEL
INTCON
RCON 1
IPR1
CCP1IP
TMR1IP
IPEN = 1: Enable priority levels
Generate high- or low-priority TMR1 interrupt
(b) Circuit

Figure 16-9 CCP1/Timer1 compare mode.

Solution

With a 2.5 MHz internal clock rate and with a Timer1 prescaler of 8, **TMR1H:TMR1L** will be incremented every 3.2 microseconds. The 65,536 count sequence takes 209,715.2 microseconds, or just over 0.2 second. If the CCP1 pin is toggled every 0.2 second, it will produce a square wave with a period of 0.4 second, or 2.5 Hz.

Example 16-8 What must be done to generate a 10 Hz jitter-free square wave?

Solution

An interrupt must be made to occur every 50 milliseconds, the duration of the desired half-period. With a ÷8 prescaler, and the attendant clocking of **TMR1H:TMR1L** every 3.2 microseconds, this leads to 50,000/3.2 = 15,625 counts of the counter. With

```
T1CON   = B'10110001'
```

and

```
CCP1CON = B'00000010'
```

the output pin will toggle with each interrupt. Within the interrupt handler do just two things: add 15,625 to **CCPR1** and then clear the **CCP1IF** flag, as shown here.

```
CCP1handler
        movlw  low 15625
        addwf  CCPR1L,F
        movlw  high 15625
        addwfc  CCPR1H,F
        bcf  PIR1,CCP1IF
        return
```

Each match between **TMR1H:TMR1L** and **CCPR1H:CCPR1L** will produce one transition of the jitter-free square wave output while also providing the notification that it is time to increment **CCPR1** by 15,625 counts.

Notice that there is no hurry in responding to the interrupt. As long as it is serviced within 50 milliseconds (the time of the next output transition), that will be soon enough.

Just as Timer1 was extended in Section 13.4 to support long time-interval measurements, so it can be extended here to support the generation of long jitter-free outputs. Consider the circuit of Figure 16-10. **TMR1X:TMR1H:TMR1L** is the 24-bit version of **TMR1** that, with its prescaler set to 1 and with the 2.5 MHz internal clock, rolls over every 6.7 seconds. **CCPR1X:CCPR1H:CCPR1L** is the 24-bit version of **CCPR1** and is able to control the time interval between changes on the RC2/CCP2 pin to any number of 0.4 microsecond clock periods up to an interval of 6.7 seconds. **DTIMEX:DTIMEH:DTIMEL** is the desired half-period of a jitter-free square wave output.

Each **TMR1** overflow causes a low-priority interrupt that increments **TMR1X** and clears the **TMR1IF** flag. Each **CCP1** compare interrupt calls for a check on the equality of the 3-byte **CCPR1** with the 3-byte **TMR1.** This reduces to a comparison of **CCPR1X** with **TMR1X**. It is crucial to know what the value of **TMR1X** was at the exact moment that the comparator signaled equality between **TMR1H:TMR1L** and **CCPR1H:CCPR1L**.

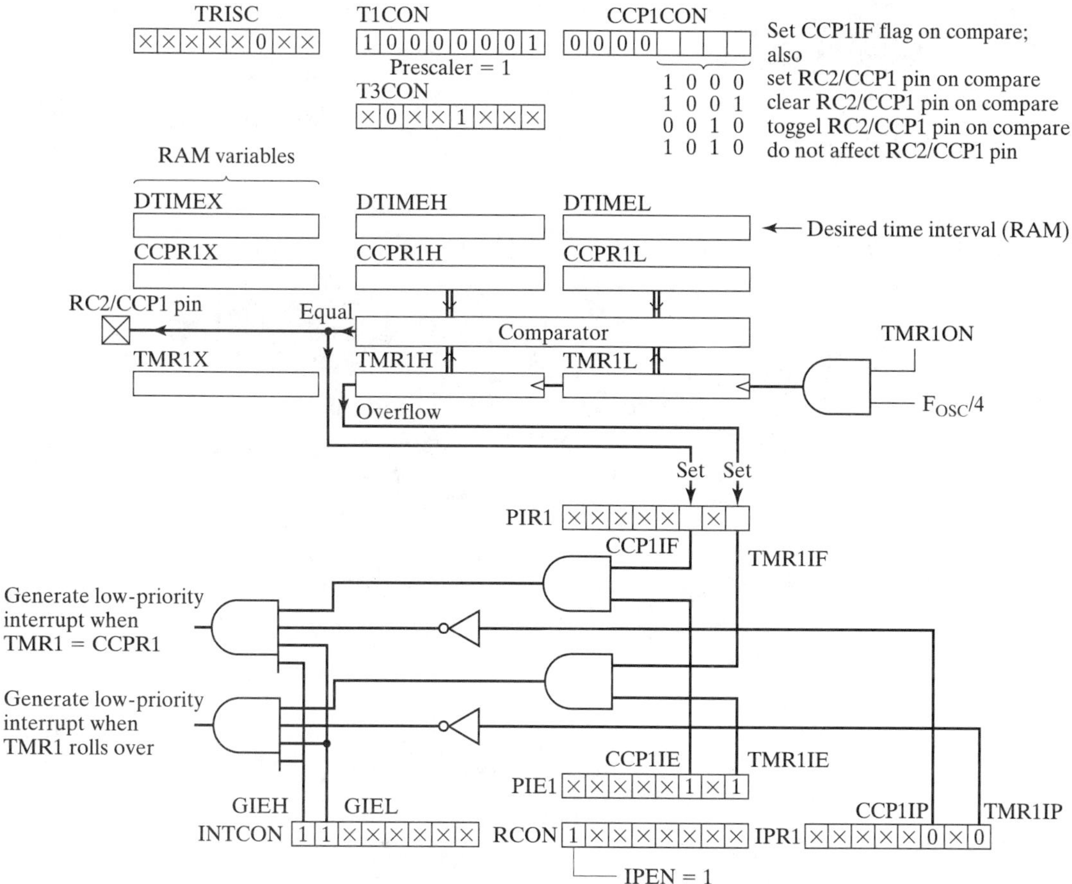

Figure 16-10 Jitter-free low-frequency square wave generation.

Example 16-9 Generate a jitter-free square wave whose half-period has been loaded into **DTIMEX:DTIMEH:DTIMEL**.

Solution

Consider the program of Figure 16-11, which initializes **DTIME** to 125,000 to generate a 10 Hz square wave. The first item to notice is that the polling routine in the low-priority interrupt service routine polls **CCP1IF** *before* it polls **TMR1IF**. This is the first step for ensuring that the **CCP1handler** reads a valid value of **TMR1X**, even in the critical case when both flags are set within a few cycles of each other.

When entering the **CCP1handler**, the **TMR1IF** flag is immediately checked to see if it is set. If not, then **TMR1X** contains a valid value to be compared with **CCPR1X** because **TMR1**'s last rollover has been handled and its flag cleared. If **TMR1IF** is set, while at the same time **CCPR1IF** is set, then **TMR1X** contains its value before the rollover occurred. This is the correct, valid value of **TMR1X** if **CCPR1H:CCPR1L** contains B'1bbb bbbb bbbb bbbb', so the

```
;;;;;;; P4 for QwikFlash board ;;;;;;;;;;;;;;;;;;;;;;;;;;;;;;;;;;;;;;;;;;;;;;
;
; Generate a jitterfree 10 Hz square wave on CCP1 output using compare mode
; with extension.
; Use 10 MHz crystal and 2.5 MHz internal clock rate.
;
;;;;;;; Program hierarchy ;;;;;;;;;;;;;;;;;;;;;;;;;;;;;;;;;;;;;;;;;;;;;;;;;;;;;
;
;Mainline
;  Initial
;
;HiPriISR (included just to show structure)
;
;LoPriISR
;  CCP1handler
;  TMR1handler
;
;;;;;;; Assembler directives ;;;;;;;;;;;;;;;;;;;;;;;;;;;;;;;;;;;;;;;;;;;;;;;;;;

        list  P=PIC18F452, F=INHX32, C=160, N=0, ST=OFF, MM=OFF, R=DEC, X=ON
        #include P18F452.inc
        __CONFIG  _CONFIG1H, _HS_OSC_1H  ;HS oscillator
        __CONFIG  _CONFIG2L, _PWRT_ON_2L & _BOR_ON_2L & _BORV_42_2L  ;Reset
        __CONFIG  _CONFIG2H, _WDT_OFF_2H  ;Watchdog timer disabled
        __CONFIG  _CONFIG3H, _CCP2MX_ON_3H  ;CCP2 to RC1 (rather than to RB3)
        __CONFIG  _CONFIG4L, _LVP_OFF_4L  ;RB5 enabled for I/O

        errorlevel -311         ;Turn off message when 3-byte variable is loaded

HalfPeriod  equ  125000         ;Number of 0.4 us clock cycles in 0.05 seconds

;;;;;;; Variables ;;;;;;;;;;;;;;;;;;;;;;;;;;;;;;;;;;;;;;;;;;;;;;;;;;;;;;;;;;;;;;;;

        cblock  0x000
        WREG_TEMP
        STATUS_TEMP
        TMR1X                   ;Eight-bit extension to TMR1
        CCPR1X                  ;Eight-bit extension to CCPR1
        DTIMEL                  ;Half-period value
        DTIMEH
        DTIMEX
        endc

;;;;;;; Macro definitions ;;;;;;;;;;;;;;;;;;;;;;;;;;;;;;;;;;;;;;;;;;;;;;;;;;;;;;;

MOVLF   macro   literal,dest
        movlw   literal
        movwf   dest
        endm

;;;;;;; Vectors ;;;;;;;;;;;;;;;;;;;;;;;;;;;;;;;;;;;;;;;;;;;;;;;;;;;;;;;;;;;;;;;;;

        org  0x0000             ;Reset vector
        nop
        goto  Mainline

        org  0x0008             ;High priority interrupt vector
        goto  HiPriISR

        org  0x0018             ;Low priority interrupt vector
        goto  LoPriISR

;;;;;;; Mainline program ;;;;;;;;;;;;;;;;;;;;;;;;;;;;;;;;;;;;;;;;;;;;;;;;;;;;;;;;

Mainline
        rcall  Initial          ;Initialize everything
        LOOP_
        ENDLOOP_
```

Figure 16-11 P4.asm file—Generates a jitter-free, low-frequency square wave.

```
;;;;;;; Initial subroutine ;;;;;;;;;;;;;;;;;;;;;;;;;;;;;;;;;;;;;;;;;;;;;;;;;;;;;;
;
; This subroutine performs all initializations of variables and registers.

Initial
        MOVLF  low HalfPeriod,DTIMEL  ;Load DTIME with HalfPeriod
        MOVLF  high HalfPeriod,DTIMEH
        MOVLF  upper HalfPeriod,DTIMEX
        MOVLF  B'11010000',TRISC  ;Set I/O for PORTC
        MOVLF  0x81,T1CON         ;Turn on TMR1
        MOVLF  B'00001000',CCP1CON  ;Select compare mode
        bsf  RCON,IPEN            ;Enable priority levels
        bcf  IPR1,TMR1IP          ;Assign low priority to TMR1 interrupts
        bcf  IPR1,CCP1IP          ; and to CCP1 interrupts
        clrf  TMR1X               ;Make first 24-bit compare occur quickly
        MOVLF  2,CCPR1X
        bsf  PIE1,CCP1IE          ;Enable CCP1 interrupts
        bsf  PIE1,TMR1IE          ;Enable TMR1 interrupts
        bsf  INTCON,GIEL          ;Enable low-priority interrupts to CPU
        bsf  INTCON,GIEH          ;Enable all interrupts
        return

;;;;;;; HiPriISR interrupt service routine ;;;;;;;;;;;;;;;;;;;;;;;;;;;;;;;;;;;;

HiPriISR                          ;High-priority interrupt service routine
;       <execute the handler for a single interrupt source>
;       <clear that source's interrupt flag>
        retfie  FAST              ;Return and restore STATUS, WREG, and BSR
                                  ; from shadow registers

;;;;;;; LoPriISR interrupt service routine ;;;;;;;;;;;;;;;;;;;;;;;;;;;;;;;;;;;;

LoPriISR                          ;Low-priority interrupt service routine
        movff  STATUS,STATUS_TEMP  ;Set aside STATUS and WREG
        movwf  WREG_TEMP

        LOOP_
          IF_  PIR1,CCP1IF == 1
            rcall  CCP1handler
            CONTINUE_
          ENDIF_

          IF_  PIR1,TMR1IF == 1
            rcall TMR1handler
            CONTINUE_
          ENDIF_

          BREAK_
        ENDLOOP_

        movf  WREG_TEMP,W         ;Restore WREG and STATUS
        movff  STATUS_TEMP,STATUS
        retfie                    ;Return from interrupt, reenabling GIEL

CCP1handler
        IF_  PIR1,TMR1IF == 1     ;If Timer1's overflow flag is set
          IF_  CCPR1H,7 == 0      ; and compare had occurred after that
            incf  TMR1X,F         ; then increment TMR1 extension
            bcf  PIR1,TMR1IF      ; and clear flag
          ENDIF_
        ENDIF_

        movf  TMR1X,W             ;Check whether extensions are equal
        subwf  CCPR1X,W
        IF_  .Z.
          btg  CCP1CON,0          ;Toggle control bit
          movf  DTIMEL,W          ;and add half period to CCPR1
          addwf  CCPR1L,F
          movf  DTIMEH,W
          addwfc  CCPR1H,F
          movf  DTIMEX,W
          addwfc  CCPR1X,F
        ENDIF_

        bcf  PIR1,CCP1IF          ;Clear flag
        return

TMR1handler
        incf  TMR1X,F             ;Increment Timer1 extension
        bcf  PIR1,TMR1IF          ;Clear flag and return to polling routine
        return

        end
```

Figure 16-11 continued

CCP2handler can proceed using this value. On the other hand, if **CCPR1H:CCPR1L** contains B′0bbb bbbb bbbb bbbb′, then the compare took place *after* the rollover occurred, but **TMR1X** has not yet been incremented to reflect its correct value at the time the compare took place. The **CCP1handler** makes the correction in this case by incrementing **TMR1X** and clearing **TMR1IF** (so that the polling routine will not find **TMR1IF** still set and call **TMR1handler**, where **TMR1X** would be incremented again).

The **CCPR1handler** now checks whether the valid **TMR1X** equals **CCPR1X**. If not, it clears the flag and returns. By using only the **CCP1CON**'s "set CCP1 pin on compare" option (**CCP1CON** = B′00001000′) and its "clear CCP1 pin on compare" option (**CCP1CON** = B′00001001′), the output will not change until bit 0 of **CCP1CON** is toggled, thereby changing this option.

If the valid **TMR1X** equals **CCPR1X**, then the 3-byte **DTIME** is added to the 3-byte **CCPR1**, bit 0 of **CCP1CON** is toggled, the **CCP2IF** flag is cleared, and the return from the handler is executed. When the *next* compare occurs, the output pin will be toggled.

PROBLEMS

16-1 Magnetic card reader

(a) Show the initialization code for a low-priority interrupt service routine triggered by rising edges on the RB2/INT2 input.

(b) Write the **INT2handler** subroutine described in Example 16-1.

16-2 Magnetic card reader

(a) Enhance the code of Problem 16-1b to check the parity of each character received. If a parity error occurs, display

```
Parity
error
```

on the QwikFlash display for two seconds.

(b) Add the LRC check. If it fails, display

```
  LRC
failure
```

16-3 Magnetic card reader When the code of Problem 16-1b completes the reading of a card, set a flag. The mainline code should then digress to a "MagCard" screen from whatever screen application was in progress, using the P3 template of Chapter 12. Display

```
MagCard1
;2163485
```

where the second row of the display is the first eight characters in CARD_BUF. As the RPB is turned CW, increment the right-most character of line 1 to

```
MagCard2
```

and show the next eight characters. Use subsequent CW and CCW increments of the RPG to display the entire CARD_BUF eight characters at a time. As the RPG is turned CCW, stop with

```
MagCard1
```

As the RPG is turned CW, stop with

```
MagCard5
```

which displays the last eight characters in the forty-character array. Blank all characters after the end sentinel. When the pushbutton is pressed, return to the formerly running "screen" application.

16-4 Timer2 interrupts The integer parameters A, B, and C associated with Timer2 can be used to obtain precisely timed interrupts. For example, with an internal clock rate of 2.5 MHz, an interrupt frequency of 1 kHz requires $A \times B \times C = 2500$. Finding suitable values for A, B, and C is simplified if 2500 is factored into its prime factors

$$\begin{aligned} 2500 &= 25 \times 100 \\ &= 5 \times 5 \times 5 \times 5 \times 2 \times 2 \end{aligned}$$

(a) Can suitable values of A, B, and C be found in this case?
(b) Do the same with an internal clock rate of 10 MHz.

16-5 Stepping rate Implement a "screen" function that can be used to vary the stepping rate of a continuously turning stepper motor. The rate is to be varied using the rate-sensitive RPG scheme of Section 8.5, where fast RPG increments change the stepping rate by increments of 10 while slow RPG increments change it by increments of 1. Display the stepping rate as

```
Steprate
 250 s/s
```

with an initial rate of 250 steps per second and ranging between 5 s/s and 2000 s/s. Use the scheme of Example 16-5 to update the CCP1/Timer1 interrupt mechanism to generate the periodic interrupts.

16-6 Stepping rate Example 16-5 discussed a code flaw that could produce a "hiccup" in the stepping rate as the rate is increased. Why does this code flaw not produce a hiccup in the stepping rate as the rate is decreased?

16-7 Fast square wave generator Create a SquareWaveOut screen for use by the QwikBug instrument for generating a jitter-free square wave output for the following output frequencies, using the PWM scheme with the internal 10 MHz clock:

5, 10, 20, 50, 100, 200, 500 kHz

and

1, 2, 5, 10 MHz

Use the RPG to select the frequency. Display

```
SQWV OUT
  10 kHz
```

varying the second line with the desired kHz or MHz value. Use a program table to hold the 11 display strings. Use another program memory table to hold the required **T2CON** value for each of the 11 frequencies. A third table should hold the 11 required **PR2** values. Derive the

CCPR1L value by adding 1 to the PR2 table entry and shifting it right one place. The bit shifted out (and collected into the carry bit) should be copied to bit 5 of **CCP1CON**, while bit 4 of **CCP1CON** can remain at its initially cleared value.

16-8 Potential glitch The interrupt handlers for both Figures 16-9 and 16-10 have a strange potential glitch problem. The problem never arises if the addition to the multiple-byte **CCPR1** is undertaken *before* the **CCPIF** flag is cleared. It also never happens when the flag is cleared first *unless* **DTIMEL** is just the right (wrong?) small value.

(a) What is going on here, and what determines the small value of **DTIMEL** that, when added to **CCPR1L**, produces the problem?

(b) If the scheme of Figure 16-10 uses the RPG to control the stepping rate of a stepper motor for every integer value from 1 step per second to 1000 steps per second, then one or more of the 1000 possible stepping rates are likely to lead to the bad value for adding to **CCPR1L**. For example, if 59 steps per second leads to the bad value, consider what will happen as the stepping rate is increased from below 59 steps per second. When the rate hits 59, what will the stepper motor do, and why?

(c) In the case just considered, a real-life example locked up the microcontroller. It would not even respond to an RPG change that attempted to recover from the problem. The chip had to be reset to recover. What was going on?

Chapter

17

SMBUS/I^{2}C FOR PERIPHERAL CHIP ACCESS

17.1 OVERVIEW

The I^{2}C (Inter-Integrated Circuit) bus was developed by Philips Semiconductors in the mid-1980s. Because of its ability to add any number of features to a microcontroller while subjecting the microcontroller to a loss of just two of its pins, the I^{2}C bus protocol has gained widespread use and has been the impetus for the development of a wealth of I^{2}C peripheral chips.

The SMBus (System Management Bus) is a recent extension of the I^{2}C bus, introduced to extend the benefits of two-wire querying and control to a breadth of applications not envisioned by the Philips designers. The original impetus for developing the SMBus came from the Smart Battery System Implementer's Forum (www.sbs-forum.org) to define a link between an intelligent battery, a charger for the battery, and a microcontroller that communicates with the rest of the system. As an example of one of the SMBus changes, it relaxes power supply requirements from the strict 5.0 V $\pm$ 10% of the original I^{2}C specification to permit it to work with batteries of lower voltage.

Upgrades to the I^{2}C specification allow a PIC18F452 to communicate with devices designed to meet either specification. Rather than having to decipher the two standards, it is only necessary to meet the more limited requirements identified by the specific SMBus/I^{2}C peripheral chips used in an application.

In this chapter, the two-wire protocol will be discussed. The support given to this protocol by the PIC18F452 and also the features of several SMBus/I^{2}C peripheral chips will be presented. Low-level subroutines will be developed that translate snippets of I^{2}C hardware support into useful entities for handling the I^{2}C message protocol. Finally, an example application will be presented that illustrates how the low-level subroutines are combined to build the I^{2}C messages needed to query and to control SMBus/I^{2}C peripheral devices.

17.2 SMBUS/I²C SPECIFICATIONS

Since its development by Philips Semiconductors in the mid-1980s, the I²C bus standard has gone through several updates (1992, 1998, and 2000). Version 2.1–2000 is available on the Internet from www.semiconductors.philips.com/i2c/support/

The System Management Bus (SMBus) Specification Version 2.0–2000 is also available on the Internet from the Smart Battery System (SBS) Implementers Forum at www.smbus.org/. In its last three pages, it describes the differences between SMBus and I²C.

17.3 I²C BUS OPERATION

Throughout the rest of this chapter, the term *I²C bus* will be used to describe the PIC18F452's interactions with peripheral chips that are designated as being either I²C chips or SMBus chips. The microcontroller's role will be the same in either case.

Each peripheral chip, as well as the microcontroller, dedicates two I/O pins to bus transfers. For the PIC18F452, these are

RC3/SCK/SCL

and

RC4/SDI/SDA

It is expected that an application using the I²C bus's SCL and SDA clock and data lines will not also be using the SPI bus's SCK, SDI, and SDO lines.

Data transfers with I²C interface chips are expected to operate at bit rates between 0 Hz and 100 kHz if designed to operate on the "standard-mode I²C bus" or between 0 Hz and 400 kHz if designed for the "fast-mode I²C bus." For the SMBus, the rate is more constrained, with bit rates between 10 kHz and 100 kHz. In this chapter, the conservative 100 kHz rate will be used for all transfers for two reasons:

- If both standard-mode and fast-mode chips are used in an application, the I²C bus transfers for *all* chips must be slowed to the 100 kHz rate.
- Peripheral chip control or status messages generally involve the transfer of only 3 or 4 bytes and, at the 100 kHz rate, may take 400 microseconds. As long as these transfers take place in the mainline code, 400 microseconds is generally inconsequential, in light of the 10 millisecond loop time.

The I²C bus takes advantage of *open-drain* output drivers for the SDA and the SCL pins for all peripheral chips and the PIC18F452 controller, as shown in Figure 17-1a. Accordingly, each of the two lines needs a pullup resistor, as shown in Figure 17-1b. Unless at least one chip is pulling a line low, the line will be pulled high by the pullup resistor.

Transfers on the I²C bus take place 9 bits at a time, as shown in Figure 17-2. The clock line, SCL, is driven by the microcontroller chip, which serves as bus master. The first eight *data* bits on the SDA

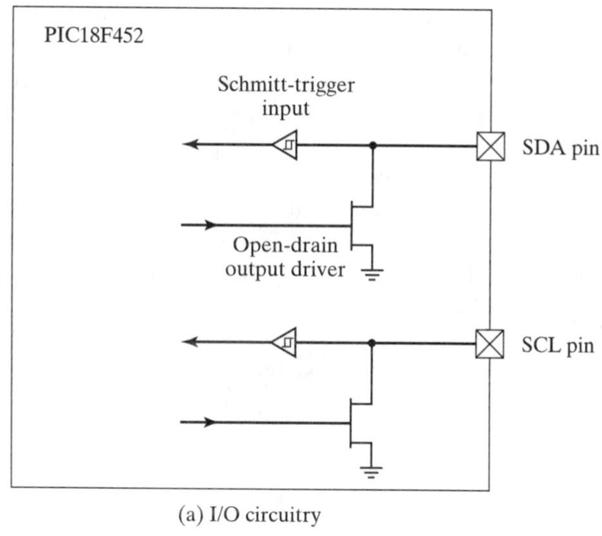

(a) I/O circuitry

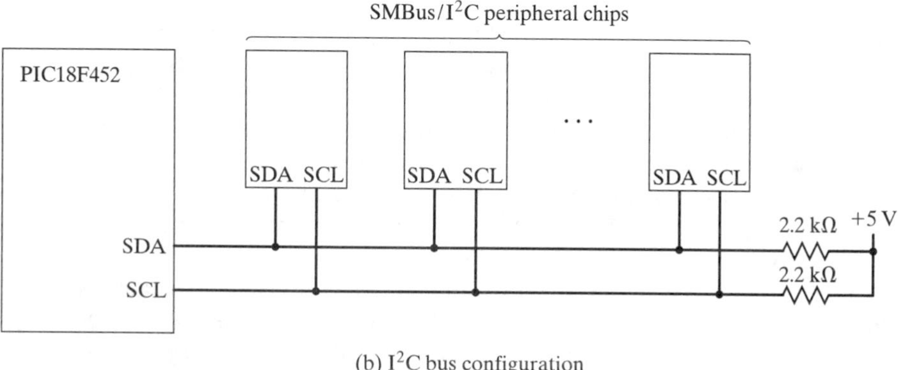

(b) I^2C bus configuration

Figure 17-1 I^2C bus hardware considerations.

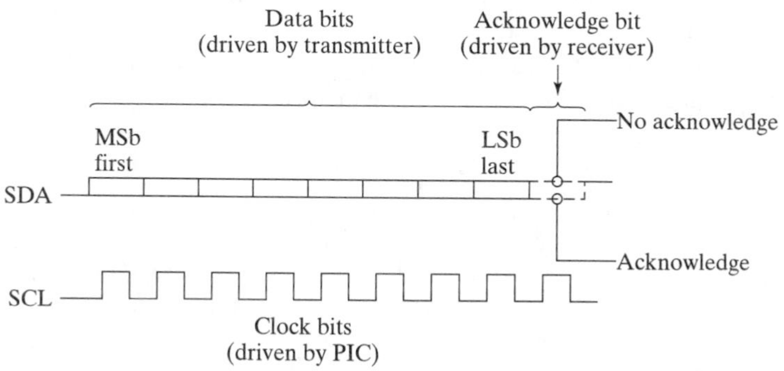

Figure 17-2 Byte transfer plus acknowledge.

line are sent by the transmitter, whereas the ninth *acknowledge* bit is a response by the receiver. For example, when the microcontroller sends out a chip address, it is a transmitter, while every other chip on the I²C bus is a receiver. During the acknowledge time, the *addressed* chip is the only one that drives the SDA line, pulling it low in response to the master's pulse on SCL, acknowledging the reception of its chip address.

When the byte transfer represents data being returned to the microcontroller from a peripheral chip, it is the peripheral chip that drives the eight data bits in response to the clock pulses from the microcontroller. In this case, the acknowledge bit is driven in a special way by the microcontroller, which is serving as receiver but also as bus master. If the peripheral chip is one that can send the contents of successive internal addresses back to the microcontroller (e.g., a serial EEPROM), then the microcontroller completes the reception of each byte and signals a request for the next byte by pulling the SDA line low in acknowledgment. After any number of bytes have been received in this way from the peripheral, the microcontroller can signal the peripheral to stop any further transfers by *not* pulling the SDA line low in acknowledgment.

Figure 17-2 also illustrates that the data bits on the SDA line must be stable during the high period of the clock. When the slave peripheral is driving the SDA line, either as transmitter or acknowledger, it initiates the new bit in response to the falling edge of SCL. It maintains that bit on the SDA line until the next falling edge of SCL.

I²C bus transfers consist of a number of byte transfers *framed* between a START condition and a STOP condition. When bus transfers are *not* taking place, both the SDA and SCL lines are released by all drivers and float high. The microcontroller initiates a transfer with the START condition. It first pulls SDA low and then it pulls SCL low, as shown in Figure 17-3a. Likewise, the microcontroller terminates a multiple-byte transfer with the STOP condition. With both SDA and SCL initially low, it first releases SCL and then SDA, as shown in Figure 17-3b. Both of these occurrences are easily recognized by the I²C hardware in each peripheral chip since they both consist of a change in the SDA line while SCL is high, a condition that never happens in the middle of a byte transfer.

The microcontroller generates the first byte after the START condition. It consists of a 7-bit *slave address* followed by an R/$\overline{W}$ bit, as shown in Figure 17-4. If the R/$\overline{W}$ bit is low, subsequent bytes transmitted on the bus will be *written* by the microcontroller to the selected peripheral. If the R/$\overline{W}$ bit is high, subsequent bytes will be sent by the selected peripheral and *read* by the microcontroller.

The I²C bus standard includes support for *10-bit* addresses. These begin with what looks like a nonstandard 7-bit address, B'11110xx'. The last two bits of this 7-bit address plus a second 8-bit address byte form the 10-bit address. Since the three peripheral chips to be discussed later in this chapter all use 7-bit addresses (as do most commodity chips having an I²C interface), the several ramifications that attend the use of 10-bit addressing will not be discussed here.

The functions of the bytes that follow the first, or control, byte are defined by the needs of the peripheral chip. For a peripheral chip that contains more than one internal register or memory address, the

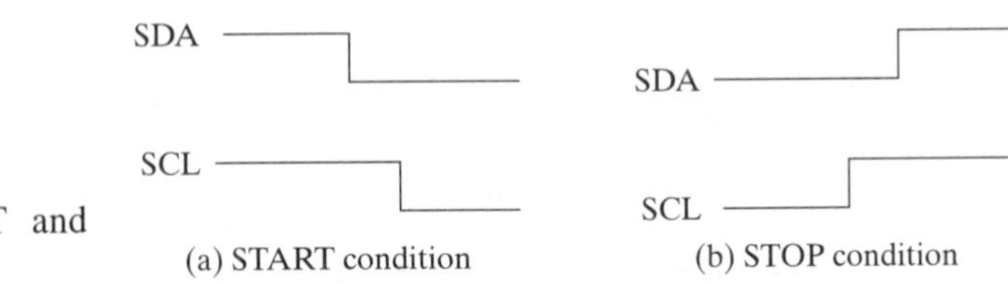

Figure 17-3 I²C START and STOP conditions.

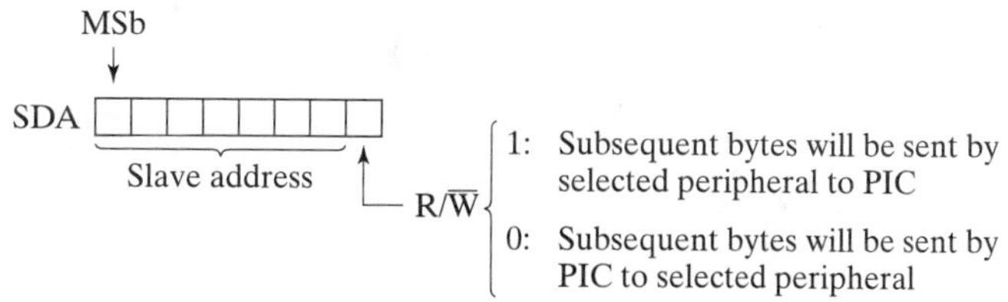

Figure 17-4 First byte of a message string.

microcontroller will typically write a second byte to the chip to set a pointer to the selected internal register or address. Subsequent bytes in the message string will typically be written to that address and then to the consecutive addresses that follow it. This is illustrated in Figure 17-5a.

A message string for reading internal peripheral registers or addresses is shown in Figure 17-5b. It begins with a 2-byte message string that selects the internal address of the selected peripheral chip. Then a RESTART condition initiates a new message string as the microcontroller raises SCL and then pulls SDA low, followed by the pulling of SCL low again. The first byte of this new message string again selects the same peripheral chip but signals that the subsequent bytes are to consist of reads from successive addresses in the peripheral chip.

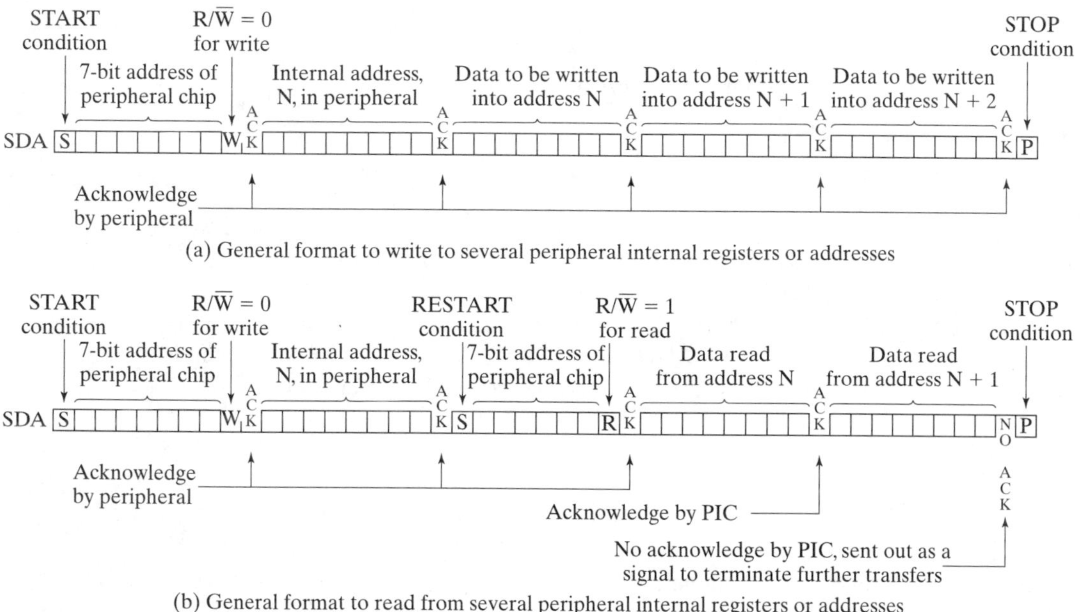

Figure 17-5 I²C typical message string formats.

17.4 PIC18F452 SUPPORT FOR I²C BUS TRANSFERS

The initialization required to use the PIC18F452 as the I²C bus master (i.e., the chip that drives the SCL clock line and that initiates all transfers) is shown in Figure 17-6a. The I²C clock rate of 100 kHz is set by scaling the internal clock rate. The relationship between the I²C clock rate, F_{I2C}, and the internal clock rate, $F_{OSC}/4$, is given by

$$\frac{F_{OSC}/4}{F_{I2C}} = \text{SSPADD} + 1$$

To obtain an F_{I2C} value of 100 kHz from a 2.5 MHz internal clock rate, **SSPADD** must be initialized to 24.

The two bits of **TRISC** that would normally control whether the general-purpose I/O pins RC3 and RC4 are inputs or outputs should be initialized as inputs. The I²C control circuitry will override this decision, switching SCL to be an output and SDA to be either an input or an output, depending on which is appropriate for each bit in a message transfer.

The **SSPCON1** register must be initialized as shown in Figure 17-6a. The lower four bits select the I²C master mode rather than any one of several I²C slave modes or SPI master or slave modes. The **SSPEN** = 1 bit switches I/O direction control of the SCL and SDA bits to the I²C control circuitry (*if* the corresponding **TRISC** bits are set as inputs). Bit 4 of **SSPCON1** must also be set to avoid its intended use of stopping the I²C clock while a peripheral chip's setup time requirements are being met. For 100 kHz transfers, setup time requirements are met by *all* I²C chips.

Once initialized, the registers of Figure 17-6b control all transfers. The message strings of Figure 17-5 are built out of seven building block commands:

- SEN, send START condition
- RSEN, send RESTART condition (i.e., release both lines with STOP condition and then send START condition)
- PEN, send STOP condition
- Write to **SSPBUF** to send an address or data byte
- RCEN, initiate the reading of a byte
- Read **SSPBUF** to read the received byte
- ACKEN, to respond to the received byte (by sending ACKDT = 0 or 1 to acknowledge or not acknowledge)

Each of these commands is paced by use of **PIR1**'s **SSPIF** flag bit. **SSPIF** is first cleared, the desired operation is initiated, and further activity is held up until **SSPIF** = 1, signaling the completion of the operation.

One further status bit, **ACKSTAT** in the **SSPCON2** register, is used to query whether a transmitted byte was received correctly, in which case **ACKSTAT** = 0. If a peripheral chip is dead (or incorrectly addressed), **ACKSTAT** = 1, signaling an unsuccessful transfer.

17.5 I/O EXPANSION

Despite a long list of over 1000 different I²C parts, the I²C bus is presently supported by only two or three I/O-expansion parts. None of these comes close to the low price of one of the generic 74HCxxx shift register parts for use with the SPI I/O port expansion circuit of Figure 15-6.

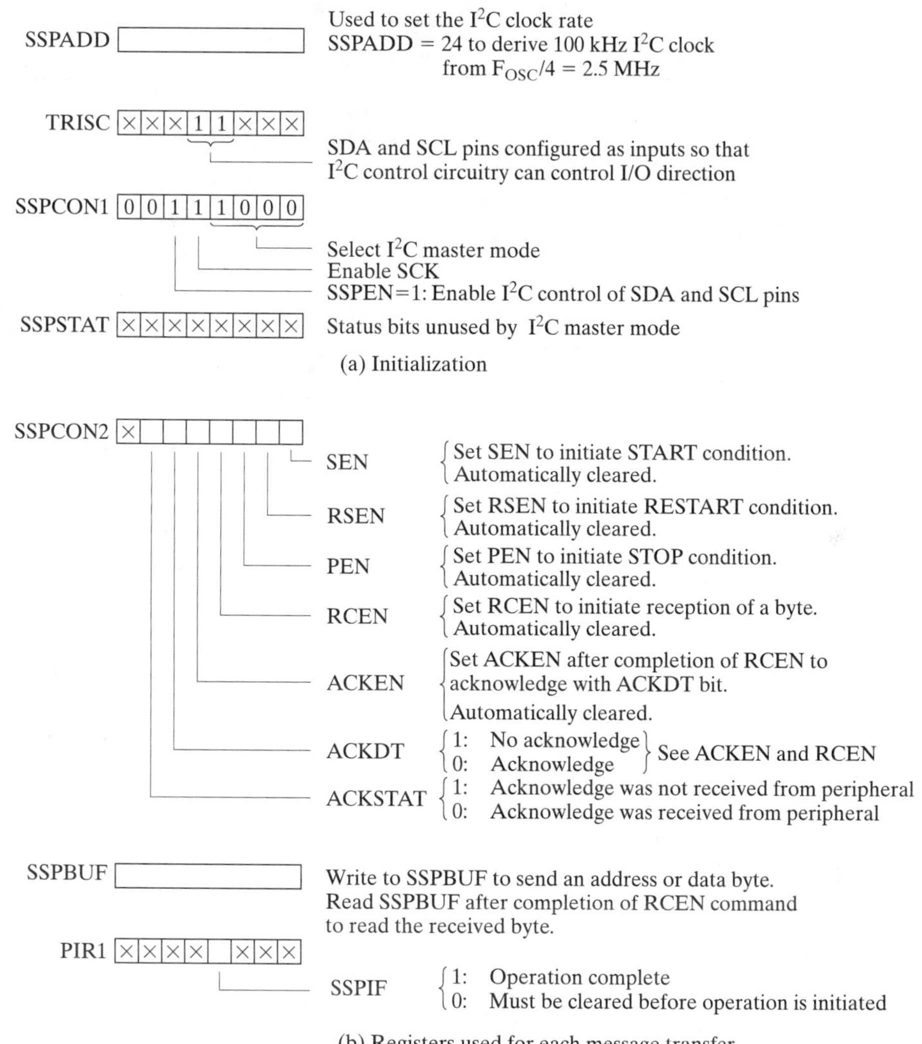

Figure 17-6 Registers for I^2C master mode.

Given this disclaimer, Philips Semiconductors' PCF8574 I/O expander of Figure 17-7 is an older part with excellent versatility and ease of use. It is available in a 16-pin DIP package as well as in two tiny surface-mount packages. Its 7-bit I^2C address is made up of two parts. The lower three bits of the 7-bit address are determined by the connection of the A2, A1, and A0 pins to any of the eight possible connections of +5 V and GND, allowing eight of the chips to be used in a single application, each with its own unique address. The upper four bits of the 7-bit address are B'0100'. Philips makes a second part, PCF8574A, identical in every respect except that the upper four bits of the 7-bit address are B'0111'. With eight of each part, the PIC18F452 can be expanded to have 128 extra I/O pins.

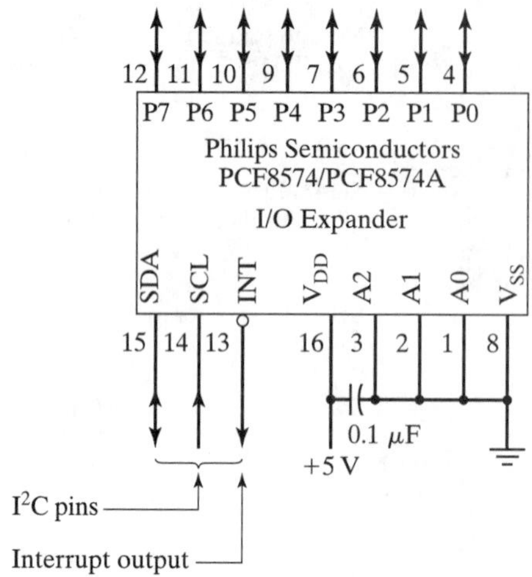

(a) Circuit

```
PCF8574  seven-bit address = B'Ø 1 Ø Ø A2 A1 AØ'
PCF8574A seven-bit address = B'Ø 1 1 1 A2 A1 AØ'
```

(b) I²C addresses

For a pin that has a 0 written to it, an output current of as much as 3 mA will raise the output pin no higher than 0.4 V.

A pin that has a 1 written to it provides a momentary drive current of about 1 mA (to charge the capacitive part of the load) and a steady-state current of less than 300 μA. This is satisfactory for driving CMOS loads.

(c) Output drive capability

Writing a 1 to a pin creates an input pin.

(d) Initialization of input pins

A rising or falling edge on any input pin (i.e., any pin that last had a 1 written to it) will cause the INT pin to be driven low. Any read or write of the port clears the interrupt, as does the return of the pin to its original state. A pullup resistor is required for this INT pin so that the INT pins from multiple chips can be tied together to generate a single falling-edge interrupt input to the PIC's INT0, INT1, or INT2 pin.

(e) Interrupt output

Figure 17-7 PCF8574 features.

Each pin can be used as an open-drain output, pulling its load low. When a 1 is written to a pin (the power-on, default state of each pin), it becomes a high-impedance input. Because of this manner of creating inputs, it is important to keep a RAM copy of what is to be written to a port, updating the RAM copy before updating the port with it.

Example 17-1 What is the problem with the read-modify-write approach to changing an output pin on a PCF8574 port?

Solution

Any pin being used as an input should have a 1 written to it. However, if external circuitry drives that pin low, a read-modify-write sequence carried out on the PCF8574 will result in the pin being driven low by *both* the PCF8574 and the external circuitry. When the external circuitry subsequently tries to drive the pin high, contention between the two drivers of the pin can lead to an ambiguous input value as well as to overloaded drivers.

The PCF8574 includes an interrupt feature that may be of less value to the PIC18F452, with its three external interrupt input pins (INT0, INT1, and INT2), than to earlier PIC microcontrollers with just one such pin. With its $\overline{\text{INT}}$ open-drain output pulled up to +5 V using a 10 kΩ pullup resistor, any externally induced change of a pin will cause $\overline{\text{INT}}$ to go low, which, in turn, can produce a falling-edge interrupt input to one of the PIC18F452's three external interrupt input pins. Multiple PCF8574 chips used in an application can translate changes on any number of input pins into a single interrupt input to the PIC18F452 by tying the $\overline{\text{INT}}$ outputs from all PCF8574 chips together. The $\overline{\text{INT}}$ output to the microcontroller can be returned high again by reading from, or writing to, the PCF8574 that pulled it low. That output will go high again, even without a read or write, if the changed pin reverts to its earlier state.

The PCF8574 is written to with the sequence:

- Initiate START condition.
- Send first byte with 7-bit address plus $R/\overline{W}$ bit = 0
  (for the connection of A2 = A1 = A0 = 0 V of Figure 17-7a, the first byte is B'0100000 0').
- Send second byte to drive pins high or low.
- Initiate STOP condition.

Each of these four operations is paced by initially clearing the **SSPIF** flag bit, initiating the operation, and then waiting for the **SSPIF** flag to be set again.

The PCF8574 is *read* with the sequence:

- Initiate START condition.
- Send first byte with address plus $R/\overline{W}$ bit = 1 (B'0100000 1').
- Initiate the reading of the byte.
- Read the received byte from **SSPBUF**.
- Initiate STOP condition.

17.6 LOW-LEVEL I^{2}C SUBROUTINES

Chris Twigg of Georgia Tech suggests the use of the low-level I^{2}C subroutines of Figure 17-8. These subroutines use the variables listed in Figure 17-8a. Note that the 7-bit address, B'0100000', is expressed in **I2CADD** as B'01000000', which is actually double the device's address. This locates the 7 bits of the address in the *upper* 7 bits of the byte, just as they must be positioned for sending to an I^{2}C device.

The **StartI2C** subroutine not only initiates the START condition, it also sends the I^{2}C address of a peripheral chip. The **SendI2C** and **GetI2C** subroutines that use the **StartI2C** subroutine set or clear the

```
I2CADD                       ;Holds left-justified 7-bit device address
I2CBYTES                     ;Indicates number of bytes to transfer
I2CBUF:4                     ;I2C buffer for multibyte transfers
I2CFLAGS                     ;Various indicator flags for I2C subroutines
                             ;bit Ø: Ø = WREG transfer, single byte
                             ;       1 = INDF transfer, I2CBYTES bytes
                             ;bit 1: Ø = Normal receive
                             ;       1 = Commanded receive
                             ;bit 2: Ø = Slave acknowledged
                             ;       1 = Slave did not acknowledge
                             ;bit 7: Previous pushbutton state
```

(a) Variables

```
;;;;;;; StartI2C subroutine ;;;;;;;;;;;;;;;;;;;;;;;;;;;;;;;;;;;;;;;;;;;;;;;;;;;;
;
; This subroutine initiates an I2C transfer by sending a start condition and
; the remote device address, I2CADD.

StartI2C
        bsf  I2CFLAGS,2          ;Reset acknowledge flag
        bcf  PIR1,SSPIF          ;Clear interrupt flag
        bsf  SSPCON2,SEN         ;Generate Start Condition
        REPEAT_
        UNTIL_  PIR1,SSPIF == 1  ;Wait until start conditioning done
        bcf  PIR1,SSPIF          ;Clear interrupt flag
        movff  I2CADD,SSPBUF     ;Send address
        REPEAT_
        UNTIL_  PIR1,SSPIF == 1  ;Wait until address sent
        bcf  PIR1,SSPIF          ;Clear interrupt flag
        IF_  SSPCON2,ACKSTAT == Ø  ;Check for acknowledge
          bcf  I2CFLAGS,2        ;Indicate that slave acknowledges
        ELSE_
          rcall  DeviceError     ;Indicate device error on LCD
        ENDIF_
        return
```

(b) StartI2C subroutine

```
;;;;;;; ReStartI2C subroutine ;;;;;;;;;;;;;;;;;;;;;;;;;;;;;;;;;;;;;;;;;;;;;;;;;;
;
; This subroutine initiates an I2C transfer by sending a start condition and
; the remote device address, I2CADD.

ReStartI2C
        bcf  PIR1,SSPIF          ;Clear interrupt flag
        bsf  SSPCON2,RSEN        ;Generate ReStart Condition
        REPEAT_
        UNTIL_  PIR1,SSPIF == 1  ;Wait until start conditioning done
        bcf  PIR1,SSPIF          ;Clear interrupt flag
        movff  I2CADD,SSPBUF     ;Send address
        REPEAT_
        UNTIL_  PIR1,SSPIF == 1  ;Wait until address sent
        bcf  PIR1,SSPIF          ;Clear interrupt flag
        return
```

(c) ReStartI2C subroutine

```
;;;;;;; StopI2C subroutine ;;;;;;;;;;;;;;;;;;;;;;;;;;;;;;;;;;;;;;;;;;;;;;;;;;;;;
;
; This subroutine ends an I2C transfer by sending a stop condition.

StopI2C
        bsf  SSPCON2,PEN         ;Generate Stop Condition
        REPEAT_
        UNTIL_  PIR1,SSPIF == 1  ;Wait until start conditioning done
        bcf  PIR1,SSPIF          ;Clear interrupt flag
        RETURN
```

(d) StopI2C subroutine

Figure 17-8 Low-level I^{2}C subroutines

```
;;;;;;; GetI2C subroutine ;;;;;;;;;;;;;;;;;;;;;;;;;;;;;;;;;;;;;;;;;;;;;;;;;;;;;;;
;
; This subroutine receives single or multiple bytes from the I2C device at
; address I2CADD.
;
; I2CFLAGS:Ø = Ø, A single byte is read into WREG
;              1, I2CBYTES are read to FSRØ
;          1 = Ø, Normal receive
;              1, Commanded receive, send command in WREG first, then read
;
; I2CADD contains an address in the upper 7 bits.

GetI2C
        IF_  I2CFLAGS,1 == 1    ;Check for commanded receive
          bcf  I2CADD,Ø         ;Clear lower bit of address to indicate Write
          rcall  StartI2C       ;Start I2C transfer
          IF_  I2CFLAGS,2 == Ø  ;Check for acknowledge
            movwf  SSPBUF       ;Send
            REPEAT_
            UNTIL_  PIR1,SSPIF == 1  ;Wait until sequence complete
            bcf  PIR1,SSPIF     ;Clear interrupt flag
            bsf  I2CADD,Ø       ;Set lower bit of address to indicate Read
            rcall  ReStartI2C   ;Start I2C transfer
          ENDIF_
        ELSE_
          bsf  I2CADD,Ø         ;Set lower bit of address to indicate Read
          rcall  StartI2C       ;Start I2C transfer
        ENDIF_
        IF_  I2CFLAGS,2 == Ø    ;Check for acknowledge
          IF_  I2CFLAGS,Ø == 1  ;Check for multibyte
            REPEAT_
              rcall  GetI2CByte  ;Get byte from device
              movff  SSPBUF,POSTINCØ  ;Store byte to FSRØ
              decf  I2CBYTES,F  ;Decrement byte indicator
              IF_ .NZ.
                bcf  SSPCON2,ACKDT  ;Send acknowledge
              ELSE_
                bsf  SSPCON2,ACKDT  ;Do not send acknowledge
              ENDIF_
              bsf  SSPCON2,ACKEN  ;Start acknowledge sequence
              REPEAT_
              UNTIL_  PIR1,SSPIF == 1  ;Wait until sequence complete
              bcf  PIR1,SSPIF   ;Clear interrupt flag
              movf  I2CBYTES,W  ;Check for last byte
            UNTIL_  .Z.
          ELSE_
            rcall  GetI2CByte   ;Get byte from device
            movf  SSPBUF,W      ;Store byte to WREG
            bsf  SSPCON2,ACKDT  ;Do not send acknowledge
            bsf  SSPCON2,ACKEN  ;Start acknowledge sequence
            REPEAT_
            UNTIL_  PIR1,SSPIF == 1  ;Wait until sequence complete
            bcf  PIR1,SSPIF     ;Clear interrupt flag
          ENDIF_
        ENDIF_
        rcall  StopI2C          ;End I2C transfer
        return

;;;;;;; GetI2CByte subroutine ;;;;;;;;;;;;;;;;;;;;;;;;;;;;;;;;;;;;;;;;;;;;;;;;;;;;
;
; This subroutine initiates the I2C receive mode and waits for completion.

GetI2CByte
        bsf  SSPCON2,RCEN       ;Enable receive
        REPEAT_
        UNTIL_  PIR1,SSPIF == 1  ;Wait until byte received
        bcf  PIR1,SSPIF         ;Clear interrupt flag
        return
```

(e) GetI2C and GetI2CByte subroutines

Figure 17-8 continued

```
;;;;;;; SendI2C subroutine ;;;;;;;;;;;;;;;;;;;;;;;;;;;;;;;;;;;;;;;;;;;;;;;;;;;;;
;
; This subroutine sends a single or multiple bytes to the I2C device at
; address I2CADD.
;
; I2CFLAGS:Ø = Ø, a single byte from WREG is sent
;              1, I2CBYTES are sent from FSR2
;
; I2CADD contains an address in the upper 7 bits.

SendI2C
        bcf  I2CADD,Ø           ;Clear lower bit of address to indicate Write
        rcall  StartI2C         ;Start I2C transfer
        IF_  I2CFLAGS,Ø == 1    ;Check for multibyte transfer
          REPEAT_
            movff  POSTINCØ,SSPBUF
            REPEAT_
            UNTIL_  PIR1,SSPIF == 1  ;Wait until start conditioning done
            bcf  PIR1,SSPIF     ;Clear interrupt flag
            decf  I2CBYTES,F    ;Decrement byte indicator
          UNTIL_  .Z.
        ELSE_
          movwf  SSPBUF         ;Send data
          REPEAT_
          UNTIL_  PIR1,SSPIF == 1  ;Wait until start conditioning done
          bcf  PIR1,SSPIF       ;Clear interrupt flag
        ENDIF_
        rcall  StopI2C          ;End I2C transfer
        return
```

(f) Send I2C subroutine

```
I2COUT  macro  address,byte     ;Single byte I2C transfer (Send)
        bcf  I2CFLAGS,Ø         ;Single byte transfer mode
        MOVLF  address,I2CADD   ;Select I2C device
        movlw  byte             ;Byte to send to device
        rcall  SendI2C          ;Transfer byte
        endm
```

(g) I2COUT macro

```
;;;;;;; DeviceError subroutine ;;;;;;;;;;;;;;;;;;;;;;;;;;;;;;;;;;;;;;;;;;;;;;;;;
;
; This subroutine displays "Device Error" on the LCD when a device does not
; acknowledge.

DeviceError
        POINT  DevE1            ;Display "Device"
        rcall  DisplayC
        POINT  DevE2            ;Display "Error"
        rcall  DisplayC
        return

DevE1   db  Øx8Ø," Device ",Ø   ;Device Error message
DevE2   db  ØxcØ," Error  ",Ø   ;Indicates device did not acknowledge
```

(h) DeviceError subroutine (called by StartI2C subroutine) and its strings

Figure 17-8 continued

LSb of **I2CADD**, as appropriate, to get ready for a read or a write operation. The **StartI2C** subroutine also checks that the designated chip acknowledges its address and calls the **DeviceError** subroutine of Figure 17-8h if the acknowledgment fails. If the address of a peripheral chip has been misidentified, this subroutine will display

```
Device
Error
```

It provides a built-in diagnostic for a common error in preparing I^{2}C application code. It also alerts a user to a dead or missing peripheral chip.

The **RestartI2C** subroutine's **RSEN** command serves the I^{2}C peripheral chips with a STOP condition (to release the SCL and SDA lines), followed immediately by a START condition. Then it sends out the I^{2}C address. The **StopI2C** subroutine initiates the STOP condition and waits for its completion.

The **SendI2C** subroutine uses a flag bit in the RAM variable, **I2CFLAGS,** to decide whether to send a single data byte from **WREG** or a string of bytes pointed to by **FSR0,** with the number of bytes to be sent stored in **I2CBYTES**. The **GetI2C** subroutine uses the same flag bit (bit 0 in **I2CFLAGS**) to decide whether to read a single byte into **WREG** or a string of **I2CBYTES** bytes into RAM, beginning at the address pointed to by **FSR0**. Another flag bit (bit 1 in **I2CFLAGS**) supports device reads of two forms. With bit 1 = 0, the address byte (address + read bit) is sent and then one or more read commands retrieve the desired data from the chip. With bit 1 = 1, the address byte (address + *write* bit) is sent followed by a command in **WREG**. After a RESTART condition, the address byte (address + *read* bit) is sent and then one or more read commands retrieve the data. This latter (bit 1 = 1) option supports reads from peripheral chips that have a command register whose contents specify which of several registers is to be read.

17.7 I/O EXPANDER CODE

The circuit of Figure 17-9 illustrates the use of two PCF8574A chips, each with its own 7-bit address. The "A" parts (see Figure 17-7b) are wired so as to have 7-bit addresses of 0x38 and 0x39. When shifted over to form the address byte sent to the parts, the two "write" address bytes will be

0x70 and 0x72

and the two "read" address bytes will be

0x71 and 0x73

The application code of Figure 17-10 checks the pushbutton every 10 milliseconds. It blinks one LED, the other LED, or both LEDs briefly every 2½ seconds. Each press of the pushbutton changes which LEDs are blinked. The **Pushbutton** subroutine queries the left PCF8574A part. It compares the MSb of the port with what it was 10 milliseconds ago (and stored in the MSb of **I2CFLAGS**, as defined in Figure 17-8a). If the pushbutton is newly pressed, it cycles an **I2CDISP** variable to the next state in the sequence

. . . 3, 2, 1, 3, 2, 1, . . .

The **Blink** subroutine acts on the value of **I2CDISP** every 2½ seconds to turn on the selected LED, or both LEDs, for 10 milliseconds, producing a brief blink. It uses the **I2COUT** macro of Figure 17-8g to set up the address and the byte to be sent to the selected PCF8574A chip.

17.8 DAC OUTPUT

Two digital-to-analog converter outputs are easily added to a PIC18F452 with the MAX518 eight-pin DIP or SO-8 surface-mount part shown in Figure 17-11. The two address inputs, AD1 and AD0, pro-

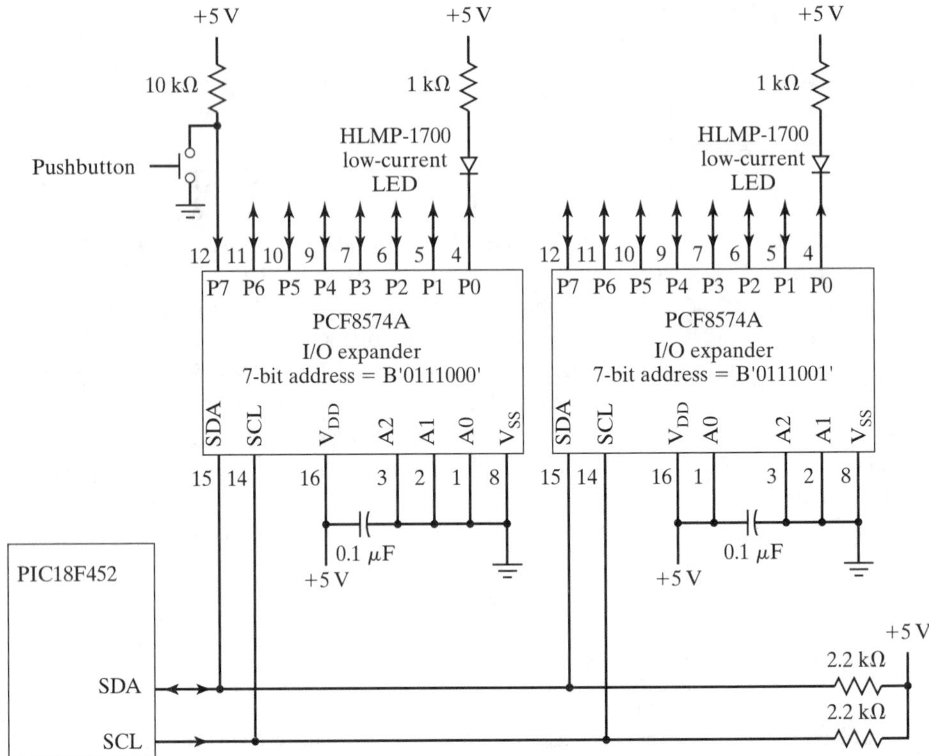

Figure 17-9 Two-port I²C expansion circuit.

vide an adjustable part of the chip's I²C address. With 5 bits fixed at 01011 and 2 adjustable bits, it is possible to connect *four* MAX518 chips to a PIC18F452.

Each output channel produces an output voltage that ranges from 0 V up to 255/256ths of the power supply voltage, giving roughly 20 mV output increments. An output of 2.50 V will appear on the OUT0 pin if the following 3 bytes are sent to the chip:

```
B'01011000'    B'00000000'    B'10000000'
```

An output of 1.25 V will appear on the OUT1 pin following

```
B'01011000'    B'00000001'    B'01000000'
```

as described in the data sheet, available at www.maxim-ic.com. The MAX518 chip includes a power-on reset circuit that drives the two outputs to 0 V initially. Because the MAX518 may come out of reset after the PIC18F452 comes out of reset, the MAX518 may ignore commands sent to it immediately after the PIC18F452 comes out of reset.

```
Mainline
        rcall  Initial          ;Initialize everything
        LOOP_
          rcall  Pushbutton     ;Check for pushbutton press
          rcall  Blink          ;Blink LED(s)
          rcall  LoopTime       ;Make looptime be ten milliseconds
        ENDLOOP_

Initial
        MOVLF  B'11011000',TRISC  ;Set I/O for PORTC
        rcall  InitI2C          ;Initialize I2C bus and devices
        return

InitI2C
        MOVLF  24,SSPADD        ;Initialize for 100 kHz I2C bus
        MOVLF  0x28,SSPCON1     ;and enable
        return

Pushbutton
        bcf  I2CFLAGS,0         ;Single byte transfer
        bcf  I2CFLAGS,1         ;Normal receive
        MOVLF  0x70,I2CADD      ;Point to first IO expander
        rcall  GetI2C           ;Read from first IO expander
        IF_  I2CFLAGS,2 == 0    ;Check for acknowledge
          xorlw  0x80           ;Check for button press
          andlw  0x80           ;Mask off button bit
          IF_  .NZ.
            xorwf  I2CFLAGS,W   ;XOR with previous state
            andlw  0x80         ;Mask off other bits
            IF_  .Z.
              bcf  PORTA,4      ;Indicate button press with LED
              bcf  I2CFLAGS,7   ;Clear previous state
              decf  I2CDISP,F   ;Decrement I2CDISP flag
              IF_  .Z.
                MOVLF  0x03,I2CDISP  ;Reset I2CDISP flag
              ENDIF_
            ENDIF_
          ELSE_
            bsf  I2CFLAGS,7     ;Set previous state
            bsf  PORTA,4        ;Clear LED
          ENDIF_
        ENDIF_
        return

Blink
        decf  BLINKCNT,F        ;Decrement loop counter and return if not zero
        IF_  .Z.
          MOVLF  250,BLINKCNT   ;Reinitialize BLNKCNT
          IF_  I2CDISP,1 == 1
            IF_  I2CDISP,0 == 1
              I2COUT  0x70,0xfe  ;Turn on both LEDs
              I2COUT  0x72,0xfe
            ELSE_
              I2COUT  0x70,0xfe  ;Turn on left LED
            ENDIF_
          ELSE_
            I2COUT  0x72,0xfe    ;Turn on right LED
          ENDIF_
        ELSE_
          I2COUT  0x70,0xff      ;Turn off both LEDs
          I2COUT  0x72,0xff
        ENDIF_
        return
```

Figure 17-10 I^{2}C port expansion code.

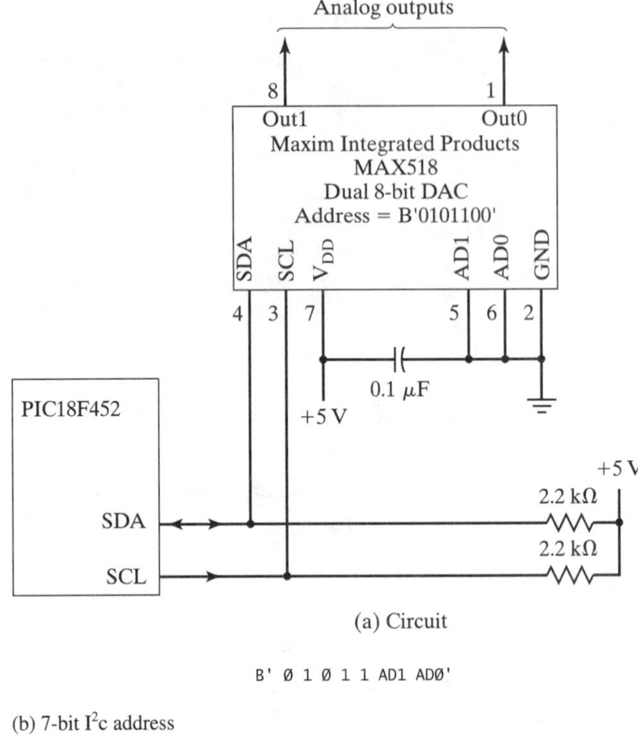

(a) Circuit

B' Ø 1 Ø 1 1 AD1 ADØ'

(b) 7-bit I²c address

Write address byte = Øx58

Figure 17-11 Dual DAC output. (c) Address byte for circuit above

17.9 DIGITAL THERMOMETER

The Dallas Semiconductor DS1621 is a versatile digital thermometer available in an eight-pin DIP package as well as two eight-pin surface-mount packages. It measures temperatures from −55°C to +125°C in 0.5°C increments as a 9-bit twos-complement-coded value. Alternatively, a 1-byte return will yield an 8-bit, twos-complement-coded value for the same range in 1.0°C increments. Examples are shown in Figure 17-12. The device includes several optional features that can be examined further from the data sheet, available at www.dalsemi.com:

- Conversions can be continuously performed (continuous mode).
- Each conversion can be individually initiated (one-shot mode) and a flag monitored for its completion after 0.4 seconds, typically.
- Higher than 9-bit resolution can be obtained from the one-shot mode by reading two counters in addition to the 9-bit value and interpolating a result.
- A thermostat output pin can be used to signal when the temperature exceeds an entered upper threshold; this output resets when the temperature drops below an entered lower threshold.

Temperature	First byte received	Second (optional byte received)
+125°C	01111101	00000000
+10°C	00001010	00000000
+2°C	00000010	00000000
+1°C	00000001	00000000
+0.5°C	00000000	10000000
0°C	00000000	00000000
−0.5°C	11111111	10000000
−1°C	11111111	00000000
−2°C	11111110	00000000
−10°C	11110110	00000000
−55°C	11001001	00000000

Figure 17-12 Bytes received in response to a "read temperature" command.

- Two flag bits in a status register retain the information that the temperature has gone beyond either of these threshold values. The two flags can only be reset by writing zeros to them or by cycling the power to the chip.

The circuit for the chip on the I^2C bus is shown in Figure 17-13a. Its 7-bit address can be configured to any one of eight values, using the A2, A1, and A0 connections to power and ground. With all three pins tied to ground, the 7-bit address is B'1001000'. Appending the $R/\overline{W}$ bit produces the write address byte and read address byte of Figure 17-13c.

In the next section, the code to initialize the chip for continuous measurements and to read and display the 1-byte (1°C resolution) value every second will be examined. This will require the following I^2C message strings:

- Send the write address of 0x90 followed by the 2-byte command, 0xac and 0x0a. This will configure the chip for continuous conversions.
- Send the write address of 0x90 followed by the 1-byte command, 0xee. This will initiate the continuous conversions.
- Send the write address of 0x90 followed by the 1-byte command, 0xaa. Restart and send the read address of 0x91 followed by a read of the upper temperature byte. This last message string will be repeated once a second and the value read will be displayed.

17.10 AN EXAMPLE

Figure 17-14 shows a circuit that includes all of these peripheral parts. The program of Figure 17-15

- Blinks one or both LEDs every 2½ seconds.
- Selects with the pushbutton which of the LEDs to blink.
- Generates slow sawtooth waveforms on the two DAC outputs.
- Updates the display of temperature every second.

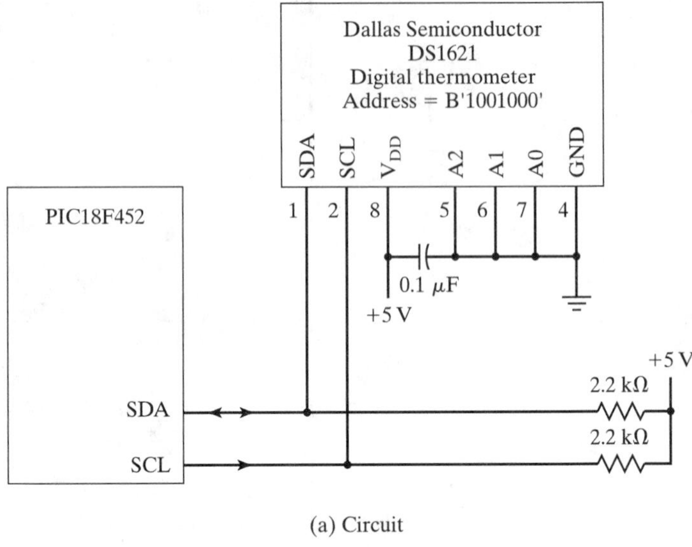

(a) Circuit

```
B' 1 Ø Ø 1 A2 A1 AØ'
```

(b) 7-bit I²C address

```
Write address byte = Øx9Ø
Read address byte = Øx91
```

(c) Address bytes for circuit above

Figure 17-13 Digital thermometer.

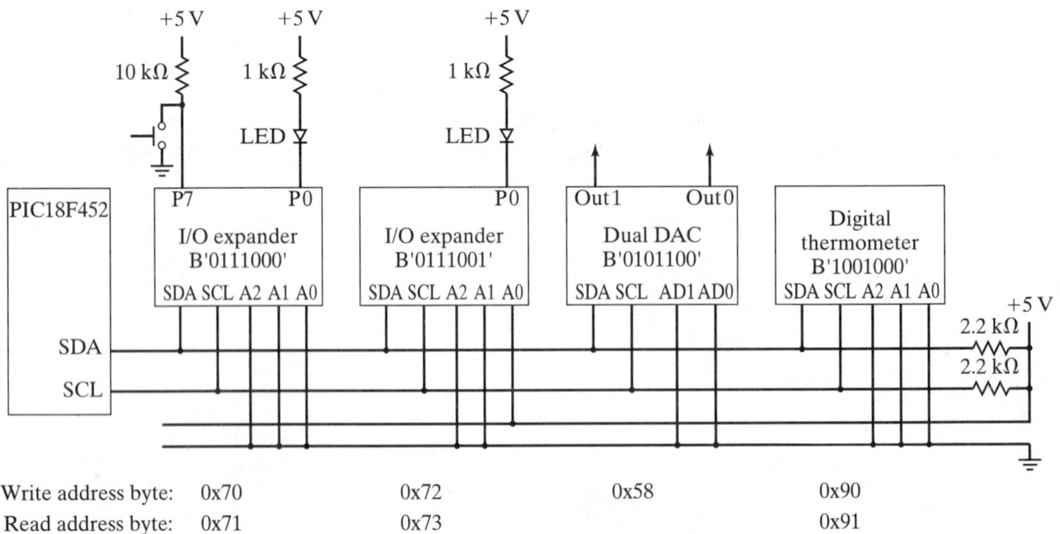

Write address byte:	0x70	0x72	0x58	0x90
Read address byte:	0x71	0x73		0x91

Figure 17-14 Addition of all four peripheral chips to the PIC18F452.

```
;;;;;;; CH17 for GT QwikPIC board ;;;;;;;;;;;;;;;;;;;;;;;;;;;;;;;;;;;;;;;;;;;;;;
;
; Chris Twigg
;
; Use 10 MHz crystal frequency and 2.5 MHz internal clock rate.
; Use I2C bus to:
;   Blink either one or two LEDs every two and a half seconds.
;   Use pushbutton to determine which LED(s) to blink.
;   Read the I2C temp sensor and display the temperature every second.
;   Output two sawtooth waveforms from the dual DAC.
;
;;;;;;; Program hierarchy ;;;;;;;;;;;;;;;;;;;;;;;;;;;;;;;;;;;;;;;;;;;;;;;;;;;;;;;
;
; Mainline
;   Initial
;     InitI2C
;       SendI2C
;         StartI2C
;           DeviceError
;             DisplayC
;               T40
;         StopI2C
;     InitLCD
;       LoopTime
;       DisplayC
;         T40
;   Pushbutton
;     GetI2C
;       StartI2C
;         DeviceError
;           DisplayC
;             T40
;       ReStartI2C
;       GetI2CByte
;       StopI2C
;   Blink
;     SendI2C
;       StartI2C
;         DeviceError
;           DisplayC
;             T40
;       StopI2C
;   Centigrade
;     GetI2C
;       StartI2C
;         DeviceError
;           DisplayC
;             T40
;       ReStartI2C
;       GetI2CByte
;       StopI2C
;     Int2ASCII
;       FXD0808U
;     DisplayV
;       T40
;   DACwave
;     SendI2C
;       StartI2C
;         DeviceError
;           DisplayC
;             T40
;       StopI2C
;   LoopTime
;
;;;;;;; Assembler directives ;;;;;;;;;;;;;;;;;;;;;;;;;;;;;;;;;;;;;;;;;;;;;;;;;;;;

        list  P=PIC18F452, F=INHX32, C=160, N=0, ST=OFF, MM=OFF, R=DEC, X=ON
        #include P18F452.inc
        __CONFIG  _CONFIG1H, _HS_OSC_1H  ;HS oscillator
        __CONFIG  _CONFIG2L, _PWRT_ON_2L & _BOR_ON_2L & _BORV_42_2L  ;Reset
        __CONFIG  _CONFIG2H, _WDT_OFF_2H  ;Watchdog timer disabled
        __CONFIG  _CONFIG3H, _CCP2MX_ON_3H  ;CCP2 to RC1 (rather than to RB3)
        __CONFIG  _CONFIG4L, _LVP_OFF_4L  ;RB5 enabled for I/O
        errorlevel -314, -315   ;Ignore lfsr messages

;;;;;;; Variables ;;;;;;;;;;;;;;;;;;;;;;;;;;;;;;;;;;;;;;;;;;;;;;;;;;;;;;;;;;;;;;;;

        cblock  0x000             ;Beginning of Access RAM
        TMR0LCOPY                 ;Copy of sixteen-bit Timer0 used by LoopTime
        TMR0HCOPY
        INTCONCOPY                ;Copy of INTCON for LoopTime subroutine
        COUNT                     ;Counter available as local to subroutines
        TEMPVAR                   ;Temporary local variable
        I2CADD                    ;Holds left-justified 7-bit device address
        I2CBYTES                  ;Indicates number of bytes to transfer
        I2CBUF:4                  ;I2C buffer for multibyte transfers
```

Figure 17-15 Example program

```
        I2CFLAGS                ;Various indicator flags for I2C subroutines
                                ;bit Ø: Ø = WREG transfer, single byte
                                ;       1 = INDF transfer, I2CBYTES bytes
                                ;bit 1: Ø = Normal receive
                                ;       1 = Commanded receive
                                ;bit 2: Ø = Slave acknowledged
                                ;       1 = Slave did not acknowledge
                                ;bit 7: Previous pushbutton state
        BLINKCNT                ;Counter for blinking LEDs
        TEMPCNT                 ;Counter for updating temperature
        I2CDISP                 ;Indicates current I2C LED Display mode, 1, 2, or 3
        DACØ                    ;DAC variables used for approximating sawtooth
        DAC1
        LCDSTRING:1Ø            ;String for LCD display
        endc
        #include <C:\MATH18\MATHVARS.INC>  ;Math routine variables

;;;;;;; Macro definitions ;;;;;;;;;;;;;;;;;;;;;;;;;;;;;;;;;;;;;;;;;;;;;;;;;;;;;

MOVLF   macro  literal,dest
        movlw  literal
        movwf  dest
        endm

POINT   macro  stringname
        MOVLF  high stringname, TBLPTRH
        MOVLF  low stringname, TBLPTRL
        endm

DISPLAY macro  register
        movff  register,BYTE
        call  ByteDisplay
        endm

I2COUT  macro  address,byte     ;Single byte I2C transfer (Send)
        bcf  I2CFLAGS,Ø         ;Single byte transfer mode
        MOVLF  address,I2CADD   ;Select I2C device
        movlw  byte             ;Byte to send to device
        rcall  SendI2C          ;Transfer byte
        endm

;;;;;;; Vectors ;;;;;;;;;;;;;;;;;;;;;;;;;;;;;;;;;;;;;;;;;;;;;;;;;;;;;;;;;;;;;;;;

        org  ØxØØØØ             ;Reset vector
        nop
        goto  Mainline

        org  ØxØØØ8             ;High priority interrupt vector
        goto  $                 ;Trap

        org  ØxØØ18             ;Low priority interrupt vector
        goto  $                 ;Trap

;;;;;;; Mainline program ;;;;;;;;;;;;;;;;;;;;;;;;;;;;;;;;;;;;;;;;;;;;;;;;;;;;;;;

Mainline
        rcall  Initial          ;Initialize everything
        LOOP_
          rcall  Pushbutton     ;Check for pushbutton press
          rcall  Blink          ;Blink LED(s)
          rcall  Centigrade     ;Check temperature
          rcall  DACwave        ;Update DAC outputs
          rcall  LoopTime       ;Make looptime be ten milliseconds
        ENDLOOP_

;;;;;;; Constant strings ;;;;;;;;;;;;;;;;;;;;;;;;;;;;;;;;;;;;;;;;;;;;;;;;;;;;;;;

LCDstr  db  Øx33,Øx32,Øx28,ØxØ1,ØxØc,ØxØ6,ØxØØ  ;Initialization string for LCD
ClrScr  db  ØxØ1,ØxØØ           ;Clear screen command
DevE1   db  Øx8Ø," Device ",Ø   ;Device Error message
DevE2   db  ØxcØ," Error  ",Ø   ;Indicates device did not acknowledge

;;;;;;; Initial subroutine ;;;;;;;;;;;;;;;;;;;;;;;;;;;;;;;;;;;;;;;;;;;;;;;;;;;;;
;
; This subroutine performs all initializations of variables and registers.

Initial
        MOVLF  B'1ØØØ111Ø',ADCON1  ;Enable PORTA & PORTE digital I/O pins
        MOVLF  B'111ØØØØ1',TRISA   ;Set I/O for PORTA
        MOVLF  B'11Ø111ØØ',TRISB   ;Set I/O for PORTB
        MOVLF  B'11Ø11ØØØ',TRISC   ;Set I/O for PORTC
        MOVLF  B'ØØØØ1111',TRISD   ;Set I/O for PORTD
        MOVLF  B'ØØØØØØØØ',TRISE   ;Set I/O for PORTE
        MOVLF  B'1ØØØ1ØØØ',TOCON   ;Set up TimerØ for a looptime of 1Ø ms
        MOVLF  B'ØØØ1ØØØØ',PORTA   ;Turn off all four LEDs driven from PORTA
        rcall  InitI2C             ;Initialize I2C bus and devices
        rcall  InitLCD             ;Initialize LCD
        return
```

Figure 17-15 continued

```
;;;;;;; InitI2C subroutine ;;;;;;;;;;;;;;;;;;;;;;;;;;;;;;;;;;;;;;;;;;;;;;;;;;;;;;;
;
; This subroutine initializes the I2C bus for 100 kHz transfers.
; The temperature sensor (0x48) is set for continuous temperature conversion.

InitI2C
        MOVLF  24,SSPADD         ;Initialize for 100 kHz I2C bus
        MOVLF  0x28,SSPCON1      ;and enable
        MOVLF  0x02,I2CDISP      ;Initialize I2CDISP flag
        MOVLF  0x80,I2CFLAGS     ;Initialize I2CFLAGS
        MOVLF  0x27,TEMPCNT      ;Initialize temperature counter
        clrf  DAC0               ;Clear DAC variables
        clrf  DAC1
        bsf  I2CFLAGS,0          ;Set for multibyte transfer
        MOVLF  0x90,I2CADD       ;I2C Thermometer address
        MOVLF  0x02,I2CBYTES     ;Set for 2 bytes
        lfsr  0,I2CBUF           ;Point to I2C multibyte buffer
        MOVLF  0xac,POSTINC0     ;Access Config byte command
        MOVLF  0x0a,POSTDEC0     ;Config byte
        rcall  SendI2C           ;Send control string
        I2COUT 0x90,0xee         ;Start conversion command
        return

;;;;;;; InitLCD subroutine ;;;;;;;;;;;;;;;;;;;;;;;;;;;;;;;;;;;;;;;;;;;;;;;;;;;;;;;
;
; Initialize the Optrex 8x2 character LCD.
; First wait for 0.1 second, to get past display's power-on reset time.

InitLCD
        MOVLF  10,COUNT          ;Wait 0.1 second
        REPEAT_
          rcall  LoopTime        ;Call LoopTime 10 times
          decf  COUNT,F
        UNTIL_  .Z.
        bcf  PORTE,0             ;RS=0 for command
        POINT  LCDstr            ;Set up table pointer to initialization string
        tblrd*                   ;Get first byte from string into TABLAT
        REPEAT_
          bsf  PORTE,1           ;Drive E high
          movff  TABLAT,PORTD    ;Send upper nibble
          bcf  PORTE,1           ;Drive E low so LCD will process input
          rcall  LoopTime        ;Wait ten milliseconds
          bsf  PORTE,1           ;Drive E high
          swapf  TABLAT,W        ;Swap nibbles
          movwf  PORTD           ;Send lower nibble
          bcf  PORTE,1           ;Drive E low so LCD will process input
          rcall  LoopTime        ;Wait ten milliseconds
          tblrd+*                ;Increment pointer and get next byte
          movf  TABLAT,F         ;Is it zero?
        UNTIL_  .Z.
        POINT  ClrScr            ;Clear the LCD
        rcall  DisplayC
        rcall  LoopTime          ;Wait 10 ms
        return

;;;;;;;DisplayC subroutine;;;;;;;;;;;;;;;;;;;;;;;;;;;;;;;;;;;;;;;;;;;;;;;;;;;;;;;;
;
; This subroutine is called with TBLPTR containing the address of a constant
; display string.  It sends the bytes of the string to the LCD.  The first
; byte sets the cursor position.  The remaining bytes are displayed, beginning
; at that position.
; This subroutine expects a normal one-byte cursor-positioning code, 0xhh, or
; an occasionally used two-byte cursor-positioning code of the form 0x00hh.

DisplayC
        bcf  PORTE,0             ;Drive RS pin low for cursor-positioning code
        tblrd*                   ;Get byte from string into TABLAT
        movf  TABLAT,F           ;Check for leading zero byte
        IF_  .Z.
          tblrd+*                ;If zero, get next byte
        ENDIF_
        REPEAT_
          bsf  PORTE,1           ;Drive E pin high
          movff  TABLAT,PORTD    ;Send upper nibble
          bcf  PORTE,1           ;Drive E pin low so LCD will accept nibble
          bsf  PORTE,1           ;Drive E pin high again
          swapf  TABLAT,W        ;Swap nibbles
          movwf  PORTD           ;Write lower nibble
          bcf  PORTE,1           ;Drive E pin low so LCD will process byte
          rcall  T40             ;Wait 40 usec
          bsf  PORTE,0           ;Drive RS pin high for displayable characters
          tblrd+*                ;Increment pointer, then get next byte
          movf  TABLAT,F         ;Is it zero?
        UNTIL_  .Z.
        return
```

Figure 17-15 continued

```
;;;;;;; DisplayV subroutine ;;;;;;;;;;;;;;;;;;;;;;;;;;;;;;;;;;;;;;;;;;;;;;;;;;;
;
; This subroutine is called with FSRØ containing the address of a variable
; display string.  It sends the bytes of the string to the LCD.  The first
; byte sets the cursor position.  The remaining bytes are displayed, beginning
; at that position.

DisplayV
        bcf  PORTE,Ø              ;Drive RS pin low for cursor positioning code
        REPEAT_
          bsf  PORTE,1            ;Drive E pin high
          movff  INDFØ,PORTD      ;Send upper nibble
          bcf  PORTE,1            ;Drive E pin low so LCD will accept nibble
          bsf  PORTE,1            ;Drive E pin high again
          swapf  INDFØ,W          ;Swap nibbles
          movwf  PORTD            ;Write lower nibble
          bcf  PORTE,1            ;Drive E pin low so LCD will process byte
          rcall  T4Ø              ;Wait 4Ø usec
          bsf  PORTE,Ø            ;Drive RS pin high for displayable characters
          movf  PREINCØ,W         ;Increment pointer, then get next byte
        UNTIL_  .Z.               ;Is it zero?
        return

;;;;;;; T4Ø subroutine ;;;;;;;;;;;;;;;;;;;;;;;;;;;;;;;;;;;;;;;;;;;;;;;;;;;;;;;
;
; Pause for 4Ø microseconds  or 4Ø/Ø.4 = 1ØØ clock cycles.
; Assumes 1Ø/4 = 2.5 MHz internal clock rate.

T4Ø
        movlw  1ØØ/3              ;Each REPEAT loop takes 3 cycles
        movwf  COUNT
        REPEAT_
          decf  COUNT,F
        UNTIL_  .Z.
        return

;;;;;;; LoopTime subroutine ;;;;;;;;;;;;;;;;;;;;;;;;;;;;;;;;;;;;;;;;;;;;;;;;;;;
;
; This subroutine waits for TimerØ to complete its ten millisecond count
; sequence. It does so by waiting for sixteen-bit TimerØ to roll over. To obtain
; a period of precisely 1ØØØØ/Ø.4 = 25ØØØ clock periods, it needs to remove
; 65536-25ØØØ or 4Ø536 counts from the sixteen-bit count sequence.  The
; algorithm below first copies TimerØ to RAM, adds "Bignum" to the copy ,and
; then writes the result back to TimerØ. It actually needs to add somewhat more
; counts to TimerØ than 4Ø536.  The extra number of 12+2 counts added into
; "Bignum" makes the precise correction.

Bignum  equu    65536-25ØØØ+12+2

LoopTime
        REPEAT_
        UNTIL_  INTCON,TMRØIF == 1  ;Wait until ten milliseconds are up
        movff  INTCON,INTCONCOPY  ;Disable all interrupts to CPU
        bcf  INTCON,GIEH
        movff  TMRØL,TMRØLCOPY    ;Read 16-bit counter at this moment
        movff  TMRØH,TMRØHCOPY
        movlw  low  Bignum
        addwf  TMRØLCOPY,F
        movlw  high  Bignum
        addwfc  TMRØHCOPY,F
        movff  TMRØHCOPY,TMRØH
        movff  TMRØLCOPY,TMRØL    ;Write 16-bit counter at this moment
        movf  INTCONCOPY,W        ;Restore GIEH interrupt enable bit
        andlw  B'1ØØØØØØØ'
        iorwf  INTCON,F
        bcf  INTCON,TMRØIF        ;Clear TimerØ flag
        return

;;;;;;; StartI2C subroutine ;;;;;;;;;;;;;;;;;;;;;;;;;;;;;;;;;;;;;;;;;;;;;;;;;;;
;
; This subroutine initiates an I2C transfer by sending a start condition and
; the remote device address, I2CADD.

StartI2C
        bsf  I2CFLAGS,2           ;Reset acknowledge flag
        bcf  PIR1,SSPIF           ;Clear interrupt flag
        bsf  SSPCON2,SEN          ;Generate Start Condition
        REPEAT_
        UNTIL_  PIR1,SSPIF == 1   ;Wait until start conditioning done
        bcf  PIR1,SSPIF           ;Clear interrupt flag
        movff  I2CADD,SSPBUF      ;Send address
        REPEAT_
        UNTIL_  PIR1,SSPIF == 1   ;Wait until address sent
        bcf  PIR1,SSPIF           ;Clear interrupt flag
        IF_  SSPCON2,ACKSTAT == Ø  ;Check for acknowledge
          bcf  I2CFLAGS,2         ;Indicate that slave acknowledges
        ELSE_
          rcall  DeviceError      ;Indicate device error on LCD
        ENDIF_
        return
```

Figure 17-15 continued

```
;;;;;;; DeviceError subroutine ;;;;;;;;;;;;;;;;;;;;;;;;;;;;;;;;;;;;;;;;;;;;;;;;;;;
;
; This subroutine displays "Device Error" on the LCD when a device does not
; acknowledge.

DeviceError
        POINT  DevE1            ;Display "Device"
        rcall  DisplayC
        POINT  DevE2            ;Display "Error"
        rcall  DisplayC
        return

;;;;;;; ReStartI2C subroutine ;;;;;;;;;;;;;;;;;;;;;;;;;;;;;;;;;;;;;;;;;;;;;;;;;;;;
;
; This subroutine initiates an I2C transfer by sending a start condition and
; the remote device address, I2CADD.

ReStartI2C
        bcf  PIR1,SSPIF           ;Clear interrupt flag
        bsf  SSPCON2,RSEN         ;Generate ReStart Condition
        REPEAT_
        UNTIL_  PIR1,SSPIF == 1   ;Wait until start conditioning done
        bcf  PIR1,SSPIF           ;Clear interrupt flag
        movff  I2CADD,SSPBUF      ;Send address
        REPEAT_
        UNTIL_  PIR1,SSPIF == 1   ;Wait until address sent
        bcf  PIR1,SSPIF           ;Clear interrupt flag
        return

;;;;;;; StopI2C subroutine ;;;;;;;;;;;;;;;;;;;;;;;;;;;;;;;;;;;;;;;;;;;;;;;;;;;;;;;
;
; This subroutine ends an I2C transfer by sending a stop condition.

StopI2C
        bsf  SSPCON2,PEN          ;Generate Stop Condition
        REPEAT_
        UNTIL_  PIR1,SSPIF == 1   ;Wait until start conditioning done
        bcf  PIR1,SSPIF           ;Clear interrupt flag
        return

;;;;;;; SendI2C subroutine ;;;;;;;;;;;;;;;;;;;;;;;;;;;;;;;;;;;;;;;;;;;;;;;;;;;;;;;
;
; This subroutine sends a single or multiple bytes to the I2C device at
; address I2CADD.
;
; I2CFLAGS:Ø = Ø, a single byte from WREG is sent
;             1, I2CBYTES are sent from FSRØ
;
; I2CADD contains an address in the upper 7 bits.

SendI2C
        bcf  I2CADD,Ø             ;Clear lower bit of address to indicate Write
        rcall  StartI2C           ;Start I2C transfer
        IF_  I2CFLAGS,Ø == 1      ;Check for multibyte transfer
          REPEAT_
            movff  POSTINCØ,SSPBUF
            REPEAT_
            UNTIL_  PIR1,SSPIF == 1  ;Wait until start conditioning done
            bcf  PIR1,SSPIF       ;Clear interrupt flag
            decf  I2CBYTES,F      ;Decrement byte indicator
          UNTIL_  .Z.
        ELSE_
          movwf  SSPBUF           ;Send data
          REPEAT_
          UNTIL_  PIR1,SSPIF == 1  ;Wait until start conditioning done
          bcf  PIR1,SSPIF         ;Clear interrupt flag
        ENDIF_
        rcall  StopI2C            ;End I2C transfer
        return

;;;;;;; DACwave subroutine ;;;;;;;;;;;;;;;;;;;;;;;;;;;;;;;;;;;;;;;;;;;;;;;;;;;;;;;
;
; This subroutine outputs an approximation of a sawtooth waveform on each DAC
; output.

DACwave
        movlw  Øx08               ;Add 8 to DACØ
        addwf  DACØ,F
        movlw  Øx1Ø               ;Add 16 to DAC1
        addwf  DAC1,F
        MOVLF  Øx58,I2CADD        ;Address DAC device (Øx2C)
        bsf  I2CFLAGS,Ø           ;Indicate multibyte transfer
        MOVLF  Øx04,I2CBYTES      ;Send 4 bytes
        lfsr  Ø,I2CBUF+3          ;Point to I2C multibyte buffer
        movff  DAC1,POSTDECØ      ;OUT1 data
        MOVLF  Øx01,POSTDECØ      ;Command to write to OUT1
        movff  DACØ,POSTDECØ      ;OUTØ data
        clrf  INDFØ               ;Command to write to OUTØ
        rcall  SendI2C
        return
```

Figure 17-15 continued

```
;;;;;;; GetI2C subroutine ;;;;;;;;;;;;;;;;;;;;;;;;;;;;;;;;;;;;;;;;;;;;;;;;;;;;;;
;
; This subroutine receives single or multiple bytes from the I2C device at
; address I2CADD.
;
; I2CFLAGS:0 = 0, A single byte is read into WREG
;              1, I2CBYTES are read to FSR0
;          1 = 0, Normal receive
;              1, Commanded receive, send command in WREG first, then read
;
; I2CADD contains an address in the upper 7 bits.

GetI2C
        IF_  I2CFLAGS,1 == 1    ;Check for commanded receive
          bcf  I2CADD,0         ;Clear lower bit of address to indicate Write
          rcall  StartI2C       ;Start I2C transfer
          IF_  I2CFLAGS,2 == 0  ;Check for acknowledge
            movwf  SSPBUF       ;Send
            REPEAT_
            UNTIL_  PIR1,SSPIF == 1  ;Wait until sequence complete
            bcf  PIR1,SSPIF     ;Clear interrupt flag
            bsf  I2CADD,0       ;Set lower bit of address to indicate Read
            rcall  ReStartI2C   ;Start I2C transfer
          ENDIF_
        ELSE_
          bsf  I2CADD,0         ;Set lower bit of address to indicate Read
          rcall  StartI2C       ;Start I2C transfer
        ENDIF_
        IF_  I2CFLAGS,2 == 0    ;Check for acknowledge
          IF_  I2CFLAGS,0 == 1  ;Check for multibyte
            REPEAT_
              rcall  GetI2CByte  ;Get byte from device
              movff  SSPBUF,POSTINC0  ;Store byte to FSR0
              decf  I2CBYTES,F  ;Decrement byte indicator
              IF_  .NZ.
                bcf  SSPCON2,ACKDT  ;Send acknowledge
              ELSE_
                bsf  SSPCON2,ACKDT  ;Do not send acknowledge
              ENDIF_
              bsf  SSPCON2,ACKEN  ;Start acknowledge sequence
              REPEAT_
              UNTIL_  PIR1,SSPIF == 1  ;Wait until sequence complete
              bcf  PIR1,SSPIF   ;Clear interrupt flag
              movf  I2CBYTES,W  ;Check for last byte
            UNTIL_  .Z.
          ELSE_
            rcall  GetI2CByte   ;Get byte from device
            movf  SSPBUF,W      ;Store byte to WREG
            bsf  SSPCON2,ACKDT  ;Do not send acknowledge
            bsf  SSPCON2,ACKEN  ;Start acknowledge sequence
            REPEAT_
            UNTIL_  PIR1,SSPIF == 1  ;Wait until sequence complete
            bcf  PIR1,SSPIF     ;Clear interrupt flag
          ENDIF_
        ENDIF_
        rcall  StopI2C          ;End I2C transfer
        return

;;;;;;; GetI2CByte subroutine ;;;;;;;;;;;;;;;;;;;;;;;;;;;;;;;;;;;;;;;;;;;;;;;;;;
;
; This subroutine initiates the I2C receive mode and waits for completion.

GetI2CByte
        bsf  SSPCON2,RCEN       ;Enable receive
        REPEAT_
        UNTIL_  PIR1,SSPIF == 1  ;Wait until byte received
        bcf  PIR1,SSPIF         ;Clear interrupt flag
        return

;;;;;;; Blink subroutine ;;;;;;;;;;;;;;;;;;;;;;;;;;;;;;;;;;;;;;;;;;;;;;;;;;;;;;;
;
; This subroutine briefly blinks one or both LEDs connected to the IO expansion
; chips via the I2C bus.

Blink
        decf  BLINKCNT,F        ;Decrement loop counter and return if not zero
        IF_  .Z.
          MOVLF  250,BLINKCNT   ;Reinitialize BLNKCNT
          IF_  I2CDISP,1 == 1
            IF_  I2CDISP,0 == 1
              I2COUT  0x70,0xfe  ;Turn on both LEDs
              I2COUT  0x72,0xfe
            ELSE_
              I2COUT  0x70,0xfe  ;Turn on left LED
            ENDIF_
          ELSE_
            I2COUT  0x72,0xfe   ;Turn on right LED
          ENDIF_
        ELSE_
          I2COUT  0x70,0xff     ;Turn off both LEDs
          I2COUT  0x72,0xff
        ENDIF_
        return
```

Figure 17-15 continued

```
;;;;;;; Pushbutton subroutine ;;;;;;;;;;;;;;;;;;;;;;;;;;;;;;;;;;;;;;;;;;;;;;;;;;
;
; This subroutine checks the pushbutton connected to the first IO expansion
; chip via the I2C bus and adjusts the I2CDISP flag accordingly.

Pushbutton
        bcf  I2CFLAGS,Ø          ;Single byte transfer
        bcf  I2CFLAGS,1          ;Normal receive
        MOVLF  Øx7Ø,I2CADD       ;Point to first IO expander
        rcall  GetI2C            ;Read from first IO expander
        IF_  I2CFLAGS,2 == Ø     ;Check for acknowledge
          xorlw  Øx8Ø            ;Check for button press
          andlw  Øx8Ø            ;Mask off button bit
          IF_  .NZ.
            xorwf  I2CFLAGS,W    ;XOR with previous state
            andlw  Øx8Ø          ;Mask off other bits
            IF_  .Z.
              bcf  PORTA,4       ;Indicate button press with LED
              bcf  I2CFLAGS,7    ;Clear previous state
              decf  I2CDISP,F    ;Decrement I2CDISP flag
              IF_  .Z.
                MOVLF  ØxØ3,I2CDISP  ;Reset I2CDISP flag
              ENDIF_
            ENDIF_
          ELSE_
            bsf  I2CFLAGS,7      ;Set previous state
            bsf  PORTA,4         ;Clear LED
          ENDIF_
        ENDIF_
        return

;;;;;;; Int2ASCII subroutine ;;;;;;;;;;;;;;;;;;;;;;;;;;;;;;;;;;;;;;;;;;;;;;;;;;;
;
; This subroutine converts an integer in AARGBØ to an ascii pointed to by FSRØ.
; FSRØ should point to the least significant digit.
; WREG should contain the number of digits - 1 to generate.

Int2ASCII
        movwf  TEMPVAR           ;Store number of digits
        movwf  COUNT
        REPEAT_
          MOVLF  ØxØa,BARGBØ     ;Divide by 1Ø to get next digit
          call  FXDØ8Ø8U
          movf  REMBØ,W
          addlw  A'Ø'            ;Convert digit to ASCII
          movwf  POSTDECØ        ;Insert into string and move to next digit
          decf  COUNT,F          ;Decrement digit counter
        UNTIL_  .Z.
        movf  AARGBØ,W           ;Get last digit
        addlw  A'Ø'              ;Convert digit to ASCII
        movwf  INDFØ             ;Insert into string
        REPEAT_
          movf  INDFØ,W          ;Check for leading zeros
          xorlw  A'Ø'
          IF_  .Z.
            MOVLF  A' ',POSTINCØ  ;Blank leading zero
          ELSE_
            movf  POSTINCØ,W     ;Advance FSRØ
          ENDIF_
          decf  TEMPVAR,F        ;Decrement digit counter
        UNTIL_  .Z.
        return

;;;;;;; Centigrade subroutine ;;;;;;;;;;;;;;;;;;;;;;;;;;;;;;;;;;;;;;;;;;;;;;;;;;
;
; This subroutine checks the temp sensor connected to the I2C bus and displays
; the reading on the LCD.

Centigrade
        decf  TEMPCNT,F          ;Decrement temperature update counter
        IF_  .Z.
          MOVLF  1ØØ,TEMPCNT     ;Reset counter
          bcf  I2CFLAGS,Ø        ;Single byte transfer
          bsf  I2CFLAGS,1        ;Commanded receive
          MOVLF  Øx9Ø,I2CADD     ;Point to temp sensor
          movlw  Øxaa            ;Read Temperature command
          rcall  GetI2C          ;Read from temp sensor
          IF_  I2CFLAGS,2 == Ø   ;Check for acknowledge
            movwf  AARGBØ
            lfsr  Ø,LCDSTRING+5   ;Point to least significant digit
            movlw  ØxØ2          ;Create 3 digits
            rcall  Int2ASCII
            lfsr  Ø,LCDSTRING+9   ;Point to last string position
            clrf  POSTDECØ       ;End of line character
            MOVLF  A'C',POSTDECØ  ;Units
            MOVLF  Oxdf,POSTDECØ
            MOVLF  A' ',POSTDECØ
            lfsr  Ø,LCDSTRING+2
            MOVLF  A' ',POSTDECØ  ;Blank first two chars
            MOVLF  A' ',POSTDECØ
            MOVLF  Øx8Ø,INDFØ    ;Update cursor positioning code
            rcall  DisplayV
          ENDIF_
        ENDIF_
        return
        #include <C:\MATH18\FXDØ8Ø8U.INC>
        end
```

Figure 17-15 continued

PROBLEMS

17-1 I^2C and SPI The PIC18F452 uses the same pin, RC3/SCK/SCL, for both the SCL clock output for the I^2C bus and the SCK clock output for the SPI bus. It also shares the RC4/SDI/SDA pin for the bidirectional SDA pin of the I^2C bus and the SDI input pin of the SPI bus. Consider the consequences of connecting the 74HC165 "input port expansion" shift register of Figure 15-5 to these two pins as well as the DS1621 digital thermometer of Figure 17-13. Consider the possibility for contention between the drivers of the RC4/SDI/SDA pin when the pin is being driven by two or more of

- The PIC18F452
- The 74HC165
- The DS1621

One consequence of contention arises when a device attempts to drive the line high while another device with lower output impedance succeeds in driving the line low. Assume that each of the devices driving low can override any of the other devices driving high. For each part that follows, determine whether contention will arise and whether the intended operation will be corrupted.

(a) In SPI mode, a byte is read from the 74HC165.

(b) In I^2C mode, a byte is written to the DS1621 to configure its mode of operation. Consider both the byte transfer and the acknowledgment.

(c) In I^2C mode, a byte is read from the DS1621. Again, consider both the byte transfer and the acknowledgment.

17-2 I^2C and SPI Assume that the RC3/SCK/SCL pin is shared between the SPI clock for the MAX522 dual DAC on the QwikFlash board, as shown in Figure 4-2b, and the I^2C clock for a DS1621 digital thermometer. The RC4/SDI/SDA pin of the PIC18F452 is connected solely to the DS1621 (and a pullup resistor). The RC5/SDO pin is connected solely to the MAX522. For this connection, contention will never occur. Assume that both SPI transfers and I^2C transfers only occur in mainline code (so that one will not interrupt the other).

(a) Will the clocking associated with SPI transfers to the MAX522 ever produce a fault in the operation of the DS1621? Explain your answer.

(b) Will the clocking associated with I^2C transfers to the DS1621 ever produce a fault in the operation of the MAX522? Explain your answer.

17-3 STOP condition During the execution of a "read" message string such as that of Figure 17-5b, the microcontroller signals the peripheral chip when it wants no further bytes by *not* pulling the SDA line low in acknowledgment of the last byte. Then the microcontroller executes the STOP condition with the SDA and SCL lines.

(a) Draw the signals on both the SDA and the SDL lines during the final acknowledge bit and the STOP condition.

(b) Now redraw these same signals at the same time, assuming that the microcontroller is supposed to pull SDA low after the last transfer. Show and describe how the response of the peripheral chip in transmitting one more byte can thwart the microcontroller's execution of the STOP condition.

17-4 I²C addressing Assume that a part has a 7-bit address of

```
B'1 Ø Ø Ø Ø A1 AØ'
```

and that the A1 and A0 pins on the chip are both tied to +5 V.

(a) Express the 8-bit write address byte as a hex number.
(b) Express the 8-bit read address byte as a hex number.

17-5 I²C clock rate If the PIC18F452 is operated with a 10 MHz crystal and its PLL clock circuit, its internal clock rate will be 10 MHz. In this case, what must be done to take code written for the PIC18F452, assuming an internal clock rate of 2.5 MHz, so that with an actual internal clock rate of 10 MHz, the I²C transfers will still occur at 100 kHz?

17-6 TRISC bits for I²C use of RC3 and RC4 Download from www.microchip.com the data manual for PIC18FXX2 microcontrollers. Find and print out Figure 9-7: PORTC BLOCK DIAGRAM (at page 91 or thereabouts). When RC3 and RC4 are used as I²C pins, it has been suggested that the corresponding **TRISC** bits should be set, to allow the I²C control circuitry to control the I/O direction.

(a) Show an example where the RC4/SDA pin cannot be switched between input and output by the peripheral control lines (i.e., the I²C control circuitry) if bit 4 of **TRISC** is cleared. Is the pin always an output if bit 4 of **TRISC** is cleared?
(b) Describe why setting bit 4 of TRISC allows the RC4/SDA pin to be switched by the I²C control circuitry between input and output, thereby overriding the **TRISC** selection.

17-7 PCF8574 I/O expander Figure 17-7c and d describe how I/O pins are configured to be either inputs or outputs. With a 1 written to a pin, the pin serves as a (relatively) high-impedance input. The description of Figure 17-7c in this case indicates that a current of less than 300 μA will be sourced by the PCF8574. This specification is actually the maximum current if the load is such that the pin voltage drops to 0 V. This is exactly what happens when the pin is used as an input. Philips is stating that the pin will serve as a satisfactory input if the device driving the input pin can sink at least 300 μA when driven low. It interprets any input of less than 1.5 V (with a supply voltage to the chip of 5 V) as logic 0.

(a) Determine the Thévenin equivalent of a PCF8574 output pin when a 1 is written to the pin by the microcontroller.
(b) The output impedance of a driver that drives a PCF8574 input pin must be less than what value to be able to drive the pin below 1.5 V?
(c) Outputs of devices are usually specified as being able to sink at least I_{OL} milliamps with the output not rising above V_{OL} volts. For $V_{OL} = 0.4$ volts, what must the I_{OL} specification be in order to work satisfactorily with the PCF8574, so as to ensure that it is able to drive the pin below the 1.5 V required by the PCF8574?

17-8 Low-level I²C subroutines Consider the **GetI2CByte** subroutine of Figure 17-8e and the **I2COUT** macro of Figure 17-8g. Both are intended to transfer a single byte between the microcontroller and an I²C chip.

(a) The **GetI2CByte** subroutine *is called* by the **GETI2C** subroutine that builds an entire message string for reading 1 or more bytes from an I²C chip. What does **GetI2CByte** actually do for **GETI2C** and why is **GetI2CByte** written as a subroutine and not a macro?

(b) The **I2COUT** macro *calls* the **SendI2C** subroutine that builds an entire message string for writing one or more bytes to an I²C chip. What does the **I2COUT** actually do and why is it written as a macro and not as a subroutine?

17-9 I2CIN macro Consider the first four lines of the **Pushbutton** subroutine of Figure 17-10. Create a macro called **I2CIN** that includes a single "address" parameter and that can be used to read a single byte from the addressed device into **WREG**. In so doing, you will create a companion macro to the **I2COUT** macro of Figure 17-8g.

17-10 Pushbutton subroutine

(a) Why does the **Pushbutton** subroutine, called each time around the mainline loop, condition its response on obtaining an acknowledgment (see Figure 17-8a for bit 2 of **I2CFLAGS**) from the PCF8574 chip to which the pushbutton is attached?

(b) The role of this subroutine is to cycle the **I2CDISP** variable to its next state, as described in Section 17.7, whenever the pushbutton is pressed. Describe, in words, what is being done by the sequence of instructions, beginning with

```
xorlw  0x80                 ;Check for button press
```

and ending with

```
MOVLF  0x03,I2CDISP         ;Reset I2CDISP flag
```

(c) Bit 4 of **PORTA** drives the "Alive" LED on the QwikFlash board. How does the **Pushbutton** subroutine use this LED?

17-11 Blink subroutine The **Blink** subroutine of Figure 17-10 takes action every 2.5 seconds.

(a) How long are selected LEDs turned on? What determines this time?

(b) Add a comment to each test of **I2CDISP** saying what its value is if the test is passed; for example,

```
IF_  I2CDISP,1 == 1         ;I2CDISP = 2 or 3
```

17-12 Dual DAC Get the data sheet for the MAX518 dual DAC from Maxim's Web site, www.maxim-ic.com.

(a) Of the three bytes sent to the chip as described in Section 17.8, the first is the write address byte. The third is the desired output voltage. What are the options made possible by the second byte?

(b) What are the full part numbers for the DIP part?

(c) One of these has a "total unadjusted error" (TUE) of ± LSb while the other has a (TUE) of ± 1.5 LSb. Check www.findchips.com for the price and availability of each of these two variations. What is the premium in the price of the more accurate part as a percentage of the less accurate part?

(d) Check the Maxim Web site for the availability of two free samples.

17-13 Digital thermometer Get the data sheet for the DS1621 from www.dalsemi.com.

(a) Describe how the temperature thresholds are set up.
(b) Write the code to set the upper threshold to the Centigrade equivalent of 110°F.
(c) Write a **HotTemp** subroutine to query the THF (Temperature High Flag), returning **Z** = 1 if THF = 1, while at the same time resetting THF if the temperature has dropped below the upper threshold.
(d) Using the fixed-point subroutines of Chapter 14, obtain the 2-byte temperature reading plus the two 1-byte counters described on page 5 of the data sheet and form the interpolated temperature value in units of 0.1°F. If the measured temperature is 71.2°F, then your calculation should produce the 2-byte value 712. Note that

$$F = \frac{18}{10} C + 32$$

While the resulting resolution is finer than the ±0.5°C absolute error of the part, it produces temperature *difference* measurements that are accurate to about 0.1°F.
(e) Check the price and availability of the DIP part (whose full part number is DS1621 with no trailing letter) on www.findchips.com.
(f) Check the Dallas Semiconductor Web site for the availability of two free samples.

17-14 Alternative I/O port expander parts

(a) Use www.findchips.com to check on the price and availability of

- 74HC595 (SPI output port expander)
- 74HC164 (SPI input port expander)
- PCF8574 (older I^2C I/O port expander)
- PCA9554 (newer I^2C I/O port expander)

(b) If the latter part is available, then download its data sheet from www.philipslogic.com. How does it handle I/O direction? What is its drive capability? What is its input loading? Is the part available in a DIP package?

Chapter

18

UART

18.1 OVERVIEW

A UART, universal asynchronous receiver transmitter, is a module in the PIC18F452 that is commonly used to create a serial interface to a personal computer. The QwikBug monitor program usurps this one resource on the PIC18F452 to create an extremely low-cost development environment. Consequently, an application that uses the UART function is better served by the PIC18F452 in-circuit debugger.

This chapter explores how the UART works, how its baud rate is derived from the microcontroller's crystal clock frequency, F_{OSC}, and how the UART is used by an application.

18.2 WAVEFORMS AND BAUD-RATE ACCURACY

When serial data is transmitted *asynchronously,* the data stream is generated with the transmitter's clock. The receiver must synchronize the incoming data stream to the receiver's clock.

An example of the transmission of 4 bytes is shown in Figure 18-1. Each 8-bit byte is *framed* by a START bit and a STOP bit. For transmission at 9600 baud, each of these bits lasts for a *bit time* (BT) of 1/9600 second. Before the first frame is transmitted, the line from the transmitter's TX output to the receiver's RX input idles high. The receiver monitors its RX input, waiting for the line to drop low because of the transmission of the (low) START bit. The receiver synchronizes on this high-to-low transition. Then the receiver reads the 8 bits of serial data by sampling the RX input at

1.5 BT, 2.5 BT, 3.5 BT, 4.5 BT, 5.5 BT, 6.5 BT, 7.5 BT, and 8.5 BT

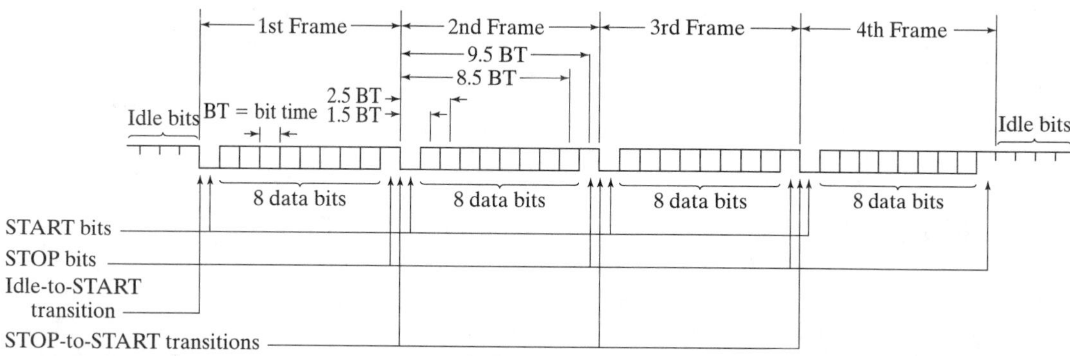

Receiver synchronizes on Idle-to-START transition
Receiver resynchronizes on each subsequent STOP-to-START transition

Figure 18-1 Four data frames having a serial protocol of 1 START bit, 8 data bits, and 1 STOP bit.

as shown in Figure 18-1. It checks that the framing of the byte has been interpreted correctly by reading what should be a high STOP bit at 9.5 BT. If the RX line is actually low at this time, for whatever reason, the receiver sets a flag to indicate a *framing error.* Regardless of whether or not a framing error occurs, the receiver then begins again, *resynchronizing* on the next high-to-low transition of the RX line. Because of this resynchronization, the receiver can generate its own baud-rate clock and yet the receiver can recover the serial data perfectly.

Example 18-1 Assume the transmitter transmits data at exactly 9600 baud and assume the receiver measures its sampling times from the exact moment when the STOP-to-START transition occurs. How far off from 9600 baud can the receiver's baud-rate clock be and still recover the data and the STOP bit correctly?

Solution

As illustrated in Figure 18-1, the STOP bit is read after 9.5 bit times. Consider the consequence if the receiver's baud-rate clock is off sufficiently to cause the sampling to be off by ± 0.5 bit time after 9.5 bit times. The sampling of the first data bit at 1.5 bit times of the receiver's baud-rate clock will occur slightly off-center of the bit time generated by the transmitter. This off-centeredness progresses with successive bits to the point where the STOP bit will be read unreliably and where the STOP-to-START transition may be missed because the receiver is not yet looking for it. This error in the receiver's baud-rate clock amounts to

$$(\pm 0.5/9.5) \times 100 = \pm 5.3\%$$

Example 18-2 The microcontroller's baud-rate clock operates at either of two ranges, called *high-speed baud rate and low-speed baud rate.* Using the *low-speed* baud rate, the receiver looks for the STOP-to-START transition by sampling its RX input every $1/16^{\text{th}}$ of one of its bit times, as shown in Figure 18-2. Then it counts six more of these sample times to a point where it reads a cluster of three closely spaced samples of RX and votes among them to ensure that

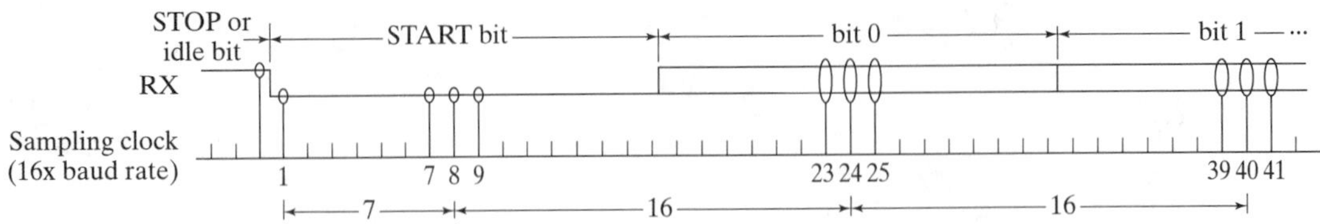

Figure 18-2 Receiver's sampling of RX using its low-speed baud-rate circuitry.

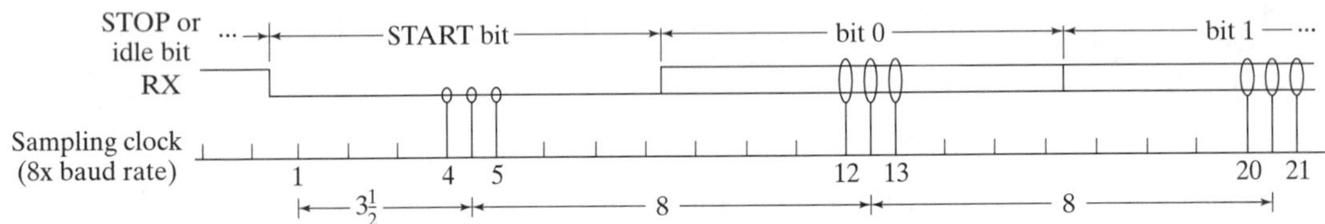

Figure 18-3 Receiver's sampling of RX using its high-speed baud-rate circuitry.

it is seeing the low START bit. Thereafter, it reads successive clusters of three samples spaced 16 sample times apart. In effect, the receiver is reading its input every 16 periods of its sample clock. How far off from 9600 baud can the receiver's baud-rate clock be and still recover the data and the STOP bit correctly?

Solution

The mechanism for detecting the STOP-to-START transition can throw the samples off from the center of each bit time by as much as 1/16th of a bit time, even if the receiver's baud rate exactly matches the transmitter's baud rate. If the receiver's baud-rate clock is off sufficiently to cause the sampling to be off by

$$\pm(0.5 \text{ bit time} - 1/16 \text{ bit time}) = \pm 0.4375 \text{ bit time}$$

after 9.5 bit times, then the error can occur. This places a baud-rate error limit of

$$(\pm 0.4375/9.5) \times 100 = \pm 4.6\ \%$$

on the receiver's baud-rate clock (assuming the transmitter's baud-rate clock matches its nominal rate exactly).

Example 18-3 Examine the baud-rate accuracy requirement for the *high-speed* baud rate. The receiver's sampling scheme is shown in Figure 18-3.

Solution

In this case, the sampling rate is 8 times higher than the baud rate. Consequently, the pinpointing of when the STOP-to-START transition occurs may be off 1/8th of a bit time. Again, if the receiver's baud-rate clock is off sufficiently to cause the sampling to be off by

$$\pm(0.5 \text{ bit time} - 1/8 \text{ bit time}) = \pm 0.375 \text{ bit time}$$

after 9.5 bit times, then an error can occur. This places a baud-rate error limit of

$$(\pm 0.375/9.5) \times 100 = \pm 3.9\%$$

on the receiver's baud-rate clock.

18.3 BAUD-RATE SELECTION

Given the considerations of the preceding section, a desired baud rate can now be approximated by the UART's baud-rate generator. If the crystal clock frequency were selected to be a carefully chosen multiple of the desired baud rate, then the baud-rate generator would produce the desired baud rate exactly. With $F_{OSC} = 10$ MHz or 40 MHz, several commonly used baud rates can be approximated sufficiently closely for use by the UART, as tabulated in Figure 18-4a. These are derived from F_{OSC} using an 8-bit presettable divider and a fixed divider of either 16 or 64, using the equations of Figure 18-4b. Even in the worst case, the percent error of the approximate baud rate is less than half of the percent error that cannot be tolerated by the UART.

18.4 UART DATA-HANDLING CIRCUITRY

The transmit data circuit is shown in Figure 18-5a. To transmit a byte of data serially from the TX pin, the byte is written to the **TXREG** register. Assuming there is not already data in the TSR (transmit shift register), the contents of **TXREG** will be automatically transferred to the TSR, making **TXREG**

Nominal baud rate	$F_{OSC} = 10$ MHz			$F_{OSC} = 40$ MHz		
	BRGH	SPBRG	% error	BRGH	SPBRG	% error
9,600 baud	1	64	+0.16%	0	64	+0.16%
19,200 baud	1	32	−1.4%	1	129	+0.16%
38,400 baud	1	15	+1.7%	1	64	+0.16%
57,600 baud	1	10	−1.4%	1	43	−1.4%
76,800 baud	1	7	+1.7%	1	32	−1.4%
115,200 baud	—	—	—	1	21	−1.4%

(a) Register contents and accuracy of approximated baud rate

	BRGH = 1 (high-speed baud rate)	BRGH = 0 (low-speed baud rate)
Baud rate =	$\dfrac{F_{OSC}}{16(SPBRG+1)}$	$\dfrac{F_{OSC}}{64(SPBRG+1)}$

(b) Relationship between BRGH, F_{osc}, SPBRG, and baud rate

Figure 18-4 Setup for some common baud rates.

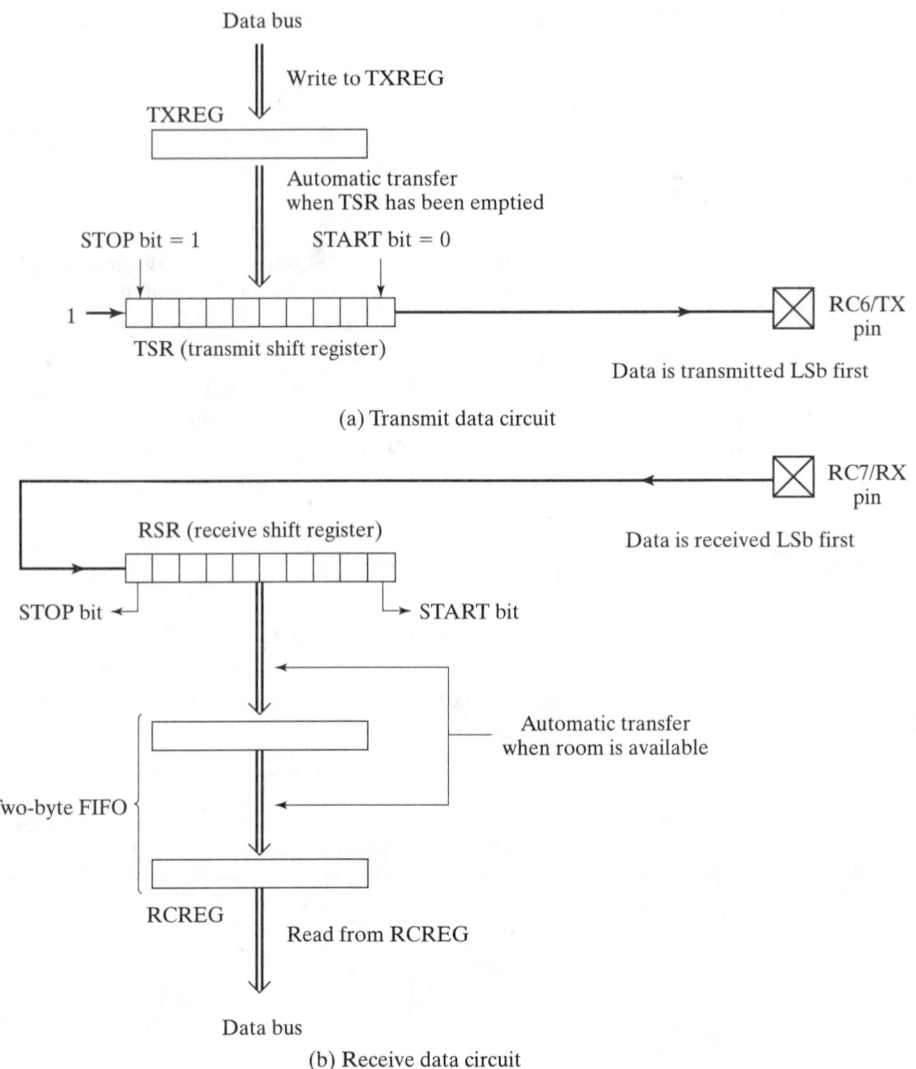

Figure 18-5 UART's data-handling circuitry.

available for a second byte even as the first byte is being shifted out of the TX pin, framed by START and STOP bits.

The receive data circuit is similar, with received data shifted into the RSR (receive shift register). When it is in place, the STOP bit is checked and an error flag is set if the STOP bit does not equal 1. In any case, the received byte is automatically transferred into a 2-byte FIFO (first-in, first-out memory). If the FIFO was initially empty, the received byte will fall through to the **RCREG** (receive register) virtually immediately, where it is ready to be read by the CPU. If the CPU is slow in reading the **RCREG**, a second byte can be received at the RX pin. When it is in place in the RSR, it will follow the first byte into the 2-byte FIFO. At that point, the FIFO is full. If a third byte enters the RX pin and is shifted all the way across the RSR before at least the first of the two bytes in the FIFO has been read, then the new byte will be lost. An *overrun* error flag will be set, alerting the receiver software of the loss of a byte of data.

At 9600 baud, it takes 10/9600 second, or just a little longer than a millisecond, to receive each byte. If the received bytes are handled under interrupt control, each byte should be easily handled in a timely fashion, well before an overrun error can ever occur. No other interrupt handler should be permitted to lock out this or any other interrupt source for anywhere near a millisecond.

18.5 UART INITIALIZATION

The registers involved with UART use are shown in Figure 18-6. The UART's baud rate and its transmit and receive functions are initialized by writes to **SPBRG**, **TXSTA**, and **RCSTA**, as shown in Figures 18-4 and 18-6. At 9600 baud, each transfer takes about a millisecond, so sending or receiving a string of characters is best carried out under interrupt control. The flag and interrupt enable bits of the **PIR1**, **PIE1**, **IPR1**, and **INTCON** registers control the timing of the CPU's interactions with the UART.

18.6 UART USE

A major application for the microcontroller's UART is to provide a two-wire (plus ground) serial interface to a personal computer. The circuit of Figure 18-7 uses a Maxim chip to translate between the 0 V and +5 V logic-level signal swings on the microcontroller's RX and TX pins and ±10 V signal swings that support the RS-232 interface requirements. Both the microcontroller and the PC should be set up for the same baud rate (e.g., 9600 baud) and for one start bit, one stop bit and no parity.

Given this setup, the microcontroller will respond to **RCIF** interrupts by reading each byte from the **RCREG** register sent by the PC. The **RCIF** flag will clear itself when the byte read from **RCREG** leaves the receive circuit's FIFO empty.

The microcontroller sends out a string of bytes by writing them, one-by-one under interrupt control, to **TXREG**. The **TXIF** flag takes care of itself, clearing automatically when **TXREG** is written to and setting again as the data written to **TXREG** is automatically transferred to the transmit shift register. At the completion of sending the string of bytes to the PC, the **TXIE** bit in the **PIE1** register is cleared to disable further "transmit" interrupts until another string needs to be sent to the PC.

Another application of the UART is to couple two microcontrollers together. In this way, some of the work that would be done by one microcontroller (if only it could do all it needs to do by itself) is off-loaded to a second microcontroller. Figure 18-8 shows this connection of two microcontrollers, using the maximum possible baud rate to obtain fast coupling between the two microcontrollers. Within 40 internal clock cycles, what is written into one microcontroller's **TXREG** register appears on the other microcontroller's **RCREG** register.

Carrying out transfers at this fast rate calls for some precautions if overrun errors are to be avoided, given microcontrollers that are trying to carry out tasks in addition to monitoring the UART's **RCREG** register. A PIC18F452 can only receive 2 bytes into its FIFO without reading them immediately. Any further bytes received will be discarded until the earlier bytes are read out of the FIFO, making room for new bytes.

A commonly used solution to the problem faced by a microcontroller receiving bytes in *bursts* is for its UART interrupt handler to *queue* the received bytes and then have its mainline program retrieve the bytes from the queue, one-by-one, acting on them as appropriate.

Example 18-4 Using the 128 bytes of RAM from 0x080 to 0x0ff as a queue, show the code to implement a **PUT** macro to enter **WREG** into the queue and a **Get** subroutine to retrieve the oldest queue entry to **WREG**. If **Get** finds the queue empty, it returns **Z** = 1.

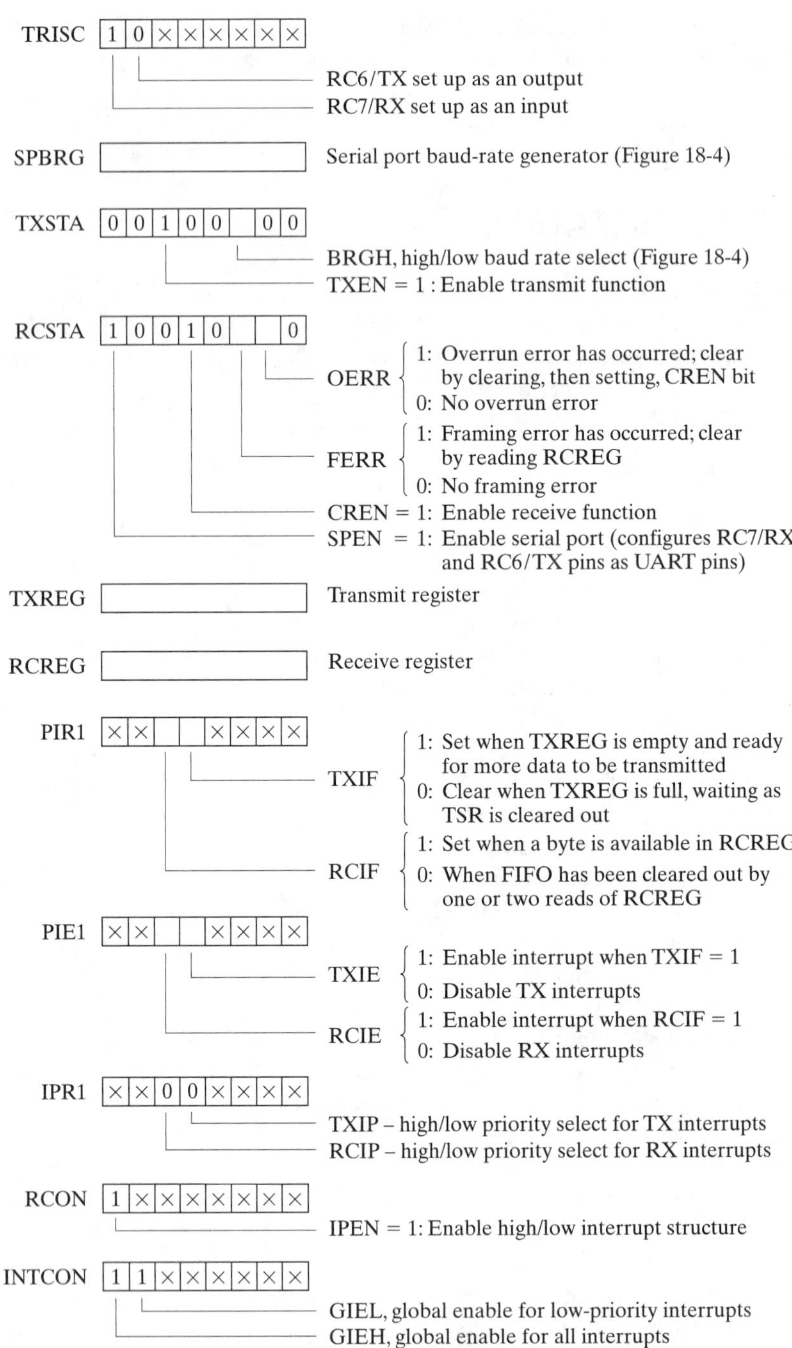

Figure 18-6 UART registers.

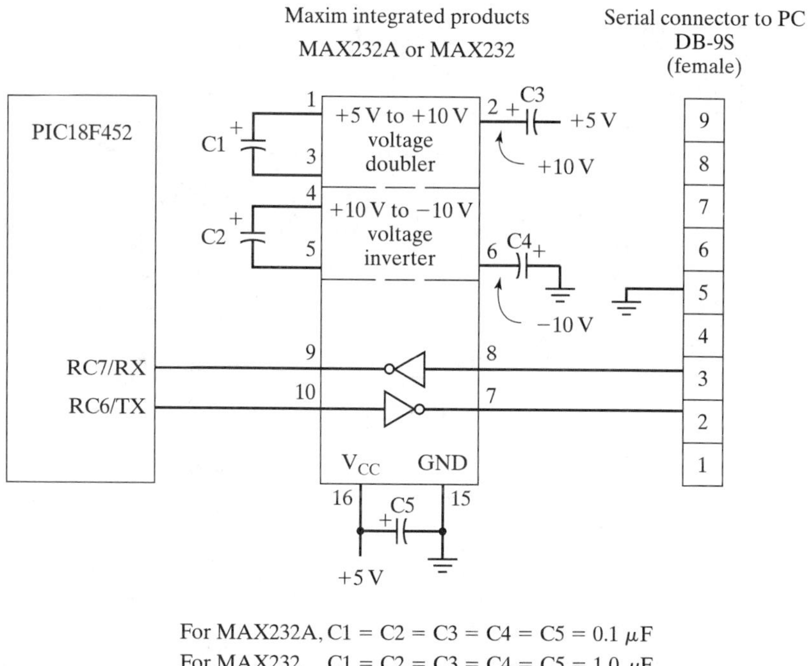

Figure 18-7 PIC's UART interface to a PC.

Solution

As befits an application in which a UART *interrupt handler* puts bytes into the queue, use **FSR2** as a pointer dedicated solely to this purpose. The corresponding pointer for the **Get** subroutine, with a value ranging from 0x080 to 0x0ff, only needs a 1-byte RAM variable, **GETPTRL**, to store its value. These are both initialized to 0x80, as shown in Figure 18-9a.

The **PUT** macro definition is shown in Figure 18-9b. Rather than auto-incrementing **FSR2**, its lower byte alone is incremented, thereby avoiding the increment from 0x0ff to 0x100. The subsequent setting of the MSb of **FSR2L** will return the pointer to 0x080 in this case.

The **Get** subroutine of Figure 18-9c first compares the two pointers. If they are equal, the queue is empty and the subroutine returns with **Z** = 1. Otherwise, **GETPTRL** is used to retrieve the oldest byte from the queue to **WREG**. The pointer is incremented and then the subroutine returns with **Z** = 0.

Example 18-5 For fast transfers between two PIC18F452's using their UARTs at the maximum baud rate, use high-priority interrupts to field the UART's reception of each byte, assuming no other interrupt sources are using high-priority interrupts. Show the high-priority interrupt service routine to put each received byte into the queue of the last example. Determine how long the CPU digresses from the mainline code and/or low-priority interrupts to handle each received byte.

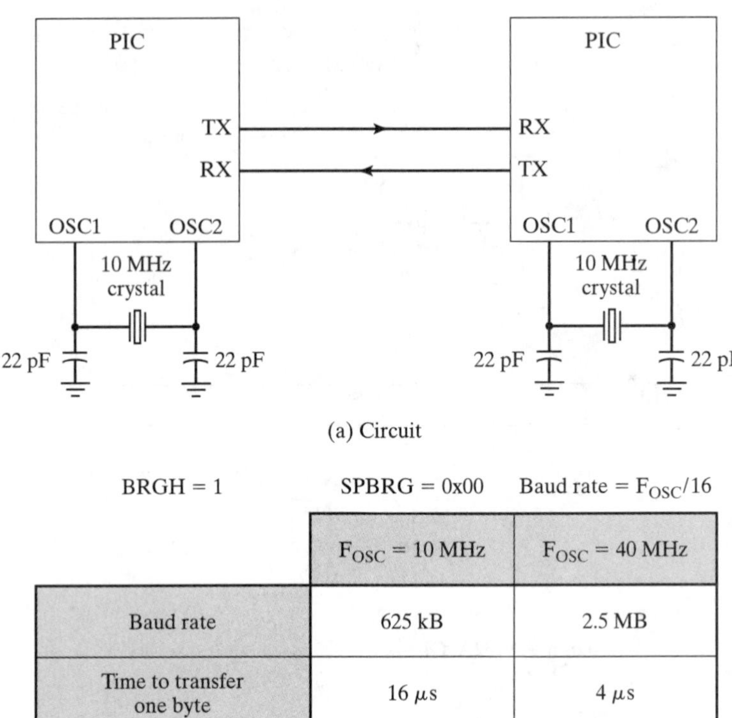

(a) Circuit

BRGH = 1 SPBRG = 0x00 Baud rate = $F_{OSC}/16$

	F_{OSC} = 10 MHz	F_{OSC} = 40 MHz
Baud rate	625 kB	2.5 MB
Time to transfer one byte	16 μs	4 μs

(b) Setup for maximum transfer rate

Figure 18-8 UART interconnection of two PIC's.

Solution

The initialization for UART "receive" high-priority interrupts is shown in Figure 18-10a. The high-priority interrupt service routine is shown in Figure 18-10b. Note that the CPU will digress for only eight cycles from what it was doing in order to handle the UART.

```
        lfsr  2,0x080             ;Initialize queue input pointer, FSR2
        MOVLF  0x80,GETPTRL       ;Initialize queue output pointer, GETPTRL
```

(a) Initialization

```
PUT     macro
        movwf  INDF2              ;Put WREG into queue
        incf  FSR2L,F             ;Increment pointer,
        bsf  FSR2L,7              ; constraining result to B'1xxxxxxx' addresses
        endm
```

(b) PUT macro

```
;;;;;;; Get subroutine ;;;;;;;;;;;;;;;;;;;;;;;;;;;;;;;;;;;;;;;;;;;;;;;;;;;;;;;;;;;
;
; If queue is empty, this subroutine returns with Z=1.
; If queue is not empty, it returns with Z=0 and with byte in WREG.
; It stores the queue output pointer in GETPTRL.
; It uses RAM ranging from 0x080 to 0x0ff for the queue.

Get
        movf  FSR2L,W             ;Compare lower eight bits of pointers
        subwf  GETPTRL,W
        IF_  .NZ.
          movff  GETPTRL,FSR0L    ;Load pointer into  FSR0H:FSR0L
          clrf  FSR0H
          movf  INDF0,W           ;Get byte
          incf  FSR0L,F           ;Increment pointer,
          bsf  FSR0L,7            ; constraining result to B'1xxxxxxx' addresses
          movff  FSR0L,GETPTRL    ;Return pointer to RAM
          bcf  STATUS,Z           ;Return from subroutine with Z=0
        ENDIF_
        return
```

(c) Get subroutine

Figure 18-9 Queue implementation.

```
        bsf     RCON,IPEN         ;Enable priority levels
        bsf     IPR1,RCIP         ;Receive interrupts have high priority
        bcf     PIR1,RCIF         ;Clear flag
        bsf     PIE1,RCIE         ;Enable local interrupt source
        bsf     INTCON,GIEH       ;Enable all interrupts globally
```

(a) Initialization of UART "receive" high-priority interrupts

```
        org  0x0008
HiPriISR                          ;2 cycles to get from interrupted code
        movf  RCREG,W             ;1 cycle (flag automatically cleared by read)
        PUT                       ;3 cycles
        retfie  FAST              ;2 cycles
```

(b) Interrupt service routine

Figure 18-10 UART high-priority interrupt service routine.

PROBLEMS

18-1 Noise spike A UART receiver is triggered by a high-to-low transition on its input. If this is a false trigger caused by an isolated noise spike, then one hopes the UART will automatically detect this and begin again to look for a new high-to-low transition upon which to trigger.

Assuming that the UART input again idles high after the noise spike, when will the UART detect the error? When it reads the START bit as a 1? When it reads the data as 0xff? When it reads the STOP bit as a 1?

18-2 Transmitter and receiver clocks Why is it that a UART transmitter can transmit data at 9500 baud, a UART receiver can receive that data with its own 9700 baud clock, and yet the data is received without error, even as hundreds of bytes of data are sent, one byte right after another?

18-3 Baud-rate selection The entry in Figure 18-4 for F_{OSC} = 10 MHz and a nominal baud rate of 9600 baud uses the high-speed baud rate choice (**BRGH** = 1) and produces an error from the nominal rate of +0.16%.

(a) Show the calculations to verify this.
(b) What value of **SPBRG** will couple with **BRGH** = 0 to approximate 9600 baud as closely as possible? What is the percent error in this case?
(c) Why does the **BRGH** = 1 choice give a lower percent error than the **BRGH** = 0 choice?

18-4 PUT macro Consider the **PUT** macro three-instruction definition of Figure 18-9b and its use in the **HiPriISR** three-line interrupt service routine of Figure 18-10b. Is there any advantage to be gained by writing **HiPriISR** as the following four-instruction sequence?

```
        org  0x0008
HiPriISR
        movff  RCREG,INDF2
        incf  FSR2L,F
        bsf  FSR2L,7
        retfie  FAST
```

18-5 Smaller queue Rewrite the **PUT** macro and the **Get** subroutine to use just the 64 bytes extending from 0x0c0 to 0x0ff.

18-6 Larger queue Rewrite the **PUT** macro and **Get** subroutine to use the 256 bytes extending from 0x100 to 0x1ff.

Chapter

19

PROGRAMMED PERIPHERAL CHIPS

19.1 OVERVIEW

The expertise gleaned in the process of learning about the PIC18F452 can be used to augment the capabilities of that chip with those of the lowest-cost PIC microcontroller family of microcontrollers. In this chapter, the limited capabilities of the 14-pin PIC16C505 will be explored. At the time of this writing, a one-time programmable, 20 MHz PIC16C505 costs $1.31 each from Digi-Key in quantities of 25–99, significantly less than most specialty peripheral chips. Given this pricing, it is worthwhile to explore its use as a programmed peripheral chip.

As an example application, the PIC16C505 will be used to decode a 12-key telephone keypad (with keys 0 to 9 plus * and #). The ASCII code for each pressed key will be sent to the UART's RX input of the PIC18F452. As will be seen, the keypad has seven pins that will be manipulated by the PIC16C505 to determine when a key is pressed and which key it is. This application, in effect, expands the PIC18F452's I/O lines to handle these seven keypad connections, using the one RX pin for the interface. In addition, the PIC16C505 becomes a smart peripheral, relieving the PIC18F452 of the job of deciphering the keypad.

19.2 PIC16C505 OVERVIEW

A block diagram of the PIC16C505 is shown in Figure 19-1. The chip has two 6-bit I/O ports, giving a maximum of 12 I/O pins. Bits 4 and 5 of **PORTB** can also be I/O pins if the internal 4 MHz $\pm 10\%$ RC oscillator is selected as the clock source. For the keypad-input/UART-output application of this chapter, this $\pm 10\%$ frequency tolerance is inadequate, so bits 4 and 5 of **PORTB** are connected to a 10 MHz, low-cost ceramic resonator having a $\pm 0.5\%$ frequency tolerance.

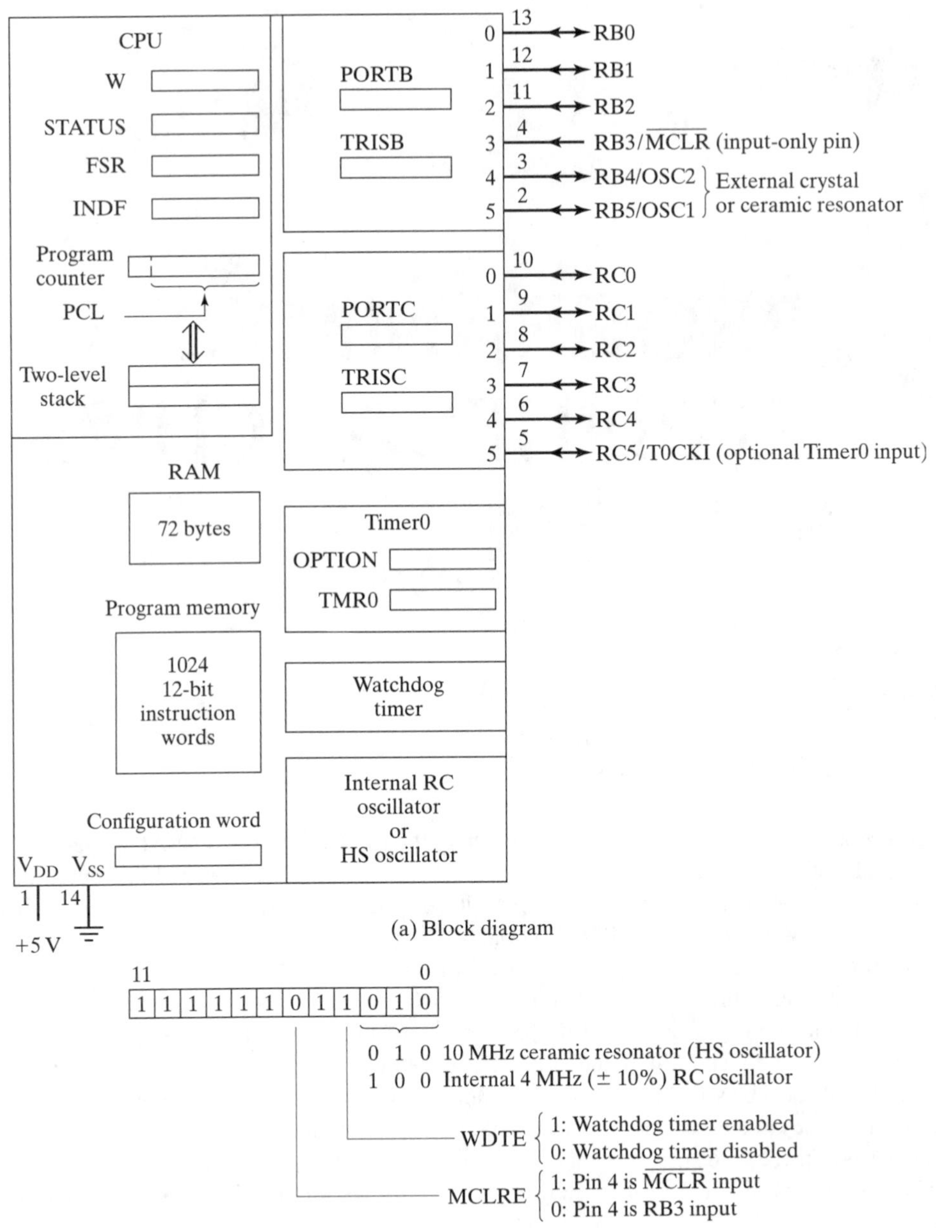

Figure 19-1 PIC16C505 block diagram.

The chip also has an optional $\overline{MCLR}$ (master clear) input. As an alternative to giving up a pin for this purpose, the *configuration word* of Figure 19-1 is shown using pin 4 (the RB3/$\overline{MCLR}$ pin) as an RB3 input. The configuration word is also used to enable the watchdog timer. Each time around the mainline loop, the watchdog timer will be reset by the application program. If the CPU ever gets *off track* so that it is no longer executing the mainline code, the chip will automatically reset itself when the

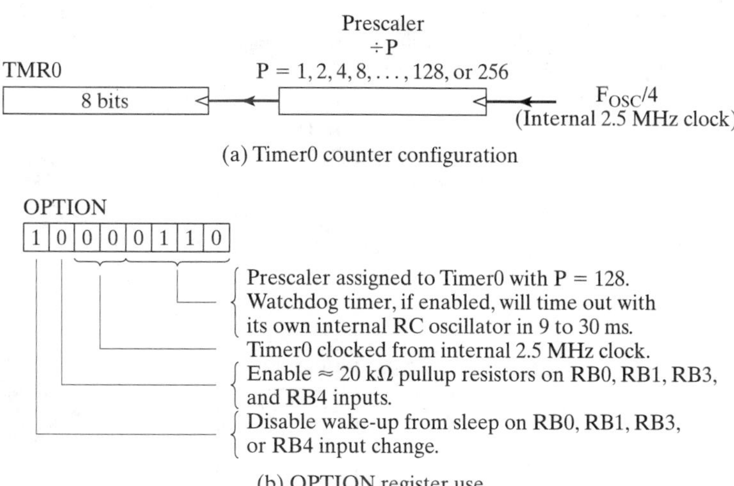

Figure 19-2 Timer0 and **OPTION** register.

watchdog timer times out (after a minimum of 9 milliseconds). Consequently, the need for a manual reset is avoided.

The PIC16C505's Timer0 is an 8-bit counter that can be clocked from the internal clock, scaled down by a prescaler, as shown in Figure 19-2a. Some of its options are illustrated in Figure 19-2b. For the keypad/UART application,

```
OPTION = B'10000110'
```

The **OPTION** register is loaded with the instruction sequence

```
movlw  B'10000110'
option
```

so that Timer0 rolls over every 13.1 milliseconds. The watchdog timer will typically time out in 28 milliseconds, but certainly no sooner than 9 milliseconds after the application program last reset it with a **clrwdt** instruction. Also pullup resistors are enabled on the RB0, RB1, RB3, and RB4 inputs.

Although the PIC16C505 has 72 bytes of RAM, only 24 bytes can be directly addressed before a bank-switching scheme must be invoked. For a small peripheral chip application, 24 bytes of RAM are likely to be sufficient for the job. If so, then the operand memory space is shown in Figure 19-3b. The indirect addressing pointer, **FSR**, must be initially cleared because its upper bits serve as the bank-switching bits for direct addressing.

The eight special-purpose registers are also shown in Figure 19-3b. The **FSR** register and the **INDF** operand serve the same function as the PIC18F452's **FSR0** and **INDF0** registers for indirect addressing. The **OSCCAL** register is used to trim the optional RC clock oscillator to within ±10% of 4 MHz.

The **STATUS** register bit definitions are shown, along with the other CPU registers, in Figure 19-4. Its **PA0** bit is used to implement the PIC16C505's awkward program memory paging scheme that affects the **goto** instruction, the subroutine **call** instruction, and any instruction that modifies **PCL**, the lower 8 bits of the program counter. These are described in Figure 19-5.. For the many applications, including the keypad/UART application, that require less than 512 instructions, **PAO** need never be changed from its power-on reset value of 0. In this case,

```
clrf FSR
```

(a) Initialization required to avoid bank switching

Address	Register
00	INDF
01	TMR0
02	PCL
03	STATUS
04	FSR
05	OSCCAL
06	PORTB
07	PORTC
08–1f	24 bytes of RAM

Figure 19-3 Direct addressing without bank switching.

(b) Special purpose registers and RAM reachable with no bank switching if FSR is constrained to the range from 0x00 to 0x1f

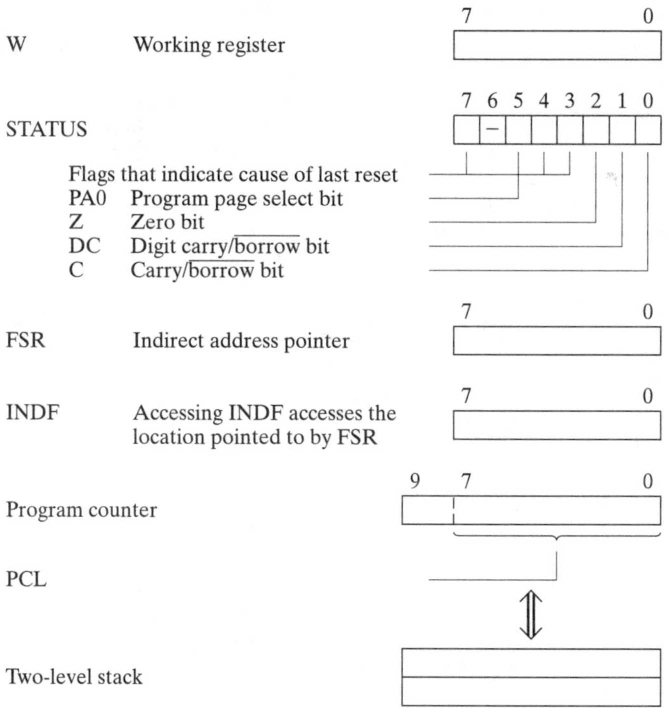

Figure 19-4 PIC16C505 CPU registers.

- A **goto** instruction will reach anywhere in the program.
- All subroutines must be located in the first 256 instructions.
- All tables, accessed by adding an offset to **PCL**, must also be located in the first 256 instructions.

Actually, with a stack only two levels deep, the subroutine constraint is not as important as it might otherwise be. Care must be taken never to call a subroutine that calls a subroutine that, in turn, calls a subroutine. The third return address will overwrite the first return address in the stack.

Missing from the list of registers are the **TRISB** and **TRISC** registers to control the input/output direction of the pins of each port. Just as an **option** instruction copies **W** into the (unaddressed) **OPTION** register, so the instruction

```
tris  PORTB
```

copies **W** into **TRISB** and

```
tris  PORTC
```

copies **W** into **TRISC**. A 0 written to a **TRISB** or **TRISC** bit causes the corresponding bit of the port to become an output, while a 1 establishes an input pin, just as for the PIC18F452.

The PIC16C505's instruction set is shown in Figure 19-6. As a greatly reduced version of the PIC18F452's instruction set, these instructions hold few ambiguities. The **rlf** and **rrf** instructions are identical to the PIC18F452's **rlcf** and **rrcf** 9-bit rotate-through-carry instructions. The only subroutine return instruction, **retlw**, not only pops the stack back into the program counter but also loads its literal

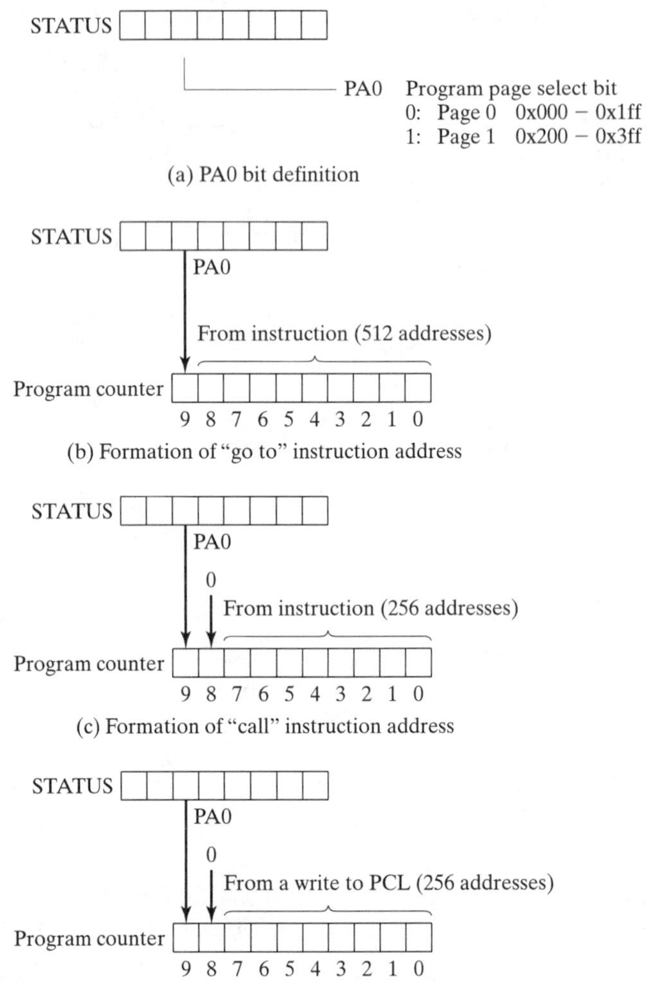

Figure 19-5 Program memory paging.

value into **W**. Since the PIC16C505 supports neither internal nor external interrupts, there is no **retfie** (return from interrupt) instruction.

19.3 KEYPAD PERIPHERAL INTERFACE

If a PIC18F452 application requires a numeric keypad and it has seven I/O pins to spare, then the frugal course of action is to connect the keypad directly to seven I/O pins. A mainline loop subroutine can decipher when a new key is pressed and determine which key it is. Without seven available pins, the "smart" I/O expansion circuit of Figure 19-7 provides an economical solution with nothing more than the PIC16C505, a 70¢ ceramic resonator, a 20 kΩ pullup resistor, and a 0.1 μf bypass capacitor. It replaces the PIC18F452's seven-pin keypad interface with a single-pin UART interface.

Mnemonic, operands	Description	Cycles	Status bits affected
bcf f,b	Clear bit b of register f, where b = 0 to 7	1	
bsf f,b	Set bit b of register f, where b = 0 to 7	1	
clrw	Clear W	1	Z
clrf f	Clear f	1	Z
movlw k	Move literal value to W	1	
movwf f	Move W to f	1	
movf f,F(W)	Move f to F or W	1	Z
swapf f,F(W)	Swap nibbles of f, putting result into F or W	1	
option	Load OPTION register from W	1	
tris PORTB (PORTC)	Load TRISB (TRISC) from W	1	
incf f,F(W)	Increment f, putting result in F or W	1	Z
decf f,F(W)	Decrement f, putting result in F or W	1	Z
comf f,F(W)	Complement f, putting result in F or W	1	Z
andlw k	AND literal value into W	1	Z
andwf f,F(W)	AND W with f, putting result in F or W	1	Z
iorlw k	Inclusive-OR literal value into W	1	Z
iorwf f,F(W)	Inclusive-OR W with F, putting result in F or W	1	Z
xorlw k	Exclusive-OR literal value into W	1	Z
xorwf f,F(W)	Exclusive-OR W with F, putting result in F or W	1	Z
addwf f,F(W)	Add w and f, putting result in F or W	1	C,DC,Z
subwf f,F(W)	Subtract W from f, putting result in F or W	1	C,DC,Z
rlf f,F(W)	Rotate f left through the carry bit, putting result in F or W	1	C
rrf f,F(W)	Rotate f right through the carry bit, putting result in F or W	1	C
btfsc f,b	Test bit b of register f, where b = 0 to 7; skip if clear	1(2)	
btfss f,b	Test bit b of register f, where b = 0 to 7; skip if set	1(2)	
decfsz f,F(W)	Decrement f, putting result in F or W, skip if zero	1(2)	
incfsz f,F(W)	Increment f, putting result in F or W, skip if zero	1(2)	
goto label	Go to labeled instruction	2	
call label	Call labeled subroutine	2	
retlw k	Return from subroutine, putting literal value in W	2	
clrwdt	Clear watchdog timer	1	TO,PD
sleep	Go into standby mode	1	TO,PD
nop	No operation	1	

Figure 19-6 PIC16C505 instruction set.

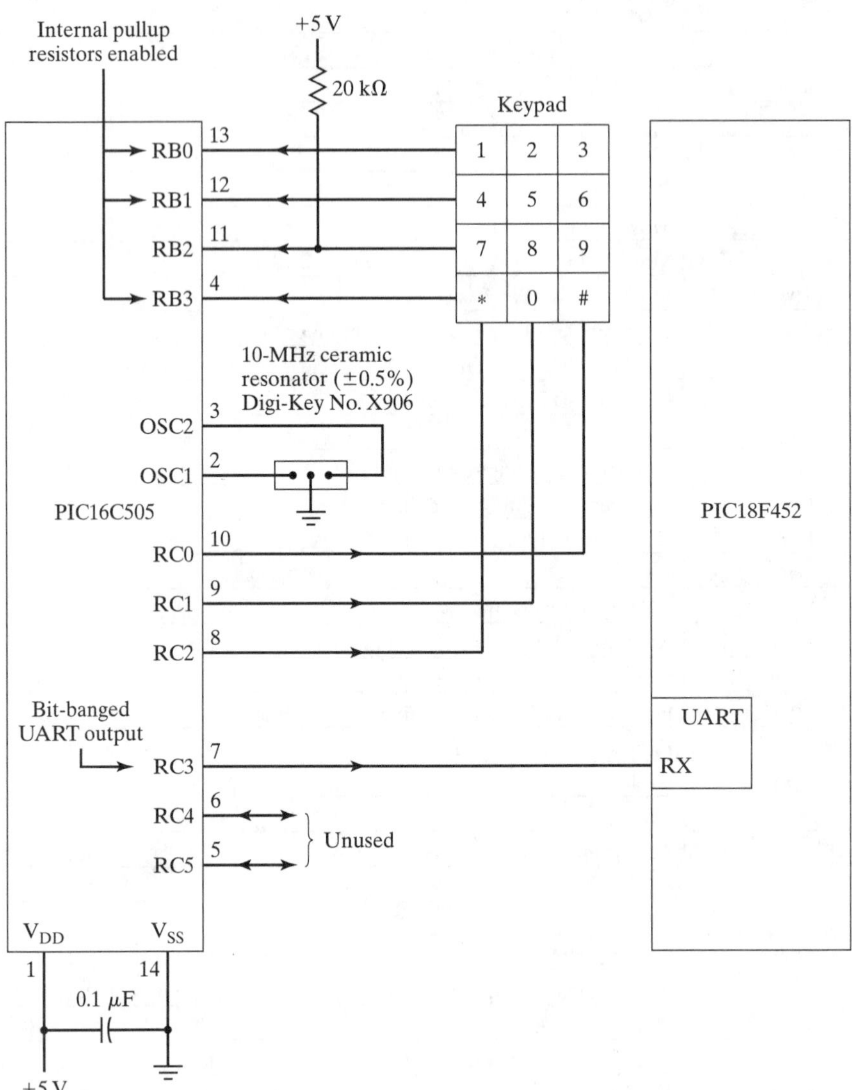

Figure 19-7 Keypad-input/UART-output interface.

Whenever a key is pressed, the PIC18F452 will find its **RCIF** flag set, with the ASCII code for the key in the **RCREG** register. Since successive key presses occur much less often than the loop time of 10 milliseconds, the PIC18F452 can simply poll **RCIF** each time around the mainline loop and act on the received character if the flag is set.

By using a 10 MHz F_{OSC} for both the PIC18F452 and the PIC16C505, the matching of transmit and receive baud rates is simplified. Figure 19-8 shows Timer0 being used to achieve three things:

- The prescaler that can be assigned to either the watchdog timer or to Timer0 is assigned to Timer0. With this assignment, the watchdog timer will time out sometime between 9 and 30 milliseconds after it was last cleared by a **clrwdt** instruction. The loop-time mechanism must execute **clrwdt** instructions with an interval that never exceeds 9 milliseconds.

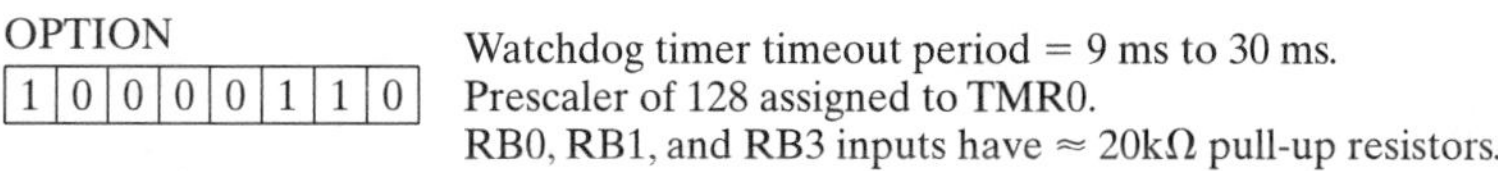

OPTION
1 0 0 0 0 1 1 0
Watchdog timer timeout period = 9 ms to 30 ms.
Prescaler of 128 assigned to TMR0.
RB0, RB1, and RB3 inputs have ≈ 20kΩ pull-up resistors.

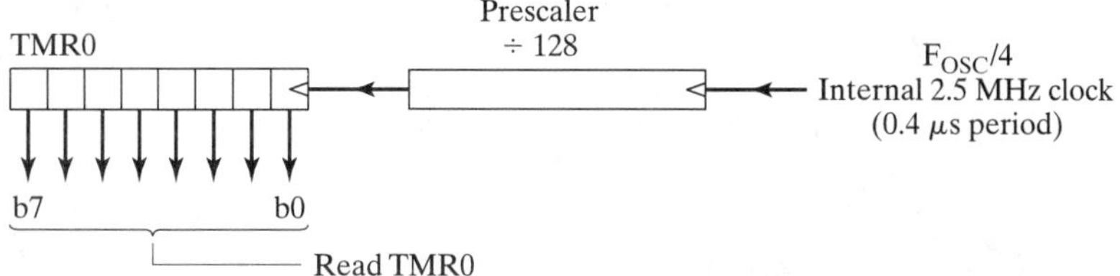

PIC16C505			PIC18F452 settings to match its UART baud rate to the PIC16C505's TMR0, b0 frequency	
TMR0 bit	Bit frequency	Bit period	BRGH	SPBRG
b0	9765.625 Hz	102.4 μs	1	63
b7	–	13.1072 ms	–	–

Figure 19-8 OPTION register and Timer0 and watchdog timer use.

- Bit 0 of **TMR0** produces a 1-to-0 transition that can be used to time successive bits of the *bit-banged* UART output on the RC3 pin when sending the ASCII code for a pressed key to the PIC18F452's UART. If the PIC18F452's UART is set up with **BRGH** = 1 and **SPBRG** = 63, then the transmitter baud rate and the receiver baud rate will be identical, at 9765.625 baud. It will take about a millisecond to transmit a character.
- Bit 7 of **TMR0** produces a 1-to-0 transition every 13.1 milliseconds. By dealing with the keypad every time this transition occurs, the keypad will be *debounced* (assuming the keypad has a worst-case debounce time of 10 milliseconds or less, which is a usual keypad specification). Consequently, this 1-to-0 transition of bit 7 of **TMR0** will be used to control the loop time. While it waits for the transition to occur, it will repeatedly reset the watchdog timer with **clrwdt** instructions.

19.4 MAINLINE PROGRAM AND LOOPTIME MACRO

A major reason for breaking a program up into a nested subroutine structure is to organize the program into understandable and testable modules. Any subroutine that is called only once can just as well be written as a macro. As such, it retains its role as a modular unit.

Consider the structure of the keypad/UART application program of Figure 19-9. Each module of the program shown is a macro, and each one is invoked only once in the program.

```
;;;;;;; Mainline program ;;;;;;;;;;;;;;;;;;;;;;;;;;;;;;;;;;;;;;;;;;;;;;;;;;;;;;;;;;;;

Mainline
        INITIAL                 ;Initialize everything
        LOOP_
          KEYSWITCH             ;Check keys
          UART                  ;Send ASCII keycode
          LOOPTIME              ;Set loop time to 13.1 milliseconds
        ENDLOOP_
```

Figure 19-9 Mainline program structure using macros.

```
;;;;;;; LOOPTIME macro ;;;;;;;;;;;;;;;;;;;;;;;;;;;;;;;;;;;;;;;;;;;;;;;;;;;;;;;;;;;;;;
;
;  This macro waits for 1-to-Ø transition on TMRØ's bit 7 that occurs every
;  13.1 milliseconds.

LOOPTIME  macro
        LOOP_
          clrwdt                ;Reset watchdog timer while waiting
          movf  TMRØ,W          ;Read TMRØ just once
          movwf  TEMP           ; and copy it to TEMP
          IF_  TMRØLAST,7 == 1  ;TMRØ's bit 7 was 1 at last check
            IF_  TEMP,7 == Ø    ; but is now Ø
              BREAK_            ; so exit loop
            ENDIF_
          ENDIF_
          movwf  TMRØLAST       ;Copy W (i.e., TEMP) to TMRØLAST
        ENDLOOP_
        movwf  TMRØLAST         ;Copy W (i.e., TEMP) to TMRØLAST
        endm
```

Figure 19-10 LOOPTIME macro

The **LOOPTIME** macro of Figure 19-10 creates a loop time of 13.1 milliseconds. As long as the **KEYSWITCH** and **UART** macros together take less than the watchdog timer's timeout period, the repeated **clrwdt** instructions in the **LOOP_. . . ENDLOOP_** construct of the **LOOPTIME** macro will hold the watchdog timer near its reset state. **TMR0** is carefully read just once within the **LOOP_. . . ENDLOOP_** construct and is copied into **W** for subsequently writing into **TMR0LAST**, and into **TEMP** for testing bit 7. When bit 7 of **TMR0LAST** equals 1 while bit 7 of **TEMP** equals 0, then 13.1 milliseconds will have passed since the last time this has occurred. The **BREAK_** construct causes execution to exit the **LOOP_. . . ENDLOOP_** construct in this case. This completes the execution of the macro. Execution continues in the mainline loop without the need for a subroutine return.

19.5 DETECTION OF KEY PRESSES

The part of the circuit of Figure 19-7 involving the keypad is shown in more detail in Figure 19-11. If all three of the **PORTC** output pins shown are driven low, then each of the **PORTB** input pins shown will be pulled high by its pullup resistor unless one of the keys is pressed. An **AnyKey** subroutine will be used to draw this distinction.

Once a key press has been found, followed by a loop time to allow any keybounce to settle out, the keys are tested, one-by-one, until the pressed key is found. The test of a key involves driving its column

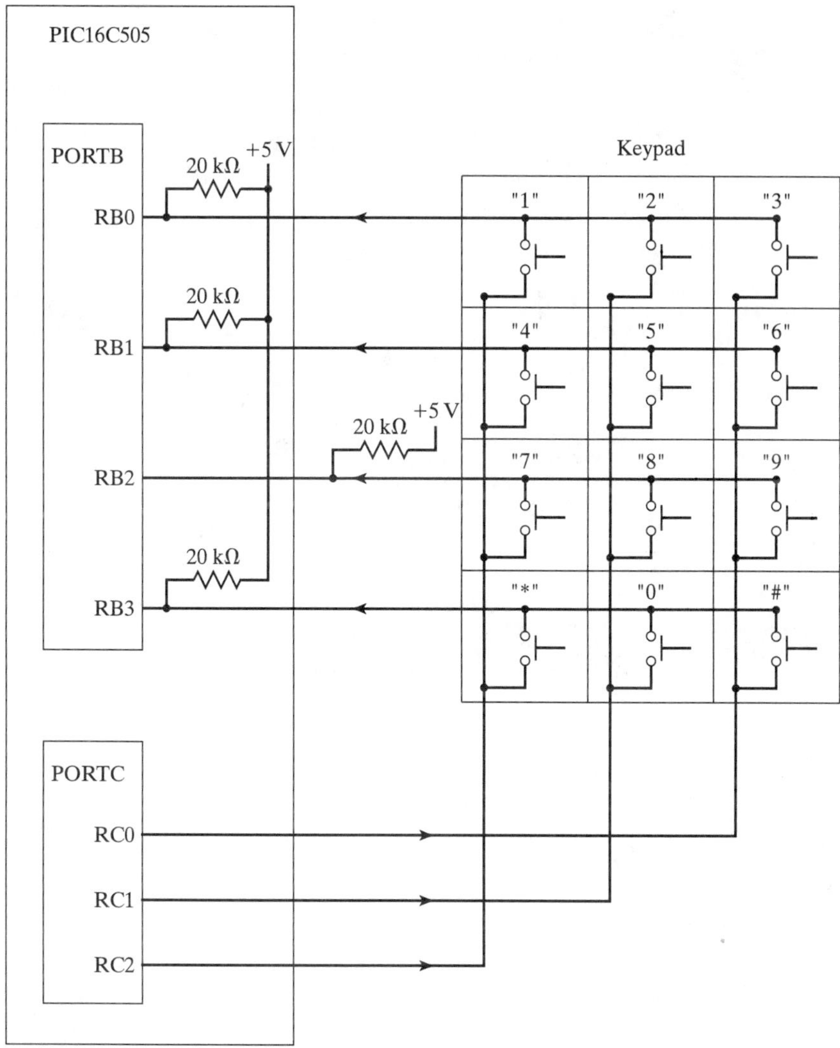

Figure 19-11 Keypad interface.

line low and determining whether its row line has followed. For example, the "0" key is tested by driving **PORTC**, bit 1 low (the column line) while driving **PORTC**, bits 0 and 2 high. If bit 3 of **PORTB** is low, then the "0" key is pressed. Its ASCII representation is sent to the PIC18F452. By waiting until the key is released before looking for a new key press, just one ASCII character is transmitted for each key press, regardless of how long a key is depressed.

19.6 KEYSWITCH STATE MACHINE

A **KEYSWITCH** macro will be executed every 13.1 milliseconds. Each time it is invoked, it must remember where it was when it left off a loop time ago. A state variable, **KEYSTATE**, will be used to maintain this information between invocations of **KEYSWITCH**. The sequence of states is

```
;;;;;;; KEYSWITCH macro ;;;;;;;;;;;;;;;;;;;;;;;;;;;;;;;;;;;;;;;;;;;;;;;;;;;;;;;;;;;;;;;;
;
; This macro implements a state machine to generate an ASCII keycode in
; response to the press of a key.

KEYSWITCH  macro
        movf  KEYSTATE,W          ;Copy KEYSTATE to TEMP; set Z if zero
        movwf  TEMP

        IF_  .Z.                  ;KEYSTATE = Ø
          call AnyKey             ;Set Z if no key is pressed
          IF_  .NZ.               ;Key is pressed so change to KEYSTATE = 1
            incf  KEYSTATE,F
          ENDIF_
        ELSE_
          decf  TEMP,F

          IF_  .Z.                ;KEYSTATE = 1
            SCANKEYS              ;Set Z if a valid KEYCODE is found
            IF_  .Z.              ;Valid keycode
              FORMASCII           ;Convert KEYCODE to ASCII
              incf  KEYSTATE,F    ;Change to KEYSTATE = 2
            ELSE_                 ;Invalid keycode
              clrf  KEYSTATE      ;Change to KEYSTATE = Ø
            ENDIF_
          ELSE_
            decf  TEMP,F

            IF_  .Z.              ;KEYSTATE = 2
              call AnyKey         ;Set Z if no key is pressed
              IF_  .Z.            ;Key has been released
                incf  KEYSTATE,F  ;Change to KEYSTATE = 3
              ENDIF_

            ELSE_                 ;KEYSTATE = 3
              call  AnyKey        ;Set Z if no key is pressed
              IF_  .Z.            ;Key has, indeed, been released
                clrf  KEYSTATE    ;Start over, looking for a new key press
              ELSE_
                decf  KEYSTATE,F  ;Aberration occurred, return to KEYSTATE = 2
              ENDIF_
            ENDIF_
          ENDIF_
        ENDIF_
        endm
```

Figure 19-12 KEYSWITCH macro.

- Until any key is pressed, **KEYSTATE** = 0. When a key press is detected, **KEYSTATE** is changed to 1.
- When **KEYSWITCH** is next invoked 13.1 milliseconds later and finds **KEYSTATE** = 1, any keybounce has settled out. The keys are tested to determine which key is pressed. If an invalid key press occurred (e.g., a lightning-fast release of the key occurred), **KEYSTATE** is changed back to 0. Otherwise, the ASCII code for the pressed key is written to the variable **ASCII**, and **KEYSTATE** is changed to 2.
- During successive loop times, **KEYSTATE** remains at 2 until the key is released, when it is incremented to 3.
- If 13.1 milliseconds later the key is still released, the **KEYSTATE** is returned to 0. However, if last time's detection of the key being released was just an aberration due to a keybounce during release, **KEYSTATE** is returned to 2.

The implementation of the **KEYSWITCH** macro is shown in Figure 19-12. Every 13.1 milliseconds when it is invoked, it checks the value of **KEYSTATE** and takes action accordingly.

```
;;;;;;; AnyKey subroutine ;;;;;;;;;;;;;;;;;;;;;;;;;;;;;;;;;;;;;;;;;;;;;;;;;;;;;;;;;
;
; This subroutine checks all keys at once and sets the Z bit if no keys are
; pressed.

AnyKey
        movlw   B'11111000'         ;Force column lines low
        andwf   PORTC,F
        movf   PORTB,W              ;Test for B'xxxx1111'
        xorlw   B'00001111'         ; by complementing lower nibble
        andlw   B'00001111'         ; and masking off upper nibble
        retlw   0
```

Figure 19-13 AnyKey subroutine.

The **AnyKey** subroutine, called from three places, is listed in Figure 19-13. It forces the three column lines low and then checks whether the four row lines are high. If so, it knows that no key is pressed, so it returns **Z** = 1. Otherwise, it returns **Z** = 0.

The **KEYSWITCH** macro also calls the **SCANKEYS** macro of Figure 19-14a to determine which key is pressed. It tests each key, starting with the "#" key, by retrieving a table entry from a table stored in the **ScanKeys_Table** subroutine of Figure 19-14b. The **KEYCODE** value (11, 10, 9, . . . , 0) is added to the program counter to jump to one of the **retlw** instructions, which returns its operand in **W**. The lower nibble of the table entry selects which column line to drive low. The upper nibble selects which row line to test. The **SCANKEYS** macro checks each key until either a pressed key is found (returning with **Z** = 1 in this case) or all keys have been checked unsuccessfully (returning with **Z** = 0).

The final macro invoked by the **KEYSWITCH** macro is the **FORMASCII** macro of Figure 19-15. It takes the **KEYCODE** value and converts it to the ASCII code for the pressed key, placing the result into a RAM variable called **ASCII**.

19.7 UART MACRO

The one remaining module in the **Mainline** program of Figure 19-9 is the **UART** macro of Figure 19-16. Each time it is invoked, it checks the value of **ASCII**. If it is 0, it does nothing. When a key is newly pressed, the ASCII code for the key will be nonzero. The **UART** macro does two things:

- It bit-bangs the ASCII code out the RC3 pin to the PIC18F452's RX input. The format is a low START bit, the 8 bits of the ASCII code (LSb first), and finally a high STOP bit. The 1-to-0 transitions of bit 0 of **TMR0**, occurring every 102.4 microseconds, are detected by the **BitWait** subroutine of Figure 19-17. These transitions are used to time the successive bits. This will produce a baud rate of exactly 9765.625 baud and will exactly match the PIC18F452 UART's baud rate (set up with **BRGH** = 1, **SPBRG** = 63, as in Figure 19-8) within the tolerance of the PIC16C505's ceramic resonator (±0.5%) and the PIC18F452's crystal (±0.005%).
- It clears **ASCII** to 0 so that nothing further will be sent to the PIC18F452 until a new key is pressed.

19.8 PIC16C505 SOURCE FILE

The complete source file for the PIC16C505 is listed in Figure 19-18 Note that each macro definition is located so as to be defined before it is invoked in another macro definition. Also note that the subroutines will all be located at the beginning of the file (as desired) because all of the macros will be invoked by the **Mainline** program, which appears at the end of the source file.

```
;;;;;;; SCANKEYS macro ;;;;;;;;;;;;;;;;;;;;;;;;;;;;;;;;;;;;;;;;;;;;;;;;;;;;;;;;;;;;
;
; This macro is invoked by KEYSWITCH macro.  It checks each key of the 3x4
; keypad to determine if a key is pressed.  If so, it returns its value in
; KEYCODE (11,...,0) and sets Z.

SCANKEYS  macro
        MOVLF  11,KEYCODE
        REPEAT_
          movlw  B'00000111'      ;Drive all column lines high
          iorwf  PORTC,F
          call  ScanKeys_Table  ;Get next table entry
          movwf  TESTVEC          ; and set it aside
          andlw  B'00000111'
          xorwf  PORTC,F          ;Drive selected column line low
          swapf  TESTVEC,W
          andlw  B'00001111'
          andwf  PORTB,W          ;Z=1 if key is pressed
          IF_  .Z.                ;Exit from REPEAT loop
            BREAK_
          ENDIF_
          movlw  0xff             ;Add -1 to decrement KEYCODE
          addwf  KEYCODE,F        ;Done when 00 + ff produces no carry
        UNTIL_  .NC.
        endm
```

(a) The macro

```
;;;;;;; ScanKeys_Table subroutine ;;;;;;;;;;;;;;;;;;;;;;;;;;;;;;;;;;;;;;;;;;;;;;;;
;
; This subroutine uses KEYCODE as an offset into its table, to return a byte
; in W that identifies the row and column of the KEYCODE key.

ScanKeys_Table
        movf  KEYCODE,W
        addwf  PCL,F              ;Jump to table entry
        retlw  B'10000010'        ;Test "0" key
        retlw  B'00010100'        ;Test "1" key
        retlw  B'00010010'        ;Test "2" key
        retlw  B'00010001'        ;Test "3" key
        retlw  B'00100100'        ;Test "4" key
        retlw  B'00100010'        ;Test "5" key
        retlw  B'00100001'        ;Test "6" key
        retlw  B'01000100'        ;Test "7" key
        retlw  B'01000010'        ;Test "8" key
        retlw  B'01000001'        ;Test "9" key
        retlw  B'10000100'        ;Test "*" key
        retlw  B'10000001'        ;Test "#" key
```

(b) The subroutine

Figure 19-14 SCANKEYS macro and its table lookup subroutine.

Because the PIC16C505 does not have in its instruction set the variety of branch instructions of the PIC18F452 (e.g., bra, bz, bnc), the use of Jess Meremonte's structured assembler requires an extra parameter:

```
sasm -16  ch19_505
```

Instead of the default use of a PIC18.cfg configuration file, the "-16" parameter invokes the use of a PIC16.cfg configuration file appropriate to the older PIC16XXX parts.

```
;;;;;;; FORMASCII macro ;;;;;;;;;;;;;;;;;;;;;;;;;;;;;;;;;;;;;;;;;;;;;;;;;;;;;;;;;;;
;
; This macro converts the KEYCODE value to the ASCII code for the pressed key
; (i.e., Ø -> Øx3Ø,...,9 -> Øx39, * -> Øx2a, and # -> Øx23)

FORMASCII  macro
        movlw  256 - 1Ø
        addwf  KEYCODE,W          ;Form 256 - 1Ø + KEYCODE
        IF_  .NC.                 ;Digit
          movlw  Øx3Ø             ;Form ASCII value
          addwf  KEYCODE,W
        ELSE_
          IF_  .Z.                ;*
            movlw  Øx2a
          ELSE_                   ;#
            movlw  Øx23
          ENDIF_
        ENDIF_
        movwf  ASCII
        endm
```

Figure 19-15 FORMASCII macro.

```
;;;;;;; UART macro ;;;;;;;;;;;;;;;;;;;;;;;;;;;;;;;;;;;;;;;;;;;;;;;;;;;;;;;;;;;;;;;;
;
; This macro bit-bangs the non-zero value of ASCII out RC3, LSb first,
; embedded between a low START bit and a high STOP bit with a bit time of
; 1Ø2.4 microseconds, derived from the 1-to-Ø transitions on TMRØ's bit Ø.

UART  macro
        movf  ASCII,F             ;Test for zero
        IF_  .NZ.
          call  BitWait           ;Wait for bit time
          bcf  PORTC,3            ;START bit
          MOVLF  8,TEMP           ;Initialize bit counter
          REPEAT_
            rrf  ASCII,F          ;Peel off a bit into C
            call  BitWait         ;Wait for bit time
            IF_  .C.
              bsf  PORTC,3
            ELSE_
              bcf  PORTC,3
            ENDIF_
            decf  TEMP,F
          UNTIL_  .Z.
          call  BitWait           ;Wait for bit time
          bsf  PORTC,3            ;STOP bit
          clrf  ASCII             ;Done with character
        ENDIF_
        endm
```

Figure 19-16 UART macro.

```
;;;;;;; BitWait subroutine ;;;;;;;;;;;;;;;;;;;;;;;;;;;;;;;;;;;;;;;;;;;;;;;;;;;;;;;;
;
; This subroutine waits for the next 1-to-Ø transition on TMRØ's bit Ø.

BitWait
        REPEAT_
        UNTIL_  TMRØ,Ø == 1       ;Wait for high TMRØ, bit Ø
        REPEAT_
        UNTIL_  TMRØ,Ø == Ø       ;Wait for falling edge
        retlw  Ø
```

Figure 19-17 BitWait subroutine.

```
;;;;;;; CH19_5Ø5 for PIC16C5Ø5 ;;;;;;;;;;;;;;;;;;;;;;;;;;;;;;;;;;;;;;;;;;;;;;;;;
;
; Scan keypad.  Bit-bang ASCII keycodes to PIC18F452's UART.
;
; Use 1Ø MHz crystal and 2.5 MHz internal clock rate.
;
; Assemble with    sasm -16  ch19_5Ø5
;
;;;;;;; Program subroutine hierarchy (one level deep) ;;;;;;;;;;;;;;;;;;;;;;;;;
;
;Mainline
;  AnyKey
;  ScanKeys_Table
;  BitWait

;;;;;;; Program hierarchy ;;;;;;;;;;;;;;;;;;;;;;;;;;;;;;;;;;;;;;;;;;;;;;;;;;;;;
;
;Mainline
;  INITIAL
;  KEYSWITCH
;    AnyKey
;    SCANKEYS
;      ScanKeys_Table
;    FORMASCII
;  UART
;    BitWait
;  LOOPTIME
;
;;;;;;; Assembler directives ;;;;;;;;;;;;;;;;;;;;;;;;;;;;;;;;;;;;;;;;;;;;;;;;;;

        list  P=PIC16C5Ø5, F=INHX32, C=16Ø, N=Ø, ST=OFF, MM=OFF, R=DEC, X=ON
        #include P16C5Ø5.inc
        __CONFIG  _HS_OSC & _WDT_ON & _MCLRE_OFF & _ExtRC_OSC_RB4EN & _CP_OFF

;;;;;;; Variables ;;;;;;;;;;;;;;;;;;;;;;;;;;;;;;;;;;;;;;;;;;;;;;;;;;;;;;;;;;;;;

        cblock  Øx08
        TEMP                    ;Temporary variable
        TMRØLAST                ;LOOPTIME variable
        KEYSTATE                ;KEYSWITCH variables
        TESTVEC
        KEYCODE
        ASCII
        endc

;;;;;;; Macro definitions ;;;;;;;;;;;;;;;;;;;;;;;;;;;;;;;;;;;;;;;;;;;;;;;;;;;;;

MOVLF   macro   literal,dest
        movlw   literal
        movwf   dest
        endm

;;;;;;; INITIAL macro ;;;;;;;;;;;;;;;;;;;;;;;;;;;;;;;;;;;;;;;;;;;;;;;;;;;;;;;;;
;
; This macro initializes everything.

INITIAL  macro
        clrf  FSR               ;Clear bank switching bits for direct addressing
        movlw  B'1ØØØØ11Ø'      ;Initialize OPTION register
        option
        movlw  B'11111111'      ;PORTB inputs
        tris  PORTB
        movlw  B'1111ØØØØ'      ;PORTC outputs
        tris  PORTC
        clrf  KEYSTATE          ;Initialize for "no keys pressed"
        endm
```

Figure 19-18 PIC16C505 source file.

```
;;;;;;; SCANKEYS macro ;;;;;;;;;;;;;;;;;;;;;;;;;;;;;;;;;;;;;;;;;;;;;;;;;;;;;;;
;
; This macro is invoked by KEYSWITCH macro.  It checks each key of the 3x4
; keypad to determine if a key is pressed.  If so, it returns its value in
; KEYCODE (11,...,0) and sets Z.

SCANKEYS  macro
        MOVLF  11,KEYCODE
        REPEAT_
          movlw  B'00000111'    ;Drive all column lines high
          iorwf  PORTC,F
          call  ScanKeys_Table  ;Get next table entry
          movwf  TESTVEC        ; and set it aside
          andlw  B'00000111'
          xorwf  PORTC,F        ;Drive selected column line low
          swapf  TESTVEC,W
          andlw  B'00001111'
          andwf  PORTB,W        ;Z=1 if key is pressed
          IF_  .Z.              ;Exit from REPEAT loop
            BREAK_
          ENDIF_
          movlw  0xff           ;Add -1 to decrement KEYCODE
          addwf  KEYCODE,F      ;Done when 00 + ff produces no carry
        UNTIL_  .NC.
        endm

;;;;;;; FORMASCII macro ;;;;;;;;;;;;;;;;;;;;;;;;;;;;;;;;;;;;;;;;;;;;;;;;;;;;;;;
;
; This macro converts the KEYCODE value to the ASCII code for the pressed key
; (i.e., 0 -> 0x30,...,9 -> 0x39, * -> 0x2a, and # -> 0x23)

FORMASCII  macro
        movlw  256 - 10
        addwf  KEYCODE,W        ;Form 256 - 10 + KEYCODE
        IF_  .NC.               ;Digit
          movlw  0x30           ;Form ASCII value
          addwf  KEYCODE,W
        ELSE_
          IF_  .Z.              ;*
            movlw  0x2a
          ELSE_                 ;#
            movlw  0x23
          ENDIF_
        ENDIF_
        movwf  ASCII
        endm

;;;;;;; KEYSWITCH macro ;;;;;;;;;;;;;;;;;;;;;;;;;;;;;;;;;;;;;;;;;;;;;;;;;;;;;;;
;
; This macro implements a state machine to generate an ASCII keycode in
; response to the press of a key.

KEYSWITCH  macro
        movf  KEYSTATE,W        ;Copy KEYSTATE to TEMP; set Z if zero
        movwf  TEMP

        IF_  .Z.                ;KEYSTATE = 0
          call AnyKey           ;Set Z if no key is pressed
          IF_  .NZ.             ;Key is pressed so change to KEYSTATE = 1
            incf  KEYSTATE,F
          ENDIF_
        ELSE_
          decf  TEMP,F

          IF_  .Z.              ;KEYSTATE = 1
            SCANKEYS            ;Set Z if a valid KEYCODE is found
            IF_  .Z.            ;Valid keycode
              FORMASCII         ;Convert KEYCODE to ASCII
              incf  KEYSTATE,F  ;Change to KEYSTATE = 2
            ELSE_               ;Invalid keycode
              clrf  KEYSTATE    ;Change to KEYSTATE = 0
            ENDIF_
          ELSE_
            decf  TEMP,F
```

Figure 19-18 continued

```
            IF_  .Z.            ;KEYSTATE = 2
              call AnyKey       ;Set Z if no key is pressed
              IF_  .Z.          ;Key has been released
                incf  KEYSTATE,F  ;Change to KEYSTATE = 3
              ENDIF_

            ELSE_               ;KEYSTATE = 3
              call  AnyKey      ;Set Z if no key is pressed
              IF_  .Z.          ;Key has, indeed, been released
                clrf  KEYSTATE  ;Start over, looking for a new key press
              ELSE_
                decf  KEYSTATE,F  ;Aberration occurred, return to KEYSTATE = 2
              ENDIF_
            ENDIF_
          ENDIF_
        ENDIF_
        endm


;;;;;;; UART macro ;;;;;;;;;;;;;;;;;;;;;;;;;;;;;;;;;;;;;;;;;;;;;;;;;;;;;;;;;;;;;;;;;;
;
; This macro bit-bangs the non-zero value of ASCII out RC3, LSb first,
; embedded between a low START bit and a high STOP bit with a bit time of
; 102.4 microseconds, derived from the 1-to-0 transitions on TMR0's bit 0.

UART  macro
        movf  ASCII,F           ;Test for zero
        IF_  .NZ.
          call  BitWait         ;Wait for bit time
          bcf  PORTC,3          ;START bit
          MOVLF  8,TEMP         ;Initialize bit counter
          REPEAT_
            rrf  ASCII,F        ;Peel off a bit into C
            call  BitWait       ;Wait for bit time
            IF_  .C.
              bsf  PORTC,3
            ELSE_
              bcf  PORTC,3
            ENDIF_
            decf  TEMP,F
          UNTIL_  .Z.
          call  BitWait         ;Wait for bit time
          bsf  PORTC,3          ;STOP bit
          clrf  ASCII           ;Done with character
        ENDIF_
        endm

;;;;;;; LOOPTIME macro ;;;;;;;;;;;;;;;;;;;;;;;;;;;;;;;;;;;;;;;;;;;;;;;;;;;;;;;;;;;;;;
;
;  This macro waits for 1-to-0 transition on TMR0's bit 7 that occurs every
;  13.1 milliseconds.

LOOPTIME  macro
        LOOP_
          clrwdt                ;Reset watchdog timer while waiting
          movf  TMR0,W          ;Read TMR0 just once
          movwf  TEMP           ; and copy it to TEMP
          IF_  TMR0LAST,7 == 1  ;TMR0's bit 7 was 1 at last check
            IF_  TEMP,7 == 0    ; but is now 0
              BREAK_            ; so exit loop
            ENDIF_
          ENDIF_
          movwf  TMR0LAST       ;Copy W (i.e., TEMP) to TMR0LAST
        ENDLOOP_
        movwf  TMR0LAST         ;Copy W (i.e., TEMP) to TMR0LAST
        endm
```

Figure 19-18 continued

```
;;;;;;; Reset vector ;;;;;;;;;;;;;;;;;;;;;;;;;;;;;;;;;;;;;;;;;;;;;;;;;;;;;;;;;;;
        org  0x0000              ;Reset vector
        nop
        goto  Mainline

;;;;;;; AnyKey subroutine ;;;;;;;;;;;;;;;;;;;;;;;;;;;;;;;;;;;;;;;;;;;;;;;;;;;;;;;
;
; This subroutine checks all keys at once and sets the Z bit if no keys are
; pressed.

AnyKey
        movlw  B'11111000'       ;Force column lines low
        andwf  PORTC,F
        movf  PORTB,W            ;Test for B'xxxx1111'
        xorlw  B'00001111'       ; by complementing lower nibble
        andlw  B'00001111'       ; and masking off upper nibble
        retlw  0

;;;;;;; ScanKeys_Table subroutine ;;;;;;;;;;;;;;;;;;;;;;;;;;;;;;;;;;;;;;;;;;;;;;;
;
; This subroutine uses KEYCODE as an offset into its table, to return a byte
; in W that identifies the row and column of the KEYCODE key.

ScanKeys_Table
        movf  KEYCODE,W
        addwf  PCL,F             ;Jump to table entry
        retlw  B'10000010'       ;Test "0" key
        retlw  B'00010100'       ;Test "1" key
        retlw  B'00010010'       ;Test "2" key
        retlw  B'00010001'       ;Test "3" key
        retlw  B'00100100'       ;Test "4" key
        retlw  B'00100010'       ;Test "5" key
        retlw  B'00100001'       ;Test "6" key
        retlw  B'01000100'       ;Test "7" key
        retlw  B'01000010'       ;Test "8" key
        retlw  B'01000001'       ;Test "9" key
        retlw  B'10000100'       ;Test "*" key
        retlw  B'10000001'       ;Test "#" key

;;;;;;; BitWait subroutine ;;;;;;;;;;;;;;;;;;;;;;;;;;;;;;;;;;;;;;;;;;;;;;;;;;;;;;
;
; This subroutine waits for the next 1-to-0 transition on TMR0's bit 0.

BitWait
        REPEAT_
        UNTIL_  TMR0,0 == 1      ;Wait for high TMR0, bit 0
        REPEAT_
        UNTIL_  TMR0,0 == 0      ;Wait for falling edge
        retlw  0

;;;;;;; Mainline program ;;;;;;;;;;;;;;;;;;;;;;;;;;;;;;;;;;;;;;;;;;;;;;;;;;;;;;;;

Mainline
        INITIAL                  ;Initialize everything
        LOOP_
          KEYSWITCH              ;Check keys
          UART                   ;Send ASCII keycode
          LOOPTIME               ;Set loop time to 13.1 milliseconds
        ENDLOOP_

        end
```

Figure 19-18 continued

PROBLEMS

19-1 PIC16C505 code debugging The code for this chapter was developed using PIC16C505 windowed EPROM parts, Microchip's PICSTART® Plus device programmer, and an EPROM eraser. Two LEDs (and their series resistors) were wired to the unused RC4 and RC5 outputs. Two macros, **TOGGLELEFT** and **TOGGLERIGHT**, were written. Inserting one or the other of these into various places in the code could indicate that execution had or had not reached that point. Repeated execution would produce either a dim LED (for fast toggling) or a flickering LED.

(a) Write the two macro definitions.

(b) For testing the **LOOPTIME** macro of Figure 19-10, the **Mainline** program of Figure 19-9 was modified by commenting out the **KEYSWITCH** and **UART** invocations and inserting in their place the **TOGGLELEFT** macro. When the code was run, it was discovered that the updating of **TMR0LAST** with

```
movwf  TMRØLAST
```

had been forgotten. What was the indication that the updating had been forgotten?

(c) A single **movwf TMR0LAST** instruction was then inserted into a position just after the **ENDLOOP_** construct. The code still did not work. What was the indication this time?

(d) Finally, both of the updates of **TMR0LAST** of Figure 19-10 were inserted. A scope connected to the RC4 output pin (the **TOGGLELEFT** pin) now showed correct operation with what frequency (or period)?

(e) Consider the sequencing of the four states of the **KEYSWITCH** macro of Figure 19-12 by inserting a **TOGGLELEFT** macro right after the line carrying the ";KEYSTATE = 0" comment and a **TOGGLERIGHT** macro right after the line carrying the ";KEYSTATE = 1" comment. When this code was run, what needed to be done with the keypad and what would you expect to see to verify proper sequencing?

(f) Answer part (e) with the two macros moved to test **KEYSTATE** = 2 and **KEYSTATE** = 3.

(g) Describe a test of the **SCANKEYS** macro of Figure 19-14a that will tell that the exit is occurring because a specific key (e.g., the "5" key) is being pressed.

(h) Describe a test that will indicate that the exit from **SCANKEYS** occurs after all keys have been tested and none have been found to be pressed. To facilitate this test, insert

```
MOVLF  1,KEYSTATE
```

just before the **KEYSWITCH** macro in the **Mainline** code of Figure 19-9.

(i) To test the **UART** macro, draw what the RC3 output should look like when the "5" key is pressed. To generate a repeated output, insert

```
MOVLF  A'5',ASCII
```

into the **Mainline** code just before the **UART** macro. Also what bit time should appear on the scope?

19-2 PIC18F452 test program Modify the P2.asm program of Figure 7-19 to do the following:

- Initialize the PIC18F452's UART to receive the ASCII characters from the PIC16C505.
- Turn off its display of **PORTD**.
- Use its **DISPLAY** macro to display (as a binary number) the UART's **RCREG** contents if its **RCIF** flag bit in the **PIR1** register is set.

19-3 Bullet-proofing application code Consider the **KEYSWITCH** macro of Figure 19-12 and what will happen if "lightning strikes" and a bit of **KEYSTATE** toggles inadvertently.

(a) Will **KEYSWITCH** ever get back on track?
(b) If so, then in the worst case, how long might this take?
(c) Modify the **KEYSWITCH** macro as simply as possible so that it gets back on track within a single pass around the mainline loop.

Chapter

20

MISCELLANEOUS FEATURES

20.1 OVERVIEW

This chapter addresses an assortment of topics of importance to the designer. The *configuration bytes* programmed into the chip enable or disable features and select parameter values. Unprogrammed bits in the configuration bytes will default to their erased state of 1. Instances where this can lead to unexpected results are mentioned.

The PIC18F452 includes eight alternatives for building the chip's clock circuitry. The chip's specification for V_{DD}, the supply voltage, is greatly enhanced for the low-supply-voltage version of the part, the PIC18LF452. The maximum clock frequency, F_{OSC}, must be derated for supply voltages down to 2.0 V.

Several mechanisms are built into the chip for ensuring desired performance as power is turned on or off. Because there are *eight* mechanisms for returning the chip to a known state through a reset, it is important to understand each one. Sometimes it is important to identify which one occurred. Knowledge of the effect of a reset on a register can simplify its initialization.

The watchdog timer can restore proper operation to a chip whose program counter has lost its way. If power to the chip comes from a battery, the watchdog timer can be used to achieve a dramatic reduction in average supply current for many applications. The designers of the PIC18LF452 were fully cognizant of the opportunities afforded by battery-supplied applications. A wealth of mechanisms can be used in combination to reduce the supply current to microampere levels.

Maintaining second, minute, hour, day, month, and year information for an application calls for special treatment. Features of the chip support such applications, even through power outages. The chip's data EEPROM gives support to the many applications that require data retention when power is removed from an application. With EEPROM built into the chip, the designer is spared the inconvenience and cost of dealing with an external eight-pin I^2C- or SPI-interfaced EEPROM.

The chapter closes with a brief look at the parallel slave port feature that permits the PIC18F452 to serve as a smart interface for a personal computer.

20.2 CONFIGURATION BYTES

When a PIC18F452 is programmed with application code (or with the QwikBug monitor code), its *configuration bytes* must also be programmed into the chip. The choices for each byte are listed in Figure 20-1. These choices can be specified in the source file for the application code using a "__CONFIG" assembler directive, as illustrated in any of the *template* files (e.g., P1.asm, listed in Figure 5-7).

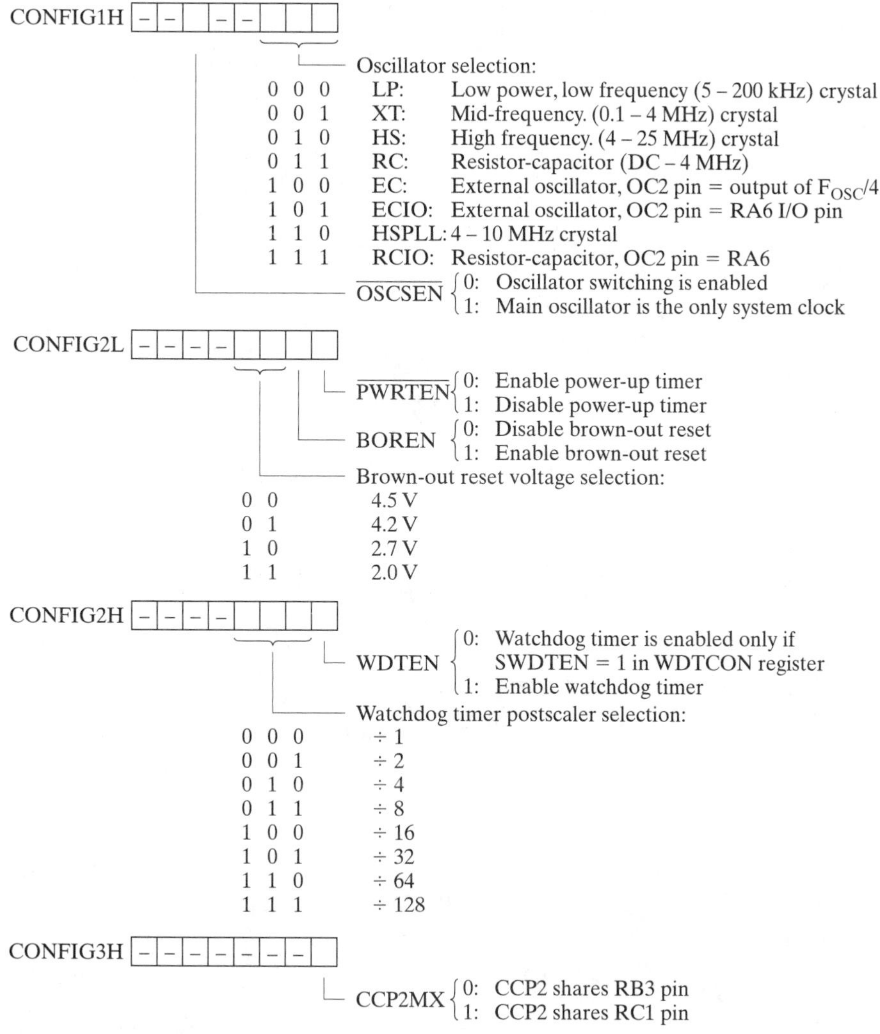

Figure 20-1 Configuration bytes.

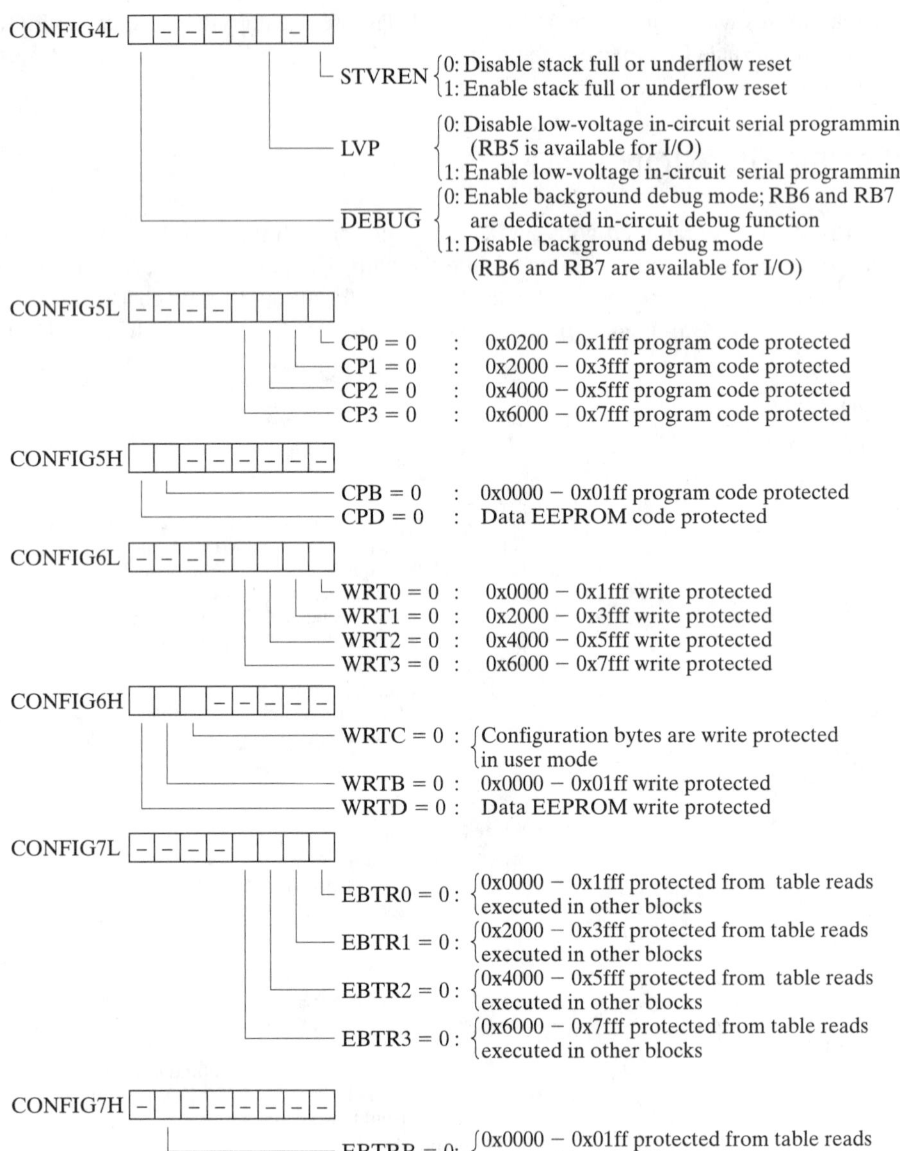

Figure 20-1 continued

The operand names (e.g., _HS_OSC_1H) are defined in the P18F452.INC file that the assembler uses for naming registers and bits when it assembles a PIC18F452 source file.

If a

```
__CONFIG  _CONFIGxx,...      ;(select an option)
```

line for one of the configuration bytes is omitted from the source file, the "1" option for its programmable bits will be programmed. Furthermore, the operand names in the P18F452.INC "include" file are defined with 1s in all undesignated bit positions. For example, with the P18F452.INC definitions

```
_HS_OSC_1H    equ B'11111010'
_OSCS_OFF_1H   equ B'11111111'
_OSCS_ON_1H   equ B'11011111'
```

the assembler directive

```
__CONFIG  _CONFIG1H, _HS_OSC_1H
```

does the same thing as

```
__CONFIG  _CONFIG1H, _HS_OSC_1H & _OSCS_OFF_1H
```

Because of this, it is important to note which configuration bits may cause a problem to the running of the chip unless these bits are intended to be left as 1s. For example:

- Unless code is written with **clrwdt** instructions being executed in timely fashion, the configuration lines should include

  ```
  __CONFIG  _CONFIG2H, _WDT_OFF_2H
  ```

- The low-voltage, in-circuit serial programming (ICSP) enable bit, LVP, should be disabled with

  ```
  __CONFIG  _CONFIG4L, _LVP_OFF_4L
  ```

  to enable the RB5 pin as a general-purpose I/O pin. Otherwise, that pin will be dedicated to the low-voltage ICSP function and lost as an I/O pin.
- The line

  ```
  __CONFIG  _CONFIG2L, _PWRT_ON_2L & BOR_ON_2L & BORV_42_2L
  ```

  enables both a power-up timer and a brownout reset threshold voltage, both of which work to ensure that the chip will start up reliably when power is applied to the chip, as will be discussed in Section 20.6.
- For use with a 10 MHz crystal, the chip needs

  ```
  __CONFIG  _CONFIG1H, _HS_OSC_1H
  ```

  for a 2.5 MHz internal clock rate, or

  ```
  __CONFIG  _CONFIG1H, _HSPLL_OSC_1H
  ```

  for a 10 MHz internal clock rate.

20.3 OSCILLATOR ALTERNATIVES

In order to be an "all things for all designers" chip, the PIC18F452 has built into it several different oscillator circuits. When one is selected, the others are shut down. Figure 20-2 illustrates some choices. For frequency accuracy, crystals provide the best solution. Ceramic resonators with built-in capacitors provide a somewhat less expensive solution. For a highly accurate clock frequency and the significantly lower power dissipation that comes from a much lower clock frequency, the 32.768 kHz watch crystal circuit of Figure 20-2d can be used. Finally, the RC oscillator of Figure 20-2e yields the lowest cost, and tiniest solution, albeit with relaxed frequency tolerance. With R = 5.1 kΩ and C = 22 pF, F_{OSC}

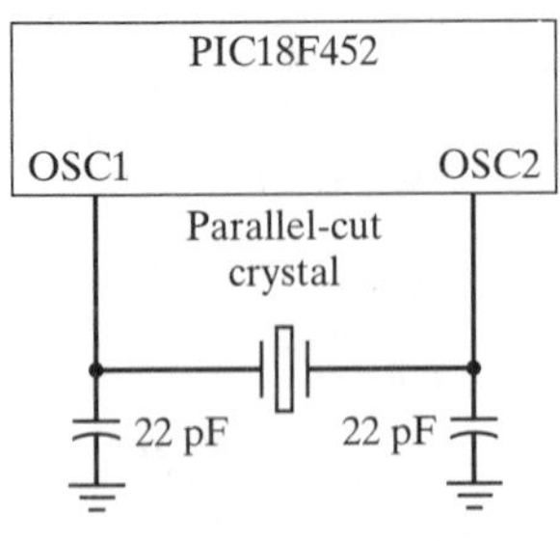

(a) Crystal oscillator
(± 0.005% tolerance)

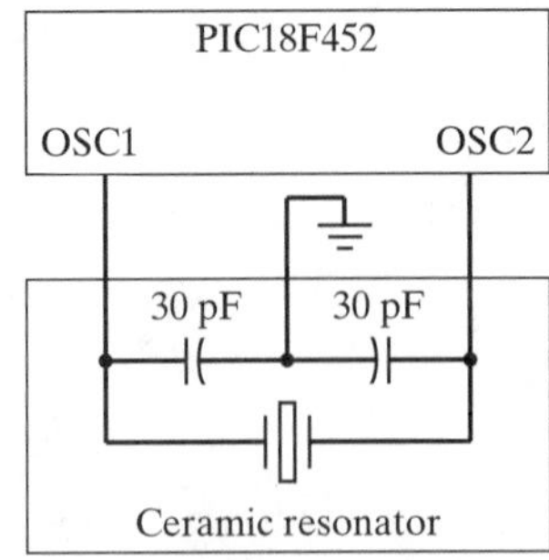

(b) Ceramic resonator
(± 0.5% tolerance)

Configuration bits in CONFIG1H	Frequency range	Specific crystal frequency	Internal clock	Digi-Key Part No.	
				Crystal	Ceramic resonator
_HSPLL_OSC_1H	4–10 MHz	10 MHz	10 MHz	X443	X906
_HS_OSC_1H	4–25 MHz	20 MHz	5 MHz	X439	X909
		10 MHz	2.5 MHz	X443	X906
_XT_OSC_1H	0.1–4 MHz	4 MHz	1 MHz	X405	X902

(c) Some alternatives.

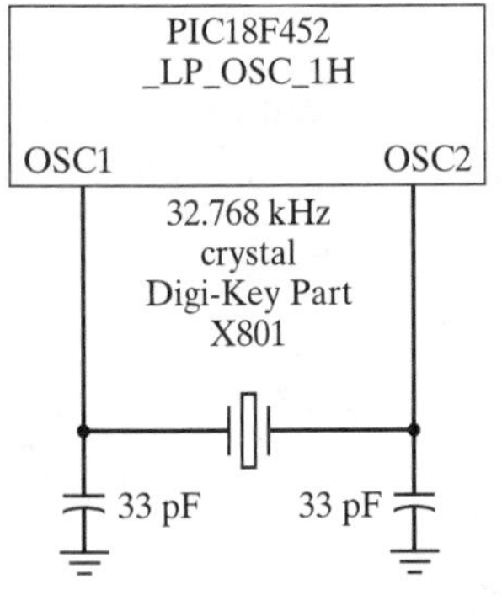

(d) Clock crystal for low power
(± 0.002% tolerance)

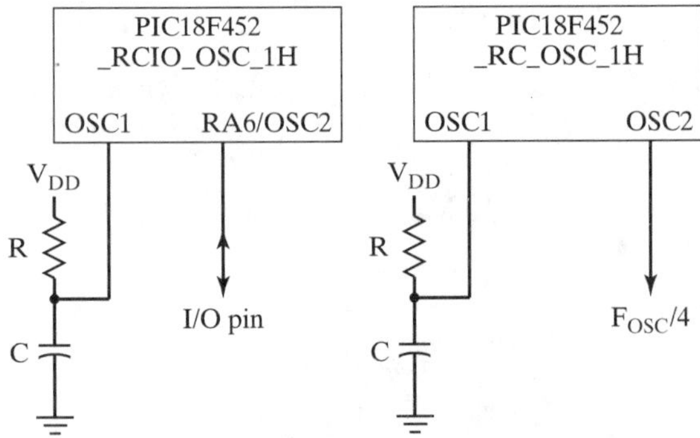

$F_{OSC} \approx 4$ MHz for R = 5.1 kΩ C = 22 pF
(e) Lowest cost mode (Frequency tolerance is due largely to tolerances in R and C)

Figure 20-2 Oscillator choices.

equals 4 MHz (for an internal clock rate of 1 MHz). This is useful to know if an alternative clock rate is desired. For example, F_{OSC} equal to 2 MHz can be obtained with

$$R = 10\ \text{k}\Omega \qquad C = 22\ \text{pF}$$

or

$$R = 5.1\ \text{k}\Omega \qquad C = 47\ \text{pF}$$

20.4 SUPPLY VOLTAGE

The PIC18F452 is designed to operate with an F_{OSC} value up to 40 MHz (using the 10 MHz oscillator and phase-locked loop combination). It is also designed to operate at any lower frequency, all the way down to 0 Hz. Thus, the clock can be stopped and subsequently started again with nothing lost. This performance is achieved over the full supply voltage range of the PIC18F452 of

$$4.2\text{ V} < V_{DD} < 5.5\text{ V}$$

For operation with a battery and a less certain value of V_{DD}, Microchip makes an extended range part, the PIC18LF452, that will operate with

$$2.0\text{ V} < V_{DD} < 5.5\text{ V}$$

However, for V_{DD} below 4.2 V, the maximum value of F_{OSC} is derated, as shown in Figure 20-3. This chart points out that the PIC18LF452 will operate satisfactorily with a V_{DD} value above 2.0 V for any value of F_{OSC} up to 4 MHz. The chip will operate with F_{OSC} up to 20 MHz if V_{DD} is assured of being greater than 3.0 V.

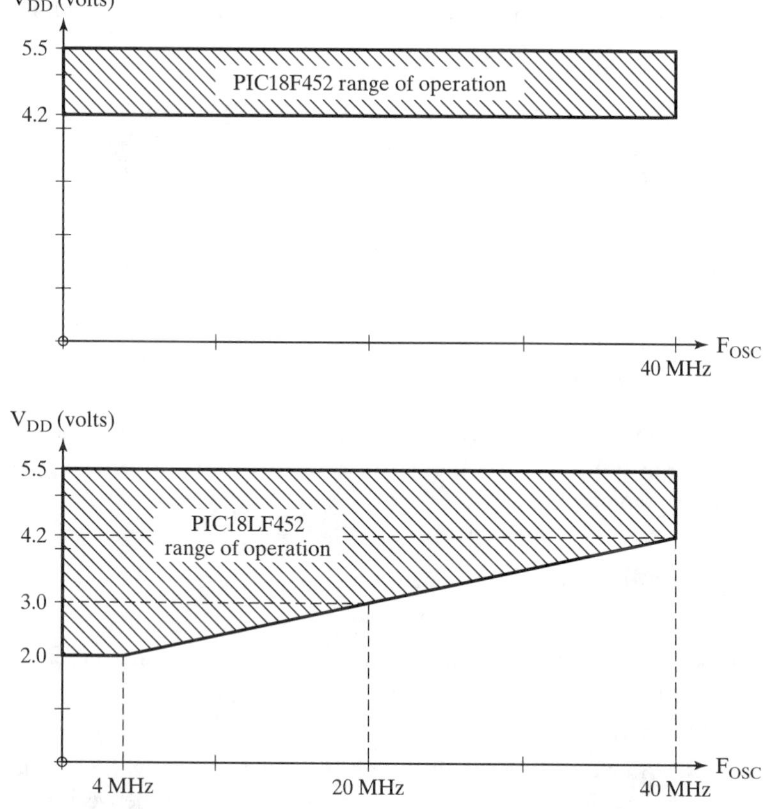

Figure 20-3 Frequency vs. power supply voltage for PIC18F452 and PIC18LF452 parts.

20.5 LOW-VOLTAGE DETECT (LVD)

Since the PIC18LF452 is really a PIC18F452 that has been tested and found to operate within specification over the extended supply voltage range of Figure 20-3, all of the features of the PIC18F452 apply to the PIC18LF452. One feature of special importance to the PIC18LF452 is the low-voltage detect circuit built into the part. It can detect when V_{DD} drops below any one of 15 threshold values. When that threshold is crossed, it can generate a low-voltage detect (LVD) interrupt that can be used to carry out any housekeeping tasks (e.g., saving state information to the nonvolatile EEPROM, discussed in Section 20.11) and then shut down the CPU by executing a **sleep** instruction.

The designers of this feature have carefully crafted it for maximum utility with regard to the V_{DD}/F_{OSC} specifications of Figure 20-3. That is, even with the tolerances of the internal voltage reference and the resistor ladder used to generate the threshold voltages, they have managed to obtain three threshold values of particular interest.

For a normal PIC18F452 part, one threshold value is particularly useful. It is specified as

$$4.2\text{ V} < \text{threshold value} < 4.45\text{ V}$$

When power is turned off to a device controlled by a PIC18F452, the LVD circuit catches the fall of V_{DD} just before it drops out of specification. By shutting down the chip at that point in time, its interrupt handler prevents the mayhem that can otherwise occur as V_{DD} drops to 0 V with a CPU that is still trying to execute millions of instructions even as the program counter drops bits.

For a PIC18LF452 (low-voltage) part, another of the threshold values is useful. It is specified as

$$2.0\text{ V} < \text{threshold value} < 2.12\text{ V}$$

With $F_{OSC} = 4$ MHz and an internal clock rate of 1 MHz, this threshold will shut down the chip for the waning supply voltage from a battery very close to the end of its life. Furthermore, even though the LVD circuitry only draws a maximum of 45 micro amperes, it can be powered up intermittently (e.g., once a second). Since it only takes a maximum of 50 microseconds for the internal reference voltage to power up and stabilize, a check of V_{DD} can take less than 100 microseconds before shutting the LVD circuitry down again. This duty cycle of 100/1,000,000 means that a check every second will draw an average battery current of

$$45 \times \frac{100}{1{,}000{,}000} = 0.0045\mu\text{A}$$

With a value so low, the LVD test will consume whatever the leakage current value is for the disabled LVD circuitry. To put this in perspective, the typical leakage current of the *entire* chip when in the SLEEP mode is 0.1 microampere.

The third threshold value of special interest is specified as

$$3.0\text{ V} < \text{threshold value} < 3.18\text{ V}$$

This is the threshold that can be used for a PIC18LF452 chip running with $F_{OSC} = 20$ MHz.

The LVD circuit is shown in Figure 20-4. It includes an option of creating a user-defined threshold, either to meet a slightly different threshold requirement or to trim a specific threshold to a tighter tolerance.

Example 20-1 An external threshold circuit is to be designed with a one-turn trimpot and two resistors that can be trimmed to produce any threshold value between about 4.1 V and 4.5 V, assuming that the internal reference voltage is exactly 1.2 V. Make the overall resistance about 10 kΩ.

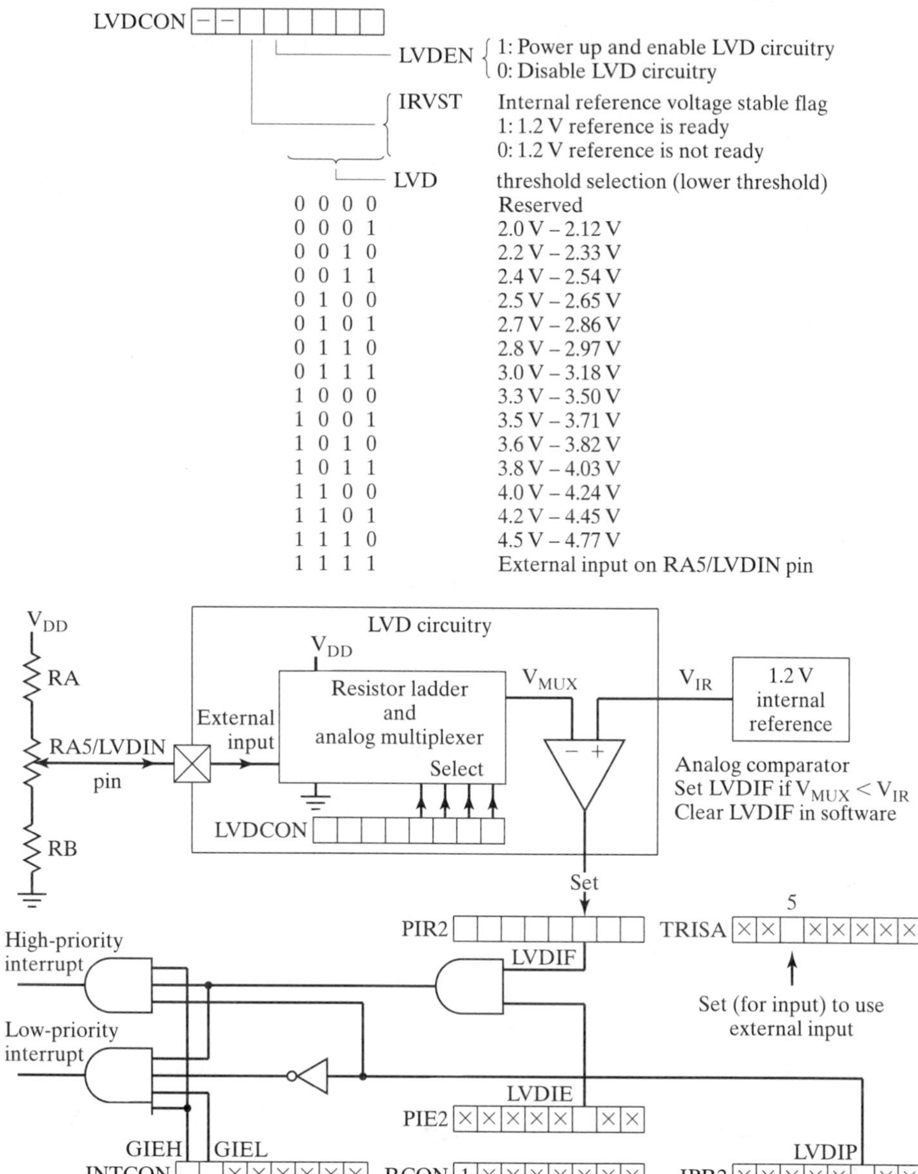

Figure 20-4 LVD operation.

Solution

Since the range 4.5 V–4.1 V = 0.4 V is about a tenth of the average (4.3 V), use a 1 kΩ trimpot. Then determine the values of two resistors that will produce 1.2 V from 4.3 V and that add up to 10 kΩ. See the solution in Figure 20-5a. Now, subtract 0.5 kΩ (half of the trimpot resistance) from each one to get the circuit of Figure 20-5b. Now look in the Manufacturer's Index in a Digi-Key catalog for Yageo metal film resistors. This will lead to a big table of 1% resistor values. Two values close to RA and RB of Figure 20-5b are

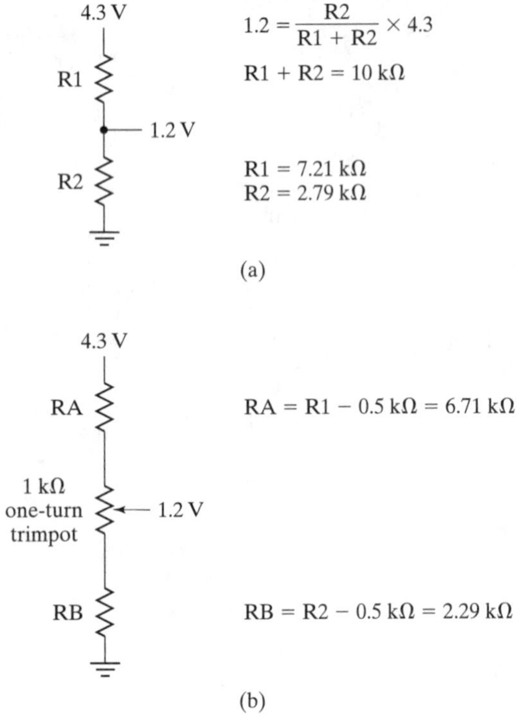

Figure 20-5 Example 20-2.

RA = 6.65 kΩ RB = 2.26 kΩ

Example 20-2 How might the threshold value of the circuit of Example 20-1 be set?

Solution

The PIC18F452 and the circuit of Figure 20-5b can be powered from a variable power supply. A digital voltmeter (DVM) can be used to monitor the voltage. However, for the purposes of building a test, note that the pot on the QwikFlash board is already connected to the RA5/LVDIN pin. A visual indication that the pot setting is at the threshold value can be obtained by making one of the LEDs on the board blink at either of two rates, depending on whether the pot's wiper is above or below the internal voltage reference. In fact, a DVM measurement of the pin's voltage will measure the microcontroller's internal reference voltage.

Write a simple test program. Upon coming out of reset, clear bit 1 of **TRISA** to set up the output to the right-hand LED and then toggle the state of the pin (just once). Write 0x1f to the **LVDCON** register of Figure 20-4 to enable the LVD circuit for the external threshold. Wait until the **IRVST** flag in the same register indicates that the internal reference has stabilized and can now be used. Clear the **LVDIF** interrupt flag and then enable a high-priority interrupt from the LVD circuitry. Finally, execute **clrwdt** instructions, while waiting for 50 milliseconds, and then go back and start all over. Include in your code the following high-priority interrupt service routine:

```
org  0x0008
<wait 0.5 second while repeatedly clearing the watchdog timer>
sleep
retfie  FAST
```

Enable the watchdog timer to time out after about 20 milliseconds with

```
CONFIG__  _CONFIG2H, _WDT_ON_2H & _WDTPS_1_2H
```

The watchdog timer will wake the chip from its SLEEP state and continue on to the

```
retfie  FAST
```

instruction, thereby returning to where the CPU left off in the program execution. The intent is to blink the LED at a 10 Hz rate if V_{DD} is above the threshold, and a 1 Hz rate if V_{DD} is below the threshold.

20.6 BROWNOUT RESET (BOR)

Whereas the LVD circuit of the last section can be used to provide a margin of time to "clean up and shut down" before V_{DD} drops out of specification, the brownout reset (BOR) circuit uses two thresholds, V_{BORU} and V_{BORL}, (nominally 65 mV apart) as follows:

- As the chip powers up, the BOR circuit holds it in reset until V_{DD} crosses the upper threshold, V_{BORU}. At that point, the BOR output releases its hold on the power-up timer (PWRT). After a typical delay of 72 milliseconds, if nothing else is holding the chip in reset (e.g., the $\overline{\text{MCLR}}$ pin), then the chip will come out of reset and begin executing instructions from the reset vector address of 0x0000.
- While the chip is executing instructions and V_{DD} drops below the lower threshold, V_{BORL}, the BOR output snaps from high-to-low regardless of how slowly the threshold was crossed. The chip is immediately thrust into its reset state, stopping the execution of further instructions. By having two thresholds plus a startup delay of tens of milliseconds, the PIC18F452 microcontroller cannot be jiggled in and out of reset within milliseconds, starting up the chip in an anomalous state.

The BOR feature provides a simple-to-use method of ensuring that the PIC18F452 microcontroller will start up reliably and shut down while the chip is still operating within specification as the power supply voltage drops to 0 V. Figure 20-6a lists the contents of the **CONFIG2L** configuration byte and the result of each option. Figure 20-6b uses the names defined in the P18F452.INC file to create the configuration line that the assembler will understand.

20.7 WATCHDOG TIMER (WDT)

The keypad-input/UART-output PIC16C505 application presented in Chapter 19 illustrated the use of that chip's watchdog timer (WDT) to keep its CPU "on track" and to negate ever having to use the chip's $\overline{\text{MCLR}}$ pin. For the little 14-pin PIC16C505, the latter feature was especially useful since the $\overline{\text{MCLR}}$ pin could then be used as an I/O pin.

While the PIC18F452 microcontroller features no such trade-off of its $\overline{\text{MCLR}}$ pin for an I/O pin, the ability of its WDT to ensure "on track" operation is invaluable. This is especially true for any application that must be left unattended for long periods of time.

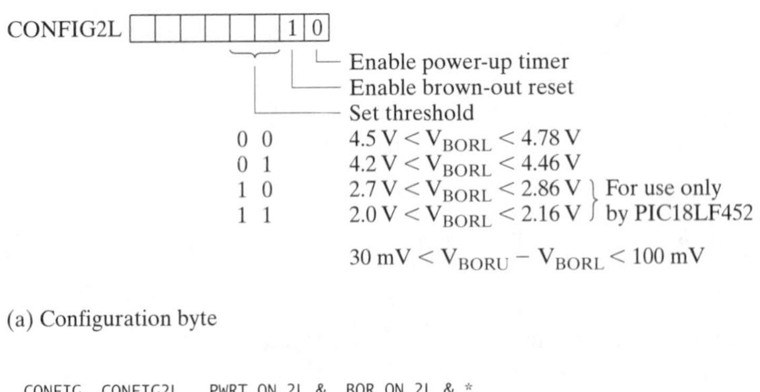

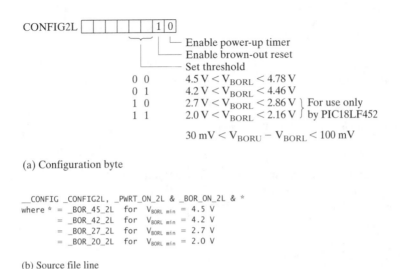

(a) Configuration byte

```
__CONFIG _CONFIG2L, _PWRT_ON_2L & _BOR_ON_2L & *
where * = _BOR_45_2L  for  VBORL min = 4.5 V
        = _BOR_42_2L  for  VBORL min = 4.2 V
        = _BOR_27_2L  for  VBORL min = 2.7 V
        = _BOR_20_2L  for  VBORL min = 2.0 V
```

(b) Source file line

Figure 20-6 Brownout reset configuration byte settings.

The WDT is used by setting its timeout interval to be greater than the loop time and then executing

```
clrwdt
```

each time around the mainline loop. The chip will reset itself and begin again from scratch if the CPU is thrown off track by any malfunction that does not return execution to the mainline loop.

The WDT operation is illustrated in Figure 20-7. It can be enabled *either* by programming the **CONFIG2H** configuration word with a 1 in bit 0 *or* by the setting of the **SWDTEN** bit of the **WDTCON** register by an application program. Unlike many earlier-generation PIC microcontroller chips (e.g., the PIC16C505 of Chapter 19), the postscaler of Figure 20-7 is not shared with Timer0. It is dedicated solely to the WDT. The timer itself also has its own RC oscillator. With manufacturing-process variations, the timeout period is somewhere between 7 and 33 milliseconds. Consequently, if a 10 millisecond loop time is being used, then a divide-by-2 (or greater) postscaler should be selected.

One interesting application of the WDT arises in battery-powered applications requiring only intermittent code execution by the CPU. Because the WDT will continue to operate when the rest of the chip is in the SLEEP mode, the WDT can awaken the chip periodically. Then the microcontroller can examine its inputs and discern whether there are matters requiring its attention. If so, it does them. If not, it executes a **sleep** instruction and returns to the SLEEP state until the next WDT "wakeup call." A PIC18F452 will draw a maximum of 4 mA of power supply current when running with $F_{OSC} = 4$ MHz (and its XT oscillator). By using the WDT to cut the usual (inactive) duty cycle down to 0.001, the average supply current is reduced to the point (4 microamperes, maximum) where it is dominated by the WDT's current (15 microamperes, maximum).

Example 20-3 The WDT's typical timeout period is specified as 18 milliseconds. After awakening from the SLEEP mode, the microcontroller pauses for 1024 F_{OSC} cycles before beginning to execute code. For $F_{OSC} = 4$ MHz, this is 256 microseconds. Assume that after wakeup,

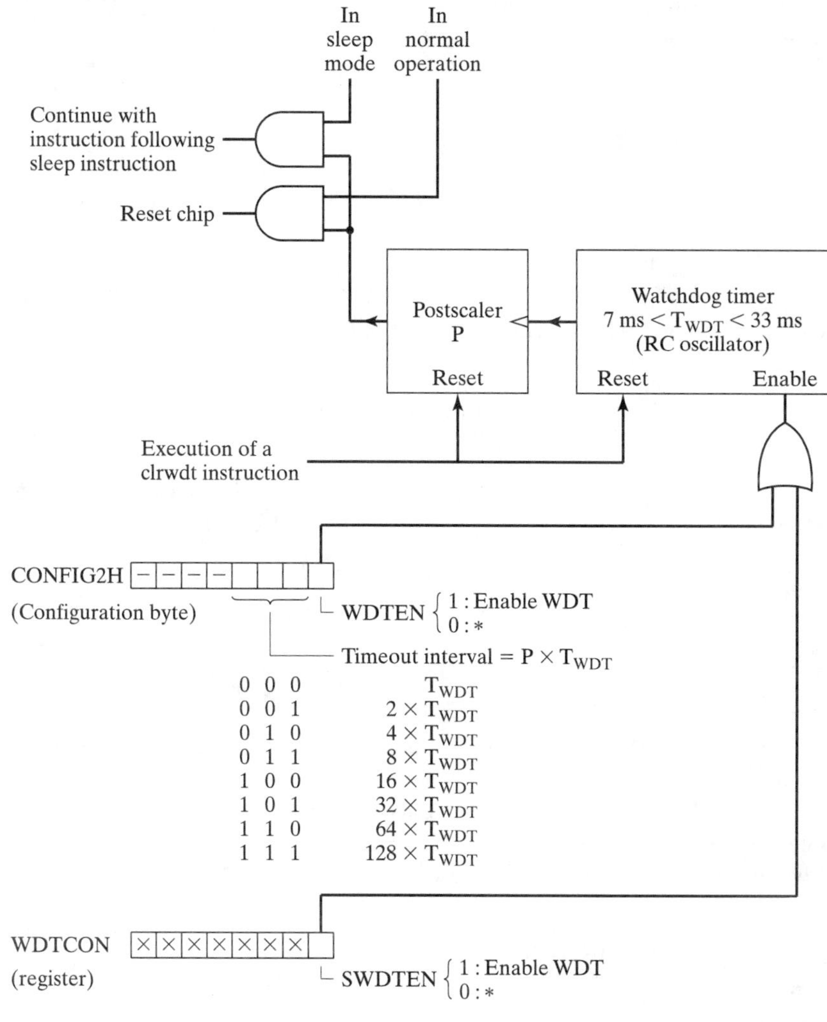

Figure 20-7 Watchdog timer use.

the CPU executes instructions for another 256 microseconds before (normally) going back to sleep. What is the minimum time between WDT awakenings to reduce the average supply current by a factor of 100? What WDT prescaler value should be used?

Solution

The microcontroller will be awake for 512 microseconds at a time. The WDT's steady current of 15 μA plus the average remaining supply current is

$$15 + \mathrm{DC} \times 4000 \text{ microamperes}$$

where DC is the duty cycle. The duty cycle is to be chosen so that this is 0.01 times the running-full-time current of 4000 microamperes. That is,

$$15 + DC \times 4000 = 0.01 \times 4000$$

and

$$DC = \frac{40 - 15}{4000} = 0.00625$$

The time between WDT awakenings must be at least

$$\frac{256 + 256}{0.00625} = 81{,}920 \text{ microseconds}$$

or 82 milliseconds. If the basic (before postscaler) WDT timeout period is 18 milliseconds, then the postscaler's divider must be at least 8. This will give a typical time between awakenings of 144 milliseconds.

20.8 RESETS

The PIC18F452 includes a variety of reset mechanisms. The role of each one is to return the chip to a known state. The cause of a reset is often important knowledge for deciding what action to take. Finally, it is useful to know what a reset does to the contents of the Special Function Registers (e.g., **TRISB**). This section will address these issues.

The following list encompasses all of the reset options of the PIC18F452:

- Power-on reset (POR)
- $\overline{\text{MCLR}}$ reset during normal operation
- $\overline{\text{MCLR}}$ during SLEEP
- Watchdog timer (WDT) reset during normal operation
- Brownout reset (BOR)
- Reset instruction
- Stack full reset
- Stack underflow reset

A power-on reset is generated if the $\overline{\text{MCLR}}$ pin is tied, or pulled up through a resistor, to V_{DD} when V_{DD} rises above 0.7 V at a rate greater than 50 mV/ms. In order to delay until V_{DD} has a chance to rise from 0.7 V to 4.2 V (or to 2.0 V for a PIC18LF452 with a 4 MHz crystal), the power-up timer (PWRT) is normally enabled by programming the **CONFIG2L** configuration bytes with B'xxxxxxx0'. This will introduce a device-dependent delay between 28 and 132 milliseconds. A further delay of 1024 crystal clock cycles (i.e., 0.1 milliseconds for a 10 MHz crystal) is inserted if one of the crystal oscillators is being used (i.e., LP, XT, HS, or HSPLL), to allow the crystal oscillator to stabilize. If the HSPLL oscillator is used to obtain a 10 MHz internal clock from a 10 MHz crystal, an extra 2 millisecond delay

```
IF_  RCON,NOT_POR == 0  ;POR has occurred
  bsf  RCON,NOT_POR     ;Set bit to distinguish from other resets
  ‹take action particular to power-on reset›
ENDIF_
```

(a) Identifying a power-on reset

```
IF_  RCON,NOT_RI  == 0  ;"reset" instruction has been executed
  bsf  RCON,NOT_RI      ;Set bit to distinguish from other resets
  ‹take appropriate action in response to "reset" instruction›
ENDIF_
```

(b) Identifying a reset due to execution of a "reset" instruction

```
IF_  RCON,NOT_TO == 0   ;WDT timeout has occurred
  bsf  RCON,NOT_TO      ;Set bit to distinguish from other resets
  ‹take action particular to a watchdog timer reset›
ENDIF_
```

(c) Identifying a watchdog timer timeout

```
IF_  RCON,NOT_BOR == 0  ;BOR timeout has occurred
  bsf  RCON,NOT_BOR     ;Set bit to distinguish from other resets
  ‹take action particular to a brown-out reset
ENDIF_
```

(d) Identifying a brownout reset

```
WHILE_  STKPTR,STKFUL == 1  ;Stack is full; stop
  bra  $
ENDWHILE_

WHILE_  STKPTR,STKUNF == 1  ;Stack underflow occurred; stop
  bra  $
ENDWHILE_
```

(e) Stack full and stack underflow traps.

Figure 20-8 Identifying the cause of a reset.

is added in, to allow the phase-locked loop circuitry to stabilize. Then the CPU begins executing instructions from the reset vector at 0x0000.

The $\overline{\text{MCLR}}$ pin has associated with it a Schmitt-trigger input so that even the relatively slow rise time generated by an opening switch, a pullup resistor, and stray capacitance will still produce a sharp edge to the reset circuitry. The master-clear input also has a noise filter to ignore small pulses. There is no appreciable delay associated with the $\overline{\text{MCLR}}$ reset mechanism.

To have a reset occur when a stack full or stack underflow condition occurs, the **CONFIG4L** configuration byte must be programmed with B'xxxxxxx1'. Because the stack contains room for up to 31 return addresses from subroutine calls or interrupts, neither condition is likely to occur with a properly operating program.

Tests for identifying the source of an interrupt are listed in Figure 20-8. The $\overline{\text{MCLR}}$ (pushbutton) reset does not produce a unique condition that can be tested. Consequently, it is identified by default after the other applicable reset flag tests have failed to identify the source of the reset.

The state of every register on reset is listed in Figure 20-9. As an example of the meaning of each table entry, consider **PORTE**, which has only three bits implemented. The "0" entry means each of these three bits is reset to 0 for power-on resets (POR), and brownout resets (BOR), as well as all other resets. Many bits come out of POR/BOR resets in a random, unknown state (represented by "x"). As an

Register	POR BOR	Other resets
ADCON0	0	0
ADCON1	0	0
ADRESH	x	u
ADRESL	x	u
CCP1CON	0	0
CCP2CON	0	0
CCPR1H	x	u
CCPR1L	x	u
CCPR2H	x	u
CCPR2L	x	u
EEADR	0	0
EECON1	m	m
EECON2	-	-
EEDATA	0	0
FSR0H	x	u
FSR0L	x	u
FSR1H	x	u
FSR1L	x	u
FSR2H	x	u
FSR2L	x	u
INDF0	-	-
INDF1	-	-
INDF2	-	-
INTCON	0	0
INTCON2	1	1

Register	POR BOR	Other resets
INTCON3	m	m
IPR1	1	1
IPR2	1	1
LATA	x	u
LATB	x	u
LATC	x	u
LATD	x	u
LATE	x	u
LVDCON	m	m
OSCCON	0	0
PCL	0	0
PCLATH	0	0
PCLATU	0	0
PIE1	0	0
PIE2	0	0
PIR1	0	0
PIR2	0	0
PLUSW0	-	-
PLUSW1	-	-
PLUSW2	-	-
PORTA	m	m
PORTB	x	u
PORTC	x	u
PORTD	x	u
PORTE	0	0

Register	POR BOR	Other resets
POSTDEC0	-	-
POSTDEC1	-	-
POSTDEC2	-	-
POSTINC0	-	-
POSTINC1	-	-
POSTINC2	-	-
PR2	1	1
PREINC0	-	-
PREINC1	-	-
PREINC2	-	-
PRODH	x	u
PRODL	x	u
RCON	m	m
RCREG	0	0
RCSTA	m	m
SPBRG	0	u
SSPADD	0	0
SSPBUF	x	u
SSPCON1	0	0
SSPCON2	0	0
SSPSTAT	0	0
STATUS	x	u
STKPTR	0	0
T0CON	1	1
T1CON	0	u

Register	POR BOR	Other resets
T2CON	0	0
T3CON	0	u
TABLAT	0	0
TBLPTRH	0	0
TBLPTRL	0	0
TBLPTRU	0	0
TMR0H	0	u
TMR0L	x	u
TMR1H	x	u
TMR1L	x	u
TMR2	0	0
TMR3H	x	u
TMR3L	x	u
TOSH	0	0
TOSL	0	0
TOSU	0	0
TRISA	1	1
TRISB	1	1
TRISC	1	1
TRISD	1	1
TRISE	1	1
TXREG	0	0
TXSTA	m	m
WDTCON	0	0
WREG	x	u

(a) Registers and their contents.

Key: 0: all zeros 1: all ones
x: unknown u: unchanged
m: mixed -: not a physical register

Register	POR BOR	Other resets
EECON1	xx-0x000	uu-0u000
INTCON3	11-00-00	11-00-00
LVDCON	--000101	--000101
PORTA	-00x0000	-00x0000
RCON	0--q11qq	0--qqquu
RCSTA	0000000x	0000000x
TXSTA	0000-010	0000-010

(b) Registers with mixed contents.

Key: q: Depends on type of reset

Figure 20-9 State of Special Function Registers after coming out of reset.

example, **TMR0L** comes out of a power-on reset in an unknown state. However, whatever is in **TMR0L** at the time of any other reset than POR or BOR, **TMR0L** will have the same unchanged contents after the reset as before the reset (represented by "u").

20.9 BATTERY-POWERED OPERATION

The PIC18LF452 (the part that can operate down to 2.0 V) is designed for low-power applications using a battery supply for V_{DD}. However, care must be taken on several fronts to conserve battery life:

- The operating frequency should be as low as is needed to handle the required tasks since the power dissipated in a CMOS part increases linearly with frequency.
- A lower supply voltage (but above 2.0 V) requires much less supply current than a higher supply voltage. For example, with a 32 kHz clock and V_{DD} = 2.0 V, the typical current is 28 μA, whereas with V_{DD} = 4.2 V, the typical current is 88 μA.
- Unused pins should be configured as outputs (left unconnected) or else as inputs that are pulled either high or low (and thereby, *not* left unconnected).
- Optional internal features that can be disabled, should be. These include the watchdog timer (which can add 1 μA at VDD = 2 V, 15 μA at 5.5 V), the brownout reset circuit (45 μA at 5.5 V), the low-voltage detect circuit (45 μA at 2.0 V), Timer1's oscillator (15 μA at 2.0 V, 100 μA at 4.2 V), and the A/D converter (15 μA at 2.0 V when enabled but not converting).
- A drastic difference in the average supply current can be produced if a feature, or the chip as a whole, can be enabled intermittently and with a low duty cycle. In Section 20.7, the use of the SLEEP mode with wakeup by the watchdog timer was seen to provide a means for reducing average supply current dramatically.

The SLEEP mode, or power-down mode, is the PIC18F452's lowest supply current state and is entered by executing a **sleep** instruction. This stops the chip's oscillator. I/O ports remain in the state they had before the **sleep** instruction was executed. Consequently, to obtain the lowest supply current, all I/O pins should be either at V_{DD} or V_{SS} with no external circuitry drawing current from any I/O pins. The optional internal features mentioned earlier should be disabled, if possible (e.g., the A/D converter). Inputs should be pulled high or low externally. The $\overline{\text{MCLR}}$ pin must be pulled high.

Awakening from SLEEP mode is accomplished by any device reset, such as the one that occurs when VDD crosses the brownout reset threshold (if BOR is enabled). If the watchdog timer is used as the wakeup mechanism, the program counter will continue where it left off when the sleep instruction was executed. This contrasts with the reset that takes place when the watchdog timer times out in normal execution mode.

Any peripheral module whose interrupt flag can be set while in SLEEP mode can awaken the chip. For this to happen, the module's interrupt enable bit must also be set. Thus, the selected edge on the INT0 input pin will awaken the chip if its **INT0IE** interrupt enable bit is set. A change (either high-to-low or low-to-high) on any of **PORTB**'s RB7, RB6, RB5, or RB4 pins set up as inputs will awaken the chip if the **RBIE** bit in the **INTCON** register is set, as described in Section 9.7.

When the locally enabled interrupting event occurs, the CPU will awaken in either of two ways:

- If interrupts are globally disabled (i.e., **GIEH** = 0), execution will proceed with the instruction that follows the **sleep** instruction.
- If interrupts are globally enabled (i.e., **GIEH** = 1), the (already prefetched) next instruction after the **sleep** instruction will be executed followed by the vectoring to the high- or low-priority interrupt service routine, whichever has been set up for that interrupt source.

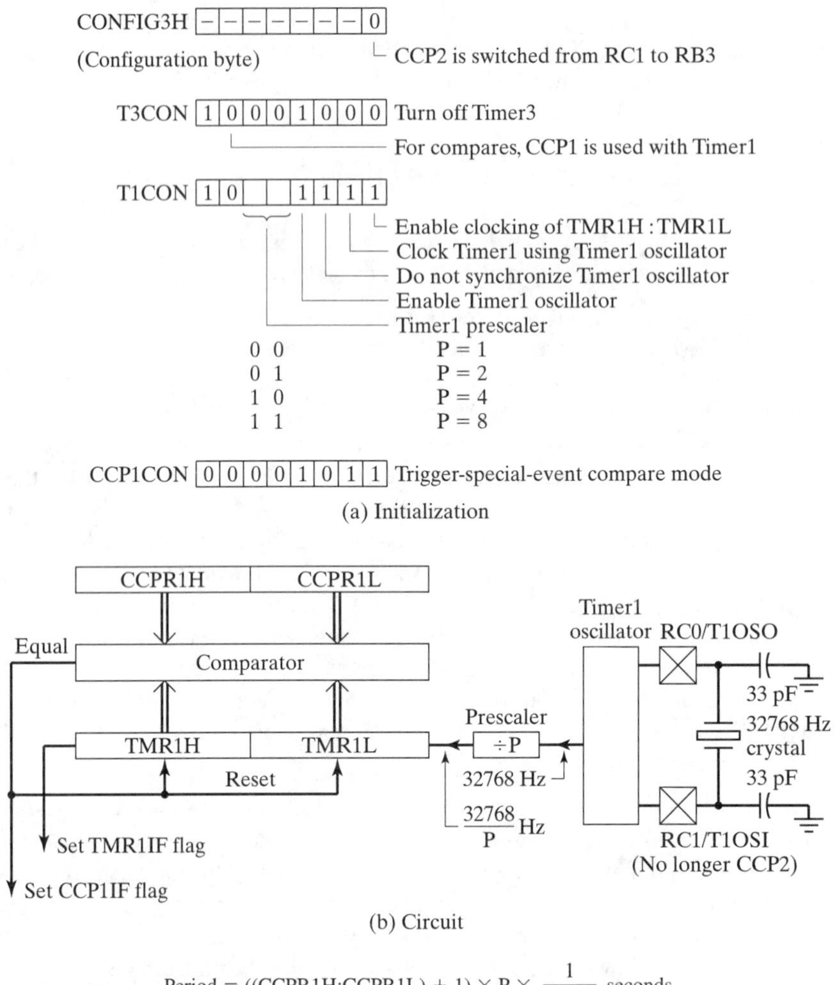

$$\text{Period} = ((\text{CCPR1H:CCPR1L}) + 1) \times P \times \frac{1}{32768} \text{ seconds}$$

(c) Period for CCP1/Timer1 circuit (see Figure 16-4)

Figure 20-10 Use of Timer1's oscillator with Timer1/CCP1 during SLEEP mode.

One interesting option for low-power operation is to use Timer1's external oscillator pins with a 32,768 Hz watch crystal, as shown in Figure 20-10. This can then be used to clock either **TMR1H:TMR1L** or **TMR3H:TMR3L**. Without using either CCP1 or CCP2, **TMR1H:TMR1L** can be used to awaken the CPU every

$$\frac{65{,}536}{32{,}768} \times P = 2, 4, 8, \text{ or } 16 \text{ seconds}$$

if the **TMR1IE** interrupt enable bit is set. By using CCP1 in the trigger-special-event mode of Figure 16-4, the CPU awakenings can be set for any interval up to 16 seconds (e.g., every second) by setting the **CCP1IE** bit to enable CCP1 interrupts.

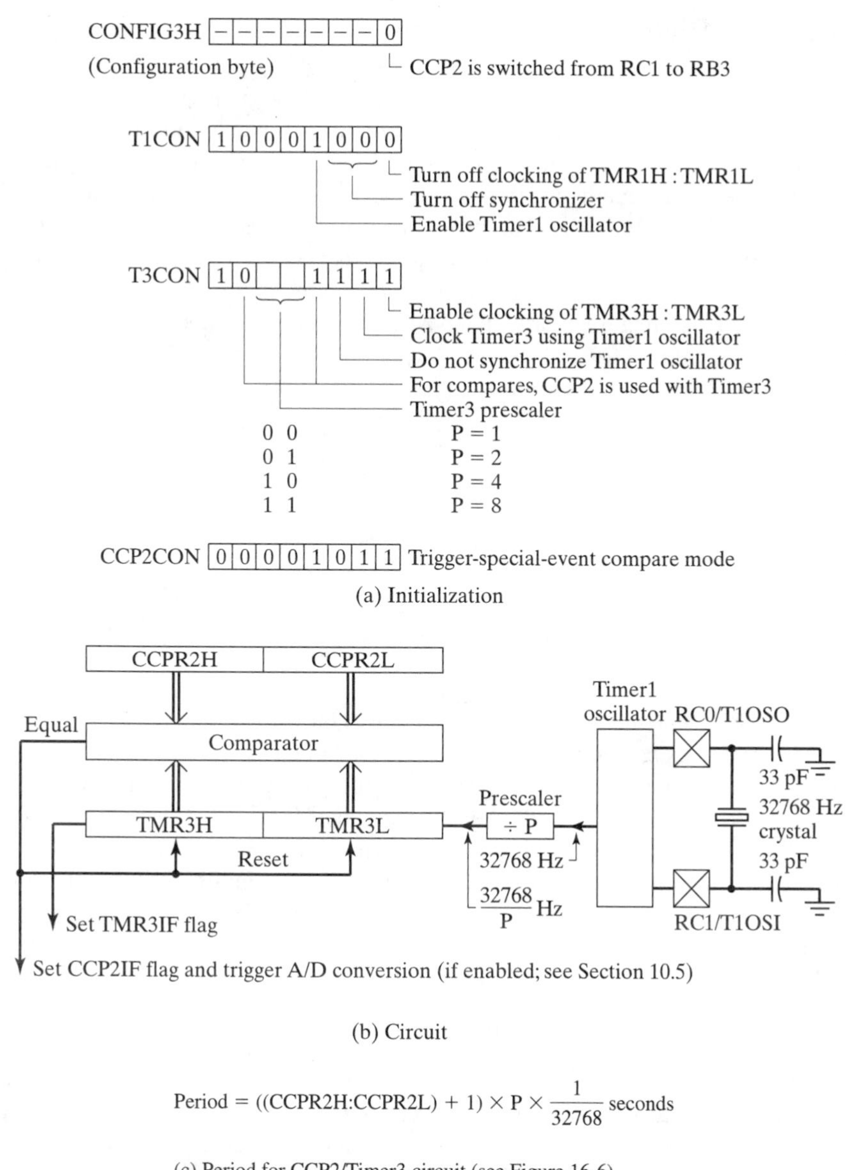

$$\text{Period} = ((\text{CCPR2H:CCPR2L}) + 1) \times \text{P} \times \frac{1}{32768}\ \text{seconds}$$

(c) Period for CCP2/Timer3 circuit (see Figure 16-6)

Figure 20-11 Use of Timer1's oscillator with Timer3/CCP2 during SLEEP mode.

Since Timer3 has the option of using the Timer1 oscillator, as shown in Figure 20-11, Timer3 offers much the same opportunity. In addition, if the analog-to-digital converter is enabled with its RC clock, then the scheme of Section 10.5 can be used to awaken the chip with an ADC interrupt. In this case, CCP2's trigger-special-event mode initiates an A/D conversion while the chip sleeps on. At the conclusion of the A/D conversion, the A/D converter interrupt (enabled by setting **PIE1** register's **ADIE** bit) will awaken the chip with a newly converted value in its **ADRESH:ADRESL** registers. CCP2 is used to set the ADC sampling rate, and thereby, the awakening rate.

20.10 TIMEKEEPING

Some applications link their actions to the outside world's clock. A lawn sprinkler controller can serve as an example. The controller is initialized with the time of day along with the watering days, start times, and sprinkling duration information. A user would then like the controller to maintain time without noticeable drift over many months and through power outages. This is an application that can be met by using the ±20 ppm (parts per million) accuracy of the watch crystal of Figure 20-2. Over a period of a month, ±20 ppm translates into ±7.5 seconds. Over a period of a year, it translates into ±1.5 minutes, a tolerance that would be satisfactory for many applications.

The problem of maintaining time through a power outage is simplified by the option of using the Timer1 oscillator as the chip's master clock, F_{OSC}, as shown in Figure 20-12. If oscillator switching is enabled in the **CONFIG1H** configuration word, programmed with

```
__CONFIG  _CONFIG1H, _RCIO_OSC_1H & _OSCS_ON_1H
```

then the chip will come out of reset ready to let **T1CON** be initialized to B'10001111'. This

- Enables the Timer1 external (32,768 Hz) oscillator.
- Enables Timer1.
- Selects the Timer1 32,768 oscillator to clock **TMR1H:TMR1L** with a 1:1 prescaler.
- Turns off synchronization of the external clock. This is needed to keep **TMR1H:TMR1L** counting during SLEEP mode.

The subsequent step of setting the **OSCCON** register's **SCS** bit will switch F_{OSC} to be the Timer1 oscillator so that the internal clock period will be 4 times the crystal's clock period, or about 122 microseconds.

Normal operation can now proceed. When the low-voltage detect circuit signals that power is about to be lost, but before the lower-voltage battery backup circuit of Figure 20-12 cuts in, the CPU can clear **TMR1IF**, clear **GIEH**, set **TMR1IE**, and execute a **sleep** instruction.

Upon awakening, the microcontroller will continue by executing the instructions following the **sleep** instruction. A check of the **PIR2** register's **LVDIF** bit will indicate whether power has been restored (**LVDIF** = 0) or not (**LVDIF** = 1). If not, then 2 seconds have passed since the last time **TMR1H:TMR1L** rolled over. The RAM variables keeping track of time,

```
YEAR:MONTH:DAY:HOUR:MINUTE:SECOND
```

can be incremented by 2 seconds and the sequence repeated to clear the **TMR1IF** flag and go back to sleep.

As long as the microcontroller is deriving its power from the ac power line, it can also derive its timekeeping information from the power line. This has the advantage, over using a watch crystal, of long-term timing accuracy. Over the long run, the power utility speeds up, or slows down, its generators slightly so as to maintain this accuracy. For example, after a year of running without a power outage, an ac-powered clock will still show the correct time. Figure 20-13 shows a simple circuit using a four-pin (DIP or surface-mount) optocoupler circuit that can be used to trigger one of the microcontroller's low-priority interrupts (e.g., RB2/INT2) every 1/120 of a second. The INT2 pin's Schmitt-trigger input will derive a sharp, unambiguous edge from the relatively slow-edged pulses occurring each time the ac line crosses 0 V. The INT2 interrupt handler simply clears **INT2IF** and increments a scale-of-120 counter. Each time this counter rolls over, it increments the "seconds" digit of the time counter stored in RAM.

Precautions are vital (literally) if 115 VAC is brought anywhere near the 5 V circuitry of a microcontroller. Before applying power, use an ohmmeter to ensure that there is no low-resistance path from the power plug to the output lines. Then cover every connection. The author uses hot glue in a lab environment. Epoxy caulk presents a more permanent solution.

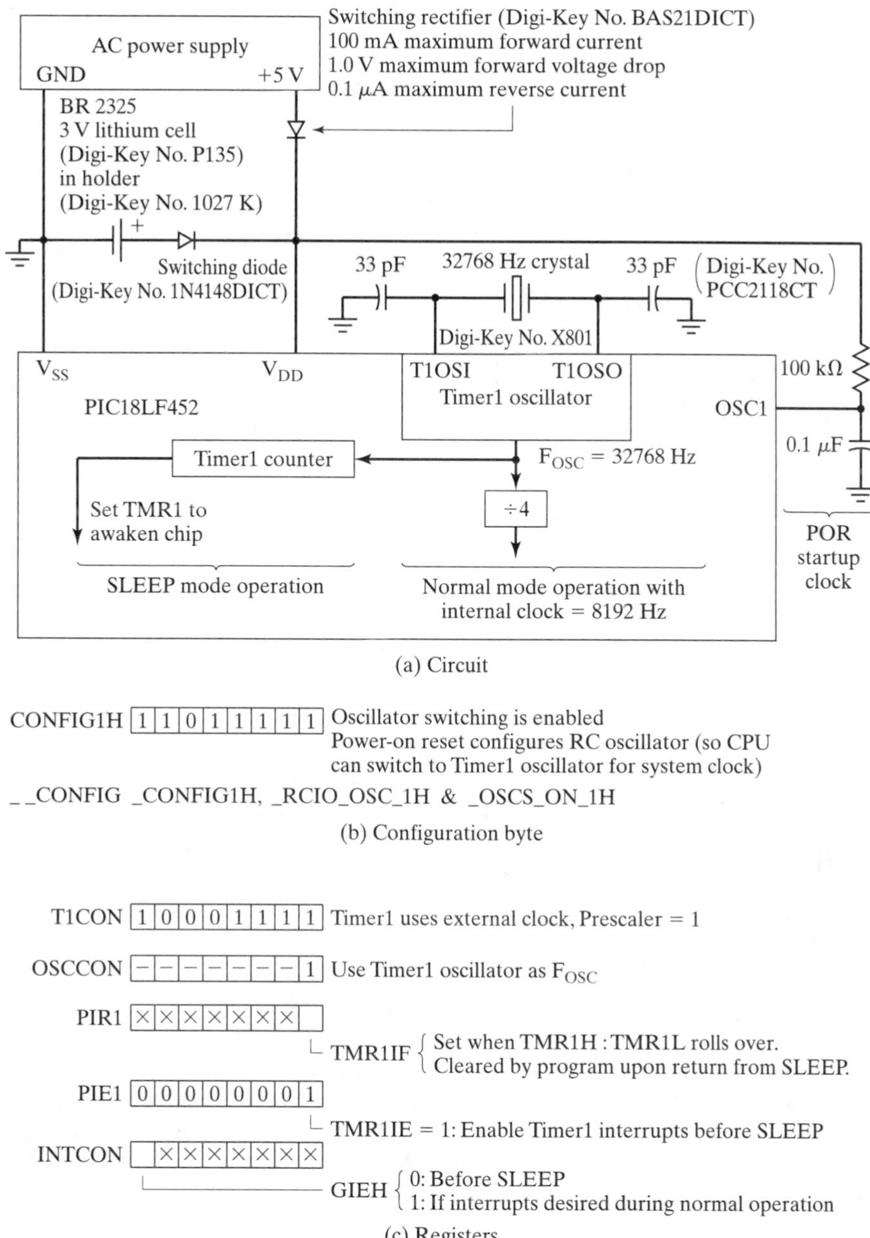

(a) Circuit

CONFIG1H | 1 | 1 | 0 | 1 | 1 | 1 | 1 | 1 | Oscillator switching is enabled
Power-on reset configures RC oscillator (so CPU can switch to Timer1 oscillator for system clock)

__CONFIG _CONFIG1H, _RCIO_OSC_1H & _OSCS_ON_1H

(b) Configuration byte

T1CON | 1 | 0 | 0 | 0 | 1 | 1 | 1 | 1 | Timer1 uses external clock, Prescaler = 1

OSCCON | – | – | – | – | – | – | – | 1 | Use Timer1 oscillator as F_{OSC}

PIR1 | × | × | × | × | × | × | × | |

TMR1IF { Set when TMR1H : TMR1L rolls over. Cleared by program upon return from SLEEP.

PIE1 | 0 | 0 | 0 | 0 | 0 | 0 | 0 | 1 |

TMR1IE = 1: Enable Timer1 interrupts before SLEEP

INTCON | | × | × | × | × | × | × | × |

GIEH { 0: Before SLEEP; 1: If interrupts desired during normal operation

(c) Registers

Figure 20-12 Battery-backed-up timekeeping circuit.

20.11 DATA EEPROM USE

Microchip Technology has a long history of making eight-pin I[2]C and SPI EEPROM (electrically erasable, programmable read-only memory) parts for miscellaneous uses. A popular application has been to provide nonvolatile memory for microcontrollers. With nonvolatile memory, a device can

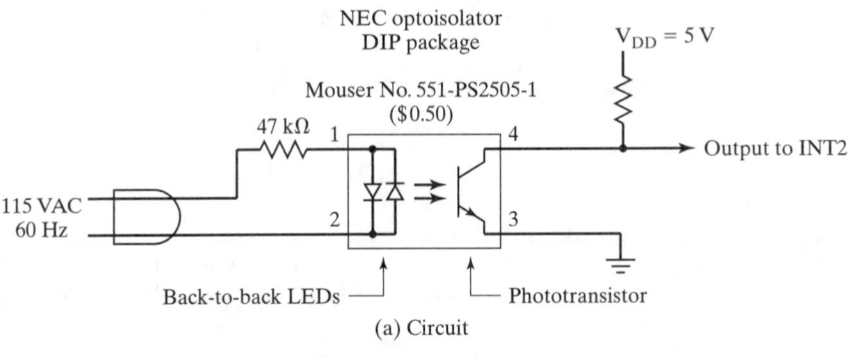

(a) Circuit

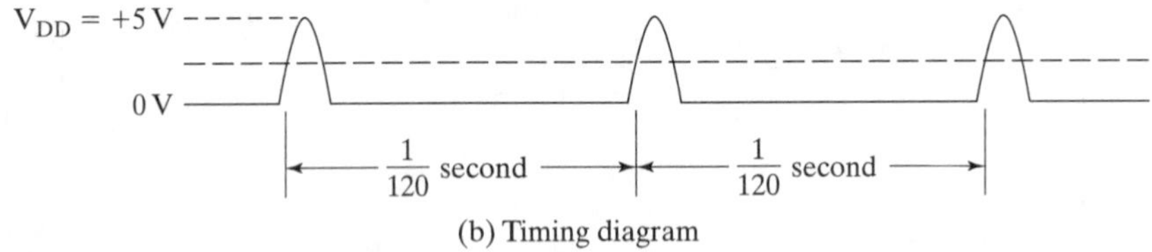

(b) Timing diagram

Figure 20-13 Derivation of time-reference pulses from power line.

remember setup information through power outages and power-cord unplugging without battery backup. In fiscal year 2001, Microchip Technology, a company that holds the number-2 spot in market share for 8-bit microcontrollers, actually earned 25% of its revenue with EEPROM parts.

A block diagram of the mechanism for accessing the 256-byte data EEPROM is shown in Figure 20-14a. As indicated in Figure 20-14b, **EECON1** should be cleared in the **Initial** subroutine. This selects subsequent accesses to be steered to the data EEPROM (rather than to the flash memory holding the program, which requires complicated multiple-byte erases and writes and which halts the CPU for milliseconds at a time).

The registers associated with the data EEPROM are shown in Figure 20-14c and d. Because a write operation takes so long (4 milliseconds, typically), a string of bytes might be written to the data EEPROM under interrupt control. Alternatively, the bytes of the string might be written into the EEPROM in the mainline code, one byte each time around the mainline loop.

Reads from the EEPROM cannot be carried out while a write is taking place. The read sequence is shown in Figure 20-14e. It begins with a check of the **EEIF** flag to ensure that a write sequence is not underway. The desired address to be read is loaded into **EEADR** and the **RD** bit is set. By the next cycle, the EEPROM data will be available in the **EEDATA** register, ready to be used.

Writing to the data EEPROM has been made more complicated, with safeguards built in to help ensure that only *intended* writes are carried out. As shown in Figure 20-14f, the write begins with the loading of the **EEADR** and **EEDATA** registers. Because a write to data EEPROM will typically last for 4 milliseconds, an **EEIF** flag is used to signal the completion of the write. This must be cleared before the write cycle begins. Writes are enabled by the setting of the **WREN** bit, a built-in safeguard against the inadvertent corruption of the EEPROM. The next sequence must be carried out *exactly,* with no gaps in the sequence, for the write operation to be successful. This is a further safeguard against inadvertent writes to the EEPROM. To ensure that the instructions are indeed carried out as intended, interrupts must be disabled for the five cycles making up the sequence. Then interrupts can be reenabled again. For the next 4 or so milliseconds, the CPU is free to do anything except modify **EEADR**, **EEDATA**, or **EECON1**.

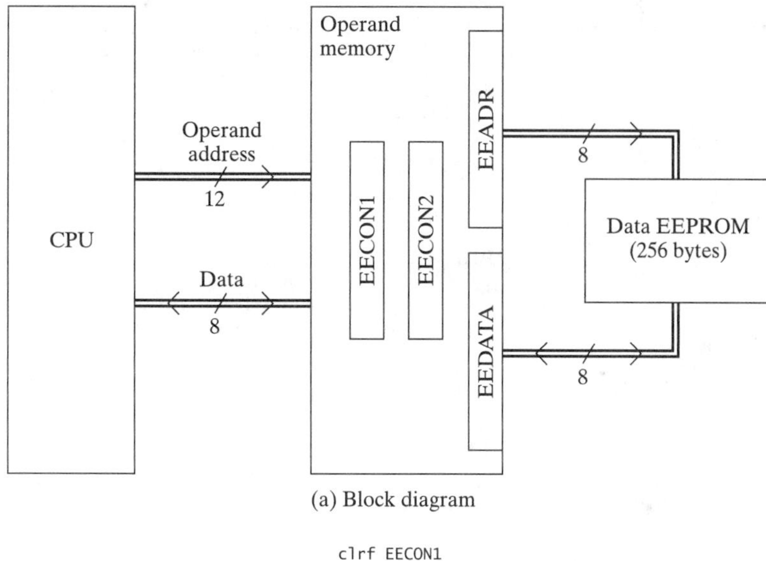

(a) Block diagram

```
clrf EECON1
```

(b) Initialization required to access data EEPROM memory

Figure 20-14 Data EEPROM.

Once the write of a string of bytes to EEPROM has been completed, further inadvertent writes to EEPROM should be prevented by the clearing of the **WREN** (write enable) bit in the **EECON1** register.

Both reads from and writes to the EEPROM can be carried out over the full frequency range of the PIC18F452. They can also be carried out over the full V_{DD} voltage range of the part, all the way down to 2.0 V for the PIC18LF452.

When updating a string of related bytes in EEPROM, interrupt control of the successive writes to the string will lock out the mainline code from reading until the entire string has been written. That is, the **EEIF** flag will always be 0 to mainline programs, from the initiation of the first write to the completion of the last write. As each write is automatically completed, the flag is set and an interrupt prevents the mainline code from seeing it set before the interrupt handler initiates the next write. Consequently, the interrupts tie up the CPU for just microseconds at a time, the string is updated in the minimum possible time, and the mainline code never reads anything but valid data from the EEPROM. This circumvents a possible erroneous interpretation of the string from occurring. If a mainline subroutine could get in and read the entire string out of EEPROM in the middle of an update of the string, that subroutine would occasionally obtain an incoherent mix of old and new data.

20.12 PARALLEL SLAVE PORT (PSP)

The *parallel slave port* is a feature that facilitates the design of PC interface circuitry by presenting an 8-bit bus interface to the PC, as shown in Figure 20-15a. The PIC18F452 can then control the complexities of the external device circuitry.

When used in this way, the PIC18F452 has its **PORTD** and **PORTE** pins dedicated solely to this parallel slave port mode of operation. As shown in Figure 20-15b, the setting of bit 4 of **TRISE** selects this mode, while at the same time giving over control of the connection between *two* **PORTD** registers

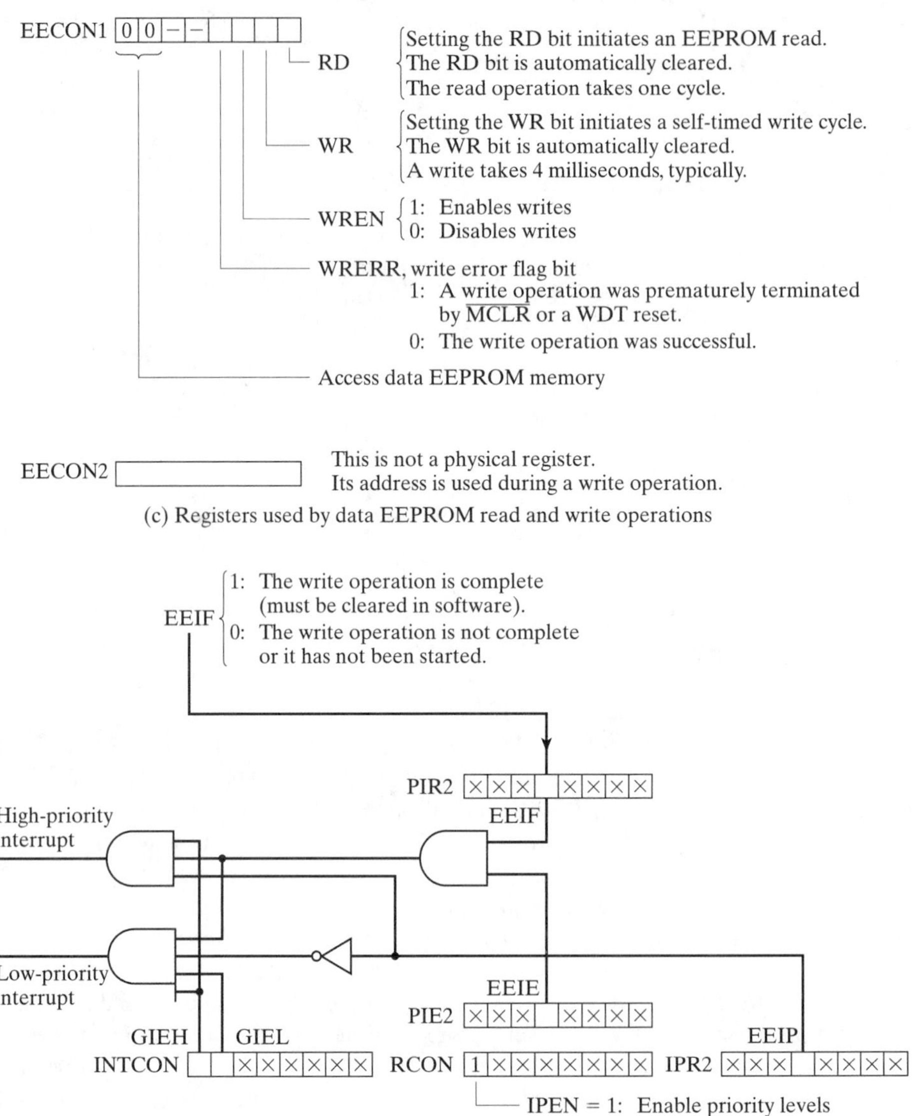

(c) Registers used by data EEPROM read and write operations

(d) Registers used during a ≈4ms write operation to signal completion.

Figure 20-14 continued

(one for input; one for output) and the **PORTE** pins to the $\overline{RD}$ and $\overline{WR}$ and $\overline{CS}$ inputs from the PC. If a PC writes to the decoded address so the microcontroller's $\overline{CS}$ input goes low, then the 8 bits of data written out by the PC will be written into the PIC18F452's **PORTD** register, and the **IBF** flag bit in the **TRISE** register will be set as well as the **PSPIF** flag bit in the **PIR1** register. If interrupts are enabled from the parallel slave port facility, then the setting of the **PSPIF** flag will interrupt the microcontroller's CPU to indicate the reception of the byte from the PC.

When the microcontroller's CPU reads the received byte in **PORTD**, the **IBF** flag is automatically cleared. The **PSPIF** flag must be cleared with a **bcf** instruction. If the PC writes a second byte to the

```
IF_  PIR2,EEIF == 1      ;No write is taking place
  ‹Load EEADR with address to be read from›
  bsf  EECON1,RD         ;Initiate read operation
  movf  EEDATA,W         ;Copy byte to WREG
ENDIF_
```

(e) Read sequence

```
‹Load EEADR with address to be written to›
‹Load EEDATA with byte to be written to this address›
bcf  PIR2,EEIF          ;Clear write-complete flag
bsf  EECON1,WREN        ;Enable writes
bcf  INTCON,GIEH        ;Disable all interrupts
MOVLF  Øx55,EECON2      ;Magic sequence to help
MOVLF  Øxaa,EECON2      ; prevent accidental writes to EEPROM
bsf  EECON1,WR          ;Trigger the (protected) write operation
bsf  INTCON,GIEH        ;Reenable interrupts
                        ; (assuming interrupts were enabled)

‹Wait until EEIF is set before writing again›

‹When writing has been completed, disable further interupts with›
bcf  EECON1,WREN        ;Disable writes
```

(f) Write sequence

Figure 20-14 continued

microcontroller before the microcontroller has read the first byte, the second byte will be lost and the **IBOV** flag will be set, marking this loss.

At the same time it is receiving bytes from the PC, the microcontroller can send a byte to the PC by writing it to **PORTD**, automatically setting the Output Buffer Full flag, **OBF**. When the PC reads from the decoded address that drives the microcontroller's $\overline{\text{CS}}$ input low at the same time that its $\overline{\text{IOR}}$ line goes low, the last byte written to **PORTD**'s output register by the microcontroller will drive the **PORTD** pins, letting the PC read the byte. At the same time, the **OBF** flag is automatically cleared and the **PSPIF** flag set, signaling the microcontroller's CPU that **PORTD** has been read by the PC.

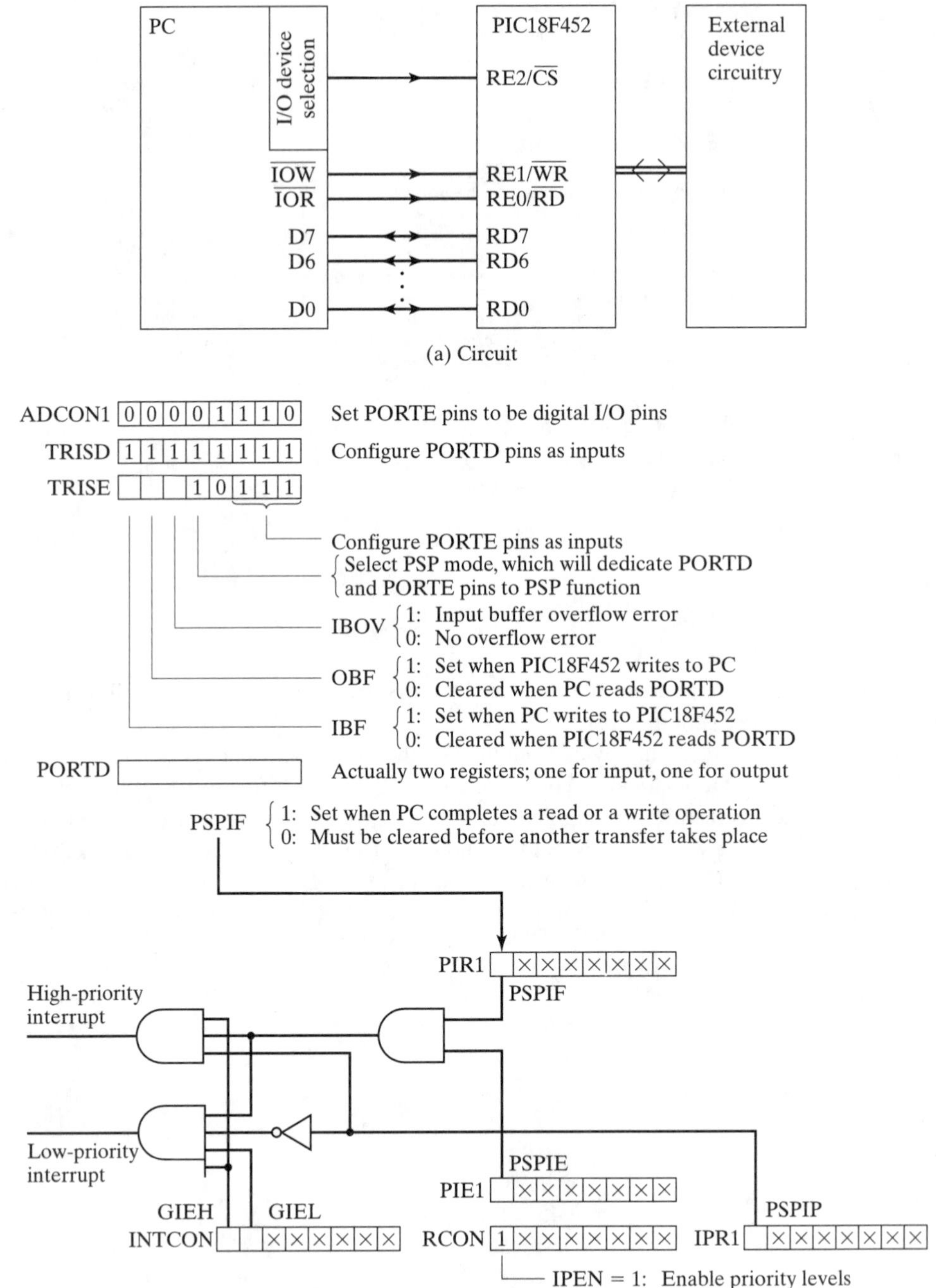

Figure 20-15 PORTE and **PORTD** use for parallel slave part.

Appendix

A1

ASSEMBLY OF THE QWIKFLASH BOARD

A1.1 PREAMBLE

Construction of the QwikFlash board will provide you with a tool to support your learning as well as arm you with a low-cost vehicle for development work for any of the many opportunities to put intelligence into a product. This appendix identifies the parts you need to purchase to populate the QwikFlash board included in the back of this first printing of the book. The board is provided, gratis, by Jim Carreker, a friend and former student of the author. In addition to these parts, you will need to purchase, or obtain access to, appropriate tools to build the board.

The lowest-cost route to development makes use of the QwikBug debugger described in Appendix A4 and programmed into the PIC18F452 microcontroller on the QwikFlash board. Before you can take advantage of this debugger, you will need to program its code into the PIC18F452. If you have access to Microchip's ICD2 in-circuit debugger, it can be used for this step, as described in Section A4.3. An ICD2 module should be available in a college or university environment supporting a course organized around this book. Alternatively, you can use the low-cost "hobby" programmer described in Section A4.4.

You will also want access to a PIC18F452 chip programmed with QFPV, a QwikFlash Performance Verification program developed by Dave Desrochers and Michael Cheng and described in Section A1.10. Both the QwikBug code and the QFPV code are available at www.picbook.com.

Before undertaking the assembly of the QwikFlash board, you might want to consider the alternative of purchasing from MICRODESIGNS Inc. (www.microdesignsinc.com) a fully functioning QwikFlash board, complete with the QwikBug monitor and the QFPV code already programmed into the chip as well as a "wall wart" power supply and a serial cable. MICRODESIGNS is a small company in the Atlanta area that has gained a reputation for quality, innovative design work over their 25 years of existence. Bill Kaduck and Dave Cornish, the principals, want to support the potential impact of this book written by their friend. They will sell the package from their web site and hope to price it at $99 plus shipping and handling.

A1.2 MICROCHIP'S ICD2 MODULE

As an alternative to the use of the QwikBug debugger, the purchase of Microchip's ICD2 will provide you with the only development tool you will ever need for working with the PIC18F452. You will be able to develop and debug program code as well as program the features of the chip controlled by the configuration options. For example, you will be able to select the chip's high-speed, phase-locked loop clock to make the board run with a 10 MHz clock rather than the 2.5 MHz clock utilized by the QwikBug debugger.

The in-circuit debugger module is available in any of three configurations. Microchip's Part Number DV164005 ($159) is just the "hockey puck" module of Figure 4-4 together with a USB cable to supply both power and communications to the ICD2 module from the PC. Part Number DV164006 ($209) comes with a DB-9 serial cable, power supply, and demonstration board. A serial cable is the connection of choice for computers without a USB port and is illustrated in Figure 4-4. Part Number DV164007 ($188) is the same as the DV164006 but without the demonstration board. For users with the QwikFlash board serving as a demonstration board and with the QFPV program serving as a demonstration program, either the DV164005 or the DV164007 unit are the parts of choice.

The module has been designed so that the firmware can be upgraded with a download from Microchip's Web site. Consequently, even early adopters of the unit need have no fear that a later revision will be a better revision.

A1.3 PARTS LIST

Figure A1-1 lists the parts needed to populate the QwikFlash board. The Digi-Key phone number for ordering parts on a credit card is 1-800-344-4539. They have set up the single identifying "kit" number, 18F452-KIT, which acts as an alias for the one-by-one enumeration of each part listed in Figure A1-1. Simplicity and accuracy in placing the order as well as significantly reduced parts cost are the result. Check the author's Web site, www.picbook.com, for possible further information.

If you do not have a serial cable available for your PC, and if you are planning to use the QwikBug on-chip monitor program, then you can either pick one up at any computer store or add Digi-Key Part Number AE1020 ($5.35) to your order. This is a standard serial cable with a male DB-9 connector on one end and a female DB-9 connector on the other end.

You may also want to add to your Digi-Key order a seven-position terminal block (Part Number 277-1252) if you want to make connections of individual wires to the board (e.g., for the wires to a stepper motor) without having the permanence of soldered connections. This terminal block can be mounted in the large holes along the top right edge of the board.

The parts list includes a 3"-long, two-conductor flex cable with two uses. First, it supports the performance testing of the on-board digital-to-analog converter, both when the board construction has been completed and later if either the Maxim DAC or the PIC18F452's ADC does not seem to be working correctly. Second, it supports the use of the board in its QwikFlash instrument role, discussed in Section 4.3, to measure the performance of code running on another QwikFlash board.

Quantity	Part number	Distributor	Part Description	Board designation	Manufacturer	Manufacturer's part number	Price each	Minimum quantity	Total price
13(20)*	1210PHCT	Digi-Key	0.1 uf ceramic capacitor	C1,2,3,4,6,7,8,9,10,11,15,16,17	BC	A104M15Z5UFVVWN		10 for 1.15	2.30
2	P835	Digi-Key	33uf @ 35V polarized electrolytic capacitor	C5,14	Panasonic	ECE-A1VKA330	0.34		0.68
2	399-1890	Digi-Key	22 pf ceramic radial capacitor	C12,13	Kemet	C315C220J2G5CA	0.28		0.56
1	A9049	Digi-Key	Modular connector - side entry, 6 position	CON1	AMP	520470-3	0.72	1	0.72
1	A23303	Digi-Key	DB-9 female serial cable connector	CON2	AMP	747844-4	1.94	1	1.94
1	CP-202A	Digi-Key	Power supply connector - 2.1 mm barrel connector	CON3	CUI Stack	PJ-202A	0.38	1	0.38
4(10)*	1839K	Digi-Key	0.25" dia. 0.625" long cylindrical threaded standoff	Corners	Keystone	1839		10 for 2.50	2.50
1 pkg.*	H342	Digi-Key	Five Phillips panhead machine screws, 4-40 X 1/4"	Corners	Building Fasteners	PMS 440 0025 PH		100 for 1.11	1.11
5	P403	Digi-Key	Red LED, high brightness, T-1 package	D1, 2, 4, 5, 6	Panasonic	LN28RAL(US)	0.38	1	1.90
1	1N4001DICT	Digi-Key	Diode rectifier	D3	Diodes Inc.	1N4001-T	0.26	1	0.26
2	1N4148DICT	Digi-Key	Switching diode	D7, 8	Diodes Inc.	1N4148-T	0.23	1	0.46
1	S1011-36	Digi-Key	Header, single row, straight solder tail, 36 pins	J1, H1, 3, LCD1S	Sullins	PZC36SAAN	1.28	1	1.28
1(10)*	929950-00	Digi-Key	Shunt	J1S	3M	929950-00		10 for 1.46	1.46
1	S2011-36	Digi-Key	Header, dual row, straight solder tail, 80 contacts	LCD1S	Sullins	PZC36DAAN	2.37	1	2.37
1	73-1106	Digi-Key	LCD module, 8X2, high contrast	LCD1	Optrex America	DMC-50448N	9.79	1	9.79
1	T402-P5P	Digi-Key	9 VDC@200 mA wall transformer, 2.1 mm barrel conn.	Plugs into CON3	CUI Stack	DPD090020-P5P	4.65	1	4.65
1	P4D2502	Digi-Key	5 kilohm thumbwheel one-turn potentiometer	POT1	Panasonic	EVL-HFAA06B53	2.07	1	2.07
3(5)*	470QBK	Digi-Key	470 ohm, 5%, 1/4W resistor	R1, 3, 15	Yageo	CFR-25JB-470R		5 for 0.28	0.28
1(5)*	3.3KQBK	Digi-Key	3.3 kilohm, 5%, 1/4W resistor	R14	Yageo	CFR-25JB-3K3		5 for 0.28	0.28
6(10)*	1.0KQBK	Digi-Key	1.0 kilohm, 5%, 1/4W resistor	R2, 5, 6, 7, 8, 12	Yageo	CFR-25JB-1K0		5 for 0.28	0.56
2(5)*	47KQBK	Digi-Key	47 kilohm, 5%, 1/4W resistor	R4, 11	Yageo	CFR-25JB-47K		5 for 0.28	0.28
3(5)*	10KQBK	Digi-Key	10 kilohm, 5%, 1/4W resistor	R9, 10, 13	Yageo	CFR-25JB-10K		5 for 0.28	0.28
1	LM340T-5.0	Digi-Key	Voltage regulator - 5V @ 1A - TO-220 package	REG1	National Semi.	LM340T-5.0	0.59	1	0.59
1 pkg.*	H216	Digi-Key	One 4-40 hex nut	REG1N	Building Fasteners	HNZ440		100 for 0.93	0.93
1	3315C-1-006	Digi-Key	RPG - Encoder 9mm, square, right angle	RPG1	Bourns	3315C-001-006	2.59	1	2.59
1	8554K	Digi-Key	RPG knob with 1/8" diameter hole and set screws	RPG1K	Keystone	8554	3.38	1	3.38
1	EG2447	Digi-Key	SPDT toggle switch	SW1	E-Switch	200MSP1T1B1M2QE	3.31	1	3.31
2	P8006S	Digi-Key	Pushbutton switch	SW2, 3	Panasonic	EVQ-PAC04M	0.29	1	0.58
1	LM34DZ	Digi-Key	Temperature sensor - TO-92 package	TMP1	National Semi.	LM34DZ	2.33	1	2.33
1	MAX232ACPE	Digi-Key	RS-232 interface chip - 16-pin DIP	U1	Maxim	MAX232ACPE	4.88	1	4.88
1	ED3116	Digi-Key	16-pin DIP socket	U1S	Mill-Max	110-99-316-41-001	0.65	1	0.65
1	MAX522CPA	Digi-Key	Dual 8-bit DAC with SPI input - 8-pin DIP	U2	Maxim	MAX522CPA	6.04	1	6.04
1	ED3108	Digi-Key	8-pin DIP socket	U2S	Mill-Max	110-99-308-41-001	0.32	1	0.32
1	PIC18F452-I/P	Digi-Key	PIC microcontroller with flash memory - 40-pin DIP	U3	Microchip	PIC18F452-I/P	9.38	1	9.38
1	ED3740	Digi-Key	40-pin DIP socket	U3S	Mill-Max	110-99-640-41-001	1.62	1	1.62
1	X443	Digi-Key	10 MHz crystal	Y1	ECS	ECS-100-18-4	0.80	1	0.80
1	A9BBG-0203F	Digi-Key	3"-long 2-conductor flex cable	H3	AMP	A9BBG-0203F	2.99	1	2.99
*designates the minimum quantity that may be ordered. This is more than the number needed for one QuikFlash board.								Total =	76.50
Digi-Key (1-800-344-4539) For latest price and description, go to www.digikey.com and enter the Digi-Key part number into the search box. Then, to see the actual catalog page, click on Technical/Catalog Information.									

Figure A1-1 QwikFlash board parts and prices

A1.4 CONSTRUCTION SUPPLIES NEEDED

Mat—An old towel or smooth placemat to work on that has been washed with a fabric softener like Downy or dried with a fabric softener like Bounce (to help keep down dangerous static). (We spray the carpet in my laboratory with half a cup of scent-free Downy in three gallons of water every couple of months to help with this same potential problem. It works well and seems to harm nothing.)

Solder—Either rosin-core solder or water-soluble-core solder is acceptable. Kester and Multicore are fine brands. I suggest thin solder (0.02″ or 0.025″ diameter, also known as 25 or 22 gauge) because it is easier to control the amount of solder used to form a solder joint. Either 63/37 (tin/lead) alloy solder with a melting point of 361°F or 60/40 alloy solder with a melting point of 361–374°F is fine.

Soldering iron—I am partial to using a soldering iron that has its temperature controlled by a temperature sensor built into its tip rather than by a dial, since I get the same reasonable temperature every time I turn it on. Weller's WTCPT soldering station with a 1/16″ (0.06″) screwdriver, 700°F tip (Weller Model PTA7 tip) is an excellent choice for a laboratory. For an individual, a 25–35 watt iron with an 0.06″ screwdriver tip and a stand to hold the hot iron and a wet sponge to clean the tip should work fine.

Desoldering braid—To remove solder that shorts two adjacent pins together or to help remove a badly placed part or remove solder from the hole on the board from which a part has been removed, I suggest that you get 0.1″-wide desoldering braid. Popular brand names are Soder-Wick and Chem-Wik. The rosin in the braid wets the connection to the solder and the capillary action of the braid sucks up the solder.

Tools—If you are building your board in a college lab, you should have the tools you need available to you. Otherwise you can go to Radio Shack and see what you are getting before you make your purchases. Alternatively, Digi-Key sells everything you'll need. See the note at the bottom of the parts list in Figure A1-1 for checking their Web site catalog pages.

Miniature pliers—For forming leads to fit through the PC board holes, it is useful to have a pair of miniature pliers. My favorite, available from Digi-Key (#232-1017), is made by Swanstrom. It is 5″- long with a 1″-long "slim nose and smooth jaw." The key parameter is its slim nose. The smooth jaw actually handles leads better than a serrated jaw.

Flush-cutting diagonal cutter—This is used to remove the soft excess leads of a component after they have been soldered to the board. I like Radio Shack's low-cost Archer 5″ Nippy Cutters (Cat. No. 64-1833C). A flush-cutting cutter will result in a smooth cut at the top of the solder blob used to join the component to the pad on the board. However, the cutting edges are so fragile that you will ding the edges if you try to cut anything hard. For example, if I have to remove a resistor from a board, I like to cut it in half first so that I can individually remove each lead from its pad. For that, I use a regular diagonal cutter, not a flush-cutting diagonal cutter.

Other miscellaneous tools—You'll need a few other tools, but only sporadically. If you don't have them, find someone who does rather than buying them. You'll need a Phillips screwdriver to tighten the machine screw that clamps the voltage regulator to the board and to tighten the corner feet on the board. You'll need a 5/16″ nut driver or a small crescent wrench to tighten the nut that clamps the RPG1 to the board. You'll need a tiny 3/64″ Allen wrench to tighten the knob onto the shaft of RPG1.

Resistor color code—It is helpful to be able to read the resistor values. A resistor has three color bars, possibly followed by a gold or silver tolerance bar. The color bars represent two digits plus an exponent. The colors are

0 — black	5 — green	no tolerance bar — 20%
1 — brown	6 — blue	silver tolerance bar — 10%
2 — red	7 — violet	gold tolerance bar — 5%
3 — orange	8 — gray	
4 — yellow	9 — white	

For example, a 10 kΩ resistor is marked with a brown bar at one end followed by a black bar followed by an orange bar. A handy calculator is found at many Internet sites, including http://www.dannyg.com/javascript/res2/resistor.htm.

A1.5 SOLDERING TECHNIQUE

When you are ready to solder the pin or the lead of a part that you have inserted onto the board, unwind enough solder from its spool to position the end so that it touches both the pin and the pad on the board. Lightly press this joint with the tip of the hot soldering iron so that the solder flows onto both the pin and the pad. Once this flow happens, remove the iron.

Leaving the iron in place too long can have the deleterious consequence of breaking the bond between the pad and the PC board. Leaving it in place even longer can destroy the part, particularly a LED or a diode. Removing the soldering iron tip before this flow occurs onto both the pad and the component's lead can produce what is called a "cold solder joint." A cold solder joint can also form if the lead moves in the hole on the board as it cools down. The connection may be good immediately but will fail as the board ages. I lean in the direction of heating a joint too long, not too little, since I cannot remember the last time I destroyed a part by overheating it.

A1.6 BOARD CONSTRUCTION

Figure A1-2 is the schematic of the board. It may be helpful to you as you build the board, giving some insight into the role of each part.

Figure A1-3 shows the board's "pads and top silk" artwork. This may be helpful, particularly after you have stuffed components and thereby obscured the labeling of a component (e.g., R3–R8).

Figure A1-4 provides a suggested sequence in which the parts might be "stuffed." As you carry out each step, you might check it off so as to ensure not missing any steps. The suggested sequence will have you stuffing the many low-profile parts first so that the board continues to lie flat (so you do not have to deal with a rocking board prematurely).

As you begin, you might insert all resistors of one value (e.g., R1, R3, and R15—the three 470Ω resistors) into the board, bend the leads to hold them snug to the board, solder them, and then cut the excess leads off. Then check off the item in Figure A1-4 before proceeding to the next item in that chart.

If you have to remove a part (e.g., a resistor soldered in the wrong place), try breaking it so that each lead can be removed one at a time. Heavy-duty diagonal cutters are good for this. Don't use the flush-cutting diagonal cutters because you'll ding the sharp edges.

There are several two-terminal components that are labeled as being "polarized" (i.e., the diodes, LEDs, and electrolytic capacitors). If these are inserted into the board with the pins reversed from what is intended, they will not work correctly. Each of these will be specifically discussed.

When soldering a multiple-pin component (e.g., the 40-pin socket or the LCD display), hold it so that it is flat and then solder just one corner pin. Check that the component is really flat on the board before soldering the opposite corner. Then check it one final time before soldering the remaining pins.

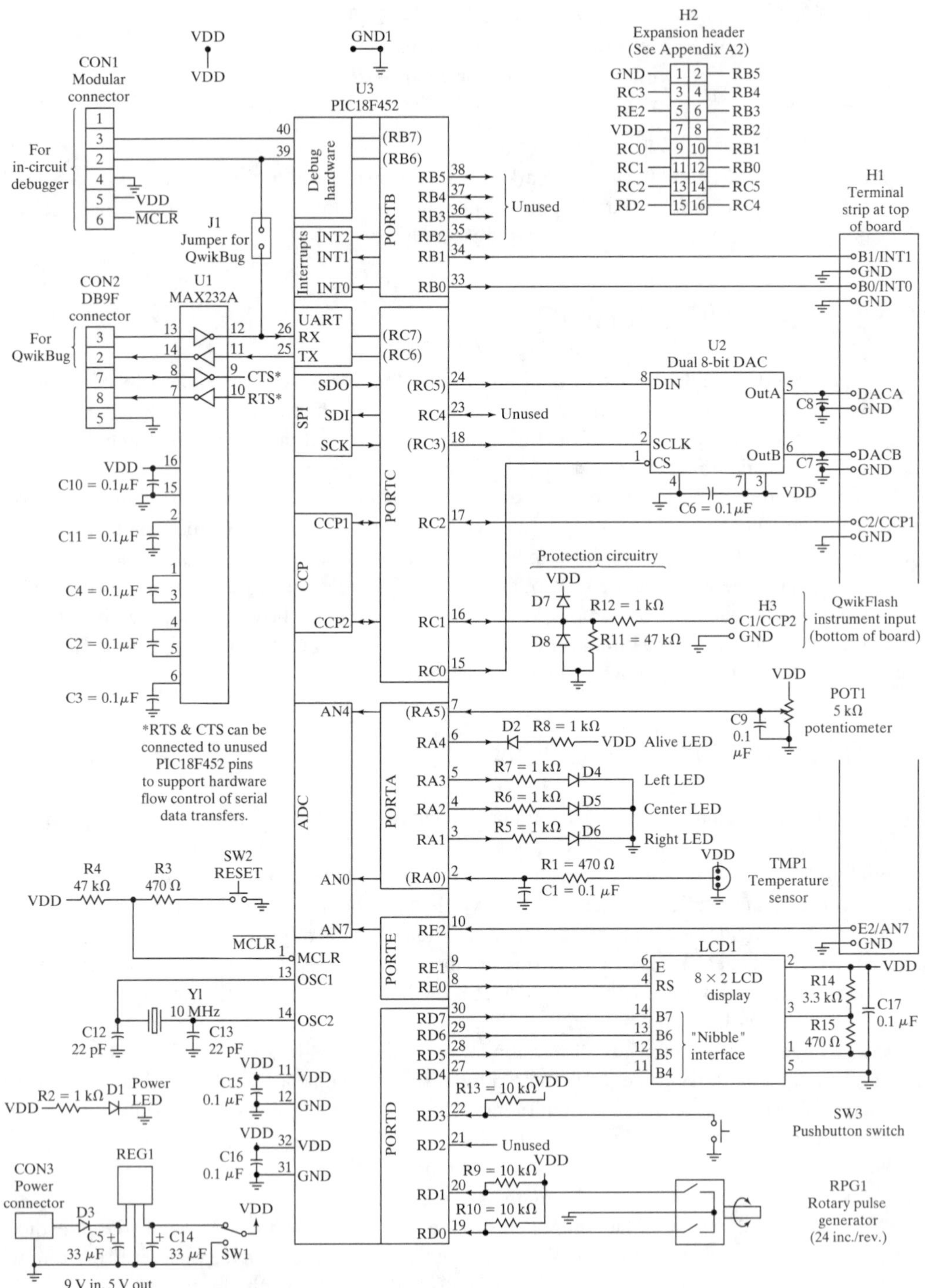

Figure A1-2 QwikFlash board schematic

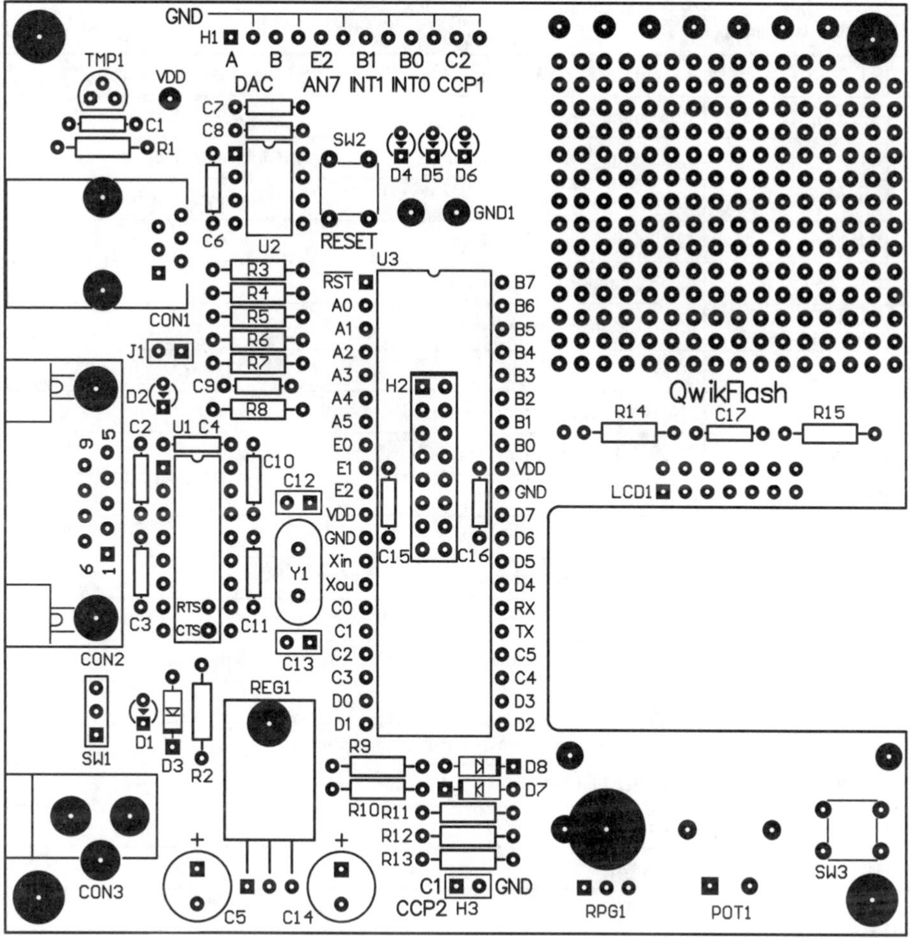

Figure A1-3 QwikFlash board's "pads and top silk" artwork

If you have an ohmmeter available to you, I suggest that you use it to check that the correct resistors have been stuffed. Also, periodically check the resistance between VDD and GND. I have checked a completed board with the ICs removed and the power supply "wall wart" removed from the board. The resistance is about 1 kΩ with the power switch turned on and 0 Ω with the power switch turned off. If you accidently create a short between power and ground, the fewer possibilities you have to look for, the better.

The two 1N4148 signal diodes, D7 and D8, have to be inserted with the bar on the end lining up with the silkscreen bar. These protect against frying the PIC18F452 with an input voltage out of the 0 V to 5 V range if such a voltage is applied to the input pin at the bottom of the board labeled CCP2/C1. One role of this board is to serve as the QwikFlash instrument, measuring frequencies and periods with the 50-parts-per-million accuracy of the crystal oscillator and measuring maximum pulse widths. If the diodes are inserted backwards, you'll know it because they'll short VDD to GND and go poof!

Checkoff	Board designation	Description	
	R1, 3, 15	470 ohm, 5%, 1/4W resistor	(yellow-violet-brown)
	R2, 5, 6, 7, 8, 12	1.0 kilohm, 5%, 1/4W resistor	(brown-black-red)
	R14	3.3 kilohm, 5%, 1/4W resistor	(orange-orange-red)
	R9, 10, 13	10 kilohm, 5%, 1/4W resistor	(brown-black-orange)
	R4, 11	47 kilohm, 5%, 1/4W resistor	(yellow-violet-orange)
	C12, 13	22 pF ceramic radial capacitor	
	C1, 2, 3, 4, 6, 7, 8, 9, 10, 11, 15, 16, 17	0.1 μF ceramic axial capacitor	
	Y1	10 MHz crystal	
	D7, 8	1N4148 switching diode (polarized)	
	D3	1N4001 diode rectifier (polarized)	
	GND1	Ground grabber — #18 wire	
	SW2, 3	Pushbutton switch	
	POT1	5 kilohm thumbwheel one-turn potentiometer	
	TMP1	LM34DZ temperature sensor — TO-92 package	
	REG1	LM340T-5.0 voltage regulator — 5 V @ 1 A - TO-220 package	
	SW1	Toggle switch	
	CON3	Power supply connector —2.1 mm barrel connector	
	D1, 2, 4, 5, 6	Red LED, high brightness, T-1 package (polarized)	
	U3S	40-pin DIP socket	
	U1S	16-pin DIP socket	
	U2S	8-pin DIP socket	
	C5, 14	33 μF electrolytic capacitor (polarized)	
	CON2	DB-9 female serial cable connector	
	CON1	Modular connector — side entry, 6 position	
	RPG1	RPG — Bourns 3315C-1-006	
	RPG1-knob	RPG knob with 1/8" diameter hole and set screws	
	J1, H3	Two 1 × 2 headers, cut from S1011-36	
	H1	One 1 × 12 header, cut from S1011-36	
	LCD1S	2 × 7 header, cut from S2011-36	
	LCD1S	Two 1 × 1 headers, cut from S1011-36	
		WASH FLUX RESIDUE FROM BOARD	
	LCD1	LCD module, 8 × 2, high contrast	
	Corners	Four 0.25" dia × 0.625" threaded standoffs and four 4-40 × 1/4" machine screws	

Figure A1-4 Suggested sequence for stuffing parts.

D3, the 1N4001 rectifier, is another polarized component. Don't cut the leads until after it has been inserted in the board and soldered in place. Save the excess leads for possible use with the GND1 (ground grabber) pads discussed in the next step. The rectifier has a bar at one end, as does the silkscreen on the board. Just insert it the same way. Its role is to keep the board from frying if a wall wart with power and ground reversed is plugged into the power jack. It is cheap insurance. The specified wall wart (Digi-Key No. T402-P5P) is neither helped nor hurt by this rectifier's presence.

The two holes labeled GND1 located above the 40-pin DIP pattern, U3, are intended to be stuffed with a piece of bare #18 AWG heavy solid wire bent into the shape of a U. After it has been soldered into the two GND1 pads, it should rise about 1/4″ above the board. It serves as a "ground grabber" for an oscilloscope's ground clip. If you have no #18 wire, use one of the excess leads left over from the rectifier, D3, discussed in the previous step. Solder each end of the wire in place on both the top and bottom pads to add sturdiness to the wire. Cut off any extra length from the wires beneath the board using a flush-cutting diagonal cutter.

The LM34DZ temperature sensor, TMP1, is mounted in the three holes in the upper left-hand corner of the board. You might mount the sensor so that its cylindrical back lies flat against the board and the "LM34" lettering is right-side up. To do this, first bend the middle lead away from the flat surface that holds the lettering, about 1/16″ away from the body of the part. Then bend the two outer leads parallel to that lead but about 1/8″ away from the body of the part. Insert it onto the board and solder just the middle lead. Now, rock the part until it is positioned with its flat surface parallel to the surface of the board and then solder the remaining two leads. Cut off the excess leads.

When you insert REG1, the 5 V voltage regulator, note that if you bend the leads in the right place, the hole in the regulator will line up with the hole in the board sufficiently closely to clamp it to the board with a 1/4″-long machine screw and nut. Do the clamping first and the soldering second so as not to stress the leads.

Mount the power switch, SW1, soldering just one pin and then looking from the top of the board to see that all four of its tiny plastic feet are in contact with the board. If not, then align the switch so that they are. If care is not taken, this is the one component on the board that can easily be askew after it has been soldered in place.

Mount the power supply connector, CON3. The holes for CON3 will require a lot of solder to fill up. However, the way the connector is built, you should not have trouble with solder slipping between the board and the connector and shorting the pins together.

Looking at the schematic of Figure A1-2, you will see that the power switch is located on the output of the voltage regulator. This is done for two reasons. First, when turning on power to the board, the input from the switch is already at 5 V, giving a fast risetime to the VDD input. This is one of the requirements for reliable startup. Second, when turning off power to the board, VDD is driven to ground, assuring the resetting of the PIC18F452 in spite of parasitic power coming in from a serial port connection to a PC.

Plug in the wall wart power supply (Digi-Key No. T402-P5P), turn on the power switch, and check that VDD is $+5$ V ($\pm 10\%$) relative to GND on the board. Remove the wall wart's plug from the board as you add parts to the board.

Be very careful with the insertion of the (polarized) LEDs, D1, D2, D4, D5, and D6. I suggest that you insert the power indicator LED, D1, first without soldering it in (yet). The long lead of the LED (the anode) should go in the hole closer to the top of the board. Before soldering it, apply power and turn on the power switch by toggling it toward the top of the board. Wiggle the LED if necessary to get it to light up. If it doesn't, reverse the leads and try again.

The remaining LEDs are driven by the PIC, so they won't light up without a little help. For every one of them, the long lead should go in the hole closer to the top of the board.

To light up D2, short the PIC's A4 pin to GND.
To light up D4, short the PIC's A3 pin to VDD.
To light up D5, short the PIC's A2 pin to VDD.
To light up D6, short the PIC's A1 pin to VDD.

Once again, check that VDD = 5 V. If you don't have a voltmeter available, just check that the power LED turns on when power is applied and the power switch is turned on. This is an important check before stuffing the 40-pin DIP socket because a short to ground beneath the socket is hard to see. If the power LED doesn't turn on after stuffing the 40-pin socket, you want to know that it did turn on before stuffing the socket and therefore the problem has to do with the soldering associated with the socket and not something you did earlier. This really shouldn't happen since the socket stands off from the board. But check it. In fact, you really should give everything a visual check. The green solder mask is designed to prevent bridging between adjacent pins, but a visual check is worth your while.

Note that all three DIP sockets have a notch at one end. The notched end should be located closest to the top of the board, aligning with the notch shown in the silkscreened DIP socket outline on the board. The notch is there to guide the insertion of the IC itself, with the IC's notch aligned with the notch on the DIP socket.

The two electrolytic capacitors, C5 and C14, are polarized. Put the side marked with the "−" in the hole closest to the bottom of the board.

Add the DB-9 connector, CON2, next. The DB-9 connector has two spring-loaded feet that help avoid strain on the actual pins. After inserting the connector in place, solder the feet to the pads that surround them. Then solder the 9 pins. This connector is used for a serial cable to a PC, for use by the QwikBug debugger program.

The modular connector, CON1, has two plastic strain-relief feet. These are hard to get through the holes. I suggest that you put the board down flat on the mat and put the 9 pins in their respective holes. Then, inclining the connector a little so that the pins remain in the holes, press hard on the top of the connector until it just snaps in place. Check that all of the pins made it through the holes. Then solder them in place. The modular connector just requires that you make sure it is flush to the board after soldering one pin and before soldering the rest. This connector is used by Microchip's ICD2, their low-cost, in-circuit debugger.

The RPG, RPG1, has a plastic pin on one side that must be put through the second hole on the board. It is designed to keep the RPG from turning and stressing the leads if the nut is a little loose. You'll have to bend the leads toward the rotating shaft of the RPG and almost to a right angle. Tighten the nut with a wrench, but not very tight. The shaft of the RPG is plastic and will break off if tightened too much. Just tighten it casually tight. If it ever seems loose, you can tighten it again, but tighter. The specified knob is a first-class knob in that it fits so well, shrouding most of the protruding shaft of the RPG. You will need a small 3/64″ Allen wrench to tighten the knob onto the shaft. Don't tighten too tight. You won't damage the knob, but you can easily round the edges of the Allen wrench so that it no longer will tighten anything. Be sure to solder each of the three RPG leads from the *back* of the board, where the soldering iron tip can come into contact with the RPG lead and the pad to which it is being soldered. I must have soldered all of the RPG leads for the boards in my lab from the front, because, one by one, the RPGs have failed with cold solder joints. Resoldering from the back cured each one, a solution that should have been carried out in the first place.

Install the single-row and dual-row headers next. There is a header, H2, inside the 40-pin DIP socket outline that you will not stuff. It is there to support the use of the QwikFlash board with additional QwikProto boards to build a college laboratory with peripheral chips and circuitry beyond that of the QwikFlash board itself. (For more information, see Appendix A2.)

There are two other headers that you may choose not to stuff. If you will be using Microchip's in-circuit debugger for the PIC18F452 and not the QwikBug debugger program, don't bother to stuff J1 with a 2-pin header. A jumper on that header lets QwikBug regain control when a user program is being executed. The pressing of any key on the PC will stop the running of the user program and return control to the QwikBug monitor program.

The other header that you may choose not to stuff is H3 at the bottom of the board. Unless you will be using your board together with another QwikFlash board, you won't be using the QwikFlash instrument option, for which this header serves as its input pins.

If you are stuffing J1 and/or H3, the optional 2-pin headers discussed above, then cut a 2-pin section from the single-row header strip. Insert the short-sided pins of the header into J1 or H3 **from above the board**. Holding the header in place with a towel (serving as a hot pad to keep your finger from being burned), solder one pin. Check the alignment carefully and fix it before soldering the other pin.

Cut a 12-pin section from a single-row header strip. Insert the short-sided pins of the header into H1 **from above the board**. Solder one end pin. Then, with the soldering iron on the same pin, make sure the pins are perpendicular to the board. (Don't leave the iron on the pin longer than is needed to loosen the solder.) Solder the other end of the strip and check the perpendicularity again. Then solder all of the pins, including the very first pin soldered (to forestall a possible cold solder joint).

If you have purchased the optional seven-position terminal block mentioned in Section A1.3, then solder it into the seven holes located at the top of the board with the seven openings for add-on wire connections directed out from the board. This terminal block supports the easy connection of external devices (e.g., a magnetic card reader or a stepper motor) to the board. Leave the excess length of the pins intact, to simplify the additional wiring needed to connect a terminal to the PIC18F452 or to a component on the QwikFlash board.

Use the flush-cutting diagonal cutters to cut off a 2×7 section of the dual-row header strip. The 2×7 pattern of holes for LCD1, the LCD display, is to be stuffed with the short-sided pins of the header **from beneath the board**. Solder a corner pin and ensure that the header is flush with the board before continuing with the opposite corner followed by another check. Then solder the remaining pins.

Cut two 1-pin sections from the single-row header strip. These will be used in the mounting of the LCD display's two bottom corners. Mount them **from beneath the board** in the same way as was done for the 2×7 dual-row header already installed for the LCD display.

A1.7 FLUX REMOVAL

Before the last construction step of mounting the LCD display, you need to clean the excess flux off both the front and the rear of the board. If you have used resin-core solder, clean the board with isopropyl alcohol, a low-cost solvent from your grocery store or drugstore. Pour some alcohol over the the rear of the board, where most of the excess flux is concentrated. Rub all contacts with an old toothbrush. Do the same on the front of the board. Pour some more alcohol over the back of the board and scrub again, to wash away as much of the dissolved flux as possible. Finally, if you have a bread pan or other small container that the board will fit into, put 1/4″ inch of alcohol in it and slosh the board around in it. You are again trying to remove the dissolved flux and make the surface of the board presentable and no longer tacky. Finally, wash the board with water under a faucet. To speed up drying, you can use a hair dryer without fear of hurting anything on the board with that amount of heat.

If you have used water-soluble-core solder such as Kester's Flux 331, the cleanup is much easier, but no less important since the residue is conductive. Just wash it under a faucet, rubbing all contacts with a toothbrush. The rubbing is very important because while the residue is water soluble, it can use a little help from you. Again, a hair dryer will speed up the drying process. Until the board is dry, it probably won't run a test program.

A1.8 PERFORMANCE VERIFICATION BEFORE LCD INSTALLATION

Before going on to mount the LCD display or to insert any of the integrated circuits, it is time to check the board for functionality. First apply power and check that you have +5 V on the pad labeled VDD in the upper left-hand corner (to the right of the TMP1 temperature sensor) relative to the GND1 ground grabber. This is really one last check against a short to ground, but you also don't want to power up the PIC18F452 if the supply voltage is anything other than +5 V. (The unregulated supply voltage coming onto the board from the "9 V" unregulated wall wart may actually be as high as 13 V or so and is higher than you want to apply accidently to the PIC18F452's VDD pins.)

With power turned off, insert a PIC18F452 programmed with the QFPV performance verification code mentioned in Section A1.1 into the U3 socket. Make sure that the notch at one end of the chip is oriented toward the top of the board (i.e., toward the GND1 ground grabber). Also make sure that each pin of the IC is centered on its socket hole so that as you insert the IC into the socket, each pin drops down into its socket hole rather than doing a "deep-knee bend" above the socket hole. Power up the board. The "Alive" LED should blink on for 2.5 seconds, off for 2.5 seconds, on for 2.5 seconds, etc. Turning the RPG should cause the D4 and D5 LEDs to count up or down in binary, depending on the direction of turning. Each press and release of the pushbutton switch in the lower right-hand corner should change the state of the D6 LED.

Remove power from the board and then remove the PIC microcontroller chip with a small screwdriver inserted from the bottom of the board. (Be careful to get between the chip and the socket and not between the socket and the board.) Twist the screwdriver to raise the bottom edge of the chip. Being careful to slide the screwdriver along the back side of the chip so as not to break a rib of the socket, twist it until the chip is loose.

A1.9 LCD INSTALLATION

Remove the piece of plastic film from the front of the LCD display. Fit the LCD display over the pins **from beneath the board**. Solder a corner pin of the 2 × 7 header and check the alignment. Then solder the diagonally opposite pin at the bottom of the LCD display, filling the mounting hole completely. Check the alignment of the LCD display relative to the slot in the board into which it fits. If the gaps between the top and bottom edges of the LCD display and the board are not uniform from left to right, then touch one of the two soldered pins and rotate the LCD display appropriately. Then solder the remaining pins. Don't bother to wash these solder joints. Keep the LCD dry from now on.

Finally, add four feet to the four corners of the board, using four standoffs and four 1/4″ -long machine screws.

A1.10 PERFORMANCE VERIFICATION

Again, install the PIC18F452 coded with the QFPV program. If you do not have such a chip available to you (e.g., in a college lab), then carry out the QwikBug installation and verification process of Section A1.11 first, subsequently using QwikBug to download QFPV.hex to the QwikFlash board and to run it.

Insert the MAX522 DAC chip in the 8-pin socket, with its notch directed toward the top of the board. Power up your board. Each component should perform as follows.

"Alive" LED—It should blink on for 2.5 seconds, off for 2.5 seconds, on for 2.5 seconds, etc.

RPG—The RPG controls the state of a two-bit binary counter, displayed on two of the three LCDs above U3. CW turning should increment the counter while CCW turning should decrement the counter.

Pushbutton switch, Potentiometer, and LCD—Each press and release of the pushbutton switch, SW3, in the lower right-hand corner of the board should toggle the right LED, D6 (from on to off or from off to on). If the LED is off, then turning the pot from fully CCW to fully CW should change the hex number displayed in the lower right-hand corner of the LCD from 00 to FF. If the D6 LED is on, then just the opposite should happen; turning the pot from fully CCW to fully CW should change the hex number displayed in the lower right-hand corner of the LCD from FF to 00.

Pot→DAC→ADC→LCD—Connect the 3″-long, two-conductor flex cable mentioned in Section A1.3 between the DAC-A/GND pins at the left end of the top terminal strip to the E2-AN7/GND pins on the same strip. Press the SW3 pushbutton to turn off the D6 LED. The pot output is converted through the PIC18F452's AN4 DAC input to the hex value displayed on the bottom row of the LCD display. It is also used to drive the DAC-A output that is fed back through the flex cable to the AN7 DAC input. The resulting value is what is displayed in the top row of the LCD display and should closely follow what is displayed on the bottom row as the potentiometer is turned. As the pot is turned from fully CCW to fully CW, the top number should track the bottom number (within a few counts) from 00 to FF.

Reconnect the flex cable between the DAC-B/GND pins and the E2-AN6/GND pins. Press the SW3 pushbutton to turn on the D6 LED. The pot output is converted through the PIC18F452's AN4 DAC input *and complemented* to form the hex value displayed on the bottom row of the LCD display. This complemented value is also used to drive the DAC-B output that is fed back through the flex cable to the AN7 DAC input. The resulting value is what is displayed in the top row of the LCD display and should closely follow what is displayed on the bottom row as the potentiometer is turned. This time, as the pot is turned from fully CCW to fully CW, the top number should track the bottom number (within a few counts) from FF to 00.

Temperature sensor verification—The LM34 temperature sensor in the upper left-hand corner of the QwikFlash board should produce a display of the room temperature in the lower left-hand corner of the LCD display. Holding a warm finger on the LM34 should cause the displayed temperature to rise.

A1.11 QWIKBUG PERFORMANCE VERIFICATION

With power turned off, put a PIC18F452 chip with the QwikBug monitor installed into socket U3. (The installation of the monitor into the PIC18F452 chip is discussed in Appendix A4 and requires access to an ICD2 in-circuit debugger or to the "hobby" PIC programmer discussed there.) Install a MAX232A chip in socket U1. Make sure that the chip has the "A" suffix because the original MAX232 chip will not work without much bigger capacitors for its dc-to-dc converters. (Refer to Figure 18-7.) Connect the QwikFlash board to the PC with a normal serial cable (with "straight through" connections of pins—2–2, 3–3, and 5–5—on the two DB-9 connectors).

Start up the Tera Term Pro terminal emulator utility as discussed in Section 5.8, with the serial port setup of Figure 5-8 (but note the comment about the "line delay" setup parameter in Section A4.5). Turn on the power to the QwikFlash board. You should see the PC display the QwikBug startup "help" message. Press the F1 key to see the "help" message rewritten. This will establish that serial communications are working in both directions.

Using the F3 key, send the QFPV.hex file to the board. Then reset the chip (F4 key) and run the QFPV program (F7 key). This will establish that you can load programs satisfactorily. As pointed out in Section A4.5, if you are using Tera Term Pro and the download is not completed successfully, increase Tera Term Pro's line delay to "20 ms/line," save this new setup, and try again. It is the author's experience that Tera Term Pro was developed several years ago and does not handle the line delay accurately for a present-generation fast computer. A setting of "20 ms/line" on this computer produced a line delay that varied somewhat from line to line but that was always more than the required 10 ms/line.

Appendix

A2

LABORATORY DEVELOPMENT WITH THE QWIKPROTO ADD-ON BOARD

A2.1 BOARD AND PARTS

In addition to the QwikFlash board described in Appendix A1, there is also a QwikProto board available for expanding I/O resources, as would be helpful for setting up a college laboratory around the PIC18F452 microcontroller. For information on how to get this board for setting up a college laboratory, check *www.microdesignsinc.com*, or contact the author at jpeatman@mindspring.com.

Figure A2-1 shows the board's "pads and top silk" artwork. The board is exactly the same 4″ × 4″ size as the QwikFlash board. It is connected to the QwikFlash board via a 16-conductor ribbon cable extending from the H2 header mounted beneath the PIC18F452 socket to a similar H1 header mounted beneath the QwikProto board, as illustrated in Figure A2-2. Additional QwikProto boards can be daisy-chained together with short jumper ribbon cables extending from the H3 header mounted beneath one board to the H1 header mounted beneath the next. In this way, a variety of laboratory projects can be "mixed and matched" together.

Figure A2-3 identifies parts that can be used to stuff the board and to implement the ribbon-cable connection between the QwikFlash board and the QwikProto board. An "IDC crimping tool" is included for squeezing the ribbon-cable connectors onto the ribbon cable. A bench vise can serve the same purpose. Cover the jaws of the vise with masking tape so as not to score the connector as you squeeze it onto the end of a piece of ribbon cable. For a lab, get lots of the 2 × 8 headers and connectors. Then, even if some are destroyed in the process of crimping the ribbon cable into a connector, others will be available. The wirewrap wire is for making connections between the H2 header and the components to

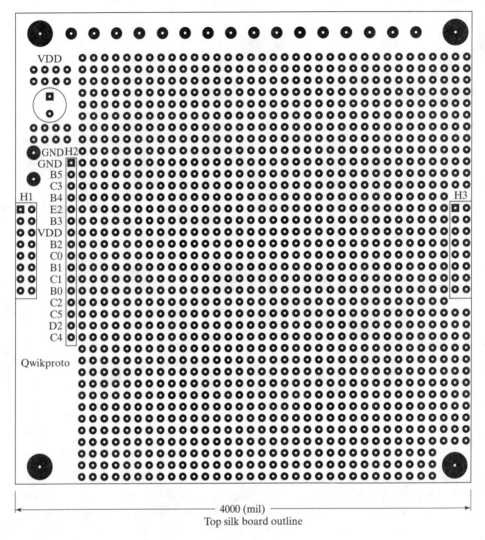

Figure A2-1 QwikProto board's "pads and top silk" artwork

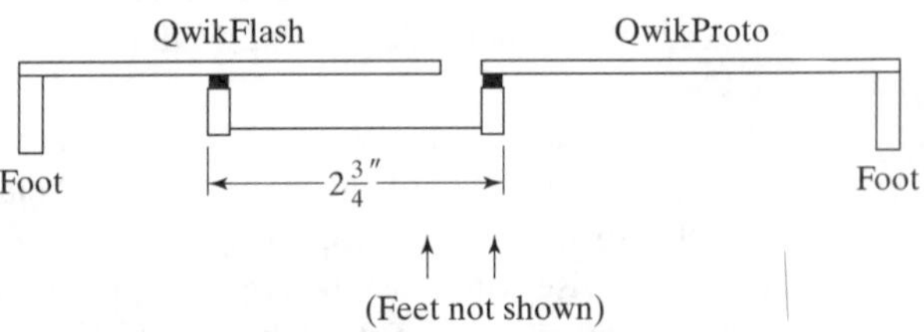

Figure A2-2 Board interconnection.

Quantity	Part number	Distibutor	Part description	Board designation	Price each	Minimum quantity	Total price
2	109567	Jameco	2 × 8 pin male header	H1 to QwikFlash	0.29	1	0.58
2	119466	Jameco	2 × 8 pin socket connector	H1 to QwikFlash	0.35	1	0.70
1	37671	Jameco	10 feet of 16-conductor gray ribbon cable	H1 to QwikFlash	1.75	10 feet	1.75
1	73251	Jameco	IDC crimping tool	H1 sockets	11.95	1	11.95
1	22664	Jameco	100 feet of white 30 AWG wirewrap wire		3.95	100 feet	3.95
1	P835	Digi-Key	33 uf @ 35V polarized electrolytic capacitor	VDD to GND	0.34	1	0.34
						Total =	**19.27**
Jameco - for price and availability information, go to www.jameco.com - add $5.00 for orders under $20.							

Figure A2-3 QwikProto board parts and prices

be added to the board. For stripping the ends of wirewrap wire, I like Radio Shack's wire-wrapping tool No. 276-1570 ($7.49). It includes an excellent little stripper stored in its handle.

A2.2 CONSTRUCTION

Before you can add the 2 × 8 header beneath the QwikFlash board, you will have to remove the two middle ribs of the 40-pin socket so that you can reach the 2 × 8 array of pins with a soldering iron. I use a soldering iron to melt a gap in the rib and then use a flush-cutting diagonal cutter to finish removing the entire rib. Just cutting the rib without first melting the gap puts a stress on the other ribs that may cause them to break. (This is not a serious problem, but it is an avoidable one.)

A2.3 CONSTRAINTS PLACED ON PIN USE

Figure A2-4 lists the pins brought over to this board from the QwikFlash board as well as any constraints on their use. Thus, the three pins used by the digital-to-analog converter on the QwikFlash board can all be used by further expansion circuitry as either inputs or outputs. Since the DAC does not *drive* any of these three pins, at most the only consequence of their arbitrary further use will be erratic output voltages appearing on the DAC outputs. Such erratic behavior is not even a possibility if only the SPI/I^2C pins are used, and not the RC0 pin. Thus, the full expansion possibilities of either the SPI bus or the I^2C bus can be exploited.

The RC0/T1OSO and RC1/T1OSI pins can be used to explore the possibilities of using a 32,768 Hz crystal as the external clock for Timer1 and thereby the clock for the chip itself, as discussed in conjunction with Figures 20-10 through 20-12. Doing this requires the removal of the DAC from the board (or rewiring its connection from RC0 to an alternative undedicated pin).

An interesting feature of the PIC18F452 is its use of either its RB3 pin or its RC1 pin as the alternative function, CCP2. The choice is made with the CCP2MX bit in one of the configuration bytes for

PIN	QwikFlash connections	Usage comments
RB0/INT0	H1 header	
RB1/INT1	H1 header	
RB2/INT2		
RB3/CCP2		Optional CCP2 pin
RB4		
RB5		
RC0/T1OSO/T1CKI	Chip select for DAC	
RC1/T1OSI/CCP2	H3 header	Optional CCP2 pin
RC2/CCP1	H1 header	
RC3/SCK/SCL	SPI clock out to DAC	OK for SPI/I^2C use
RC4/SDI/SDA		OK for SPI/I^2C use
RC5/SDO	SPI data out to DAC	OK for SPI use
RD2		Best used as input, not output (because of LCD) — see text
RE2/AN7	H1 header	
VDD	Most of 200 ma supply current available here	
GND		

Figure A2-4 QwikFlash connections and usage comments

the chip (refer to Figure 20-1). If RC0 and RC1 are used as 32,768 Hz crystal inputs to Timer1, the CCP2 function can be moved to the RB3 pin so as not to lose *its* functionality.

Figure A2-4 also lists RD2 as best serving as an input, not an output. The rationale for this statement lies in the use of RD4 . . . 7 as outputs to the LCD display. The other three pins of PORTD serve as dedicated inputs from the RPG and the pushbutton. As presently written, the routines that write to the LCD display blindly write to PORTD as if all four lower bits are inputs and will not be affected if garbage is written to them. Should RD2 be set up as an output, then the LCD display routines would need to be rewritten so as not to affect the output on RD2.

A2.4 PROJECT IDEAS

Several project ideas have been considered in earlier chapters, including the stepper motor drive of Figure 16-5. The stepper motor and its drive chip can be mounted on the QwikProto board, as shown in Figure A2-5, with connections made to the PIC18F452 through the ribbon-cable connection to the QwikFlash board.

The Analog Devices' 3-pin TMP04 temperature sensor circuit of Figure 13-14 is also shown in Figure A2-5. It provides a vehicle for using CCP1 or CCP2 to capture input time intervals, converting them to either Fahrenheit or Centigrade temperature, with arbitrary resolution, with the help of the math subroutines of Chapter 14.

Agilent Technologies' HLCP-J100, ten-segment, low-current bar graph display and a 1 kΩ SIP resistor pack driven from two 74HC595 double-buffered shift registers provide a good example of SPI use.

The QwikProto board can serve as the home for a second PIC18F452 (or the 28-pin PIC18F252) connected to the PIC18F452 on the QwikFlash board using the SPI in a master–slave relationship. The slave PIC microcontroller can decipher a keypad into keycodes using the circuit of Figure 19-11 and returning the keycode of a newly pressed key in response to periodic queries from the master PIC microcontroller. This serves as a fine example of master–slave interactions on the SPI bus.

Sharp Microelectronics' IS1U60 is a low-cost, three-terminal device for demodulating the 38 kHz output of a TV/VCR/etc. remote into 5 V pulses that can be deciphered by the CCP1 or CCP2 capture input of the PIC18F452. It makes an interesting keypad input to the PIC microcontroller and uses only a single pin to do so. A digital scope can capture the IS1U60 output for each of the digit keys on the remote so that you know what you are trying to do to distinguish one pattern from another. The inner tube from a paper towel roll slid over the end of the remote can be used to confine the IR output to a single QwikFlash board and prevent the output from being picked up by other QwikFlash boards in a lab.

Figure A2-5

For short-range wireless control using RF data transmission, RF Modulation (www.rfm.com) makes low-cost transmitters and receivers. Check their TX5003 and RX5003 303.825 MHz transmitter and receiver modules. Also check Microchip's rfPIC12C509 "AF Enhanced Microcontroller with UHF ASK/FSK Transmitter" and related parts just being introduced as this book is being completed.

Another low-cost, interesting device is the Model 1490 eight-direction digital compass sensor made by Dinsmore Instrument Company.

A search for "robotics" and "RC control" on a search engine like www.google.com will turn up a variety of low-cost devices.

The same Jameco mail-order distributor and source of the materials of Figure A2-3 is also a good source of miscellaneous kits and parts for getting a head start on some project ideas.

Two other sources of unusual I/O devices at relatively low cost are B. G. Micro, www.bgmicro.com and Marlin P. Jones & Assoc., Inc., www.mpja.com. These companies buy surplus electronic parts that companies sell before the end of their fiscal year to reduce their year-end tax on inventory. Thus, for example, the Magtek magnetic card reader discussed in Section 16.2 was a $5 surplus item from B. G. Micro.

A2.5 THE AUTHOR'S LABORATORY STATIONS

For our instructional laboratory at Georgia Tech, we have mounted a QwikFlash board and a QwikProto board side by side on the little stand shown in Figure A2-5. The stand is formed from an 8¼″ wide × 8½″ sheet of aluminum with eight ⅛″-diameter mounting holes, four for each of the boards and drilled so as to align each board with an upper corner of the stand. The aluminum has been folded on a line 4½″ from the top, with an angle of about 45°. Finally, the stand has been commercially anodized to give it a black finish. Four rubber feet (Digi-Key No. SJ5523) on the bottom give the stand a solid feel.

The 0.625″ standoffs listed in Figure A1-1 provide sufficient clearance for the connectors used with the ribbon cable between the two boards. If any other holes are needed (e.g., to provide clearance for a stepper motor that is deeper than the 0.625″ allowed by the standoffs), these are most easily punched out before the aluminum has been folded.

My favorite add-on device is a stepper motor. With the drive circuit of Figure 16-5, it is easy to add to the QwikProto board. It provides a range of lab projects, starting with stepping it once per loop time (i.e., 100 steps/second), then reversing direction with each push of the pushbutton. CCP1 or CCP2 "compare" interrupts can be used to step the motor at a variable rate set in with the RPG, up to the point where the motor drops out and dithers without stepping. It can be stepped down to just one step per second by using the 24-bit version of Timer1/CCP1 (or Timer3/CCP2), discussed in Section 16.5, to support an interrupt handler that pulses the driver chip's "step" input at the end of each timer-derived step period.

The driver chip of Figure 16-5 will handle stepper motors with four unipolar windings. In contrast to a stepper motor with two bipolar windings (that requires an "H-bridge" controller to be able to reverse the direction of current in each winding), a stepper motor with four unipolar windings only requires the driver to drive each winding to ground. The UCN5804B driver chip can handle a wide range of motor voltages and motor currents. With luck, 5 V unipolar stepper motors appear on the pages of surplus distributors like Marlin P. Jones & Assoc., Inc. (www.mpja.com). I found some listed at $1.95 each. Since the surplus market leads to "here today, gone tomorrow" (they had 403 of the motors in stock), I asked about price breaks and was given a price of $0.50 each for 100 units. So I bought 100 units! One of these is shown in exploded form in Figure A2-6.

This motor's winding resistance of 20 ohms means that the motor will draw 250 mA from the power supply. I use the motor with the "full-step, wave-drive sequence" shown in Figure 16-5 so as to limit the draw on the power supply to just 250 mA, rather than the 500 mA resulting from either of the other two

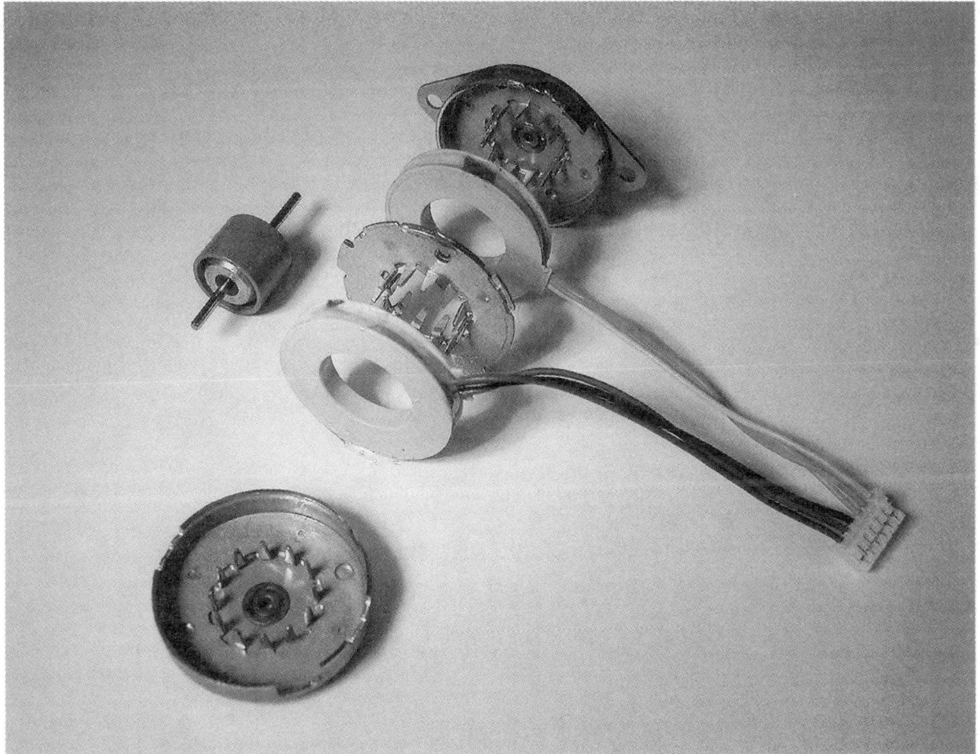

Figure A2-6

operating modes of that figure. I also have changed from the 9 V @ 200 mA wall transformer of Figure A1-1 to a 9 V @ 300 mA wall transformer (Mouser No. 412-109034). A heavier-duty wall transformer might be used (e.g., 9 V @ 500 mA) since the voltage regulator on the board is rated for up to 1 ampere.

To find a source for the Allegro Microsystems UCN5804B stepper motor translator/driver chip, go to www.findchips.com and enter UCN5804B. This is a wonderful Web site for finding distributors for any chip and for being steered to each distributor's pricing and availability information. (Newark Electronics should be listed as one of the sources.)

Also shown in Figure A2-5 is the magnetic card reader of Figure 16-1, with the simple connections to the PIC18F452 microcontroller shown in Figure 16-2. Once again, these card readers were obtained from a surplus distributor—B. G. Micro in this case (www.bgmicro.com)—and for less than $5.00 each. The card reader affords the opportunity to retrieve characters bit by bit under interrupt control. The little 8 × 2 LCD can be used to display eight characters at a time:

```
MCR    1
;1234567
```

The RPG can be used to cycle among five groups of eight characters making up the card's contents of up to 40 characters. Alternatively, the PIC18F452's UART can be used to display each successive character in sequence on the PC's monitor. As a character is formed into ASCII code in **WREG**, a call of the following **TXbyte** subroutine will send it to the PC's monitor. At 19,200 baud, the transmission of each character takes only about half a millisecond. The example magnetic card scan of Figure 16-2c takes about 6.5 milleseconds to read in each character, so this subroutine will keep up with the input rate of new characters without requiring buffering.

```
TXbyte
        REPEAT_
        UNTIL_  PIR1,TX1F     ;Wait, if necessary, on previous transfer
        movwf  TXREG          ;Send character
        return
```

Be sure to include in the **Initial** subroutine the initialization of the UART, as described in Chapter 18.

Appendix

A3

USE OF STRUCTURED ASSEMBLER WITH MPLAB USER INTERFACE

James M. Eubanks

*MPLAB software does not have to be used in order to create a .hex file. If sasm.exe and mpasmwin.exe are both present on your machine, you may type **sasm ‹filename›** at the DOS prompt in order to create a .hex file. In this example, ‹filename› refers to the .asm file, but the .asm extension can be left off.*

A3.1 INSTALLING SASM

Five files will be added to the MPLAB folder in order to enable the use of the structured assembler. The files can be found at www.picbook.com and are contained in a .zip file called **SASM.zip.** Locate the MPLAB folder, and put the five files that were extracted from the .zip file directly **in the MPLAB folder**. The five files that will be added are listed here.

- Tlsasm.ini—defines the tool suite in the MPLAB program
- Sasm.mtc—tool configuration
- sasm.exe—converts a structured source file to mpasmwin.exe assembler-compatible format
- PIC18.cfg—configuration file for PIC18 series microcontrollers
- PIC16.cfg—configuration file for PIC16 series microcontrollers

After the files are placed in the MPLAB folder, start the MPLAB program. Select **Project > Install Language Tool. . .** from the menu bar. Change the **Language Suite:** to **SASM Suite**. Change the

Tool Name: to **SASM**. For the **Executable:,** click **Browse:** and locate the MPLAB folder. Find and click **sasm.exe**, and then click **OK**. Finally, click the **Windowed** option and click **OK.**

A3.2 SETTING UP THE PROJECT

Open the MPLAB program and select **Project > New Project.** Find the folder where you want to create your project. (This will be the folder containing your .asm file; e.g., C:\Work.) Enter the name of your project as ‹filename›.pjt. It is a good idea to name your project according to your .asm file. (If your .asm file is called Project1.asm, your project will most likely be called Project1.pjt.) Click **OK**. An **Edit Project** window should appear and the **Target Filename** field should show ‹filename›.hex. Pick the **Development Mode:** you need (editor, ICD2, etc.). Change the **Language Tool Suite:** to **SASM Suite**. Under the **Project Files** field, click on the [.hex] file shown and then click **Node Properties. . . .** Make sure the correct part is selected (e.g., click 18 for 18F452.) Click **OK.** Now click **Add Node . . .** and locate the .asm file you are working with. Click on the .asm file and click **OK.** Now click **OK** in the **Edit Project** window. Select **Project > Make Project**, and the file should be assembled properly. The .hex file has been created and is ready to be programmed into the PIC18F452.

A3.3 USE OF THE QWIKADDRESS UTILITY

- An error file with extension .err will be created if any errors occur in either the .asm file or the .apr file. Use David Flowers' QwikAddress utility (described in Appendix A5) to obtain the line number of each error reflected back to the .asm file, regardless of whether it was generated by the structured assembly preprocessor or the assembler.
- If the ICD2, in-circuit debugger, is being used, the same QwikAddress utility can be employed to translate any point in the source file into its corresponding program memory address. This capability is useful when setting a breakpoint address.

Appendix

A4

QWIKBUG MONITOR PROGRAM

Burt Sims

A4.1 INTRODUCTION

QwikBug is a resident monitor program for the Microchip PIC18F452 microcontroller with its flash program memory and its built-in "background debug mode." QwikBug supports the downloading of a user program from the PC to the QwikFlash board. The CPU can be reset and the program then run from reset. For debugging, a breakpoint address can be entered and the program again run from reset to the breakpoint. The value of a variable or SFR can be modified before continuing. Selected variables and SFRs can be set up as watch variables and displayed in response to running again to the breakpoint or single-stepping from the breakpoint.

The installation of QwikBug into a PIC18F452 chip currently requires the one-time use of Microchip's ICD2 in-circuit debugger for programming the QwikBug code into the PIC18F452 chip, to enable the background debug mode and to set up the vectoring that causes the chip to respond to a power-on reset by ignoring a user program's reset vector at address 0x0000 and instead vector automatically into the QwikBug monitor code. This programming operation using the ICD2 module is discussed in Section A4.3.

As this book was being completed, David Flowers (creator of the QwikAddress utility described in Appendix A5) had begun working on a QwikProgram utility that could make use of a low-cost, widely available "hobby" programmer called the P16PRO PIC Programmer to program QwikBug into a PIC18F452. His QwikProgram utility is described in Section A4.4.

A4.2 RESOURCES USED

QwikBug resides in the high addresses of the program memory. Since the PIC18F452 has a huge program memory of 16,384 16-bit words, QwikBug's residence in upper memory will not cramp the space needed for most user programs. QwikBug shares the program stack with the user program, but since the PIC18F452 supports a large stack of 31 levels, this should never cause a user program to run out of stack space. QwikBug reserves the last 256 bytes of RAM (i.e., Bank 5) for its own use, leaving the remaining 1280 bytes of RAM for use by the user program. When a user program is downloaded to the PIC18F452, the code intended to set the configuration bytes (e.g., to select the oscillator type) is ignored. The configuration bytes will have already been programmed along with the programming of QwikBug into the chip. QwikBug takes over the on-chip UART, and thereby pins RC7 and RC6, to support serial communication with a PC at 19,200 baud. It also takes away pins RB7 and RB6 from the user. Microchip's ICD2 in-circuit debugger uses these two pins for its own special communication protocol with the chip. Because QwikBug uses the background debug mode built into the chip to support ICD2, these pins are lost to the user. The one use made of these pins by QwikBug occurs when executing a user program. With the J1 jumper in place on the QwikFlash board, a falling edge occurring as a character is received into the PIC18F452's UART is steered to the RB6 pin (see the schematic for the board, Figure A1-2). This causes the switch from user program execution to QwikBug monitor execution.

Whereas the MPLAB interface to the QwikFlash board via the ICD2 module supports the setting of watch variables with an internally displayed list, Tera Term Pro's interface to the QwikFlash board provides no such support. However, David Flowers' QwikAddress utility, discussed in Appendix A5, provides this support in a separate window. It also supports the setting of breakpoints by quickly helping to identify the program address of any subroutine and from there to any point in a subroutine. This utility is also a help to MPLAB users who have source code written with the structured assembly constructs of Chapter 6, since MPLAB deals with the .apr file that generated the assembler output files, whereas a user is more familiar with the original .asm file. QwikAddress deals with the .asm file and the .lst file to produce its concise lists of addresses.

Neither the user program's use of the reset vector address 0x0000 nor its interrupt vector addresses are affected by QwikBug. The template programs in this book show a "nop" instruction followed by a "goto Mainline" instruction at address 0x0000. These were inserted before it was fully understood how the background debug mode in this new chip would work. The earlier-generation PIC16F877 microcontroller's background debug mode did require a "nop" at address 0x0000. We postulated that we might have to copy the user program's reset vector code to a high memory address when downloading the user program and then initiate execution from there to run the user program from reset. Doing this would require a "goto Mainline" instruction rather than a "bra Mainline" instruction. The designers of the background debug mode for the PIC18F452 microcontroller allow the user program's reset vector to be downloaded and installed directly at address 0x0000 and executed from there, so none of our precautions turned out to be necessary.

A4.3 INSTALLATION OF QWIKBUG USING ICD2 MODULE

Download the QwikBug monitor from www.picbook.com. A new PIC18F452 chip will have its pins flared out, to support their use with automatic insertion equipment. After placing the chip on a conductive surface like a sheet of aluminum foil placed on a flat surface and touching the conductive surface with both hands to discharge any static electicity, rock one side of pins against the surface to bend them in, all at one time. Do the same on the other side of pins so that the two rows of pins are bent until they are parallel to each other, rather than flared out. With the power plug disconnected from the QwikFlash board, the PIC18F452 chip can be inserted into the 40-pin IC socket, with the chip's notch oriented toward the top of the board. Connect the QwikFlash board's power supply and turn on its power.

Connect Microchip's ICD2 in-circuit debugger to the PC with either its serial cable or its USB cable. If the serial-cable configuration is used, the ICD2 module must be powered by its own 9 V unregulated supply, included with the DV164007 packaging of the ICD2 module. Although the barrel connector for the QwikFlash board's 9 V unregulated supply looks almost identical to the supply that comes with the ICD2 module (and needed for the serial connection but not for the alternative USB connection to the PC), they actually differ in the inside diameter of the "barrel." Electrically they could be interchanged, but mechanically they cannot.

Connect the 9″ cable with modular plugs on each end between the ICD2 module and the QwikFlash board's CON1 connector. Open the MPLAB program installed on the PC. Click on the **Options** pulldown menu and then click on **Development Mode. . . .** Select PIC18F452 from among the choices in the **Processor** window. Select **MPLAB ICD Debugger** and click **OK**. This will open a window labeled MPLAB ICD 2. Click on the **Advanced . . .** button to open the **Configuration Bits** options, the **Programming Options**, and the **Communications** options. In the MPLAB ICD 2 window, you should see a series of diagnostic messages: "Reading MPLAB ICD 2 module product ID; MPLAB ICD 2 Detected; Reading MPLAB ICD 2 firmware version." If you do not get this message, then check that the **Communications** section is correct for your serial or USB cable connection. If you are using the serial cable and communication fails at 57,600 baud, select 19,200 baud and click on the **Reconnect** button to try again.

Having established the connection between ICD2 and the PIC18F452, click on MPLAB IDE's **Window** pulldown menu and click on **Program Memory**. Click on

File → Import → Import to Memory

and go to the directory holding the QwikBug.hex file downloaded from www.picbook.com and select it. Click **OK**. This will download two programs into the **Program Memory** window. One is the code for QwikBug, residing at high memory addresses. The other is a little program called ModifyBDMvector.

Return to the **MPLAB ICD 2 Advanced** window. If the configuration bits have not already been set by the downloading of QwikBug, then select the following:

Oscillator	HS
Watchdog Timer	Disable
Power Up Timer	Enable
Stack Reset	Enable
Osc. Switch Enable	Enable
Brown Out	Enable
Brown Out Voltage	4.5V
Low Voltage Program Disable	
CCP2 Mux	RC1

In the **Programming Options** section, enter

Start Address	0x0000
End Address	0x7bff

This "End Address" will be above the end of the QwikBug code and below the section of memory reserved for ICD2 when **Enable Debug Mode** is selected.

Select **Program Memory** and **Enable Debug Mode**. Click on **Program** at the bottom of the **MPLAB ICD 2 Advanced** window. Programming will take a minute or so. Upon completion the **MPLAB ICD 2 Version . . .** status window should show a series of messages, ending up with ". . . Programming Debug Executive; . . . Programming Configuration Bits; . . . Program Succeeded." (As a further error check, make sure that the "Error" LED on the ICD2 module has not turned on.) This step has enabled the background debug mode used by ICD2 and used by QwikBug when the ICD2 module is no longer attached to the QwikFlash board.

With background debug mode enabled, the PIC18F452 will subsequently come out of power-on reset into the ICD2's "Debug Executive." The next step is to change this so as to come out of power-on reset into QwikBug. In the **MPLAB ICD 2 Version . . .** window, press the **Reconnect** button. In the **MPLAB IDE** window, click on

Debug → Run → Reset

Make sure that the **MPLAB ICD 2 Version . . .** window's last message is "Resetting Target." If, instead, it indicates that this operation failed (or if the ICD2 module's Error LED has turned on), then click on the **Reconnect** button and try again. Then

Debug → Run → Run

The right LED on the QwikFlash board should turn on immediately as a sign that it has completed its job successfully. Immediately remove the modular cable from the QwikFlash board while the program is still running (as indicated by the yellow strip across the bottom of the **MPLAB IDE** window). Then turn off the power to the QwikFlash board. Exit from **MPLAB**.

By letting ICD2 run what it thinks is a user program that it has loaded into program memory, it will actually run a little "ModifyBDMvector" program that will do nothing more than rewrite the power-on vectoring into the QwikBug monitor program rather than into the ICD2's Debug Executive program.

Finally, remember to install the J1 jumper so that control of the board from the PC is not lost once the PIC18F452 chip begins execution of a user program. A press of any PC key returns control to the QwikBug monitor program.

A4.4 INSTALLATION OF QWIKBUG USING THE P16PRO PIC PROGRAMMER

Before ordering this programmer, check www.picbook.com for David Flowers' successfully completed QwikProgram utility. The free utility will program PIC18F452 parts with any program, including QwikBug, using the P16PRO PIC Programmer.

The P16PRO PIC Programmer is a "hobby" programmer that attaches to a PC through the parallel port and makes use of a wall transformer ("wall wart") to supply a high enough dc or ac voltage to generate both the +5 V and the +13 V supplies that it needs to program a part. It is widely available both as an assembled, working board and also in kit form (saving only $4). One source is Amazon Electronics (www.electronics123.com). Their toll-free number is 1-888-549-3749 (USA and Canada). The assembled board is their part CPA96, costing $17.95. The recommended 14 VAC wall transformer is their part BB041, costing $5.95. While some PCs have enough clearance to plug the board directly into the printer port, most users will probably require a DB-25 "straight-through" extension cable, available here as part BB040, costing $4.95. They ship from Ohio by priority mail. All told, the cost is about $30–35, depending on the need for the extension cable.

This programmer can also be used to program many other types of PIC microcontroller parts. A free programming utility is available through Amazon Electronics. A registered version is also available that removes the file-size limitation of the free utility.

To use this programmer, a PIC18F452 is inserted into the programmer and then the programmer is connected to the PC's parallel (i.e., printer) port, either directly or through a cable, but without power applied to the board. The QwikProgram utility is then launched. It begins by prompting for the desired hex file to be programmed into the part. If the QwikBug.hex file has been downloaded from www.picbook.com to the desktop, then it can be selected. It next requests that power be applied to the P16PRO PIC Programmer board followed by the press of any key. The utility then begins programming the part, providing feedback:

```
User program ..................................................
Configuration bytes programmed
QwikBug vector programmed
```

The QwikBug hex file specifies the programming of the DEBUG bit in the CONFIG4L byte (see Figure 20-1). When QwikProgram detects this, it also programs a

```
goto QwikBug
```

instruction into address 0x200028, the BDM (background debug mode) vector address used at power-on reset, breakpoints, and single stepping. It is this last step that is difficult to achieve with standard PIC microcontroller programmers. Finally, the user is prompted to remove power from the programmer, disconnect the programmer from the PC, remove the PIC18F452 from the programmer, and insert it into the socket on the QwikFlash board.

A4.5 QWIKBUG VERIFICATION

Having exited from MPLAB, the PC's serial port is free for use by Tera Term Pro (or another terminal emulator). Set up Tera Term Pro with the serial port setup of Figure 5-8, described in Section 5.8. Connect the QwikFlash board to the PC via a serial cable and begin the execution of QwikBug by turning on the power to the QwikFlash board. You should see QwikBug's start-up "help" message. If a user program is already installed (e.g., the ModifyBDMvector program of Section A4.3), press any key on the PC within four seconds to enter QwikBug. Obtain the QwikFlash Performance Verification file, QFPV.hex, available at www.picbook.com. Using the F3 key, download the QFPV.hex file to the board. Then reset the chip (F4 key) and run the QFPV program (F7 key). This will establish that you can load and run programs satisfactorily. If the download is not completed successfully, increase Tera Term Pro's line delay to "20 ms/line," save this new setup, and try again. It is our experience that Tera Term Pro was developed several years ago and does not handle the line delay accurately for a present-generation fast computer. A setting of "20 ms/line" on this computer produced a line delay that varied somewhat from line to line but that was always more than the required 10 ms/line. There is nothing mysterious about this process that cannot be clarified by connecting a digital scope to the PIC18F452's RX input. By setting the scope to capture a single trace and starting the download, the gaps in the waveform corresponding to pauses between the PC's sending of each line of the .hex file can be examined to verify that these gaps are longer than 10 milliseconds. If not, then increase the line-delay parameter of the terminal emulator to meet this requirement.

A4.6 AUTOSTART FEATURE

If a user program is already resident in the PIC18F452 when power is applied to the QwikFlash board, then QwikBug will pause for about four seconds, waiting to see if a user wants to intervene by pressing any key on the PC. If so, then the QwikBug "help" screen will be written to the PC's screen followed by the QwikBug prompt:

```
QB>
```

If no key is pressed, then execution of the resident user code will begin.

A4.7 COMMAND KEYS

All of QwikBug's commands begin with the "QB>" prompt. The function keys, F1 to F9, can initiate each of the commands. The F1 key provides a brief help screen of the commands. Each command can also be initiated from the uppercase letter listed in the response to the the F1 key. For example, the "Modify" command can be initiated in response to the "QB>" prompt by either the F9 key or the "m" key.

For a command with a complex syntax, QwikBug displays a brief synopsis of the syntax. For example, in response to the F5 or "b" command to deal with a breakpoint, QwikBug displays

```
<aaaa> to set breakpoint, 'R' to remove breakpoint, 'D' to display breakpoint
```

followed by an

```
F5>
```

prompt, looking for either the entry of a breakpoint address, or the press of the "r" key to remove the breakpoint, or the press of the "d" key to display a previously entered breakpoint address (or a message indicating that no breakpoint address is set). In any case, in response to the command, a message indicates the result of the command followed by a new "QB>" prompt.

A4.8 Help COMMAND (F1 or H)

The F1 function key or the "h" key displays the QwikBug user menu. At any time during the running of the monitor, F1 can be pressed to display the list of function keys along with the operation of each key. Figure A4–1 shows the help message and the power-on start-up message that is displayed when no user code resides in program memory.

A4.9 reseT COMMAND (F2 or T)

Pressing the F2 or "t" key while at the "QB>" prompt executes the PIC18F452's reset instruction. This instruction affects all registers and flags in the same manner as would occur if the master-clear pin on the chip were toggled low and then high again by pressing and then releasing the QwikFlash board's RESET button (See "Other resets" in Figure 20-9.)

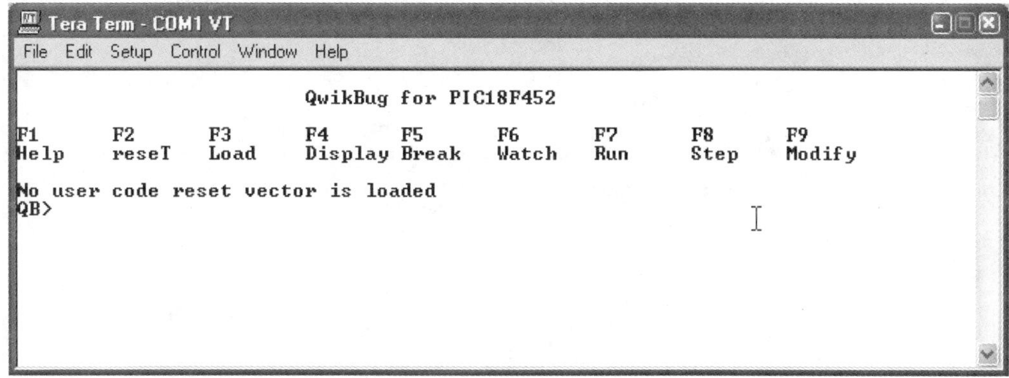

Figure A4-1 Help message at power-on with no user code loaded

A4.10 Load COMMAND (F3 or L)

This command supports two actions:

The erasing of user program memory
The loading of a new user program into the erased memory

To erase the entire user program memory, just press the F3 key (or the "l" key) and then turn off power to the board. To download the "hex" file for a user program, press the F3 key. QwikBug will respond with

```
QB> User program memory erased - Send HEX file now
```

Tera Term Pro supports the sequence

```
File → Send file... → <select drive, folder, hex file>
```

to select the file. Alternatively, and more easily, if a desktop window is opened to the folder holding the hex file (e.g., C:\Work), then simply click on the hex file to select it and drag it into the **Tera Term Pro** window. In either case, QwikBug will respond by displaying a series of periods while the hex file is downloaded. Upon completion, it returns with

```
Download successful
```

followed by a new "QB>" prompt, as shown in Figure A4-2.

If the download is unsuccessful, try again. If still unsuccessful, check that the Tera Term Pro's setup is correct with

```
Setup → Serial port... →
```

Compare the setup with that of Figure 5-8, with the possible exception of the line delay mentioned in Section A4.5. That is, because of a Tera Term Pro quirk, the line-delay parameter may need to be entered as a larger value than "10 ms/line" in order to obtain an actual pause after each line of the hex file of at least 10 milliseconds.

If the downloaded file does not execute in response to the Run command, check that the source file includes the reset vector at address 0x0000. That is, the user program should begin at address 0x0000, perhaps with a "goto Mainline" instruction, a "bra Mainline" instruction, and perhaps preceded by a "nop"

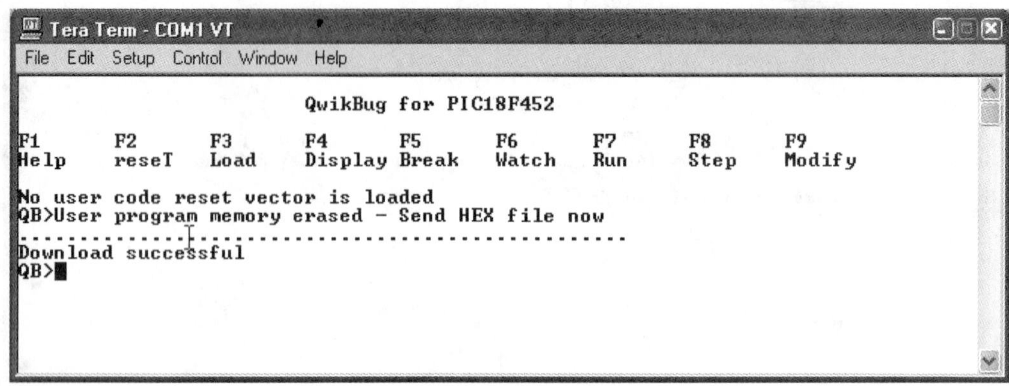

Figure A4-2 Response to load command

instruction. For a user program that employs interrupts, the normal interrupt vectors must be present at 0x0008 and/or 0x0018.

A4.11 Display COMMAND (F4 or D)

This command is an adjunct to the Step command or the Run (to breakpoint) command. The first time that a step is taken, the watch variable labels (i.e., PC, W, etc.) are listed, followed on the next line by the state of each watch variable. Each subsequent step results only in the display of the state of each watch variable. After many steps, the labels will have scrolled out of view. Pressing the F4 key or the "d" key, rewrites the watch variable labels.

The same behavior occurs when a breakpoint has been set and successive presses of the Run command return to QwikBug with a display of the watch variables. When the watch variable labels have scrolled out of view, execute the Display command to rewrite the labels.

A4.12 Break COMMAND (F5 or B)

See Section A4.7, where this command was described as an example of how commands operate. The QwikAddress utility, described in Appendix A5, can be used to get the hex address of a desired location for a breakpoint by double-clicking on a subroutine name in one window. This opens a second window showing the source file with the subroutine name highlighted. Move to the desired line in the subroutine and double-click on it to obtain its address. The execution of the Break command is illustrated in Figure A4-3.

A4.13 Watch COMMAND (F6 or W)

The following registers and bits are automatically displayed in response to each Step command (F8) or to the stop at a breakpoint in response to the Run command (F7):

PC W Z C N FSR0 FSR1 FSR2

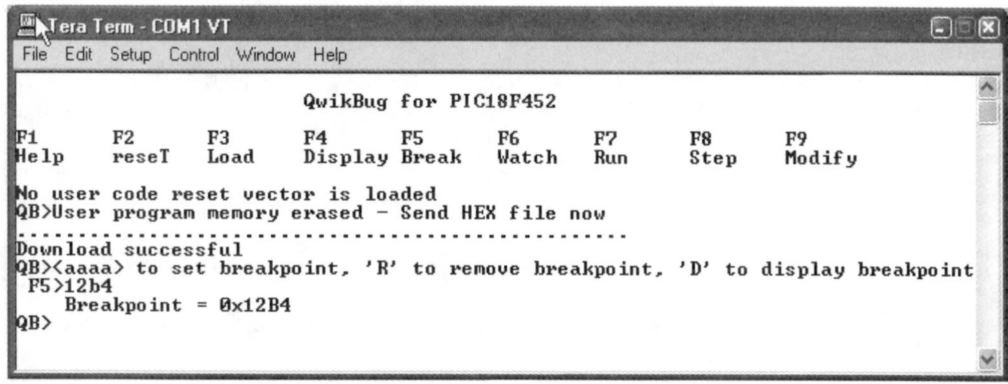

Figure A4-3 Response to break command

Additional RAM variables or SFRs can be added to this list. Because of its many useful variations, this is the most complex of the commands. QwikBug expects a hex address to be entered for a RAM variable or a Special Function Register. The QwikAddress utility described in Appendix A5 supports this process by listing within one window the addresses of all RAM variables and within an alternative window all of the SFRs.

If nothing further is entered, then the variable will be displayed as a hex byte. If that variable is already set up as a watch variable, then it will be removed. For example, if the variable with address 0x012 has not already been set up as a watch variable, then the entry

```
012
```

will set it up, to be displayed as a 1-byte number, expressed in hexadecimal code.

If the hex address is followed by a space and then a "b", the variable will be displayed in binary format. For example, the entry of

```
012 b
```

will set up the contents of address 0x012 as a watch variable, to be displayed as an 8-bit binary number.

If the hex address is followed by a space and then an "a", then the variable will be treated as an ASCII value. For example, the entry of

```
012 a
```

will set up the contents of address 0x012 as a watch variable, to be displayed as a single displayable ASCII character. If the variable does not represent a displayable ASCII character, then the variable will be represented by "*".

Adding a space followed by a digit *N* (ranging from 2 to 8) after either the preceding hex or ASCII entry will result in the display of *N* bytes, beginning at the entered address. For example, the entry of

```
012 a 8
```

will set up the contents of eight addresses beginning at 0x012 to be displayed as an ASCII string.

The entry of

```
012 2
```

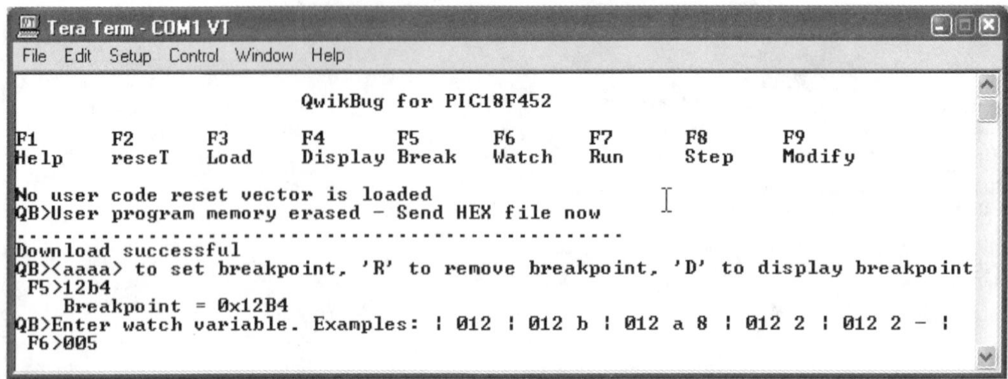

Figure A4-4 Response to watch command

will set up the contents of addresses 0x012 and 0x013 to be displayed as a 2-byte hex number, with 0x012 being treated as the most-significant byte.

Following this with a space and a "-" will result in the bytes being displayed in reverse order. Thus, the entry of

```
012 2 -
```

will set up the contents of addresses 0x012 and 0x013 to be displayed as a 2-byte hex number, with 0x013 being treated as the most-significant byte.

An example of a watch variable entry is shown in Figure A4-4.

A4.14 Run COMMAND (F7 or R)

Execution of this command switches the CPU from the execution of the QwikBug monitor to the execution of the user program. If the user program has just been downloaded or if the Reset command has just been executed, then execution begins at address 0x0000. Otherwise, execution picks up where it left off when a breakpoint or a step or a press of a PC key switched the CPU from the execution of the user program to the execution of the QwikBug monitor.

A4.15 Step COMMAND (F8 or S)

This command switches the CPU from the execution of the QwikBug monitor to the execution of one instruction of the user program before bouncing back into the QwikBug monitor. Successive presses of either the F8 key or the "s" key will single-step through the user program, instruction by instruction.

A4.16 Modify COMMAND (F9 or M)

This command brings up the message:

```
QB>Display/Modify contents of RAM or register address:
<aaa> to Display, <aaa xx> to Modify
```

Both the address and the contents are expected to be expressed as hexadecimal numbers.

A4.17 MODIFYING QWIKBUG

Several minor changes can be made to the QwikBug source code (available at www.picbook.com) to alter the operation of the monitor. These changes can be made by altering the following constants found at the beginning of the source code file: BAUD_CONSTANT, STARTDELAY, and WATCHDEPTH. By altering the BAUD_CONSTANT (set to 32 for a baud rate of 19,200 and a crystal frequency of 10 MHz), the user can change the baud rate. Refer to Figure 18-4a. The STARTDELAY constant determines the number of seconds before QwikBug automatically starts. STARTDELAY is presently set to 4 for a four-second delay. WATCHDEPTH determines the maximum number of user-added watch variables that can be added to the watch list. It is presently set to ten watch variables.

A4.18 ACKNOWLEDGMENT

The features of QwikBug were defined by the following students during the spring of 2001. Since this was prior to the introduction of the "first silicon" PIC18F452 parts, the code they wrote executed on the PIC16F877, with Backbround Debug features only discussed but not implemented.

Thomas Backus
Rafael Ballagas
Brandon Cromer
James Eubanks
Darren Gerhardt
Mayuresh Gogate
Lawrence McDonald
Barreus Sims
Christopher Stephens

During the summer of 2001, Mayuresh and Larry translated the code to PIC18F452 code, getting it running on a PIC18C452, an EPROM program memory predecessor of the PIC18F452 that did not support Background Debug Mode features. In was not until August 2001 that we received several first silicon PIC18F452 parts. During the fall of 2001, I developed enough further modifications to support QwikBug as a "load and go" tool (i.e., the implementation of the F3 and F7 functions). Then during the spring of 2002, Rawin Rojvanit, with the help of Drew Maule, got the remaining features of QwikBug working, including a creative use of the Background Debug Mode's "FREEZE" feature to keep the PIC18F452's counters from running while in BDM and yet to overcome the FREEZE feature's stopping of the UART. The UART is needed in BDM to accept commands and return results to the PC. Stopping the counters in BDM is needed to support single-stepping through mainline code in the presence of enabled timer interrupts.

This development would not have been possible without the help of Al Lovrich, Greg Robinson, and Craig Miller of Microchip Technology. They supported our understanding of a subset of the BDM features built into the hardware of the chip to support their ICD2 module and needed by QwikBug.

Appendix

A5

QWIKADDRESS AND QWIKPH UTILITIES

A5.1 OVERVIEW

This appendix describes two utilities of value in debugging code. Both are available from the author's Web site, www.picbook.com. The QwikAddress utility was developed by David Flowers of Georgia Tech to deal with several issues that arise as a result of using the structured assembly preprocessor of Chapter 6. The error file generated by the assembler includes a line number for each error that points back into the .apr file generated by the preprocessor, whereas what is needed is the corresponding line number in the original .asm source file. By dragging the .err file from the folder containing the source file (e.g., C:\Work), into the QwikAddress window, each of the error line numbers is translated back to its source file line number.

Subsequently, when debugging user code with the QwikBug monitor program described in the previous appendix, this QwikAddress utility serves two further roles. When setting a watch variable, the RAM or register address of the variable is needed. When setting a breakpoint, its program memory address is needed. This capability is also of value when using Microchip Technology's ICD2 in-circuit debugger and the MPLAB environment with code generated using structured assembly constructs. In this case, QwikAddress reaches a breakpoint address via the selection of a desired subroutine in one table followed by the switching to a listing of that subroutine in the source file. When the desired line in the subroutine is selected, its address is displayed.

The QwikPH utility was developed by Chris Twigg of Georgia Tech to generate and insert a Program Hierarchy into a source file. The Program Hierarchy lists the relationships between all of the subroutines in the source file. An accurate Program Hierarchy for a large program is difficult to generate manually with complete accuracy. It is helpful in several ways, including the tracking down of the corruption of a variable being used by several subroutines.

A5.2 DAVID FLOWERS' QWIKADDRESS UTILITY

This utility is normally opened at the same time that a folder is opened showing the source and listing files being debugged. Figure A5-1 shows the files generated by the assembler for the template program, P3.asm. Clicking on this and dragging it into the **QwikAddress** window triggers QwikAddress to act upon this file. A watch variable address can be found by selecting **Variables** in the **View** pulldown menu, as shown in Figure A5-2. It may be easier to find the address of a variable using the alphabetized list obtained by selecting **Sort Lists** in the **Sort** pulldown menu, as shown in Figure A5-3. The address of one of the Special Function Registers is found as shown in Figure A5-4.

Obtaining a breakpoint address begins by selecting **Labels** in the **View** pulldown menu, as shown in Figure A5-5. For a specific address within the **Pbutton** subroutine, for example, the **Pbutton** subroutine address is double-clicked in this window, as shown in Figure A5-6. This opens the source file shown in

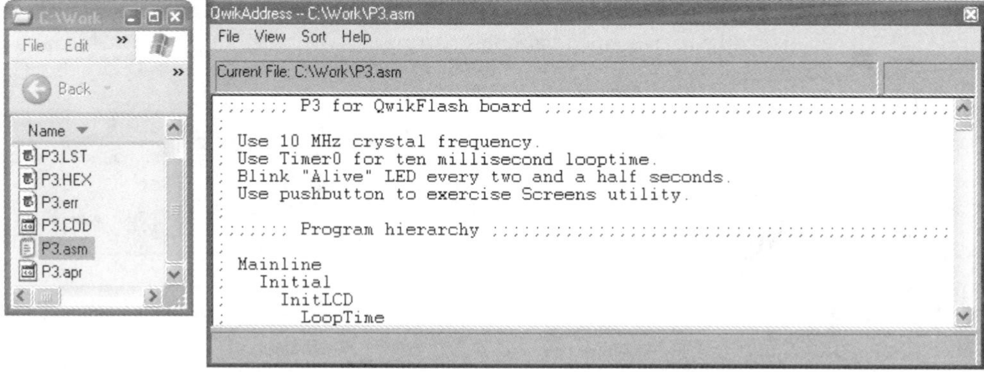

Figure A5-1 Selecting a source file to be operated upon by QwikAddress

Figure A5-2 The display of all user-defined variables and their addresses

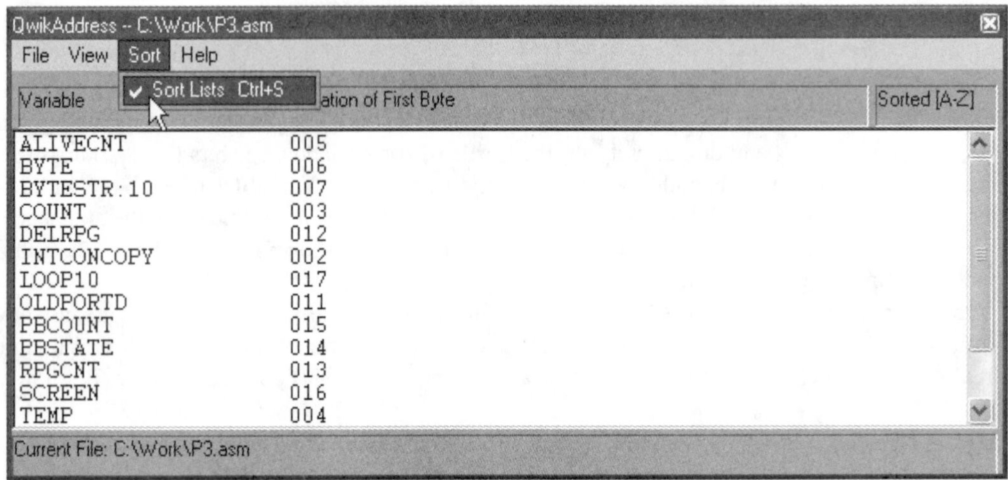

Figure A5-3 Alphabetizing the user-defined variables

QwikAddress -- C:\Work\P3.asm
File View Sort Help
Variables Ctrl+V
SFRs Ctrl+R
Labels Ctrl+L
Find Line Ctrl+F
Sorted [A-Z]
ADRESL FC3
BSR FE0
CCP1CON FBD
CCP2CON FBA
CCPR1H FBF
CCPR1L FBE
CCPR2H FBC
CCPR2L FBB
EEADR FA9
EECON1 FA6
Current File: C:\Work\P3.asm

Figure A5-4 The display of the Special Function Registers

Figure A5-7, scrolled down to the **Pbutton** subroutine. Further scrolling into this subroutine is shown in Figure A5-8. Double-clicking on the line shown leads to the display of the address of the first instruction generated by the macro, **MOVLF**.

A5.3 CHRIS TWIGG'S QWIKPH UTILITY

This utility opens to a tree of file folders that is navigated to the folder holding the source (.asm) file of interest. Thus, in Figure A5-9, the Work folder with the pathlist C:\Work has been opened. It is shown holding two source files, P3.asm and P4.asm. Before selecting one of these to be operated upon, the

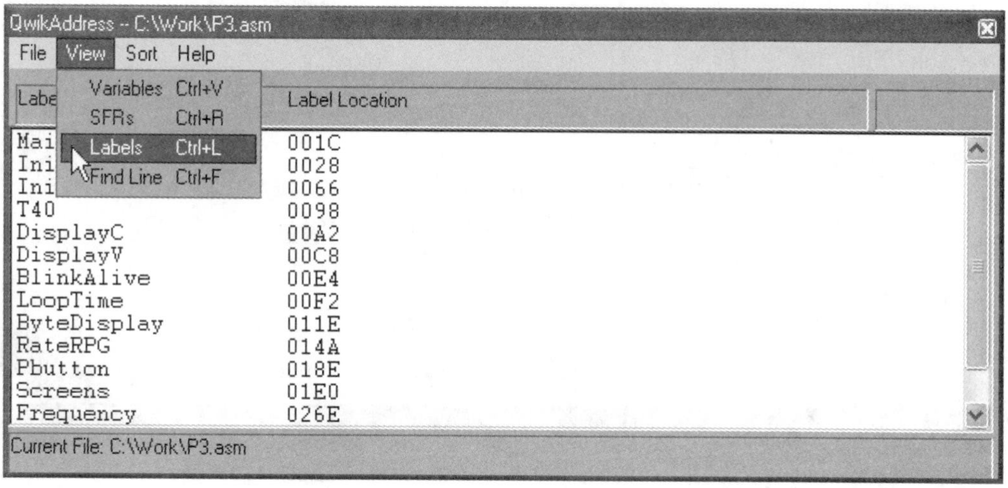

Figure A5-5 Addresses of all subroutines

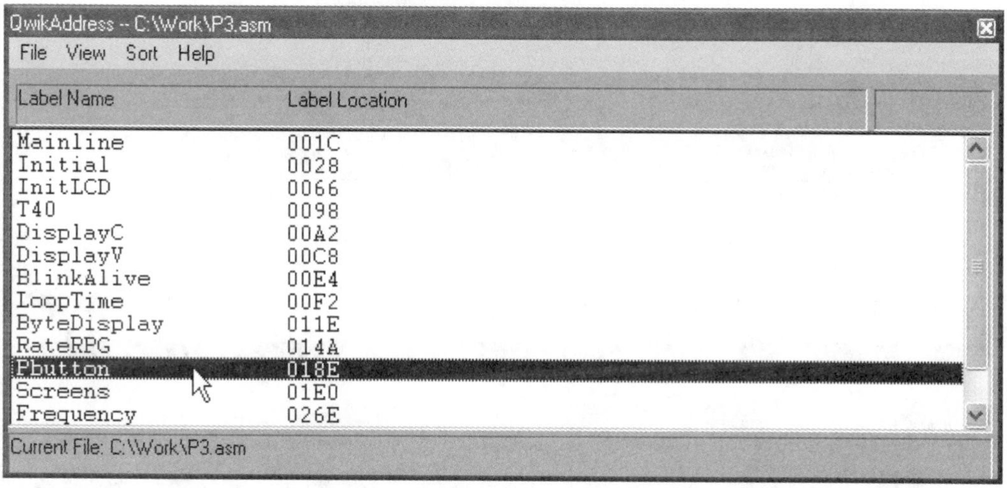

Figure A5-6 Selection of a specific subroutine

Config pulldown menu and the **Special Labels** window can be opened, as shown in Figure A5-10 and A5-11. This window allows a user to name the mainline program and the interrupt service routine(s) with arbitrary names such that the QwikPH utility will handle them appropriately.

The **Config** pulldown menu also permits the choice of having the QwikPH utility write the Program Hierarchy to the clipboard for manual inspection and manual insertion into the source file. Alternatively, by checking the AutoUpdate ASM entry, the Program Hierarchy already in the file will be updated with the new results. As a backup, the original file is first renamed with a numerical suffix and then the utility generates the new .asm file. When using the AutoUpdate ASM feature, the utility looks for "Program Hierarchy" in a comment line. After finding this comment line, QwikPH replaces all lines between

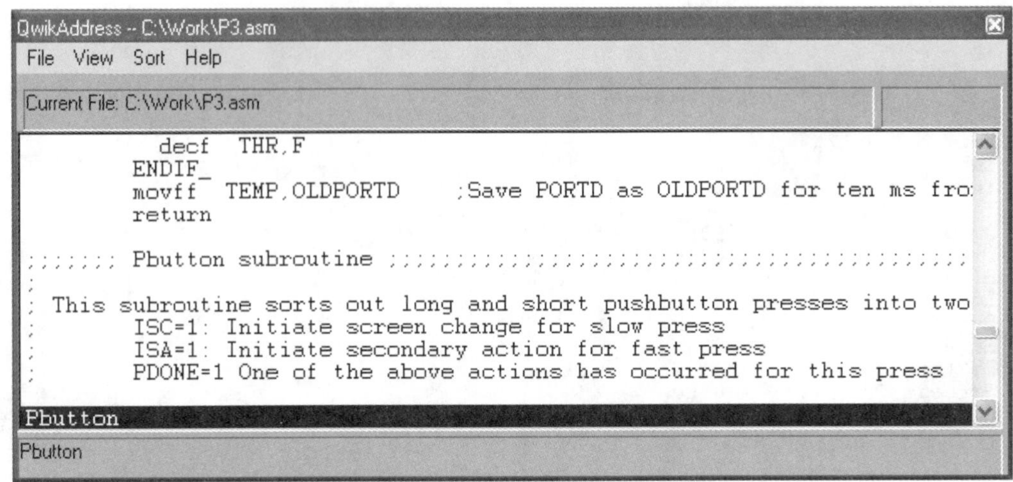
QwikAddress -- C:\Work\P3.asm
File View Sort Help
Current File: C:\Work\P3.asm
decf THR,F
ENDIF_
movff TEMP,OLDPORTD ;Save PORTD as OLDPORTD for ten ms fro
return
;;;;;;; Pbutton subroutine ;;;
;
; This subroutine sorts out long and short pushbutton presses into two
; ISC=1: Initiate screen change for slow press
; ISA=1: Initiate secondary action for fast press
; PDONE=1 One of the above actions has occurred for this press
Pbutton
Pbutton

Figure A5-7 Source file display of the selected subroutine

```
QwikAddress -- C:\Work\P3.asm
File  View  Sort  Help
Current File: C:\Work\P3.asm

          bsf   PBSTATE,NEWPB
        ELSE_
          bcf   PBSTATE,NEWPB
        ENDIF_

        IF_   PBSTATE,OLDPB == 1 ;Look for leading edge (OLDPB=1, NEWPB
          IF_   PBSTATE,NEWPB == 0
            MOVLF  PBthres,PBCOUNT   ;Start counter
          ENDIF_
        ENDIF_

        IF_   PBSTATE,NEWPB == 0 ;Pushbutton is still pressed
          movf   PBCOUNT,F
Address of line: 01A4
```

Figure A5-8 Obtaining the address of a specific instruction within the selected subroutine

it and the next comment line or blank line with the newly generated program hierarchy. If QwikPH fails to find this comment line, it will copy the generated hierarchy to the clipboard.

Double-clicking the selected file in the menu initiates the utility's activity. Upon completion, the action taken is written in the status bar of the QwikPH utility, as shown in Figure A5-12. The resulting section of the source file is shown in Figure A5-13.

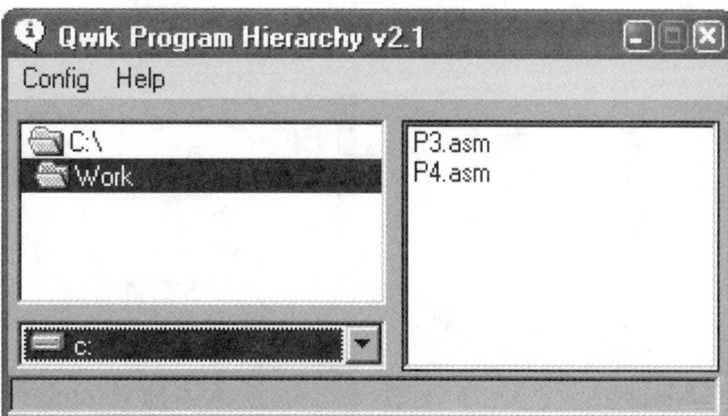

Figure A5-9 Selection of source file for Program Hierarchy generation

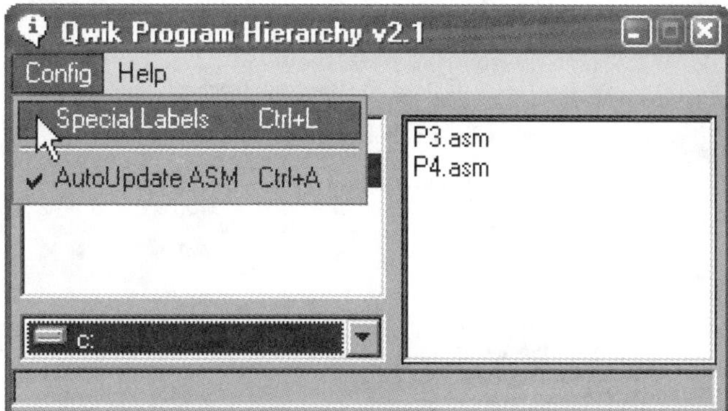

Figure A5-10 Configuration of QwikPH to identify vector labels

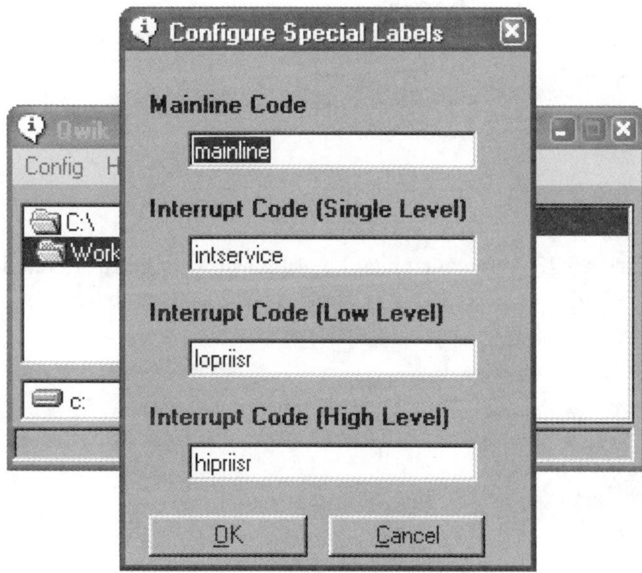

Figure A5-11 Entry of vector label names

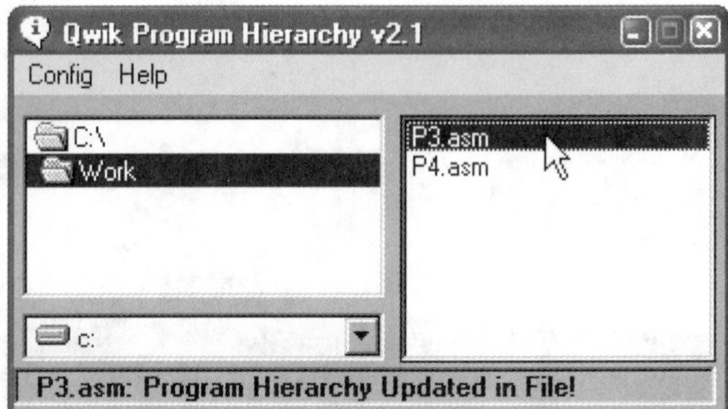

Figure A5-12 Initiating Program Hierarchy generation

```
;;;;;;; P3 for QwikFlashboard ;;;;;;;;;;;;;;;;;;;;;;;;;;;;;;;;;;;;;;;;;;;;;;;;;
;
; Use 10 MHz crystal frequency.
; Use Timer0 for ten millisecond looptime.
; Blink "Alive" LED every two and a half seconds.
; Use pushbutton to exercise Screens utility.
;
;;;;;;; Program hierarchy ;;;;;;;;;;;;;;;;;;;;;;;;;;;;;;;;;;;;;;;;;;;;;;;;;;;;;
;
; Mainline
;   Initial
;     InitLCD
;       LoopTime
;     DisplayC
;       T40
;   BlinkAlive
;   Pbutton
;   Screens
;     DisplayC
;       T40
;     Frequency
;     Period
;     PWmax
;     RateRPG
;     ByteDisplay
;       DisplayC
;         T40
;       DisplayV
;         T40
;   LoopTime
;
;;;;;;; Assembler directives ;;;;;;;;;;;;;;;;;;;;;;;;;;;;;;;;;;;;;;;;;;;;;;;;;;;
```

Figure A5-13 Automatic updating of P3.asm's Program Hierarchy

Appendix

A6

VERIFICATION OF MATH SUBROUTINES

Chris Twigg

All of the math routines described in Chapter 14 were verified by executing the selected math routine on the PIC and transferring all resulting data to a PC using the UART. The data transferred included the math routine arguments, the results of the execution, and the execution time of the subroutine. A program running on the PC stored the raw data to a temporary file on the disk. Once the transfer was completed, the program read this temporary file, verified the math, calculated the minimum, maximum, and average execution times, and wrote the data and verification results to a new file. If errors were found, the arguments resulting in the error could easily be located within this file to help determine the cause of the error.

Each of the math routines was executed 100,000 times using pseudo-random numbers for the arguments. The only exceptions were the 8-bit routines in which there were only 65,536 possible combinations of arguments. These routines were evaluated using all possible combinations of input arguments. Execution times for the math subroutines were calculated for the instructions within the math subroutine only; the **call** of the subroutine was not included.

The division routines were verified on the PC by multiplying the quotient by the divisor and adding the remainder. The result should have been the dividend if the divide subroutine performs correctly. Multiply routines were tested in a similar fashion by multiplying the two arguments and comparing the result to the product generated by the multiply routine.

$\frac{dividend}{divisor} = quotient + \frac{remainder}{divisor}$	$divisor*quotient + remainder = dividend$
Typical divide routine results	**Test to determine divide routine validity**

A couple of interesting cases occur within the signed divide subroutines. The first is an exception caused by dividing the smallest representable value by -1. For instance, consider the FXD0808S subroutine. Mathematically, -128 divided by -1 should be $+128$. However, $+128$ cannot be represented as an 8-bit twos-complement-coded number. The divide routines account for this by setting the **NAN** flag in the **FPFLAGS** RAM variable.

The second interesting case occurs in the sign of the remainder. Consider again the FXD0808S subroutine and divide $+1$ by -128. By our mathematical test above, we expect to see a quotient of 0 and a remainder of $+1$. However, the earlier versions of the math routines from Microchip's C18 compiler would yield a quotient of 0 and a remainder of -1. Testing of the signed subroutines revealed this phenomenon. The math subroutines used within this book have been corrected to provide the expected results.

Appendix

A7

USE OF C PROGRAMMING FOR THE PIC18F452

Mike Chow

If you are already familiar with assembly language coding, then the use of C should not be too difficult a transition. However, one has to keep in mind that writing C code for a *microcontroller* is different than writing C code for a *personal computer*. For example, Microchip Technology's MCC18 compiler and Hi-Tech Software's PICC-18 compiler both translate C code into assembly language for the PIC18F452 microcontroller. Visual C++ also translates C code into assembly code to run on a PC, but most programmers do not concern themselves with the assembly code, given the relatively unlimited resources of the PC. However, with a microcontroller, one must take care not to overrun its limited resources, especially its RAM memory, or to use variable lengths or expressions that unduly extend execution time. The following are some issues to keep in mind while programming:

- Always use the smallest possible variable necessary.
- Whenever possible, use constant strings that reside in program memory rather than variable strings that reside in RAM.
- Multiplies and divides are slow. If time efficiency is of concern, try using a combination of left-shifts, right-shifts, adds, or subtracts. For example, to multiply a number by 10 try

  ```
  number = (var<<3)+(var<<1)
  ```

  instead of

  ```
  number = 10*var
  ```

- Do not confuse the notation for a bitwise operation with that for a logical operation. For example, a double ampersand, &&, is a logical AND while a single ampersand, &, is a bitwise operator.
- In general, keep in mind how your C code will compile into assembly code.

This appendix derives the C code version for two template programs presented earlier in this book:

- P3.asm, the "Screens" example of Chapter 12
- P4.asm, the interrupt-driven, square wave generator example of Chapter 16

So as to illuminate a few differences in the requirements of Microchip Technology's MCC18 compiler and Hi-Tech Software's PICC-18 compiler, each of these programs has been written for each of these compilers. As you examine both the assembly code and the C code in each case, notice the many parallels that exist between them. The general structure of the program remains the same. For example, there is still a Mainline routine that repeatedly executes the subroutines within its loop every 10 milliseconds.

Very few significant differences between the source code requirements for the two compilers have been observed. One obvious difference deals with bit manipulation. In standard C, a *bit* type is not truly defined; however, it is very useful to have when programming a microcontroller. For Microchip Technology's compiler, the preferred method of defining bits is to use their "struct" construct. For example, to define bits you must create them in your variable declaration area as

```
struct {
        unsigned ISC:1;
        unsigned ISA:1;
        unsigned PDONE:1;
        unsigned OLDPB:1;
        unsigned NEWPB:1;
} PBSTATEbits;
```

As an example, to use the bit named PDONE, you would refer to the bit as PBSTATEbits.PDONE.

```
PBSTATEbits.PDONE = 1;  // example of setting the PDONE bit

if (PBSTATEbits.PDONE)  // example of using the PDONE bit in a test statement
{
   <task>
}
```

Hi-Tech Software's compiler defines a *bit* type and allows you to use it directly as you would any other variable type. For example, you can define the same bits above as follows:

```
bit ISC;
bit ISA;
bit PDONE;
bit OLDPB;
bit NEWPB;
```

To access the bits, you simply refer to them by name.

```
PDONE = 1;    // example of setting the PDONE bit

if (PDONE)    // example of using the PDONE bit in a test statement
{
   <task>
}
```

Hi-Tech Software's compiler performs bit "packing." That is, bits are defined successively in 8-bit bytes so that eight individual bits can be defined using only a single byte of memory.

Both versions of C compilers are ANSI C compliant. Along with the standard functionality of C, the compilers also include added support that is specific for microcontrollers. There is, however, some divergence from standard C, such as the inability to perform function recursion due to hardware limitations relating to the stack and limited memory. Further details can be found in the user's manual of their respective versions.

Additional information on Microchip Technology's MCC18 compiler can be found at the Web site, http://www.microchip.com The specific URL for the MCC18 compiler (generally referred to as their MPLAB® C18 compiler) is http://www.microchip.com/1010/pline/tools/picmicro/code/mplab18/index.htm

Additional information on Hi-Tech Software's PICC-18 compiler can be found at the Web site, http://www.htsoft.com The specific URL for the PICC-18 compiler is http://www.htsoft.com/products/pic18/manual

```
/******* P3_MCC18.c *****************************************************************
 *
 * Use 10 MHz crystal frequency.
 * Use Timer0 for ten millisecond looptime.
 * Blink "Alive" LED every two and a half seconds.
 * Use pushbutton to exercise Screens utility.
 *
 ******* Program hierarchy *****************************************************
 *
 * Mainline
 *   Initial
 *     InitLCD
 *       LoopTime
 *     DisplayC
 *       T40
 *   BlinkAlive
 *   Pbutton
 *   Screens
 *     DisplayC
 *       T40
 *     Frequency
 *     Period
 *     PWmax
 *     RateRPG
 *     ByteDisplay
 *       DisplayC
 *         T40
 *       DisplayV
 *         T40
 *   LoopTime
 *
 ********************************************************************************
 */

#include <p18cxxx.h>

/*******************************
 * Assembler directives
 *******************************
 */

/*******************************
 * Definitions and equates
 *******************************
 */

#define PBthres 30       // Pushbutton threshold for a long press

/*******************************
 * Global variables
 *******************************
 */

char TMR0LCOPY;          // Copy of sixteen-bit Timer0 used by LoopTime
char TMR0HCOPY;
char INTCONCOPY;         // Copy of INTCON for LoopTime subroutine
char COUNT;              // Counter available as local to subroutines
char TEMP;               // Temporary local variable
char ALIVECNT;           // Counter for blinking "Alive" LED
char BYTE;               // Eight-bit byte to be displayed
char OLDPORTD;           // Holds previous value of inputs
char DELRPG;             // Generated by RPG
char RPGCNT;             // Used to display RPG changes
char PBCOUNT;            // Counter for measuring duration of press
char SCREEN;             // State of LCD subroutine
char LOOP10;             // Scale of ten loop counter
char THR;                // Threshold value used by Pbutton
```

Figure A7-1 P3_MCC18.c (P3 template recast for Microchip's C compiler).

```
struct {                // Control/status bits for pushbutton
    unsigned ISC:1;     // Initiate screen change for slow press
    unsigned ISA:1;     // Initiate secondary action for fast press
    unsigned PDONE:1;   // Pushbutton action has been taken
    unsigned OLDPB:1;   // Old state of pushbutton
    unsigned NEWPB:1;   // New state of pushbutton
} PBSTATEbits;

/********************************
 * Constant strings
 ********************************
 */

// For stability reasons, create an EVEN number of elements in any given array
const char LCDstr[]  = {Øx33,Øx32,Øx28,ØxØ1,ØxØc,ØxØ6,ØxØØ,ØxØØ};// LCD Initialization string
const char StrtStr[] = {Øx8Ø,'P','u','s','h',' ','P','B',' ',Ø};// Startup screen
const char BYTE_1[]  = {Øx8Ø,'B','Y','T','E','=',' ',' ',' ',Ø};// Write "BYTE=" 1st line of LCD
const char Clear1[]  = {Øx8Ø,' ',' ',' ',' ',' ',' ',' ',' ',Ø};// Clear line 1
const char Clear2[]  = {ØxCØ,' ',' ',' ',' ',' ',' ',' ',' ',Ø};// Clear line 2
const char FreqStr[] = {Øx8Ø,'F','r','e','q',' ','k','H','z',Ø};// Frequency instrument
const char PerStr[]  = {Øx8Ø,'P','e','r',' ',' ',' ','u','s',Ø};// Period instrument
const char PWmaxStr[] = {Øx8Ø,'P','W','m','a','x',' ','u','s',Ø};// Max pulse width instrument

/********************************
 * Variable strings
 ********************************
 */

char BYTESTR[] = {Ø,Ø,Ø,Ø,Ø,Ø,Ø,Ø,Ø,Ø}; // Display string for binary version of BYTE

/********************************
 * Function prototypes
 ********************************
 */

void Initial(void);
void InitLCD(void);
void Looptime(void);
void T4Ø(void);
void DisplayC(const char *);
void DisplayV(char *);
void BlinkAlive(void);
void LoopTime(void);
void ByteDisplay(void);
void RateRPG(void);
void Pbutton(void);
void Screens(void);
void Frequency(void);
void Period(void);
void PWmax(void);

/////// Mainline program ////////////////////////////////////////

/********************************
 * main()
 ********************************
 */

void main()
{
        Initial();      // Initialize everything
        while(1)
        {
          PORTBbits.RBØ = !PORTBbits.RBØ;  // Toggle pin, to support measuring loop time
          BlinkAlive();                   // Blink "Alive" LED
          Pbutton();                      // Check pushbutton
          Screens();                      // Deal with SCREEN state
          LoopTime();                     // Make looptime be ten milliseconds
        }
}

/********************************
 * Initial()
 *
 * This subroutine performs all initializations of variables and registers.
 ********************************
 */
```

Figure A7-1 continued

```
void Initial()
{
        ADCON1 = 0b10001110;            // Enable PORTA & PORTE digital I/O pins
        TRISA  = 0b11100001;            // Set I/O for PORTA
        TRISB  = 0b11011100;            // Set I/O for PORTB
        TRISC  = 0b11010000;            // Set I/O for PORTC
        TRISD  = 0b00001111;            // Set I/O for PORTD
        TRISE  = 0b00000000;            // Set I/O for PORTE
        T0CON  = 0b10001000;            // Set up Timer0 for a looptime of 10 ms
        PORTA  = 0b00010000;            // Turn off all four LEDs driven from PORTA
        OLDPORTD = PORTD;               // Initialize "old" value
        RPGCNT   = 0;                   // Clear counter to be displayed
        PBCOUNT  = 0;                   // and pushbutton count
        SCREEN   = 0;                   // Initialize LCD's SCREEN variable
        THR = 0;                        // Initialize Pbutton's THR variable
        PBSTATEbits.ISC = 0;            // Initialize pushbutton state
        PBSTATEbits.ISA = 0;
        PBSTATEbits.PDONE = 0;
        PBSTATEbits.OLDPB = 1;
        PBSTATEbits.NEWPB = 0;
        InitLCD();                      // Initialize LCD
        DisplayC(StrtStr);              // Display startup message
}

/*******************************
 * InitLCD()
 *
 * Initialize the Optrex 8x2 character LCD.
 * First wait for 0.1 second, to get past display's power-on reset time.
 *******************************
 */
void InitLCD()
{
        char currentChar;
        char *tempPtr;

        COUNT = 10;                     // Wait 0.1 second
        while (COUNT)
        {
          LoopTime();                   // Call LoopTime() 10 times
          COUNT--;
        }

        PORTEbits.RE0 = 0;              // RS=0 for command
        tempPtr = LCDstr;

        while (*tempPtr)                // if the byte is not zero
        {
          currentChar = *tempPtr;
          PORTEbits.RE1 = 1;            // Drive E pin high
          PORTD = currentChar;          // Send upper nibble
          PORTEbits.RE1 = 0;            // Drive E pin low so LCD will accept nibble
          LoopTime();
          currentChar <<= 4;            // Shift lower nibble to upper nibble
          PORTEbits.RE1 = 1;            // Drive E pin high again
          PORTD = currentChar;          // Write lower nibble
          PORTEbits.RE1 = 0;            // Drive E pin low so LCD will process byte
          LoopTime();                   // Wait 40 usec
          tempPtr++;                    // Increment pointer to next character
        }
}

/*******************************
 * T40()
 *
 * Pause for 40 microseconds  or 40/0.4 = 100 clock cycles.
 * Assumes 10/4 = 2.5 MHz internal clock rate.
 *******************************
 */

void T40()
{
        // Measured with oscilloscope to be about 42.80 us
        // including the time to call this routine.  Decrementing each
        // "cCOUNT" takes approximately 4 us.

        unsigned char cCOUNT = 7;
        while (cCOUNT)
          cCOUNT--;
}
```

Figure A7-1 continued

```
/*******************************
 * DisplayC(const char *)
 *
 * This subroutine is called with the passing in of an array of a constant
 * display string.  It sends the bytes of the string to the LCD.  The first
 * byte sets the cursor position.  The remaining bytes are displayed, beginning
 * at that position.
 * This subroutine expects a normal one-byte cursor-positioning code, 0xhh, or
 * an occasionally used two-byte cursor-positioning code of the form 0x00hh.
 *******************************
 */

void DisplayC(const char * tempPtr)
{
        char currentChar;

        PORTEbits.RE0 = 0;              // Drive RS pin low for cursor-positioning code
        while (*tempPtr)                // if the byte is not zero
        {
          currentChar = *tempPtr;
          PORTEbits.RE1 = 1;            // Drive E pin high
          PORTD = currentChar;          // Send upper nibble
          PORTEbits.RE1 = 0;            // Drive E pin low so LCD will accept nibble
          currentChar <<= 4;            // Shift lower nibble to upper nibble
          PORTEbits.RE1 = 1;            // Drive E pin high again
          PORTD = currentChar;          // Write lower nibble
          PORTEbits.RE1 = 0;            // Drive E pin low so LCD will process byte
          T40();                        // Wait 40 usec
          PORTEbits.RE0 = 1;            // Drive RS pin high for displayable characters
          tempPtr++;                    // Increment pointer to next character
        }

}
/*******************************
 * DisplayV(char *)
 *
 * This subroutine is called with the passing in of an array of a variable
 * display string.  It sends the bytes of the string to the LCD.  The first
 * byte sets the cursor position.  The remaining bytes are displayed, beginning
 * at that position.
 *******************************
 */

void DisplayV(char * tempPtr)
{
        char currentChar;

        PORTEbits.RE0 = 0;              // Drive RS pin low for cursor-positioning code
        while (*tempPtr)                // if the byte is not zero
        {
          currentChar = *tempPtr;
          PORTEbits.RE1 = 1;            // Drive E pin high
          PORTD = currentChar;          // Send upper nibble
          PORTEbits.RE1 = 0;            // Drive E pin low so LCD will accept nibble
          currentChar <<= 4;            // Shift lower nibble to upper nibble
          PORTEbits.RE1 = 1;            // Drive E pin high again
          PORTD = currentChar;          // Write lower nibble
          PORTEbits.RE1 = 0;            // Drive E pin low so LCD will process byte
          T40();                        // Wait 40 usec
          PORTEbits.RE0 = 1;            // Drive RS pin high for displayable characters
          tempPtr++;                    // Increment pointer to next character
        }
}

/*******************************
 * BlinkAlive()
 *
 * This subroutine briefly blinks the LED next to the PIC every two-and-a-half
 * seconds.
 *******************************
 */
void BlinkAlive()
{
        PORTAbits.RA4 = 1;              // Turn off LED
        if (!(--ALIVECNT))              // Decrement loop counter and return if not zero
        {
          ALIVECNT = 250;               // Reinitialize ALIVECNT
          PORTAbits.RA4 = 0;            // Turn on LED for ten milliseconds every 2.5 sec
        }
}
```

Figure A7-1 continued

```
/********************************
 * LoopTime()
 *
 * This subroutine waits for TimerØ to complete its ten millisecond count
 * sequence. It does so by waiting for sixteen-bit TimerØ to roll over. To obtain
 * a period of precisely 10000/0.4 = 25000 clock periods, it needs to remove
 * 65536-25000 or 40536 counts from the sixteen-bit count sequence.  The
 * algorithm below first copies TimerØ to RAM, adds "Bignum" to the copy ,and
 * then writes the result back to TimerØ. It actually needs to add somewhat more
 * counts to TimerØ than 40536.  The extra number of 12+2 counts added into
 * "Bignum" makes the precise correction.
 ********************************
 */

void LoopTime()
{
  #define Bignum  65536-25000+12+2

        while (!INTCONbits.TØIF);       // Wait until ten milliseconds are up
        INTCONCOPY = INTCON;            // Save INTCON bits
        INTCONbits.GIEH = 0;            // Disable all interrupts from CPU
        INTCONbits.GIEL = 0;
        TMRØLCOPY = TMRØL;              // Read 16-bit counter at this moment
        TMRØHCOPY = TMRØH;
        TMRØLCOPY += Bignum & 0x00FF;   // add LSB
        if (STATUSbits.C)               // If Carry, increment high byte
          TMRØHCOPY++;
        TMRØHCOPY += (Bignum>>8) & 0x00FF;  // add MSB
        TMRØH = TMRØHCOPY;
        TMRØL = TMRØLCOPY;              // Write 16-bit counter at this moment
        WREG = INTCONCOPY & 0b11000000; // Reenable interrupts to CPU if enabled prior
        INTCON = INTCON | WREG;         // to LoopTime
        INTCONbits.TØIF = 0;            // Clear TimerØ flag
}

/********************************
 * ByteDisplay()
 *
 * Display whatever is in BYTE as a binary number.
 ********************************
 */
void ByteDisplay()
{
        DisplayC(BYTE_1);               // Display "BYTE=".

        COUNT = 8;                      // 8 bits in BYTE
        while (COUNT)
        {
          TEMP = (BYTE & 0b00000001);   // Move bit 0 of BYTE into TEMP
          TEMP |= 0x30;                 // Convert to ASCII
          BYTESTR[COUNT] = TEMP;        // and move to string
          BYTE = BYTE>>1;               // Right shift bits in BYTE by 1
          COUNT--;                      // Decrement COUNT;
        }
        BYTESTR[0] = 0xC0;              // Add cursor-positioning code
        BYTESTR[9] = 0;                 // and end-of-string terminator
        DisplayV(BYTESTR);              // Display the string
}

/********************************
 * RateRPG()
 *
 * This subroutine deciphers RPG changes into values of DELRPG.
 * DELRPG = +2 for fast CW change, +1 for slow CW change, 0 for no change,
 *          -1 for slow CCW change and -2 for fast CCW change.
 ********************************
 */

void RateRPG()
{
  #define Threshold 3                   // Value to distinguish between slow and fast
  char W_temp;

        PORTAbits.RA2 = 0;              // Turn LED off
        DELRPG = 0;                     // Clear for "no change" return value
        W_temp = PORTD;                 // Copy PORTD into W_temp
        TEMP = W_temp;                  // and TEMP
        W_temp = W_temp ^ OLDPORTD;     // Any change?
        W_temp = W_temp & 0b00000011;   // If not, W_temp = 0
        if (W_temp != 0)                // If the two bits have changed then...
        {
```

Figure A7-1 continued

```
            W_temp = OLDPORTD>>1;           // Form what a CCW change would produce
            if (OLDPORTD & 0x01)            // Make new bit 1 = complement of old bit 0
              W_temp &= 0b11111101;
            else
              W_temp |= 0b00000010;
            W_temp = (W_temp ^ TEMP);       // Did the RPG actually change to this output?
            W_temp &= 0b00000011;           // Mask off upper 6 bits
            if (W_temp == 0)                // If so, then change  DELRPG to -1 for CCW
            {
              DELRPG--;
              if (THR != 0)
              {
                DELRPG--;                   // If fast turning, decrement again
                PORTAbits.RA2 = 1;          // Turn LED on
              }
            }
            else
            {
              DELRPG++;                     // Otherwise, change DELRPG to  +1 for CW
              if (THR != 0)
              {
                DELRPG++;                   // If fast turning, increment again
                PORTAbits.RA2 = 1;          // Turn LED on
              }
            }
            THR = Threshold;                // Reinitialize THR
          }
          if (THR != 0)                     // Does THR equal zero
            THR--;                          // If not, then decrement it
          OLDPORTD = TEMP;                  // Save PORTD as OLDPORTD for ten ms from now
}

/*******************************
 * Pbutton()
 *
 * This subroutine sorts out long and short pushbutton presses into two outputs:
 *      ISC=1: Initiate screen change for slow press
 *      ISA=1: Initiate secondary action for fast press
 *      PDONE=1 One of the above actions has occurred for this press
 *******************************
 */

void Pbutton()
{
        PBSTATEbits.ISC = 0;              // Clear Initiate Screen Change bit (if set)
        PBSTATEbits.ISA = 0;              // Clear Initiate Secondary Action bit (if set)

        if (PORTDbits.RD3 == 1)           // Copy pushbutton state to NEWPB
          PBSTATEbits.NEWPB = 1;
        else
          PBSTATEbits.NEWPB = 0;

        if (PBSTATEbits.OLDPB)            // Look for leading edge (OLDPB=1, NEWPB=0)
        {
          if (!PBSTATEbits.NEWPB)
            PBCOUNT = PBthres;            // Start counter
        }

        if (!PBSTATEbits.NEWPB)           // Pushbutton is still pressed
        {
          if (!PBCOUNT)                   // and counter has passed threshold
            if (!PBSTATEbits.PDONE)       // and no action has yet been taken
            {
              PBSTATEbits.ISC = 1;        // Initiate screen change
              PBSTATEbits.PDONE = 1;      // Done with pulse
            }
        }
        else                              // Pushbutton has been released
          PBSTATEbits.PDONE = 0;          // so clear PDONE

        if (!PBSTATEbits.OLDPB)           // Look for trailing edge (OLDPB=0, NEWPB=1)
          if (PBSTATEbits.NEWPB)
          {
            if (PBCOUNT)                  // Fast pulse
              PBSTATEbits.ISA = 1;        // Initiate secondary action
            PBSTATEbits.PDONE = 0;        // Done with pulse
            PBCOUNT = 0;                  // Finish counting
          }
```

Figure A7-1 continued

```
        if (PBCOUNT)                    // Has counter reached zero?
          PBCOUNT--;                    // If not, then decrement it

        if (PBSTATEbits.NEWPB)          // Copy NEWPB to OLDPB
          PBSTATEbits.OLDPB = 1;
        else
          PBSTATEbits.OLDPB = Ø;
}

/*******************************
 * Screens()
 *
 * This subroutine uses the ISC bit from the Pbutton subroutine to cycle the
 * state of SCREEN and to take action based upon its value.
 * Initially SCREEN=Ø, so that whatever screen is displayed by the Initial
 * subroutine is not changed until a PB switch press.  Then the screen
 * corresponding to SCREEN=1 is displayed.  Subsequent PB switch
 * presses cycle through SCREEN=2, 3, etc., recycling back to SCREEN=1.
 *******************************
 */

void Screens()
{
  #define NumberOfScreens  4            // Change this value if new screens are added

        if (PBSTATEbits.ISC)
        {
          SCREEN++;
          if (SCREEN == (NumberOfScreens+1))  // Check if past last screen
            SCREEN = 1;                 // Cycle back to SCREEN = 1

          DisplayC(Clear1);             // Clear the display when switching screens
          DisplayC(Clear2);
        }

        if (SCREEN == 1)
        {
          if (PBSTATEbits.ISC)
            DisplayC(FreqStr);
          Frequency();
        }

        if (SCREEN == 2)
        {
          if (PBSTATEbits.ISC)
            DisplayC(PerStr);
          Period();
        }

        if (SCREEN == 3)
        {
          if (PBSTATEbits.ISC)
            DisplayC(PWmaxStr);
          PWmax();
          if (PBSTATEbits.ISA)          // Fast pulse, toggle PORTAbits.RA1
            PORTAbits.RA1 = !PORTAbits.RA1;
        }

        if (SCREEN == 4)
        {
          RateRPG();                    // Decipher RPG inputs into DELRPG
          RPGCNT += DELRPG;             // Increment or decrement RPGCNT from RPG
          BYTE = RPGCNT;                // Point BYTE to RPGCNT
          ByteDisplay();
          if (PBSTATEbits.ISA)          // Fast pulse, reset RPGCNT
            RPGCNT = Ø;
        }
}

/////// Stubs for measurement subroutines //////////////////////////////////////


void Frequency() { }
void Period()    { }
void PWmax()     { }
```

Figure A7-1 continued

```
/******* P3_PICC-18.c *******************************************************
 *
 * Use 10 MHz crystal frequency.
 * Use Timer0 for ten millisecond looptime.
 * Blink "Alive" LED every two and a half seconds.
 * Use pushbutton to exercise Screens utility.
 *
 ******* Program hierarchy **************************************************
 *
 * Mainline
 *   Initial
 *     InitLCD
 *       LoopTime
 *     DisplayC
 *       T40
 *   BlinkAlive
 *   Pbutton
 *   Screens
 *     DisplayC
 *       T40
 *     Frequency
 *     Period
 *     PWmax
 *     RateRPG
 *     ByteDisplay
 *       DisplayC
 *         T40
 *       DisplayV
 *         T40
 *   LoopTime
 *
 ****************************************************************************
 */

#include <pic18.h>

/********************************
 * Assembler directives
 ********************************
 */

/********************************
 * Definitions and equates
 ********************************
 */

#define PBthres 30      // Pushbutton threshold for a long press

/********************************
 * Global variables
 ********************************
 */

char TMR0LCOPY;         // Copy of sixteen-bit Timer0 used by LoopTime
char TMR0HCOPY;
char INTCONCOPY;        // Copy of INTCON for LoopTime subroutine
char COUNT;             // Counter available as local to subroutines
char TEMP;              // Temporary local variable
char ALIVECNT;          // Counter for blinking "Alive" LED
char BYTE;              // Eight-bit byte to be displayed
char OLDPORTD;          // Holds previous value of inputs
char DELRPG;            // Generated by RPG
char RPGCNT;            // Used to display RPG changes
char PBCOUNT;           // Counter for measuring duration of press
char SCREEN;            // State of LCD subroutine
char LOOP10;            // Scale of ten loop counter
char THR;               // Threshold value used by Pbutton

                        // Control/status bits for pushbutton
bit ISC;                // Initiate screen change for slow press
bit ISA;                // Initiate secondary action for fast press
bit PDONE;              // Pushbutton action has been taken
bit OLDPB;              // Old state of pushbutton
bit NEWPB;              // New state of pushbutton

/********************************
 * Constant strings
 ********************************
 */

// For stability reasons, create an EVEN number of elements in any given array
const char LCDstr[]  = {0x33,0x32,0x28,0x01,0x0c,0x06,0x00,0x00};// LCD Initialization string
const char StrtStr[] = {0x80,'P','u','s','h',' ','P','B',' ',0};// Startup screen
const char BYTE_1[]  = {0x80,'B','Y','T','E','=',' ',' ',' ',0};// Write "BYTE=" 1st line of LCD
const char Clear1[]  = {0x80,' ',' ',' ',' ',' ',' ',' ',' ',0};// Clear line 1
const char Clear2[]  = {0xC0,' ',' ',' ',' ',' ',' ',' ',' ',0};// Clear line 2
```

Figure A7-2 P3_PICC-18.c (P3 template recast for Hi-Tech's C compiler).

```
const char FreqStr[] = {0x80,'F','r','e','q',' ','k','H','z',0};// Frequency instrument
const char PerStr[]  = {0x80,'P','e','r',' ',' ',' ','u','s',0};// Period instrument
const char PWmaxStr[] = {0x80,'P','W','m','a','x',' ','u','s',0};// Max pulse width instrument

/*******************************
 * Variable strings
 *******************************
 */

char BYTESTR[] = {0,0,0,0,0,0,0,0,0,0}; // Display string for binary version of BYTE

/*******************************
 * Function prototypes
 *******************************
 */

void Initial(void);
void InitLCD(void);
void Looptime(void);
void T40(void);
void DisplayC(const char *);
void DisplayV(char *);
void BlinkAlive(void);
void LoopTime(void);
void ByteDisplay(void);
void RateRPG(void);
void Pbutton(void);
void Screens(void);
void Frequency(void);
void Period(void);
void PWmax(void);

/////// Mainline program ////////////////////////////////////////

/*******************************
 * main()
 *******************************
 */

void main()
{
        Initial();                      // Initialize everything

        while(1)
        {
          RB0 = !RB0;                   // Toggle pin, to support measuring loop time
          BlinkAlive();                 // Blink "Alive" LED
          Pbutton();                    // Check pushbutton
          Screens();                    // Deal with SCREEN state
          LoopTime();                   // Make looptime be ten milliseconds
        }
}

/*******************************
 * Initial()
 *
 * This subroutine performs all initializations of variables and registers.
 *******************************
 */

void Initial()
{
        ADCON1 = 0b10001110;            // Enable PORTA & PORTE digital I/O pins
        TRISA  = 0b11100001;            // Set I/O for PORTA
        TRISB  = 0b11011100;            // Set I/O for PORTB
        TRISC  = 0b11010000;            // Set I/O for PORTC
        TRISD  = 0b00001111;            // Set I/O for PORTD
        TRISE  = 0b00000000;            // Set I/O for PORTE
        T0CON  = 0b10001000;            // Set up Timer0 for a looptime of 10 ms
        PORTA  = 0b00010000;            // Turn off all four LEDs driven from PORTA
        OLDPORTD = PORTD;               // Initialize "old" value
        RPGCNT   = 0;                   // Clear counter to be displayed
        PBCOUNT  = 0;                   // and pushbutton count
        SCREEN   = 0;                   // Initialize LCD's SCREEN variable
        THR = 0;                        // Initialize Pbutton's THR variable
        ISC = 0;                        // Initialize pushbutton state
        ISA = 0;
        PDONE = 0;
        OLDPB = 1;
        NEWPB = 0;
```

Figure A7-2 continued

```
        InitLCD();                      // Initialize LCD
        DisplayC(StrtStr);              // Display startup message
}

/*******************************
 * InitLCD()
 *
 * Initialize the Optrex 8x2 character LCD.
 * First wait for 0.1 second, to get past display's power-on reset time.
 *******************************
 */

void InitLCD()
{
        char currentChar;
        const char *tempPtr;

        COUNT = 10;                     // Wait 0.1 second
        while (COUNT)
        {
          LoopTime();                   // Call LoopTime() 10 times
          COUNT--;
        }

        RE0 = 0;                        // RS=0 for command
        tempPtr = LCDstr;

        while (*tempPtr)                // if the byte is not zero
        {
          currentChar = *tempPtr;
          RE1 = 1;                      // Drive E pin high
          PORTD = currentChar;          // Send upper nibble
          RE1 = 0;                      // Drive E pin low so LCD will accept nibble
          LoopTime();
          currentChar <<= 4;            // Shift lower nibble to upper nibble
          RE1 = 1;                      // Drive E pin high again
          PORTD = currentChar;          // Write lower nibble
          RE1 = 0;                      // Drive E pin low so LCD will process byte
          LoopTime();                   // Wait 40 usec
          tempPtr++;                    // Increment pointer to next character
        }
}

/*******************************
 * T40()
 *
 * Pause for 40 microseconds  or 40/0.4 = 100 clock cycles.
 * Assumes 10/4 = 2.5 MHz internal clock rate.
 *******************************
 */

void T40()
{
        // Measured with oscilloscope to be about 42.80 us
        // including the time to call this routine.  Decrementing each
        // "cCOUNT" takes approximately 4 us.

        unsigned char cCOUNT = 7;
        while (cCOUNT)
          cCOUNT--;
}

/*******************************
 * DisplayC(const char *)
 *
 * This subroutine is called with the passing in of an array of a constant
 * display string.  It sends the bytes of the string to the LCD.  The first
 * byte sets the cursor position.  The remaining bytes are displayed, beginning
 * at that position.
 * This subroutine expects a normal one-byte cursor-positioning code, 0xhh, or
 * an occasionally used two-byte cursor-positioning code of the form 0x00hh.
 *******************************
 */

void DisplayC(const char * tempPtr)
{
        char currentChar;

        RE0 = 0;                        // Drive RS pin low for cursor-positioning code
        while (*tempPtr)                // if the byte is not zero
```

Figure A7-2 continued

```
        {
          currentChar = *tempPtr;
          RE1 = 1;                    // Drive E pin high
          PORTD = currentChar;        // Send upper nibble
          RE1 = Ø;                    // Drive E pin low so LCD will accept nibble
          currentChar <<= 4;          // Shift lower nibble to upper nibble
          RE1 = 1;                    // Drive E pin high again
          PORTD = currentChar;        // Write lower nibble
          RE1 = Ø;                    // Drive E pin low so LCD will process byte
          T4Ø();                      // Wait 4Ø usec
          REØ = 1;                    // Drive RS pin high for displayable characters
          tempPtr++;                  // Increment pointer to next character
        }
}

/********************************
 * DisplayV(char *)
 *
 * This subroutine is called with the passing in of an array of a variable
 * display string.  It sends the bytes of the string to the LCD.  The first
 * byte sets the cursor position.  The remaining bytes are displayed, beginning
 * at that position.
 ********************************
 */

void DisplayV(char * tempPtr)
{
        char currentChar;

        REØ = Ø;                      // Drive RS pin low for cursor-positioning code
        while (*tempPtr)              // if the byte is not zero
        {
          currentChar = *tempPtr;
          RE1 = 1;                    // Drive E pin high
          PORTD = currentChar;        // Send upper nibble
          RE1 = Ø;                    // Drive E pin low so LCD will accept nibble
          currentChar <<= 4;          // Shift lower nibble to upper nibble
          RE1 = 1;                    // Drive E pin high again
          PORTD = currentChar;        // Write lower nibble
          RE1 = Ø;                    // Drive E pin low so LCD will process byte
          T4Ø();                      // Wait 4Ø usec
          REØ = 1;                    // Drive RS pin high for displayable characters
          tempPtr++;                  // Increment pointer to next character
        }
}

/********************************
 * BlinkAlive()
 *
 * This subroutine briefly blinks the LED next to the PIC every two-and-a-half
 * seconds.
 ********************************
 */

void BlinkAlive()
{
        RA4 = 1;                      // Turn off LED
        if (!(--ALIVECNT))            // Decrement loop counter and return if not zero
        {
          ALIVECNT = 25Ø;             // Reinitialize ALIVECNT
          RA4 = Ø;                    // Turn on LED for ten milliseconds every 2.5 sec
        }
}

/********************************
 * LoopTime()
 *
 * This subroutine waits for TimerØ to complete its ten millisecond count
 * sequence. It does so by waiting for sixteen-bit TimerØ to roll over. To obtain
 * a period of precisely 1ØØØØ/Ø.4 = 25ØØØ clock periods, it needs to remove
 * 65536-25ØØØ or 4Ø536 counts from the sixteen-bit count sequence.  The
 * algorithm below first copies TimerØ to RAM, adds "Bignum" to the copy ,and
 * then writes the result back to TimerØ. It actually needs to add somewhat more
 * counts to TimerØ than 4Ø536.  The extra number of 12+2 counts added into
 * "Bignum" makes the precise correction.
 ********************************
 */

void LoopTime()
{
```

Figure A7-2 continued

```
#define Bignum  65536-25000+12+2
        while (!T0IF);                   // Wait until ten milliseconds are up
        INTCONCOPY = INTCON;             // Save INTCON bits
        GIEH = 0;                        // Disable all interrupts from CPU
        GIEL = 0;
        TMR0LCOPY = TMR0L;               // Read 16-bit counter at this moment
        TMR0HCOPY = TMR0H;
        TMR0LCOPY += Bignum & 0x00FF;    // add LSB
        if (STATUS & 1)                  // If Carry, increment high byte
          TMR0HCOPY++;
        TMR0HCOPY += (Bignum>>8) & 0x00FF; // add MSB
        TMR0H = TMR0HCOPY;
        TMR0L = TMR0LCOPY;               // Write 16-bit counter at this moment
        WREG = INTCONCOPY & 0b11000000;  // Reenable interrupts to CPU if enabled prior
        INTCON = INTCON | WREG;          // to LoopTime
        T0IF = 0;                        // Clear Timer0 flag
}

/*******************************
 * ByteDisplay()
 *
 * Display whatever is in BYTE as a binary number.
 *******************************
 */

void ByteDisplay()
{
        DisplayC(BYTE_1);                // Display "BYTE="

        COUNT = 8;                       // 8 bits in BYTE
        while (COUNT)
        {
          TEMP = (BYTE & 0b00000001);    // Move bit 0 of BYTE into TEMP
          TEMP |= 0x30;                  // Convert to ASCII
          BYTESTR[COUNT] = TEMP;         // and move to string
          BYTE = BYTE>>1;                // Right shift bits in BYTE by 1
          COUNT--;                       // Decrement COUNT;
        }
        BYTESTR[0] = 0xC0;               // Add cursor-positioning code
        BYTESTR[9] = 0;                  // and end-of-string terminator
        DisplayV(BYTESTR);               // Display the string
}

/*******************************
 * RateRPG()
 *
 * This subroutine deciphers RPG changes into values of DELRPG.
 * DELRPG = +2 for fast CW change, +1 for slow CW change, 0 for no change,
 *        -1 for slow CCW change and -2 for fast CCW change.
 *******************************
 */

void RateRPG()
{
  #define Threshold 3                    // Value to distinguish between slow and fast
  char W_temp;

        RA2 = 0;                         // Turn LED off
        DELRPG = 0;                      // Clear for "no change" return value
        W_temp = PORTD;                  // Copy PORTD into W_temp
        TEMP = W_temp;                   // and TEMP
        W_temp = W_temp ^ OLDPORTD;      // Any change?
        W_temp = W_temp & 0b00000011;    // If not, W_temp = 0
        if (W_temp != 0)                 // If the two bits have changed then...
        {
          W_temp = OLDPORTD>>1;          // Form what a CCW change would produce
          if (OLDPORTD & 0x01)           // Make new bit 1 = complement of old bit 0
            W_temp &= 0b11111101;
          else
            W_temp |= 0b00000010;
          W_temp = (W_temp ^ TEMP);      // Did the RPG actually change to this output?
          W_temp &= 0b00000011;          // Mask off upper 6 bits
          if (W_temp == 0)               // If so, then change  DELRPG to -1 for CCW
          {
            DELRPG--;
            if (THR != 0)
            {
              DELRPG--;                  // If fast turning, decrement again
              RA2 = 1;                   // Turn LED on
```

Figure A7-2 continued

```
            }
          }
          else
          {
            DELRPG++;                   // Otherwise, change DELRPG to  +1 for CW
            if (THR != Ø)
            {
              DELRPG++;                 // If fast turning, increment again
              RA2 = 1;                  // Turn LED on
            }
          }
          THR = Threshold;              // Reinitialize THR
        }
        if (THR != Ø)                   // Does THR equal zero
          THR--;                        // If not, then decrement it
        OLDPORTD = TEMP;                // Save PORTD as OLDPORTD for ten ms from now
}

/*******************************
 * Pbutton()
 *
 * This subroutine sorts out long and short pushbutton presses into two outputs:
 *      ISC=1: Initiate screen change for slow press
 *      ISA=1: Initiate secondary action for fast press
 *      PDONE=1 One of the above actions has occurred for this press
 *******************************
 */

void Pbutton()
{
        ISC = Ø;                        // Clear Initiate Screen Change bit (if set)
        ISA = Ø;                        // Clear Initiate Secondary Action bit (if set)

        if (RD3 == 1)                   // Copy pushbutton state to NEWPB
          NEWPB = 1;
        else
          NEWPB = Ø;

        if (OLDPB)                      // Look for leading edge (OLDPB=1, NEWPB=Ø)
        {
          if (!NEWPB)
            PBCOUNT = PBthres;          // Start counter
        }

        if (!NEWPB)                     // Pushbutton is still pressed
        {
          if (!PBCOUNT)                 // and counter has passed threshold
            if (!PDONE)                 // and no action has yet been taken
            {
              ISC = 1;                  // Initiate screen change
              PDONE = 1;                // Done with pulse
            }
        }
        else                            // Pushbutton has been released
          PDONE = Ø;                    // so clear PDONE

        if (!OLDPB)                     // Look for trailing edge (OLDPB=Ø, NEWPB=1)
          if (NEWPB)
          {
            if (PBCOUNT)                // Fast pulse
              ISA = 1;                  // Initiate secondary action
            PDONE = Ø;                  // Done with pulse
            PBCOUNT = Ø;                // Finish counting
          }

        if (PBCOUNT)                    // Has counter reached zero?
          PBCOUNT--;                    // If not, then decrement it

        if (NEWPB)                      // Copy NEWPB to OLDPB
          OLDPB = 1;
        else
          OLDPB = Ø;
}

/*******************************
 * Screens()
 *
 * This subroutine uses the ISC bit from the Pbutton subroutine to cycle the
 * state of SCREEN and to take action based upon its value.
 * Initially SCREEN=Ø, so that whatever screen is displayed by the Initial
```

Figure A7-2 continued

```
 * subroutine is not changed until a PB switch press.  Then the screen
 * corresponding to SCREEN=1 is displayed.  Subsequent PB switch
 * presses cycle through SCREEN=2, 3, etc., recycling back to SCREEN=1.
 ********************************
 */

void Screens()
{
  #define NumberOfScreens  4            // Change this value if new screens are added

        if (ISC)
        {
          SCREEN++;
          if (SCREEN > NumberOfScreens) // Check if past last screen
            SCREEN = 1;                 // Cycle back to SCREEN = 1

          DisplayC(Clear1);             // Clear the display when switching screens
          DisplayC(Clear2);
        }

        if (SCREEN == 1)
        {
          if (ISC)
            DisplayC(FreqStr);
          Frequency();
        }

        if (SCREEN == 2)
        {
          if (ISC)
            DisplayC(PerStr);
          Period();
        }

        if (SCREEN == 3)
        {
          if (ISC)
            DisplayC(PWmaxStr);
          PWmax();
          if (ISA)                      // Fast pulse, toggle RA1
            RA1 = !RA1;
        }

        if (SCREEN == 4)
        {
          RateRPG();                    // Decipher RPG inputs into DELRPG
          RPGCNT += DELRPG;             // Increment or decrement RPGCNT from RPG
          BYTE = RPGCNT;                // Point BYTE to RPGCNT
          ByteDisplay();
          if (ISA)                      // Fast pulse, reset RPGCNT
            RPGCNT = 0;
        }
}

/////// Stubs for measurement subroutines ///////////////////////////////////////

void Frequency() { }
void Period()    { }
void PWmax()     { }
```

Figure A7-2 continued

```
/****** P4_MCC18.c *****************************************************************
 *
 * Generate a jitterfree 10 Hz square wave on CCP1 output using compare mode
 * with extension.
 * Use 10 MHz crystal and 2.5 MHz internal clock rate.
 *
 ******* Program hierarchy *****************************************************
 *
 * Mainline
 *   Initial
 *
 * HiPriISR (included just to show structure)
 *
 * LoPriISR
 *   CCP1handler
 *   TMR1handler
 *
 ********************************
 */
#include <p18cxxx.h>
/*******************************
 * Definitions and equates
 *******************************
 */
#define HalfPeriod  125000      // Number of 0.4 us clock cycles in 0.05 seconds
/*******************************
 * Global variables
 *******************************
 */
char WREG_TEMP;
char STATUS_TEMP;
char TMR1X;                     // Eight-bit extension to TMR1
char CCPR1X;                    // Eight-bit extension to CCPR1
char DTIMEL;                    // Half-period value
char DTIMEH;
char DTIMEX;

/*******************************
 * Function prototypes
 *******************************
 */
void Initial(void);
void CCP1handler(void);
void TMR1handler(void);
void HiPriISR(void);
void LoPriISR(void);

#pragma code highVector=0x08
void atHighVector(void)
{
 _asm GOTO HiPriISR _endasm
}
#pragma code

#pragma code lowVector=0x18
void atLowVector(void)
{
 _asm GOTO LoPriISR _endasm
}
#pragma code

/*******************************
 * main()
 *******************************
 */
void main()
{
     Initial();                 // Initialize everything
     while(1) { }
}
/*******************************
 * Initial()
 *
 * This subroutine performs all initializations of variables and registers.
 *******************************
 */
void Initial()
{
     DTIMEL = HalfPeriod;       // Load DTIME with HalfPeriod
     DTIMEH = (HalfPeriod>>8);
     DTIMEX = (HalfPeriod>>16);
     TRISC = 0b11010000;        // Set I/O for PORTC
     T1CON = 0x81;              // Turn on TMR1
     CCP1CON = 0b00001000;      // Select compare mode
     RCONbits.IPEN = 1;         // Enable priority levels
     IPR1bits.TMR1IP = 0;       // Assign low priority to TMR1 interrupts
```

Figure A7-3 P4_MCC18.c (P4 template recast for Microchip's C compiler).

```
     IPR1bits.CCP1IP = 0;       //  and to CCP1 interrupts
     TMR1X = 0;                 // Make first 24-bit compare occur quickly
     CCPR1X = 2;
     PIE1bits.CCP1IE = 1;       // Enable CCP1 interrupts
     PIE1bits.TMR1IE = 1;       // Enable TMR1 interrupts
     INTCONbits.GIEL = 1;       // Enable low-priority interrupts to CPU
     INTCONbits.GIEH = 1;       // Enable all interrupts
}
/****** LoPriISR interrupt service routine ************************************/
#pragma interrupt HiPriISR      // High-priority interrupt service routine
void HiPriISR(void)             // Included to show form
                                // Supports retfie FAST automatically
{

}

#pragma interruptlow LoPriISR   // Low-priority interrupt service routine
void LoPriISR(void)
{
     while(1)
     {
       if (PIR1bits.CCP1IF)
       {
         CCP1handler();
         continue;
       }
       if (PIR1bits.TMR1IF)
       {
         TMR1handler();
         continue;
       }
         break;
     }
}
void CCP1handler()
{
     if (PIR1bits.TMR1IF)       // If Timer1's overflow flag is set
       if (!(CCPR1H & 0b10000000))  // and compare had occurred after that
         {
           TMR1X++;             // then increment TMR1 extension
           PIR1bits.TMR1IF = 0;  // and clear flag
         }
     if (TMR1X == CCPR1X)       // Check whether extensions are equal
     {
       CCP1CON = CCP1CON ^ 1;   // Toggle control bit (bit 0)
       CCPR1L += DTIMEL;        // and add half period to CCPR1
       if (STATUSbits.C)
         CCPR1H++;
       CCPR1H += DTIMEH;
       if (STATUSbits.C)
         CCPR1X++;
       CCPR1X += DTIMEX;
     }
     PIR1bits.CCP1IF = 0;       // Clear flag
}
void TMR1handler()
{
     TMR1X++;                   // Increment Timer1 extension
     PIR1bits.TMR1IF = 0;       // Clear flag and return to polling routine
}
```

Figure A7-3 continued

```
/****** P4_PICC-18.c ************************************************************
 *
 * Generate a jitterfree 10 Hz square wave on CCP1 output using compare mode
 * with extension.
 * Use 10 MHz crystal and 2.5 MHz internal clock rate.
 *
 ******* Program hierarchy ******************************************************
 *
 * Mainline
 *   Initial
 *
 * HiPriISR (included just to show structure)
 *
 * LoPriISR
 *   CCP1handler
 *   TMR1handler
 *
 ********************************************************************************
 */

#include <pic18.h>

/*******************************
 * Definitions and equates
 *******************************
 */

#define HalfPeriod  125000      // Number of 0.4 us clock cycles in 0.05 seconds

/*******************************
 * Global variables
 *******************************
 */

char WREG_TEMP;
char STATUS_TEMP;
char TMR1X;                     // Eight-bit extension to TMR1
char CCPR1X;                    // Eight-bit extension to CCPR1
char DTIMEL;                    // Half-period value
char DTIMEH;
char DTIMEX;

/*******************************
 * Function prototypes
 *******************************
 */

void Initial(void);
void CCP1handler(void);
void TMR1handler(void);

/*******************************
 * main()
 *******************************
 */

void main()
{
        Initial();              // Initialize everything

        while(1) { }
}

/*******************************
 * Initial()
 *
 * This subroutine performs all initializations of variables and registers.
 *******************************
 */

void Initial()
{
        DTIMEL = HalfPeriod & 0xFF;  // Load DTIME with HalfPeriod
        DTIMEH = (HalfPeriod>>8) & 0xFF;
        DTIMEX = (HalfPeriod>>16) & 0xFF;
        TRISC = 0b11010000;     // Set I/O for PORTC
        T1CON = 0x81;           // Turn on TMR1
        CCP1CON = 0b00001000;   // Select compare mode
        IPEN = 1;               // Enable priority levels
        TMR1IP = 0;             // Assign low priority to TMR1 interrupts
        CCP1IP = 0;             //  and to CCP1 interrupts
        TMR1X = 0;              // Make first 24-bit compare occur quickly
        CCPR1X = 2;
```

Figure A7-4 P4_PICC-18.c (P4 template recast for Hi-Tech's C compiler)

```
        CCP1IE = 1;             // Enable CCP1 interrupts
        TMR1IE = 1;             // Enable TMR1 interrupts
        GIEL = 1;               // Enable low-priority interrupts to CPU
        GIEH = 1;               // Enable all interrupts
}

/****** HiPriISR interrupt service routine ************************************/

void interrupt HiPriISR()       // High-priority interrupt service routine
{
//        <execute the handler for a single interrupt source>
//        <clear that source's interrupt flag>
//        Note that HiTech has not implemented the retfie FAST instruction as
//        of this writing.  However, saving and restoring of registers are
//        said to be handled automatically by the compiler.
}
/*** LoPriISR interrupt service routine ************************************/

void interrupt low_priority LoPriISR()  // Low-priority interrupt service routine
{

        while(1)
        {
          if (CCP1IF)
          {
            CCP1handler();
            continue;
          }

          if (TMR1IF)
          {
            TMR1handler();
            continue;
          }

          break;
        }
                                // Return from interrupt, reenabling GIEL
}

void CCP1handler()
{
        if (TMR1IF)             // If Timer1's overflow flag is set
          if (!(CCPR1H & 0b10000000))  // and compare had occurred after that
            {
              TMR1X++;          // then increment TMR1 extension
              TMR1IF = 0;       // and clear flag
            }

        if (TMR1X == CCPR1X)    // Check whether extensions are equal
        {
          CCP1CON = CCP1CON ^ 1;  // Toggle control bit (bit 0)
          CCPR1L += DTIMEL;       // and add half period to CCPR1
          if (STATUS & 1)        // if CARRY, increment high byte
            CCPR1H++;
          CCPR1H += DTIMEH;
          if (STATUS & 1)
            CCPR1X++;
          CCPR1X += DTIMEX;
        }

        CCP1IF = 0;             // Clear flag
}

void TMR1handler()
{
        TMR1X++;                // Increment Timer1 extension
        TMR1IF = 0;             // Clear flag and return to polling routine
}
```

Figure A7-4 continued

Appendix

A8

PIC18F452 SPECIAL FUNCTION REGISTERS AND THEIR BITS

The purpose of this appendix is to identify the name of each bit in each Special Function Register of the PIC18F452 microcontroller, as defined by the P18F452.INC "include" file used by the assembler. Whereas these names are generally identical to the bit names used in the PIC18F452 data sheet, in those few cases where a difference exists, the name used here is the name that will allow assembly to proceed. Some bits have multiple names in the PIC18F452.INC "include" file. For these, the name listed here is the name used throughout this text.

Another purpose of this appendix is to provide a debugging aid to the reader. Throughout this text, not all bits of all registers have been identified. Loading a value into a register to initialize certain bits may inadvertently change other bits residing in that same register from their power-on reset value. Figure A8-1 lists all Special Function Registers and their bit names. Figure A8-2 repeats the table of Figure 20-9 listing the power-on reset value of every register.

It should be noted that whereas the role of the data sheet is to describe *every* available feature of the PIC18F452 microcontroller, this text has dealt with a somewhat reduced set of features in the interests of simplicity. Accordingly, there are bits that are listed in Figure A8-1 that are not otherwise described in this text. For example, the UART description of Chapter 18 ignores the *synchronous* feature of what is actually a USART module having both master and slave capabilities. Thus, if the **SYNC** bit in the **TXSTA** register were to be set inadvertently, the UART would suddenly become a synchronous serial transfer module having a clock line and a bidirectional data line.

REGISTER	ADDRESS	B7	B6	B5	B4	B3	B2	B1	BØ
ADCONØ	FC2	ADCS1	ADCSØ	CHS2	CHS1	CHSØ	GO_DONE	–	ADON
ADCON1	FC1	ADFM	ADCS2	–	–	PCFG3	PCFG2	PCFG1	PCFGØ
ADRESH	FC4	A/D RESULT REGISTER – HIGH BYTE							
ADRESL	FC3	A/D RESULT REGISTER – LOW BYTE							
BSR	FEØ	–	–	–	–	BANK SELECT REGISTER			
CCP1CON	FBD	–	–	DC1B1	DC1BØ	CCP1M3	CCP1M2	CCP1M1	CCP1MØ
CCP2CON	FBA	–	–	DC2B1	DC2BØ	CCP2M3	CCP2M2	CCP2M1	CCP2MØ
CCPR1H	FBF	CAPTURE/COMPARE/PWM REGISTER 1 – HIGH BYTE							
CCPR1L	FBE	CAPTURE/COMPARE/PWM REGISTER 1 – LOW BYTE							
CCPR2H	FBC	CAPTURE/COMPARE/PWM REGISTER 2 – HIGH BYTE							
CCPR2L	FBB	CAPTURE/COMPARE/PWM REGISTER 2 – LOW BYTE							
EEADR	FA9	DATA EEPROM ADDRESS REGISTER							
EECON1	FA6	EEPGD	CFGS	–	FREE	WRERR	WREN	WR	RD
EECON2	FA7	DATA EEPROM CONTROL REGISTER 2 (not a physical register)							
EEDATA	FA8	DATA EEPROM DATA REGISTER							
FSRØH	FEA	–	–	–	–	INDIRECT ADDRESS POINTER Ø – HIGH BYTE			
FSRØL	FE9	INDIRECT ADDRESS POINTER Ø – LOW BYTE							
FSR1H	FE2	–	–	–	–	INDIRECT ADDRESS POINTER 1 – HIGH BYTE			
FSR1L	FE1	INDIRECT ADDRESS POINTER 1 – LOW BYTE							
FSR2H	FDA	–	–	–	–	INDIRECT ADDRESS POINTER 2 – HIGH BYTE			
FSR2L	FD9	INDIRECT ADDRESS POINTER 2 – LOW BYTE							
INDFØ	FEF	USES CONTENTS OF FSRØ TO ADDRESS DATA MEMORY – VALUE OF FSRØ NOT CHANGED (not a physical register)							
INDF1	FE7	USES CONTENTS OF FSR1 TO ADDRESS DATA MEMORY – VALUE OF FSR1 NOT CHANGED (not a physical register)							
INDF2	FDF	USES CONTENTS OF FSR2 TO ADDRESS DATA MEMORY – VALUE OF FSR2 NOT CHANGED (not a physical register)							
INTCON	FF2	GIEH	GIEL	TMRØIE	INTØIE	RBIE	TMRØIF	INTØIF	RBIF
INTCON2	FF1	RBPU	INTEDGØ	INTEDG1	INTEDG2	–	TMRØIP	–	RBIP
INTCON3	FFØ	INT2IP	INT1IP	–	INT2IE	INT1IE	–	INT2IF	INT1IF
IPR1	F9F	PSPIP	ADIP	RCIP	TXIP	SSPIP	CCP1IP	TMR2IP	TMR1IP
IPR2	FA2	–	–	–	EEIP	BCLIP	LVDIP	TMR3IP	CCP2IP
LATA	F89	–	–	READ/WRITE PORTA DATA LATCH					
LATB	F8A	READ/WRITE PORTB DATA LATCH							
LATC	F8B	READ/WRITE PORTC DATA LATCH							
LATD	F8C	READ/WRITE PORTD DATA LATCH							
LATE	F8D	–	–	–	–	–	READ/WRITE PORTE DATA LATCH		
LVDCON	FD2	–	–	IRVST	LVDEN	LVDL3	LVDL2	LVDL1	LVDLØ
OSCCON	FD3	–	–	–	–	–	–	–	SCS
PCL	FF9	PROGRAM COUNTER – LOW BYTE – PC<7:Ø>							
PCLATH	FFA	HOLDING REGISTER FOR PROGRAM COUNTER BITS PC<15:8>							
PCLATU	FFB	–	–	–	HOLDING REGISTER FOR PROGRAM COUNTER BITS PC<2Ø:16> (maintain all zeros for PIC18F452)				
PIE1	F9D	PSPIE	ADIE	RCIE	TXIE	SSPIE	CCP1IE	TMR2IE	TMR1IE
PIE2	FAØ	–	–	–	EEIE	BCLIE	LVDIE	TMR3IE	CCP2IE
PIR1	F9E	PSPIF	ADIF	RCIF	TXIF	SSPIF	CCP1IF	TMR2IF	TMR1IF
PIR2	FA1	–	–	–	EEIF	BCLIF	LVDIF	TMR3IF	CCP2IF
PLUSWØ	FEB	USES FSRØ PLUS WREG (as a signed number) TO ADDRESS DATA MEMORY – VALUE OF FSRØ NOT CHANGED							
PLUSW1	FE3	USES FSR1 PLUS WREG (as a signed number) TO ADDRESS DATA MEMORY – VALUE OF FSR1 NOT CHANGED							
PLUSW2	FDB	USES FSR2 PLUS WREG (as a signed number) TO ADDRESS DATA MEMORY – VALUE OF FSR2 NOT CHANGED							
PORTA	F8Ø	–	–	READ FROM PORTA PINS; WRITE TO PORTA DATA LATCH					
PORTB	F81	READ FROM PORTB PINS; WRITE TO PORTB DATA LATCH							
PORTC	F82	READ FROM PORTC PINS; WRITE TO PORTC DATA LATCH							
PORTD	F83	READ FROM PORTD PINS; WRITE TO PORTD DATA LATCH							
PORTE	F84	–	–	–	–	–	READ FROM PORTE PINS; WRITE TO PORTE DATA LATCH		

Figure A8-1 PICI 8F452 registers and their bits

REGISTER	ADDRESS	B7	B6	B5	B4	B3	B2	B1	BØ
POSTDECØ	FED	USES CONTENTS OF FSRØ TO ADDRESS DATA MEMORY; THEN CONTENTS OF FSRØ ARE DECREMENTED							
POSTDEC1	FE5	USES CONTENTS OF FSR1 TO ADDRESS DATA MEMORY; THEN CONTENTS OF FSR1 ARE DECREMENTED							
POSTDEC2	FDD	USES CONTENTS OF FSR2 TO ADDRESS DATA MEMORY; THEN CONTENTS OF FSR2 ARE DECREMENTED							
POSTINCØ	FEE	USES CONTENTS OF FSRØ TO ADDRESS DATA MEMORY; THEN CONTENTS OF FSRØ ARE INCREMENTED							
POSTINC1	FE6	USES CONTENTS OF FSR1 TO ADDRESS DATA MEMORY; THEN CONTENTS OF FSR1 ARE INCREMENTED							
POSTINC2	FDE	USES CONTENTS OF FSR2 TO ADDRESS DATA MEMORY; THEN CONTENTS OF FSR2 ARE INCREMENTED							
PR2	FCB	TIMER2 PERIOD REGISTER							
PREINCØ	FEC	CONTENTS OF FSRØ ARE INCREMENTED AND THEN USED TO ADDRESS DATA MEMORY							
PREINC1	FE4	CONTENTS OF FSR1 ARE INCREMENTED AND THEN USED TO ADDRESS DATA MEMORY							
PREINC2	FDC	CONTENTS OF FSR2 ARE INCREMENTED AND THEN USED TO ADDRESS DATA MEMORY							
PRODH	FF4	PRODUCT REGISTER - HIGH BYTE							
PRODL	FF3	PRODUCT REGISTER - LOW BYTE							
RCON	FDØ	IPEN	-	-	NOT_RI	NOT_TO	NOT_PD	NOT_POR	NOT_BOR
RCREG	FAE	UART RECEIVE REGISTER							
RCSTA	FAB	SPEN	RX9	SREN	CREN	ADDEN	FERR	OERR	RX9D
SPBRG	FAF	UART BAUD RATE GENERATOR							
SSPADD	FC8	FOR I^2C SLAVE MODE, SLAVE ADDRESS; FOR I^2C MASTER MODE, BAUD RATE RELOAD REGISTER							
SSPBUF	FC9	FOR BOTH SPI AND I^2C BUS OPERATION, RECEIVE BUFFER/TRANSMIT REGISTER							
SSPCON1	FC6	WCOL	SSPOV	SSPEN	CKP	SSPM3	SSPM2	SSPM1	SSPMØ
SSPCON2	FC5	GCEN	ACKSTAT	ACKDT	ACKEN	RCEN	PEN	RSEN	SEN
SSPSTAT	FC7	SMP	CKE	D_A	I2C_STOP	I2C_START	R_W	UA	BF
STATUS	FD8	-	-	-	N	OV	Z	DC	C
STKPTR	FFC	STKFUL	STKUNF	-	RETURN STACK POINTER				
TØCON	FD5	TMRØON	TØ8BIT	TØCS	TØSE	PSA	TØPS2	TØPS1	TØPSØ
T1CON	FCD	RD16	-	T1CKPS1	T1CKPSØ	T1OSCEN	T1SYNC	TMR1CS	TMR1ON
T2CON	FCA	-	TOUTPS3	TOUTPS2	TOUTPS1	TOUTPSØ	TMR2ON	T2CKPS1	T2CKPSØ
T3CON	FB1	RD16	T3CCP2	T3CKPS1	T3CKPSØ	T3CCP1	T3SYNC	TMR3CS	TMR3ON
TABLAT	FF5	PROGRAM MEMORY TABLE LATCH							
TBLPTRH	FF7	PROGRAM MEMORY TABLE POINTER - HIGH BYTE - TBLPTR<15:8>							
TBLPTRL	FF6	PROGRAM MEMORY TABLE POINTER - LOW BYTE - TBLPTR<7:Ø>							
TBLPTRU	FF8	-	-	PROGRAM MEMORY TABLE POINTER - UPPER BYTE - TBLPTR<21:16> (A value of Øx2Ø allows access to the configuration bits)					
TMRØH	FD7	TIMERØ REGISTER - HIGH BYTE							
TMRØL	FD6	TIMERØ REGISTER - LOW BYTE							
TMR1H	FCF	TIMER1 REGISTER - HIGH BYTE							
TMR1L	FCE	TIMER1 REGISTER - LOW BYTE							
TMR2	FCC	TIMER2 REGISTER							
TMR3H	FB3	TIMER3 REGISTER - HIGH BYTE							
TMR3L	FB2	TIMER3 REGISTER - LOW BYTE							
TOSH	FFE	TOP-OF-STACK - HIGH BYTE - TOS<15:8>							
TOSL	FFD	TOP-OF-STACK - LOW BYTE - TOS<7:Ø>							
TOSU	FFF	-	-	-	TOP-OF-STACK - UPPER BYTE - TOS<2Ø-16>				
TRISA	F92	-	-	DATA DIRECTION CONTROL REGISTER FOR PORTA					
TRISB	F93	DATA DIRECTION CONTROL REGISTER FOR PORTB							
TRISC	F94	DATA DIRECTION CONTROL REGISTER FOR PORTC							
TRISD	F95	DATA DIRECTION CONTROL REGISTER FOR PORTD							
TRISE	F96	IBF	OBF	IBOV	PSPMODE	-	DATA DIRECTION CONTROL BITS FOR PORTE		
TXREG	FAD	UART TRANSMIT REGISTER							
TXSTA	FAC	CSRC	TX9	TXEN	SYNC	-	BRGH	TRMT	TX9D
WDTCON	FD1	-	-	-	-	-	-	-	SWDTEN
WREG	FE8	WORKING REGISTER							

Figure A8-1 continued

Register	POR BOR	Other resets
ADCONØ	Ø	Ø
ADCON1	Ø	Ø
ADRESH	x	u
ADRESL	x	u
CCP1CON	Ø	Ø
CCP2CON	Ø	Ø
CCPR1H	x	u
CCPR1L	x	u
CCPR2H	x	u
CCPR2L	x	u
EEADR	Ø	Ø
EECON1	m	m
EECON2	–	–
EEDATA	Ø	Ø
FSRØH	x	u
FSRØL	x	u
FSR1H	x	u
FSR1L	x	u
FSR2H	x	u
FSR2L	x	u
INDFØ	–	–
INDF1	–	–
INDF2	–	–
INTCON	Ø	Ø
INTCON2	1	1

Register	POR BOR	Other resets
INTCON3	m	m
IPR1	1	1
IPR2	1	1
LATA	x	u
LATB	x	u
LATC	x	u
LATD	x	u
LATE	x	u
LVDCON	m	m
OSCCON	Ø	Ø
PCL	Ø	Ø
PCLATH	Ø	Ø
PCLATU	Ø	Ø
PIE1	Ø	Ø
PIE2	Ø	Ø
PIR1	Ø	Ø
PIR2	Ø	Ø
PLUSWØ	–	–
PLUSW1	–	–
PLUSW2	–	–
PORTA	m	m
PORTB	x	u
PORTC	x	u
PORTD	x	u
PORTE	Ø	Ø

Register	POR BOR	Other resets
POSTDECØ	–	–
POSTDEC1	–	–
POSTDEC2	–	–
POSTINCØ	–	–
POSTINC1	–	–
POSTINC2	–	–
PR2	1	1
PREINCØ	–	–
PREINC1	–	–
PREINC2	–	–
PRODH	x	u
PRODL	x	u
RCON	m	m
RCREG	Ø	Ø
RCSTA	m	m
SPBRG	Ø	u
SSPADD	Ø	Ø
SSPBUF	x	u
SSPCON1	Ø	Ø
SSPCON2	Ø	Ø
SSPSTAT	Ø	Ø
STATUS	x	u
STKPTR	Ø	Ø
TØCON	1	1
T1CON	Ø	u

Register	POR BOR	Other resets
T2CON	Ø	Ø
T3CON	Ø	u
TABLAT	Ø	Ø
TBLPTRH	Ø	Ø
TBLPTRL	Ø	Ø
TBLPTRU	Ø	Ø
TMRØH	Ø	Ø
TMRØL	x	u
TMR1H	x	u
TMR1L	x	u
TMR2	Ø	Ø
TMR3H	x	u
TMR3L	x	u
TOSH	Ø	Ø
TOSL	Ø	Ø
TOSU	Ø	Ø
TRISA	1	1
TRISB	1	1
TRISC	1	1
TRISD	1	1
TRISE	1	1
TXREG	Ø	Ø
TXSTA	m	m
WDTCON	Ø	Ø
WREG	x	u

(a) Registers and their contents.

Key: Ø: all zeros 1: all ones
x: unknown u: unchanged
m: mixed –: not a physical register

Register	POR BOR	Other resets
EECON1	xx-ØxØØ	uu-ØuØØØ
INTCON3	11-ØØ-ØØ	11-ØØ-ØØ
LVDCON	--ØØØ1Ø1	--ØØØ1Ø1
PORTA	-ØØxØØØØ	-ØØxØØØØ
RCON	Ø--q11qq	Ø--qqquu
RCSTA	ØØØØØØØx	ØØØØØØØx
TXSTA	ØØØØ-Ø1Ø	ØØØØ-Ø1Ø

Key: q: Depends on type of reset

(b) Registers with mixed contents.

Figure A8-2 State of Special Function Registers after coming out of reset

Appendix

A9

PARTS AND PACKAGES

This appendix lists, in Figure A9-1, the part numbers for each of the family parts. This is useful when buying parts, helping to forestall the purchase of the right part in the wrong package. The QwikFlash board uses the PIC18F452-I/P part in its 40-pin DIP package. Alternatively, the PIC18LF452-I/P part operates over the extended supply voltage range shown in Figure 20-3 and will, of course, work with the 5 V supply of the QwikFlash board.

Part number	Program memory (16-bit words)	RAM bytes	Total pins	I/O pins	Package size (length × width, including pins)				
					Part number, including package identification				
					40-pin DIP	44-pin PLCC	44-pin TQFP	28-pin DIP	28-pin SOIC
PIC18F452	16384	1536	40/44	33	2.058" × 0.600"	0.690" × 0.690"	0.472" × 0.472"		
					PIC18F452-I/P	PIC18F452-I/L	PIC18F452-I/PT		
PIC18F442	8192	768	40/44	33	2.058" × 0.600"	0.690" × 0.690"	0.472" × 0.472"		
					PIC18F442-I/P	PIC18F442-I/L	PIC18F442-I/PT		
PIC18F252	16384	1536	28	22				1.345" × 0.300"	0.704" × 0.407"
								PIC18F252-I/SP	PIC18F252-I/SO
PIC18F242	8192	768	28	22				1.345" × 0.300"	0.704" × 0.407"
								PIC18F242-I/SP	PIC18F242-I/SO

Figure A9-1 Alternative family member parts and their package identification

Appendix

A10

EXAMPLE OF COURSE ORGANIZATION AND LAB PROJECTS

A10.1 COURSE CALENDAR

Georgia Tech operates on a semester schedule consisting of 45 fifty-minute class periods. An example course calendar is shown in Figure A10-0. A new project generally comes due each week. The class is divided into teams of two and the lab projects are sized taking this into account. Over the course of the semester, students undertake ten or so lab projects. The semester ends with each group taking on a design project of its own selection.

While the course calendar is handed out at the beginning of the semester and while it lists the subjects studied during the semester, the *order* in which topics are discussed in class is actually driven by the needs of the lab projects. The projects that we use at Georgia Tech take advantage of the resources on the QwikFlash board plus the three added resources of our QwikProto board, as indicated in conjunction with Figure A2-5.

A10.2 BUILDING A LABORATORY

The laboratory for another course at another university would be augmented with whatever popular add-on resources a professor has used in the past. I would welcome suggestions using such other resources and would plan to add references to creative ideas being used elsewhere via the URL to Web sites describing them on my own Web site, www.picbook.com. Also, check www.microdesignsinc.com to obtain the extra QwikFlash and QwikProto boards needed for building a lab. Alternatively, e-mail me at john.peatman@ece.gatech.edu.

Class	Text	Topics
1	Ch. 1	Introduction
2	2.2, 2.3, 2.7, 2.8, Ch. 3	Harvard architecture; Direct addressing; CPU and status bits; Instruction set
3	Ch. 3	Instruction set
4	Ch. 3, 4, 5.2–5.4	Instruction set; QwikFlash board; Timer0; LoopTime subroutine
5	5.5, 2.4, 5.6	BlinkAlive subroutine; Indirect addressing; Macros
6	Ch. 6	Structured assembler preprocessor
7	2.5, 7.2–7.5	Reading operands from program memory; LCD initialization; Display strings
8	7.5, 7.6	DisplayC and DisplayV subroutines; LCD character set
9	7.8	DISPLAY debugging aid
10	7.9	P2 template code
11	Ch. 8	Rotary pulse generator
12	9.2	Interrupt timing
13	9.3, 9.4	Low-priority and high-priority interrupt structures
14	9.5, 9.6	Critical regions; External Interrupts
15	Ch. 10	Analog-to-digital conversion
16	Ch. 11	I/O pin considerations
17	12.2	Pbutton subroutine for short and long presses of a pushbutton
18	12.3	Screens subroutine
19	13.2, 13.3	Timer1 for internal time-interval measurements
20	13.4	Extended time-interval measurements
21	13.5	CCP1/Timer1 combination for external time-interval measurements
22	13.7, 13.8	Extended time-interval measurements; Timer3/CCP2 use
23	13.9, 4.3	Frequency measurements; QwikFlash instrument
24	14.2–14.4	Multiplication and division subroutines and their use
25	A6	Chris Twigg's verification of math subroutines; PRBS generators
26	14.5–14.8	Floating-point subroutines; Normalize subroutine
27	15.2	Serial peripheral interface (SPI) operation
28	15.3–15.6	SPI output and input port expansion
29	15.7, 15.8	DAC output, Temperature Input
30	15.9	Multiple PIC operation via SPI connection
31	16.2	Magnetic-card reader use
32	16.3	Periodic interrupt generator; Stepper motor control
33	16.4	Fast jitter-free square wave output via the pulse-width modulation (PWM) facility
34	16.3, 16.5	General output timing control with CCP1/Timer1 or CCP2/Timer3
35	19.2	Programmed peripheral using the PIC16C505 microcontroller
36	19.3–19.6	Keypad interface
37	18.1, 18.2, 19.7	UART operation; Bit-banged UART output
38	20.2, 20.3	Configuration bytes; Oscillator alternatives
39	20.4, 20.5	Supply voltage requirements; Low-voltage detection
40	20.6, 20.7	Brownout reset; Watchdog timer use
41	20.8, 20.9	Resets; Battery-powered operation
42	20.11	Nonvolatile memory use

Figure A10-0 Course Calendar

Even without the addition of the QwikProto board, a versatile lab can be developed by adding interesting I/O parts in the 1¼″ × 1½″ pattern of 100-mil-spaced holes in the upper right-hand corner of the QwikFlash board. For example, Maxim makes a thermocouple converter, the MAX6675, that comes in an SO-8 surface-mount package. Digi-Key carries a little adapter (Part No. A724) that converts this package into a standard 8-pin DIP package. This combination is shown on the cover of this book. The seven-position terminal block listed in conjunction with the parts list of Figure A1-1 can be used to connect a Type-K thermocouple to the board. An oven calibrator can be implemented having a range up to 700°C with ±3°C accuracy (which can, of course, be displayed as a Fahrenheit temperature using the math subroutines of Chapter 14). Many specialty I^2C parts are also available only as surface-mount parts and can be handled in the same way.

One of my former students, Rick Farmer, is responsible for the fine layout and production of the QwikFlash and QwikProto boards as well as many of the design ideas incorporated in them. He has indicated his willingness to field requests from professors who want to make modifications to either board for their use. However, as is true for the production of any printed circuit board, the board house that actually makes the boards for Rick has setup charges that make small runs of boards expensive (in addition to Rick's charge for his work). Rick presently lives in Portland, Oregon. His present e-mail address is rfarmer@skyweb.net. If you have trouble contacting him, check my Web site, www.picbook.com.

A10.3 LAB EQUIPMENT

For tools in the lab, we begin with the PIC18F452 part programmed with the QwikBug monitor described in Appendix A4. This lets students load and run their code as well as run to a breakpoint, single-step, and monitor "watch" variables. To measure time intervals, I have students drive a pin high at the beginning of the event I want them to measure (e.g., the call of a subroutine) and drive it low at the end of the event. The top strip of pins is particularly useful for this purpose (e.g., "C2" or "B0" or "B1" or "E2"). One of them can be easily probed and displayed with a digital scope like that shown in Figure 5-11. Alternatively, it can be coupled with the two-conductor flex cable listed in Figure A1-1 to another board used as the QwikFlash instrument described in Section 4.3. The loop time can be verified by toggling one of these pins and measuring the period of the waveform (i.e., 20 milliseconds for a 10 millisecond loop time).

While I am a believer in the efficacy of low-cost tools like the QwikBug monitor and the QwikFlash instrument described briefly in Chapter 4, we eventually switch to Microchip's ICD2 in-circuit debugger. Its connection to the QwikFlash board is already in place with a 6-pin modular connector included specifically for this purpose. This gives students experience with this important tool. Even if a lab has just one of these versatile tools, it will provide the laboratory with a versatile PIC18F452 programmer that can be used to program the QwikBug monitor code into PIC18F452 parts.

A10.4 ASSEMBLY CODING VS. STRUCTURED ASSEMBLY CODING VS. C CODING

We quickly get to the use of the structured assembler described in Chapter 6 so students can write code and have self-evident control flow. With this structured assembler comes the need for the QwikAddress utility described in Appendix A5. For simplicity, we automatically open six separate windows on the desktop for student use:

A:\ folder	For a student's floppy disk.
C:\Work folder	To copy a source file from the floppy to the hard drive, and vice versa, for work in the lab by dragging the source file from one window to the other.
Text editor	For editing the source file and for easily viewing the .err, .apr, and .lst files in the C:\Work folder. Again, a file name in the C:\Work folder can simply be dragged into the text editor window to open that file in the text editor.
C:\Work>	DOS prompt to process a student source file with the sasm structured assembler.
Tera Term Pro	The terminal emulator, to communicate with the QwikBug monitor program residing in the PIC18F452 chip on the target board.
QwikAddress utility	When assembling with sasm, this utility translates error line numbers back to the .asm source file. When using QwikBug, this utility quickly presents any address needed to set a watch variable or a breakpoint address.

Eventually, at some point in the semester we switch over to the use of a C compiler. At the time of this switch, we begin again with the "screens" template code, P3.asm, converted into C. The file we use is listed in Appendix A7. While it would be possible to start the lab work with the use of the C compiler, students would lose insight into the workings of the microcontroller and control over the generated code and its timing. When using a C compiler, MPLAB and the ICD2 in-circuit debugger become the tools of choice because of their smooth handling of watch variables and breakpoint addresses. In contrast, QwikBug reverts to being pretty much of a "load and go" tool for compiled C code.

A10.5 TEN PROJECTS

What follows, as separate figures, are a set of projects that might be used to get a lab started. Each project description might be accompanied by a checkout sheet indicating what a student team must do to demonstrate the effectiveness of the code they have prepared. I often work in a timing measurement that gives insight into the power of the microcontroller to carry out rather extensive code execution in a tiny fraction of the loop time. A maximum pulse-width measurement can be used to indicate how little time *all* of the code execution within the mainline loop plus that for interrupt service routines generally takes—only a fraction of the loop time. The "infinite persistence" feature of a digital scope or the "maximum pulse width" feature of the QwikFlash instrument can capture this time, even when the maximum rarely occurs (as long as it occurs even once).

ECE 4175
Project One
Introduction to the Microcontroller Development Environment

References:

Sections 2.1, 2.2, 2.3, 2.7, 2.8
Chapter 3 - skim
Chapter 4 - skim
Chapter 5 - this chapter explains the P1.asm code for this project
Appendix A4 - skim

Before Lab

[ ] Attend the demo.

[ ] On the "team" signup sheet, put a "handle" together with your name and that of your partner. You will need one or two floppy disks. You will want to get lined up with a lab partner even though I suggest that you work on this specific project individually.

Using QwikBug

[ ] The QwikBug monitor, described in Appendix A4, supports the use of the F3 key to load your assembled user code, P1.HEX. The F7 key will then run your program. It can also be run, once loaded, by toggling the power switch or by pressing the reset pushbutton, SW2.

[ ] Turn on one of the PCs, if necessary.

[ ] Log on the PC using the user id "4175" (without quotes) and password "4175" (without quotes). The login process will take 30-60 seconds while the PC's hard disk is scanned for viruses. If a warning or error occurs during login or bootup, please contact the TA.

[ ] Click on the "Development" icon on the desktop to open the six windows that we use for development. These are the A:\folder, the C:\WORK folder, the text editor, a DOS prompt in the C:\WORK folder, Tera Term Pro, and the QwikAddress utility.

[ ] We suggest that you do all of your work from files temporarily loaded into the C:\WORK folder while at the same time maintaining (and updating often) a copy of your source file on a floppy disk. In this way you will gain the speedy execution of the assembler. Copy P1.asm from a floppy available in the lab to the C:\WORK folder. Then replace the lab floppy with your own floppy in the A:\drive. As you change your source file, remember to periodically slide the P1.asm file name in the C:\WORK folder to the A:\folder on the desktop, thereby maintaining an up-to-date copy of your source file on your floppy disk.

Figure A10-1 Project One: Microcontroller Development Environment (Page 1 of 4)

WARNING: All user files are deleted from the PC's hard disk whenever the computer is rebooted or a new user logs on. **If you ever quit your work and then realize that you have not saved your source file to your floppy, DO NOT log on again. As long as the computer is not rebooted or logged onto again, the TA can retrieve your source file for you.**

[ ] Open the P1 source file (P1.asm) into the editor by sliding the P1.asm icon on the desktop into the open editor window. Move and/or resize the resulting window to make it easy to read and use.

[ ] Insert your handle and name(s) somewhere within the first few lines of the program. Be sure that a semicolon is placed at the beginning of the line so that your handle and name(s) will be considered to be comments by the assembler. Also, change line 17 from X=ON to X=OFF to turn off "macro expansion." Macro expansion shows the lines of code generated by a macro, as is done in the P1.LST file in Figure 5-10. Turning off macro expansion reduces the size of your list file.

Add a line to the **Initial** subroutine to initialize the **ALIVECNT** variable to a value of 250 with the line

```
MOVLF 250,ALIVECNT
```

[ ] Save your updated source file to your floppy disk by again sliding the P1.asm label from the C:\WORK folder to the A:\folder.

[ ] To assemble your P1 source file, go to the DOS window in the C:\WORK folder and type

```
mpasm p1
```

Press the Enter key to invoke Microchip's free assembler, mpasm.exe. This will produce the ".HEX" file needed by the monitor program, the ".LST" file to get a hardcopy printout of the assembled output, and an ".ERR" file for a concise listing of assembly errors (if any occurred). Modify the source file, save it, and reassemble until all errors have been corrected.

NOTE:Treat all warnings generated during assembly as errors. Several forms of "typos" will result in warnings being generated during assembly rather than errors. The warnings often result in assembled code that does not perform as expected.

[ ] Drag the P1.LST desktop icon into the editor window and print a copy of it to familiarize yourself with the printing process.

[ ] Use the mouse to select the Tera Term Pro terminal emulation window. The target board should have the serial cable from the PC connected to its DB-9 socket. Turn on power to the target board using the toggle switch located in the lower left-hand corner of the board.

Figure A10-1 Project One: Microcontroller Development Environment (Page 2 of 4)

You should get the QwikBug help screen that ends with the message

QwikBug is autostarting user code

Press any key to abort:[#]

Within four seconds press any key on the PC's keyboard to avoid running previously loaded user code. If you don't do this quickly enough (and if user code was previously loaded), you will get the message

Running . . .

Just press the white reset button (SW2) or toggle the power switch to start over, this time with faster reaction time in pressing a PC key. Now you will get the QwikBug prompt

QB>

[ ] Press the F1 key at any time to repeat the brief reminder of QwikBug commands.

[ ] To load your new file, press the F3 key, resulting in the query

Send HEX File Now

Do not press any PC keys. Rather, just drag the P1.HEX label from the C:\WORK directory into the Tera Term Pro window to send it to the target board.

[ ] When the

. . . .

feedback stops with the message

Loading successful

press the F7 to switch from the QwikBug monitor program to the running of your user program. Note that the "Alive" LED located to the left of the PIC18F452 blinks briefly every 2½ seconds. Referring to Figure 4-2, note that the Alive LED is driven from bit 4 of PORTA.

[ ] QwikBug will let you selectively monitor the execution of the P1 program. Hit any key on the PC to return control to the QwikBug monitor program. Press the F1 key if you need to refresh the help message. Go to the QwikAddress window to obtain the address of the **ALIVECNT** variable. Note that it has been assigned to hex address 003. Then press the F6 key to add the address of the **ALIVECNT** variable to the watch list with

003

Now return to the QwikAddress window to obtain the address represented by the program label **Loop**. This address is shown to be 001E. Press the breakpoint key, F5, and enter a breakpoint at this address. Then press the F2 key to reset the CPU followed by the F7 key to run from reset to the breakpoint. Note the displayed value of **ALIVECNT**, represented as the hex value FA. Pressing the F7 key repeatedly will result in the display of the successive values of **ALIVECNT** each time around the mainline loop: F9, F8, F7, etc.

Figure A10-1 Project One: Microcontroller Development Environment (Page 3 of 4)

[ ] Use the F9 "Modify" key to change the value of **ALIVECNT** to 1. Again, run to the breakpoint by pressing the F7 key. This time around the mainline loop, the **BlinkAlive** subroutine will decrement **ALIVECNT** from 1 to 0 and will turn on the Alive LED. Press the F7 key again. This will result in another call of the **BlinkAlive** subroutine, turning off the Alive LED.

[ ] Set the breakpoint at the address represented by the subroutine label **BlinkAlive**. Again modify the value of **ALIVECNT** to 1. Run to the breakpoint. Using the QwikAddress utility, note that **PORTA** has address F80. Add this address to the list of watch variables with the F6 key. Now press the F8 key to step through the successive instructions of the **BlinkAlive** subroutine, noting when the Alive LED turns on and what instruction is indicated by the program counter value at that point.

[ ] Use the HP54645A scope's channel 1 probe to monitor bit 2 of PORTC (connected to the pin located on the H1 header of pins at the top of the board and labeled C2/CCP1). Connect the scope's ground clip to the GND1 "ground grabber" loop of wire located just above the PIC chip. The code for this project toggles this pin every 10 milliseconds, each time around the mainline loop. In this part you are to verify this loop time.

Press the scope's "Setup" key followed by the "Default Setup" softkey to get the scope back to its default state. Next, press the "Autoscale" key to get a waveform on the scope. Now press the "Time" key followed by the "Next Menu" and the "+Width" softkeys. What is the measured time?

___________ms

Winding Up

[ ] Be sure to save your file(s) onto your floppy disk.

[ ] Turn off power to the target board, using the toggle switch in the lower left-hand corner of the board.

[ ] Log off of the computer.

[ ] Tell the lab TA to check you off as having completed Project One. You need not turn in anything for this first project.

Figure A10-1 Project One: Microcontroller Development Environment (Page 4 of 4)

ECE 4175
Project Two
Slow Rate Control

References:

Figure 3-1 Instruction set
Figure 4-2 QwikFlash I/O
Handout QwikProto I/O

Overview

For this project, the code for Project One should continue to work. Add to this the following:

For the first 2560 milliseconds after reset, cycle the three LEDs as follows:
Lcr (turn on the left LED for 640 milliseconds)
lCr (turn on the center LED for 640 milliseconds)
lcR (turn on the right LED for 640 milliseconds)
lcr (turn on no LED for 640 milliseconds)
In addition, step the stepper motor clockwise every 640 ms.

For the next 2560 milliseconds after reset, cycle the three LEDs as follows:
Lcr (turn on the left LED for 320 milliseconds)
lCr (turn on the center LED for 320 milliseconds)
lcR (turn on the right LED for 320 milliseconds)
lcr (turn on no LED for 320 milliseconds)
Repeat this sequencing for the rest of the 2560 ms interval.
In addition, step the stepper motor clockwise every 320 ms.

Continue halving the LED "on" time and the step period every 2560 milliseconds until the "on" time and step period are 10 milliseconds. At that point, continue indefinitely with the 10 millisecond LED "on" time and step period.

Procedure

Write a **SequenceLEDs** subroutine which, when called, produces the next state of the LEDs. That is, if the present state is lCr, then **SequenceLEDs** will change this to lcR.

Write a **Halve** subroutine that, when called, halves a variable called **LED_PER.** This variable is to be initialized to 64 in the **Initial** subroutine. When **LED_PER** reaches a value of 1, leave it at that value thereafter.

Define three 1 byte variables, **BIG_CNT, LED_CNT,** and **LED_PER.** The **BIG_CNT** variable is to be decremented every time around the 10 millisecond mainline loop so that it goes through its full 256 count sequence every 2560 milliseconds. Each time that **BIG_CNT** reaches zero, call the **Halve** subroutine. The **LED_CNT** variable is to be initialized to equal the value of **LED_PER** in the **Initial** subroutine. Each time around the mainline loop, call a **LEDcounter** subroutine that decrements **LED_CNT.** When **LED_CNT** reaches zero, reload it with the value of **LED_PER,** call **SequenceLEDs,** and pulse the clock input to the stepper motor. Also, toggle the output, pin RB0 (i.e., PORTB, bit 0), which must be initialized to be an output, as must pin RB4 and RB5 for the stepper motor.

Figure A10-2 Project Two: Slow Rate Control (Page 1 of 1)

ECE 4175
Project Three
Enhanced Slow Rate Control

Reference:

Chapter 6 Structured Assembly Preprocessor

Overview

Your code for the last project is to be modified so that, depending on the state of a **STATE** flag bit, the sequencing is the same as the last project or just the opposite. Toggle the state of **STATE** after each complete sequence of counting; that is, after having stepped every 10 milliseconds for 2.560 seconds (after the sequence of increasing stepping rates) and after having stepped every 0.640 seconds for 2.560 seconds (after the sequence of decreasing stepping rates).

Thus, depending on the state of **STATE:**

-the sequencing should either speed up or slow down
-the LED sequencing should either be from left to right or from right to left
-the stepper motor should either step CW or CCW

Part A

You are to rewrite the code for Project Two, translating all code to use the structured assembler constructs of Chapter 6. Your modified code should not include any conditional or unconditional branches or "goto" instructions other than the "goto Mainline" instruction used as the reset vector. See Figure 6-7 for the rewritten version of the code.

From now on, all your assembly code should be written in this way. Note that Jess Meremonte's structured assembler preprocessor can be used to carry out automatic indenting.

Part B

Carry out the rest of the code development. The "Alive" LED must still blink every 2.5 seconds.

Figure A10-3 Project Three: Enhanced Slow Rate Control (Page 1 of 1)

ECE 4175
Project Four
New DISPLAY Utility

References:

Figure 7-19	P2.asm file
Chapter 14	FXD0808U.INC subroutine
	MATHVARS.INC file

For this project the code for Project Three should continue to work. In addition, you are to modify the **DISPLAY** macro (i.e., the **ByteDisplay** subroutine called by it) so that when the following line is executed

```
DISPLAY   <variable name>
```

the LCD display will express the variable in hex, decimal, and binary form with the format

```
hh   ddd
bbbbbbbb
```

where bbbbbbbb is the 8-bit binary representation of the variable, hh is the two-hex digit hexadecimal representation of the variable, and ddd is the decimal representation of the variable (with leading zeros suppressed).

Thus, 254 will produce a display of

```
FE   254
11111110
```

while 64 will produce a display of

```
40    64
01000000
```

and 0 will produce a display of

```
00     0
00000000
```

Use this to display the value of **LED_PER,** updating its value every 2.56 seconds.

As always, from the last project on, use only the structured assembly constructs to deal with conditional branches. Also use it to obtain the indenting for your file.

Use Chris Twigg's QwikPH utility of Appendix A5 to obtain your Program Hierarchy.

Figure A10-4 Project Four: New DISPLAY Utility (Page 1 of 1).

ECE 4175
Project Five
Square Wave Generator - Part 1

References:

Figure 2-8	Reading operands from program memory
Sections 20.2 and 20.3	HS+PLL oscillator
Figure 16-6	Making a scale-of-25000 counter

Overview

For this project, keep blinking the "Alive" LED every 2.5 seconds and keep stepping each time around the mainline loop. Also, toggle B0 (instead of C2) each time around the mainline loop. You might keep the **DISPLAY** macro and its subroutine to help with debugging. Otherwise, clean up the file for this project so that it becomes a file dedicated to the implementation of a square wave generator.

With this project, we are going to begin the development of the code for a square wave generator. It will run on a QwikFlash board having the modification that the internal clock will be 10 MHz, not the 2.5 MHz used in the lab. The higher clock rate is obtained by programming one of the "configuration words" (CONFIG1H) to select the use of a phase-locked loop working with the 10 MHz crystal to obtain F_{OSC} = 40 MHz and an internal clock rate of 10 MHz.

With your "user program", you cannot change the configuration bytes. You are to write code assuming the chip is running at an internal clock rate of 10 MHz. The consequence of this is that when we eventually generate a square wave output on one of our normal lab stations, it will have a frequency of one-fourth the displayed frequency. With slight modification, the code will run on the board having F_{OSC} = 40 MHz, producing the displayed frequency.

LoopTime subroutine modification

For Project Six, the next project, this square wave generator design will make use of Timer1 and the "capture/compare/PWM" module, CCP1, to produce a jitter-free square wave on the C2/CCP1 output pin located on the strip at the top of the board. This will leave Timer3 and CCP2 free for us to use to generate a 10 millisecond loop time with much more simplicity than has been done using Timer0. Initialize T3CON and CCP2CON as shown in Figure 16-6 to implement a scale-of-25000 counter. The prescaler divider for Timer3 should be set to 1. When we switch to an internal clock rate of 10 MHz, we will change this prescaler divider to 4 and thereby maintain a loop time of 10 milliseconds. The new **LoopTime** subroutine is simply

```
LoopTime
      REPEAT_
      UNTIL_  PIR2, CCP2IF == 1  ;Wait until the CCP2IF flag is set
      bcf PIR2, CCP2IF           ;Then clear it and return
      return
```

Figure A10-5 Project Five: Square Wave Generator—Part 1 (Page 1 of 3)

RPG use

You are to initially display the following LCD message:

```
SQWV OUT
   1 kHz
```

Then, using the **RPG** subroutine of Figure 8-3, each RPG increment should rewrite the second line of this display to the next frequency value in the sequence shown below. Each clockwise increment should display the next-higher frequency value, stopping at 10 MHz. Each counterclockwise increment should display the next-lower frequency value, stopping at 0.1 Hz.

DisplayFrequency subroutine

Each time around the mainline loop, this subroutine should look at the **RPG** subroutine's **DELRPG** variable. If a change has taken place, then the display is to be updated accordingly.

Output frequency values

These are the values to be displayed as the RPG is turned.

```
Ø.1  Hz
Ø.2  Hz
Ø.5  Hz
  1  Hz
  2  Hz
  5  Hz
 1Ø  Hz
 2Ø  Hz
 5Ø  Hz
1ØØ  Hz
2ØØ  Hz
5ØØ  Hz
  1 kHz
  2 kHz
  5 kHz
 1Ø kHz
 2Ø kHz
 5Ø kHz
1ØØ kHz
2ØØ kHz
5ØØ kHz
  1 MHz
  2 MHz
  5 MHz
 1Ø MHz
```

FreqDisplay table

Shown below is a **FreqDisplay** table to be stored in program memory. Each entry in the table consists of a 10 byte display string. If the **DisplayC** subroutine is called with **TBLPTRH:TBLPTRL** pointing to the beginning of one of these strings, it will display that desired message on the second line of the display. Note that

Figure A10-5 Project Five: Square Wave Generator—Part 1 (Page 2 of 3)

POINT FreqDisplay

will set up **TBLPTRH:TBLPTRL** to point to the base address of the table. If **FREQ** is a 1 byte variable representing which of the display strings should be used, then 10 times **FREQ** can be added to the base address of the table, moving the pointer to the desired string to be displayed.

```
;;;;;;; Constant strings ;;;;;;;;;;;;;;;;;;;;;;;;;;;;;;;;;;;;;;;;;;;;;;;

FreqDisplay
        db "\xcØ Ø.1  Hz\xØØ"      ;Display string to display " Ø.1 Hz"
        db "\xcØ Ø.2  Hz\xØØ"
        db "\xcØ Ø.5  Hz\xØØ"
        db "\xcØ   1  Hz\xØØ"
        db "\xcØ   2  Hz\xØØ"
        db "\xcØ   5  Hz\xØØ"
        db "\xcØ  1Ø  Hz\xØØ"
        db "\xcØ  2Ø  Hz\xØØ"
        db "\xcØ  5Ø  Hz\xØØ"
        db "\xcØ 1ØØ  Hz\xØØ"
        db "\xcØ 2ØØ  Hz\xØØ"
        db "\xcØ 5ØØ  Hz\xØØ"
        db "\xcØ   1  kHz\xØØ"
        db "\xcØ   2  kHz\xØØ"
        db "\xcØ   5  kHz\xØØ"
        db "\xcØ  1Ø  kHz\xØØ"
        db "\xcØ  2Ø  kHz\xØØ"
        db "\xcØ  5Ø  kHz\xØØ"
        db "\xcØ 1ØØ  kHz\xØØ"
        db "\xcØ 2ØØ  kHz\xØØ"
        db "\xcØ 5ØØ  kHz\xØØ"
        db "\xcØ   1  MHz\xØØ"
        db "\xcØ   2  MHz\xØØ"
        db "\xcØ   5  MHz\xØØ"
        db "\xcØ  1Ø  MHz\xØØ"
```

Figure A10-5 Project Five: Square Wave Generator—Part 1 (Page 3 of 3)

ECE 4175
Project Six
Square Wave Generator - Part 2

References:

Section 16.4	PWM output (Figures 16-7 and 16-8)
Section 16.5	Extended compare output (Figure 16-10)
Figure 16-11	P4.asm template file

Overview

For the last project you related a number in the variable **FREQ** to the display of the desired frequency. For this project you will use the PIC18F452's PWM mechanism to generate outputs of 5 kHz and above. You will use its extended compare mechanism to generate outputs of 2 kHz and below. Note that the PWM mechanism is the easier of the two mechanisms to implement. Just load the registers of Figure 16-7 with appropriate values for a given frequency and no further interactions are required. As shown in Figure 16-8, the output period can extend from 0.1 microseconds (with **PR2** = 0 and Timer2 prescaler = 1) to 409.6 microseconds (with **PR2** = 255 and Timer2 prescaler = 16). A value of **PR2** = 124 and Timer2 prescaler = 16 gives 2000 cycles (i.e., 200 microseconds), or a frequency of 1,000,000/200 = 5000 Hz (i.e., 5 kHz).

The extended compare mechanism of Figure 16-10 will be used for all lower frequencies, the highest of which is 2 kHz (with a period of 500 microseconds). For that value, the CPU needs to be interrupted by a CCP1 interrupt every half period, or every 250 microseconds. This gives 2500 internal clock cycles between interrupts. Even at this highest compare rate, the CPU will spend only a minuscule percentage of its time servicing interrupts. Furthermore, if Timer1's prescaler is set to 4 (with **T1CON** = 0xa1), the maximum obtainable period will be 2 × 4 × 256 × 256 × 256 = 134,217,728 cycles = 13,421,772.8 microseconds, or 13+ seconds. For our lowest frequency, the period will be 100,000,000 cycles, obtained with DTIME = 100,000,000/8 = 12,500,000 = 0xbebc20. For our highest frequency using the compare mechanism, the period will be 5000 cycles, obtained with DTIME = 5000/8 = 625 = 0x000271.

Initial subroutine

Initialize any new variables appropriately. Initialize the registers used by the extended compare mechanism to generate a 1 kHz output including **T1CON** = 0xa1 to set the Timer1 prescaler to 4. Set the **CCP1IE** local interrupt enable bit in the **PIE1** register to enable the CCP1 interrupt source. Set the **GIEL** and **GIEH** bits in the **INTCON** register as the last two instructions before the final **return** instruction from the **Initial** subroutine.

ChangeFrequency subroutine

The last project's **DisplayFrequency** subroutine changes the display in response to a nonzero value of the **DELRPG** variable generated by the **RPG** subroutine. A new **ChangeFrequency** subroutine, also called each time around the mainline loop, is to change the frequency of the square wave on the CCP1 output if **DELRPG** has a nonzero value. Also, for the old value corresponding to 2 kHz and the new value corresponding to 5 kHz, clear the **CCP1IE** local interrupt enable bit in the **PIE1** register to disable CCP1 interrupts. Then for *any* new value corresponding to a frequency of 5 kHz or above, call a **PWM** subroutine. This subroutine is to initialize the PWM registers: **T2CON, PR2, CCPR1L,** and **CCP1CON** with values taken from a table called **PWMtable** and having one 4 byte table entry for each frequency:

Figure A10-6 Square Wave Generator - Part 2 (Page 1 of 2)

```
PWMtable
        db 6, 124,  62, 0x2c          ;T2CON, PR2, CCPR1L, CCP1CON, for 5 kHz
        db 5, 249, 125, 0x0c          ;10 kHz
        db 5, 124,  62, 0x2c          ;20 kHz
        db 5,  49,  25, 0x0c          ;50 kHz
        db 5,  24,  12, 0x2c          ;100 kHz
        db 4,  49,  25, 0x0c          ;200 kHz
        db 4,  19,  10, 0x0c          ;500 kHz
        db 4,   9,   5, 0x0c          ;1 MHz
        db 4,   4,   2, 0x2c          ;2 MHz
        db 4,   1,   1, 0x0c          ;5 MHz
        db 4,   0,   0, 0x2c          ;10 MHz
```

Refer to Section 16.4 and especially Figures 16-7 and 16-8 for the derivation of these values.

For a change from 5 kHz to 2 kHz, set the **CCP1IE** local interrupt enable bit in the **PIE1** register to turn on the CCP1 interrupts needed by the extended compare mechanism. Then for *any* new value corresponding to a frequency of 2 kHz or below, call a **Compare** subroutine. Each time that the value of **FREQ** changes (and only then), this subroutine is to initialize the compare mode registers, **DTIMEX, DTIMEH, DTIMEL,** and **CCP1CON,** with values taken from the **COMPAREtable** listed below.

```
COMPAREtable
        db 0xbe, 0xbc, 0x20, 0x08     ;DTIMEX, DTIMEH, DTIMEL, CCP1CON for 0.1 Hz
        db 0x5f, 0x5e, 0x10, 0x08     ;0.2 Hz
        db 0x26, 0x25, 0xa0, 0x08     ;0.5 Hz
        db 0x13, 0x12, 0xd0, 0x08     ;1 Hz
        db 0x09, 0x89, 0x68, 0x08     ;2 Hz
        db 0x03, 0xd0, 0x90, 0x08     ;5 Hz
        db 0x01, 0xe8, 0x48, 0x08     ;10 Hz
        db 0x00, 0xf4, 0x24, 0x08     ;20 Hz
        db 0x00, 0x61, 0xa8, 0x08     ;50 Hz
        db 0x00, 0x30, 0xd4, 0x08     ;100 Hz
        db 0x00, 0x18, 0x6a, 0x08     ;200 Hz
        db 0x00, 0x09, 0xc4, 0x08     ;500 Hz
        db 0x00, 0x04, 0xe2, 0x08     ;1 kHz
        db 0x00, 0x02, 0x71, 0x08     ;2 kHz
```

Refer to the P4 template program shown in Figure 16-11 that uses the extended compare mechanism to generate a 10 Hz output from a 2.5 MHz internal clock rate. You will modify this code, using the selected 4 byte entry in **COMPAREtable** to provide the 4 bytes needed to initialize the registers that will produce the new rate.

Modifications to run with F_{OSC} = 40 MHz

When you are ready to modify your code to run on the board we have set up with the 40 MHz oscillator frequency and an internal clock rate of 10 MHz, modify two things. To keep a 10 millisecond loop time, change the Timer3 prescaler so as to insert an extra scale-of-4 divider into its counting chain. Also change the initialization of **COUNT** within the **T40** subroutine from

```
        movlw 100/3
        movwf COUNT
```

to

```
        movlw 400/3
        movwf COUNT
```

Figure A10-6 Square Wave Generator - Part 2 (Page 2 of 2)

ECE 4175
Project Seven
RateRPG/ADC Use

References:

Section 8.5 Rate-sensitive RPG
Chapter 10 Analog-to-Digital Conversion
FXD1608U.inc subroutine

Overview

For this project you will produce a stepping rate value controlled by slow and fast turning of the RPG. The potentiometer on the board will be used to set the threshold distinguishing between slow and fast turning with a value between 1 and 8. The stepping rate is to vary from 10 to 1990, with an initial value of 50.

The LCD display should display this information using the following format:

```
  THR=4
240 s/s
```

The parameter value on the second line is to be initialized to 50 and is to extend from 10 up to 1990 in increments of 10. Each slow increment of the RPG is to change the value by 10. Each fast increment is to change the value by 100. In either case, stop at 10 on the low end and 1990 at the high end. Blank leading zeros. Initialize the THR= on the first line and the s/s on the second line just once in the **Initial** subroutine.

THRSTG and SRATESTG display strings

Create and initialize a 3 byte variable display string called **THRSTG** that will be used to write the value of the **THRESHOLD** in the upper right-hand corner of the display. Create and initialize a 6 byte variable display string called **SRATESTG** that will be used to write the four-digit value (perhaps with leading blank characters) of **SRATE** to the display.

RateRPG subroutine

Modify the **RateRPG** subroutine presented in the text so that when it needs to use the value of **THRESHOLD,** it calls a **ConvertPot** subroutine and then uses the value formed by that subroutine. Call the **RateRPG** subroutine each time around the mainline loop to update **DELRPG** to a value of 0 if no RPG change is seen, ±1 for a slow change, and ±2 for a fast change.

ConvertPot subroutine

Figure A10-7 Project Seven: RateRPG/ADC Use (Page 1 of 2)

In your **Initial** subroutine, initialize **ADCON1** to B'11001110' and **ADCON0** to B'01100001'. Create a **ConvertPot** subroutine that initiates a conversion by setting the **GO_DONE** bit in the **ADCON0** register. Test this bit to wait the 20 microseconds used by the ADC to carry out the conversion. The result will have the form shown in Figure 10-5a. Just rotate **ADRESL** left through the carry bit, rotate **ADRESH** left through the carry bit (putting the result into **WREG),** increment the resulting 3-bit value (0-7), and store the result into **THRESHOLD** (whose value will now range between 1 and 8). Update the **THRSTG** display string with the ASCII representation of this value. Then call **DisplayV** with **FSR0** pointing to **THRSTG** to update the display.

FormSRATE subroutine

This subroutine is to be called in the mainline loop after the **RateRPG** subroutine is called. If the variable **DELRPG** has a value other than zero, then update the value of **SRATE** appropriately and display the value. Mike Chow suggests that you maintain the stepping rate as a 2 byte binary number, **SRATEH:SRATEL.** When you are ready to display its value in a display string, just carry out successive divisions by ten to break out the digits. For example, if the rate is 1230, then division by 10 will produce a quotient of 123 and a remainder of 0. Dividing 123 by 10 will produce a quotient of 12 and a remainder of 3. Dividing 12 by 10 will produce a quotient of 1 and a remainder of 2. Convert each 0-9 value to its ASCII representation by inclusive-ORing it with 0x30 (since, for example, 0x35 is the ASCII code for the digit 5).

Stepping the stepper motor

Modify your code to cause the stepper motor to step at the displayed stepping rate using any of our normal stations (where the internal clock rate of the chip is 2.5 MHz). Note that if the stepping rate is N steps/second and if the clock input to the stepper motor controller is toggled every P internal clock cycles, then

```
2 x P x Ø.ØØØØØØ4
```

represents the time per step, in units of seconds/step. N times this value equals 1. Thus, the number of cycles between each toggling of the controller's clock input is given by

```
P = 1,250,ØØØ/N = Øx1312dØ/N
```

Use the FXD2416U subroutine described in Figure 14-4 to obtain the 3 byte period between steps and use this value to control the stepping rate. Remember to treat the three **movff** instructions wherein you update the value of **DTIMEX:DTIMEH: DTIMEL** as a critical region. Why should this be done and what might the consequence be if this is not done?

To verify the stepping rate, toggle RB1 each time that the clock input to the stepper motor controller is toggled. This pin is brought out on the top strip of test points on the board where it can be grabbed with the scope probe.

Figure A10-7 Project Seven: RateRPG/ADC Use (Page 2 of 2)

ECE 4175
Project Eight (two-week project)
MaxPW

References:

Section 4.3	QwikFlash instrument description
Figure 12-4	The "Screens" implementation of the QwikFlash instrument
Sections 13.7, 13.8	Timer3/CCP2 use
Sections 9.3, 9.4	Interrupts

Overview

For this project, begin anew using the "Screens" template program, P3, of Chapter 12. Using the "C1/CCP2" input at the bottom of the board (i.e., the QwikFlash Instrument input), you are to capture the time of occurrence of each rising edge on CCP2, the time of occurrence of the subsequent falling edge, form the difference, compare with the previous highest value, and replace that value if this time is larger. All of this is to be done in the high-priority interrupt service routine. The low-priority interrupt service routine is to be used to implement a 3 byte version of Timer3 that will be used with CCP2 to capture time intervals with 3 byte resolution. Ensure the *correct* reading of **TMR3X** every time with the special precautions discussed below.

Every tenth of a second, rewrite the second line of the LCD with the maximum pulse width, to date, producing a screen of the form:

```
MaxPW us
   234.4
```

That is, display the maximum pulse width with a resolution of the internal clock period and blanking leading zeros. The maximum time interval to be measured is about 0.99 seconds. Note that the 3 byte Timer3 counter counting at a 2.5 MHz rate will roll over every 256x256x256x0.4 microseconds, or every 6.7108864 seconds. Upon each rising edge, clear a one-byte **LOOPTIMES** counter. Upon each falling edge, check to see if **LOOPTIMES** equals 99. If so, display

```
MaxPW
  >1 sec
```

and turn on the three "annunciator" LEDS, waiting for a short press of the pushbutton to begin again. In fact, begin the maximum pulse width measurement again in response to *any* short press of the pushbutton switch.

Interrupts

Since you will be using low-priority interrupts for nothing but to increment **TMR3X** and to clear **TMR3IF,** there is no need to execute a polling routine or to set aside, and subsequently restore, any registers *if* you use the following sequence to do the incrementing:

```
incfsz TMR3X, F     ;Increment, skip if zero; change no flags
nop
```

Figure A10-8 Project Eight: MaxPW (Page 1 of 2)

Likewise, if you use a high-priority interrupt with the **FAST** return from interrupt, the shadow registers will automatically take care of preserving **WREG** and **STATUS.**

Don't worry about having a pulse width so narrow as to be too fast for this measurement technique. As part of the checkout, you will determine the minimum pulse width that you can measure.

LoopTime subroutine

Change the implementation of the **LoopTime** subroutine to use the otherwise unused Timer1/CCP1 scale-of-25000 counter approach of Figure 16-4 to get a 10 millisecond loop time from the 0.4 microsecond internal clock period.

TMR3X handling

The RAM variable, **TMR3X,** is not automatically incremented as Timer3 rolls over from 0xffff to 0x0000. As a consequence, the **HiPriISR** (high-priority interrupt service routine) has the (rare) possibility of obtaining an erroneous reading of the 3 byte value of time, **TMR3X:CCP2H:CCP2L.** Furthermore, because the MaxPW mechanism ratchets up to a maximum value, even a single erroneously large value will invalidate the entire measurement of maximum pulse width.

If an erroneous reading occurs, it will be because an input edge occurred at almost exactly the same time that Timer3 rolled over. Accordingly, take the following steps:

1. Within the **HiPriISR,** check whether the Timer3 rollover flag, **TMR3IF,** is set. If so, and if the most-significant bit of **CCP2H** = 0, then the input edge occurred *after* the rollover, but **TMR3X** has not been incremented to the correct value. So, increment **TMR3X** and clear the **TMR3IF** flag before reading **TMR3X** as the upper byte of the 3 byte value of time.
2. Within the **LoPriISR,** disable high-priority interrupts momentarily by clearing the **GIEH** bit. Then increment **TMR3X** (using the **incfsz** scheme discussed above so as not to change any **STATUS** bits), clear **TMR3IF,** reenable **GIEH** and return from the interrupt. Note that this incrementing of **TMR3X** and the clearing of **TMR3IF** constitute a critical region for high-priority interrupts. Consider what can possibly happen if high-priority interrupts are not disabled during the execution of these two events.

Figure A10-8 Project Eight: MaxPW (Page 2 of 2)

ECE 4175
Project Nine
DAC Output

References:

Chapter 15	Serial Peripheral Interface
Section 15.7	Digital-to-analog converter output

Overview

On the DAC-A output on the top strip of pins, generate a sawtooth output waveform. The waveform should rise linearly from 0 V to a value wherein the 8-bit input to the DAC equals the upper 8 bits from the ADC register that contains a digital number corresponding to the potentiometer output. The waveform should have as short a period as you can achieve while at the same time assuring that every step of the waveform has exactly the same duration. However, if you need a slight pause at the end of each sawtooth before beginning the next sawtooth, that is fine. Note that the period of the waveform will be proportional to the potentiometer output.

Figure A10-9 Project Nine: DAC Output (Page 1 of 1)

ECE 4175
Project Ten
Temperature Display

References:

Section 10.3	LM34 temperature sensor
Section 10.4	ADC use
Figure 7-12b	Display of special characters

Overview

The LM34 temperature sensor located in the upper left-hand corner of the QwikFlash board produces an output of 10 millivolts per degree Fahrenheit. Using the 5 volt power supply voltage as the reference voltage, the analog-to-digital converter's AN0 input will convert the LM34 output to an 8-bit number (using the lower 8 of the 10 output bits) for temperatures up to 125°F. Use the output of the one-turn pot to trim the value ±2°F so you can calibrate the temperature against an external reference thermometer at room temperature. Update a display of the resulting value every second, with a display of the form

```
Temp
  73.5°F
```

Round the result to the nearest 0.5°F. For temperatures above 100°F, add in the extra hundreds digit (that should be blanked for temperatures below 100°F).

Be sure to pause for at least 15 microseconds after changing the ADC's multiplexer and before initiating a conversion by setting its **GO_DONE** bit.

To display the "°" degree symbol, use the ASCII code 0xdf, as indicated in Figure 7-12b.

For testing, use a hair dryer to raise the temperature above 100°F.

Figure A10-10 Project Ten: Temperature Display (Page 1 of 1)

INDEX

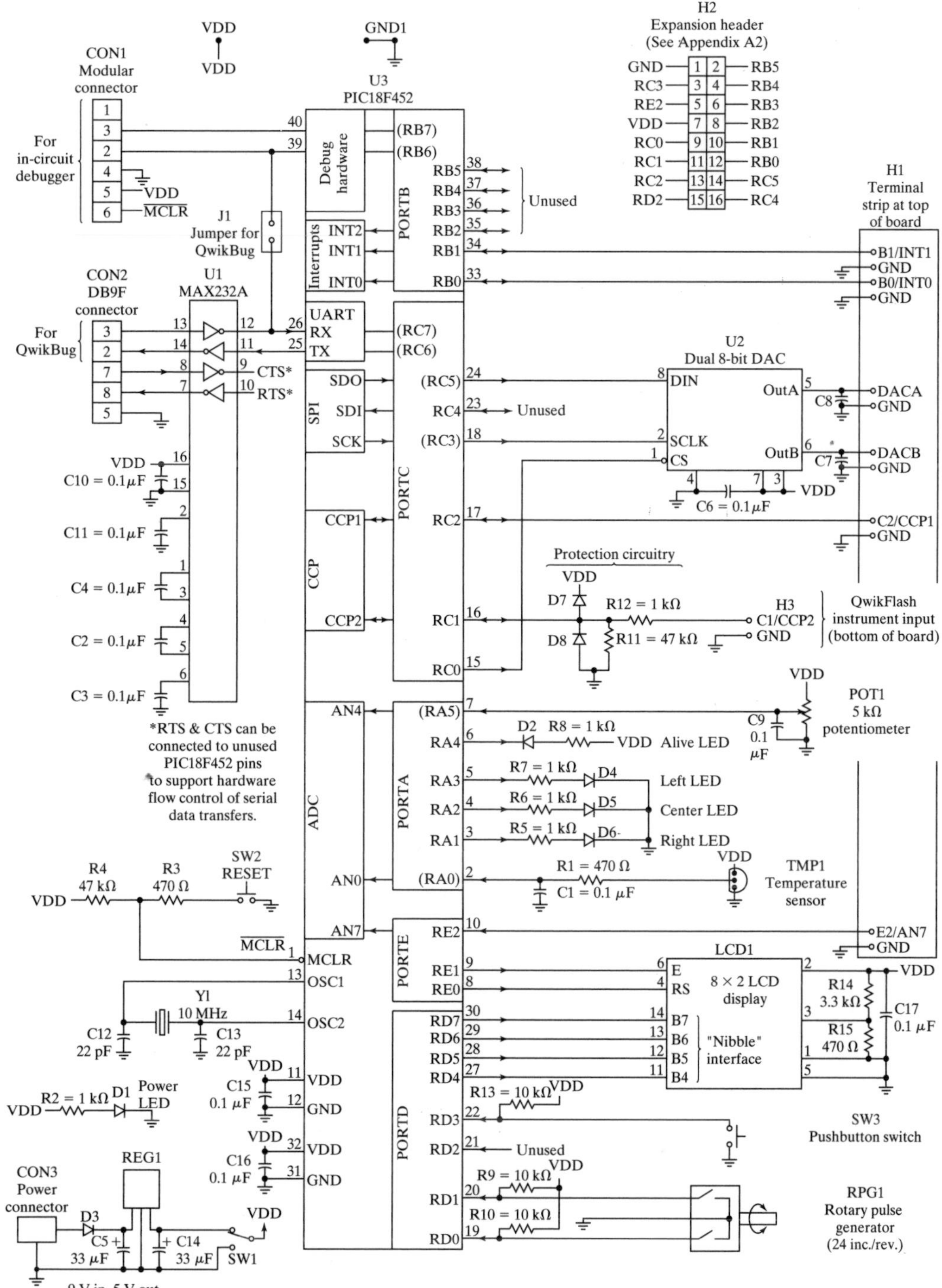

VDD
VDD
GND1
H2
Expansion header
(See Appendix A2)
GND 1 2 RB5
RC3 3 4 RB4
RE2 5 6 RB3
VDD 7 8 RB2
RC0 9 10 RB1
RC1 11 12 RB0
RC2 13 14 RC5
RD2 15 16 RC4
CON1
Modular
connector
For
in-circuit
debugger
1
3
2
4
5 VDD
6 MCLR
U3
PIC18F452
40
39
Debug
hardware
(RB7)
(RB6)
PORTB
RB5 38
RB4 37
RB3 36
RB2 35
Unused
RB1 34
RB0 33
Interrupts
INT2
INT1
INT0
J1
Jumper for
QwikBug
H1
Terminal
strip at top
of board
B1/INT1
GND
B0/INT0
GND
CON2
DB9F
connector
U1
MAX232A
For
QwikBug
3
2
7
8
5
13
14
8
7
12
11
9 CTS*
10 RTS*
26
25
UART
RX
TX
(RC7)
(RC6)
SPI
SDO
SDI
SCK
(RC5) 24
RC4 23
Unused
(RC3) 18
U2
Dual 8-bit DAC
8 DIN
2 SCLK
1 CS
OutA 5
OutB 6
4
7
3
VDD
C6 = 0.1 μF
C8
C7
DACA
GND
DACB
GND
VDD
16
C10 = 0.1μF
15
C11 = 0.1μF
C4 = 0.1μF
C2 = 0.1μF
C3 = 0.1μF
PORTC
CCP
CCP1
CCP2
RC2 17
C2/CCP1
GND
Protection circuitry
VDD
D7
D8
R12 = 1 kΩ
R11 = 47 kΩ
H3
C1/CCP2
GND
QwikFlash
instrument input
(bottom of board)
RC1 16
RC0 15
*RTS & CTS can be
connected to unused
PIC18F452 pins
to support hardware
flow control of serial
data transfers.
ADC
AN4
(RA5) 7
VDD
POT1
5 kΩ
potentiometer
C9
0.1
μF
PORTA
RA4 6
D2
R8 = 1 kΩ
VDD
Alive LED
RA3 5
R7 = 1 kΩ
D4
Left LED
RA2 4
R6 = 1 kΩ
D5
Center LED
RA1 3
R5 = 1 kΩ
D6
Right LED
R4
47 kΩ
R3
470 Ω
SW2
RESET
VDD
AN0
(RA0) 2
R1 = 470 Ω
C1 = 0.1 μF
VDD
TMP1
Temperature
sensor
AN7
PORTE
RE2 10
E2/AN7
GND
MCLR
1 MCLR
13 OSC1
RE1 9
RE0 8
LCD1
6 E
4 RS
8 × 2 LCD
display
2
VDD
R14
3.3 kΩ
3
R15
470 Ω
1
5
C17
0.1 μF
Yl
10 MHz
14 OSC2
C12
22 pF
C13
22 pF
PORTD
RD7 30
RD6 29
RD5 28
RD4 27
14 B7
13 B6
12 B5
11 B4
"Nibble"
interface
VDD
11 VDD
C15
0.1 μF
12 GND
R2 = 1 kΩ
D1
Power
LED
VDD
R13 = 10 kΩ
VDD
RD3 22
SW3
Pushbutton switch
RD2 21
Unused
VDD
32 VDD
C16
0.1 μF
31 GND
CON3
Power
connector
REG1
R9 = 10 kΩ
VDD
RD1 20
R10 = 10 kΩ
RD0 19
RPG1
Rotary pulse
generator
(24 inc./rev.)
D3
C5
33 μF
C14
33 μF
VDD
SW1
9 V in, 5 V out